Employment in Developing Nations

REPORT ON A FORD FOUNDATION STUDY

EDGAR O. EDWARDS
Editor

COLUMBIA UNIVERSITY PRESS
NEW YORK AND LONDON 1974

THE FORD FOUNDATION
320 East 43rd Street, New York, N.Y. 10017

© Copyright 1974 by The Ford Foundation
All rights reserved

Library of Congress Catalog Card Number: 74-16724
Printed in the United States of America

ISBN 0-231-03873-9 Clothbound
ISBN 0-231-03874-7 Paperback

Contributors

Partap C. Aggarwal has been associated with the Shri Ram Centre for Industrial Relations and Human Resources in New Delhi since 1971. Prior to that appointment, he served on the faculty of Colgate University for four years, and continues to hold an appointment here as adjunct professor of anthropology. He has written two books, *Caste, Religion, and Power* (1971) and *The Green Revolution and Rural Labour* (1973), and a number of articles. At present he is investigating the impact of special privileges on the scheduled castes of Haryana.

Vincent M. Barnett, Jr., is James P. Baxter III Professor of History and Public Affairs. He has taught at Harvard and Colgate, been visiting professor at Stanford and UCLA, and was president of Colgate University (1963-69). He served in Washington during World War II (OPA and WPB), and later as deputy chief, Marshall Plan Mission to Italy (1948-53), and as counselor economic affairs, U.S. Embassy, Rome (1958-60). In 1971-72, he was director of the Harvard Advisory Group in Malaysia. He has contributed extensively to professional journals in political science, public administration, economics and law.

Henry J. Bruton has been a member of the Department of Economics and the Center for Development Economics at Williams College since 1962. Prior to Williams he taught at Yale University. He has served as visiting professor at the University of Bombay and the University of Chile and as the joint director of the Pakistan Institute of Development Economics. He has worked as an economic consultant for extended periods in Iran, Malaysia and Indonesia. He has published books and articles on most aspects of the development process.

Edgar O. Edwards has been economic advisor to the Asia and Pacific Program of the Ford Foundation since 1970. He served earlier to associate professor at Princeton University and then as Hargrove Professor and chairman at Rice University. On leave from Rice he acted for four years as principal economic advisor to the Ministry of Planning of the Government of Kenya (1963-68). He has written on various development matters, macro- and micro-economic theory, and income theory and measurement.

D.J.C. Forsyth is senior lecturer, David Livingstone Institute of Overseas Development Studies, University of Strathclyde, and member of the appropriate technology research team there. He has worked at the Universities of Virginia, Aberdeen and Strathclyde, spent a year as visiting senior academic at the University of Ghana, and acted as consultant to the U.N. Economic Commission for Africa. His recent publications include *U.S. Investment in Scotland* and *The Appraisal of Proposals for Foreign Participation in Manufacturing Industry in Africa*.

iii

Carl H. Gotsch is a fellow of the Harvard Institute of International Development and a lecturer in the Department of Economics, currently on leave with the Ford Foundation's Middle East Regional Office as project specialist in agriculture. He has written extensively on the effects of green revolution technology in the irrigated and semi-arid areas of Pakistan and India.

Keith Griffin has been a fellow of Magdalen College, Oxford, and tutor in economics since 1965. He has served as advisor to the Pakistan Institute of Development Economics (1965 and 1970), advisor to the Algerian Government on agricultural planning (1963-64), and visiting professor at the University of Chile (1962 and 1964). His publications include *The Political Economy of Agrarian Change, Underdevelopment in Spanish America,* and articles in various journals.

John G. Gurley is professor of economics at Stanford and vice-president of the American Economic Association. Earlier he taught economics at Princeton University and the University of Maryland, and was a senior fellow at the Brookings Institution. He was managing editor of the *American Economic Review* from 1963 to 1968. He has written extensively on monetary theory, Chinese economic development, Marxian economics, and public finance.

L.S. Jarvis is assistant professor at the University of California, Berkeley. On leave from July 1972 to December 1973, he served as program advisor for the Ford Foundation in Chile. He has published several articles and has a book forthcoming on Argentine development which will be published by the University of California Press.

Amir Khan is head of the Agricultural Engineering Department, The International Rice Research Institute, Los Banos, Philippines, currently on leave with the Denver Research Institute as a senior research fellow. He owned and operated a farm machinery manufacturing business in India from 1952 to 1958 when he became a deputy director in the Ministry of Commerce and Industry. In 1959 he joined Voltas Ltd., Bombay, as head of their agricultural machinery development program. He migrated to the USA in 1964, obtaining his Ph.D. in agricultural engineering at Michigan State University. He joined IRRI in 1967, and has since written several articles on appropriate technology.

Raj Krishna is senior economist, Development Economics Department, International Bank for Reconstruction and Development, Washington, D.C. He was earlier Council of Economic and Cultural Affairs fellow at the University of Chicago (1958-61), senior research fellow at the Institute of Economic Growth, University of Delhi (1961-65), and professor and head of the Department of Economics, University of Rajasthan, Jaipur, India (1967-73). He has published extensively—on agrarian reform, agricultural policy and employment problems—in Indian, British and American journals.

N.S. McBain is senior research fellow (engineer), David Livingstone Institute of Overseas Development Studies, University of Strathclyde, and a member of the appropriate technology research team there. He has served as development engineer, Giddings & Lewis-Fraser Ltd., Scotland (1962-64); manufacturing engineer, The Boeing Co., Seattle (1966-68); and resident consultant, Project Planning Division, P.A. Management Consultants Ltd., London (1968-71). His articles have been published in *Accountancy* and *Journal of Business Finance*.

Manning Nash has been with the University of Chicago since 1957 and professor of anthropology since 1964. He has been visiting professor at the University of Washington on two occasions and at Harvard University in 1968. He has done field work in Mexico, Guatemala, Burma, Malaysia and Indonesia. He is author of six books and numerous scholarly articles.

James Pickett is director of the David Livingstone Institute of Overseas Development Studies, University of Strathclyde, and heads a major research project on appropriate technology. He has served as special economic advisor, U.N. Economic Commission for Africa (1965-68), and as consultant to the ECA/OAU/ UNIDO Conference of African Ministers of Industry (Addis Ababa, 1971, and Cairo, 1973). He has published in such journals as the *Canadian Journal of Economics,* the *Journal of Economic Studies,* and the *Journal of Modern African Studies*.

Mohammad Sadli has been Minister of Manpower, Government of Indonesia, since 1971. His education has taken him to such universities as Gadjah Mada, Indonesia, M.I.T., California (Berkeley) and Harvard. He served from 1957 to 1963 as director of the Institute of Economic and Social Research at the University of Indonesia and then as assistant to the president of that institution. He has been a member of the Governing Council, Asian Institute of Development and Planning (1963-64), chairman, Indonesian Economists Association (1966-67), and chairman, Technical Committee for Foreign Investment (1967).

Frances Stewart has been a senior research officer at the Institute of Commonwealth Studies, Oxford, since 1972. She has also served in Whitehall—in the Treasury, the National Economic Development Office and the Department of Economic Affairs—as a lecturer in the University of East Africa, and as a member of the ILO/UNDP Employment Mission to Kenya. Her publications have appeared in *Oxford Economic Papers, Journal of Development Studies* and *World Development*.

George J. Stolnitz is professor of economics at Indiana University. He was earlier on the staff of Princeton University and associated with the Office of Population Research. He has lectured at Michigan, Vanderbilt, Minnesota, Emory, and New Delhi universities, been visiting scholar at Kiel University, Resources for the Future and the University of Sao Paulo, and served as a consultant to many national and international organizations. He has published widely on population, economic development and statistical methodology, and is currently engaged in a study of "U.S. and Regional Manpower Movements in the 1960s."

John Woodward Thomas is a member of the Harvard Institute for International Development. He served earlier as a representative of CARE in Sri Lanka, the Philippines and East Pakistan, and as a member of the Harvard Advisory Group in Pakistan (1968-70). He has advised on rural development problems in Bangladesh,

Ethiopia, Mauritius and Pakistan. At present he is directing a comparative study of special employment creating public works programs. His papers and articles have focused on issues of organization and technology as applied to rural development and to special public works programs.

Michael P. Todaro has been with the Rockefeller Foundation since 1968—first as a research fellow at the Institute of Development Studies (Nairobi), then in New York becoming associate director of Social Sciences, and again at the IDS beginning July 1974. He is widely known for his work on rural-urban migration and employment. His other publications include *Economic Theory* (with P. Bell) and *Development Planning: Models and Methods.*

Constantine V. Vaitsos is head of the Department on Policies on Science and Technology of the Junta del Acuerdo de Cartagena (Secretariat of the Andean Common Market), and holds the position of fellow of the Institute of Development Studies, Sussex. He has served as principal advisor for the preparation of the Common Treatment on Foreign Investments of the Andean Pact countries, a member of the Harvard Advisory Group in Colombia, and as teaching fellow at Harvard. He has written extensively on the importation of technology, foreign investments, and issues of industrial property, most recently, *Intercountry Income Distribution and Transnational Enterprises.*

Alberto Valdés, a Chilean, has been on the staff of the Centro Internacional de Agricultura Tropical (CIAT), Colombia, since May 1973. Formerly, he has served in the Faculties of Economics and Agriculture of Universidad Católica where he created and chaired the Department of Agricultural Economics, was dean of agriculture and, in 1971 became director of the Post-Graduate Program in Economics. As consultant, he has served in Argentina, Colombia, Peru, Bolivia and Ecuador. His writings include articles on agricultural trade policy, labour markets, land reform and farm management.

William N. Wamalwa has been chairman of the Public Service Commission of Kenya since 1968. He joined the Kenya Civil Service in 1962, became clerk to the Kenya Cabinet in 1963 and permanent secretary to the Ministry of Economic Planning and Development in 1966, a post which included responsibility for manpower planning and the Central Bureau of Statistics. He is a founder member of the African Association for Public Administration and Management and has, on several occasions, acted as consultant to the African Training and Research Centre in Administration for Development (CAFRAD), Tangier, Morocco.

Foreword

The study of which these selected papers were a part was initiated by the Ford Foundation because we shared in the growing worldwide concern over the pervasiveness and intractability of unemployment in the less developed countries.

Secretary Kissinger this past spring told the United Nations that hunger and unemployment are the two most fundamental problems of the poor countries. The Foundation has long been engaged with both, but with differences of approach that derive from different characters of the two problems. No one needs to be told how formidable the task of feeding the world now is, but awareness of the size and persistence of unemployment in the less developed countries has come more slowly and uncertainly. Programs for increasing food production and limiting population growth are natural and straightforward parts of a war on hunger, however difficult they may be to carry out effectively. Unemployment seems a rather more elusive evil, and discouragingly unresponsive to the direct "make-work" programs that have been tried in many countries. The search for its true causes leads deep into the analysis of strategies for economic growth and questions of the distribution of its benefits. Like others, we have been unclear about the best approaches to this problem; hence this study.

Two outcomes have been sought. The first was a wider understanding among our own Foundation staff, both in New York and in our field offices overseas, of promising ways toward generating more emloyment (or other opportunities to earn income) in the impoverished circumstances of most developing countries. The spectrum of possibilities is a long one, from basic research on the development process through to pilot action programs. The measure of our enlightenment will not come immediately, but in the wisdom of our choice of projects in the next years.

A second outcome is exemplified by this publication. From the outset of this study we have intended to share its results with those outside the Foundation who might be interested. Much of the improved understanding our own staff has gained came about through the circulation of papers written for the study. We hope that this publication of a selection of those papers will enable others to benefit from them as we have.

McGeorge Bundy
President
The Ford Foundation

Preface

The papers selected for this volume are revised versions of some of those prepared for three international seminars conducted by the Ford Foundation in 1973 as part of its study of employment problems in developing nations. Nearly a hundred professional people and policy makers from several disciplines and many countries have been drawn directly into the study. To lend focus to their efforts, the employment problem has been approached from five different but overlapping points of view—policy, technology, rural development, international issues and education. These had been identified as especially significant issues for employment during the course of preliminary surveys of the employment problem beginning in 1964 with the planning for the Conference on Education, Employment and Rural Development held in Kenya in 1966,* and later through a series of seminars within the Foundation. These disclosed the complexity of the employment problem and affirmed the wisdom of exploring it in some depth.

The effects of international economic activities on employment problems in developing countries were reviewed in conjunction with Fred Bergsten's study of the international economic order; the supporting paper on "third world" considerations prepared by the Overseas Development Council was particularly helpful.** Simultaneously, the interaction between education and development (including employment) has been explored in two meetings of heads of donor agencies held in Bellagio, Italy, in May, 1972 and November, 1973.***

The study of policy, technology and rural development in relation to employment was conducted over the course of 1973 with the aid of Norman Dahl and David Heaps of the Ford Foundation staff and an internal advisory committee composed of Clark Bloom, Norman Collins, Norman Dahl, Peter deJanosi, Craufurd Goodwin, David Heaps, Lester Porter, Ozzie Simmons, Mitchell Sviridoff and Robert Tolles. Three principal consultants were engaged and, with their assistance, three international seminars were arranged. Henry Bruton of Williams College provided guidance for the first. Held in Bogota, Colombia, on February 21-23, 1973, it dealt with employment policies and their feasibility. The second, led by Frances Stewart of Queen

---

* James R. Sheffield, ed., *Education, Employment and Rural Development: The Proceedings of a Conference Held at Kericho, Kenya, in September 1966* (Nairobi, East African Publishing House, 1967).

** C. Fred Bergsten, *The Future of the International Economic Order* (New York, D.C. Heath, 1973), esp. Chapters 1 and 7.

***F. Champion Ward, ed., *Education and Development Reconsidered* (New York, Praeger, forthcoming).

Elizabeth House, Oxford University, took place in New Delhi on March 21-24, 1973, and explored the role of technology and technological change in the creation of employment opportunities. The third, under the leadership of Carl Gotsch of Harvard University was held in Ibadan, Nigeria, April 9-12, 1973, in facilities provided by the International Institute of Tropical Agriculture; the seminar took rural development and employment as a theme. (Lists of papers and participants in the three seminars can be found in the appendices.)

About one-third of the papers prepared are included in this volume. These are not organized by seminar but rather by the ways in which the authors have chosen to approach employment as a problem, running roughly from the comprehensive to the specific. The first paper attempts to digest the insights gained from the several aspects of the employment study, of which the three seminars were a major part. This is followed by the papers prepared by our three principal subject matter consultants. The next seven papers deal with a number of fundamental issues which cut across sectors into the institutional settings which seem to govern the pace and pattern of development. Then five papers have been grouped together which focus more sharply on sectoral policies and problems, including agriculture, public works, education, foreign investment and public sector employment. The final set of four papers brings together several country experiences with employment and development problems, including Indonesia, India, China and Chile.

I would like to express appreciation to the authors of these papers who, though scattered throughout the world, have without exception responded to my every query quickly, constructively and graciously. Jocelyn Saitta performed under difficult circumstances the arduous task of guiding the manuscript through its composition and typesetting stages. My greatest debt, however, is to Edith Reckholder, who, with excellence, patience and good humor, helped with the preparation and management of the seminars, retyped many of the revised papers in final form, and read diligently the many pages of proof.

Edgar O. Edwards
June, 1974

Contents

I. Basic Discussion Papers

Economic Development and Labor Use: A Review   **49**
Henry J. Bruton

Technology and Employment in LDCs   **83**
Frances Stewart

Economics, Institutions and Employment Generation in Rural Areas

Carl Gotsch

II. Selected Papers on Generic Issues

Implementation of Policies for Fuller Employment in Less Developed Countries 247

Vincent M. Barnett, Jr.

III. Some Sectoral Considerations

Employment Effects of Foreign Direct Investments in Developing Countries

Employment in Developing Countries

Edgar O. Edwards*

Ford Foundation

Introduction

The cumulative experience of the last two decades has demonstrated that the development strategies pursued by most developing countries have *not* produced the wide distribution of benefits some thought would follow naturally from the attainment of reasonable rates of growth. One of those benefits—the opportunity to earn a living—has turned out to be particularly elusive to growing numbers of people. As a result, many governments in developing countries have become deeply concerned with the increasingly troublesome problem of creating constructive employment opportunities for their rapidly growing populations.

The violence in Sri Lanka three years ago is clear evidence of the troubles which can ensue when large numbers of the educated in cities are confronted with a shortage of job opportunities; and some of the difficulties between East (now Bangladesh) and West Pakistan can be traced to the slower rate of growth in employment opportunities in the East as compared with the West, as well as to an inequitable sharing between the two wings of other benefits of national growth. These experiences, and spreading student unrest, have disturbed other governments throughout Asia who are aware that their own employment problems are reaching magnitudes of major consequence. Even in Africa, where one might think that the more favorable population/land ratios would keep unemployment within reasonable bounds, Tanzania has forcefully removed unemployed from the cities, Kenya has resorted to a tripartite agreement to expand employment artificially, and a number of countries have established youth corps to keep at least some of the unemployed actively engaged. It has now become clear that such measures are not a solution to an employment problem which threatens to be chronic as well as acute, but are more on the order of stop gap measures.

The roots of the problem go much deeper and any effective and lasting treatment of it will require substantial changes in the economic policies pursued in the past. As governments have become aware of this, they have turned to a number of sources, internal and external, for analysis and advice. One notable external response has been the International Labor Organization's Employment Program through which large, short-term missions have been sent to Colombia, Sri Lanka, Iran, Kenya and the

* The author has drawn on the views of an advisory committee and participants in three seminars, and acknowledges helpful comments on an earlier draft by David Bell, Henry Bruton, Norman Dahl, Carl Gotsch, Frances Stewart and Francis Sutton. The parenthetical references scattered through the text relate to other articles in this book.

1

Philippines with the express purpose of making recommendations for dealing effectively with the employment problem in these countries.[1] In every case the missions have been led by the pervasive nature of the problem to undertake sweeping reevaluations of the entire policy spectrum embraced by development strategy.

These several experiences, among others, have led us, in the course of this study, to look at the employment problem as a symptom of more far-reaching economic and social disturbances. The study has explored the characteristics and dimensions of the problem, its relationship to other development objectives, the suitability of past and prospective development strategies, and the feasibility of various strategy options in different social, political and economic settings. Its aim has been to identify issues in need of research, loci of decision making most crucial to the generation of productive employment opportunities, and the institutional, organizational and training needs most essential to the wider sharing of the benefits of development.

The paper begins with substantive issues and their analysis. We discuss the nature and dimensions of the employment problem, the environmental factors which constrain the choice of employment strategies, and the nature of strategy options which seem promising or in need of investigation. The final section is devoted to program options for donor agencies, particularly as these might relate to research, institution-building, and training activities, and to the means by which these might be organized and conducted; it is natural that this section reflects a Ford Foundation perspective.

The Nature of the Employment Problem

We have come to recognize during the course of this study that the problem of generating more employment opportunities in developing countries involves a substantial redefinition of appropriate development strategies, and indeed considerably more than that. There are probably many mixes of policies and structural changes which could in a technical sense yield improved employment in most developing countries. Knowing which of these, if any, is feasible in a particular social, political and economic setting requires in addition a deep and intimate understanding of the values, institutional framework and stage of development of each nation (and indeed of its subdivisions) and of the nature of its relationships with the rest of the world (Gotsch, Griffin). The study suggests that considerations of feasibility have received much less attention in the past than they deserve, particularly in the course of framing development strategies for particular settings, and that they should be matters of more serious concern in the future.

A Scenario of the Underutilization of Labor

This rather wide view of employment problems in developing nations has led us to explore, though in a somewhat superficial fashion, the historical roots of the problem in order to identify some of the principal causes of the symptoms we have only recently begun to perceive. The scenario may run something like this: There has been in nearly all developing nations, precedent to any important efforts at modernization, a sleeping giant called the underutilization of labor. Its principal form was underemployment, people finding that only limited work effort could be productively combined with the meager resources of land and capital at their disposal; moreover, the scarcity of markets in which people could buy and sell goods and services limited both their incentives and opportunities. Very few lived well by modern standards and most lived in conditions of abject poverty (as many of them still do), but long hours of work were usually futile in their circumstances. Thus, apparent leisure and obvious poverty ran hand in hand. Possibly, in some premodernization situations, a growing population meant that scarce land and capital had to be shared with a larger labor force so that both leisure and poverty tended to increase as the limited output and restricted employment opportunities both had to be divided among larger numbers of people.[2]

All of this has about it a Malthusian air of the inevitable, complicated in different ways in different settings by the "rules" which have governed the distribution of resources and output. The communal use of land in African tribal settings probably meant a relatively equitable distribution of work and output, whereas the landlord/tenant relationship in many other parts of the third world tended to aggravate poverty and limit opportunities among the many in favor of benefits for the few. Clearly political and economic power were for the most part very unequally distributed in most traditional settings, meaning that the many lived in even more serious poverty than the averages might suggest, their numbers being constrained through various Malthusian checks to those who could subsist in the setting available to them. Thus limitations on average living standards imposed by *technical* relationships among land, capital and population were aggravated for most people by *social* arrangements which permitted the few to enhance their own welfare at the expense of the many, and to extend this advantage as modernization proceeded.

As elements of modernization were introduced into the system—mainly in the form of injections of capital (through domestic savings, foreign investment, and foreign aid) in new technological dress—our sleeping giant, itself growing at nearly the rate of population growth, began to make its presence known. In the first place, the scarcity of indigenous planning, management and professional talent meant that efforts to assimilate the new capital tended to be concentrated geographically and in large projects so as to conserve scarce domestic talent and to attract supplementary talent from abroad. This meant that capital was not spread widely among those who needed it, the bulk of the population receiving little in the way of additional resources which might help them to make a better living; meanwhile, the security of parents seeming to depend on the raising of children, population continued to grow. Moreover, much of the technology imported from abroad was designed for large scale activities and seemed to work best when assembled in clusters of mutually supportive activities. This new technology often did not require very many people to make it productive and many of the few who could be productively employed had to be highly skilled, and, for a time at least, imported from abroad (Stewart).

This act of the scenario, too, has an element of inevitability about it. If talent was scarce, and new technology was available largely from advanced countries where labor was expensive and where large scale could reduce the wage bill, the concentration of capital was a "logical" consequence. But this "natural" outcome, too, was aggravated in intensity by the colonial propensity for "white highlands," the donor preference for large, visible projects and tied aid, and the tendency of indigenous elites to consolidate and expand their own positions of political and economic power. The social overlay strengthened and exaggerated the technical constraints limiting equitable development (Gotsch).

At the same time, certain advanced country institutional and incentive arrangements were imported along with capital and technology. Capital subsidies, intended to attract capital from abroad, had also the unwanted effects of stimulating capital intensive production and encouraging excess capacity (Bruton). Standard work weeks became common in urban centers of developing nations when the previous custom had been one of sharing available work widely among those seeking it. Wage rates and fringe benefits for those employed in modern activities reflected in some measure advanced country standards, partly to induce labor to accept advanced country styles of discipline and partly to prevent, through legislation and labor union activity, the "exploitation" of domestic labor. The combination of high wages and the standard work week meant that incomes for those fortunate enough to be employed in urban areas were substantially higher than the incomes which could be earned in traditional occupations in rural areas. Indeed, many landlords (and possibly indigenous businessmen) who had earlier felt a social obligation to share work among their constituents were strengthened in their new conviction that "excessive" employment, even at distorted prices, was socially harmful. Moreover, high modern sector wage rates, in combination with the subsidies to capital, fortified the positions of both indigenous elites and multi-national corporations and encouraged both to "save labor." The stage was set for our sleeping giant to stir himself.

The tendency to concentrate infrastructure and industry, and all the other trappings of modernization, in the cities, coupled with a continuing rapid growth of population in rural areas, had the natural and dual consequence of making the rural areas less attractive (population was growing more rapidly than capital and land) and the urban areas more enticing. The underemployed in rural areas began to move to the cities in larger and larger numbers where many of them unfortunately became openly unemployed and dependent on transfer payments from friends and rural families for their support. While the terms of urban employment were attractive, the forms in which new capital was being invested and the nature of the new technologies being installed did not create new jobs anywhere nearly as rapidly as people sought to fill them. The fact that many of the jobs in the modern sector required skills not naturally acquired in rural areas contributed to the rapid expansion of formal education (which provided the necessary credentials if not always the skills) and the tendency for the better educated to concentrate in the urban areas (Edwards and Todaro). Thus, increasing numbers of those openly unemployed in the cities came to be reasonably well educated and posed a growing problem for those in authority. It is more clearly seen now than it was a decade ago that efforts to deal with the visibly unemployed in the city may only stir the giant further while he continues to grow in size.

This is not to say that the elimination of socio-political constraints on development would mean sudden affluence for all, but rather that in seeking to improve employment opportunities for the many it seems necessary to move constructively against both the technical and socio-political conditions which limit choices of development strategies. If the employment problem can be traced to (1) rapid rates of population growth, (2) the introduction of new technologies which soak up limited capital but create few employment opportunities in the process, and (3) the related failure to disperse new capital widely throughout a nation so as to use existing labor and land more productively, to what extent are these phenomena technically or politically determined? In Tanzania, for example, technical constraints seem to be most binding; on the other hand in neighboring Kenya the sharply skewed income distribution which seems to be appearing among Africans may be traceable largely to policy decisions taken in both colonial and post-Independence settings.[3] Unemployment is a problem in both countries.

We shall return frequently to these issues throughout the paper, but in the remainder of this section we shall attempt a more analytical look than our scenario has permitted at relationships between employment and other complementary objectives, at the dimensions of the employment problem, and at the limited evidence which suggests its magnitude.

Employment and Other Objectives

Economists have long regarded increases in the general welfare as being the ultimate objective of development. The direct measurement of such increases in welfare is hazardous at best and has usually foundered on the rock of interpersonal comparisons, which are logically required whenever an improvement in one's welfare is accompanied by a decrease in another's. Thus social scientists and policy makers have often shifted their focus from this analytically complex objective to intermediate objectives, such as employment, growth, productivity, income distribution, and the elimination of poverty, progress toward which can be more clearly measured. None of these alone is a good proxy for increases in the general welfare, although the glamour of growth as a popular substitute has only recently been tarnished. Nevertheless, several perceptive scholars have raised with us, during the course of our seminars, the question as to why we should focus in this study on employment rather than on growth, income distribution, or the elimination of poverty (Jarvis). The relationships among these several objectives are obviously of critical importance to the shape of development.

Employment and growth. The relationship between employment and growth has probably excited most discussion. Will every set of policies intended to increase employment above present levels necessarily result in a lowering of the growth rate? (Is there a necessary tradeoff between the two?) Or are there policies which, if introduced, will increase both employment and growth? The collective insights of our many discussants suggest a two-part hypothesis.

That judgment suggests in the first place that a considerable portion of under-utilized labor does represent at once a diminution of the national income, a symptom of an inefficient economy and an opportunity to promote both growth and employment. The argument is that there are ways of organizing a nation's resources—land, labor and capital—so that output, employment and growth would all be increased relative to existing magnitudes (Bruton).[4] In such circumstances technical conditions do not prevent increases in either employment or growth; inefficiency must be traced to other sources, mainly to the social and political setting in which choices about development strategies are made. It is suggested that, while it may be technically and economically possible to improve *both* employment and growth by correcting price distortions and undertaking structural reforms, the political will is lacking to pursue those strategies. Instead, development strategies are adopted which benefit and strengthen vested interests and which may indeed maximize the growth and welfare of a favored social minority. If the political will could be found, both employment and growth could be increased. There is no tradeoff problem—only the (serious) problem of making the political structure more responsive to the general welfare.[*]

Nevertheless, even in the most favorable of political circumstances, actual employment may fall short of a full utilization of available labor time because other, technical factors limit the work which can be productively performed. The nature of natural resources may limit employment opportunities; or the technologies known to

---

[*] If political considerations do not limit development strategy, growth can be pressed toward its technical limits. There may be, however, several sets of policies which would yield the *same* rate of growth, each having *different* consequences for employment and income distribution. A concern for employment implies that policy makers would prefer that policy set which maximizes employment. There is, however, no tradeoff in this choice, only the exercise of a preference.

be available for development may not encompass labor intensive choices. If, in these circumstances, further employment is sought, it must come at the expense of growth—there is a tradeoff. But the tradeoff means, if exercised, that a country's population will work harder and longer in the aggregate and share a smaller material income—a rather dismal and nonsensical prospect, unless work is to be valued for its own sake. Far better perhaps to find means of sharing the available productive work more widely so that the distribution of income and leisure is improved without reducing aggregate material welfare. Such an approach would require more flexible working arrangements both in and among enterprises, and in particular a skeptical view of overtime and standard-work-week practices which have been borrowed from advanced countries where labor is in relatively short supply. When one considers that the ratio of population to land in most developing countries will certainly double by the end of the century, the burden placed on capital growth and use as a means of creating jobs can be seen to be enormous. The need to find effective means for sharing productive work may loom even larger than it does today.*

The distinction just drawn between situations in which there is and is not a tradeoff between growth and employment is basic to the analytical approach followed in this paper, but it is also too clearly drawn, too pat, to accord with reality. The model assumes a faultless definition of technical and economic policies so that the presence or absence of a tradeoff situation depends solely on Political Will. In reality, of course, the other actors on the stage may not play their parts all that perfectly either. Take one example which happens also to be a critical matter in most developing nations with mixed economies, namely, the problem of defining economic policies which will induce the private sector to behave in a socially circumspect manner.

In the typical developing country there is often an inherent conflict of interest between social welfare and private interests.[6] Such a society must, for example, attempt to provide minimum subsistence for its population, preferably by creating productive jobs for all in its labor force. Private employers in that society, on the other hand, may regard their own mini work forces as variables which, if they can be reduced, may enhance profits and simplify management. The social problem then is to find policies which will induce employers to act in the public interest, i.e., policies which will make it profitable for them to offer productive work to more of the labor force by encouraging them to economize in their use of capital (Bruton). In the absence of constructive policies of these kinds, the growing public concern with unemployment—a strong public-welfare-motivated political will, if you wish—may manifest itself in policies which will force employers, both public and private, to employ more labor even in unproductive circumstances. There is then a tradeoff—not because political will is lacking, but because economic policies are not up to the task at hand.

---

* The productivity of labor is normally defined in terms of those who are employed. So long as full employment obtains—a situation which economists readily assume in conventional theory and one which has been closely approximated in advanced countries since the great depression of the 30's—efforts to increase productivity will normally increase both total output and per capita incomes, and permit the employed to reduce their hours of work and enjoy more leisure.

In circumstances where labor is substantially underutilized, blind efforts to raise the productivity of those employed may increase the numbers unemployed and possibly even reduce levels of output and per capita incomes. When labor is underutilized, the productivity of the entire labor force, whether employed or not, is a more constructive policy guide, because increases in employment which raise the average productivity of the total labor force, and increase total output and per capita incomes—all desirable outcomes—may nevertheless reduce the average productivity of those employed. Such increases in employment would not be sought at all if policy makers were being guided in their decisions by the criterion of average worker productivity.[5]

The balance of this paper is based on the premise that the tradeoff situation in which technical and economic policies are well defined and political will is not an obstacle to their adoption is analytically an arid one—even though increasing employment at the expense of growth in some of these situations may be politically expedient in the short run. The analytically interesting and politically challenging situation is that in which there is no necessary tradeoff between employment and growth but in which the achievement of increased employment and better growth requires improved technical and economic policies and greater political commitment to the general welfare. It is in advances along these lines that lasting employment opportunities and genuine participation in the benefits of growth are to be found, not in make-work expediencies, doles and famine relief.*

An obvious question arises: Is this decision tantamount to advocating more of the same, namely, the pursuit of growth as in the past? I think not. Growing problems of labor utilization suggest that while growth has been *measured* in terms of gross national product in the past, growth has been *pursued* in a much more partial sense. It has been urban in character, to the neglect of rural areas; modern sector oriented, at the cost of the traditional sector; frequently industrial in content, at the expense of agricultural development; usually large scale and capital intensive in nature, instead of small scale and employment creating; and the benefits have tended to accrue to foreign investors and a growing indigenous upper class whose views are influential in the making of policy decisions. It can be argued that growth in the past has been sought for only a privileged segment of the population; the assumption that aggregate growth can be maximized by tending mainly to the welfare of a privileged group is very probably misplaced.[7]

Moreover, past strategies for development have focused on the relief of perceived *scarcities,* not on the utilization of obvious *surpluses.* The most notable scarcities attacked have been domestic savings (often through regressive tax systems) and foreign exchange, usually for the express purpose of increasing the *availability* of capital, the factor of production in shortest supply. But subsidies to capital have encouraged its *use* in capital intensive ways so that the factor in surplus, labor, instead of being drawn into the growth process in ever greater numbers, was often displaced.

An emphasis on employment creation means a focus in designing development strategies on the efficient utilization of factors of production in apparent surplus. This does not mean that capital flow should not be stimulated but it does shift the weight of development strategies to the real purpose of doing so, namely to use and distribute it—geographically, sectorally, temporally, and by scale—so as to absorb surplus factors in productive employment and further growth. That represents a substantial departure from traditional strategies for development in which problems of enlarging the pool of scarce resources have been emphasized, while problems of improving the social efficiency of resource use have received a second order of attention or been assumed to take care of themselves.

Employment and income distribution. Increasingly, income distribution is being regarded as an essential dimension of national welfare and development (Stewart, Jarvis), a view which we share. Let no one be misled, however: the reorientation of

---

* The decision to pursue longer term objectives in this paper should not be mistaken to mean a lack of humanitarian concern for shorter term needs which society should of course attempt to meet. But feeding the unemployed through transfer mechanisms does not create jobs; nor does such sharing mean genuine participation in development.

development strategies toward a fuller utilization of labor along the lines sketched above will not automatically settle problems of income distribution. We can also say with safety that the achievement of an equitable income distribution (however defined) will not automatically ensure that those who are able will have an opportunity to use their capacities in production; participation in the *distribution* of the benefits of growth does not necessarily mean participation in the *production* of those benefits. But the two are related and that relationship merits brief exploration if only to ensure that neither is accepted as a proxy for the other in the design of development strategies.

Income distribution in a country depends on (1) the distribution of income-earning assets—jobs, land, and capital, (2) the provision and distribution of public goods —education, health services, housing, etc., (3) the direction and size of transfer payments, both public and private, and (4) the tax system—through which government activities, including but not limited to activities (2) and (3) just mentioned, are financed. Of these four layers, the first alone acts directly on the distribution of *earned* incomes; the direct effects of the other three are to *redistribute* those earned incomes. Let's peel these layers off in reverse order to end up with employment opportunities, an element in item (1) above.

The tax system is a potential means for modifying inequalities in the distribution of earned incomes. To do so, it should be progressive in nature. Unfortunately, most observers have concluded that tax systems in developing countries are not very progressive, and in some cases may be essentially regressive in nature. The nature of the tax system is an important ingredient in assessing the redistributional effects of transfer payments and public goods, those effects depending not only on who benefits but also on who pays.

Transfer payments are a means of transferring income from those who earn it to others. Public transfer payments are normally intended to provide a minimum income to the needy—the aged, the disabled, the malnourished, the temporarily unemployed—who can then spend to satisfy their needs or suit their preferences. For many, the mechanism is a necessary means of subsistence; for some it is a means of increasing employability and therefore the labor supply. But some public transfer payments may take the form of subsidies to large farmers, plantation owners and industrialists and, if financed through even a mildly progressive tax system, may tend to worsen income distribution.

Much of the social burden of the needy in less developed nations is managed through private transfer payments, largely within the extended family. These transfers probably move mostly from the poor (but active) to the needy—from the small farm family to parents or to children seeking employment in the city—rather than from the rich to the poor. Transfer payments are necessary mechanisms, but they should not be regarded as a long-term substitute for employment opportunities or as a complete solution to problems of income distribution.

The provision of public goods is essentially a transfer payment in kind. The means ensures that the transfer is not dissipated on "non-social" goods and services. The services supplied are normally intended to meet urgent social needs and to improve the *capacity* of people to participate in development through better nutrition, health, education and housing. Public goods tend to increase labor supply; the effect on labor demand depends on how the funds required might otherwise have been used. Moreover, some public goods affect income distribution adversely, as when university level education is heavily subsidized and health facilities are concentrated in urban areas. The need for public goods does not diminish the need for employment opportunities and the provision of necessary public goods is not in itself a basic solution to problems of income distribution.

The roots of the income distribution problem lie in the distribution of *earned* incomes and lasting solutions must come to grips with that issue. The creation and distribution of jobs is one element affecting the distribution of earned incomes. A focus on the creation of employment opportunities, as outlined earlier, will not in itself achieve equity in income distribution but it should help substantially to improve the distribution of earned incomes, partly through direct employment effects and partly because real resources complementary to labor will have to be more widely dispersed as a means of generating employment opportunities.

An employment effort is, of course, no substitute for a progressive tax system or the widespread distribution of essential public goods. On the other hand, overzealous attention to income distribution may lead to concentration on transfer payment mechanisms which may seem to be more easily and quickly achieved than the creation of more job opportunities. But transfer payments do not carry with them three important characteristics which do adhere to employment as a means of generating incomes, namely: (a) productive employment directly increases output; (b) employment is an essential means of providing learning experiences; and (c) employment is a means of relieving the growing frustration often associated with prolonged unemployment. Even in circumstances where full employment cannot be achieved, the latter two of these criteria suggest that work-sharing mechanisms may have substantial social advantages over income-sharing mechanisms.

Employment seems to us to be a critical issue in its own right. Considered in a wide development context, employment-oriented policies should also improve the distribution of earned incomes, particularly if such policies are understood to embrace technological choice and the geographic, sectoral and scalar distribution of capital. Properly conceived, employment and income distribution objectives are complementary to each other, not substitutes to be confused with one another.

Employment and poverty. The alleviation of poverty, usually expressed as a concern for those receiving the lowest incomes in the nation, say the lowest third, is also a very different objective from employment.[8] In the first place, many of the very poor work very long hours but with inadequate skills or resources with which to make even a minimum living. On the other hand, some of those who are openly unemployed may in fact be receiving incomes through the extended family system which would put them above the minimum income line in very poor countries. The creation of more employment opportunities should not be viewed as a solution to the poverty problem, not only for these reasons but also because in the short-run it is unlikely that sufficient employment opportunities can be created for all of those willing and able to work. Moreover, even the creation of ample opportunities for employment cannot help those who are unemployable for one reason or another. We argue only that the provision of more work and the wider sharing of the work that is available would make an important and positive contribution to the alleviation of poverty.

Finally, we should note that these substantive reasons for dealing in this paper with the employment problem have been substantially reinforced by political considerations. Policy makers in many less developed countries are quite clearly concerned with growing problems of employment and indeed in many cases are taking active, if sometimes ill-considered, steps to deal with the most obvious of these problems. Efforts by donor agencies to respond to this need need not portend a slackening of efforts directed at other intermediate objectives, such as growth and a more equitable distribution of its benefits, but rather may demonstrate a recognition that these several objectives are interrelated and often complementary.

Dimensions of the Underutilization of Labor

As our scenario may have indicated, the dimensions of the employment problem in developing countries are not yet well understood. This is partly because the framework used for most analyses so far has been that developed for the analysis of employment problems in the advanced countries, and partly because efforts to gather more appropriate data have been for the most part sporadic, lacking both continuity in collection over time and the discipline of cross-country comparisons. It appears, however, that the most visible dimension of the underutilization of labor in developing countries, namely, open unemployment in the modern sector, is but the tip of an iceberg resting on a stratum of underemployed outside the modern sector, both obscuring larger numbers of others who are visibly active, as in education or civil service employment, but really underutilized. Efforts to clear away the visible portion of the iceberg may simply motivate other layers to emerge; for example, efforts to provide jobs for the unemployed in urban areas may simply entice others from the countryside to take their places, for a time at least. Not surprisingly, our study confirms that the employment problem is likely to be one of long duration and any lasting and comprehensive solution must be one which pervades the entire economy.

In addition to the numbers of people unemployed, many of whom may receive minimal incomes through the extended family system and therefore not rightly classified with the very poor, it is also necessary to consider the dimensions of (1) time (many of those employed would like to work more hours per day, per week or per year), (2) intensity of work (which brings into consideration matters of health and nutrition), and (3) productivity (lack of which can often be attributed to inadequate, complementary resources with which to work). Even these are only the most obvious dimensions of effective work, and factors such as motivation, attitudes, and cultural inhibitions (as against women, for example) must also be considered. Our discussions have thrown up the following forms of underutilization of labor, which may indicate the diversity of the phenomenon but which further study will probably show to be incomplete:

1. *Open unemployment*—both voluntary (people who exclude from consideration some jobs for which they could qualify, implying that they have some means of support other than employment) and involuntary.
2. *Underemployment*—those working less (daily, weekly, or seasonally) than they would like to work.
3. *The visibly active but underutilized*—those who would not normally be classified as either unemployed or underemployed by the above definitions, but who in fact have found alternative means of "marking time," including
   (a) *Disguised underemployment.* Many people seem occupied on farms or employed in government on a full-time basis even though the services they render may actually require much less than full time. Social pressures on private industry also may result in substantial amounts of disguised under-employment. If available work is openly shared among those employed, the disguise disappears and underemployment becomes explicit.
   (b) *Hidden unemployment.* Those who are engaged in "second choice" nonemployment activities, perhaps notably education and household chores, primarily because job opportunities are not (i) available at the levels of education already attained, or (ii) open to women, given social mores.

Thus, educational institutions and households become "employers of last resort." Moreover, many of those enrolled for further education may be among the less able, as indicated by their inability to compete successfully for jobs before pursuing further education.

(c) *The prematurely retired.* This phenomenon is especially apparent, and apparently growing, in the civil service. In many countries, retirement ages are falling at the same time that longevity is increasing, primarily as one means of creating promotion opportunities for some of the large numbers pressing up from below.*

Even a cursory consideration of this preliminary analytical framework suggests complex interrelationships and how little is really known either quantitatively or qualitatively about how these dimensions have changed over time or how and why they vary from one country to another. A clear need exists in our view for new concepts, basic data, and empirical analyses related to the underutilization of labor in developing countries; hopefully as such investigations are pursued, they will include common elements on which comparative studies can be based.

The several studies already completed or currently underway on rural-urban migration and open unemployment in the cities suggest that there is substantial substitutability among these several dimensions of underutilization of labor and that one form can easily and quickly be transformed into another.[9] Thus, efforts to relieve open unemployment in the cities seem to create a vacuum which is quickly filled by others from rural areas who in turn become openly unemployed in the cities. This transformation may not be direct; some who leave rural areas in favor of the cities may leave jobs behind to be filled by others who exchange underemployment or schooling for the jobs vacated. (Calcutta provides an interesting example of reverse migration during the latter half of the decade of the 60's. The lack of development activity in Calcutta throughout the decade apparently caused some to give up their hopes in the cities for the slender existence available in the rural hinterland.)[10] Moreover, while education is often regarded as a necessary means of qualifying for a job, there is growing evidence to suggest, notably in India, that it is increasingly regarded as a desirable substitute for unemployment. But this may at best be a temporary (and expensive) storage place for the unemployed until the growing numbers so occupied begin to emerge at the other end of the system with credentials but not jobs.

These examples of substitutability suggest the iceberg phenomenon alluded to before, and an important policy consequence which may follow from it. Much of the rising political concern with the so-called employment problem is a reaction to the visible political threat posed by growing open unemployment, particularly in urban areas and among the better educated. But to measure the depth of the problem by the number openly unemployed is to underestimate it, leading very likely to policies which are inadequate in both scope and magnitude. Chipping away at the problem in this way is not likely to make a visible dent and may indeed only prolong and possibly magnify the extent of both the economic and political problems to which the policy is directed.

---

* Some would add the following to this list:
  4. *The impaired*—those who may work full time but whose intensity of effort is seriously impaired through malnutrition or lack of common preventive medicine.
  5. *The unproductive*—those who can provide the human resources necessary for productive work but who struggle long hours with inadequate complementary resources to make their inputs yield even the essentials of life.
  This has not been done in the text because neither of these categories represents an underutilization of available work effort. Both are, however, employment problems.

An essential characteristic of the employment problem is the way in which it permeates the whole economy. It is therefore only through revision of total development strategy and its application to rural and urban areas, modern and traditional sectors, public and private activities, and education and job creation that lasting solutions can be found. But to imagine that complete solutions are likely to be found over any short time horizon such as the next decade is wishful thinking. Given rapid rates of population growth and the pervasiveness and enormity of the problem, it is probably more realistic to think of the employment problem in many of the developing countries which adopt only limited employment strategies as surviving the population problem.

TABLE 1

ESTIMATES OF GROWTH OF THE LABOR FORCE IN
LESS DEVELOPED COUNTRIES: 1950-1980

	Annual percentage rates		
	1950-1965	1965-1980	1970-1980
Developed countries	1.1	1.0	1.0
Less developed countries	1.7	2.2	2.3
Regions			
Other East Asia	1.8	3.0	3.1
Middle South Asia[1]	1.4	1.9	2.0
South East Asia[2]	1.9	2.4	2.5
South West Asia[3]	1.9	2.8	2.8
West Africa	2.2	2.3	2.3
East Africa	1.3	1.8	1.8
Central Africa	1.0	1.2	1.2
North Africa	1.1	2.5	2.6
Tropical South America	2.7	3.0	3.0
Central America	2.8	3.3	3.4
Temperate South America	1.5	1.5	1.5
Caribbean	1.8	2.3	2.3

SOURCE: David Turnham (with assistance of I. Jaeger), *The Employment Problem in Less Developed Countries*, O.E.C.D., June 1970, derived from data given in J.N. Ypsilantis, "World and Regional Estimates and Projections of Labour Force" ISLEP/A/VII.4/Add.1, 1966 (mimeo.). (Excludes Sino-Soviet countries.)

NOTES: [1]Includes Ceylon, India, Iran and Pakistan.

[2]Includes Burma, Cambodia, Indonesia, Malaysia, the Philippines and Thailand.

[3]Middle East countries.

The Supply of Labor and the Extent of its Underutilization

The number of people seeking work in a developing country depends mainly on the size and age composition of its population; the rate of growth in the labor force depends mainly on the rate of growth in population, other factors such as participation rates of women, playing a relatively minor role (Stolnitz). We also know that labor forces in advanced countries have over the last decade grown at approximately one percent per year while the labor force in less developed countries has been growing at approximately twice that rate. We also know that the rate of growth of the labor force in developing countries has itself been growing from approximately 1.6 percent per annum in the decade of the 50's to approximately 2 percent per annum in the decade of the 60's. Present reasonably based projections—after all, those who enter the labor force over the next 15 years have already been born—suggest a growth of 2.3 percent for the decade of the 70's. (See Table 1) At this rate the labor force would nearly double in size over the next 30 years and as arable land will not grow substantially over that period, the burden imposed on the wise use of increases in capital as a means of creating employment opportunities is very substantial indeed. In these circumstances, the importance of reducing the rate of population growth as a means of easing employment problems can hardly be questioned even though the first impact of such reductions on the labor force cannot possibly be felt until 15 years after an initial reduction in birth rates.

TABLE 2

RATES OF URBAN UNEMPLOYMENT BY AGE

	15-24	15 and over
Ghana, 1960 Large towns	21.9	11.6
Bogota, Colombia, 1968	23.1	13.6
Buenos Aires, Argentina, 1965	6.3[1]	4.2[2]
Chile, 1968 Urban areas	12	6[3]
Caracas, 1966	37.7	18.8
Guyana, 1965 Mainly urban areas	40.4	21.0[4]
Panama, 1963/64 Urban areas	17.9[5]	10.4
Uruguay, 1963 Mainly urban	18.5	11.8
Venezuela, 1969 Urban areas	14.8	7.9
Bangkok, Thailand, 1966	7.7	3.4
Ceylon, 1968 Urban areas	39.0	15.0
India, 1961/62 Urban areas	8.0	3.2[6]
Korea, 1966 Non-farm households	23.6	12.6
Malaya, 1965 Urban areas	21.0	9.8
Philippines, 1965 Urban areas	20.6[7]	11.6[8]
Singapore, 1966	15.7[9]	9.2
Tehran City, Iran, 1966	9.4	4.6

SOURCE: David Turnham, *op. cit.*

NOTES: [1] 14-29 age group   [4] over 14 age group   [7] 10-24 age group
        [2] 14 plus   [5] 15-29 age group   [8] 10 plus
        [3] 12 plus age group [6] 15-60 age group   [9] 15-29 age group

Current rates of open unemployment in the cities of less developed countries vary substantially but an average rate for the major cities might run as high as 10 percent. The full gravity of the problem is not exposed, however, until one examines the age distribution of those who are unemployed in the cities. Table 2 shows that the rates of urban unemployment in the age group 15 to 24 are just about double the rates of unemployment among the urban labor force as a whole. Moreover, increasing numbers of those who are unemployed are reasonably well educated and many of the educated who have taken jobs are over qualified for the jobs that they have been able to get. Dissatisfaction is not restricted to those who are entirely without work.

These data relate mainly to the tip of the iceberg, the openly unemployed, whereas the underemployed in both urban and rural areas are themselves a serious measure of the degree of underutilization of labor in developing countries. Unfortunately, the evidence on underemployment is not good, and its measurement is both difficult and costly. The ILO Employment Study in Colombia suggested that perhaps 30 percent of the available labor, counting open unemployment and various kinds of under-employment, was unutilized.[11] Similar figures could be cited for Sri Lanka and Kenya and several other countries, but the definitions being used are ambiguous, the concepts employed are not comparable, and the data on which they are based are sketchy indeed.

Information on unproductive employment, hidden unemployment and the prematurely retired is simply not available but it is the judgment of those who know the less developed nations well that these too represent serious components of labor underutilization (Wamalwa).

The One-Sector Fallacy

Given the severe data limitations, our efforts during the course of this study to describe the magnitude and complexity of the employment problem in quantitative terms have not met with great success. This area emerges instead as one in which donor support may be particularly valuable and constructive. Nevertheless, the information which is available does support the judgment of our consultants that the employment problem is so complex and pervasive that it is unlikely to yield to relief measures directed at any one sector of economic activity alone, even when so-called multiplier effects are taken into account (Krishna, Thomas). This is in our view an important policy conclusion supported by experiences with limited efforts in a number of different countries.

If indeed the underutilization of labor pervades the entire economy in one form or another and opportunities for employment are less than they might be in all sectors (because of inappropriate policies with respect to factor prices, investment, and technology), efforts to relieve the employment problem by stimulating work opportunities in one sector alone are likely to be inadequate and may indeed penalize that sector while others continue to be favored. Take rural public works programs, which have frequently been suggested as a principal means of alleviating employment problems, as an example. Rural public works, properly planned and efficiently administered, are a form of investment, and even a massive public works program probably could not absorb as much as 10 percent of gross national product. Yet the proposed policy is really to suggest that the underutilization which pervades the entire economy should find its principal relief in the creation of employment opportunities related to the production of only 10 percent of GNP. In these circumstances, the producers of the other 90 percent—agricultural products, manufactured goods, other construction, and trade and other services—are left to make their employment decisions, as before, on the basis of distorted factor prices, etc. The expansion of what is in most developing countries a relatively small rural infrastructure "industry" is generally regarded as a step in the right direction, but it is too much to expect that such programs alone can absorb the underutilized labor which exists throughout the economy.

Even programs aimed at improving employment opportunities in agriculture, which in many developing countries produces perhaps 50 percent of the gross national product and employs 70 percent of the labor force, are not likely to be sufficient by themselves (Krishna). Similarly, the industrial sector, which will undoubtedly continue to grow more rapidly than the agricultural sector in less developed countries, cannot be viewed as an employer of last resort without discouraging the very growth on which additional employment opportunities depend.[12] Some countries have attempted to use the civil service as an employer of last resort, but the effect is usually one of providing a facade for unproductive work (Wamalwa).

Table 3 contains data for the decade of the sixties displaying relationships between output and employment for major economic sectors in Latin America. In general output has grown twice as fast as employment, though the relationship varies considerably from one sector to another. While employment in agriculture has not kept pace with population growth, the dominance of the sector has meant that most new jobs have been created in agriculture. Apparent employment creation in services probably reflects largely the failure of other sectors to create productive jobs rapidly enough to absorb increases in the labor force. The service sector is in a sense an employer of last resort; those who cannot find other jobs press themselves into domestic service and government employment, often with very low social productivity.

TABLE 3

ANNUAL GROWTH RATES IN EMPLOYMENT AND OUTPUT BY SECTOR
IN LATIN AMERICA, 1960-1969

	Employment (1)	Output (2)	Elasticity of Employment (1)/(2)
Agriculture	1.5	4.0	0.4
Mining	2.2	4.2	0.5
Manufacturing	2.3	5.9	0.4
Construction	4.0	5.0	0.8
Transport and public utilities	3.4	5.4	0.6
Commerce and finance	4.1	5.1	0.8
Miscellaneous services	4.0	3.9	1.0
Unspecified (services)	8.2	7.3	1.1
Aggregate employment and output	2.8	4.8	0.6

SOURCE: *Economic Survey of Latin America 1968* (New York, United Nations, 1970), Tables I-22 and I-23.

If our judgment is correct that the emerging visible form of labor underutilization is but a single manifestation of a latent problem of long standing, great magnitude, and many dimensions, and that its alleviation is fundamental to the achievement of greater equity in the distribution of the benefits of growth, the modification of development strategies in order to generate increasing numbers of productive employment opportunities becomes a matter of major importance. Whether or not effective strategies exist or can be found depends in part on the technical, social and political constraints which bind them and the extent to which development strategies themselves can loosen those bonds within reasonable time horizons. The nature of those constraints is an essential part of the diagnosis of the employment problem.

The Limits to Feasibility

The eventual resolution of the ldc employment problem depends not only on the direct employment effects of the year-to-year choice of development strategies but also on how effectively these strategies widen the field of choice in subsequent years by pressing back presently inhibiting conditions. The distinction between constraint and strategy variables is essentially arbitrary depending as it does primarily on judgments as to how quickly substantial change can be effected and what instruments of change it is reasonable to entertain. Our discussions have disclosed eight environmental constraints which in most ldc situations are likely, even with constructive effort, to change very slowly over time: (1) the rate of population growth; (2) the physical and technological characteristics of production; (3) the technical form and location of resources; (4) the behavioral and cultural characteristics of households and communities; (5) the organization and capacity to plan and implement; (6) the international setting; (7) the ownership and management of resources; and (8) the internal structure of political and economic power. Policies intended to affect these conditions cannot be expected to yield visible results quickly, but to move them in right directions is essential to any lasting employment solution. In a very loose sense, the first six of these can be regarded as essentially technical in nature while the last two represent social and political conditions subject to more rapid change (favorable and unfavorable) if indeed a will and a force for change exist.

Population Growth

The direct relationship of population growth to employment is through its effect on the labor force, on the supply of labor (Stolnitz). Its effect on employment opportunities is less clear depending as it does on what happens to national income and capital accumulation. The ratio of dependent to working population rises with increases in fertility (in many ldcs 40 to 50 percent of the population is below the age of 15). Those who are working must share their incomes with more people leaving less for saving and capital accumulation. Moreover, with high rates of population growth, a larger share of the reduced saving may have to be devoted to the provision of social services, such as education, health care and nutritional supplements, leaving even less saving to be invested in more immediately productive ways.

There is little doubt that reducing the rate of population growth is a principal means for alleviating the employment problem in developing countries, both because of the direct effect it would have on reducing the rate of growth in the numbers seeking work and because of its indirect effects on national income and capital accumulation permitting more of the nation's resources to be devoted to the creation of jobs. But because of the lag between birth and the attainment of working age, the impact of any such reduction on the rate of growth of the labor force will be substantially delayed. In what promises to be a very long interim period, it will be especially critical to find means of increasing the stock of capital and yields and employment per acre of land at rates significantly greater than population growth, if the necessary conditions for improving job opportunities are to be met.

Technology and Employment

The availability of natural resources and the circumstances of climate and rainfall obviously condition the kinds of products that can be produced in a nation and provide certain limits to the ways in which production can be carried out. While discovery may lead to dramatic changes in some natural resources, such as petroleum and metal ores, in agriculture for the most part ecological conditions can only gradually be modified through irrigation, clearing and replenishment of soils (Gotsch).

To create jobs for a large labor force with limited supplies of both capital and land is a challenging task because the amount of land and capital available per worker in the event that everyone is to be given employment is so very small by the standards prevailing in advanced countries (Stewart). The burden in these circumstances falls on the physical, biological and chemical technologies available for combining small amounts of complementary resources with large amounts of labor in ways which are productive in the physical, economic and cultural circumstances of the country. The critical role of technology in increasing agricultural output in ldcs has been recognized by the Foundation and other donor agencies, and their interest has been reflected in continuing support of the several international agricultural research institutes. In recent years these institutes have also turned their attention to the critical problem of creating agricultural technologies which can enhance employment as well as output.

The need to develop appropriate technologies in fields other than agriculture seems clearly important (Khan), but the kind of systematic response which might be effective is a much more controversial question and our seminars revealed no definitive solution. It is a fact that over 95 percent of the research and development funds devoted to the development of new technologies, to new methods of combining capital and labor, are spent in the advanced countries, usually under the instruction to save labor because capital is relatively cheap and labor is relatively expensive. But the relative scarcity of labor and capital is reversed in developing countries and their own poverty prevents them from allocating substantial resources to the discovery of new technologies which can combine the resources at their disposal in ways which are domestically productive and internationally competitive.

Unfortunately, we cannot sort out to what extent the use of capital intensive technologies can be attributed to (a) the unavailability of labor intensive alternatives (Stewart), (b) inappropriate conditions of choice (information, prices, etc.) (Bruton), and (c) irrational preferences for sophisticated methods of production (Pickett et al, Sadli). Examples of all of these have come to our attention during the course of our study. Employment considerations suggest that social choices should reflect preferences for products which are labor intensive in their production and in any configuration of output for those methods of production which generate most employment. But the task of ensuring that sound social choices are indeed made is extremely complex.

Evidence is also beginning to emerge which suggests that much of the limited capital equipment available in developing countries is in fact idle most of the time and often for more of the time than comparable capital would be idle in advanced countries (Bruton). Much of it is operated for only one shift, five days a week; much of it is used only seasonally; much of it is idle awaiting parts and repair. The reasons are not yet entirely clear but may include inefficiency in repair and maintenance; inefficient means for delivery of inputs; insufficient public infrastructure, such as street lighting and public transportation, which may limit multiple-shift work; and daily and seasonal price variations which may make the more intensive use of capital unprofitable.[13]

Some of our participants felt that "technology" should include not only biological, chemical and physical types—the "hard" technologies—but also "soft" technologies such as administrative and management structures and organizational means for delivering services (health, education, credit, inputs and advice). These forms of technology, when borrowed from advanced country social and cultural settings for which they have been developed, have also often turned out to be inefficient in other social settings. Thus soft and hard technologies alike may require modification to make them efficient in new situations and at the same time impose new disciplines on old cultures.

The Technical Distribution of Resources

The distribution of resources takes one form which is largely technical in nature. If capital is congealed in the form of large tractors and combines on large farms or has taken the shape of oil refineries, automobile assembly plants, or fertilizer factories, it cannot be changed by legislation into small, hand and power tools for craftsmen and small farmers. It can only be changed gradually as depreciation makes funds available for replacement or other uses. Moreover, the freedom to choose among future uses of capital is seriously impeded by the commitments which existing forms of capital imply to owners, buyers, employees, and suppliers. Policies on capital allocation are best introduced before such commitments are so large as to impede change.

Behavior, Skills and Social Organization

Policies, other than those introduced and enforced by fiat, depend for their effectiveness on their influence on decision making units, be they individuals, households, employers, villages or communities, or associations of farmers, workers, the landless, and the unemployed. To design effective policies, it is necessary to understand to which variables decision making units react and how their behavior will be altered when these variables are changed (Nash, Aggarwal). A better understanding of decision making units in developing countries, particularly in traditional settings where change is most needed and modern sector experience is least applicable, is essential to the design and enforcement of constructive development policies.[14]

The behavior of households with respect to the supply of labor, production, new technologies and patterns of consumption is perhaps the most pervasive element conditioning social and economic development. The dominance of the family as a decision making unit in most developing countries is not a matter of serious challenge. Thus it may be the family which inventories its human resources, decides who will work on the farm, who will go to the school, who will work for the next door neighbor, and who will be sent to the city to seek money income for the family. In this way, the family can distribute its resources in search of several opportunities for advancement, can spread its risks, and hopefully maximize its gains. Ceremonial occasions and religious festivals can provide an incentive for production even without access to outside markets, though when access to outside markets is provided, the persistence of such customs may act to reduce investment in methods which would increase productivity. Traditions such as the extended family may mean that increases in production must be widely shared with non-participants in the production process thus reducing incentives to increase productivity. Similarly, respect for burial plots in widely scattered locations may make efforts to consolidate landholdings extremely difficult. And efforts to create cooperatives in settings in which people are highly suspicious of one another are not likely to be very successful. Many of these attitudes and cultural conditions affect also the ability of communities to absorb and manage industrial and agricultural technologies. We are persuaded that a better knowledge of household behavior would help in the construction of improved development policies, particularly those directed at rural development.

The traditional functions of communities and villages are also often constraints on development and transformation. In the traditional setting, community and village organization is usually introverted, concerned with internal law and order (mainly the settlement of disputes), the arrangement of community festivals, and the administration of mechanisms for sharing work and income. As external relationships assume greater importance, internal cohesion may be threatened. The integration of the community into a wider circle of social and economic activity may tend to break down feudal landlord/peasant relationships in favor of more horizontal, class oriented associations which may in turn threaten local positions of power and create in the process opposition to further change (Thomas). Indeed, the growing value of external links of transport and communications may threaten the very existence of the community if it is disadvantageously located by the new criteria.

The Organization and Capacity to Plan and Implement

Widespread development requires a capacity to plan and implement at all levels of government (Barnett, Valdes). If this capacity is overestimated, policies may be established which have no chance of success; if this capacity is underestimated, many feasible policies may be ruled out of consideration. That capacity is made up of appropriate organization and the existence and proper placement of planning and management skills.

It is understandable that in the search for national unity, stability, and control, newly independent nations would seek a high degree of centralization. This tendency was reinforced in most cases by the recognition that the nation's capacity to plan and implement was limited, and that scarce domestic planning and management skills could be most easily supplemented from abroad by offering expatriates attachments to central government ministries and large, attractively located projects. This combination of circumstances has contributed to the centralization of power, the concentration on and development of large projects clustered together as a means of conserving scarce managerial resources, and the relative neglect of the rural hinterland. Thus, the natural disparities between urban and rural settings have been exaggerated. Even though planning and management skills have grown substantially over the years, little has been done to provide an organization for and placement of personnel which would promote more widespread development through greater decentralization. Instead, increasing numbers of qualified people have been placed in central government positions which are often supernumerary in character, and which have been created more to provide employment than to find productive uses for the skills acquired. Thus, today underestimations of the capacity to plan and implement at local levels in conjunction with strong vested interests in centralization probably rule out of consideration many constructive policies for rural development. Moreover, one finds large numbers of educated people employed in the urban centers of nations when the need for such people in the rural areas goes unmet.

Centralized planning has naturally concentrated on the formation of macro-economic policies, such as tax rates and structures, tariffs and foreign exchange rates, pricing policies for agricultural inputs and outputs, and interest rate and monetary policies, and on sophisticated project evaluation techniques appropriate for large projects and necessary for obtaining foreign aid. The concentration on these kinds of issues is reflected as well in special training programs for planners established both in less developed countries and abroad, thus strengthening the idea that planning is essentially a macro-economic exercise. Planning at lower levels of government must take most of these variables, such as support prices, exchange rates, interest rates, and the location of large projects, as given. The task at local levels is to assess the availability and quality of resources, to absorb and assess available technologies, to establish patterns of infrastructure and development, to identify and establish priorities among social needs, such as nutrition, health and education, and to decide what to produce given opportunities, support prices, and the availability of inputs and markets. These levels of planning are obviously not independent of each other and the need for an efficient two-way flow of information and for action on new information is a necessary ingredient of an efficient planning process (Gotsch, Thomas). This requires an organization for local outreach and feedback which does not exist in most developing countries. Indeed, little attention has been devoted by development planners anywhere in the world to the problems involved in creating the methodology and organization necessary for effective multi-level planning.

A critical problem in local level planning is the integration of the economic, physical and social aspects of planning. These different functions are typically separated, indeed one might say isolated, in central governments and the separation there may not be too costly. But at the local level the integration of these functions, and indeed of the functions of the several ministries which may extend into the local level, is absolutely necessary if effective and coordinated development is to be pursued. The problems of integration at the local level are obviously great, involving as they do the disciplines of different subject matters and the highly valued autonomies of many central ministries. Means for overcoming these difficulties will entail both research and practical experimentation (Barnett).[15]

The International Setting

There is growing concern in the less developed countries that participation in international economic affairs may offer less potential for domestic development than it was once thought to have. This disillusionment may result from a combination of high expectations and poor performance, but it should not disguise the fact that a country with links to the rest of the world has opportunities open to it which would not exist if it were closed. The rest of the world is at once a market for products, a source of raw material, machinery and consumer goods, a reservoir of technological knowledge and experience, and a source of capital and human resources. The problem is to use these opportunities selectively and wisely to promote development and employment, to reduce the barriers which limit participation, and to cushion the shocks which sometimes accompany international involvement (Sadli, Vaitsos). We assume that the advantages of international participation are substantial; otherwise a consideration of the risks, costs, and constraints associated with involvement in international economic affairs would be pointless.

The extent to which a country chooses to involve itself in international economic affairs is not simply a matter for economic analysis. The gains from trade and other international economic activities must be balanced against the risk that supplies may be cut off and markets foreclosed for political reasons. Indeed, the concern with self-sufficiency apparent in the development policies of most less developed countries, in common with the advanced countries, is essentially politically derived. Thus, self-sufficiency arguments are normally addressed to the production of essential foods, basic minerals and raw materials, and the means of defense. But political and economic affairs are much more intertwined than this simple example would suggest. Until we understand better how political affairs influence economic policies, we can say little more than that, as political stability increases throughout the world, the opportunities for moving away from self-sufficiency in favor of more employment-oriented development strategies should increase.

Barriers to trade, migration, and the flow of capital and information represent perhaps the most serious international constraint on the generation of employment opportunities in developing countries. Many of the barriers to trade thrown up by advanced countries are intended to protect long established industries which have nevertheless demonstrated their inability to compete in world markets. It is ironic that the ingenuity in advanced countries which has so successfully created new products and new markets has never been successfully turned to the problem of eliminating, with equity, inefficient industries. Typically, these industries have become inefficient because their methods of production are relatively labor intensive, precisely the kind of industry in which developing countries have a comparative advantage. The gradual elimination of such inefficient industries in advanced countries should free resources for more productive uses in the advanced countries and at the same time provide substantial and expanding markets for many of the products which less developed countries can produce competitively.

Of the other barriers, perhaps the most serious are those which limit the flow of technological information and experience. The patent system in particular, originally intended to provide limited exclusive rights in exchange for disclosure of information, seems often to be abused and on occasion to have precisely diametric effects, namely to provide perpetual rights with no disclosure. As the patent system should in theory be the main method for disseminating information internationally, serious study of its operation and effects as a basis for modification seems long overdue.

An international constraint which is less susceptible to relaxation no matter how great goodwill might be is that of natural biases in the products and technology which can be borrowed from the advanced countries (Stewart). Per capita incomes in advanced countries are perhaps on the average about twenty times per capita incomes in the less developed countries and the products produced in the advanced countries are naturally those which will appeal to people whose incomes are substantially higher than those in the less developed nations. Moreover, there is some evidence to suggest that these kinds of products in general require capital intensive methods of production because of the low tolerances and high quality standards demanded. When such products are introduced into less developed countries they can be afforded by perhaps only the top ten percent of income receivers. When their production is taken up in the less developed countries, the methods used must be capital intensive in nature drawing scarce investment funds from the production of other products which might be produced by more labor intensive means. Whether the degree of such biases will diminish over time depends very much on whether the gap between per capita incomes in less developed nations and those in advanced countries diminishes. Present evidence suggests that the gap continues to widen so that the outlook, at least for the next decade or so, is that such biases will increase, not decrease.

Even if capital and expatriate skills and experience can be attracted to developing countries on favorable terms, there is the risk that such resources will not add to domestic supplies, at least not in their entirety, but will rather substitute for supplies that might otherwise have been forthcoming domestically. There is some evidence to suggest for example that domestic savings rates are somewhat less in countries which receive large amounts of foreign capital and that learning opportunities for indigenous people may be reduced by the substantial import of expertise from abroad. Avoiding these kinds of substitution effects is obviously a primary responsibility of less developed nations; foreign capital and expertise should not be regarded as an unblemished blessing.

The magnitude of explicit international economic activities, such as trade and capital movements, is growing much more rapidly than domestic economic activities. The trend is clearly in the direction of greater interdependence among nations, not less. But there are signs that interdependence takes other less explicit forms as well and these seem to be less well understood. Many domestic economic activities have unintended spillover effects on other nations and as the bulk of the world's economic activity takes place in advanced countries, the direction of flow of these spillover effects is largely from advanced countries. The advanced countries are using up a disproportionate share of the world's irreplaceable resources, and in the process, the off flow of waste from their economic activities, through the oceans and air space, limits the economic opportunities open to far distant countries. The Scandinavian experiment in which citizens of one country may bring damage suits in the courts of another will be interesting to watch.

Ownership and Management of Resources

The present pattern of resource distribution (land and capital) in any nation is a net result of a wide array of past decisions both public and private, and therefore may differ widely from one nation to another. But just as it derives from the past it conditions the future. The distribution of income, which depends in part but not entirely on the distribution of resources, affects employment opportunities primarily by modifying the pattern of domestic demand, possibly by changing the magnitude of savings, the proportion invested at home, and the form and location of that investment, and by modifying the efficiency of the labor force at work.

It is perhaps most common to view distribution in terms of ownership, though that concept varies considerably from one country to another, comprising different bundles of rights with respect to use, disposition, duration, comprehensiveness (surface, mineral and/or water rights), and access to income earned. A second dimension of resource distribution is control and management. In what organization, family or individual resides the power to make decisions over resource use?

Ownership can be public or private, diffused or concentrated; management can be large scale or small scale. Ownership and management can be coincident, as in the case of owner managed, public or private, farms and enterprises, or these functions can be separated, as in the case of absentee landlords, corporations with widely diffused stock ownership, or state owned lands leased to individual farmers or cooperatives. Moreover, ownership may be concentrated while units of management are small scale, as when state owned lands are leased to small individual farmers, or ownership may be diffused with management large scale, as in the case of many corporations in the private sector. Which configurations of ownership and management are most favorable to employment?

Among our seminar participants and with respect to agriculture, most felt that small family owned farms, supported by efficient delivery systems for inputs, credit and advice, provided both the right level for management decisions and the incentives necessary for the full and constructive use of land resources (Gotsch, Griffin). There was general agreement that a system of absentee landlords was most injurious to both employment and efficient land use because the high rentals charged eliminated tenant incentives for both innovation and employment, the gains from either activity accruing normally to the landlord.

The obstacles to constructive change in forms of ownership and management were regarded as mainly political in nature, such changes being technically feasible through the passage and enforcement of appropriate legislation regarding nationalization, land ceilings, and landlord/tenant relationships. While problems of enforcement and implementation were often serious, these difficulties, too, often had political origins (Valdes).

The distribution of income depends, of course, on the ownership of resources and the ways in which the earnings of resources are divided between ownership and management; it also depends on the array of employment opportunities, earning differentials by occupation and location, transfer payments whether through government or the extended family, and the provision of public goods, such as health and education services. Positive incentive effects are associated with those incomes which derive from participation in production, that is, earned incomes. Transfers and public goods may improve the working efficiency of the labor force by raising levels of nutrition and skills, but to the extent that they can be substituted for earned incomes, they probably diminish incentives.

A more debatable effect of a more equal income distribution is its influence on aggregate savings and the form and location of investment. In recent years the argument that people with higher incomes save a greater proportion of their incomes and that therefore an unequal distribution of income increases aggregate saving has been challenged, though not conclusively. A more powerful argument is that more of the savings of the wealthy in developing countries finds its way abroad or is invested in unproductive forms such as jewelry and precious metals, whereas the savings of those of lower income groups is normally invested domestically, usually to improve small scale farms and enterprises, and may be more widely and effectively distributed throughout a nation.

Perhaps the main employment argument advanced for a more equal income distribution is its effects on patterns of consumption. The argument is really twofold, namely, that the consumption patterns of the wealthy tend to favor products which must be imported and therefore draw foreign exchange away from more essential uses, and that the domestic products demanded by the wealthy are weighted toward luxury goods which by their very nature require more capital intensive methods to produce and therefore reduce the employment opportunities which could be generated with greater equality (Stewart). The first of these arguments is reasonably well substantiated; the second requires further investigation and empirical research. The weight of the evidence now available does suggest that greater equality of income distribution would increase employment opportunities in most developing countries. The question is, by how much?

The Political Structure and Policy Formation

Most changes in government policy with respect to development improve the economic situation of some members of society at the expense of others. These shifts in economic advantage may be direct and obvious, as in the case of land reform or higher support prices for food crops, or indirect and indeed unclear, as in the case of a general increase in income taxes where the incidence of the associated benefits of government services is difficult to trace. Similarly, efforts to reduce the employment problem in developing countries will generate conflicts of interest ranging from the subtle to the explicit between such groups as the rich and the poor, the employed and the unemployed, local and central authorities, rural and urban dwellers, and industry and agriculture.

Policy makers who must resolve or override such conflicts of interest can be neither independent of nor objective about the conflicts they perceive. The circumstances which limit their freedom of choice and the factors which influence their decisions are important elements in determining what is or is not feasible in a particular setting

(Griffin). That political structure and political behavior differ widely from one situation to another is clear. How these conditions can be changed in order to widen the range of feasible policies which can be considered in constructing employment strategies is not so well known.

It is, however, precisely the problem of political feasibility which accounts for much of the observable gap between professional knowledge about employment strategies and the programs which are in fact introduced, enforced and implemented. It is at political levels that policies are decided (if not determined) and it is at other points in the political apparatus (the civil service and local authorities, for example) that policies can be implemented, deflected or scuttled (Gotsch, Thomas). The set of political institutions (and the powers reflected through them) is the amorphous locus within which the attitude of government to employment is determined and then reflected in the extent to which development strategies are permitted to pursue employment and growth to technical as opposed to political limits (Gurley, Valdes).

The political choice is often one between satisfying social needs and protecting individual rights. While the circumscription of individual rights in favor of general welfare is a recognized role of government, most political processes are more responsive to the wishes of the wealthy than to the needs of the poor. The emerging employment problem is a striking example of the kind of dilemma social problems can pose for governing elites. Growing unemployment threatens political stability and the power of elites, but effective policies for alleviating the problem may themselves erode vested interests. Not surprisingly, governments respond differently to this dilemma, some exercising more police power, others betting on surface remedies and emergency schemes and still others searching for fundamental changes in development policies.

Problems of political feasibility are not, of course, limited to the center. They exist as well at state, provincial, and urban levels of decision making. Local elites may be reluctant to initiate local programs which will erode their own positions and indeed may siphon away from the local poor many of the benefits of well intentioned programs initiated at national levels. Examples were also cited of instances in which constructive, locally initiated projects were stymied by lack of support from the center.

A Note of Optimism

There is naturally a note of pessimism emerging from this discussion of the bounds imposed on development by the settings in which less developed nations find themselves. The purpose is not to smother optimism with gloom but rather to temper it with reality, so that assessments about both problems and opportunities can be more soundly based.

The evidence of the past decade suggests that many of the constraints identified above are less binding today than they were a decade ago. Some growth rates of population have already been reduced and many population programs are in place that did not exist ten years back; the scope for technological choice has also widened, perhaps primarily as a result of successful research in a number of the international agricultural research institutes; the five percent rate of growth for less developed countries, once regarded as an optimistic figure, was achieved on the average during the decade of the 60's and as population grew less rapidly than income, per capita incomes are now larger and there is more capital available per member of the labor force; the management and other professional skills necessary to multi-level planning and implementation have grown rapidly in developing countries over the past decade; and recognition that the employment problem is both serious and lasting has been growing among policy makers. As some of the constraints limiting feasibility have been relaxed, a somewhat wider range of development and employment strategies can now be entertained. Thus, while the employment problem has almost certainly increased in magnitude over the last decade, opportunities for dealing with it constructively are also greater.

Strategies for Improving Employment

Technical strategies for improving employment in developing nations require continuing research and empirical study, but the state of knowledge about them is relatively advanced. The more critical problems have been and continue to be (1) to modify ideal strategies to conform to the settings in which they must be implemented (that is, to consider more carefully and systematically than heretofore the particular dimensions which limit feasibility in specific situations), (2) to find means of transferring the knowledge and information about development strategies to policy makers and other interested groups in a form which they can absorb and translate into specific policies, and (3) to widen the range of development strategies which can be labelled ''politically feasible'' in specific national settings.

Development strategies themselves comprise two different but closely related efforts, one being to work directly on those technical and political constraints which limit choice, the other being to devise policies within existing constraints and with given resources which will ease the employment problem keeping in mind the probable effects such policies will have on the setting in which they are introduced. These two components are closely interrelated if only because resources allocated to direct efforts to improve the setting reduce the resources available for increasing employment opportunities within the setting. Moreover, the time horizon within which policy makers can safely work may limit the amount of resources which can be assigned to the task of environmental change simply because the visible effect of such efforts is not likely to emerge until after a long period of gestation.

Direct Efforts to Modify Settings

Measures to affect directly the social and technical constraints which limit development are generally less well understood than those elements of development strategy which are intended to achieve an optimum path within those constraints. The dicta are often clear—reduce population growth, develop appropriate technologies, reduce constraints on trade, etc.—but the underlying processes which should be understood if effective policies are to be defined and implemented, are for the most part simply not well known. When uncertainty looms so large it may be well to match efforts of a practical sort to promote constructive change with efforts of a research and experimental nature to promote understanding.

Population growth. Efforts to reduce the rate of population growth have spread rather widely throughout the world, and experience with family planning programs has both advanced knowledge and revealed unanticipated difficulties. The close association of family planning programs with medical services and the ''patient'' complex it generates is increasingly being questioned as an excessively narrow approach. Our social scientist consultants have felt that a disproportionate share of the funds going into population are devoted to the search for new technologies and that too little is devoted to studies of family planning behavior and motivation with respect to fertility, particularly as modes of behavior may differ so widely from one cultural setting to another. The modes of control acceptable today are generally much more numerous than was the case a decade ago, vasectomies being commonplace in some countries and the legalization of abortion spreading slowly but surely. The use of compulsion is still not a feasible policy in most countries and indeed in many, strong and open official support for voluntary programs is still lacking. Yet today's rate of population growth is perhaps the most important single determining factor of the magnitude of the employment problem which will be faced in developing countries a quarter of a century hence. Stem population growth—yes; but do we understand—socially, as opposed to technically—how to go about it?

Appropriate technology. The problem of generating and diffusing appropriate technologies is one about which much less is known. The International Rice Research Institute (IRRI) and the International Maize and Wheat Improvement Center (CIMMYT) have demonstrated the important role which international institutes can play in improving the agricultural production of food crops, but the possibility of replicating these experiences in industry, and even in other more complex agricultural situations, is not at all clear. It is clear that perhaps little more than three percent of the world's expenditure on technological research and development is in fact spent in the circumstances of developing nations where the employment problem is still critical, and that the means for transferring even this information to the less developed countries are not only limited but possibly inhibited by self interest and the practical operation of the international patent system.[16] Moreover, the conditions which influence choice of technology, a matter discussed more fully later, are often prejudicial to employment. Finally, the process of technological change is not well understood even in advanced countries and the problems of creating such a process in the thin economic atmosphere of developing countries have not yet been systematically investigated.[17] They should be.

Social behavior. Direct efforts to modify social behavior and human skills have largely taken the form of the provision of health and education services and occasionally nutrition programs. The strategy elements here are largely twofold, namely, how many resources can be reasonably allocated to the provision of such services and at what cost in terms of other development activities, and what form and location should these services take. There seems to be wide agreement on three features, namely, that such services should be more widely distributed throughout rural areas, that health and nutrition measures should be largely preventive rather than curative, and that primary education should be given priority over higher levels. But these represent a minimal program for transforming traditional household behavior and village life into modern sector counterparts. What will stimulate that change? Are economists learning from their other social science colleagues?

Multi-level planning. Matters of planning and implementation capacity seem especially susceptible to direct efforts in the current circumstances of most less developed nations today. More people need to be trained in planning and management skills; existing skills need to be turned to the task of developing appropriate methodologies and organizations for decentralized planning and implementation; and more of those skills now unemployed in urban areas need to be redeployed in rural directions. As the organization and methodology for multi-level planning are developed and rural programs are expanded, the demand for relevant skills in outlying areas is likely to increase rapidly, possibly exhausting the reservoir of unemployed who have management and planning skills and requiring the training and retraining of others. In common with population and technology, this constraint might be eased in many countries through appropriate donor agency support which would be both acceptable and welcomed. This constraint may yield to such action-oriented efforts.

International constraints. Perhaps one of the greatest frustrations for the governments of developing countries over the last decade has been their inability to find acceptable means for influencing the nature of international constraints which limit their own choice of development policies. Developing countries are often consulted superficially, if at all, when critical international policy issues are negotiated. The recent discussions on the succession of monetary crises which have exploded on the international scene over the last three years are only the latest of several, including the Kennedy round of discussions on trade barriers, in which participation by less developed countries has been minimal. Important progress toward world harmony is unlikely to be made without taking into account more fully the interests of the ldc's, in which, after all, most of the people of the world live. How to achieve more effective and responsible ldc participation in world councils is the perplexing problem.

There is also a growing awareness in developing nations that their welfare is often very directly and significantly affected by many domestic policy decisions taken in advanced countries or other ldc's. The protection of inefficient industries through tariffs and quotas may limit markets for ldc products; and the manipulation of domestic supplies and stockpiles may affect international prices and the ability of poor nations to finance necessary imports. Perhaps many traditionally "national" policies may in the future have to be submitted to international forums for discussion and agreement.[18]

Redistribution. The scope for the direct redistribution of resources and incomes varies considerably from one country to another but it is not large in most of the less developed nations, being limited partly by technical constraints, such as the shape and location of physical capital, but mostly by political considerations, including built-in safeguards of individual rights. The tools available are mainly those of nationalization, with or without compensation, and the redistribution of land. Land reform seems most essential in many developing countries as a means of ensuring its full use in combination with more labor. Several countries have undertaken land reform measures and others have introduced ceilings on land ownership, partly as a tool of land reform and partly to prevent future growth in the concentration of landholdings. Experience has been very uneven (Valdes, Gotsch, Gurley).

Power and politics. Development strategies composed within the planning apparatus of a country cannot normally contain explicit ingredients intended to change the political structure or the behavior of policy makers. Advice from outside may touch on such issues depending upon the person being advised and the terms of reference given to the advisor. So far as external donor agencies are concerned, such as the Ford Foundation, changes in political structure and behavior are primarily matters for research support, not subjects of action programs. In particular, the interaction between development policies and the state of political feasibility merits serious study. Are there currently feasible policies which if adopted in a country would widen the field of choice in subsequent periods? Will most currently feasible policies simply strengthen the status quo and curtail future choice? Comparative studies of actual social systems (as opposed to idealized versions) may shed light on the forms most responsive to social need and on the factors which may induce favorable change.

Principal Elements of Feasible Employment Strategies

A systematic analysis of the employment implications of development strategies should undoubtedly have been a principal concern of development planners and policy makers long before the underutilization of labor began to take the form of open urban unemployment—rather than basing strategies on other factors under the implicit assumption that the generation of employment opportunities would naturally follow. To a large extent this neglect has been a natural consequence of the character of economic analysis which typically concentrates on those factors of production which are most limited in supply, the assumption being that abundant factors will not limit output. In a situation of surplus labor in developing countries, this approach has run aground on two connected reefs.

In the first place, unlike other factors of production which are normally not paid when idle over prolonged periods of time, the labor force and its dependent population normally exercise a first social claim on the nation's income through such mechanisms as the extended family, feudal landlord-peasant relationships, and explicit government subsidies. Labor is in effect "paid" at the minimum subsistence level whether it is employed or not. But if it is to be paid whether employed or not, it makes sense to employ the labor force as fully as possible because any addition to total output which such employment may contribute is a net social gain.[19]

Secondly, the products and techniques imported from abroad and the incentives used to stimulate the inflow of capital have all contributed to capital intensity of the means of production in developing countries. This, too, would not matter particularly if the social cost of idle labor was zero, but when it is not, employment at any positive marginal product becomes an economic, as well as a social, consideration. Moreover, when the underutilization of labor begins to take the form of educated unemployed concentrated in the cities, the political costs of such neglect become an overriding concern.

Admittedly, economists have only recently begun to enter into their calculus the social, economic and political costs associated with the employment problem. The problems of doing so are not simple, but the modified development strategies which are emerging from such efforts should contribute both to an improved rate of growth in output and to higher and more rapidly growing levels of employment. Employment strategies are essentially development strategies in which such assessments have been attempted. Some of the critical elements in these strategies are explored briefly in the following paragraphs as they relate to product mix, technology, the flow and use of capital, the rural-urban balance, and education and development. Emergency employment measures are not discussed.

Product mix. Product composition has obvious effects on the magnitude of employment opportunities which can be generated with a given level of output (Stewart). Some products require more labor per unit of output than do others and, if total costs are comparable, more labor per unit of capital employed in production. There is then prima facie evidence favoring the production of more labor intensive products, assuming, of course, that markets can be found to absorb the increased output (Khan). But each product also requires for its production other materials and capital equipment, and may itself be an input in the production of another product. When these secondary employment effects are taken into account, product preferences may have to be reordered.

The principal markets which can be served by domestic production are located either abroad or at home. The share of the domestic market available to domestic producers can be enhanced through import substitution activities; alternatively, the resources needed for that purpose might be used to expand production for export markets. The argument has been made that employment considerations tend to favor import substitution over export promotion because per capita incomes are lower at home, and the products produced to meet lower income needs may on the average employ more labor in their production than products produced for higher income groups (Khan). This argument is less persuasive when secondary employment effects are introduced, when it is applied to intermediate products, perhaps particularly capital goods, and when export markets are only selectively entered. More study is needed of these effects.

Domestic income distribution affects the product mix demanded within a nation, those in higher income groups typically demanding more products which must be imported from abroad or which must be produced at home with relatively capital intensive methods. This, too, requires further research before quantitative effects on employment can be determined. There are, of course, many policy tools which can be used to modify income distribution and the product mix purchased domestically. These include progressive taxation, the subsidized distribution of public goods and essential commodities, the establishment of high tariffs on luxury consumer goods, and the use of excise taxes to limit the domestic production of luxury goods. The extent to which these and other measures can be applied depends, of course, upon the willingness and ability of decision makers to establish appropriate policies and on their ability to enforce such policies and to prevent their circumvention through such means as tax avoidance, corruption, and smuggling.

Technology. Evidence suggests that in many instances in which labor intensive and efficient technologies are available, more capital intensive technologies are nevertheless chosen for production. The reasons given are extensive and include subsidized capital prices, wages in excess of the marginal productivity of labor, the ease of importing packaged technologies which are generally capital intensive in nature, lack of information about alternative technologies, the desire to minimize management problems associated with the employment of labor, and the pride which engineers and top management may associate with sophisticated methods of production (Pickett et al). All of these then automatically become action variables which employment strategies should attempt to modify in order to improve the employment generated through choice of technologies in the private sector.

Government decisions on technology and its geographic location are undoubtedly influenced by some of the same considerations. They seem to have contributed in the past, in conjunction with the short time horizon within which policy makers have worked, to the apparent preference for large, urban-located projects constructed and operated with imported technologies (Sadli). It is the consensus of our consultants that the balance of future infrastructure developments should be noticeably biased in favor of many small rural-located infrastructure needs, such as rural roads, rural electrification, small irrigation and drainage schemes, and essential health and education services (Nash). Moreover, for many agricultural and industrial labor intensive technologies to be employed in rural areas, it is essential that delivery systems for inputs and other complementary services, such as credit, advice, and storage facilities be provided on a dependable basis and by means which reach small farmers and industries, the intended beneficiaries (Gotsch). Finally, science policy should not be restricted to matters of scientific research as defined by academics but should extend to the practical development of appropriate technologies and to improving the conditions which influence technological choice.

The flow and use of capital. The relative prices of capital and labor are obviously central to the creation of employment opportunities not only because of their influence on choice of technology but also because of their effects on the way in which technology is used once it is in place (Bruton). Early desires to stimulate capital inflows from abroad led, in most developing nations, to policies which provided extravagant subsidies for capital. While these did encourage much foreign capital to be invested in developing countries, they also encouraged the use of that capital in capital intensive means of production. Moreover, many of these incentives were made available to domestic firms as well (for example, investment allowances) and thus domestic capital, too, tended to find its way into capital intensive methods of production. At the same time, minimum wages and labor unions tended to raise the price of labor in urban areas substantially above wages prevailing in rural areas. These efforts to improve the welfare of the employed have had the natural consequence of increasing the numbers who are completely without work. One even finds in many urban areas the anomalous situation, supported by both management and labor, in which overtime is being worked while large numbers of the labor force are unemployed. Possibly the ingenuity of some economists could profitably be turned to the task of devising administratively feasible systems of dual wages, particularly at the lower wage levels, so that employers pay less than workers receive and are thus encouraged to offer employment to additional numbers of people.

There is evidence to demonstrate that setting prices right would undoubtedly increase employment opportunities, but by how much and how quickly we do not know. Given the shape and form of existing capital equipment, it does not seem that immediate effects would be large, but cumulative effects over time could be substantial since the new factor prices would favor the investment of new capital in more labor intensive industries and within each industry in more labor intensive technologies if such are available. Moreover, correcting factor prices should tend to raise the prices of capital intensively produced goods relative to labor intensively produced goods, thus shifting the composition of output in favor of goods with a higher employment content.

There is one important external effect which should be noted. Attempts to set prices right in one country, say by eliminating subsidies on capital, may dry up sources of outside capital and stimulate the outflow of domestic capital as both seek investment in other countries where capital subsidies have been retained. In this, as in some other areas of policy, the less developed nations might benefit from common as opposed to independent actions.

We noted earlier that the limited stock of capital in developing countries appears to be considerably underutilized in terms of its technical potential to employ labor. Policies designed to increase the degree of utilization of capital should increase employment not only by encouraging more efficient utilization of existing capital, but also by permitting new capital to be allocated to other employment generating activities. Setting prices right should, of course, have a favorable effect, but there may be other policies which research would disclose that might also improve capital utilization.

Rural-urban balance. All three seminars exposed serious concerns about problems of achieving an appropriate rural-urban balance of job opportunities and development activity within a nation. Indeed, the most persuasive and widely expressed view was that the root of the employment problem lay in the fact that modern economic activity is not being diffused to the countryside (Gurley, Griffin). The need to extend planning, infrastructure, appropriate technology, and complementary resources and services to the rural areas was stressed as a matter of the highest priority. The hurdles which have stood in the way of such development in the past—vacillating political will, the shortage of managerial resources, and the weakness of decentralized administrative structures—seem to have diminished in recent years and appropriate strategies for improving the rural-urban balance may have some chance of success in at least some countries over the next decade.

Unfortunately, the concentration of planners and central government policy makers on macro-economic considerations and on large projects which might attract foreign aid has meant that the basic homework necessary to define practical strategies for balanced rural-urban development have been in most cases seriously neglected. Are commodity pricing and subsidy policies well understood in terms of their effects on rural-urban terms of trade and their differential impact on large farmers, peasants and the landless (Griffin)? How can rural, non-agricultural work opportunities be generated? What is the cost of creating a job in the cities as compared to the rural areas when capital per worker and new infrastructure requirements (including social services) per family, etc. are included in the calculus? Indeed, what are the full costs of providing basic infrastructure and social services in cities as compared with rural areas? Why do people migrate and what are the full benefits and costs of their doing so considering that their arrival in a new location may increase the need for social and physical infrastructure? What are the patterns of rural-urban transfer payments which migration generates and what are their effects on development? Can simple methodologies be formulated for evaluating the many small projects which represent development opportunities in rural areas? These are some of the problems of rural-urban balance with which development planners and decision makers must grapple if the general strategy of diffusing economic activity more widely throughout a nation is to be pursued in a practical manner. Moreover, if more funds are allocated to rural development, the problem of rearranging urban priorities will arise.

Similar problems arise in determining appropriate balance between the "informal" and "formal" sectors of economic activity (Stewart). The small, "barefoot" indigenous entrepreneurs who practice, often illegitimately but ingeniously, in both urban and rural areas do not usually qualify for government protection and subsidy (except, of course, for their ingenuity in escaping taxation). Yet their potential for growth and the creation of employment opportunities may be substantial (as the ILO Employment Mission to Kenya has noted). Empirical studies are needed to assess the potential of the informal sector and to define appropriate means to foster this development.

Education and learning. Another important shift in development strategies which appears necessary over the next decade relates to education and the learning opportunities implicit in employment (Edwards and Todaro). The very substantial quantitative deficiencies in education which existed two decades ago in less developed nations have to a large extent been overcome. Indeed, there is a growing body of evidence in the form of the educated unemployed which suggests that the enthusiasm and subsidies for higher education have led to a rate of growth of higher education which cannot possibly be sustained over the next decade. This recent experience also implies that educational systems are not the engines of growth they were once considered to be. Those systems are mainly shaped by the societies they must serve and should not be expected to modify those societies in fundamental ways.[20]

The principal elements of educational strategy for the next decade are beginning to emerge from several ongoing studies. First, a larger share of the educational budgets in most developing countries should be allocated to the expansion of primary education, particularly in rural areas. Second, those benefitting from higher education should be required to pay for that education either at the time it is received or later through loan repayments or service in rural areas. Third, educational budgets should grow more slowly than in the past permitting more funds to be used for the creation of employment opportunities. Fourth, the internal efficiency and quality of educational systems should be given higher priority than quantitative expansion. Fifth, nonformal means of education intended to bring practical knowledge to people who need it—extension services and adult education are examples—should increase in importance. Sixth, the learning opportunities inherent in employment experience should be recognized as a fundamental value of employment, lending strength to efforts to increase employment opportunities and possibly to arrangements for work sharing and the provision of a wider variety of employment experiences to members of the labor force.

The extent to which these kinds of considerations can be entertained in designing future development strategies intended to relieve employment problems will vary considerably from one country to another. Moreover, the brevity of the summary here cannot expose the full complexity involved in defining appropriate development strategies and the oversimplification entailed may suggest a degree of certainty and knowledge which is misleading. Nevertheless, the lines of change indicated seem to us to be soundly based and worth testing over the next decade.

Program Options for Donor Agencies

The foregoing discussion discloses how very pervasive and complex the employment problem in developing countries is, encompassing as it does (a) a wide array of resistant variables from household behavior through population and technology to the international market framework and (b) a range of employment strategies which may differ widely in feasibility from one setting to another. The sprawling nature of the animal makes it especially difficult to identify specific points of substantive contact on which program actions of donor agencies might focus. There are, however, four considerations which enable us to narrow the many possibilities to a subset which seems both practical and promising.

The first reflects a decision to exclude recommendations concerning major loan programs of donor agencies. Obviously the criteria followed by donors in responding to requests for project aid must have important implications for employment—indeed many of the substantive issues raised in earlier sections are pertinent to the definition of such criteria—but project loans are simply not important foundation-type activities. The second consideration is that external agencies are at least one step removed from the locus of decision making, namely governments, in which principal employment policies are decided. The scope for donor agencies to initiate action on the employment problem is therefore limited, most donor assistance being a response to recognized needs. The third consideration is that some important needs, limiting population growth, for example, are already being addressed more actively and widely than others. The fourth consideration is relative importance itself, a matter on which our consultants have been particularly helpful.

With the assistance of these criteria, we have identified five major areas in which Foundation activities, alone or in conjunction with other donor activities might be welcomed and which should make a significant and lasting contribution to the relief of employment problems. The five areas are: (1) concepts and dimensions of the employment problem and its relationship to other development objectives, (2) the rural-urban balance in development, (3) comparative studies of development efforts, (4) the promotion of appropriate technological change, and (5) the easing of international tensions and constraints. We conceive of each of these five areas as entailing actions which range, hopefully in an interrelated fashion, from basic and empirical research to assistance with practical programs, from institutional development to essential training needs, though the proportions among these will certainly differ from one area to another.

The Concepts and Dimensions of the Employment Problem

The problems of measurement are in themselves more complex than we at first thought. In the first place, the concepts needed to analyze the underutilization of labor in developing societies seem to be more numerous and varied than the concept of open unemployment on which most analyses in advanced countries are based. In the second place, in order to define concepts whose measurement would assist in devising useful employment policies, a much better understanding is needed of the behavior of households with respect to the disposition of the human resources they control and of the factors which affect that behavior.

The basic measurement problem therefore encompasses studies of family and enterprise behavior, the design of concepts which will have policy relevance, and the measurements which these concepts suggest and require. The need to add time dimensions to these measurements in order to determine how the several kinds of labor underutilization are changing, suggests that a number of retrospective studies and the periodic repetition of surveys will be essential elements in the measurement process. Some valuable insights about how the underutilization of labor and its composition may vary from one stage of development to another can be gained by ensuring some commonality in the concepts used in different countries and by undertaking comparative studies. Finally, employment should not become an exclusive and isolated concern, as may have been the case with growth in the last several decades, but rather should be dealt with in relation to other development objectives, such as growth, income distribution and the quality of life, and as an integral as well as an essential part of the development process.

As the bulk of these several kinds of activities must be conducted within individual countries, the bulk of the funds required should undoubtedly come from the individual governments concerned, with supplementary assistance, largely for survey financing, research support, technical assistance, and training, coming from outside agencies as interest inspires them.

The need to develop concepts which have common elements from one country to another and the importance of comparative research as a means of promoting understanding suggest the desirability, particularly in the early stages of conceptual development, of having a small core of analytical and linking activities which is international in scope. One possibility worthy of consideration is the formation of a team of three professional scholars and statisticians, perhaps one from each of the three major less developed continents, which would be given a clear and definitely limited life of, say, three years. The group itself would work on the development of concepts in consultation with interested government agencies and university and research institute staffs, and as experience was generated, advise in specific countries on the elaboration and implementation of such concepts. The team would need funds to bring in occasional consultants, to finance experimental surveys and related (particularly comparative) analyses, to finance occasional workshops among ldc professionals actively engaged in similar work, and to promote selected ldc exchanges of personnel. The financing for such a core group might be shared with other donor agencies and interested governments of less developed countries.

The efforts of such a group would be considerably diminished if complementary activities at the national level were not supported both by ldc governments and external donor agencies. Such nation-related activities should embrace analysis, survey and census measurement, technical assistance when necessary, and training. Adequate staffing of departments of statistics in central governments may be a critical need in many countries, but training needs related to the program may also arise in such fields as anthropology, sociology, demography, and economics.

The Rural-Urban Balance

We are firmly persuaded that the most fundamental and promising attack on employment problems in developing countries is in efforts to redress the present urban bias in development strategies and the consequent need to disperse economic activity much more widely than heretofore. This shift in development strategy seems to us central to the widespread creation of employment opportunities and to the more effective use of the limited capital available in developing countries. Moreover, the interest in developing countries in the dispersion of economic activity has grown rapidly and widely over the last decade. The problem, however, is not simply one of generating activity in rural areas but rather of balancing development between rural and urban sectors. The two sectors are intimately related in their economic activities, and any diversion of national development efforts to rural areas will require careful reassessment of urban priorities.

We see three principal lines of effective action relative to the rural-urban balance problem—support for behavioral research, support for strategy research and experimentation, and support for multi-level planning and implementation, i.e., decentralized decision making. Of these three the latter is perhaps most practical and important, and possibly essential to the stimulation of relevant empirical research.

Behavioral research. As efforts are made to define appropriate policies for dispersing economic activity, the need to understand the factors which influence the behavior of households, small farms and enterprises, and rural elites assumes greater importance. These are major actors on the rural development stage and their decisions and activities are crucial to the transformation of essentially traditional, inward-looking communities to more modern, exchange-oriented farms, villages and towns. To speed the transformation process it seems to us necessary to improve understanding of basic behavioral patterns as it is in these that both the obstacles to and opportunities for constructive change lie. Efforts to diffuse multiple cropping technologies, for example, have disclosed that the scheduling, management, marketing and coordination problems encountered require a discipline and attention to detail to which many communities are unaccustomed by past experience. Most behavioral research must be location-specific and should focus on incentives and motivations, attitudes toward risk and innovation, determinants of spending patterns and employment decisions, patterns of income and work sharing, the identification of critical bottlenecks to development, and management requirements of alternative patterns of development. Some of the research might profit from multidisciplinary inputs, particularly from economics, anthropology, sociology, and psychology, though the possibility of mounting successful multidisciplinary efforts will depend on the human resources available in each country and their ability to coordinate such research. Most behavioral studies should be planned and executed in specific country settings, but some related studies which are methodological or comparative in nature would also be useful.

Strategy research. There are a number of primarily economic issues related to the rural-urban balance in development about which further research and experimentation are needed. Well focused behavioral studies would make useful contributions to understanding these economic issues but would fall far short of resolving them. We are convinced that the concentration of planners on macro and international development variables has resulted in serious neglect of the development strategies which would improve rural-urban relationships and generate employment opportunities. The problems which seem to us to have been inadequately addressed thus far include how to generate nonagricultural, rural work opportunities; the causes and effects, and the costs and benefits of rural-urban migration; the relative costs of creating jobs in urban and rural areas; the relative costs of providing minimal infrastructure and social services in the two situations; the extent to which the private benefits of social and physical infrastructure are subsidized in both rural and urban areas and the locational effects of differential rates of subsidy; the economic effects of rural-urban transfer payments; and the development potential of the informal sector in both rural and urban areas.

Closely related to these essentially economic issues is the growing awareness in poor countries of the need to introduce into development discussions and the evaluation of prospective development programs a number of social and humanitarian considerations which economists have tended to neglect in pursuing their planning functions in the past—partly perhaps because the relationships of these factors to economic development are not all that well understood. Alternative rates of population growth, for example, are seen to affect development opportunities, but development strategies and their component policies and programs are seldom analyzed carefully for their likely effects on population growth. Similarly, development policy consequences for employment, family security, nutrition, income distribution, leisure-time activities, access to minimal public services, opportunities for self improvement, and other dimensions of social and human welfare are seldom entered systematically into the planning calculus.

The need is not simply to finance rurally and socially oriented research but also to link it closely with policies designed to deal with the issues concerned. Indeed, such policies should be regarded as essentially experiments whose careful evaluation should shed valuable light on the design of future policies. While many of these kinds of research must be national in orientation, it is worth noting that many of the issues involved, perhaps particularly those relating to the relative costs of infrastructure and job creation in rural and urban areas and the social consequences of economic development, are not much better understood in advanced countries. Comparative research which embraces similar problems in both advanced and less developed countries may well accrue to the benefit of policy makers in both worlds.

Decentralized decision making. But the most pressing need in improving the rural-urban balance in less developed countries is support for provincial planning and implementation in both methodological and organizational aspects. After all, it is in practical encounters with development problems in the field that real learning opportunities are generated and urgent research needs identified. The principal needs perceived in the area of multi-level planning involve increased decentralization of planning and implementation functions and their coordination at local levels, be these urban or rural. The methodological issues which emerge in multi-level planning are essentially of three kinds, namely to identify the variables for which decision responsibility is appropriate at each level, to define the functional relationships among these variables, and to find means of integrating the methodologies associated with economic, physical and social planning, particularly at lower planning levels. The organizational problems parallel the functional or methodological problems, but are further complicated by the needs to man the organizational apparatus with skilled personnel at every level, to ensure that power hungry central ministries will indeed delegate to lower levels appropriate decision responsibilities, and to provide for coordination across ministries at both central and local levels.

The nature of the involvement of external agencies in supporting provincial planning efforts requires careful thought because the opportunities likely to emerge over the next few years run well beyond the financial competence of most agencies. Agencies like the Ford Foundation simply cannot afford to involve themselves on a broad scale, for example, in the provision of provincial planning teams. On the other hand, technical assistance and finance in support of indigenous efforts to design multi-level planning methodologies and organizations would use accumulated experience and competence, as would support for systematic evaluation of multi-level planning efforts. Moreover, experience with provincial planning in a number of countries has reached a stage where serious comparative study might reveal some ingredients which are essential for success and some pitfalls which might wisely be avoided in other countries.

But it is the training demands which will emanate from the wider application of multi-level planning that provide perhaps the most serious challenge and one with which external agencies could be particularly helpful. The Ford Foundation in particular has been actively engaged in developing central planning expertise in many countries; it has also been deeply involved in support of special development planning courses both in the United States and developing countries. It seems clear that the large training requirements which will be associated with multi-level planning should be met largely through internal training programs, the expense of foreign training programs being much too high and their suitability being questionable. There is now considerable experience in establishing training programs in development planning and administration (the Philippines, Indonesia, Thailand, India, Kenya and Nigeria are examples) but for the most part these have catered to the needs of central planning agencies and therefore have concentrated on macro and international policies devoting little space in the curricula to regional planning problems. This lacuna is already being noticed in some countries and pressures to modify curricula or establish supplementary training programs with more emphasis on economic and physical planning needs at provincial levels are mounting. Opportunities to assist in the design and initiation of such training programs are likely to grow rapidly and we would recommend strongly that external agencies consider such opportunities sympathetically.

Comparative Studies of Development Efforts

In terms of rates of growth a number of developing countries have achieved some success. Taiwan, South Korea, Malaysia, the Philippines, Kenya, Mexico, Brazil, and recently Indonesia are examples. One or two of these and a few others have taken steps to share the progress being made rather widely among their citizens. Taiwan, Malaysia, China, Tanzania and Chile are perhaps the prominent examples. In both of these sets and in most of the rest of the third world, employment problems persist or grow except among a very few countries most of which are relatively well advanced, such as Taiwan and Singapore.

Some of the more "successful" countries by standards of growth and equity appear to have had "natural" advantages of location, natural resources, or cultural traits; others have benefitted from massive foreign aid; some have at least the facade of democracy; other governments are clearly totalitarian in form and substance; some pursue socialism as an ideal system; others adhere to capitalist principles; but most can be described as "mixed economies," traceable more to historical and colonial experience than to the texts of Marx or Marshall.

If it could be demonstrated that growing employment problems are but a natural consequence of "technical" considerations, it would be right to concentrate on the necessarily slow modification of such variables as natural resources, population, technology, and the availability of capital—and to accept employment problems as both inevitable and persistent. But the element of truth which lurks in this overstatement should not obscure the fact that policies, even with respect to technical variables, are "chosen." Because policies are chosen, it is likely that employment can be promoted and more equitably shared by (1) extending the range of choice of development strategies through research and experience, (2) easing political constraints on feasibility, and (3) improving economic conditions of choice in both public and private sectors. These are mainly matters of political economy, not matters of technical capacity.

While much has been learned about the development process over the last several decades, the employment problem, perhaps more than any other, has exposed a serious deficiency in our understanding of the mutual interaction between economic policies on the one hand and the nature of political constraints on the other. Economists seem to have focused their attention on the design and analysis of policies intended to alleviate technical limitations to growth and, more recently, employment, but the problems encountered in getting effective policies chosen and implemented and in understanding how policy choices may widen or narrow future conditions of political feasibility seem to have escaped serious and concerted effort. Some have argued that the conditions of political choice in most systems inevitably lead to policy choices which increasingly restrict future opportunities and strengthen the elites in positions of power. Others have suggested that authorities must try to cope with emerging problems, such as employment, in order to retain their political, social, and economic power, and that even marginal concessions to social needs will erode the roles of elites in favor of greater equity. The point is that neither the evidence nor the hard analysis seems to be available from the real world to carry such questions much beyond the level of opinion or the theoretical constructs of Marx and Marshall.

The need is not, however, to promulgate further studies of ideal, hypothetical systems, but rather to learn from the rich and varied array of practical development experiences what seems to work and why, particularly in terms of the dynamics of employment, distribution, growth, and the political process. A program, possibly competitive in nature, in support of comparative studies of development efforts seems to us worthy of consideration. Sponsoring such a program would involve many problems, including the sensitivity of much of the subject matter and the consequent need for the credentials of objectivity, the needs for ldc scholar participation and for access to in-country data and decision makers, and the challenge of building into much of the research multidisciplinary considerations.

The risk in such a program is large. The Economic Growth Center at Yale once had aspirations to do comparative studies but has produced mainly country studies, and the Development Advisory Service at Harvard has had planning experience in many countries but definitive comparative studies have not emerged. More recently the Institute of Development Studies at Sussex has initiated efforts to draw together the comparative experience gained through participation in ILO Employment Missions to Colombia, Sri Lanka and Kenya, but it is too early to judge the outcome. Nevertheless, the promise of comparative studies—of Taiwan and South Korea, of Tanzania and

Kenya, of Thailand and Malaysia, of Thailand and Ethiopia, of Malaysia, Kenya, and Colombia, of Brazil, China and India—in which conditions of political feasibility play a major role is an exceptionally attractive lure.

Technological Change

The promotion of appropriate technological change in developing countries involves three related functions—the generation of technologies suitable to the resource endowment of a country or region including its natural resources, infrastructure, labor force skills and capital; the effective transfer of technological information from source to potential user; and the establishment of local conditions for the choice and use of technologies which will induce users to adopt those known methods which are most socially beneficial. There is wide agreement that none of these functions is currently performed well in developing nations. On the other hand, there is considerable uncertainty (but not a shortage of ideas) as to how the performance of these several functions might be improved.

New technology. In principle, modern knowledge applied to technological problems in many sectors of developing nations should generate technologies which are (1) appropriate to national needs, cultural conditions and resource endowments, and (2) competitive in the local setting with those technologies currently being borrowed from advanced countries. How to harness that knowledge effectively is, however, unclear. IRRI and CIMMYT are outstanding demonstrations of the feasibility and value of such efforts in the field of agriculture; public efforts to assist small industry with technology problems and to identify labor intensive methods of constructing public sector infrastructure have not achieved comparable success.

Many questions have been raised concerning the appropriate focus of national or regional institutes which take the generation of appropriate technology as a purpose. Most of the so-called industrial institutes in developing nations today have been concerned with responding to the apparent needs of small industries in the private sector. Evidence suggests that these institutes have become essentially service organizations and indeed that none of them has really had as its primary purpose the development and extension of competitive, labor intensive methods of production. It can be argued, therefore, that this approach has not really been given a fair test. Some have argued that the client relationship typical of industrial institutes inevitably subordinates the social need for appropriate technology to the private need for greater profit. On the other hand, such a conflict may suggest that it is the conditions of technological choice which are at fault; appropriate technology *should* be profitable.

Several other foci for technological institutes have been suggested as being more promising than the industrial approach. An institute might be "demand-oriented," for example, focusing on perceived economic needs. It might concentrate on the design and development of technology for small farms whether that technology is biological, chemical, electrical or mechanical; or it might fix on the design of low cost consumer products to be produced with local materials. Others have argued that institutes should be designed for internal efficiency, specializing in a particular kind of technology—biological, electronic, mechanical or chemical—and assembling staff accordingly. Such an institute might respond to needs in several industries or demand situations providing only that its technological specialization offers promise for the task at hand. Institutes might also be "material" or "process" oriented; some industrial institutes started in these ways.

We have not been able to evaluate these different approaches to the development of appropriate technologies and are not convinced that the necessary evidence and experience exists to do so. Experiments seem necessary, but unfortunately experiments with research institutes are expensive and it takes time to generate the experience needed for evaluation. Moreover, it is unlikely that the diverse technological needs of developing countries can be met through one kind of research institute alone. Given this present state of uncertainty, we urge that investigations of possible experimental institutes, such as those conducted by the East-West Center and the National Academies of Engineering and Sciences, be continued and as more definitive and promising opportunities emerge, that these be considered for the joint financing they may require.

Means of generating appropriate technologies which are both less organizationally formal and less financially massive than the institute device also merit investigation. In particular, the broker function—through which technological needs and opportunities in less developed countries might be brought to the attention of existing private and public centers of technological research—may merit expansion and support. In this regard, the growing experience of the Intermediate Technology Group in London seems especially promising.

Technological transfer. Probably the most effective means of transferring existing technological knowledge from one location to another is the market process itself. Those interested in initiating production or increasing efficiency seek means of doing so and either transfer knowledge they already have, as, for example, in the case of multinational corporations, retrieve it from public sources, pay royalties for it or hire knowledgeable people. While most technological information is transferred by these means, the system works imperfectly, often slowly and with many impediments. To improve the speed of transfer of relevant information, supplementary institutional means may be required as proposed, for example, by the UN Industrial Development Organization and the Ad Hoc Panel of the National Academies of Engineering and Sciences, and as practiced on a small scale by the Intermediate Technology Group. In any event, efforts are required to improve the effectiveness of the market system itself, particularly by reducing existing impediments such as secrecy and abuses of the international patent system.

Donor agencies need obviously to consider where they have comparative advantage in assisting efforts to establish institutional means for storing, retrieving and transferring technological knowledge. In the meanwhile, a particular need exists for research on the international patent system to determine how it might be modernized in order to disseminate technological information more quickly and effectively in the emerging circumstances of a new international economic order.

Conditions of choice. The need to improve conditions of choice and use of technology in less developed countries is an extremely important part of the larger problem of improving the price signals and incentive structure to which all modern-sector-related economic activities respond. That wider need requires continuing improvements in planning and policy-making processes and, as we have discussed, the generation of political processes which are increasingly responsive to the general welfare. There is some interesting and needed research going on on the use of technology in developing countries and external agencies have supported much of this work.

The uncertainty which prevails concerning the means for generating appropriate technologies and transferring technological information suggests clearly that knowledge about the whole process of technological change is limited. This is not to disparage the substantial research which has been done on this subject since the Industrial Revolution but rather to note that it has not reached definitive conclusions—NASA's effort over the last decade to disperse its new technologies to private industry is a compelling example—and has been concentrated on and in advanced countries. What are the respective roles of competition and past and prospective profits in the production of technological change? In industries where firms and profits are small how can research on technological change be most effectively organized? From which sources have most technological changes been produced—producers of materials, producers of final products, or independent research organizations? Do patent systems stimulate or inhibit technological change? What has compelled the public sector in advanced countries to become such a major financier and manager of research and development expenditures? How does initial research, private or public, get transferred and diffused to other potential users of new technologies? What are the essential ingredients of science policy at the national level which will promote the production and diffusion of technological change? If knowledge of ongoing processes of technological change in advanced countries are not well understood, how much more needs to be known in order to initiate an effective process of technological change in the impoverished circumstances of developing nations? This is a challenging problem which should be addressed by some of the best research talent available. Support for such research is one important line that should be pursued in the technology field.

All three of our seminars and some of the papers prepared for them have noted the critical role which engineers in government, the private sector, universities, and research institutes play in both the development and choice of technology. Our attention has also been called to the propensity of engineers to prefer sophisticated technologies. It has been suggested to us that this propensity derives from two closely related factors, namely, the experience of advanced countries with sophisticated technologies and the tendency for engineering schools to focus on the more sophisticated technologies. Many felt that some reorientation of engineering education in the less developed nations was a matter of considerable urgency. It was not suggested that curriculum content should be downgraded but rather that modern scientific knowledge should be directed increasingly at the problems which developing nations face in the field of technology. The consensus was that this might well require more imagination and deeper perception than that entailed in simply replicating the sophisticated hardware which has been designed to meet the needs of advanced countries.

Perhaps the most promising suggestion for improving the training of engineers so that they can deal more effectively with the practical engineering problems which arise in both rural and urban areas was to improve the social science content in engineering curricula, and in particular to devote much more attention in teaching engineering to the social and economic criteria which should govern technological change and choice in the circumstances of developing nations. If regional planning and rural development do receive increasing attention during the next decade, the need for engineers who are conversant with such social science matters will increase substantially. Fortunately, there is growing evidence that engineers themselves perceive this need. Agencies that have experience in the social sciences should consider sympathetically opportunities to intensify the social science training available to engineers whether through regular curricula of engineering colleges and universities or through the establishment of refresher training programs for engineers already engaged in both the public and private sectors.

The International Setting

The international scene has demonstrated clearly over the past decade that when crunches and crises occur the less developed nations of the world lack the monetary power and the political clout to be invited to those councils attempting to grapple with important international problems, much less to influence the shape of the outcome. Though the bulk of the world's population resides in developing countries and will be affected by the shape of the international economic order, they are essentially disenfranchised when major international economic policies are decided, the "voting" on such issues being weighted more by national incomes than by national populations.

We would encourage those donor agencies which are multi-national in character and have a field presence in developing countries to be both alert and sympathetic to opportunities which may arise to promote professional and policy level discussions among less developed nations, to encourage research intended to clarify and make known the effects of the international economic order on the welfare of less developed nations, and to support interchanges which may serve to educate advanced country scholars and policy makers in the major interest which less developed nations have in the form of the international economic order.

A second important need is to reduce a wide range of barriers which limit the access of less developed nations to the markets of the advanced countries. It seems to us that the most constructive thing to be done here is to get at the very root of the problem, namely, the continuing existence behind those barriers of inefficient industries located in the advanced countries. Experience has clearly demonstrated that inefficient industries do not automatically succumb to competition, the councils of economic theory notwithstanding. Many groups—labor, management, stockholders, and the communities affected—have a vested interest in the continuation of inefficient industries, and the ability to draw protection around them. As a practical matter, it may be necessary to seek means of compensating these groups for the burdens disinvestment in those industries would impose on them. The social cost of such compensation—whether it takes the form of financial reimbursement, the provision of alternative employment opportunities, or subsidies to enter new lines of economic activity—could be recovered over time through the more efficient use of the capital and labor freed from inefficient activities.

There are many other aspects of the international economic order which are of importance and concern to the less developed nations of the world, including foreign aid, exchange rate policy, the role of the multi-national corporation, international migration, industrial location among developing nations, and export/import biases in development strategy. Opportunities to help with such matters may merit selective support.[21]

Some Supplementary Considerations and Opportunities

There are two matters to which we would like to draw attention before concluding this paper. The first relates to certain characteristics which might enhance the value of much of the research which would be required in conjunction with the five major areas of activity identified above. The second relates to the importance of developing closer communication between policy makers on the one hand and social science research on the other and in particular the potential of the press and other news media as means of promoting such communication, a potential which we think is greatly underplayed.

Development research characteristics. We have been persuaded, primarily by the participants in our seminars from the less developed nations, that more research support should be directed to and through ldc scholars so that they not only participate in research but also gain experience in the design and management of more complex research projects. The urgent needs for expertise in the rapidly changing environments of most less developed countries over the last two decades elicited a generous response from many donor agencies. To help as quickly as possible, many scholars in advanced countries were trained for, or diverted from other activities to, research on development problems. While originating in a sincere desire to assist the ldcs, the consequence has been, as seen from the perspective of today, to build up in the advanced countries a large pool of scholarly resources interested in problems of development, possibly at the expense of training larger numbers of ldc scholars. Moreover, the advanced country scholars, by reason of their early involvement, have a natural advantage over their less experienced ldc counterparts in the conduct of further research. Indeed these scholars now have an understandable vested interest in continuing to use their hard earned expertise, an interest which is currently reinforced by the apparent decline in their alternative opportunities at home. In addition, the advanced country scholars, through their cumulative experience with donor agencies and in the coordination of ldc research, have developed very substantial expertise in preparing proposals for research and in managing complex research projects. Finally, there has been a tendency for advanced country scholars, international donor agencies, and less developed countries to place a higher value on the absolute quality of research than on opportunities to improve research experience and capability in less developed countries.

These arguments suggest that the research capacity in the advanced countries devoted to developing country problems has been overbuilt and that its comparative advantage over scholarly resources in less developed countries may increase even further if research funds continue to be allocated according to standards of quality instead of by measures of the extent to which quality can be increased in the ldcs themselves. Ldc scholars need not only to gain research experience by participating in relevant projects but also to gain experience in the design and management of research projects, activities from which they are often excluded through the application of high quality standards. The need to provide a richer array of research experiences to ldc scholars is considerably strengthened when the policy implications of research are introduced into the picture. Policy makers may regard research by their own nationals, particularly on sensitive issues, as being better grounded in local knowledge and possibly, though not necessarily, more concerned with national welfare and long-term implications than research conducted abroad or by visiting scholars.

A note of caution is in order, however. The suggestion that more research should be designed, managed, and conducted by ldc scholars should not be construed as an exclusion of others. The argument is that an imbalance needs to be redressed, not that a different one should be created. Indeed, much theoretical and comparative research, and research on international problems may naturally fall to advanced country scholars (though one would hope not exclusively) simply because urgent needs in ldcs for research on internal applied problems outrun the limited supply of local research talent. Thus visiting scholars will continue to be drawn upon, but increasingly at the initiative and request of indigenous researchers who themselves provide the leadership and management for the projects. But the major need for technical research assistance from the advanced countries will in the next decade be in the design and management of research.

There will also be growing opportunities for promoting ldc managed workshops and conferences and for arranging exchanges among ldc scholars and the use of professionals from developing countries as sources of technical assistance in other nations. A few organizations which may promote such interchanges are already in being or in the process of development. They include the Latin American Council of Social Sciences (CLACSO) and The Program of Joint Studies on Latin American Economic Integration (ECIEL) in Latin America, and the Council on Asian Manpower Studies (CAMS) and the Organization of Demographic Associates (ODA), both in Asia. There is also an International Association of Directors of Development Research and Training Institutes which has three regional organizations for Asia, Africa, and Latin America. In addition, the International Economic Association, which has occasionally conducted useful conferences involving professional economists from both less developed and advanced nations, might assume a more active development role, though the bulk of its work today is oriented towards advanced countries, the scholars in them, and the quality standards to which they aspire. All of these organizations have the potential for managing, and in most cases conducting, comparative research in many of the major areas in which we feel externally financed activities would be appropriate.

In addition to giving greater research responsibilities to scholars from developing countries, we also feel that much of the research financed with Foundation funds would benefit from a problem focus, a characteristic which carries with it four implications. The first is that several dimensions of problem analysis—concepts, empirical data, behavioral relationships, formulation of policy options, the exploration of feasibility and, where possible, empirical testing—should not be segregated but rather managed as part of a research package. An increase in problem-oriented research might help to avoid two pitfalls now associated with much ongoing research related to developing countries, namely, data gathering as an end in itself and the production of policy recommendations without reference to feasibility. A second implication is that research would be much more policy oriented than much of it is at present, if only because many of the problems perceived in developing countries are those having policy significance. A third implication is that more research would be location-specific, problems having to be defined in relation to the setting to which they apply. Of course, the "location" appropriate to the analysis of a particular problem may vary from the village to the nation and indeed to the international arena. The fourth implication is that much more research would be multidisciplinary in character, not because it is an important end in itself but rather because the comprehensive analysis relevant to a problem may require inputs from several different disciplines. Relating multidisciplinary analysis to problem research is based on the judgment that researchers from different disciplines may work better together when they share a common interest in a problem than they would if they were simply assembled in an institution having multidisciplinary research as an objective in itself.

Public media. For several years, those who follow development problems have been increasingly concerned with promoting communication between policy makers on the one hand and social science researchers on the other, but programs have met with varying degrees of success. Most of these efforts have been devoted to the promotion of direct links between the two groups through the financing of workshops and conferences, support for consultancy services, and help for research centers which have direct links with various government ministries. The role of the press and other news media as intermediaries for conveying social science research information to both policy makers and the public has been generally neglected. Yet the media are major conveyors of information and the possibility of raising the analytical content of the material conveyed seems to us to be a promising though indirect way for indigenous researchers to reach influential government and non-government leaders, even in those situations where the press is fairly tightly controlled.

Direct efforts to raise the quality of news media would take the form of providing appropriate training in the social sciences for professional media people either by enrollment in degree courses or by the establishment of special short courses which could be offered at night or in short packaged courses of four to eight weeks. Most of such training should take place in the country concerned, not abroad, and should be conducted by indigenous social scientists who are themselves actively engaged in policy-oriented research. The connections thus established between journalist and scholar would in themselves improve communication. University people in the social sciences might also be supported in local efforts to hold short workshops and perhaps briefing sessions on sharply focused issues of current concern so that these matters can be better analyzed in the media.

Finally, there may be in some countries opportunities for supporting the establishment of special purpose publications such as the *Economic and Political Weekly* in India which it seems to us performs a very important function in presenting scholarly views in laymen's language on many current issues in India and which is widely read by civil servants and policy makers.

One advantage of using news media as a means of communication between research scholars and policy makers is the requirement they impose on researchers to translate research into a language which can be readily assimilated by policy makers who have neither the time nor the professional expertise to cope with technical jargon.

Conclusion

This agenda for donor assistance with employment problems in developing countries is both insufficient to cope with those problems and too extensive for the Ford Foundation alone to finance. The first point is only a reminder that the crucial decisions on employment must be taken in the countries concerned. Donor activities, even of the most promising kinds, will largely expand understanding and identify new opportunities and approaches; assistance with implementation depends upon prior national decisions having been taken.

The second point suggests that there may be on this agenda opportunities for many donor agencies interested in employment problems, some of which could be pursued independently, others of which may require joint financing or more complex forms of cooperation. The extent to which there is interest among donors in exploring productive forms of cooperative effort is a matter for continuing investigation.

Less ambitious agenda items may be pursued by the Foundation itself. Indeed, several of these, like training for provincial planning and employment-related research, are already receiving support from field offices and others may readily be absorbed in ongoing programs. Some, like comparative studies, may require fresh initiatives.

There are two characteristics of the Foundation's style of operation in the international field to which attention might be drawn as employment-related programs are considered within the Foundation. The first of these is its network of field offices throughout the world. This network, being well and professionally staffed, has accumulated a rich experience in the "ways and means" of developing nations. The field offices are not only closely linked with each other, but also, through related activities of the Foundation, with strong research and area studies centers in advanced as well as developing countries. This network, extending as it does from research bases to field activities, gives the Foundation a strong comparative advantage in supporting effectively not only in-country programs, but also comparative studies.

The second characteristic is the Foundation's strong professional capacity and experience, in New York and the field, in the social sciences. Moreover, its social science expertise has been brought to bear on a number of practical problems, such as population growth, the consequences of agricultural change, education for development, and the formulation of socially responsive strategies for development. Those several program options discussed above which require more imaginative uses of the social sciences in mitigating future employment problems in developing countries would seem to be natural extensions of an already substantial experience.

The opportunities for sensitive external agencies to assist nations as they struggle to understand and cope with the employment aspects of development seem to us to be significant, substantial and possibly vital. But whatever the form external agency support takes, it is in the last analysis only assistance. To be effective there must be a mass of indigenous effort—social, political and economic, and encompassing both research and policy—seeking to ensure that the poor not only share in the benefits of development, but also participate in the development process itself. That commitment of will and resources is a matter of national decision for which external assistance cannot substitute.

Notes

1. See U.N. International Labour Office, *Towards Full Employment* (Geneva, 1970); *Matching Employment Opportunities and Expectations* (Geneva, 1971); *Employment, Incomes and Equality* (Geneva, 1972); *Sharing in Development* (Geneva, 1974). For a discussion of research priorities of the ILO's World Employment Programme, see Louis Emmerij, "Research Priorities of the World Employment Programme," *International Labour Review* (May, 1972).

2. For analyses of traditional settings see particularly J.H.Boeke, *Economics and Economic Policy of Dual Societies*, (New York, Institute of Pacific Relations, 1953); Clifford Geertz, *Agricultural Involution: The Process of Ecological Change in Indonesia* (Berkeley, University of California Press, 1963); and Everett E. Hagen, *On the Theory of Social Change* (Homewood, Illinois, Dorsey, 1962).

3. UNILO, *Employment, Incomes and Equality, op. cit.*

4. See also Frances Stewart and Paul Streeten, "Conflicts between Output and Employment Objectives in Developing Countries," *Oxford Economic Papers* (August, 1971); Nurul Islam, "Employment and Output as Objectives of Development Policy," paper for Fifteenth International Congress of Agricultural Economists (Sao Paulo, Brazil, August, 1973); Howard Pack, "The Employment-Output Trade-off in LDC's: A Microeconomic Approach," Yale University, Economic Growth Center Discussion Paper No. 179 (June, 1973); and Erik Thorbecke, "The Employment Problem: A Critical Evaluation of Four ILO₁ Comprehensive Country Reports," *International Labour Review*, Vol. 107, 5 (May, 1973).

5. Edgar O. Edwards, "The Problem of Labor Utilization in Developing Countries," mimeo (Ford Foundation, June, 1971).

6. Edgar O. Edwards, "Work Effort, Investible Surplus and the Inferiority of Competition," *The Southern Economic Journal*, XXXVIII, 2 (October, 1971).

7. James P. Grant, "Equal Access and Participation vs. Trickle Down and Redistribution—The Welfare Issue for Low-Income Societies," prepared for One Asia Assembly (New Delhi, India, February, 1973).

8. V.M. Dandekar and N. Rath, *Poverty in India* (Bombay, Indian School of Political Economy, 1971); and B.S. Minhas, "Rural Poverty, Land Redistribution and Development Strategy: Facts and Policy," *Indian Economic Review* (1970).

9. For a review of recent work, see Michael P. Todaro, "Rural-Urban Migration, Unemployment, and Job Probabilities: Recent Theoretical and Empirical Research," International Economic Association Conference on Economic Aspects of Population Growth, Valescure, France (September, 1973).

10. Harold Lubell, "Urban Development and Employment in Calcutta," *International Labour Review* (July, 1973).

11. UNILO, *Towards Full Employment, op. cit.*

12. See, for example, Peter Dorner, "Land Reform, Income Distribution and Employment: Conceptual and Empirical Relationships," paper for Fifth Conference of the Harvard Development Advisory Service (September, 1972); Walter P. Falcon, "The Green Revolution: Generations of Problems," *American Journal of Agricultural Economics* (December, 1970); Edgar O. Edwards, "Researching the Social and Economic Consequences of the Green Revolution," mimeo (Ford Foundation, July, 1970); Randolph

Barker, William H. Meyers, Cristina M. Crisostomo, and Bart Duff, "Employment and Technological Change in Philippine Agriculture," *International Labour Review* (August-September, 1972); Lester R. Brown, *Seeds of Change* (New York, Praeger, 1970); Bruce F. Johnston and J. Cownie, "The Seed Fertilizer Revolution and Labor Force Absorption," *American Economic Review* (September, 1969); and Robert d'A. Shaw, *Jobs and Agricultural Development*, Monograph Number Three (Washington, D.C., Overseas Development Council, 1970).

13. See Gordon Winston, "The Theory of Capital Utilization and Idleness," *Journal of Economic Literature* (forthcoming); Gordon Winston and Thomas O. McCoy, "Investment in the Optimal Idleness of Capital," *Review of Economic Studies* (forthcoming); and Daniel M. Schydlowsky, "Putting Existing Capital in Latin America to Work," A Collaborative Research Project of the Center for Latin American Development Studies, Boston University (October 24, 1972).

14. On this point, see J.H. Boeke, *op. cit.;* and Manning Nash, "Social Prerequisites to Economic Growth in Latin America and Southeast Asia," *Economic Development and Cultural Change* (April, 1964).

15. See also Rajni Kothari, "Political Economy of Development," R.R. Kale Memorial Lecture (Poona, Gokhale Institute of Politics and Economics, 1971).

16. Hans W. Singer, "The Development Outlook for Poor Countries: Technology Is the Key," *Challenge* (May/June, 1973).

17. See, however, W.P. Strassman, *Technological Change and Economic Development* (Ithaca, New York, Cornell University Press, 1968).

18. C. Fred Bergsten, *The Future of the International Economic Order* (New York, Heath, 1973).

19. See Harvey Leibenstein, *Economic Backwardness and Economic Growth* (New York, Wiley, 1957); and Edwards, "Work Effort . . .," *op. cit.*

20. Edgar O. Edwards and Michael P. Todaro, "Education, Society and Employment: Some Main Themes and Suggested Strategies for International Assistance Efforts," *World Development* (January, 1974); and Jagdish Bhagwati, "Education, Class Structure and Income Equality," *World Development* (May, 1973).

21. For a more detailed and extensive discussion of current needs and opportunities in the international sphere, see Bergsten, *op. cit.*

I

Basic Discussion Papers

Economic Development and Labor Use:
A Review*

Henry J. Bruton
Williams College

Introduction

Experience during the 1960's revealed a variety of aspects about development that were inadequately appreciated at the beginning of that period. In the broadest terms what became clear was that the mere achievement of an acceptable rate of growth of Gross Domestic Product—say 5 per cent or more per year—was not assurance that development was proceeding in a satisfactory fashion. It now seems clear that good growth rates of GDP can be achieved for 5 or 10 years by means that create a set of conditions that in effect impede or prevent continued growth. We have also seen that just any sort of growth does not necessarily resolve a number of vital social and economic problems. Among such unresolved problems is that of unemployment. There are others, e.g., income distribution (not unrelated to employment) and regional balance. In general terms we have learned that we must generate a growth process that rests on a more effective use of domestically available resources than was the case in most countries during the 1960's.

In the present paper attention is devoted to the employment issue. There is no need to justify concentration on this issue. Unemployment has both economic and social implications that are universally recognized as harmful both to society at large and to the individual who is without work. A development process that fails to produce sufficient employment opportunities is therefore not one that is acceptable. As noted above development must meet other requirements as well, and the possibility of trade-offs between the employment content of development and these other objectives (income distribution, regional balance, rate of growth of GDP) will be noted below. In general however the possibility of important and inevitable trade-offs appear infrequent, *if* we can find the right mix of policy and strategy.

The argument in the preceding paragraph may be restated in a slightly different way. The difficulties with the employment (and other) issues is not due to a mistaken emphasis on aggregate measures of growth such as Gross Domestic Product. It is rather due to an inadequate appreciation of the development process and how that process can be directed. It also seems clear that to attack the unemployment problem only by seeking a markedly higher rate of growth of output than that achieved over the 1960's is not satisfactory. (Although for some countries getting the growth rate up is an essential ingredient of an effective employment policy.) Thus the conclusion, that we must seek a development that in some sense is built around a more effective use of domestic resources and that does not thereby penalize the growth rate.

* This paper has been published in *World Development* (December, 1973).

49

Over the past five years considerable work has been done on the employment question in developing countries. This work ranges from efforts to measure its extent and to describe the characteristics of the unemployed (as to age, education, skill, experience) to the construction of theoretical models designed to show why recent development has not in and of itself solved this problem. Despite this work it is fair to say that little in the way of a consensus has emerged, and that we are still groping toward a set of arguments that will illuminate both the sources of the difficulties and provide guides to corrective policy. It is also correct to say that the understanding of various parts of the problem has increased, and we know things now that we didn't know five years ago. The present exercise is not a review of the literature, but an effort will be made to note what we know or what seems to be emerging as the prevailing view and what remains indefinite or controversial.[1]

The major purpose of the paper is to try to put the employment issue into a context that will enable us to see its nature and its relationship to growth and development more clearly than we do now. From such an effort some policy implications may be derived, but mainly the objective is to show where and what kinds of work must now be done in order to establish a development process that does build on the particular advantages that a given economy offers.

The paper is divided into six sections. The first is a discussion of definition and measurement questions. As will be seen such questions have to do not only with measurement itself, but also with conceptual issues that help to put the employment issue in a policy oriented perspective. The second reviews those aspects of development policy that are most frequently found in developing economies and how such policies have affected labor adsorption. Included here is an effort to explain or justify why these policies have been pursued, and the kind of modifications in them that appear necessary if headway on employment is to be made. The third section reviews the specific aspects of the traditional sector that are of special relevance to employment, and the fourth does the same for the modern sector. In the fifth section links between the sectors and how such links affect labor adsorption are considered. In the concluding section an attempt is made to suggest directions—immediate and longer range—that our efforts should now take.

Who Are the Unemployed?

Explanations of unemployment occupy attention throughout the paper. It is however useful to begin with a categorization of explanations that will help in the discussion of definitional and measurement issues and prove useful in later arguments as well. On the one hand there are explanations in which cultural and social and institutional matters play a crucial role. Characteristics that are frequently included have to do with land ownership arrangements, attitudes toward competition, response to market or other incentives, work-leisure trade-offs, value systems, and technological rigidities. Such characteristics change slowly, or not at all, and are little subject to the conventional instruments of economic policy. If the major explanation of unemployment in the developing countries is to be found in these slow changing, policy impervious characteristics, then resolution is either long in the future or demands revolutionary measures.

On the other hand there are explanations of unemployment which place primary or exclusive emphasis on the economic policies that most of the less developed countries have followed over the 1950's and 1960's. If it is believed—if it were discovered —that economic policies of the usual variety can solve the problem, the time horizon within which the problem is manageable becomes considerably shorter, and the problem more tractable to the economist's tools. With this emphasis, analysis and policy prescription concentrates on factor prices, tariff and exchange rates, investment incentives, agriculture mechanization measures, infrastructure location, and other similar issues that employment models identify as relevant.

One can isolate two general evolutionary strands in recent thinking on this distinction. An increasing number of investigators are finding evidence that conventional policies are, if not paramount, certainly crucial to understanding and to policymaking. Even those economists who would place principal emphasis on the social and institutional factors would, for the most part, acknowledge that getting conventional policies consistent with employment creation is a necessary ingredient to any successful attack on the problem. More generally, however, a more satisfactory combining of the two categories is emerging. Policies are indeed crucial, but they are to be used in an employment environment that both imposes constraints and offers opportunities, neither of which is fully understood nor clearly defined. The more complete description and analysis of this employment environment therefore is a prerequisite to the design and implementation of economic policies. Emphasis is placed on policies in the conventional sense, but on policies designed to fit a situation that is apparently different in key respects from the unemployment that existing models examine. Included among the differences is that of the capacity and willingness of government to implement new measures.[2]

Part of this employment environment description is most clearly reflected in efforts to identify and measure the unemployed. The discussion in this section is directed toward measurement issues, but with the larger objective revealing some of the more relevant aspects of the employment environment in which policy is to function.[3] Certain other aspects can be most conveniently considered later.

The Poor and Unemployed

An initial question is simply who is or should be included in unemployment in the contemporary developing country. Several points make this more than an elementary question. The conventional notion of course is that an unemployed person has no job and is actively seeking one (although "actively" is not a very helpful notion). Unemployment surveys usually ask essentially whether the individual had worked one day or regularly over the past week or possibly the past few weeks. While data on such questions are useful, neither the magnitude nor the nature of the problem may be satisfactorily identified by such questions. Several points may be noted.

The unemployed may not be the economically worst off in the society.[4] An unemployed person must have some means of support, or otherwise he could not long survive. A man with a wife and children who cannot move in with working relatives or friends simply cannot be unemployed. He must work even if only at the least productive activities. On the other hand, an individual who has means of support may opt not to accept a low paying, undesirable job, even when it is available. The latter would be counted as unemployed, the former not. Yet the former is evidently much the worst off economically. In attacking the unemployment problem, as conventionally defined, we may therefore not be directing attention to the area where economic hardship is most severe. This simple point also emphasizes the importance of the means of support or sharing mechanism issue in the employment problem.[5] Several aspects may be mentioned here to illustrate the kinds of empirical and policy questions that emerge in this particular context.

In almost all countries measured unemployed rates are much higher among younger age groups than among older persons. This is often explained in terms of younger persons having less experience, fewer contacts, and less knowledge of the labor market. While these arguments are doubtless often valid, it is also correct that younger people are much more likely to have means of support, and can thereby "afford" to be unemployed until a job that they want becomes available. Difficult entry into the labor force may really be ease of obtaining support from relatives. Evidently, this distinction is important for a variety of policy issues. It could even mean that raising wages in activities where they are very low could increase social welfare (via an income distribution effect) even if employment growth among those with means of support were penalized.

The importance of the sharing mechanism can be illustrated in another way. Suppose that in a particular country the diagnosis of the situation indicated a worsening of the unemployment problem over the approaching decade or two. Then the question of means of support of the unemployed becomes acute. It is especially acute when note is taken of the great increases in absolute numbers that are involved and the apparently continuous eroding of traditional arrangements of providing for the unemployed. The extended family is often cited as a means by which poverty is shared, but even in the most convenient of circumstances it worked only adequately. As numbers increase, it becomes an increasingly doubtful means of caring for those with no jobs. In many countries the single most important reason to define and project estimates for the number of unemployed is in order that some attention may be given to finding new and effective sharing mechanisms.

This point also brings out the importance of thinking now about emergency measures to meet these problems. "Emergency" in this instance refers to temporary measures designed essentially to provide jobs and income, without much concern for the social productivity of the work. In many instances the result is largely a transfer payment, but the social and political implications of providing work in one form or another are such that limiting the exercise to transfer payments probably is not satisfactory. For some countries the machinery for making transfer payments is less effective and less available than it is for mounting large-scale make-work schemes. Evidently if such emergency measures do produce something of social value so much the better. Indeed one of the major reasons for considering emergency measures now is to try to make them as productive as possible.

Such measures often place heavy demands on organizational skills, and of course add to the government's financing problems. In some countries the armed forces may be an existing institution that could be used for these purposes. In those cases where the organizational skills in the armed forces are underemployed or are employed in less urgent tasks, a ready made agency may be available for an emergency effort of significant size. It is also frequently easier to get funds to the armed forces than to new agencies. It may be emphasized that the argument here is not to make the armed forces larger, but rather to use the skills frequently found there to organize and carry out emergency employment activities.[6]

There are reports that China has had considerable success in organizing large work crews that not only provide emergency employment, but also result in the creation of social capital. Greater understanding of how the Chinese have accomplished this might provide suggestions and policies applicable in other countries.[7] Work brigades are also used in several countries as are youth corps of various kinds, and we do not know very much about how effective they are or exactly how they work. Such measures or organizational approaches to the employment problem may be more than emergency, more than temporary, and serve as longer run means of meeting the issues. As emphasized later, it is important to recognize that the kind of wage employment dominant in the United States and Western Europe must not be looked upon as the only route to resolving the employment problem in the developing countries.

These issues have led a number of observers to include in the unemployment definition those members of the labor force whose income is below some stated level. In this event, such workers would be treated simply as having no job at all. To do this has certain appeal and certain practical advantages. Individuals earning less than the stated minimum usually require additional income to survive. Also such persons are usually readily available for more productive employment, and therefore from the supply side it seems reasonable to count them in the unemployed category. Evidently this approach would include the disguised as well as open unemployed. It is the number of people in this group that constitutes a measure of the magnitude of the economic problem, and an estimate of the supply of labor that is available. Evidently such an approach implies that some or all members of the labor force would agree to work more hours and/or at a more sustained rate. The projection into the future (not impossible) of estimates of the size of this group would indicate the kinds of demands for sharing that would prevail over the future.

There are however difficulties with the counting of low productivity people as unemployed. These difficulties have chiefly to do with matters of policy. Suppose there was no unemployment, but productivity was very low throughout the labor force. Most economists would agree that to raise productivity in this situation calls for a different set of policies from that useful in attacking conventional unemployment. In this event, the task would be that of generating growth. The existence of unemployment—of fewer jobs than there are people seeking work—implies, as noted in the introduction, that the development process has been defective in some respects, and it is at the correction of this defect that policy is aimed. Low productivity itself is not evidence of distortion or of defective policy. The classical stationary state is one of low productivity, where all are employed in an essentially competitive equilibrium. Moving up from that equilibrium is not the same problem as creating a growth process that does in fact resolve the unemployment problem.

A less important difficulty arises from the fact that the size of the labor force itself is, probably, a function of the demand for labor. Thus the level of unemployment and its projection depends to some extent on the demand for labor. Evidently this complicates the definition of unemployment, and its projection.

These various points have a number of implications for the way we think about employment policy and the way we measure unemployment rates. The sharing arrangements are relevant both in terms of helping to account for who is without any work at all, and in terms of providing for those who cannot find work. The latter point emphasizes that an essential aspect of the unemployment problem is the finding of ways to provide for those who are not able to obtain a job. The other major issue suggested by the preceding discussion concerns the low productivity worker. The low productivity worker is an important part of the problem, but it is necessary to keep in mind that policy implications of a low income society without unemployment in the usual sense are different from those for a society dominated by such unemployment.

Work Preferences

The measurement problem is further complicated by certain structural and behavioral characteristics in developing countries. Two examples illustrate the complication.

In an economy in which there are several high wage activities and a number of lower wage activities a rational calculation might show that it pays one to leave voluntarily the low wage job in order to make himself available to and thereby to increase the probability of getting a job in the higher wage area. The person may then remain unemployed for some time (depending on means of support available to him) before getting a new job or before becoming convinced that it was impossible to get such a job.[8] Such a person is unemployed, but again the policy implications as well as the social and economic consequences of this kind of unemployment are different from those associated with strictly involuntary idleness. Much of the movement to urban from rural areas falls in this category. So too does some of the "educated unemployed," who, at least for a time, are willing to accept only the job for which they have trained. If other jobs are available, should such persons be defined as unemployed or as something else?

This argument illustrates an important way in which matters related to education and to labor markets create a situation in which private and social costs and returns may differ. Evidently from society's point of view idleness of labor for the reason just stated constitutes an unqualified loss. These sorts of adjustments by individuals are in response to market imperfections as reflected by the structure of wages. The wage differential between urban and rural areas is especially important and occupies attention later. The point here is to emphasize the role of means of support in this kind of situation, and how individuals respond to wage rate differentials due to the specific nature of the employment environment. In a later section, attention is allocated to why the structure of wage rates seems to be conducive to unemployment in the developing countries.

A rather similar case is often implicit in trade-offs between leisure and work and in the choice of job. In virtually all less developed countries there are shops filled with clerks who are idle a major part of the time. The choice of this type job—if other jobs are available—implies that the person consciously chooses underemployment to full employment. There is also some evidence that seasonal idleness frequently represents no more non-work days than are usual for a "full time" worker.

Another behavioral matter that affects both measurement and policy matters arises out of the fact that a very large proportion of the labor force are own account workers. Work is spread among family members, generally unpaid. Some members cannot work other than in a family situation. Similarly, family members are rarely released. In the same kind of environment, there is modest evidence that family members stretch their work to cover the time available. For example, a man with four acres of land may work as many hours on the four acres as does a man with eight acres. There are other examples of the way in which the large number of "own account workers" complicate the measurement problem in both advanced and less developed countries.[9] The issue is more acute in the latter group of countries simply because such a large proportion of the work force falls in this category. It is surely inadequate to assume that own account workers—even the sidewalk peddler—represent pure unemployment.

The Locus of Labor Supply Decisions

There is a more general point that is helpful. In most really traditional societies there is "full employment" in the sense that each member has a role, a role recognized by all members of the society as justifying a share of the economy's product. This role did not necessarily involve full time work in any conventional sense, but it did involve performing a recognized function. In these circumstances it does not make much sense to speak of employment or of a full employment objective. Traditional societies are now changing, but many of the characteristics remain to the extent that the exact nature of the employment situation is difficult to pin down. At the same time many of the characteristics of the traditional societies are disappearing. Especially relevant are those characteristics having to do with sharing mechanisms or (more revealing words perhaps) the recognition that each person's performance of an accepted role justified his claim to livelihood. [10] The disappearance of these traditionally accepted modes of behavior are due to many things: the opening up of villages to greater outside contacts, increased education, and, most important of all, increased population. The kind of social arrangements which worked for one level of population may not function effectively for a higher level. Yet no new, workable arrangement has emerged. Especially, no new tradition of widespread wage earning has evolved. It has not evolved partly because demand for hired labor has not grown rapidly enough. Partly, however, it has not evolved because of the kind of complications on the supply side, on the employment environment side, that were alluded to in the preceding paragraphs. Many countries now seem to be in a state of limbo. Traditional arrangements that effectively solved the employment problem can no longer do so, yet effective new arrangements have not emerged. It is worth repeating a point made earlier to the effect that the possible new arrangements are not limited to Western-type widespread wage employment complemented by relatively small numbers of own account workers.

There is some evidence to suggest that in this kind of situation the appropriate economic unit to study is not the individual but the household. In instances where traditional arrangements can no longer provide acceptable forms of activities for all members of the family, the family may then act as a unit in finding new roles for its members. This procedure also provides a means of meeting the risk associated with rapid structural changes in the society. Consider a simple example. A rural family cannot find "employment" for all its members in traditional activities. The family as a unit—or its head—selects one or two members of the family to seek employment outside traditional areas. The family continues to support these members until they find employment or become convinced that there is no hope and return home. If employment is found by those who leave, earnings are shared with those who remain in the traditional activities. In this way risks associated with seeking new employment are shared among all members of the family, and the procedure also permits a somewhat more satisfactory response to employment (and income) difficulties than would be possible on an individual basis.

It is likely that in this kind of situation, the decision making process is significantly different from that that characterizes an individual acting on his own. It is also likely that incentives that act on a family unit are different from those that act on an individual. Hence policy that meets acceptable social criteria in a situation where family decision making dominates may need to be different from that for a situation in which individual decision making prevails.[11]

This argument leads to another point associated with family decision making and family activities. There are in almost all villages, towns, and cities numerous one family non-agricultural activities. These informal activities are rarely included in any censuses, but what evidence there is suggests that they are empirically of considerable importance. They offer a kind of employment opportunity that is quite suitable in many respects to the prevailing economic and social environment, and often a level of income above average. Rarely do they profit from government subsidies and regulations, and indeed often are penalized in one way or another by government. Yet they now serve an important role in the employment picture and could, in many instances, serve an even more important role. Small scale activities are now being studied with increasing diligence. While these informal activities are always small scale, their important characteristic is not their size, but their indigenous nature and their unaided response to observed opportunities. We need more details on these activities, but even in our present state of knowledge, we are surely safe in saying that government policies that actually penalize or harass such informal activities are misguided. It should also be noted that providing assistance—funds, technical advice, marketing aids—to such activities has been found to be extremely difficult.[12]

Japan may offer an example of a fairly painless shift to new social organizations as existing ones became evidently obsolete. There the kinship and hierarchical order of society were not really overthrown by the industrialization process. Indeed these were strengthened by political means and by policies of individual industrial firms which offered a kind of security not unlike that supplied by traditional society. Labor recruitment continues to be carried on through families, and even in large establishments paternalism is evident and a real security thereby created, and recognized. Japan, as in so many other ways, found a means of adapting and modifying an important traditional arrangement so that it was consistent with new economic activities.[13]

This discussion of definition and measurement problems began with the distinction between explanations of unemployment resting mainly on conventional economic policy matters and those based on more fundamental aspects of the society. In trying to identify exactly what is meant by unemployment and who it is that is unemployed, attention was called to a variety of characteristics that make it evident that conventional definitions are not adequate. Yet no neat definition that lends itself to quantification emerged. We are interested in definition and measurement for three broad reasons. In the first place some feel for the "magnitude of the problem" is necessary in the design of all kinds of policy. Secondly, as noted above, we need to have a much improved understanding of the problems that arise if unemployment increases over the next decade. Problems include not only those having to do with providing a means of support for the unemployed, but with the social and political problems that seem to accompany widespread unemployment. Finally, the way we define and identify the unemployed evidently affects the approach to policy that is chosen. We need to be able to predict how people respond to various incentives and penalties. How people do respond depends in part on the kinds of issues referred to above.

Estimates of open unemployment particularly in urban centers remains an important issue. It seems clear however that spending more time and resources refining these estimates is hardly justified given that our understanding of the nature of the labor market is so inadequate. Two sets of issues in particular stand out: The first has to do with the kinds of sharing arrangements that now prevail and other kinds that might be developed. (Evidently, the kind and extent of the sharing arrangement itself affects whether people consider themselves unemployed, and hence whether and how they respond to incentives and opportunities.) The other issues are those bearing on the behavioral and structural characteristics noted above. To provide a clearer way of thinking about and classifying these various groups—households, firms, elites, government—will help our understanding as to policy and our appraisal of the seriousness of the problem.

Development Policy and Employment Growth

Consider now the relationship between employment growth and development strategy, or more specifically between employment growth and economic policy. The current literature is filled with discussions of how the policies followed in a large number of countries have penalized employment growth. Almost all of these discussions are concerned with the growth of the demand for labor, and therefore imply some sort of explanation of why the demand for labor grows less rapidly than does output or less rapidly than necessary to make a satisfactory dent in the problem. It is therefore convenient to begin with a discussion of those explanations that are concerned primarily with the demand for labor.

Underutilization

The kind of unemployment that economists understand the best and have the most unambiguous policy recommendation for is that due to a deficiency of aggregate demand, the kind of situation out of which Keynesian economics was born. While there may be individual developing countries here and there or now and then where this explanation is generally relevant, few economists would accept it as widely applicable.[14] Aggregate supply is rarely perfectly elastic in a developing country, so that pushing ahead with deficit financing would be expected to produce inflation or balance of payments problems, or both. It would however be wrong to dismiss the aggregate demand argument completely. Increased "aggregate" demand does not necessarily mean greater demand for each commodity, and there are some commodities the supply of which is perfectly elastic. In particular it is frequently the case that more demand would elicit more output and more employment without problems, *if* it could be directed at specific sectors. Two examples may be noted.

a. Some capacity to produce non-food items usually consumed by low income groups is idle in many countries. Measures that raise the incomes of these low income groups would then increase the demand for labor without creating inflation or balance of payments problems, or by creating only minor problems of this kind.[15] Increased demand in this sense has a role to play, but evidently simple deficit financing models are not adequate for the problem.

b. The second point is a bit more complex though similar. We observe that capital is idle a great deal of the time in developing countries. This idle capital is in many forms, tractors, factories, machines, transportation equipment. There are of course many reasons for this, but in some cases aggregate demand is an important part of the explanation. For example, a country may have several textile mills each of which operates 30 hours per week simply because if all mills operated at full capacity all the time, the output could not be disposed of in the domestic market at cost-covering prices. Also costs are too high for this activity to export. Yet if more demand were forthcoming at cost-covering prices, output and employment would increase. This situation may indicate that wage rates are too high or it may represent a situation in which entrepreneurs refuse to write down capital values commensurate to actual values. It may also indicate an overvalued exchange rate. In this case the idle capacity may be turned into working capacity, not by deficit financing, but rather by measures that result in relative prices changing in such a way that cost curves fall. (In the case of a devaluation the foreign demand curves, measured in domestic currency, rise.) Evidently (to repeat) *all* observed idleness of capital is not due to the kind of situation just described.[16]

In both of the arguments just considered, idle capacity is presumed to exist. In the one case it could be eliminated by increasing the incomes of the specific groups (or redistributing income) and in the other case by a change in relative prices. While the simple Keynesian argument does not apply, the frequent existence of idle capacity in a number of sectors does tell us that increments in demand of a certain kind or composition would result in increased output and increased employment; i.e., it isn't only labor that is idle. Therefore studies that examine how demand may be increased in certain sectors may have great usefulness. Rural works programs or rural industrialization of a variety of kinds may offer considerable promise in these areas. Similarly, studies of tax policies that reward utilization (or penalize non-utilization) may be effective in uncovering ways to increase utilization and thereby increase employment.

In more general terms the fiscal machinery of most developing countries does not usually allow for anything approaching fine tuning. Thus countries that are cautious or who find (or imagine) inflation and balance of payments problems to be especially damaging must necessarily operate well below limits that could be reached were the taxing and fiscal systems more effective. There is little evidence to suggest that the use of direct controls can do an acceptable job in replacing tax and fiscal policy. Countries who are not cautious and who seek the limit of capacity by increasing demand often produce an inflation or balance of payments situation that is more harmful to employment than underutilization would be. Improvements in fiscal capacity may therefore be an important means of effecting and maintaining fuller utilization than now exists. This is a relatively neglected area of research, partly because it has as much to do with implementation and administration as with economics, and partly because of the common practice—until quite recently—to assume that all kinds of capacity, except labor, were fully utilized.[17]

Capital Formation

In many economic growth models, especially of the pre-1960 period, primary, even exclusive, emphasis was placed on increasing the rate of capital formation. Evident also was (and is) the fact that the most apparent difference between rich countries and poor countries is the amount of available capital per laborer. For these and possibly other reasons, development policy has placed, and continues to place, great emphasis on capital formation. In pursuit of higher rates of capital formation a great variety of inducements have been offered the inventor. Such inducements have taken the form of tax holidays, tariff exemptions, overvalued exchange rates, import licensing advantages, and many other arrangements. In almost all cases the inducement takes the form of making the cost of capital lower than it would otherwise be. Evidently this type of approach to encouraging investment created incentives to use capital at the expense of labor, where such was technologically possible.

The appropriateness of such measures depends on one or both of two assumptions. The first is that there is little or no substitution between capital and other inputs, especially labor and domestically produced inputs. If such substitution were technologically impossible, then policy measures that reduce the cost of capital relative to labor would not penalize employment. It was in this context that the capital output ratio became such a strategic parameter, and on which so many development plans relied so heavily.

This set of policies to raise the investment rate may also be defended on the grounds that, though it may sacrifice employment in the short run, the greater capital intensity will produce both a higher growth rate and a higher saving rate from a given level of income, and thereby lead to a higher rate of capital formation (than would be achieved with less capital intensive techniques). Over a period of several years therefore more employment opportunities will be generated than would be the case were capital formation not subsidized.

Empirical and qualitative evidence accumulated by a large number of investigators suggest that substitutability between capital and other inputs is substantial, and economic agents do respond to factor price signals.[18] Therefore policies that result in reducing the cost of capital relative to other inputs will result in increased capital intensity. The assumption of rigidities that underlies capital-output and foreign exchange-saving gap models and policies built from those models are now rather widely believed to have penalized employment growth. The sources of substitution are not only within the same activity, but among activities as well. Thus, the measures aimed at increasing the rate of capital formation have contributed to the emergence of types of activities—as well as techniques of production—that are alien to the resource endowment of the developing countries. This alienness seems to have penalized further the kind of adaptations and modifications that might have produced greater labor absorption.

While many observers now believe that the form that the emphasis on capital formation has taken has penalized employment growth, there is less evidence on how much the penalty has in fact been. Estimates of the elasticity of substitution and of the wage coefficient in demand-for-labor regressions suggest considerable variation among sectors. This variation suggests that had more suitable factor prices prevailed, a different set of activities would have emerged as well as less capital intensity in all activities. The question of how much the subsidizing of capital has penalized employment is important because we need to know the extent to which simple elimination of capital subsidies would help. Also, of course, there may be costs involved that would have to be weighed against the increased employment.

Evidence on the second rationale of subsidizing capital accumulation—a positive effect on saving—is less clear. There is little to indicate that saving rates are—or are not—positively related to capital intensity.[19] If factor substitution is substantial, then a capital intensity unjustified by factor endowment will mean lower output than is technologically possible. Saving potential is usually greater, the greater is total income. If income is penalized (a result that depends on substitutability of factors), then total savings may be lower with the higher capital intensity than with a more nearly optimal (in the conventional sense) allocation. This could be correct even if the saving rate itself were higher, the greater the capital intensity. More important however is the argument that the saving (and investment) objective should be met by other instruments, e.g., tax policy, interest rate policy, asset offerings, rather than by seeking to distort in a particular way the productive process.

Wage Policy

Along with policies that reduce the cost of capital there are many developing countries that seek actively to raise wage rates. Among such practices are minimum wage laws, laws that make dismissal difficult and expensive, laws that require many fringe benefits, and extra legal pressures to keep wage rates rising. Such practices are often motivated by the most humanitarian reasons, and do in fact usually help those who work. But the same arguments and evidence referred to above indicate that rising wage rates do hold down the growth of employment. However, the design of a correct wage policy does not immediately follow from this fact.[20] Wage earners are, in most developing countries, a minority, and it is not clear how labor payments affect the various other categories of work. Public sector employment, often large, may also be affected in a variety of ways by wage rate changes. Employment in the service sector is also affected, probably negatively, but we do not really know exactly how. Rising wage rates also produce a more rapid rate of obsolescence of physical capital than is the case with constant wage rates. Wage rates—or other forms of payment to labor—are also income, and doubtless under some assumptions as to the composition of consumption of wage earners, it would pay in employment terms to raise wages even if the direct employment effect were negative. Under any circumstance it is difficult to discuss the effect of wage rates on employment independently of an analysis of product prices.

Despite all these qualifications and complexities, most observers would agree that both employment and output objectives are furthered by constant wage and other labor payments. Therefore, those policies that push up wage rates are generally regarded as harmful to the employment objective. Similarly, where incentives seem necessary, a system based on the rate of increase in employment, rather than the level of investment is preferred. Still we do not know how harmful it might be, or indeed exactly how the employment picture would look, if payments to labor were constant over time. This too would be useful to know. Similarly, urban wage rates in many countries are rising in the face of increasing numbers of unemployed. The exact process by which wage rates are pushed up in such circumstances is not completely clear.[21]

Another side of the wage picture has to do with the structure of wages. Structure here has two dimensions. The first has to do with relative wage rates among various skills. Such variation often misrepresents both relative supply and social productivity. Governments in particular are often guilty of setting educational requirements for positions, and then offer a salary to justify that education. One observes salaries of e.g. extension workers very much below those of Ministry of Agriculture office workers, even where extension worker services are apparently much more productive, and much more essential to the creating of labor intensive agriculture. Other examples could be cited.

Wage rates that are simply "too high" can be corrected to some extent by devaluation, but where the labor market is so imperfect that the relationship among wage rates in different activities is distorted, devaluation is not the appropriate instrument. The existence of high wage and low wage sectors is commonly observed. Less frequently noted are the distortions in wage rates among several sectors due to a variety of causes. The policy objective should be to eliminate these sources of distortions, but such a statement does not help much until we can pinpoint the source of the distortions. The literature and the policymaker have concentrated on "the" price of labor relative to "the" price of capital. This of course is a fundamental question, but it now also seems that the structure of wage rates in the economy is important in understanding employment issues. Finding ways to correct this structure may be more difficult than correcting the average labor-capital price ratio.

The other dimension of the structure of wages has to do with urban-rural differences. Discussion of this question is included in a later section.

Import Substitution

The most frequently found approach to development policy is that characterized as import substitution. The details of this approach have been explored at length by numerous economists, and attention here is limited to the employment effects of that approach.[22] The essential nature of import substitution is simply the imposing of impediments on the importation of certain products, particularly manufactured consumer goods. It is immediately evident that such an approach means that new investible resources are allocated very much on the basis of demand conditions, with little reference to supply capabilities. In particular, there is the presumption that the imports being curtailed are *less* demanding of those resources with which the developing countries are most abundantly endowed. Otherwise such products would, presumably, have already been produced domestically. For such an approach to be very satisfactory requires significant adaptation as to techniques of production as well as increases in overall productivity.[23] Such adaptation has occurred rarely, partly because of the kind of factor pricing noted above, and generally the import replacement activity remains a virtual mimic of that in the advanced countries. The issue of the adaptation of imported technology is however more complicated than simply factor price distortion, and we need much more understanding of the process by which countries modify imported technology to fit their factor endowments more satisfactorily.

Import substitution has affected employment in another important way. As a new activity is created behind protective barriers, a growth rate of output in excess of that of GDP is expected. After this import replacement is accomplished however, the growth rate will decline. Further growth will depend primarily on the rate of growth of GDP, since only now and then have these new activities been able to enter the export markets. At the same time some more or less regular increase in labor productivity is expected. Such increases are due to a learning effect (on the part of both labor and management), economies of scale, and occasionally new technology embodied in new machines. The consequence of this increased productivity on employment depends on what happens to wage rates and to output and the value of the elasticity of substitution between capital and labor. Note has already been taken of the evidence that the substitutability between capital and labor is much higher than was generally thought during the 1950's. The point now is that as the growth of output in an import replacing activity slows down and the rate of growth of productivity tends to rise, then the growth of employment—possibly even the absolute numbers employed—must decline. Evidently if productivity increases more rapidly than demand in a given activity, then employment must fall in that activity.[24] Evident too is the fact that rising wage rates will in this circumstance reduce the demand for labor even further, and will also prevent costs from falling. Finally, if productivity increases rapidly enough and if costs do decline, then entry into the export market is considerably facilitated. As noted above, entry into the export markets is an exceptional event. Thus the creation of a set of new activities that continue to require protection and to depend primarily on the domestic market will, except under strong assumptions as to the continuing appearance of new activities, result in declining labor absorption in the import replacing activities.[25]

The import substitution strategy has also accounted for a considerable part of the factor price distortion previously noted. This approach to development has had other consequences for employment, but the points made above are surely fundamental. The great policy moral of the import substitution experience seems to be that a development strategy that links directly with domestic factor supplies and indigenous institutions is necessary. That this involves much greater attention to exports is generally agreed, but it is less clear what else is involved, and less clear exactly how to establish a development strategy that is more indigenously oriented than is import substitution.

Productivity Growth

In recent work on the sources of growth, increases in productivity have been shown to be as or even more important than increasing inputs. A growing economy is therefore necessarily one in which the productivity of labor is growing, and policies or circumstances that dampen productivity growth necessarily dampen output growth. Also it has been shown that productivity growth, with wage rates (deflated by product prices) constant, should encourage employment growth. A rise in productivity with wage rates constant is equivalent (and more practical) to a decline in real wages with constant productivity. But if the rising productivity is to produce increased employment, not only must wage rates be constant but output must expand. The policy objective then must be to increase productivity within a context that permits growing output. The productivity growth must also be such that it does not favor the use of capital more than that of labor. The problem of growth of demand has already been noted. Consider now some of the issues associated with technical change as a major source of increased productivity.

The frequently noted point that the technology of the advanced countries is not suited to the factor supply situation in the developing countries is of course vital. Therefore the simple borrowing of technology creates many problems, among which are those having to do with employment.

Technological change that penalizes employment must take one of two forms. It must affect more favorably those activities that already make use of relatively more capital than do other available techniques. In this event, optimal techniques at prevailing factor prices become even more capital intensive than they were. Conventional wisdom has it that technology has developed in this fashion in the West largely because of increasing costs of labor. When such technology is transferred to a labor surplus economy, it means that even with a much lower wage-capital cost ratio the relatively more capital intensive technique may still be optimal. Thus getting factor prices to reflect relative factor supplies may not be sufficient to prevent increasing capital intensity, if technology is imported from capital rich countries and no modifications or adaptations are made in that technology. In this case the technological change eventually makes the more labor intensive techniques technologically inefficient, i.e., they are no longer economic at any set of factor prices. To choose a technique that is technologically inefficient would, in this event, mean using not only more labor, but also more capital. It is indeed difficult to define a situation in which sacrificing output to get greater employment does not also result in a higher capital-output ratio. If choosing a more labor intensive technique does in fact result in a lower output than is possible with another technique and less labor, the marginal product of labor must be negative. This result almost necessarily implies differing technologies between the relatively more and less capital intensive techniques, and therefore creates a strong likelihood that capital productivity also falls if the relatively more labor intensive technique is used.[26]

The second form that technological change may take that can affect employment is through its impact on produced inputs. Usually emphasis is placed on the substitutability between capital and labor with no reference to produced inputs. Changes in the produced inputs or changes in their quality may however impose technological restrictions on productive processes. Raw material processing and handling is sometimes in this category. Changing speeds of operation in one part of a process often require changes elsewhere that substitute capital irrespective of changes in wage and capital costs. Similarly, the argument is often noted that tractors do not so much replace labor as that they are land using. It is this latter characteristic that penalizes employment. On the other hand, an improved seed that results in quicker maturing and permits two crops per year is in effect equal to an increase in land and thereby is employment creating.

Several general conclusions on the technology issue seem fairly widely accepted. Considerably more resources should be applied to technical research in developing countries than now is the case. This research should be of a very applied nature, and concerned largely with the adaptation of existing technology to the factor endowment of the developing countries. This is clear enough, but less clear is the exact means by which this objective can be achieved.

The incentive to search out new techniques is not always present. A firm, domestically owned or foreign owned, has access to a particular technique of production to produce a given commodity. It also is well protected from foreign competition. Why should such a firm seek to find techniques that are more suitable for the economy than those readily available? It must make some search, incur some outlay to find a new input combination. The new input combination will—by definition—reduce costs. Evidently a sufficient reduction in cost would justify the increased outlay. If the firm were already making acceptable profits, it may not respond to an opportunity to make more profits. If the prospects for increased output seem favorable, the incentive may be greater. If the reduced costs would enable the firm to export or to increase local sales by a substantial margin the likelihood of making an effort appears greater. There is some evidence that firms that face a rather elastic demand curve for their product tend to adapt imported technology to the domestic factor supply situation more often than those that face an inelastic demand curve. In general, the widespread practice of protecting to the extent necessary to ensure satisfactory profits discourages search for new techniques on the part of most producers.

These same policies plus those noted above that affect relative input prices have some effect on the kind of technological change which proves profitable. The kind of innovations most appropriate are those that facilitate the greater use of those resources in most abundant supply. If the prices of such resources are rising relative to other input prices, then research activity aimed at reducing costs will tend also to aim at reducing the quantity of inputs whose prices are expected to rise.

What we think we now know is that the kind of protection that more or less guarantees profits and the policies that distort factor prices also tend to direct the research that does take place into directions that are not favorable to the use of the relative abundant factors. No one argues however that just eliminating these two categories of policies would thereby relieve the difficulties. It is however an important first step.

There are examples of apparently successful formal research efforts. The work summarized by "Green Revolution" is generally regarded as employment creating. It imposes other requirements, especially availability of fertilizer and water control, and a range of problems connected with distribution, storage, financing, and so on. Results so far however indicate that the Green Revolution can increase yields per acre and labor input per acre. This result is in sharp contrast to many of the results of tractorization and other forms of mechanization. Some of the results of research on rubber production are also labor using as well as yield increasing.[27]

The research institute approach to the problem seems to work reasonably well in agricultural activities. The evidence of the effectiveness of this approach is not so favorable in the case of industrial technology. Some institutions have turned out useful findings, but in general what little evidence there is supports the view that industrial research is best done in the context of the producing unit, whether public or privately owned. This general position, of course, emphasizes the importance of the protection and factor price distortion issues noted above. It also would doubtless require some form of public subsidy to encourage research activity.

Foreign Trade Policy

There are a wide range of ways in which foreign trade policy has affected employment growth. As already noted, import replacement activities are generally less labor intensive than are export activities, and the common neglect of exports has doubtless produced an employment growth rate below what it would have been had exports grown along with output. Two specific areas of policy are especially important —exchange rate policy and policy toward foreign investment.

Exchange rate policy. The ubiquity of the overvaluation of domestic currency and the consequent employment and export penalizing effects have been emphasized often. Less attention has been given to what constitutes the "right" exchange rate. It is generally recognized of course that with any form of protection, an exchange rate that equates demand and supply for foreign exchange will be less favorable to exports than would the rate prevailing under free trade. (This fact means incidentally that when capital goods are admitted free of duty, they are admitted at exchange rates more favorable than would have been the case with free trade.) There are however more complicating difficulties. A country that depends heavily on one or two export commodities that are doing well can support an exchange rate that puts the costs of a large part of the activities of the economy above foreign prices. The problem is more severe if the export sector has few technical links with the rest of the economy. The extreme example of this phenomenon is Kuwait where virtually everything tradable is imported. Kuwait is almost unique of course, but it does illustrate the nature of the problem. Substantial inflows of aid and foreign investment also help support an exchange rate that emits misleading signals. Thus defining an "equilibrium exchange rate" in terms simply of maintaining a strong balance of payments position is generally not a sufficient definition of a correct exchange rate for allocative purposes. The set of circumstances that can produce an overvaluation also of course militate against exports and add to the inducements to use foreign inputs at the expense of domestic ones.

Much of exchange rate discussion is pitched in terms of elasticities. Elasticities are difficult to measure, and low values are often found. From this finding, it is sometime concluded that the exchange does not really matter insofar as exports and imports are concerned. Recent measures are increasingly turning up higher values of elasticities. But measured elasticities do not tell us everything we need to know. They do not tell us much about new products that might become tradable because of devaluation. More important they tell us little about the allocative effects of a changed exchange rate. The exchange rate has the advantage of being more easily affected by government than wage rates, capital costs, and other factor prices. Further understanding of the definition of the appropriate exchange rate is therefore especially relevant.

There is another issue that is linked—a bit vaguely—to the exchange rate. The import substitution approach to development provides protection for infant import replacements. It does not provide protection for infant exportables, but of course penalizes them. There is no a priori reason why current imports are more suitable for protection than are new exports. But export protection is rare. In some sense what is needed is protection for domestic activities, but we are not very clear on how to devise policies that do that. This point has implications for exchange rate policy as one form of export protection is an "undervalued" domestic currency. Undervalued is in quotes to emphasize that the definition of equilibrium exchange is ambiguous in the context of the developing country.[28]

Policy toward foreign investment. Foreign investment has many links with employment. When capital formation was viewed as the primary or exclusive source of growth, foreign investment was considered simply another source of capital and thereby a source of employment. Questions that have arisen recently concern the extent to which foreign investment is of a form and content that is most suitable for the economy. In many respects the employment problems caused by foreign investment are the consequence of the kinds of policies reviewed in the preceding pages. There are indeed reasons to believe that these policies affect employment in foreign firms more directly than domestic firms because the former are better equipped to evaluate opportunities and explore alternatives. Some evidence exists to suggest that foreign owned firms are likely to choose more labor intensive techniques, where these are profitable, than is the domestic firm.

The chief source of difficulties arises from the fact that the foreign firm often has access to funds and to raw materials at prices different from those faced by domestic firms. In this event domestic policies may not be very relevant to the decision making of the foreign firm. This is surely correct to some extent. It is however equally important to emphasize that in many instances, probably in most, the various incentives offered to foreigners are unnecessary to attract them, and do encourage activities which are less domestic resource using than they would be in the absence of the incentives. These incentives also tend to encourage firms (domestic and foreign) to locate in central cities where access to imports is relatively easy. (This location effect is increased if the central city is the seat of government.) It is also apparent that foreign firms find it politically convenient, and economically possible, to pay wages that are generally higher than would be necessary to attract their required labor force.

Two generalizations appear justified as far as the relationship between foreign investment and employment are concerned. First, the whole range of policies described earlier as dampening labor absorption affect foreign firms in a direct way. Modification of these policies therefore should relieve some of the difficulties associated with the foreign firm. Second, the foreign firms are strategic agents in exporting. Encouraging them to establish in an economic environment that is essentially discouraging to exports means that one of the foremost advantages from foreign investment is lost. This second point is especially important as technology increasingly permits single aspects of processing activities to be done in different countries. Declines in the relative costs of international transportation have also added to profitability of firms performing one step in a manufacturing process in one country, and a second step in another. This kind of processing can be especially labor using, and a number of countries—Korea, Hong Kong, Mexico (along the border with the United States)—have found this activity to be an effective way to use labor. The central objective should therefore be to affect the impact foreign investment has, rather than to seek to curtail its total.[29]

Education Policy

In few countries has education policy been related very closely to employment.[30] The result has been not only the appearance of educated unemployed, but also bottleneck shortages in various parts of the economy. As noted earlier the fact that people with some education are unemployed is, if unskilled jobs are available, a behavioral phenomenon. Such workers are able to choose unemployment rather than take a job which they feel does not make satisfactory use of their training. It is not their education that makes them unemployed; it is their refusal to accept jobs other than those for which they have specific training. To accept lower level jobs would mean that the return on the investment in education is lower than if the person could get a job commensurate with his training. But that is another matter. If the individual accepts a job for which he is overeducated or if he remains unemployed after completing his education, the resources allocated to education are less than optimally used, i.e., too many resources are engaged in educational activities, and the rate of return on investment in education falls. The problem is made more severe if those who are unemployed simply remain in school because they can find no jobs. In this case the demand for education increases because there are no jobs for the unemployed. If some of the resources allocated to education had been used in other forms of capital formation, the demand for educated manpower would in fact be greater. The analysis however is further complicated by two additional considerations: the fact that educational opportunities are not uniform around most countries, e.g., rural areas are almost always neglected. Also many educational institutions are quite ineffective in training, e.g., persons taking engineering do not learn engineering, persons attending elementary school do not really learn to read and write, and so on. Concrete evidence is hard to come by, but there is little doubt that one reason for educated unemployed is that many persons who attended school acquired so little from the experience.

Again the exact policy to follow is not completely clear. Simply cutting back on educational opportunities has numerous social and political implications. So too would increasing the cost borne directly by the individual attending the school. Evidently a reduction in demand for places in educational institutions would be the most satisfactory way to meet the difficulty. Three general points are relevant in this connection. To a very large extent demand for education beyond elementary school is a demand for a job in modern, urban activities. Some of this demand is due to absence of opportunities and to unpleasant living conditions in rural areas. One attack on the problem might then be to try to make rural activities more appealing and more remunerative. This might mean a greater effort in education in particular areas than now, but considerably less in urban areas. It would probably also mean decidedly less emphasis on university level work.

The second general point has to do with the role of on the job training. Greater emphasis on this form of training greatly facilitates meshing supply and demand for specific skills and reduces the likelihood of "too much" or misdirected training. There are problems of course, and doubtless some form of subsidy or tax relief is essential. Finally, high wage rates in jobs that (as noted earlier) carry an educational prerequisite (frequently arbitrary) make such jobs unduly attractive. If wage rates in jobs calling for education can be established more nearly in accord with the prevailing demand and supply of educated labor, they (wages) would surely fall relative to other wages. This too may tend to discourage people from seeking as much education as they now do.

These various arguments approach the problem from the demand side. Another key element would be simply more employment opportunities for the less well educated, thereby raising the opportunity cost of attending school. All of these devices would dampen demand for education possibly significantly, with less social and political consequences than would accompany attacking the problem simply by reducing supply of educational opportunities.

Population Policy

Rapid rates of growth of population produce rapid rates of growth of the labor force, and the latter add to the employment problem. Population policies are found less infrequently now than a decade ago, but because of age distribution effects the labor force growth even in such countries is yet to be affected. Thus the failure of countries to pursue an effective population policy in the past is now penalizing employment. One can, of course, design assumptions as to substitutability, market mechanisms, and technology such that rapid population growth rates produce low incomes, not unemployment. Few observers would so argue now, and a population policy then becomes part of the attack on unemployment. This area of the problem has been explored so frequently that further comment here is unnecessary.

Conclusions

There are many other policies that have affected employment growth, but those just reviewed appear most important quantitatively and are common to more countries than others that might be discussed. It appears beyond doubt that this set of policies has significantly penalized the growth of employment opportunities in all sectors of the economies of the less developed countries, and has encouraged a movement of labor from rural or traditional sectors into seeking jobs in urban, modern activities. It also seems reasonably well established that modifications in these policies in the directions indicated above would have significant positive effects on labor use. The evidence supporting this latter point is both quantitative and descriptive. Several papers by Professor Gustav Ranis provide a large number of examples of practices that have encouraged labor absorption in countries where the commitment to the policy package outlined above has been less strong.[31] Similarly there are numerous studies published in the *International Labour Review* discussing labor intensive techniques in a wide range of activities, including public works, agriculture, and industry. On the quantitative side, regression equations of a great variety of shapes and forms have demonstrated the vulnerability of employment growth to increases in wage rates, the substitutability among inputs, and the way in which the policies outlined above create price signals that penalize employment growth.

What kinds of additional work in this area appear most useful at the present time? Three areas seem hopeful.

a. We need a great deal more quantification of the effects of such policies. If it were possible to show in a fairly convincing fashion that employment growth would be increased by x percentage points by doing something or by ceasing doing something, then it may be more feasible to influence policy makers or at least those who do influence the policy maker. So one aspect of work that may bring major returns would be empirical work that leads to quantitative conclusions as to the cost or the benefit for employment of existing and new policies.

b. We need study of alternative policy measures. It is helpful, but not helpful enough, to argue for emphasis on exports or an outward looking (in place of an inward looking) policy. Exactly how is this to be done? The design of policies is difficult, and calls for attention to many factors specific to the individual country. But even when working at fairly general levels, economists should be able—must become able—to suggest blueprints for the design of a policy. Coming to grips with this issue is similar in effect to improved quantification in that it gives the policymaker something concrete on which to focus his attention and energy.

c. We need to look more carefully at the implementation side of the employment policy problem. Why is it, for example, that countries almost inevitably swing into action as a balance of payments problem appears, but do so very little when employment difficulties arise? This is partly a matter of implementation machinery, but it is surely due to other things as well. Matters such as communication and explanation are important as are the nature and interests of those in power. In any event further work in this area must be part of the attack on the employment objective.

The analysis just completed is applicable, in broad terms, to all sectors of the economy. At the same time there are certain aspects of both the traditional sector and the modern that merit notice in connection with employment generation. It is useful therefore to look at these sectors separately to try to isolate those aspects, peculiar to the sector, that may have policy implications.

The Traditional Sector

Most attention (until quite recently) both in the professional literature and in practical policy decisions has been concerned with employment in the industrial and service sectors. To a lesser extent attention has been given to employment in modern sector agriculture, and much less effort has been expended on traditional agriculture and village life in general. This emphasis is due to a number of factors. In the 1950's it appeared possible that development in the modern sector could proceed rapidly enough and in such a manner that the labor surplus pool in the traditional sector would be absorbed within acceptable time spans. The unlimited supply of labor models of Arthur Lewis and Fei and Ranis, while not specifying actual periods of time, did fasten attention on capital formation in modern sector activities which would pull labor from the traditional sector. As labor moved out of traditional activities into the modern sector, rationalization of the economy of the former sector would occur thereby increasing productivity and output there as well. This argument, the details of which are the most generally known of development models, has surely affected the emphasis not only in models but also in practice.

Added to this reason are others as well. Modern sector industry lends itself to international investment much more than does agriculture. In all developing countries some new industry was (and is) certainly in order. Civil servants live in urban areas, and rarely enjoy rural life. Approaches to rural development have tended to take the form of giant dams and irrigation works, market roads, and other activities that were assumed to provide an environment within which village life would develop somehow on its own. All of these elements have contrived to direct attention away from employment possibilities in rural areas and to justify the assumption that employment growth in the modern sectors will be adequate to eliminate the problem.

It is now abundantly clear that if the employment problem is to be manageable, ways must be found to absorb much more labor in the rural areas than has been the case in the recent past. This follows from the fact that such a large proportion of the labor force is now engaged in rural activity and the rate of growth of population is so high that even the most optimistic assumptions about urban employment growth will leave huge and growing numbers to find some acceptable role in agriculture and other rural activities. Emphasis is placed on finding an acceptable role, not simply on the continued use of the rural sector as some sort of survival reservoir of labor. Also the term "role" is used rather than "employment" to call attention to the arguments, noted earlier, that forms of earning a claim on resources other than conventional employment are included.

It is convenient to separate the discussion into three sections, employment in agriculture itself, non-agricultural rural activities, and the more nebulous issues surrounding the efforts to make life a bit more appealing in rural areas.

Agricultural Employment

The policies reviewed in the preceding section have dampened employment growth in agriculture no less than in other sectors of the economies. Examples abound of product and factor pricing practices that encourage substitution of capital for labor and do little to raise yields.[32] There are several studies that demonstrate that prices of machinery relative to that of labor affects in a significant way techniques used in agriculture. These machines are almost invariably more labor-replacing than output-increasing. They also benefit large farms substantially more than the smaller farms, and it is the latter in most countries that are most desirable from a social and employment point of view. The various aspects of the import substitution strategy that have dampened export possibilities have in many cases penalized agricultural (including forestry and fishing) output and employment in a rather obvious way. Also credit procedures to finance fertilizer, new seeds, and local water distribution arrangements almost always favor the larger units, which in turn have the greater incentive to seek ways to substitute machinery for labor. In most countries the fiscal systems are frequently ineffective in agriculture, both with respect to land and agricultural incomes. This has resulted not only in substantial profits going untaxed, but also creates difficulties for affecting the techniques used and the products produced in agriculture.

Perhaps the most important element acting on agricultural employment is technological and seed development. When the labor force in agriculture is rising rapidly but the quantity of land under cultivation is increasing slowly (or not at all), rising output per man implies rising yields per hectare. If yields per hectare increase more rapidly than output per worker, then employment per hectare rises. Thus in this situation (rapidly growing labor force and slow growing area under cultivation) any innovation that raises yields per hectare without reducing labor per unit of output will increase employment per hectare. Yield increasing innovations are therefore equivalent to an increase in land. Such an innovation then would have the effect of requiring more use of the relatively abundant factor (labor) and less use of the relative scarce factor (land). As noted earlier, it is this category of technical change that is most effective in attacking the employment problem in any sector.[33]

The evidence available to date indicates that the new high yielding seed varieties (the Green Revolution) are land augmenting in the sense just described. The new high yielding varieties of seeds affect yields in a number of ways: they are more responsive to fertilizer, they respond better to improved cultivation and weeding practices, and in some instances are better suited to double cropping than previous seeds were. (Farm machinery that speeds land preparation and other processes also facilitates multiple cropping.) These results make profitable the use of greater labor input and the higher yields also help the farmer finance his purchase of new inputs. They do however seem to place greater importance on water than ordinary varieties.

Available studies of Taiwan, Japan, Thailand, Philippines, and Mexico suggest the importance of this kind of picture of the technological evolution of the agriculture sector. Even now with her significantly higher wage rates, Japanese rice production is more labor intensive than that in a number of other rice growing areas. In Mexico the modern agriculture sector has applied both yield increasing and labor displacing technologies, and the larger traditional sector, being poorly placed to adopt or compete with them, weakens as a provider of livelihoods.

In the agricultural sector, the diffusion of new technical knowledge is especially relevant because of the large numbers involved and because farmers are frequently uninformed, illiterate, and difficult to teach. These observations apply most directly to the small scale operator. It is also clear that small scale operators are usually less able to risk losses and to keep informed on new technical developments. Similarly credit, marketing, and storage arrangements can apparently be designed more easily for large scale than for small scale operators. At the same time the most favorable effects in terms of employment and income distribution of the new technologies depend on their being suitable and available to the small farmer.

The seeds themselves are as applicable to small as to large producing units. There are then the kinds of things just noted, credit, etc. plus some things to be noted later (e.g., land reform) that require additional work. Also, and perhaps most important at the moment, is the need for a new type farm machinery. If farm machinery suitable only for large scale operators develops, then it is increasingly difficult to meet other needs—e.g., credit, marketing, land reform—of small scale farmers. That it is not utopian to assume that it is possible to develop suitable agricultural machinery and thereby facilitate selective mechanization is suggested by the experiences of Taiwan and Japan. A by-product of using machines designed especially for a given area is a much lower rate of breakdown than is observed where inappropriately modified, imported machines are used. More importantly of course ready availability of labor displacing machines that affect yields per acre only slightly will result in the larger farms becoming more and more profitable relative to the small farmer. In this event the small farm has less and less chance of survival as a viable institution, and the larger units are becoming less labor absorbing.

It is in the area of selective mechanization that technical research seems most urgent. Such technical research would have to be organized and financed by governments, the World Bank, United Nations, foundations, or other such organizations. It obviously cannot be arranged and carried out by the small farmers themselves. Of equal importance is a change in lending policies of international financial agencies toward understanding more clearly the implications of what the impact of their policies is on the development of agricultural activities and employment.

In those parts of the world where land relative to population is abundant, the problems just alluded to are of course less urgent. In many such places, e.g., Malaysia, parts of South America, and Africa, a higher rate of growth of employment in agriculture depends more immediately on making land available for cultivation. In some instances land reform is a necessary part of doing this, while in others better tax measures might do it, and in still others changed pricing policies may do the trick.

Other Rural Economic Activities

If the rural areas of the developing countries are to be more than simply reservoirs where unemployed and low productivity labor is hidden, rural activities in addition to agriculture must also be given a chance to grow. Of special importance is the question of increased industrial activities in small towns. The most obvious of such industrial activities are those having to do with processing agricultural products and the manufacture of agriculture inputs. Still, there is no a priori reason why some other non-agricultural activities would not also be possible.

Some of the development policies discussed earlier have had effects on the location of new activities. Especially do exchange rate policy and other import substitution measures that result in the new activities relying heavily on imported inputs and imported physical capital encourage their location in port cities. So too does the widespread use of imported technology. Where direct government controls are common, it is also convenient to a producer to be located near the control agency.

Few data are available that tell us much about factors that affect the location of new activities (except in the obvious case of natural resource based activities). Evidently infrastructure deficiencies in many rural areas penalize location away from major cities. It is extremely doubtful, however, that simply building infrastructure into rural areas to match that in urban areas would do much. At the same time the very building of infrastructure—roads, power facilities, irrigation, school buildings—plus rural housing offers significant employment opportunities for wage labor in themselves. These activities are, or can be, very labor intensive, and use other domestic resources quite intensively. It may be noted that labor used for these purposes should be paid money wages, not asked to work for no wage. Wage payments to people in these activities will often stimulate secondary demands for goods and services, and hence employment. Increments in consumption induced by such wage payments will frequently be concentrated in areas where excess capacity or easily increased capacity exists. This applies not only to food products, but to other consumer products as well, textiles, simple wood products, and so on. So independent of the industry inducing effect of such infrastructure expenditure, it should offer direct employment opportunities accompanied by some multiplier effect on output and employment. These expenditures will also help make the rural areas somewhat more pleasant, and the opportunity cost of leaving somewhat higher than it would otherwise be. Difficulties usually cited as to why these activities are not more common have to do with finance and organizational capacity. Also it is doubtless correct that fears of inflation or balance of payments problems emerging are not completely unfounded.[34]

There is relatively little work on rural industrialization. If infrastructure were provided and if appropriate modifications in general policy were made, what else is required? The major cost advantage of areas away from central cities is lower wage rates for unskilled labor. Professional labor may however be more expensive as such labor may require a premium to move away from an urban center. Very large scale operations are also evidently unlikely to succeed in areas where population is widely dispersed. Small scale operations that have a high ratio of unskilled to skilled labor, that use inputs and produce outputs that are easily and cheaply transported do offer considerable opportunity. Putting out systems of one kind or another also may be possible in some areas. Such a description does not lead directly to specific projects, but it does suggest that the idea of rural (perhaps non-central city is a better term) industry is not complete nonsense. Some direct help (or direct investment) from the government is sure to be required, especially at the outset. More importantly at the moment is simply the acceptance of the necessity of promoting rural non-agricultural activities, and that it makes sense to try to do something in this area.

The Rural Social and Political Setting

It is in the rural areas that such issues as work sharing and group decision-making are most apparent and most frequently encountered. The institutions that help shape the way people respond to various incentives are even less well understood and less defined in rural than in urban areas. In particular the nature of the household decision-making process and how it affects individual behavior and individual response to incentives and opportunities is not very well understood. Also ambiguous are the exact form of sharing mechanisms and, equally important, how much strain such mechanisms can absorb. In general terms the rural society is being subjected to tradition upsetting and destroying developments. These developments affect not only the number of income earning jobs, but also the number of people in the labor force, the sharing arrangements, attitudes toward work and leisure and toward whether one considers oneself unemployed, and the definition of the good life. New arrangements must therefore be sought that will provide opportunities (or roles, of which conventional jobs are one example) sufficiently attractive to dampen markedly urban migration. At the same time, as noted above, the traditional sector must not be—indeed can not be—considered simply a place to keep that part of the population that is unable to find a place in the modern sector.

A number of specific aspects of all this are generally regarded as important. Rural education and health facilities are, almost everywhere, less satisfactory than in urban areas. So too are most recreation and entertainment facilities. Although there is little solid empirical evidence on this question, it seems clear that improved education and health are necessary ingredients of the new rural environment. The difficulties due to educational policies noted above may well have been avoided had fewer resources been allocated to higher level education programs and more to the establishing of effective elementary educational programs in rural areas. This however is simply an hypothesis that needs to be researched, rather than a clear cut policy guideline.

A second specific aspect of the rural scene that surely matters greatly is land ownership arrangements. An enormous amount of work has been done on matters concerning land reform and related problems.[35] These investigations demonstrate the virtually unlimited implications of trying to remodel existing land ownership systems. One evident point may be noted: providing ownership rights is hardly enough and perhaps the easiest part of the problem. The problems noted above of making available to small scale operators appropriate technology, water, seeds, marketing arrangements, credit, and extension services are much less readily accomplished.

The third aspect to which attention is directed has to do with the "rural power structure." Traditional societies have a well defined social structure. As this structure deteriorates and some increased fluidity emerges, to whom economic and social advance is open becomes important. If land ownership declines as the chief source of power, if moneylending loses out to improved credit facilities, if improved education makes some inroads on fear and superstition, and if new opportunities emerge in rural areas what is necessary to ensure that this social and economic fluidity remains? Included in this range of issues is family organization and the extent to which individuals within the family can respond to opportunities that are seen. Here again is an area that appears crucial and yet about which our understanding is so limited that policy or approaches to policy are virtually non-existent.

The points briefly noted in the preceding paragraphs take us well beyond the notion of job creation. They do however point up the way in which the employment environment extends well beyond that of simply the number of jobs available. As the analysis is widened in this way, evidently the conventional tools of the economists become less adequate. Unfortunately the tools of other disciplines have, at least to date, appeared almost equally wobbly.

The Modern Sector

Employment in the modern sectors of the less developed economies can generally be treated in a more orthodox fashion than is the case in traditional sectors. Open unemployment is a useful notion here, and there is ample evidence that such open unemployment exists in urban areas. There is also much more wage employment in the modern sector than in traditional sectors. More conventional development policies therefore act more or less directly on employment in the modern sector activities. Perhaps the major disappointment on the employment side in development in the 1950's and 1960's has been the failure of modern sector activities (especially new manufacturing activities) to absorb labor at satisfactory rates even though output was often growing at relatively high rates. The kinds of policies discussed above, especially those that affect factor prices and export potential, have surely been responsible for a significant part of this failure. It is of course unlikely that the growth of employment in manufacturing and other modern sectors would have been high enough to solve the problem. The point however is that with a rate of growth of employment in the modern sector approximating that of output plus a concentration of effort in rural areas along the lines noted in the preceding section, considerable progress is possible. (The problem of the flow of labor from rural to urban centers is reviewed later.) The question now is what are those conditions that have to be met in order that employment growth, relative to output, be much higher than it now is.[36] There are several issues on which attention should be fastened.

Wage Setting

The single most important issue is probably the wage setting mechanism in the urban sector. As already noted, urban wage rates are higher than average rural income in almost all developing countries, and in many the differential is increasing. Clearly the determinants of wage rates in most urban centers is not a simple matter of supply and demand of labor. There are numerous explanations offered of which three seem the most frequently encountered.

One frequently finds arguments that wages *should* rise as productivity rises. This argument is sometimes based on the notion that competitive pressure will in fact push wages up as productivity rises, but such an argument is clearly false if there is unemployed labor available. It is also frequently based on the notion that unless wages do rise with productivity, profits will shoot up in a manner that is socially and politically unacceptable. This argument is also invalid if (as already noted) some substitutability exists, and if demand for the product is growing more rapidly than productivity. Nevertheless, both these arguments have been used to support a wage policy or an attitude toward wages that tends to push them up.

The second argument rests on the role of the foreign enterprise (and possibly the more aggressive domestic firms). These firms often increase wage rates rather routinely, partly because they do so in their home country, partly to gain political favor, partly because productivity increases allow it with no reduction in profit per unit of output, and partly because it is a fairly painless way to ensure getting the best labor available and avoiding labor difficulties. There is some empirical evidence that suggests that wage rates in manufacturing in the less developed countries grow at about the same percentage rate as those in the more developed countries.[37] Increased wage rates in these firms will tend to pull all urban wages up. In so doing not only are more labor intensive techniques and products discouraged, but those firms where productivity is rising less rapidly (frequently smaller, domestically owned firms) are penalized. In encouraging (or not discouraging) wage increases in the foreign firms, governments tend thereby to dampen employment growth of such firms, and, more importantly, to make the development of indigenous firms more difficult.

The third general argument that is often offered as to why urban wage rates rise has to do with the skill mix and educational requirements of the urban labor force. The qualifications are frequently higher than for rural jobs, therefore wages should be higher. Again this is not a valid normative argument, and if it is indeed descriptive of the labor market, then the latter is simply not working very effectively. This is especially the case as it becomes increasingly evident that learning-by-doing is a fairly effective device, and many of the stated educational requirements are unnecessary.

Earlier it was concluded that exactly the correct wage behavior was not unambiguously clear, though there was a strong presumption that fairly constant wages will make the most significant contribution to employment growth. Within the modern, urban sector however, a further specific objective is that the average wage rate in this sector should certainly rise no more rapidly than average rural income. To accomplish this objective would require, in most countries, an explicit wage policy. But the formulation of such a policy will remain difficult until we have a clearer explanation of the exact mechanism by which urban wage rates are pushed up. As noted above, one evident thing to do is to change the investment incentive package away from the now common practice of encouraging the most capital intensive activities available. Incentive systems that rest on increments in employment are easily designed, and even where their objective impact is modest, they can have an important effect by creating a much more employment conscious atmosphere.

The wage rate issue bears directly on another aspect of urban employment, namely the role of small scale firms. Such firms are essential not only in rural areas (as emphasized above), but in the modern, urban sector as well. Smaller firms are generally more labor intensive and hence rising wage rates penalize them more. Incentives based on size of investment also discriminate against the small units. Just as in rural areas therefore explicit attention needs to be given to the creation of an economic environment in which small units are not penalized.

Foreign Enterprises and Technology

The foreign firm is usually found in urban areas (except those concerned with using natural resources), and the question of technology is perhaps most immediately apparent here. The general argument made earlier that foreign firms have more information and are better able to appraise options than are domestic firms bears repeating. They therefore are often more responsive to market signals, and are more affected by those policies that do in fact result in misleading price signals. There is some evidence, though neither systematic nor extensive, that urban foreign firms do employ more suitable techniques when it pays them to do so. It is however a complex question to untangle the exact circumstances which make it pay. Domestically owned firms on the other hand are less well informed and less able to appraise the options that they do know about. They also are more susceptible to salesmen of foreign, shiny equipment of which the world has an ample supply. There are also many examples of aid agencies providing financing arrangements and imposing restrictions on purchases that result in firms in the developing countries being barred from the most suitable markets. Finally where the firms are owned or effectively controlled or operated by civil servants the pressure and incentives to seek out a range of options from which to choose is generally less.[38]

These various points suggest that the foreign firm itself is not a major culprit insofar as urban employment is concerned in that they do not willy-nilly violate the domestic factor supply guides as they see them. The problem here is to make sure that the signals are right, and as noted this is not an easy matter. Firms that have easy access to foreign funds and technology may in fact require signals of a particular kind to induce them to use appropriate techniques and product mix. On the other hand domestic firms in the modern sector appear less able to appraise and respond to market signals and to search out methods that work effectively in a given environment. In this respect modern sector entrepreneurs and managers are probably less qualified, less well prepared for their duties than are their counterparts in the traditional sectors. In the latter sector available evidence indicates that the economic "agents do understand their position well enough to know when and how to react to changing opportunities.

Part of the attack on the employment problem in urban industrial activity therefore is the training of managers, foremen, entrepreneurs in such a way that they are better able to appraise their own interests, as well as search out new ideas and techniques. This need is somewhat different from that to which attention is usually placed, that of technical training. One of the reasons that employment incentive systems are important then is that they call extra attention to the advantages of the adaptation and modification of the more readily available technology.

Virtually all countries have special incentive systems aimed at encouraging the establishment of new industrial activities. As has been noted in several places almost all of these incentive systems (they are usually tax holidays) make capital cheaper and more easily available than it would otherwise be. The simple elimination of such incentive systems would have some favorable effect, but probably not enough to overcome all of the biases that exist against the choice of the most labor using technique that is technologically efficient. The point made in the preceding paragraph that domestic entrepreneurs and managers need extra strong signals is one reason why special incentives to seek and use the most labor intensive techniques are necessary. Foreign firms also have, as noted, many economically rational reasons to choose techniques less suitable than they could be under different circumstances. Also an incentive system that rewards the use of labor should affect not only the choice of techniques, but also affect the efforts to search for, and to design, new labor using techniques. (Incentive systems are not suitable means of affecting the level of investment. This objective must be attacked by other means.) Given this conclusion, a study of specific incentive arrangements is useful. Most economists steer clear of such tasks, and conceptually there is not much involved. Practically however there are a lot of difficulties in terms of implementing and financing. It may be noted again that tax holidays are not very powerful instruments.

Service Activities

The service sector in the urban community includes both a modern part and a part that serves somewhat as a reservoir or hiding place for some members of the labor force. Some of the issues raised earlier about traditional agriculture apply here as well. In general however we are safer in saying that most of this labor is forced into these activities—sidewalk selling, shoe shining, car washing, pedicabs, etc.—because of lack of alternative opportunities. To the extent that a livelihood is earned in this way, these activities serve an important function. It is a commonplace of the development literature that the widespread use of personal and household servants (in both rural and urban areas) is, to a significant degree, a recognition of the importance of sharing arrangements. Supporting sidewalk hawkers and similar "service" activities is often in the same category.

Modern service activities are generally induced activities, rather than leading sectors. Their growth therefore depends on the overall growth of the economy, especially that of the modern sector. It is evident of course that most service sectors are, almost by definition, relatively labor intensive. Expansion of this sector is therefore an important source of employment creation.

There are two notable exceptions to the notion of the growth of service activities being dependent on the growth of other sectors. One is the tourist industry about which much is known and little more need be said. The other has to do with a specific service that for reasons never fully explored is neglected in most developing countries, repair and maintenance. Repair is an activity that is almost by definition very labor intensive although in some cases it may demand considerable skill. Improved and increased repair and maintenance will not only provide jobs as such, it will mean more capital available directly because of the repair, and indirectly because good, inexpensive repair can help to delay economic obsolescence. In this connection the point made earlier that declining relative costs of international transportation make tradable much that previously was not tradable is also relevant. There is some evidence to suggest that some repair work is now, in fact, exported. Some watch repair is in this category as also are certain kinds of health services, i.e., stays at spas, resorts, etc., though where tourism ends and health services begin is difficult to ascertain.

The peculiar neglect of repair and maintenance deserves remedy, and studies that seek out new exportable services are to be encouraged.

Links Between Traditional and Modern Sectors

The two preceding sections considered the traditional and modern sectors in isolation, and sought to identify those characteristics that appear most important in understanding labor use within these sectors. The two sectors are of course not independent, and movement of persons and products between the sectors is a major element in the picture. Although there are many strands worthy of exploring, attention may be limited to two: the flow of labor between the sectors and the internal terms of trade between the rural and urban sectors.

The Flow of Labor Between the Sectors

In almost all developing countries, there has been a marked flow of labor from rural areas to cities. Some evidence indicates that labor moves first from farms to smaller towns, then to larger towns, and eventually on to cities. In almost all situations this movement worsens the employment problem and adds to congestion and other problems of developing urban areas in a more rational way. There is indeed some evidence that creating one new job in a city may worsen urban unemployment because labor flows to cities as word gets around that employment is increasing.[39] The creation of one new job may therefore induce more than one additional worker to move to town. In the larger urban centers the means of caring for the unemployed are generally less satisfactory than they are in rural areas, and the social and political implications of open urban unemployment are more far reaching than those of rural idleness. In any event the movement is generally undesirable. How may it be slowed down?

A central argument in our discussion of the traditional sector was that rural and small town life could be made more appealing and more satisfying by a set of policies ranging from the establishment of new industries to land reform measures. In addition it was argued that a fundamental objective of urban wage policy should be that wage rates in urban centers should not exceed average income in rural areas. Suppose these things could in fact be done, would it stem the tide? All presumptions indicate that the flow would certainly be slowed down, but again measurement is virtually non-existent.

The key explanatory variables are wage rates differentials between urban/modern and rural/traditional and the relative rates of job creation (at these wage rates) in these two sectors. If the wage rate differential is given and the probability of employment after various periods of waiting given, then one may still find it profitable to move to town and accept unemployment for specified periods. Profitable here would mean that the present value of one's future income would be higher if one opts for initial unemployment followed by high wage employment than it would be if he opts for continued employment at lower wage rates. Evidently if the probability of finding a high wage job approaches zero over any reasonable time period, then moving to town does not pay. Similarly if the wage differential is very small, it will not pay to do so. To seek simply to reduce the probability of finding a job is hardly a sensible approach, thus the emphasis must be on reducing the wage rate differentials and on creating increased job opportunities in the rural/traditional sector.

In some conflict with this approach is an argument that explains the movement of labor from rural to urban in much more institutional and sociological terms. Such arguments emphasize the appeal of urban living to those who are educated, well informed, and ambitious. If improved education in rural areas does take place, if new acquaintances with the rest of the world do occur, then those who can will move to the city irrespective of wage differentials and job probabilities. In this way of thinking the urban movement is very much a part of the development process, and to stop it without stopping development is virtually impossible.

It is doubtless correct to include in the dynamics of development an increase in the proportion of the population living in urban areas. But the rate of this flow is surely not fixed beyond any policy measure. Nor does it appear inevitable that one or two cities get larger and larger, while the rest of the countryside remains largely rural and small townish. The policy objective then is to affect the rate of flow of labor and to seek to induce it to settle in smaller urban centers and rural towns. In trying to do this the wage rate differential, job probability model seems crucial. In any event, it is generally correct to say that of greater importance than an inherent dynamism of urbanization residing in the development process is the relentless pressure of population growth. In some countries population growth may so dominate the situation in rural areas, that no manageable policy can be expected to have much of an impact.

Research in these areas appears very fruitful. We need to know much more about the empirical magnitudes of labor movements and the extent of responsiveness of these movements to employment opportunities in rural areas and to wage differentials. Considerable research is being done on this problem now. Also important in this (and other) areas is the household decision making process. As the traditional arrangements break down, and it becomes economically imperative to find new ways of earning a livelihood, the search for these new ways and new arrangements is rarely a simple individual action. But what kind of action it is, where and how decisions are made, and therefore how inducements and incentives must operate to affect decisions is less clear; and of course economists are less equipped to investigate. In this area the question of the employment environment in especially important.

The Internal Terms of Trade

The simplest measure of internal terms of trade is that between agricultural and non-agricultural products. The simplest argument making use of these terms of trade is that rising food prices in urban areas tend to justify and to contribute to pushing urban wage rates up. And this upward push then dampens demand for labor. At the same time these increases in agricultural prices have not had the kind of impact on rural incomes necessary to encourage people to remain on the farms. Part of the difficulty is that of institutional arrangements for distribution, the usually criticized middleman. But also the kinds of difficulties mentioned earlier as to credit, cost of fertilizer, water availability make it difficult for the small scale operator to exploit rising agriculture prices.

The other side of the coin is also relevant. The creation of high cost industries, mainly supplying consumer goods, often means that prices paid by all consumers —rural and urban—go up even more than agriculture income. The way in which government policies have in fact squeezed agriculture is described for a number of countries. In those countries (e.g., Pakistan) where the discrimination of government policy against agriculture, especially small scale agriculture, has been most thoroughly studied, it seems clear that that policy itself has been most crucial in accounting for the failures on the agricultural side. Thus the worst of two worlds happens. Agricultural prices rise and urban wage rates are affected, but the rise in agricultural prices does little for the farmer. Such an extreme case is not completely realistic, but this kind of problem is frequently observed.[40]

The general point to be emphasized is that changing internal terms of trade over extended periods indicate first of all that allocation may not be working well. While it is probably wrong to argue that in all cases a different set of policies would have prevented any change in terms of trade, it is correct to argue that policies in many countries have contributed to this end. The institutional rigidities and more entrenched social and economic organizations are also at work, but they often have been strengthened by government policies rather than worn away by such policies. Still another side, bearing more directly on the employment issue, is the relationship between product prices in urban and rural areas and how these prices affect the urban-rural wage differential. And these issues too take us into the economic policy area as well as into the employment environment area.

Conclusions

One conclusion that emerges is reasonably clear: the economic policies followed in many less developed countries have significantly dampened the rate of growth of employment. The general nature that policy change should take to increase the rate of growth of employment relative to output is also fairly clear. There are at least two major unknowns: we have relatively little empirical evidence that shows how much effect a major redirection of policy would have on the rate of labor absorption. To accumulate such empirical evidence should be a high priority objective.

The second major unknown has to do with the design and implementation of policy. There are many reasons why governments make the kind of economic policy that they do.[41] Availability of convincing economic argument supported by empirical evidence is doubtless helpful, but surely is not enough. What kinds of policy are most easily and effectively implemented by governments with few well educated, well trained civil servants? More specifically, what kind of implementation problems would be faced in trying to induce governments of less developed countries to re-orient their policies in the direction the preceding discussion points toward? Still more specifically, what are the major difficulties in implementing a set of policies that would make the rural areas and smaller towns more interesting and hopeful places in which to live and work? These kinds of questions are as crucial as is the determination of the correct policy. It may well be found in a number of instances that certain measures simply can not be carried through, and such a conclusion evidently affects the employment strategy that is suitable. At the same time, it is unacceptable simply to say of any change in direction of policy that it is politically unfeasible, i.e., that the policies adopted are in fact the only ones that were politically feasible. Investigations that lead to greater understanding of organizational and administrative machinery of implementation and of mechanisms by which governments can be convinced of the validity of economic arguments would also yield high pay offs.

The preceding argument leads to a more general point: what are the real constraints in a given economy? Or, what do we accept as given and beyond our capacity to influence and therefore must work around, and what is it that we recognize as changeable, i.e., as subject to policy? The answer to this question may vary from country to country and in the same country over time. In a number (possibly large) of instances, the economist seeks to get policies enacted that are essentially so alien to the community that the whole effort is futile.[42] Just as steel mills can be alien to an economy so can an economic policy that is in some sense technically correct be inappropriate, given certain other characteristics of the system. It has been observed that economics is a study of the implications of choice, and sociology the study of why we have no choice. While this statement exaggerates the argument, that choice is not everywhere a point of substance, and an important empirical question is where can we change things and where we can not. There are then really two questions: what are the obstacles to a satisfactory resolution of the labor use problem and which of these obstacles lend themselves to surmounting? The answer to the second question is not only a matter of government implementation capacity, but links up directly with a wide range of characteristics of a society that are conventionally defined as non-economic.

These latter characteristics have been referred to above as the employment environment, and a major research objective is the more systematic definition of the precise content of this environment. Certain of these characteristics now seem especially important, and warrant important research efforts. Perhaps most important are matters having to do with sharing arrangements. Associated with this are the various issues involved in understanding the decision making processes of households, about which we now know very little. A third aspect of the employment environment that appears crucial has to do with incentive systems in general, particularly their operation in rural areas. Especially do we need to know more about inducement variables other than wage rates and income. For example, does land ownership as such (in contrast to tenancy of one kind or another) induce people to be more satisfied with rural life and lower real income. Does participation in government affect one's efforts, one's willingness to save, one's commitment to change? A fourth area that is important to the employment issue, and that now seems researchable, is that of implementation capacity. Needed is not so much additional studies on skills and training as researches on how government policy is determined and why (as asked above) some types of policies seem easier to implement than do others. Studies of how a government's capacity to implement should affect policy recommendations, and in what way should that capacity be introduced as a constraint are surely issues that merit a great deal of attention.

A great number of other topics could be mentioned, but the argument is that with a clearer understanding of the nature of the employment environment we can design policies that will move us a long way toward reducing the acuteness of the problem. This amounts to arguing that given a more accurate description than we now have of the several points noted above the general policy prescriptions outlined in the preceding sections can be made concrete enough to be applied, and will have a considerable impact. It also argues that we can do much more than has been done by fairly orthodox policy instruments. This does not mean that structural and institutional changes are not relevant and important. Rather the point is that until we have exploited the usual policy measures more fully than we now have, the specific content of much of direct government action cannot be defined. This is a generally optimistic conclusion: if improvement in the employment situation must wait until there are major structural and social revolutions and disinterested, socially minded leaders take over, then there are grounds for considerable pessimism.

Notes

1. The literature is of course vast, and I cannot claim to have read everything that would be helpful. I have tried to be selective in my references, and to limit them to those that appear most original or that state an argument in an especially clear fashion. Most of the references cited contain many additional references.

2. The distinction drawn in these paragraphs is relevant to a number of issues in development economics. The distinction was formerly usually identified as the "structural approach" vs. the "policy approach." For example, explanations of Latin American inflation were identified as either structural or monetary. See Dudley Seers, "A Theory of Inflation and Growth in Underdeveloped Countries Based on the Experience of Latin America," *Oxford Economic Papers* (February, 1962). The term "radical" is now more often used in place of structural implying rather drastic (in some sense) and direct action, rather than reliance on conventional policies. The text seeks to avoid these terms, and to try to examine the effectiveness of all policies—conventional and radical—in the context of the prevailing environment.

3. On general issues associated with identifying and measuring unemployment see David Turnham and Ingelies Jaeger, *The Employment Problem in Less Developed Countries* (Paris, Organization for Economic Co-operation and Development, 1971), and the literature cited there.

4. The recent studies of unemployment of the International Labor Organization define as the unemployed those whose income is very much below the country's average. See *Towards Full Employment: A Programme for Colombia* (Geneva, 1970); *Matching Employment Opportunities and Expectations: A Programme for Action in Ceylon* (Geneva, 1971); and *Employment, Incomes and Equality: A Strategy for Increasing Productive Employment in Kenya* (Geneva, 1972).

5. See Gene M. Tidrick, "Wage Spillover and Unemployment in a Wage Gap Economy," Research Memorandum No. 47, Center for Development Economics, Williams College (Williamstown, Massachusetts, 1972) for further elaboration of the means of support point. See also Michael Todaro, "A Model of Labor Migration and Urban Unemployment in Less Developed Countries," *American Economic Review* (March, 1969) and John R. Harris and Michael Todaro, "Wages, Industrial Employment and Labor Productivity," *Eastern Africa Economic Review* (June, 1969).

6. On the question of the role of public works in creating employment and reducing poverty see the especially helpful articles John P. Lewis, "The Public-Works Approach to Low-End Poverty Problems: The New Potentialities of an Old Answer," mimeo (Princeton University, 1973) and S. V. Sethuraman, "Underemployment in Rural India: Implications for Rural Works Programme," Economic Affairs Division Staff Paper, United States Agency for International Development (New Delhi, 1972).

7. Some discussion of China's early efforts along these lines is found in Christopher Howe, *Employment and Economic Growth in Urban China* (Cambridge, England, Cambridge University Press, 1971).

8. See the Tidrick and Todaro articles cited in footnote 5 for further elaboration of the point raised here.

9. The preponderance of own account workers in most developing countries is an important aspect of the employment environment that has not been discussed as much as it deserves. The ILO Report on Kenya (see footnote 4) has a chapter on the "Informal Sector" that brings out a number of arguments relevant to this issue.

10. Some further discussion of this point is found in S.N. Eisenstadt, "Breakdowns of Modernization," *Economic Development and Cultural Change* (July, 1964) where numerous further references are cited. David C. McClelland, *The Achieving Society* (New York, Van Nostrand, 1961), also is helpful.

11. There is not much literature on decision making in the household in the less developed countries. Eisenstadt, *op. cit.*, has some interesting points and useful hypotheses.

12. See Chapter 22 of the I.L.O. Kenya Report, *op. cit.*, for an elaboration of this argument.

13. There is of course much material on Japan. The most inclusive is William W. Lockwood, *The Economic Development of Japan* (Princeton, Princeton University Press, 1954).

14. An early and very clear discussion of the applicability of the conventional Keynesian model to a less developed country is V.K.R.V. Rao, "Investment, Income and the Multiplier in an Underdeveloped Economy," *The Indian Economic Review* (February, 1952).

15. Empirical work on this argument is just beginning. Ronald Soligo and James W. Land have done some especially helpful work on this and related issues. See especially Ronald Soligo and James W. Land, "Models of Development Incorporating Distribution Aspects," Paper No. 22, Program of Development Studies, Rice University, (1972) and Ronald Soligo, "Factor Intensity of Consumption Patterns, Income

Distribution and Employment Growth," Economic Growth Center, Yale University (New Haven, 1972). Also useful are W.R. Cline, *Potential Effects of Income Redistribution on Economic Growth* (New York, Praeger, 1972) and Harold Lubell, "Effect of Distribution of Income on Consumers' Expenditures," *American Economic Review* (March, 1947).

16. The implication of writing down capital values and the means to bring such a writing down about have been little discussed in the literature. The problem would seem to warrant more attention than it has received. Gordon C. Winston has studied the capacity utilization question from a variety of angles. See his "Capital Utilization in Economic Development," *Economic Journal* (March, 1971).

17. A summary of available research on the incidence of fiscal policy on income distribution in the less developed countries is Jacob Meerman, "Fiscal Incidence in Empirical Studies of Income Distribution in Poor Countries," Agency for International Development, Discussion Paper No. 25 (1972). A more general discussion of fiscal policy and employment is Alan Peacock and G.K. Shaw, *Fiscal Policy and the Employment Problem* (Paris, Organization for Economic Co-operation and Development, 1971).

18. The literature on substitutability of inputs and the responsiveness of economic agents to price signals has grown rapidly in recent years. See especially Jere Behrman, *Supply Response in Underdeveloped Agriculture* (Amsterdam, North-Holland, 1968); Jeffery G. Williamson, "Capital Accumulation, Labor-Saving, and Labor Absorption Once More," *Quarterly Journal of Economics* (February, 1971); Henry J. Bruton, "The Elasticity of Substitution in Developing Countries," Research Memorandum No. 45, Center for Development Economics, Williams College (Williamstown, Massachusetts, 1972); and Mark R. Daniels, "Differences in Efficiency Among Industries in Developing Countries," *American Economic Review* (March, 1969).

19. See H.S. Houthakker, "On Some Determinants of Saving in Developed and Under-developed Countries," in *Problems in Economic Development,* edited by E.A.G. Robinson (London, MacMillan, 1965).

20. Good discussions of the wage rate issue are found in papers by Elliott Berg, "Wage Structures in Less Developed Countries," in *Wage Policy Issues in Economic Development,* edited by A.D. Smith (London, MacMillan, 1969), and by Lloyd G. Reynolds, "Wages and Employment in a Labor Surplus Economy," *American Economic Review* (March, 1965).

21. A satisfactory formal theory of wage rate determination in labor surplus economies is not available, and is badly needed. A most interesting and provocative article on this subject is H.A. Turner and D.A.S. Jackson, "On the Determination of the General Wage Level—A World Analysis," *Economic Journal* (December, 1970).

22. See for example, Ian Little, Tibor Scitovsky, and Maurice Scott, *Industry and Trade in Some Developing Countries* (London, Oxford University Press, 1970), and references included there and Henry J. Bruton, "The Import-Substitution Strategy of Economic Development: A Survey," *The Pakistan Development Review* (Summer, 1970).

23. For the relationship between import substitution and productivity growth see Henry J. Bruton, "Import Substitution and Productivity Growth," *The Journal of Development Studies* (April, 1968).

24. This argument is spelled out in more detail in Henry J. Bruton, "Employment, Productivity and Import Substitution," Research Memorandum No. 44, Center for Development Economics, Williams College (Williamstown, Massachusetts, 1972).

25. The argument about the role of productivity and employment growth in the text states that with product wage rates constant (or growing less rapidly than productivity) employment growth is encouraged by increases in productivity. The size of the employment effect also depends on the elasticity of substitution and growth in the demand for the product. In this case productivity growth, at given capital labor ratios, will produce an increase in employment that is greater, the greater is the elasticity of substitution and the greater the growth in demand. This result also means that the productivity of the labor force, i.e., output divided by the total labor force, not just total employment, *rises* to the maximum extent. We can then say that in the employment context, interest focusses on the productivity of the entire labor force, rather than of the employed portion. See Edgar O. Edwards, "The Problem of Labor Utilization in Developing Countries," mimeo (June, 1971).

26. A most useful examination of the nature of conflicts between growth of output and growth of employment is Paul Streeten and Frances Stewart, "Conflicts between Output and Employment Objectives in Developing Countries," *Oxford Economic Papers* (July, 1971).

27. Experience with the use of the high-yielding seeds is now such that some important conclusions are possible. See Walter P. Falcon, "The Green Revolution: Generations of Problems," *American Journal of Agricultural Economics* (December, 1970), for a good, general picture of the current state.

28. Discussions of the role of the exchange rate may be found in Little, Scitovsky and Scott, *op. cit.;* John Sheahan and Sara Clark, "The Response of Colombian Exports to Variations in Effective Exchange Rates," Research Memorandum No. 11, Center for Development Economics, Williams College (Williamstown, Massachusetts, 1967); Carlos Diaz-Alejandro, *Exchange Rate Devaluation in a Semi-Industrialized Country* (Cambridge, Massachusetts Institute of Technology Press, 1966); and Richard N. Cooper, "An Assessment of Currency Devaluations in Developing Countries," in *Government and Development,* edited by Gustav Ranis, (New Haven, Connecticut, Yale University Press, 1971).

29. The multinational firms have been examined in great detail by numerous economists. For the effect of the multinational firm on exports and employment a good place to begin is with two papers by Gerald K. Helleiner, "Manufacturing for Export, Multinational Firms, and Economic Development," *World Development* (July, 1973), and "Manufactured Exports from Less Developed Countries and Multinational

Firms," *Economic Journal* (March, 1973), and one by Paul Streeten, "The Multinational Enterprise and the Theory of Development Policy," mimeo (1973).

30. The paper by Edgar O. Edwards and Michael P. Todaro, "Educational Demand and Supply in the Context of Growing Unemployment in Less Developed Countries," *World Development* (March/April, 1973) discusses the education-employment issue in some detail. See also Mark Blaug, *An Introduction to the Economics of Education* (Middlesex, England, Penguin Books, 1970), for a general review.

31. See especially, Gustav Ranis, "Industrial Labor Absorption," *Economic Development and Cultural Change* (April, 1973).

32. Papers by Walter Falcon, *op. cit.,* Carl H. Gotsch, "Tractor Mechanization and Rural Development in Pakistan," Economic Development Report No. 227, Center for International Affairs, Harvard University (1972) and Robert E. Evenson, "Labor in the Indian Agriculture Sector," Economic Growth Center, Yale University (1972), are good places to begin on this subject. The excellent book by Vernon W. Ruttan and Yujino Hayami, *Agricultural Development: An International Perspective* (Baltimore, Johns Hopkins, 1971), is more comprehensive and has extensive references.

33. This argument is developed in very effective detail by Montague Yudelman, Gavan Butler and Ranader Banerji, *Technological Change in Agriculture and Employment* (Paris, Organization for Economic Co-operation and Development, 1971).

34. Keith Griffin, "Rural Development: The Policy Options," this book, provides an excellent general discussion of many aspects of rural development, and defends a variety of concrete policy recommendations.

35. A recent paper that discusses explicitly the relationship between land reform and employment is Peter Dorner, "Land Reform, Technology, Income Distribution and Employment: Conceptual and Empirical Relationships," mimeo, paper presented at the Torremolinos Conference of the Development Advisory Service, Harvard University (1972). See also the I.L.O. reports on Colombia and Kenya cited in footnote 4.

36. Charles R. Frank, "Urban Unemployment and Economic Growth in Africa," *Oxford Economic Papers* (July, 1968), reviews a variety of issues associated with urban unemployment.

37. Turner and Jackson, *op. cit.*

38. "Intermediate technology" is frequently discussed as a solution to a range of problems usually traced to the use of inappropriate technology. Though the term "intermediate technology" is not very clear, various analyses of its impact are often helpful. See for example Keith Marsden, "Progressive Technologies for Developing Countries," in *Essays on Employment,* selected by Walter Galenson (Geneva, International Labour Office, 1971), and E.F. Schumacher, "Industrialization through Intermediate Technology," in *Industrialization in Developing Countries,* edited by Ronald Robinson (Cambridge, England, Cambridge University for Old Schools, 1965).

39. See the papers by Michael Todaro and Gene M. Tidrick cited in footnote 5.

40. A discussion of the role of the terms of trade between agriculture and manufacturing in Pakistan is found in Stephen R. Lewis, *Economic Policy and Industrial Growth in Pakistan* (London, Allen and Unwin, 1969).

41. See the study, "Implementation of Policies for Fuller Employment in Less Developed Countries," this book, by Vincent M. Barnett.

42. What is futile and what isn't is indeed a difficult question. The ILO report on Colombia rules out a wage policy and improvement in land tax in that country as being politically unfeasible, but does press strongly for a thoroughgoing reform in land ownership arrangements. The ILO report on Kenya rules out as administratively unfeasible an industrial subsidy based on employment, but plugs throughout a limitation on salary payments and income. Rarely does one find a discussion of why the observer believes one policy is possible and another not.

Technology and Employment in LDCs

Frances Stewart
Institute of Commonwealth Studies
Oxford University

Introduction

The magnitude of un and underemployment in developing countries appears to be enormous and growing. Despite conceptual and measurement difficulties in identifying precise quantities, it is undoubtedly true that in many (probably most) LDCs the numbers of people seeking modern sector jobs far exceeds the jobs available.[1] This growing problem has arisen despite substantial investment and fairly rapid rates of growth of output in many countries. It is natural to conclude from this that something must be wrong with the nature of investment carried out—or put in another way, the wrong technology must have been adopted. This paper is concerned to examine the relationship between technology and employment; to identify the ways in which technology might be changed in the light of the employment problems, and how such changes might be brought about.

Technology has been defined as the "skills, knowledge and procedures for making, using and doing useful things."[2] This broad definition will be adopted in this paper. Technology thus includes knowledge of organisation and methods of production in all economic activities, public and private. Vertically, it includes administration and management systems as well as types of machinery. It covers knowledge about the structure of production—in terms for example of scale, and the nature of ownership—as well as the nature of the processes adopted. Horizontally, it includes the production of services—e.g. banking, education and health—as well as goods; and it covers the nature of the goods and services produced—the different ways in which needs are fulfilled—as well as the different ways in which these goods are produced. Technology often tends to be identified with the hardware—the machines and processes. This is to restrict the field too much, leaving out many important aspects. But using the broader definition has its difficulties. In particular, it will be impossible to give all aspects full coverage; and what can be correctly said about one aspect of technology, may be untrue of others. Both these factors should be borne in mind, and allowed for, in what follows.

A distinction needs to be made between technological possiblities available —which is a form of *knowledge* about methods of production, and the technology in use, or the methods actually being used. Often *technology* is used interchangeably for these two aspects and this can result in confusion. The technology in use is limited (obviously) to known methods. Normally only some of the known methods are

83

actually being used. Thus, the technology in use may be changed by adopting a different subset of the known methods, without changing knowledge at all. In arguing that LDCs have adopted inappropriate technology it is the technology in use that is normally being described as inappropriate. This situation could arise because the wrong methods were being selected from all the known methods, and could be put right by changing the selection. Or it might arise because appropriate knowledge was not available. In the latter situation no amount of change in the system of selection would bring about the appropriate technology in use. Here it is necessary to create new technology, since the inappropriate technology in use is a reflection of inappropriate technological knowledge whereas in the former case it resulted from inappropriate selection systems.

The knowledge possessed by different people/institutions/countries is not only a function of total world knowledge in the area in question but also of how much of that world knowledge has got through to the institution in question. Technology may be inappropriate because of weak communications.

Possessing or not possessing knowledge is not always a simple thing like knowing or not knowing the distances between the main capitals of the world. It is more often a question of knowing where to go to acquire the detailed knowledge; and it is also a question of price. If the price of acquiring the knowledge is prohibitive it may not be communicated for that reason alone.

Thus inappropriate technology may arise in a number of ways:
1. through wrong selection systems;
2. through weak communication systems—this may be at an inter-country level, or within the country;
3. through expensive technology transfer;
4. through inadequate supply;
5. through inadequate world knowledge.

Item 4 above—inadequate supply—describes a situation where appropriate methods are known, but the inputs, particularly machinery, essential for adopting them are unavailable: e.g. where production of 19th century appropriate machines has ceased. The solution to the problem of inappropriate technology in use will differ according to which of these factors is primarily responsible. As we shall see the use of inappropriate technology in developing countries, may in part be due to each of these factors, though observers differ on the weight to be attributed to each, and the methods to be used to change the situation in each case.

Employment Problems in LDCs

There is no single employment (or unemployment) problem in LDCs, rather a syndrome of interrelated problems, displayed in different ways, and to different degrees in different countries. The employment problem cannot be simply identified as one of insufficient employment opportunities, and measured by the rate of open unemployment. For one thing only the (relatively) rich can afford to be unemployed, in societies without systematic provision for the unemployed, where those who are seeking work have to rely on support from their relations or their past savings. For another thing, in many societies which are clearly exhibiting employment problems, there is work to be done. The ILO Mission to Ceylon[3] found agricultural employers unable to hire the workers they needed, fields that required weeding, and numbers of workers imported from South India as toddy tappers, despite 550,000 (or 14% of the labour force between 15 and 59) who were openly unemployed. Recently many observers[4] have suggested identifying the employment problem with low incomes. This classification then automatically includes the openly unemployed, and also those scraping a living in rural or urban areas with inadequate equipment and markets. Poor societies are, by definition, characterised as having low incomes and productivity *on average*. To identify an employment problem, as against a general problem of poverty, the incomes approach to employment problems suggested a criterion of low incomes, *in relation to the rest of the society*.

The incomes approach to employment problems suggests that the key problem is one of *differential access to income earning opportunities*. The relative poverty of some members of society is due to their relatively poor access to good income earning opportunities. High levels of open unemployment, massive rural-urban migration,* the very high ratios of applicants to modern sector jobs,** the main symptoms of the employment problem, can all be seen as a consequence of the large differences in productivity and earning opportunities between the modern sector and the rest of the economy. They are signs that people are trying to shift into the modern sector. Thus the employment problem is not a matter of an absolute lack of useful things that might be done, but a shortage of modern sector jobs in relation to the number of people who would like them. The employment opportunities that exist are in the informal or traditional sector and offer only relatively low incomes.

This view of the employment problem is presented graphically below. LL' represents the total labour force in a developing country. It is assumed that the economy is neatly divided into two sectors—the 'modern' and the traditional or informal. LM shows how output changes as employment in the modern sector increases. (It shows diminishing marginal productivity as employment increases; the dotted line LM' shows an alternative, fixed proportion case where the employment/output ratio does

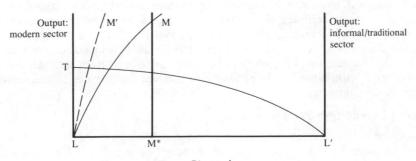

Diagram 1

not vary). Let us assume that modern sector employment is limited to LM*. We discuss below the factors that might limit it in this way. Then the remaining labour force, M*L', may be totally absorbed into the traditional sector, or may be partially absorbed and partially unemployed. In either case there will be big differences between average (and marginal, as shown by the slopes of the output curves) productivity in the two sectors, and between incomes in the two sectors. Open

---

* The well known Harris-Todaro model of migration attributes open unemployment to the difference in income expectations between the modern sector and other opportunities.[5]

** The high ratio was indicated by analysis of the impact of the Tripartite Agreement in Kenya, when Government and employers agreed to expand employment by 10%, first in 1964 then in 1970. On both occasions there was massive registration for the promised jobs—amounting to over 45% of employees in the modern sector in 1970.[6]

unemployment, rural-urban migration and other symptoms of pressure for modern sector employment can be seen as attempts to shift into the higher income modern sector. Anyone using low productivity (relatively) as a guide to underemployment will tend to include many of those employed in the traditional sector. This approach is of course a tremendous oversimplification of reality. Economies do not fall into two easily differentiated and internally homogeneous sectors. However, it is possible crudely to classify employment opportunities in many economies, in this sort of way.

In the modern sector the technology is imported from developed countries—not just the machinery but also the systems of management, ownership, labour relations, etc. The informal or traditional sector tends to use local technology and local systems of ownership, control and management. In the modern sector wages are subject to Trade Union and Government regulation. In the traditional sector incomes are determined competitively or on traditional lines. Thus the major distinguishing characteristic between the two sectors is the nature of the technology. This explains the differences in labour productivity shown in the diagram. The imported technology exhibits higher labour productivity than local technology for two reasons: first, because it is generally associated with much higher levels of expenditure on capital equipment per employee; and secondly, because the methods of production have high factor productivity because they have been developed using the scientific and technological resources of developed countries.

There are of course all sorts of marginal firms, and employment opportunities, which do not easily fit into either category. However, so long as the broad distinction remains relevant this need not invalidate the approach.

The Unsuitability of Technology

The dualism exhibited by many developing economies—which it is argued here is responsible for the complex of employment problems—is in large part due to the nature of imported technology. The technology available from the developed countries is technology which was designed primarily *for* the developed countries, in the light of their conditions. In a number of respects these conditions are such that the technology is unsuitable for developing countries and contributes to the dualistic nature of development.

Capital Expenditure Per Head

Perhaps the most important respect in which the technology is unsuitable—and one most often noted—is in terms of capital expenditure per head. The resources a country can afford to spend on capital equipment are broadly proportionate to its income. Savings ratios do differ and foreign savings reduce the connection between domestic income and total savings. Nonetheless these variations operate within rather narrow limits. Among 21 developing and developed countries, 15 had savings ratios (gross savings as a proportion of gross domestic product) of between 15 and 25%. Savings per head can be taken as broadly proportionate to income per head. In developed countries, with incomes per head of the working force of five to fifty times that of the developing countries the level of investment per head of the work force will be five to fifty times that of developing countries.

Technology emanating from developed countries is designed in the light of the investment resources *they* can afford. Assuming that investment each year equips one twentieth of the labour force, the rest of the labour force being equipped or requipped in the following nineteen years, that a country's saving ratio is 20%, and one-quarter of this is required for infrastructural investment, then resources available for (non-infrastructoral) capital equipment per head,

$$k = 20 \cdot 3/4 \cdot 1/5 \cdot O/L = 3(O/L).$$

With these crude assumptions a country can afford to provide every member of its work force with equipment (and buildings) worth 3 times the value of output per head per member of the workforce. Table 1 illustrates the value of k, or what we might describe as 'appropriate' capital per head for various selected countries.

Technology designed in and for a country will, on average, be in line with what that country can afford, that is in line with the figures in Table 1. Obviously, there are

TABLE 1

INVESTMENT COSTS PER MAN

	"Appropriate" capital stock per man (assumed = $3O/L$)	Actual capital stock per man in manufacturing (excluding working capital)
	(1)	(2)
U.S.	$28,965	$24,100
U.K.	12,519	10,608+
France	16,695	13,050
Japan	6,759	
Argentina	5,154	
Brazil	3,606	
Jamaica	4,110	
Nigeria	639	
Ceylon	1,458	
India	551	

NOTE: These figures in Column (1) are calculated on the basis of the formula:

$$\bar{k} = \propto /n \cdot s \cdot O/L$$

where $\bar{k}$ = investment costs per man;

$\propto$ = fraction of investment resources devoted to buildings and equipment (and not to infrastructural investment);

n = fraction of labour force equipped or reequipped each year;

s = gross savings ratio;

O/L = output per head of labour force

and $\propto$ = 0.75

n = 1/20

s = 1/5

SOURCES: Column (1) World Economic Survey, 1969-1971, *ILO Statistical Year Book,* 1971.

Column (2) for U.K., *The British Economy Key Statistics.* For France and U.S. figures are derived from the British figure applying the ratios for net stock of non-residential structures and equipment in E. Denison, *Why Growth Rates Differ* (Brookings Institution, 1967), p. 166. The figures exclude working capital. According to Denison inventories "typically represent one-third or one-fourth as much as non-residential structures and equipment." Making adjustments for working capital would bring the two columns closer together.

variations between industries, and equally obviously, the assumptions behind the calculations are extremely crude. Nonetheless in a very rough way they may provide orders of magnitude for the type of technology likely to be produced. That these rough orders of magnitude have some verisimilitude is suggested by the actual figures for capital intensity for the U.S. and U.K. shown in the Table, and the fact (which is another aspect of the same thing) that the capital-output ratio in aggregate in advanced countries is between 2.5 and 3, as suggested by the above formula.

Poor countries obtaining technology (unmodified) from rich countries may thus receive technology whose cost is in line with the resources of the advanced countries, not with what they can afford. To the extent that they do spend their resources on advanced country technology, their limited investment resources will mean that only a fraction of their labour force can be equipped. Table 2 calculates the proportion of the work force that a few countries could afford to equip, using the assumptions of Table 1, and assuming that each country adopts, in unmodified form, the technology Table 1 suggests the U.K. would be likely to design. (The U.K. is selected as providing a less extreme case than other advanced countries, particularly the U.S.) On these assumptions a dualistic form of development is an inevitable result of adopting advanced country technology without major modifications.

TABLE 2

FRACTION OF LABOUR FORCE THAT CAN BE
EQUIPPED WITH U.K. LEVELS OF INVESTMENT PER HEAD
(Selected Countries)

	%
Argentina	41.2
Brazil	28.7
Jamaica	32.9
Nigeria	5.1
Ceylon	11.6
India	4.4

It must be emphasized that capital costs per head are not the only relevant dimension to be examined in choosing techniques. Among the other factors discussed below, the efficiency of the investment is an important characteristic. Thus equipment in line with the costs suggested as appropriate above is not a sufficient reason for choosing it; it may well involve substantially less output per unit of investment and be an inappropriate choice for this reason. There are circumstances in which the advanced country technology, however inappropriate in relation to these figures, is nonetheless the best choice given the range of possibilities. These figures are simply intended to show that if such advanced technology is adopted, dualism is unavoidable.

Labour Productivity

Modern developed country technology is associated with relatively high rates of labour productivity which is essential if it is to be viable in the developed countries, because of the high wages involved. If transferred unchanged to developing countries it leads to high rates of labour productivity, and hence very wide divergences between labour productivity in the modern sector and incomes in the rest of the economy. Such high labour productivity must be reflected either in high rates of profits or in high wages and salaries (or both) relatively to incomes elsewhere in the economy. (Though the profitability may be offset by low rates of capacity utilisation.) Conditions of production are such that employers are liable to give way to pressure from Trade Unions and/or the Government for higher incomes. The dualistic nature of production tends therefore to be reflected in a dualistic distribution of income. In so far as the firms are foreign owned—as, at least in the early stages of development, they often are—the LDC government has an interest in ensuring that the high rates of labour productivity are kept in the country in the form of wages rather than retained and remitted by the Companies in the form of profits.

Other Inappropriate Characteristics

Other important ways in which the transferred technology may be inappropriate are in *scale, skill* requirements (including management), *input* requirements, and *product* nature.

Scale. In most developed countries the typical size of the firm has grown dramatically from the cottage industry of the 18th century. In Britain in 1963 the largest 50 firms accounted for one quarter of total employment in manufacturing industry. In 1958 27% of employment arose in plants employing more than 1,500,[7] compared with 15% in 1935.

Successive plants have thus been designed for increasingly large scale production. The increasing scale has normally resulted in substantial economies in cost, in part because of physical scale economies, in part because larger scale allows machine specialisation, and in part because the large scale plants are often the most recently designed and hence reflect a greater technical sophistication. The resulting scale economies are well documented.[8] Some examples are contained in Table 3.

TABLE 3

VARIATION IN PRODUCTION COST IN RELATION TO
DIFFERENT SCALES OF OUTPUT IN SELECTED INDUSTRIES

Product	Unit	Variation in capacity and production cost			
Steel					
Capacity	Thousands of tons per year	50	250	500	1,000
Cost per ton	1948 U.S. dollars	209.4	158.8	137.5	127.2
Cement					
Capacity	Thousands of tons per year	100	450	900	1,800
Cost per ton	1959 U.S. dollars	26.0	19.8	16.4	13.9
Ammonium nitrate					
Capacity	Short tons per day	50	100	150	300
Cost per ton	1957 U.S. dollars	190.4	145.1	125.6	101.5
Beer bottles					
Capacity	No. of moulding machines	1	2	6	12
Cost per gross	1957 U.S. dollars	8.51	7.25	6.13	5.69
Glass containers					
Capacity	No. of moulding machines	1	2	6	12
Cost per gross	1957 U.S. dollars	8.66	7.77	6.78	6.33

SOURCE: *Industrialisation and Productivity*, No. 8 (see note 8), Table 1.

The transfer of modern developed country technology thus involves the transfer of large scale units of production. This tends to be inappropriate to the needs of developing countries for a number of reasons. Generally, the size of their markets is relatively small, and hence if the domestic market only is to be supplied, underutilised capacity, and/or an oligopolistic production structure (often both), is inevitable. The large scale also makes local development of entrepreneurial abilities much more difficult. In the developed countries the increasing scale was achieved gradually and the entrepreneurs grew with the job, so to speak. There was a natural evolution in the appropriate form of production. In Japan the local small scale sector played an essential role in development. In many LDCs the transfer of modern large scale technology involves a complete scale break with the local entrepreneurial and managerial resources. There is no role therefore for local evolution, and foreign managers and/or foreign managerial training is required. The scale of modern technology also contributes to the dualistic nature of development.

Skill requirements. Again developed country technology has been developed against a background of (and called forth) rising supplies of skilled labour, with increasing sophistication of the skills involved. In the U.S. for example unskilled labour accounted for 36% of the work force in 1910 and 25% in 1968. Professional and technical workers accounted for 4½% in 1910, and over 11% in 1968. These data indicate how skill composition of the labour force has changed in the U.S. The transfer of the technology tends to require similar skills in the LDC; these are in scarce supply. The skill requirements tend therefore to lead to high skill differentials (contributing to inequality of income distribution), concentration of educational resources on a fortunate minority, while limiting the area in which a country can afford to introduce modern technology because of scarcity of the required skills.

Input requirements. Technological developments occur in the light of the resource availability of the rich countries. The local materials possessed by many poor countries are often ignored, and the technology designed to use materials abundant in the rich countries. Thus in Kenya imported corrugated iron sheets are used for roofing: there has been no attempt to develop local materials into viable cheap roofing. Bamboo has been ignored as a source of building material and furniture. Plastics, often imported, are used widely instead of local resources of wood etc. Pulping technology has been based on conifers as a raw material. These are generally scarce or absent in developing countries. Consequently research is needed to adapt the technology to make use of local materials such as sugar cane bagasse. The neglect of local LDC materials is indicated by the lists of research priorities for LDCs which almost invariably start with proposals for the use and development of local materials.[9] Although the use of local materials is not directly related to employment, it may have considerable indirect employment implications through employment generation in the material supplying industry, and through balance of payments savings.

Products. Among the most important, and least emphasised, ways in which imported technology may be inappropriate lies in the nature of the products.

The basic human needs—for food, drink, shelter, warmth, entertainment and companionship—are broadly common to all mankind. But the ways in which these needs are fulfilled (and the extent to which these and others are fulfilled) is dependent in large part on the amount, characteristics and distribution of goods in a society. Products can be regarded as bundles of characteristics fulfilling various needs (and wants) more or less efficiently.[10] The characteristics of a product are its attributes: its colour, weight, size, function. A list of the characteristics of a product indicates the various needs it may fulfil. Thus a shirt may provide protection against cold or heat, may demonstrate by its cleanliness and smartness, a certain status in society, may impress potential employers, may by its colour and decoration give pleasure to onlookers, and may, if drip dry, avoid the need for ironing. It may fulfil these needs more or less well and may be acquired for any or all of these reasons.

Products are indivisible. If one acquires a particular product for one of its characteristics one unavoidably has to acquire the other characteristics too. The only way to avoid unwanted characteristics is to find some product without them (e.g. a non drip dry shirt). A particular product may be described as having excessive characteristics or embodying excessive standards, in relation to a particular consumer, or set of consumers, when it has characteristics which the consumer does not want, or standards in excess of those needed to fulfil the purpose for which the product is required. An example of excess standards is of a brick strong enough to support a four storey building, used for a single storey house.

Just as any one product fulfils a number of needs, so any one need can normally be fulfilled by a variety of products. The need for accommodation may be fulfilled (more or less well) by the pavements of Calcutta, caves, mud huts, multistorey apartments, or a palace; the need for transport, by a basket, a wheelbarrow, an airplane or a space ship. The number and nature of the products fulfilling a particular need depend on the specific nature of the need: the more narrowly it is specified the fewer products which fulfil it. An airplane is no good for transporting bricks from one end of a village to the other; a wheelbarrow may be of some use for collecting rocks on the moon, but not for bringing them back to earth.

As people (and societies) get richer they do not simply consume the same as before but more of it—10 maunds of rice a year instead of 2; the nature of the products they consume changes. The same broad needs are fulfilled by a different set of products, embodying a different (on the whole more satisfying, more sophisticated) set of characteristics, with higher standards. Rice tends to be replaced by wheat and by meat; Jatra by movies and by radio; radio is replaced by television, first black and white and then in colour. Cars take over from horse or human powered vehicles, and the cars become more sophisticated, faster, quieter, even safer. Changes in the nature of products consumed is an essential aspect of getting richer; long before modern science and technology made possible the sort of product replacement described above, richer societies and people were distinguished from their poorer contemporaries by the nature of the goods they consumed, as well as by their quantity—by their silks and their palaces. Modern science and technology made possible various products which were previously unknown, even unthinkable, and it put the search for new products on a systematic basis. These new products are both cause and consequence of higher incomes; higher incomes provide the purchasing power and hence the markets which make it worth developing new products; and the technological developments make possible the mass production of sophisticated goods, embodying new materials, which are the basis of the increases in incomes.

The diagram illustrates the nature of technological developments in developed countries. Three interconnecting cycles have been distinguished. First, on the left, that of increases in per capita incomes providing an incentive for technological developments which lead to higher labour productivity, thus making possible further increases in incomes. Secondly, on the right, higher incomes providing an incentive for technological developments involving new and improved products, while these new products are in turn an essential aspect of further increases in incomes. Thirdly, in the centre, higher incomes leading (with constant propensity to save) to higher savings per man and consequently greater capital accumulation per man, thus influencing and making possible technological developments of both types, techniques and products. In practice it is not easy to distinguish between these types of technological developments, since many changes in techniques also involve new products—new machines or other inputs, or changed characteristics of old products. The evidence suggests that the bulk of technical developments involve new products (and *ipso facto* changed methods of production).* Most products change, at least in terms of detailed physical characteristics, in a dynamic economy over time. Product developments like technique developments reflect the society in which they are developed. They do so in two ways. On the side of production they require capital intensive techniques related to the resource availability of the economies at the time when they are first produced. On the demand side they are products designed for

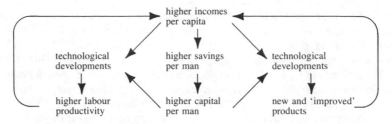

Diagram 2: Technological developments in a (dynamic) closed system
NOTE: The arrows indicate the direction of causality.

levels of income typical in the societies in which they are developed. With technological developments in products, as well as in techniques, almost entirely confined to the rich countries, the products developed are inappropriate to poorer countries, being designed for much higher income levels, and embodying therefore many characteristics which are excessive in relation to what average consumers in poorer countries can afford. For example, detergents possess various advantages over soap—they are labour saving and produce a 'whiter' wash. But they also involve a far more capital-intensive technology than some methods of producing soap, and their additional qualities may not be a sensible way for a poor society to spend its income. Such a society might well be better off with a poor quality soap that everyone could afford than sophisticated detergents whose consumption must be confined to a rich minority.

Developing countries are thus just as much in need of appropriate products, as of appropriate techniques. Inappropriate products are products with excessive characteristics and standards in relation to needs and income levels of the country in question. Some characteristics may be excessive in the sense that they are neither useful nor wanted, but since they come in one indivisible bundle with the other characteristics, they have to be acquired. In this they resemble the appendix in the human body—more expensive to remove than to ignore. Much more common are products whose characteristics are excessive in relation to the poverty of society but which are nonetheless desired by those who consume them. Cars, washing machines—almost any of the products of modern developed country consumer durable industries provide examples. They are not confined to consumer durables: the

---

* For example one study found that for 90% of manufacturing firms the main aim of their research programmes was the development of new products or improvement of old products.[11]

standard of durability and strength of textiles may be excessive; similarly of building materials and also other qualities such as heat and sound insulation.

Consumption of rich country products *requires* an unequal income distribution in a much poorer country. Take the example of housing. Most people can afford to spend about one fifth of their income on housing. In the U.K. with average earnings per man of around £1,500 this is consistent with a typical house with a capital value of around £5,000. But if similar housing standards were adopted in India, with average incomes about one twentieth of those in the U.K. each person would need to spend £300 a year, which is more than the average income, on housing. Obviously this is impossible. There are two alternatives: modifying housing standards so that the cost of an average house is consistent with expenditure of one fifth of average income—i.e. providing houses in India whose purchase price was around £200. Or, providing £5,000 houses identical to those produced in the U.K. and allowing (or generating) sufficient inequality of income distribution to enable some of the population to enjoy incomes at least as high as the average in the U.K. and so be able to afford the £5,000 houses.

Houses are not, in general, transferred lock, stock and barrel to developing countries, though many building standards are. But other products are transferred complete with all characteristics. The consumption of such products raises the same issues. Either standards have to be modified so that less costly products can be consumed by all, or the products are transferred intact and their consumption by a few deprives the rest of the population of the possibility of consumption. Private cars are an example. In most developed countries a family with average income can afford a car. In developing countries a market for cars for private consumption is only possible with a highly unequal income distribution—the cheapest car available costs about ten times the average income per head in India.

Medicine provides an example. Most research has been devoted to high income medicine in the developed countries. Medicine of similar standards and nature has been adopted in many developing countries, with the result that medical facilities tend to be concentrated in the towns and on the relatively rich. Drug production is capital intensive,[12] while its administration and other medical attention is highly skill intensive. Unequal access to medical facilities is the inevitable result of providing developed-country-type facilities for some.[13] China, in contrast, with a far more equal income distribution, has made a determined attempt to develop a more appropriate pattern of medicine, making selective use of modern and traditional techniques, and introducing 'barefoot doctors.'[14]

The example illustrates the close connection between income distribution and the nature of products. Once an unequal income distribution is established, emanating from the system of production, it is extremely difficult to make a radical change towards more appropriate products which are consistent with quite different and more egalitarian income distribution. Traditional products, and those recently developed in and for the poorer sections of the community, are much more appropriate in characteristics and in methods of production. They are so by necessity. The labour intensity of traditional forms of entertainment, of housebuilding and of road construction, of carpentry and of spinning, arose from the fact that the people who used and developed them could afford only very limited amounts of capital. Similarly, traditional products are designed for poor consumers and do not contain excessive standards. There have also been some product developments in the poorer sectors, also of an appropriate nature. In Kenya used tyres are used to manufacture sandals, and also the base of

beds. But lacking all resources—of capital and science—they are inevitably out-
shadowed by developments in the modern sector of the economy.

The transfer of developed countries' products, reinforces the dualistic nature of
development, and the unequal income distribution between the two sectors, described
earlier.

Assumptions of the Dualistic Model

The dualistic model rests on the assumptions that the modern sector in developing
countries uses only the most recent technology from developed countries, that the
factor requirements of that technology are rigidly determined, and that no adaption or
innovation in the LDC takes place. We shall discuss each of these assumptions.

Old technology. Developing countries may use old technologies from developed
countries. Older technologies are in general associated with lower capital expenditure
per employee, smaller scale production units, less sophisticated products. Table 4
illustrates how capital equipment per employee has risen in the developed countries

TABLE 4

CAPITAL STOCK PER HEAD—U.K., U.S. AND NORWAY
(1920 = 100)

Around	U.K. (Fixed capital per man, manufacturing)	U.S. (H.P. per man, manufacturing)	Norway (Real capital per man per year)
1900		61.5	74.6
1910		86.7	
1920	100	100	100
1930	125.1	145.3	
1940	115.0	206.4	137.3
1950	129.1	341.5	141.8
1960	156.8		181.3*
1970	210.0		

*1955

SOURCES: The British Economy: *Key Statistics 1900-1970*, Tables E.I.; *Income and Health Series II*, ed. S. Kuznets
(Cambridge, 1952), Table 11; and *Income and Health Series VIII*, ed. Goldsmith and Saunders (Cambridge, 1959),
Table IV, p. 97.

since the 19th century, and other data, noted above, indicates that scale was smaller
and skill abundance less in earlier periods; conditions were generally more similar to
those of present developing countries. However, there are factors which often rule out
the use of old technologies. In the first place, very often the machinery for such
technology is no longer being produced. Hence it does not present an alternative,
unless production is resuscitated. Secondly, the old methods are often more expensive in terms of capital costs per unit of output as well as labour costs. This arises
because technological developments may take the form of a saving of capital as well
as labour.

Suppose 1972 developed country technology requires OL' labour, and OI' investment expenditure to produce a particular quantity of output. If the old technology to
produce the same output was as 1900b in the diagram its use would enable the LDC to
economise on investment and use more labour in relation to output. If, on the other

hand, the old technology was 1900a then investment requirements per unit of output would be greater and its use would involve a loss of output (as compared with 1972 technology) for any given expenditure on investment. Old technologies emanate from an earlier period, scientifically, and for this reason may be more inefficient all round, using more capital, as well as labour, than the new technologies.

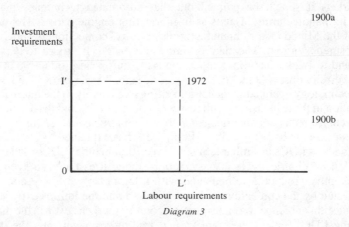

Diagram 3

Thirdly, as argued above technological developments are accompanied by product developments. Thus the 1900 technology is almost certain to be associated with a different product from the 1972 technology. The LDC will only find it worth going back to the 1900 technology if it is prepared to go back to the 1900 product. This product may have become genuinely obsolete: the penny-farthing bicycle, though undoubtedly associated with a more 'appropriate' technology, is substantially less efficient, as a bicycle, than modern vehicles. The functions of modern electronic desk computers cannot be performed fully either by mechanical calculating machines or by the abacus. It may be impossible to go back to old products on a piece meal basis because of the links between different parts of the productive structure: like wine and bottles, modern vehicles require modern roads, some modern production methods require computer control. Not only are there links on the production side so that one part of the production process determines the choice of inputs and methods of production elsewhere, there are also links in consumption patterns, or complementarities—cars and petrol, cans and can openers, ties and suits, cocktails and cocktail bars.[15] Some of these links are obviously stronger than others. The basic point is that production—products and techniques—and consumption are both packages (themselves interlinked), and not a series of isolated decisions. Consequently, marginal change may be impossible; one may have to change the system as a whole to secure a different type of product consumption. Such wholesale change includes change towards more equal income distribution, because, as argued earlier, the later products are designed for, and demanded by, richer consumers.

A country's position in international trade also limits its freedom to use old (or adapt new) products. This operates through both exports and imports. If LDCs are to make real inroads into developed country markets they have to produce the sort of products that are consumed in developed countries. Though such products may well be labour-intensive as compared with other products produced and consumed in developing countries,[16] the standards required of goods imported into developed countries are higher, and the technology associated more capital intensive, than those of similar goods purely for home consumption. The exporting country also has to keep abreast with product and technology changes over time if it is to maintain its position in export markets. In empirical studies of the choice of technique one continually finds that a more capital intensive technology has to be adopted so as to maintain standards for exports. This is Baranson's conclusion.[17] "In considering export markets it should be pointed out that automated techniques may be as warranted in manufacturing biscuits as in fabricating engine parts." He quotes the example of the Minoo factory manufacturing biscuits, confectionery, pharmaceuticals and cosmetics in Iran. The plant is highly automated. It exports to Persian Gulf countries and to Afghanistan in competition with European producers. In a recent seminar[18] Ferreira observed that in Latin America small scale firms with less capital intensive technology operated in industries selling exclusively in the internal market. "The situation in these industries with respect to productivity and the use of labour is quite different from that of industries *which use capital intensive technologies to meet international standards.*" (my italics). Philips Co. has explained their production of the latest goods of LDCs in similar terms. Competition in other LDCs—where goods from developed countries were also available—made it essential to keep up with advanced country product developments, with a lag of only a few years.

As suggested by the confectionery factory in Iran and the Philips experience it is not just a question of competing *in* developing country markets: even in the markets of neighbouring LDCs, unless there are special trading arrangements, the incoming products have to compete with developed country technology, and the best way of doing so seems to be to adopt it. Similarly, competition with imports from countries using advanced technology may require the adoption of advanced country products.

Despite these obstacles to the use of old technologies in LDCs, there is a technological lag between developed countries and most LDCs. This lag in large part consists of a lag in industrial structure, so that LDC production has much less, proportionately, (and in many cases none) of some of the latest products and industries. The industrial structure lag accounts for some at least of the observed differences between aggregate ratios—capital-labour, skill use etc.—between developed and developing economies. But there are also lags within industries; typically developing countries do use older technology than developed countries and normally, to some extent, rely on second hand equipment imported from developed countries. In Kenya, Pack[19] found that almost all plants bought some used equipment, and when purchasing new equipment "many firms purchase older, slower models where these are available." Nonetheless this equipment used only slightly more labour than modern equipment. The selective use of older equipment was a feature of Japanese economic development, also.[20]

Rigid factor requirements. It is assumed in the discussion above that factor requirements of each technology of any given vintage are rigidly determined. In fact what has been described as the *core*[21] equipment and the associated labour requirements may be fairly rigidly determined for any given process. But there is considerable choice in the technology to be adopted, and the consequent factor requirement in ancillary activities. A good deal of the variation in factor use in Japan, S. Korea and Kenya found by Ranis and Pack took the form of variations in methods used in ancillary activities. According to Pack, "The major scope for substituting labor for capital is in peripheral activities and these account for a major part of the work force in most plants."[22] Peripheral, non-process activities include transport to and within the factory, mixing, filling and packing. In contrast, Pack concluded that "in primary production processes there are relatively limited substitution possibilities." Ranis came to similar conclusions for many of the industries he examined in Japan and S. Korea. He quotes Orchard,[23] "at one of the largest copper smelters in Japan, clay for the lining of the furnaces is carried down from the nearby hillside on the backs of women. At the plant of the Tokyo Gas Company, coke is put in kegs by hand and then carried by coolies, some of them women, to the barges in the adjacent canal. Coal, even in the larger Tokyo plants, is unloaded by hand and carried in baskets to the power houses."

Ranis concludes: "In sum, the quantitative importance of this ability to substitute labor for capital in activities peripheral to the machine proper was apparently quite substantial." However, the scope for such substitution may be limited by quality considerations. An investigation into cement block manufacture[24] found that machine mixing and transport of the mixture from mixer to block maker greatly increased the uniformity of the strength of blocks. Pack found that mechanical unloading was being introduced to reduce the high percentage loss of damaged fruit caused by manual handling. Scale is also an important factor. "Efficient substitution is possible even in peripheral activities only at low volumes relative to those in the developed nations." At high levels of output (3 to 10 times actual levels) it was argued, for example, that automatic filling machines would be profitable to introduce *regardless of the level of wages*.

Another way in which the coefficients of imported technology may be altered is through the more intensive use of capital equipment through time. This has the effect of reducing the capital-output ratio and the capital-labour ratio—though it does require increased inputs of other scarce factors, such as supervision and maintenance. In some countries—e.g. Japan and S. Korea—much equipment does appear to be used for a larger proportion of the time than in developed countries. However, in many other LDCs rates of capacity utilisation are notoriously low. Winston found that in West Pakistan industrial equipment was idle two thirds of the time.[25]

Adaption and innovation in LDCs. Adaption consists in taking modern developed country technology and adapting it to the special conditions of the country in which it is introduced. Sometimes physical conditions make this necessary (e.g. climatic differences), or it may occur in response to Government regulation—the Indian Government restrictions on importing various oils led to the development of methods of making soap with local oils;[26] or in response to differences in the quality, availability and price of local resources. Thus in Japan coarser cotton was used than in the U.S., and more labour used to allow for the consequent breakages.[27] Some of the examples discussed above—selective use of old machinery, the use of labour-using methods in ancillary activities, as compared with those normally used in developed countries and the more intensive use of equipment through time—are of course one form of adaption to the different conditions found in developing countries. However, since they do not in general involve any innovation in the developing country, but consist in a *selective* use of advanced country technology, here they will be described not as *adaption*, but as *appropriate selection* and use. *Adaption* of developed country technology is defined here as requiring some form of change in the imported technology. Adaption, thus defined, requires some form of innovation; but innovation covers a wider field than adaption since it includes improvement of traditional methods, and the development of entirely new methods, as well as the adaption of imported technology.

One can find many examples of adaption and innovation. The Ambar Charkha provides a well known (and on balance unsuccessful)[28] attempt to improve traditional methods. In India in the fifties an improved hand rice pounding equipment was introduced. In Vietnam in the early 1960's two local engineers developed a small motor pump for raising water.[29] The Agricultural Engineering Department of the International Rice Research Institute in the Philippines has developed a number of small scale agricultural machines, including a 1-H.P. rotary power weeder, a 3-H.P. table thresher.[30] Many other examples could be cited.[31] Different types of innovation have different origins: some come from outside, from the multinational corporation, or international research projects; others are imposed from above, via national research institutes; and others are the local response to local conditions. But though there are numerous examples of adaption and innovation, they are insufficiently numerous or significant to alter the overall picture. For the most part technology is imported and introduced into the modern sector in unmodified form. Although ancillary activities are on the whole carried out more labour intensively than in developed countries, this does not sufficiently alter the aggregate results. That this is so is borne out by the employment situation itself, and by the aggregate data available. The data are weak, and subject to conceptual difficulties. Thus they must not be interpreted precisely. For what it is worth they show that capital labour ratios, while lower than in the developed countries, are not nearly as much lower as the ratio of income per head.[32]

Table 5 compares ratios between plants. The comparisons must be treated cautiously because scale, output and age differences may be responsible for the differences. Exactly the same technology can be associated with radically different ratios of investment cost to labour because of differences in infrastructural investment requirements (or overhead investment) and differences in efficiency of plant management.*

TABLE 5

EQUIPMENT LABOUR RATIOS
(U.S. $, 1971)

Country	Paint Production	Cotton Textiles
India - Plant 1	672	2,072
India - Plant 2	1,110	1,484
India - Plant 3	4,620	2,212
India - Plant 4	-	1,722
India - Plant 5	-	6,120
Israel	8,632	8,318
Japan	1,958	-
Kenya (average of several plants)	2,063	2,044

SOURCES: H. Pack, "Employment and Productivity in Kenyan Manufacturing," August 1972, Tables I and II based on Pack's own sample for Kenya; and UNIDO, *Profiles of Manufacturing Establishments,* Vol. I and II.

The data[34] reinforce the more impressionistic evidence, quoted earlier, that typically developing country methods are more labour intensive, in terms of capital-labour ratios, than advanced countries.[35] These differences are probably partly due to differences in the scale of production and the nature of output, partly to

---

*   This was illustrated in a very detailed comparison between two cement plants, one in Indonesia and one in the U.S. which used the 'same' technology but had widely different ratios.[33]

less efficient management leading to the greater use of labour with the same equipment,[36] and partly to the use of different techniques, particularly in ancillary activities. However, though there are some differences in capital-labour ratios these are not proportionate to the differences in availability of savings. For example according to the Netherlands Economic Institute estimates for 1955, capital-labour ratios in Mexico were about 40% of those in the U.S. while output per member of the work force was (in 1967) 17% in India, capital-labour ratios were about 29% of those of the U.S. (1955); output per member of the labour force was 29% of the U.S. in 1967.

There are disparities between different plants in the same country, different LDCs* and different advanced countries. More careful analyses of particular cases are needed to ascertain how real these differences are, and the reasons for them. Such analyses might throw considerable light on the question of technological choice.

Trends in Technology Over Time

Technology, as emphasised above, changes over time; this applies as much (possibly more) to the future as the past. Generally, in the developed countries technology becomes increasingly capital intensive over time, and increasingly large scale, as was suggested by the earlier tables.** Comparisons within developing countries over time suggest that their technology changes in the same direction.[39]

The way in which technology develops over time may be illustrated in the case of textiles.[40] A study of choice of techniques for Latin America compared three technologies, a 1950 vintage, a 1960 vintage and a 1965 vintage. Table 6 shows how some of the key variables changed with technological developments between these years.

TABLE 6

EFFECTS OF TECHNOLOGICAL DEVELOPMENT ON KEY VARIABLES
1950 = 100

	1950 vintage	1960 vintage	1965 vintage
Investment per unit of equipment of minimum economic size	100	127	146
Investment per worker	100	190	310
Value added per worker	100	145	211
Output per $ of investment	100	76	68

SOURCE: ECLA Report (see note 40), Table 17.

Scale, capital per employee and labour productivity increased during this period. In this case the capital requirements per unit of output also increased, though rather

---

* Variations between LDCs are also shown in a recent comparison between India and Ethiopia showing Ethiopia to use substantially more capital-intensive methods than India.[37]

** Most historical series show a well defined increase over time in capital per employee for the same industry.[38]

little between the 1960 and 1965 vintages. Changes in the skill composition of the labour force were also marked, as Table 7 shows.

Labour requirements fell at all levels, but the fall was far more marked in the case of unskilled labour (the automated machine required only 38% of the requirements of the

TABLE 7

LABOUR REQUIREMENTS IN TEXTILE INDUSTRY

	Conventional	Intermediate	Automated
	As % of total requirements:		
Administrative	5.6	6.9	8.1
Skilled	24.5	31.5	32.3
Semi-skilled	41.9	41.5	41.4
Unskilled	28.0	20.0	18.2
Total	100	100	100
Total requirements per unit equipment	100	76.6	58.4
Total requirements per $ investment	100	63.7	31.9

SOURCE: UNIDO Report (see Table 5).The conventional/intermediate/automated classification roughly corresponds to the vintage classification used by the ECLA Report.

conventional machine) while the proportionate importance of administrative and skilled labour increased.

With the massive expenditure on r. and d. in developed countries, past trends are likely to be intensified in the future. New increasingly capital and skill intensive technologies will be developed. They may well make current methods appear labour intensive; they may also make them inefficient, as compared with the new methods. New products will also tend to make current technology obsolete, particularly if LDCs pursue a free trade strategy. Thus adaption and innovation in the LDCs is required for them to keep in the same place, and prevent the new methods overtaking the more labour intensive methods. The current balance of world r. and d. shows that by far the greater innovative effort (about 98% of all expenditure) is being devoted to advanced country technology. This is likely to mean that any labour intensive innovations of the LDCs will be dominated by developments in the advanced countries, almost before they are introduced.

While these figures suggest that it may be difficult for developing countries to maintain their current levels of labour intensity in the face of new developments, labour supply projections suggest the increasing need for employment opportunities over time. Rapid rates of growth of population will be reflected in rapid rates of growth of the working force. Increasing levels of education will make the unemp-loyed more vocal and possibly more powerful. Simply to absorb the *additions* to the work force in the modern sector will require, for most countries, an unprecedented rate of growth of employment. India, for example, would require an annual growth of 30% in modern sector employment if the modern sector were to absorb all the additions to the work force arising from the growth in population. In the past modern sector employment was expanded by 4% per annum.

The transfer of advanced country technology is in large part responsible for the growing employment problem. Not only has it limited the possibility of job expansion, it has also contributed to the growing demand for jobs, both by providing the conditions leading to the acceleration in population growth and contributing to the explosion in aspirations.

The question of technology is thus central to that of employment. The rest of this paper will be concerned with analysing in what direction, and how, changes might be made.

Direction of Change in Technology

It may be helpful to go back to Diagram 1 as summarising some important dimensions of the employment problem. The diagram emphasises unequal access to productive employment opportunities, as an essential aspect of this. There are three directions in which improvements might be made, as shown in Diagram 4.

First, if the numbers employed in the modern sector could be extended, the numbers dissatisfied in the traditional sector would be reduced; and ultimately when the modern sector absorbed the whole labour force the problem would be eliminated. Secondly, modification of modern sector technology would reduce disparities in the modern sector and could also be combined with an expansion in the size of the sector. Thirdly, improvements in traditional sector technology, raising productivity there, would reduce the gap between the sectors, and hence the desire to shift between them. If the gap in incomes between the sectors were eliminated then a very important aspect of the employment problem would also be removed. We shall discuss each of these approaches separately.

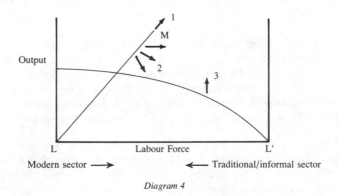

Diagram 4

Expanding the modern sector. The curves in the diagram show what happens to output as employment increases. They contain nothing directly about investment requirements or technology used, though they are of course based on assumptions about these, as discussed at length earlier. The reason the modern sector productivity is much above the traditional sector is that the technology it uses is both more expensive per employee, and more productive—because it embodies recent scientific developments. Any expansion in modern sector employment requires a parallel expansion in investment resources, if unmodified imported technology is to continue to be the basis of modern sector employment. Hence this possibility is excluded by the very nature of the problem—that the LDCs cannot afford the resources to employ its whole population with that technology and associated productivity. Indeed once one introduces dynamic aspects, as discussed above, most LDCs cannot keep pace with the expansion of the work force let alone absorb those at present in the traditional sector. An expansion in the modern sector might even increase the gap between the two sectors, assuming, which is likely, that there are increasing returns (not constant as in the diagram) to expansion of the sector. Past policies—e.g. as summarised in the I.L.O. Colombia Report[41]—have in many cases taken the form of making output growth (in the modern sector) the primary objective of development, and seeking to raise investment, by increasing internal and foreign savings to achieve this objective. In terms of the employment problem this strategy assumes that the modern sector expansion will involve an expansion in employment which will ultimately absorb the whole workforce, as in developed countries. Thus the strategy has been along the lines of alternative (1). While it looks as if this strategy may succeed in a few countries (combined to some extent with strategy (2)), for many others employment problems have worsened rather than improved with this approach.

Harris and Todaro have also pointed out that expansion of modern sector employment may increase overall unemployment by encouraging people to leave the traditional sector to seek jobs.* This is a weakness of any strategy involving expansion of the modern sector which is only partially successful—i.e. which does increase jobs but not enough to make real inroads into traditional sector activities, yet enough to raise aspirations within the sector. It must be emphasised that we are discussing here increasing complementary resources *parri passu* with employment in the modern sector; it is this which makes the policy unviable. The alternative, more often discussed, is expanding employment in the modern sector without expanding the complementary resources in line. This requires modification of technology and is therefore discussed under alternative (2).

Modifying modern sector technology. This would achieve two objectives: first, to reduce the disparity between the two sectors; and secondly, to enable the modern sector to expand faster, as the same investment resources could then employ a larger number of people. Thus the technology needs to be modified in a direction which reduces capital per head and output per head of employee, and produces output which is consistent with a smaller disparity in incomes. Such modification might be achieved:

(a) by improving the selection of current technologies—e.g. making better use of second hand equipment, shopping around more for more appropriate technology, and making more use of labour intensive ancillary activities, and fuller time use of existing technologies. Strategies (currently much favoured) involving export orientation—leading to a more labour-intensive technology via a more labour-intensive product mix, both of complete goods, and of processes may be classified as coming under improved selection, since they do not involve technological adaption.

(b) adapting existing technologies, and creating new appropriate ones.

Improved selection is a function of two variables—knowledge of the alternative available and incentives. Neither is effective in the absence of the other. Adaption and innovation may require more substantial institutional and other changes. Incentives may be important here too—as providing a necessary condition of development. But more substantial social and institutional change is needed.

---

* In a recent (unpublished) paper M.FG. Scott has challenged this conclusion, applying empirically derived parameters to a Harris-Todaro type model, and showing that, on what appear as reasonable assumptions, expansion of employment in the modern sector will reduce open unemployment.

Improving traditional technology. In many developing countries very large proportions of the population are employed in the traditional or informal sector, both rural
and urban, and are likely to continue in that sector—in some countries in Africa as
much as 90%. From the point of view of human welfare this sector is of overriding
importance. It is here too that the real poverty in developing countries is to be found.
Any policy concerned with poverty and income distribution must give this sector
priority. Low incomes in this sector derive from inadequate complementary resources, and low productivity of the resources there are. With few resources, people
cannot afford substantial expenditure on equipment. What is needed is low cost
technology, using the resources of modern science and technology to improve the
production possibilities of the sector. It is not just a question of the development of
new technology—though clearly this is key—but of its diffusion to literally thousands
of millions of families, who are often illiterate and may be conservative, for whom a
new and risky opportunity may not appear as presenting a possibility of gain, but
rather a probability of starvation. Social and cultural knowledge is essential in
addition to technical development. Outside subsistence activities, income earning
technology will only create incomes given markets. The problem of gearing markets
to technology is therefore an important one.

Improving technology in the informal/traditional sector thus requires: (a) search
for appropriate improved technology around the world; (b) creation of new technology either by institutional r. and d. or by creating the right conditions for local
developments; (c) diffusion of knowledge of the alternatives, and (d) creation of the
conditions, attitudes, markets and incentives, which will lead to its adoption.

Income Distribution

The analysis of the employment problem adopted has taken unequal access to income
earning opportunities as the key to the problem. The last two of the three approaches
suggested above—modification of modern sector technology and improvement in
traditional sector technology—would, it is believed, help to reduce disparities, by
raising incomes in the traditional sector and reducing incomes in the modern sector. A
more direct attack on unequal incomes is also needed, for two reasons. First, a direct
and substantial attack on income inequalities would contribute to removal of much of
the problem. If income earning opportunities in the modern sector were little greater
than those outside, there would be little incentive to seek modern sector employment,
and many of the symptoms of the employment problem would disappear. New
technology would be required to increase the productivity of the labour force as a
whole—by enabling more to benefit from latest developments in science—but not to
deal with the problem of unemployment, as such. The Chinese example shows that
the employment problem in LDCs is in large part a product of a particular set of
political and social and economic institutions. In a society in which rewards are, to a
much greater extent, divorced from activity, employing the whole work force becomes a question of organisation rather than incentives. Many public works programmes involve little capital equipment, but they cannot be undertaken on a sufficient
scale in many countries because of the cost in terms of wages. If incomes were
determined separately from employment, there need be little consumption cost in
providing extra employment. China has also pursued an active technology policy.[42]
This is important in increasing the productivity of the labour force, and of investment,
and in achieving self-reliance. But for the employment problem per se, substantial
reduction in wage differentials and in the system of rewards, accompanied by radical
changes in the organisation of production, were enough without major changes in

technology. Similarly, though with some loss in efficiency, Cuba has turned an apparently chronic unemployment situation into one of overfull employment. The existence, in some LDCs at least, of some obvious unfilled work opportunities side by side with massive open unemployment, also suggests the problem is at least in part one of incentives and organisation.

A direct attack on income distribution is also required, if the technology policy is to be successful. This arises because appropriate technology involves appropriate products as well as techniques. Such products would be products designed to cater for the average incomes earned in LDCs, rather than products designed to cater for the consumers of rich countries. The market for such products would only be forthcoming with more equal income distribution. Thus an essential aspect of China's textile technology has been to produce large quantities of standardised cotton outfits, rather than higher quality textiles in a variety of colours and styles. But this required a market for such cottons.

Similarly, more appropriate medical facilities involve the widespread provision of fairly elementary services. They are not consistent with the provision of modern hospitals which provide the latest care and attention for a small minority. But with unequal income distribution, the market will demand just such hospitals.

Causality works both ways; the technology adopted helps determine the income distribution also. This is partly a question of product availability. If only cheap standardised clothing and universal elementary medical services were provided, this would have an important impact on the real distribution of income, irrespective of the money distribution of income. Technology also influences income distribution because wages are positively related to labour productivity. In a decentralised system, in which incomes are determined privately, income distribution is heavily influenced by technology. Policy towards technology then becomes an important instrument of policy towards income distribution, as well as the other way round; and it is difficult to tackle either technology or distribution on its own.

Prices and Incentives

The system of prices may be of importance in two respects—in helping determine which techniques are selected, within the choice available, and in providing some incentive for appropriate technical innovations. However, so long as the main source of technology is the developed countries, the role of LDC incentive systems is modified, in both respects. The dominance of the latest technology means that often choice of technique is determined by scale and product considerations. The range of efficient choice available is too limited to make the system of selection (of which the price system is one part) of substantial importance. Much of the empirical evidence supports this conclusion.* Similarly, though the price system may play some role in leading to appropriate local innovations, so long as most innovational activity comes from outside, the significance of the LDC price system may be only slight.

While a change in the price and incentive system is unlikely to be a sufficient condition for securing the appropriate technology it may well be a necessary condition. It would be pointless to develop a new technology, while simultaneously operating an incentive system which discriminated against its use, and there is likely to be little local adaptive and innovative effort while the incentive system guarantees the highest profits to those introducing unmodified advanced country technology.

---

*   In one of the case studies I conducted (cement blocks) scale was the key determinant of choice of technique; in the other (maize grinding), the nature of the product. Other studies also show the importance of scale.[43]

The system of prices cannot be treated as an independent parameter, which may be altered at a stroke. It is in part a reflection of the technology adopted (as well as in part a cause). Prices, which here include wages received by different groups of workers and the profits received by different groups of entrepreneurs, are themselves the consequence of a particular production structure, arising from technology and historical developments in the society in question. Though this does not mean they are unalterable, it does mean that they are not amenable to change in the way that, for example, one can change Hire Purchase regulations.

Industrialisation based on the use of advanced country technology (particularly in the context of an import substitution strategy, but also with a more open strategy) tends to lead to high (relatively to the rest of the economy) real wages in the sector affected, and subsequently to powerful interests concerned to maintain those wages, and therefore that technology.

While an appropriate technology policy would require incentives consistent with its development and use, once widely introduced such a technology would also tend to *lead* to an appropriate system of incentives. Lower labour productivity associated with such technology would not permit the massive differentials currently paid in the modern sector. The effect of technology on wages can be seen in the differences in wages and incomes currently paid in different parts of the same economy, varying according to the technology adopted. The differentials between wages in large and small scale industry in Japan and India have been well documented. Table 8 below gives some figures for Kenya.

TABLE 8

WAGE AND INCOME DIFFERENTIALS—KENYA, 1969

Modern sector	Index
Overall average	100
Manufacturing - urban	149.2
- rural	92.7
Informal sector	
Non-agricultural (regular employees)	26.2
Self-employed	17.4
Wages in maize grinding	Shillings per month
Water mills	45/-
Hammer mills	99/-
Roller mills	293/-

SOURCES: F. Stewart, "Maize Grinding" (unpublished case study); *Kenya Statistical Abstract*.

Many would argue that the causality works the other way—with independently determined wage differentials giving rise to technology differences. Although the causality probably works both ways, the fact that in many cases it is difficult to find an independent explanation of the wage differences, while the technology *is* independently determined, by scale, markets etc., suggests that the technology adopted may in large part be responsible for the income differentials rather than the other way round.

Those who stress price 'distortions' as a prime cause of many of the problems of

LDCs, including inappropriate technology and employment problems, are generally primarily concerned with the following 'distortions':

(a) relatively high wages in the modern sector;

(b) relatively low price of capital, caused by low interest rates, tax incentives related to investment, and overvaluation of the exchange rate;

(c) overvalued exchange rates combined with high levels of protection.

It should be noted that (a) and (b) are modern sector phenomena only. In the informal sector access to funds for investment expenditure is limited, and expensive, and wages (as shown above) are low. Thus these policy changes are directed at the modern sector. They might even have deleterious effects on the informal sector, by making the modern sector more competitive with the informal sector, thus destroying employment opportunities in that sector. The net effect on employment in the economy as a whole as a result of a reduction in modern sector wages may in some circumstances be negative.[44] (c) does apply to some extent to the informal sector too. However, protection from international competition can permit continued existence and development of labour-intensive technologies, which might not be viable with a more outward looking policy. Thus removal of any of the 'distortions' may not invariably have a net expansionary effect on employment.

Conflicts

This last point suggests some of the conflicts implicit in the different strategies possible. Vigorous promotion of appropriate technology would involve losers as well as gainers. Those currently employed in the modern sector (workers and employers) would be the main losers from a successful strategy including redistribution of income, substantial change in differentials throughout the economy, and in the productiveness of different sectors' technology. These include the decision makers in politics and the civil service. There are a number of conflicts in policy which may be worth bringing out more explicitly. First, there is a conflict between modern and traditional sectors in resource allocation, both investment and r. and d. Until now the conflict has been solved largely by ignoring the traditional sector. Strategy (2) above involves using resources for the modern sector adapted technology; strategy (3) for the traditional sector. Conflicts between the sectors also arise in terms of markets. In many places the introduction of modern sector technology has destroyed the markets of the traditional sector. Keith Marsden has shown how the introduction of modern methods of shoe production and baking in various countries has destroyed substantial jobs in the traditional sector.[45] The policy of walking on two legs is an attempt to resolve some of these conflicts by allocating different and complementary activities to the two sectors. Whether it does more than replace an obvious dilemma by a convenient phrase has yet to be seen. There is a conflict also in policies towards prices in the two sectors as suggested above.

International Trade

Some see participation in international trade as the most promising employment creating avenue. With comparative advantage in labour-intensive goods and activities this ought to increase the employment content of activities. But the policy is likely to require increasing capital intensive technology to produce the kind of quality required by international markets, while free trade in imports is likely to lead to the continued consumption of inappropriate goods.[46] An alternative policy, where trade with LDCs is emphasised, but not trade with developed countries, offers more possibility of equal income distribution and continued labour intensive technology.

Technology Policy: Three Schools of Thought

In pulling together the threads of this discussion three sharply constrasting views of effective policy lines to pursue in promoting appropriate technological change in the LDCs can be identified.

One is the *price incentive school*. Some believe that "getting prices right," and "letting factor endowments speak" will be enough. The problem will then solve itself. The assumption behind this school is that there is a substantial amount of choice in technology available from the developed countries. With the 'right' incentives the correct choice will be made, and there will also be incentives for any needed adaption. Consequently a minimum of institutional intervention is required. The examples of Taiwan and S. Korea are quoted as examples. This school ignores (or believes unimportant) the fact that with the source of most technology in the advanced countries, the scope for technological choice is itself becoming increasingly inappropriate.

Another is the *radical reform school*. This school believes that radical transformation in the structure of societies in LDCs is required. Given such transformation— along the lines of the Chinese revolution—correct technology policy will follow automatically. Without such transformation no amount of institutional and incentive changes will bring about the correct technology.

A third is the *technologist school*. This school believes that institutional changes and changes in expediture on r. and d. may themselves be enough to bring about the required transformation. There is an inclination to believe that the problem is amenable to the same sort of effort as putting a man on the moon; indeed some of these resources are being switched to this end. The Intermediate Technology Development Group in London, the U.S.A.I.D. and the World Bank appear to share this sort of view.

It should by now be clear that the analysis in this paper suggests *a combined view*. The creation of a new technology is needed, as well as improved diffusion and selection of existing technologies. Such a change will not come about automatically, even with a reformed price structure. It requuires institutional changes to bring about. But a new technology is not, in itself, enough to cure the employment problem. Changed income distribution, and the devotion of much greater resources to the traditional sector are also required. More than straight forward technological research is also needed to bring about the widespread diffusion of a new technology. Technological change needs to become an intrinsic part of the economic development of the countries concerned, so that innovations become self-generating, as they were in Britain in the 19th century, and do not need to be continually imposed from above. This is not a once and for all problem but a continuing one.

Appropriate Types of Institutional Change

The rest of this paper will be primarily devoted to types of institutional change that might lead to the creation of improved technologies. This emphasis follows from the aim of the paper—to look at possible contributions by donor agencies. But this does not mean that the required changes in income distribution, and in resource allocation, are regarded as unimportant, or less important. They are almost certainly more important, but there is little that outside donor agencies can do to bring them about. However, without such changes anything that a donor agency does is unlikely to be effective.

Characteristics of More Appropriate Technologies

Dr. Schumacher—who first introduced the concept 'intermediate technology,' and is founder and co-director of the Intermediate Technology Development Group (ITDG) summarised the criteria he believes are necessary for appropriate technologies as follows:

> they must be cheap enough for jobs to be provided in very large numbers and simple enough to be used and maintained by rural and small town populations without sophisticated technical or organisational skills and with very low incomes. It follows that equipment of this kind will have to be provided largely from indigenous resources and employed largely to meet local needs.[47]

Dr. Schumacher and his group are almost entirely concerned with rural/village industry. They use a three-fold classification in searching for appropriate technologies:

> 1. Home industry: local resources, hand tools, family members, up to £20 per work position, handmade articles generally for local use.
> 2. Village industry: more a community operation, small groups of artisans, co-operatives, basic technical terms capable of translation into the vernacular, locally purchased materials, hand and simple machinery, up to £100 per work position, production for the local and surrounding communities.
> 3. Small industry: local companies, bigger co-operatives, normal technical terminology, indigenous or imported materials, powered machinery, relatively skilled labour, up to £500 per work position, machine products for district or national markets.[48]

In the earlier discussion we used a two-fold classification—'modern' and 'non-modern,' and this classification is adopted in Chart 1 which summarises requirements of an appropriate technology. The ITDG's first two categories fit into the improving non-modern technology classification. Their category (3) can be similarly viewed, or regarded as modifying modern sector technology.

It is worth commenting briefly on this chart. First, of all it is impossible to say exactly what the requirements of *the* appropriate technology would be. This depends on the objectives a country has (and the weighting attributed to them), technical possibilities (which we do not know), and the implications for development of different technologies, many of which we only know very sketchily. What one can do is sketch the direction in which technology should be changed, not the exact requirements.

Secondly, new developments in technology might be in the 'right' direction for some characteristics, and in the wrong direction for others. It is then a matter of judgement, viewed against the resources—of skills and of savings—of the society in question, which technology is more appropriate.

Thirdly, countries differ in the stage of development and their resources, so that there is no such thing as a technology appropriate for the third world as a whole. In Africa, where the urban population accounts for a small proportion of the total, improvements in rural technology are likely to bring the most benefits. In Latin America, in contrast, modification of modern urban technology is likely to be of greater importance.

Fourthly, as argued above, there may be conflicts between the sectors. Modifying modern sector technology may improve its competitiveness with the traditional sector, and thus on balance eliminate jobs.

Fifthly, there may be conflicts through time. A more appropriate technology secured immediately may be at the expense of some future improvements. The classic

CHART 1

REQUIREMENTS OF AN APPROPRIATE TECHNOLOGY

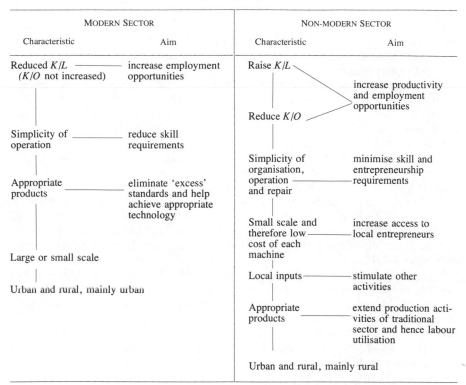

MODERN SECTOR		NON-MODERN SECTOR	
Characteristic	Aim	Characteristic	Aim
Reduced K/L (K/O not increased)	increase employment opportunities	Raise K/L	increase productivity and employment opportunities
		Reduce K/O	
Simplicity of operation	reduce skill requirements		
		Simplicity of organisation, operation and repair	minimise skill and entrepreneurship requirements
Appropriate products	eliminate 'excess' standards and help achieve appropriate technology		
		Small scale and therefore low cost of each machine	increase access to local entrepreneurs
Large or small scale		Local inputs	stimulate other activities
Urban and rural, mainly urban		Appropriate products	extend production activities of traditional sector and hence labour utilisation
		Urban and rural, mainly rural	

case of this arises from savings.[49] If a more capital intensive technology—involving less immediate jobs—leads to higher profits and more savings—then in the long run the higher rate of investment, and consequent higher rate of growth of output, may lead to more jobs than the labour-intensive alternative.[50] Time conflicts may work in other ways than through savings. For example the introduction of modern technology might be an essential aspect of spreading attitudes to production and machinery, which in turn are essential prerequisites of development of local technical capacity, and hence development of appropriate, locally developed, methods.

Most of the essential characteristics of appropriate technologies have been discussed above in the context of discussing why developed country technologies are inappropriate. Little further discussion is therefore required.

The requirement—in both sectors—that capital productivity should not be reduced (that K/O should not be increased) is essential if developing countries are not to suffer a loss in output. Such a sacrifice of output, though it might be justified by immediate distributional considerations, and by employment creation, is likely to lead to reduced savings and growth of output. It may, therefore, ultimately lead to fewer jobs, as well as a lower level of output. Given that investment resources are scarce in LDCs what is required is to maximise its productivity, not reduce it.

There are many dimensions to simplicity. Some of these may be in conflict.

Machines which are simple to operate are often difficult to manufacture and repair, like many household appliances. Simplicity of manufacture has not been included as a characteristic, but it must be one, if local manufacture is desired. Simplicity of organisation is often in conflict with the other characteristics. The most simple operation, organisationally, is the turn key factory, where all that is required is a single contract with a foreign firm. Contrast this with the manifold decisions, explanations, communication and persuasion needed to spread a new form of technology to every village.

The need for appropriate products has been discussed at length earlier. This implies an inward looking LDC trade strategy. The alternative strategy of promoting trade with developed countries involves production of commodities required by the developed countries. In this case the appropriate products are those for which there are international markets. The appropriate strategy is likely to differ among countries, with the smaller LDCs who are already developing fast on the basis of developed country exports, more suited to a continuation of this trend.

Scale is not an objective in itself, but it has important implications some of which were discussed earlier: (a) on capacity utilisation, if internal markets are small; (b) on the ability of local entrepreneurs to take over fully; (c) on the possibilities of production in rural areas, and by small entrepreneurs. For village technology, small scale is essential; for the development of local dynamic enterprise, small scale may also be important.

Many observers have put emphasis on the need for rural industry. While it seems sensible and desirable to prevent the development of huge urban conglomerations, and essential to provide some productive opportunities for the masses in the rural areas, the emphasis on rural industry does sometimes seem to hark back to the delights of rural eighteenth century England, without any real attempt to look at the relative costs and benefits of urban and rural development, and without allowing for the desire apparent among many, to get away from their rural surroundings. The rural-urban question is an area in which research is much needed.

The exact description of requirements of appropriate technology differs among observers. (Contrast the Schumacher classification with that discussed here). The requirements in Chart 1 are only intended to provide a rough guide to the direction in which the search for more appropriate technology should go.

Non-Production Technology

Technology covers many areas in addition to processes, plant and machinery primarily discussed above. For many of these similar arguments apply. The methods—of public administration, and private management, of communication and for the provision of services—tend to be inappropriate for LDCs in two respects. In the first place, in many cases these services provide complementary inputs with other services. Thus a good deal of public administration is concerned with enabling private production to take place: managerial services are complementary to the plant and labour requirements of production. Where they provide complementary services to production structures which are themselves inappropriate, they may be inappropriate for this reason. For example, banking systems were developed to cater for developed country business and have been transferred to developing countries to deal with similar business there. Although they are efficient in working in that way, they are inimical to the development of local small scale activities. They tend to provide low cost loans to modern firms, particularly if run by foreigners, while their surety and character requirements are such that they find few good risks among the local and as yet unproven small scale entrepreneurs. Hence when placed in the rural areas they tend to tap rural savings, and lend them in the urban areas. Systems of management, accounting and law are similarly designed for the structure of society and production found in developed countries. One of the first activities of the ITDG was to develop three manuals of simple accounting techniques for co-operatives.[51] Similarly, in looking at appropriate methods in the building industry, one of the first needs was found to be for simple systems of management, rather than plant or machinery.[52] The development and communication of appropriate systems of management, banking etc. may be an essential complement to more appropriate machinery.

The second reason why such services may be inappropriate is that, like other products, they have been developed for consumers who are, typically, much richer than the consumers, on average, in developing countries. Hence they tend to embody standards in excess of those that LDCs can afford. Take housing: until recently, £1,000 was the minimum price house provided by the Nairobi City Council, which effectively ruled out this form of housing for most of the population. Some services are both inputs and output. Education is an obvious example. Here standards may be inappropriate because they produce the wrong sort of education viewed as an input—with formal knowledge of the sort required in the formal sector, but with little of use for the vast majority who will be working outside this sector—and because they are too high standard and expensive for the whole of the population to be able to enjoy, viewed as a consumption good. Buildings for administration, for offices and for factories are similarly consumption goods as well as inputs and are often inappropriate from both points of view. The development of appropriate technology in these fields and of mechanisms for ensuring that where available it is in fact chosen, is of equal importance with, and may indeed be an essential prerequisite of, the development and introduction of more appropriate machinery.

Sources of Appropriate Technology

It seems clear that, left alone, insufficient effort is likely to be devoted to the creation of appropriate technologies. This may in large part be due to the social, economic and political structure of society that has developed in response to (and been reinforced by) the import of advanced country technology. It is also in part due to the inappropriate factor prices that have developed, partly in response to technological imports, but partly the reason for those imports. Reforms, which virtually amount to revolutions, are needed to put these right. But there is also a need for a conscious technological effort—to counter the trends of current technological developments in the developed countries, and to provide the third world with the possibility of a more appropriate technology.

Information. The necessary effort is in part one of collection and dissemination of existing information. In various parts of the world, and at various times in history, more appropriate technologies have been developed, but have not been communicated to those who need the information. Much of the technological information communicated to the third world comes from the salesmen of machinery manufactures in the developed countries.

"Equipment salesmen sometimes tend to offer to developing countries the most expensive models which, in some cases, may be . . . even more labour saving than equipment currently in use in typical plants in the country of origin."[53] Consulting engineers from the developed countries are also in general familiar with the equipment in use in developed countries. Judet has emphasised[54] the need for developing countries to develop their own engineering consultants, to reduce their dependence on the developed countries, and to bring about a more appropriate choice of technology.

The two other major sources of technical information also tend to promote the use of recent developed country capital equipment: multinational companies and aid donors. Multinational companies in general (with some exceptions to be discussed more below) tend to introduce similar equipment in whichever part of the world they operate. This is partly because they aim to produce standard products, and these normally require standard equipment, partly because their engineers and managers tend to be familiar with their main office technology, and partly because they are not, normally, machinery manufacturers, but machinery users. It is rarely the case that their operations in LDCs are sufficiently important to justify requests for major adaptions in machinery, particularly when they can make perfectly adequate profits with existing technology. Aid donors too have been responsible for introducing modern and capital intensive technology.[55] Tying aid to the donor countries' own products tends to restrict the search for appropriate technology. Failure to provide local cost finance automatically favours capital-intensive projects which have a lower labour (local cost) element. Despite aid donors' recent attention to questions of employment and choice of technique, both types of tying in large part persist.

The effect of aid on technology was illustrated in a case study of Swedish aid by M. Radetzki. He shows that in the two projects examined the aid strengthened dualistic tendencies in the economy. In one case—grain storage—more centralised and capital intensive methods were proposed than might have been appropriate. In the other the benefits of the project—in increased milk production—were concentrated on a small minority of the population. The cases are interesting in showing how apparently well motivated and disinterested aid efforts may nonetheless lead to the transfer of inappropriate technology.

The *sources* of information about methods of production are thus biased against any search for appropriate technology. Among UNIDO technical consultants, who have no direct interest in promoting capital intensive technology, the largest group of experts are involved in technology transfer: "In most cases the technologies are applied without significant modification."[56]

"The prevailing methods for the transfer of technology from the developed to the developing countries sometimes impose serious constraints on the possibilities of choosing the most appropriate technology for any given line of production, and of adapting existing technologies."[57]

UNIDO also believes that inadequate information is responsible for many of the wrong decisions: "Unfortunately primary information needed to make correct choices of equipment is often lacking; many enterprises looking for a new production-technology or for industrial equipment do not even know whether such technology can be found, who are the suppliers and on what terms the purchase can be done."[58]

In general, in developed as well as developing countries, small firms find it most difficult to acquire knowledge about alternatives, and are most in need of special services. Obstacles to the communication of knowledge about appropriate technology thus occur at both ends: at the supplying end most of the information about alternatives comes from those who are selling large scale modern equipment; at the buying end, the small entrepreneurs are in a particularly weak position to look for appropriate technology.

Various information collecting centres have been established. These include VITA—Volunteers in Technical Assistance—set up in 1960, and the ITDG.

UNIDO provides industrial and technical information in a set of services that they describe as the "Clearing House for Industrial Information." There are numerous other information services though few concerned specifically with collecting and disseminating information on appropriate technology. For example, the Tropical Products Institute in the U.K. answers technical queries on food processing. However, the present services are on far too small a scale. Their net impact is smaller than might appear because of the system of handing queries on from one service to another. The need for action on a larger scale was indicated in the Council of Europe recommendation for an International Information Centre for Intermediate Technology (1971) which was welcomed by UNCTAD and, with qualifications, by UNIDO.

It may be that the various embryonic institutions around the world, will, when fully developed, prove adequate. But at the moment there is a real gap here. It is therefore worth discussing more fully the sort of thing that is needed.

First, any information collecting centre must be in a position to collect information from suppliers all over the world, and particularly from machine producers in LDCs. Hence an International Centre is required, rather than a national centre in a developed country. International centres tend to belong to no nation, belonging to all. Close contact with industries in machine-producing and machine-using nations is essential, however.

Second, more is needed than simply a catalogue of existing machinery. Detailed economic information on different alternatives—scale, labour requirements, skill requirements, product nature, input requirements, likely repair cost—is needed as well as technical details and plant cost. Information on working capital requirements are also needed, as these can outweigh fixed capital, and reverse conclusions based on fixed capital costs alone.

Third, particular emphasis on the search for information about *appropriate* and *small-scale* technology is needed. There is something to be said for having a special Intermediate Technology Centre—in addition to a broader service such as UNIDO's ACE (Appropriate Choice of Equipment) extended—so that this part of the field will not be neglected.

Fourth, it is difficult to distinguish sharply between collection of existing information and technical innovation. Almost all the queries answered by the ITDG have consisted of a combination of the two; no major technical break-through has been achieved but innovations have occurred by the ingenious use and combination of existing information. For example, in answer to an enquiry about a cheap method of weighing babies, the unit in combination with Salter, manufacturers of weighing equipment, modified a spring scale and designed plastic trousers and straps, which would support the child while being weighed. The cost of this equipment was £6.75, as compared with £25 for the cheapest scale available without modification. Innovation needs to be combined with information collection from the point of view of efficient innovation as well—there is no need to redesign the wheel, as has often been pointed out. Thus any information collection centre needs to have close links with, or be part of, a technical innovation centre. The requirements for innovation will be discussed more below.

Fifth, the Centre needs to do more than simply respond to formal requests. Identifying the areas which are most in need of innovation and information, and the nature of those needs, is a required innovation. People tend to request information about subjects about which they already have a vague idea. The Centre would need to do more positive pushing to get the right sort of requests.

Information collection includes past techniques, processes and products as well as those currently in use. Some old techniques and products may be economical in LDCs with their much lower labour costs, although obsolete in developed countries. More often it is likely that the old products and processes will point the way to possibly appropriate innovations, rather than themselves providing the whole answer. This is because many modern discoveries have undoubtedly much to contribute to developing as well as developed countries. Almost all the examples of innovation in an appropriate direction use some modern methods or materials. For example, plastics form an essential part of the ITDG water catchment tank, and its attempt to develop waterproof roofing material. Similarly, the diesel engine is a key part of many appropriate technologies. The small scale water pump, the hammermill for grinding maize, and the ITDG proposal for small scale production of gur all make use of small diesel engines.

It is unlikely that an International Information Centre, on its own, will have adequate contacts with national industries in either developed or developing countries. The requirements thus point to the need for a kind of federal structure, with the International Centre acting as a clearing house, passing queries on to different national and regional centres in developed and developing countries, while initiating enquiries itself only where there are obvious gaps, or where the national centres seem blind to possibilities in other countries. Links between information collection and innovation could then be maintained through the national (and specialist) institutions.

Innovation. The earlier discussion about technology and employment suggested that information collection alone would not be enough. A major effort of innovation is also required. This is recognised in the global targets for research and development set out in the World Plan of Action for the second development decade.

One reason why general targets for expenditure may not achieve much is that they ignore the quality of the research undertaken. According to John Lewis, ''It cannot be denied that much if not most of the research going on in LDC's is irrelevant to the development needs of the countries, and much too much is second rate.''[59] In many developing countries, little research is concerned with industrial development. It is estimated[60] that in Pakistan less than one per cent of the industrial programme stems from research carried out by Pakistan's Council for Scientific and Industrial Research; and UNESCO estimated that in 1963 only 71 of Africa's 3,428 research workers were engaged in industrial research. Even where sizeable expenditure is concentrated on industrial research, innovation does not necessarily follow.

A recent report[61] discusses and analyses the relative failures of many research institutes in LDCs. These are in part due to organisational and similar factors —particularly insufficient contact between the research institutes and industry, as will be discussed more below. But it is also due to the nature of innovation. Innovation consists essentially of looking at old things in new ways; the ability to do this is difficult to institutionalise. Nelson[62] has emphasised the diversity and unpredictability of technological advance in the U.S.:

New products, processes, inputs, and equipment for an industry have come from established firms in the industry, from suppliers, purchasers, new entrants to the industry, individual investors. Many developments that seemed to be promising did not pan out. Many important breakthroughs were relatively unpredicted and were not supported by the recognised experts in the field.

Analysis of historical experience in other countries experiencing rapid technological advance gives a similar picture of diversity of source of innovation, and of unpredictability. In Britain in the early 19th century a very large proportion of the technological developments came from small entrepreneurs. In general technological advance preceded, and was not based on, scientific explanation. Formal research and development was virtually unknown.[63] Recent development in the Punjab, although based on the formally organised and researched seed revolution, is now evolving into a process of local innovation and interaction, carried out by numerous small mechanics.

There are of course examples of technical innovation that have been organised from above. The seed revolution, the space race, and the arms race provide spectacular examples. On a less grandiose scale, the success of the Leather Research Institute in Madras, the Rubber Industry in Malaysia and the Korean Institute of Science and Technology (KIST) are examples. The nature of these success cases will be discussed more below. They are exceptions. Recently an analysis of the projects supported by The Fundicao A Apara Ampara E Pesquisas do Estado do Sao Paolo (FAPESP) in Brazil showed that "only one out of 1,000 projects, funded during the past several years really had practical direction or application."[64] That they are exceptions is in part due to the fact that there is more to technical innovation than the disbursement of funds. Given the right social and economic conditions technical dynamism will occur without prodding from above; without the right atmosphere conditions for success are much more difficult to achieve. The right conditions are difficult to pin down. They include general attitudes and atmosphere—in which innovation is expected, not just in one or two places, but throughout society at all levels; in which technology is not simply imported ready made from abroad, but foreign technology is regarded as a source for new ideas, rather than the end product; in which technical innovation is rewarded, in the sense that there is a market for the new products, whether they are machinery or final consumer goods. A (mechanically) skilled labour force seems to be an essential prerequisite, as the examples of Japan, S. Korea and Taiwan suggest. For major local innovation, a local capital goods industry is required. The tubewell revolution in the Punjab could not have occurred without mechanical production capacity. But equally the Punjab shows that market conditions—in this case transformed by growing farm incomes as a result of the Green Revolution—must also stimulate technical developments.

As so often, the question is, in part, one of chicken and egg. While some local mechanical skills are needed, and some local capital goods capacity, these themselves expand (in the right sort of society) in response to technical innovations, and this expansion in turn breeds further innovation. This was the story of the European Industrial Revolution, and also seems to be the story of current developments in the Punjab. "In West Pakistan, small-scale manufacturers of tube-wells and irrigation pumps not only helped train machinists and other metal working crafts-men, it also provided important inputs towards increased agricultural productivity."[65]

While mechanical skills, and some capital goods production capacity, appear to be necessary conditions for local innovation they are not in themselves sufficient. Both India and Brazil have sizeable capital goods industries; neither have made major innovations in a labour-using direction.[66] Pack and Todaro have emphasised the need for capital goods capacity, so that old capital goods (designed e.g. in the 19th century) may be reproduced.[67] In China, it seems, capital goods industries are being used in this way. Elsewhere too, on a more moderate scale, local engineering machine shops are reproducing small scale equipment, which is now obsolete in developed countries. Research on cement block making machines, mixing machines and local hammer mills in Kenya,[68] showed that small scale machines—almost exact copies of machines previously imported from the developing countries, and now obsolete in developed countries (though still being produced for sale in LDCs)—were being produced locally. On the whole it seems that engineering workshops originating in a small way are more likely to copy old designs and innovate, on a minor scale, than larger scale capital goods firms.

Every developing country needs mechanical repair capacity—and this often develops into manufacture, first of spare parts and then of machinery. But each country cannot expect to have a full scale capital goods industry. Those who do not, can, however, benefit from those that do through international trade. Already machinery made in LDCs tends to be somewhat more appropriate than machinery made in the developed countries.* With correct policies towards capital goods industries in the countries with capital goods capacity this tendency should increase. Hence developing countries should give trading preference to machinery from other LDCs.

The three targets of the World Plan of Action correspond to three areas where innovation may originate and which require exploration:

1. through increased expenditure on r. and d. by the developing countries themselves (target 1);
2. through developments in the LDCs financed and assisted by the developed countries (target 2); and
3. through research in the developed world, on behalf of developing countries (target 3).

Both the latter two provide a potential role for outside agencies. Before discussing them in more detail something should be said about their relative merits. Scientific, technical and machinery producing capacity undoubtedly exists to a massive extent in the developed countries; in contrast the capacity of most developing countries is puny. In North America there are 37 people with science degrees for every 100,000 people; in Africa there are 0.2 (though it should be noted that, according to these UNESCO figures, Asia with 22 has more than Europe, with 13 per 100,000). The ITDG has found that "for this kind of work to be fruitful a considerable part of it must of necessity be done in the developed countries."[69]

In the first place arguments based on capacity and specialisation are essentially static; they dwell on comparative advantage today, not on the potential for development. But capacity is itself largely a function of past development. Today's limited research capacity in LDCs is due to the fact that past r. and d. has been concentrated in developed countries. The relative weakness of LDC scientific and technical potential will continue, if the argument based on current capacity leads to continued emphasis on developed country research. The brain drain is in part due to lack of opportunities for research at home. KIST has managed to staff itself with a reverse brain drain (of scientists who would not otherwise have returned) from the U.S., by offering special opportunities and incentives. One aspect of underdevelopment lies in the LDC's attitude to science and technology—"the weak development of local scientific institutions and their marked susceptibility to orient their activities in line with external influences."[70] This attitude will be reinforced if the source of appropriate technology comes from the developed countries. Scientific and technological capacity in the LDCs should be (and is at least verbally) a major objective.[71]

The work should be carried out in LDCs, wherever possible, even if it means some

---

* A preliminary research report on intermediate technology in Indonesia, by Lou Wells, suggests that intermediate techniques were associated with 2-3 times more employment than advanced techniques, and that machinery imported from other developing countries was always associated with intermediate techniques.

initial loss in efficiency. Quite apart from the need to build up local scientific capacity, it would be extremely difficult otherwise to maintain the required interaction between industry, economic and social conditions, and research that is required for the successful promotion of appropriate innovations.

Action in developed countries. Broadly, this may be divided into r. and d. financed by non-profit making agencies, and r. and d. financed by the private sector. Research financed by the private sector, whether by potential exporter or investors, is primarily determined by the expected profitability of the research, which in turn depends partly on the facts of the situation, and partly on how these facts are viewed. Thus getting a more active policy of r. and d. on the part of the private sector may require a change in the objective situation, and may require a change in the sector's appreciation or viewing of the facts.

The multinational corporation. The evidence, though sketchy, points in one direction. Multinational corporations have been responsible for transferring modern technology to developing countries, with very little modification to the core plant or process and product, but with some variation in labour use in ancillary activities. Baranson concludes, on the basis of a survey of 50 multinational firms with automotive parts manufacturing affiliates in developing countries, "there has been very little in the way of technical adjustments in product designs or production techniques."[72] Hughes and Seng,[73] in a study of foreign investment in Singapore, conclude that foreign firms had shown little replacement of capital by labour in comparison with techniques used by firms in their own home countries. Similarly, Reynolds and Gregory found that in Puerto Rico in the early fifties, "the production operations in the Puerto Rico branch plants were usually engineered in much the same way as on the mainland."[74]

Although multinational companies have carried out little modification in the basic technology, they do seem often to use more labour in ancillary activities, as compared with their home activities, and also in some cases to use more labour than locally controlled enterprises in similar activities. Pack found this sort of adjustment in Kenya[75] in both local and foreign firms, but he suggests that "foreign plants are more likely to be directed by those with considerable technical expertise, while locally owned ones are more likely to be run by owners who have extended their selling operations backwards." He argues that managers with technical expertise are more likely to adapt the technology, "Those without technical background rely on capital goods salesmen—with predictable results." The evidence contained in the Kenya ILO Mission Report[76] supports Pack's hypothesis. The Mission found that though, on aggregate, foreign investment was more capital intensive in Kenyan manufacturing industry than local enterprise, "In sectors where foreign and locally owned enterprises co-exist, foreign enterprises are less capital intensive than locally owned firms." The explanation suggested is that "foreign firms have more skilled supervisory staff, and that this allows them to use production techniques which use low-cost unskilled labour." This explanation is supported by the evidence showing that foreign firms have lower labour cost per worker than local firms, in those sectors where both operate. Strassman, in Mexico, also found that foreign (U.S.) firms were more likely to adopt labour-intensive techniques than the Mexican firms he questioned. Hal Mason got very similar results in the Philippines to those in Kenya. On aggregate the foreign firms were more capital intensive; among the 200 largest firms examined, he found assets of $11,400 per employee for U.S. firms, as compared with

$9,600 for non-U.S. firms. However, the discrepancy was due to the greater propor-
tion of U.S. activity in capital-intensive products, and disappeared (but was not
reversed) when this was allowed for. Mason found, as hypothesised in the Kenya
Report, that the U.S. firms had a higher proportion of executive skilled and unskilled
workers; the non-U.S. firms a greater proportion of professional and skilled workers.
The U.S. firms generally manufactured products "which are technically more refined
than those produced by the local counterpart."[77]

The net effect on factor use must include the effect of product mix as well as factor
use for a given product. It should also include the effect of scale on factor use. Thus,
despite the fact that foreign firms appear to use more labour-intensive techniques for
given products at a (relatively) large scale,* because they tend to produce more
capital intensive products and operate at a large scale, they are likely, in aggregate, to
be more capital-intensive than local firms. This is a field where more systematic
research is needed.

Multinational companies are primarily interested in making profits. Hence their
choice of technique, and product, is at least partly a response to the structure of factor
prices, tariffs and import restrictions, taxes and subsidies and income distribution that
they find. But they also individually, and more as a sector, contribute to this structure
in a way that makes their activities profitable. One essential characteristic of multinational companies has been, until now, that they produce the same product irrespective of location. This contributes to the capital intensive nature of the products they
produce and to their high income characteristics. However, some multinationals are
changing their strategy. In the first place the growth of runaway industries—where
labour-intensive processes are located in low labour cost countries[78] allows labour
intensive production. Estimates for the Kaohsiung export processing zone in Taiwan
show capital per employee of £520.[79] Secondly, there seems to be increasing
awareness of the need for r. and d. in techniques and products for developing
countries.

Philips' Utrecht Pilot Plant, established in 1961, provides a pioneering
example—but one which to date does not seem to have been copied. The Plant, which
is deliberately placed some way away from the main Philips factories, with communication with the Head Office only (in theory anyway) by letter, is an attempt to
duplicate in Holland the conditions of a developing country and develop techniques
and methods of organisation appropriate to those conditions. Administrative procedures have been adapted as well as production activities; for example the manager's
secretary is also the receptionist at the main gate, and the accountant looks after
personnel affairs. "Production tools and equipment, administrative procedures,
documentation methods, stores organisation and stock control systems were all
studied and simplified. The assembly line itself was found to be unsuitable in small
manufactured exports."[80]

The net result of the changes made has been to reduce capital costs and increase
labour costs. A conventional T.V. assembly line would require capital investment of
around fl.160,000 and each product would take around 3.2 hours of labour time. The
Pilot Plant operations designed for a volume of output 1/50 of the conventional plant
requires fl.60,000 investment, and each unit needs 4.8 hours of labour.[81] Capital
costs per unit are thus still substantially higher than with conventional methods
operating at full capacity, but much lower than with the use of conventional methods
to produce very low production runs.

---

*   The evidence of Strassman and Mason was for large (relatively) scale activities, selected so as to get
comparability; that for Kenya was also for firms with more than 50 employees.

A few facts are worth noting about the Philips operation. First, the Pilot Plant scheme does not seem to be obviously profitable. It is maintained on the assumption that adjustments of this kind will be required before long if foreign enterprises are to be allowed to operate in developing countries. Secondly, technical change in processes and products in radio, T.V. etc. is occurring fast, and rapidly overtakes any adjustments made, so continual modifications are required to keep the labour intensive methods competitive. Thirdly, the plant uses highly skilled manpower to obtain its results, and makes considerable use of the research facilities of the main part of Philips. The manager thought the operations would be difficult to carry out in a developing country. Fourthly, no attempt at all has been made to modify the products, only the processes. It is accepted that market forces will require developing countries to produce the latest products, if they are to compete in export markets, and nearly the latest if they are to have a contented local market. Thus short time lags are allowed in the introduction of product modifications in developing countries. Even the (apparently) metal decorations around T.V. sets, which are purely decorational and perform no function, are carefully included in the Pilot Plant operations. The Pilot Plant makes no effort to devise the kind of simple radio in simple casing that might be appropriate to many low income countries. This, together with the need to keep up with technical change in processes as well as products, severely limits the usefulness of the operation. It supports the view that modification of technology alone is difficult without simultaneous modification of the structure of demand. Fifthly, perhaps the major contribution of the Pilot Plant lies in the structure of administration and organisation of production, rather than the production processes.

The Philips case provides an example of modification of technique but not product. At the other extreme are the recent attempts by Ford and General Motors to design a much modified vehicle. Ford recognised that conventional cars were unsuitable for Southeast Asia, both because physical conditions differed and because "their high price tag limited the availability of imported cars to a small number of people."[82] They recognised the need for an intermediate vehicle "more efficient than the traditional animal or human-powered vehicles but less expensive than the imported vehicles designed for use in developed country markets."[83] The production requirements were also for appropriate technology—low cost, at low volume, using local materials, simple equipment and local labour. "Fabrication of the body had to be simple enough to be done on equipment as basic as a 70-ton brake press, a manually operated screw press, and simple jigs and fixtures which can be welded together out of readily available materials."[84] The *Fiera* was produced. It is a basic vehicle consisting of a simple cab and chassis. Model variations are possible so that it can be used as a truck, a passenger minibus, a van; it can be used to drive a rice husking machine, power a water pump or a saw. Manufacture is planned in the Philippines this year. The total research investment for the vehicle was $700,000.

There are other examples of products designed specially for the developing countries. Ford has designed a Developing Nation Tractor which is a low cost one-man tractor intended to replace the ox or buffalo. This has been tested in Jamaica. The National Cash Register Company has designed a simple machine in Argentina suitable for family businesses.[85]

These examples are exceptions. This might appear surprising in view of the size of the markets the developing countries as a whole possess, and the small size of the research required, as the Ford experience showed. Indeed Ford believed itself to be responding to a commercial challenge. Multinational companies are more likely to make contributions of this kind if (a) there is a market for appropriate products, which means that the increase in incomes is widely spread and not concentrated on an elite, who can afford conventional Western products; thus the development of *Fiera* has been attributed to "rising incomes in rural areas resulting from higher agricultural productivity from the Green Revolution,"[86] and (b) the profitability of more conventional operations is in doubt. Tariffs, taxes and income distribution are the determinants.

Multinational companies appear to locate most of their research in the advanced countries. This in itself makes research *for* developing countries less likely. Even Ford and Philips located their developing country oriented research in developed countries, limiting the learning effect of the research. The multinational company would justify this policy with reference to economies of scale and diseconomies of fragmentation. Developing countries can counter this by *requiring* multinationals to locate r. and d. in their territory. This the Andean Pact countries have already done. Although of course they cannot make this particular horse drink, this at least may prevent it drinking elsewhere. In general developing countries probably can do more in laying down requirements of various kinds. Many of the adaptions in process that have taken place have been in response to insurmountable obstacles—differences in climate, availability of materials, and in Government regulations. Price differences—not insurmountable, just costly—seem to be less effective.[87] The requirements for local resource content have caused adaptions in Indian manufacturing. It would be worth investigating the possiblity of establishing standards institutes whose job is to lay down product and technique requirements that lead to more appropriate technological research.

Machinery suppliers. Developing countries' investment forms about 15% of world investment. In 1971 their imports of engineering products from U.S., W. Europe and Japan amounted to 22% of total exports of these areas. There must be profitable opportunities for manufacturers of capital equipment to design equipment specially for developing countries. To some extent this happens. Massey-Ferguson and other farm machinery manufacturers do design machinery for use in LDCs; other firms maintain production of equipment now obsolete in the developed countries for use in LDCs. The market for such appropriate equipment is determined by the structure of production and credit in the developing countries. For example, with a combination of large farmers who can afford to invest and wish to use the latest techniques, and subsistence farmers who can afford no equipment, there is no market for appropriate equipment even if it were available. Hence there is no incentive to make it available. But this is a vicious circle. So long as such equipment is not available, the position of the large farmers is reinforced while the subsistence farmers have no hope of raising themselves from their poverty, since no suitable machinery is available even if they do raise a little cash. Hence the lack of incentive to develop appropriate equipment remains. It is this sort of vicious circle, in industry as well as agriculture, that needs to be broken through simultaneously in terms of available technology, and distribution of purchasing power for that technology. Breaking through the circle in one place only—be it technology or distribution—will not be enough.

Non-profit making r. and d. In a small way Governments and others have supported research for developing countries for some time. The Tropical Products Institute and the Road Research Laboratory in Britain have been involved in work of this kind. Some of the results of such research have been successfully adopted—e.g. the cashew nut processing machine, developed by the TPI. Others have not: the coconut protein extractor developed at the TPI has not yet been introduced; nor has the USAID financed hand pump, or plastic roof. "While the technical aspects of these projects were sound, the economic realities of developing country manufacturing interests were less well understood.[88] The failure to implement, despite technical success, illustrates the drawbacks of locating research in the developed countries (though as will be shown below research results in developing countries are also often unexploited.

More recently, there have been more direct attempts to use developed country resources for the creation of appropriate technologies. USAID has financed a five year project at MIT for adaption of industrial and public works technology to the conditions of developing countries. The ITDG has set up an agricultural tools and equipment service unit at the National College of Agricultural Engineering, Silsoe. The unit combines collection of information on intermediate technology with innovation. The unit has designed and fabricated an improved fiddle seed-broadcasting machine, and a metal bending machine (scaling down a conventional machine costing £700 to a manually operated machine, costing £7).

Although work on appropriate technology is now becoming fashionable in developed countries it is still on a very small scale. Some have suggested that environmental problems in developed countries will necessitate a more intermediate technology there too—such technology has been described as a *soft* technology.[89] Work on environmental technology in developed countries *may* throw up ideas of relevance to developing countries, but often environmentally oriented technology proves to be more expensive then dirty technology.

Clearly, efforts in advanced countries to promote appropriate technology could easily be extended. But a major effort financed by aid agencies to promote the development of appropriate technology *in* developed countries will be inevitably —and in my view rightly—under suspicion from developing countries, as representing another aspect of a neo-colonial determination to maintain technological dominance, and to promote the interests of multinational corporations and advanced country machinery producers.

Research and development in LDCs. The record of r. and d. expenditure by companies in LDCs is on the whole a weak one.* Although, tax incentives can be used to encourage such expenditure, in the short run the main thrust of additional search for appropriate technology must come from the public sector.

There is no shortage of institutions concerned with research and development, but there has been little successful innovation in relation to the efforts expended. A low proportion of research expenditure goes on applied research and technology projects—the National Council for Scientific and Technological Investigations in Argentina spends less than 3% of its funds on applied projects. There is considerable replication of projects in different institutes, and "nearly every research center has a sizeable collection of completed research projects waiting exploitation by an entrepreneur. . . . So far, contribution of much of this research has to be considered as a form of education for indigenous research staffs with very little input in industrial growth and development."[91]

Analysis of the piecemeal evidence available both about the research institutes that

---

* A survey on large enterprises (with more than 500,000 new cruizeiros capital, or more than 100 employees) showed that less than one quarter of the enterprises conducted research. More than half of the enterprises claiming to do research employed no more than three researchers with professional training. Traditional industries (textiles, leather, etc.) employing the bulk of the labour force, accounted for the smallest part of the research effort.[90]

have "failed," and those that have "succeeded" allows one to draw some general conclusions.[92] First isolation from industry is an almost universal characteristic of the failures; and contact with industry an essential characteristic of success. "In each of the 50 research centers visited to date the concern is commonly expressed that much greater interaction is urgently required with industry and with government enterprise . . . In observing the research activities of these centers it is apparent that such activities are often not relevant to the real world problems around them, . . . industry lacks confidence in the ability of the research centers to perform; the research centers lack knowledge of the needs of their potential clients."[93] Nayudamma aptly sums up the situation: "Research and industry run parallel to each other but, like the two banks of a river they never meet."

The more successful institutes have all actively pursued close cooperation with local industry. KIST surveyed the needs of 600 enterprises before designing its programme. The IRRI provides designs free of cost to any firm demonstrating a genuine interest in commercial production and marketing. The history of the development of the small tractor in India was one of close and continuous contact with Indian industry. The need for close contact with industry is perhaps too obvious to need elaboration; it may also, arguably, be a symptom or result of success rather than a cause. What is of interest is how such industrial liaison is best brought about. One method widely advocated is the use, in part at least, of contract finance, on the dual argument that one only values what one pays for, and one only pays for what one values. Contract finance is used in part in KIST. But there are objections to its exclusive use. In the first place, it requires a degree of scientific sophistication among potential clients that is often lacking. This environment means that technological innovations have to be pushed actively. One cannot wait for industry to request and finance them. Of course, the scientific environment differs between countries. There are numerous firms in S. Korea able and willing to contract research. But this is not true elsewhere. Contract research, as a system, is suited only to the type of research where results can be more or less foreseen. More dramatic innovations require originality and creativity outside the limits of such contracts. The demonstration pilot plant is seen, by a USAID report, as "the major potentially successful link that joins industrial research institute to the industrial development process."[94] The report quotes a number of examples.

A second apparently universal characteristic of successful institutes is dynamic leadership. In the description of success stories all concur in pointing to a single individual combining entrepreneurial, administrative and scientific ability. In one case (the Central Mechanical Engineering Research Institute) the rise and fall of the success of the institute was directly attributed to the arrival and subsequent departure of one man. The story of the development of the small Swaraj tractor is interesting also in illustrating the inhibiting effect on local technological development of imported technology.* "Collaborative arrangements which bring about an unequal competition between foreign and indigenous technology are likely, therefore, to be detrimental to the growth and skill and confidence in the indigenous industry."[95]

A strictly *selective* attitude to foreign technology is essential for successful local technology development. The Japanese policy provides a very good example of successful selection.

Most of the research institutes in developing countries are not primarily concerned with the development of appropriate technology. Where successful the innovations are

---

* K.K. Subramaniam has listed large numbers of processes where the private firms have bought foreign technology, although the technology was also available from C.S.I.R. laboratories.

often not in the sort of direction described as appropriate in this paper. Strassman has done a detailed investigation of innovations in the construction industry in LDCs.[96] Among the 16 off-shelf innovations (i.e. innovations in production of off-site inputs) he examined, 81% *saved* labour, and none increased the use of labour. In half of the innovations this was the only innovation and was accompanied by an *increase* in the use of materials or foreign exchange. Thus in essence these innovations were labour saving and capital (or materials) using, the opposite of what might be thought appropriate in adaptions of developed country technology. In some of the innovations there was an increase in quality (accompanied by an increase in cost)—again the opposite of what might be thought of as appropriate product innovation.

The Korean Institute of Science and Technology provides an example of a successful research institute in an LDC, which has not been primarily concerned with *appropriate* innovations. The Institute was designed to apply current world technology to the problems of the Korean economy; "it presents the professional staff with a working environment comparable to the better outfitted research laboratories to be found anywhere."[97] The research results from the Institute, while undoubtedly helping S. Korean industry to solve technical problems arising in the use of advanced country technology, and themselves contributing to improved techniques and products which will enable S. Korea to compete on world markets, have not been particularly appropriate, in the sense in which the concept has been used in this paper.

This does not, of course, mean that the results are inappropriate to the S. Korean economy, which with its rapid rate of industrialisation, heavy export orientation and emerging labour shortage, and scientific and technical (relative) sophistication may benefit substantially from the type of innovation achieved. But KIST does not provide a model for many other developing countries in search of appropriate technology.

The point was put graphically by Mr. Bav Dev Singh:[98]

Science in most developing countries and likewise in India has two faces. One face is turned expectantly towards the achievements of the advanced nations in regard to the fantastic progress that science has made in landing a man on the moon, sending missiles to objects in the solar and extraterrestrial systems, the harnessing of atomic energy and powerful generation; advances in civil aviation; electronics, communication, synthetic fibres . . . The cost of these achievements and of an r. and d. system to maintain this progress is fantastic and beyond the means of the developing countries. . . . The other face of science in developing countries is towards the utilisation of science and technology for improving the welfare of the common man. This effort includes the introduction of new technologies for agriculture and small/medium scale industry, the dissemination of scientific knowledge to overcome superstitions and prejudice, the creation of job opportunities and the achievement of greater economic and social justice.

Generally speaking, for appropriate employment-creating innovations it is the second type of innovation that is primarily needed. To achieve these, the research institutes themselves must be using the right face: this is a question of the industry, and the nature, product and scale of production, for which their innovations are primarily intended. Appropriate innovations derive in large part from institutes which have been primarily concerned with small scale and traditional production, as shown in the case of the Indian Leather Research Institute and the agricultural mechanisation programme at IRRI. A higher proportion of r. and d. resources needs to be devoted to this type of research institute, rather than to institutes mainly concerned with advanced technology. Such institutes need to be located in the area where most of the relevant industry is and to maintain continuous contact with local industry.

One way of maintaining relevance and contact is to combine problem solving service with r. and d. An institute prepared to answer technical queries will then automatically have an outlet for innovation, and contact should ensure relevance.

Selection of areas. Institutes can be too narrowly focused and thus miss relevant alternatives. On the other hand if too widely based they may miss everything, seeing no trees for the wood. There are a number of criteria which may be used as a basis of selection:

1. Needs oriented. There are various broad needs—for food, shelter, clothing, transport—which may be met in various ways and by all sorts of products using all sorts of techniques. Institutes which are set up to cover a single need, with three main functions—investigation and collection of information on a world wide basis, industrial and technical problem solving and innovation on a low income basis, may avoid these twin dangers and also avoid excluding alternatives because they are a different type of product. For example, an appropriate rural transport institute would collect information on different methods of transport, and develop further what appear to be the most appropriate forms.
2. Resource based. Such institutes as the Leather Research Institute and the Malayan Rubber Institute are concerned with developing the use of a local resource.
3. Employment based. These are institutes which are intended to develop methods in industries which already employ substantial numbers of people. Agriculture, construction and textiles are obvious candidates.

Clearly there are some overlaps: thus a shelter oriented institute would overlap with one for the construction industry; agriculture with one based on raw materials e.g. sisal. These are just ideas, not proposals. The important things are: (i) to select the areas in such a way that they are sufficiently focused to be productive, but not so narrowly focused that they exclude important alternatives; (ii) that the areas are selected in such a way that appropriate innovations are the natural outcome. For example, any institute whose main function is to improve traditional housing, is almost certain to come up with some appropriate innovations. On the other hand an institute to adapt advanced country technology may well produce important scientific results, but may actually have negative employment and income distribution effects. Development requires ''walking on two legs;'' successful and self-sufficient innovation requires machinery inputs; it requires a machine tools industry, and some advanced technology input into the industry. The idea is not to exclude such research but rather to see that it is justified with reference to the overall objectives of the policy, and not simply because this appears to be what r. and d. is normally about; (iii) to ensure that the whole of the *innovative chain*, which includes scientific research, marketing research, invention, development, design, tooling, and early production and marketing of the product or process, is carried out, not simply the first scientific part, which is often the easiest and the cheapest.*

The success of the International Rice Research Institute suggests a possible parallel development in technologies. There are obvious advantages in terms of avoiding duplication, and avoiding concentration of development in a single LDC. Such international institutes may more easily generate international finance than

---

* It has been estimated that for the U.S. typically expenditure on innovation was broken up as follows: [99]

r. and d.	5-10%
Engineering and design	10-20%
Tooling	40-50%
Manufacturing start up	5-15%
Marketing start up	10-25%

national institutes and may contribute to the easier international dissemination of results. On the other hand it may be more difficult to get continuous industrial contact going with an international institute.

Lessons of the Green Revolution. In some ways the Green Revolution appears to provide a prototype. After the need for agricultural change was identified, Rockefeller, Ford and others cooperated over a ten-year period, in financing research into seed developments in a number of international institutions located in the developing countries. The results, which enabled output per acre to increase in some cases by as much as 30-fold, were rapidly introduced.

Technologically, the possibility of seed revolution presented a unique opportunity. Because of the very large areas devoted to growing rice, wheat and maize, a few technological developments could have enormously wide implications and effect. There is no industrial parallel because of the non-homogeneity of industrial production: a hundred, at least, revolutions would be required, not a single one. Moreover, physical conditions in the tropics presented an obstacle to the transfer of existing advanced country technology. Developing seeds to suit these conditions could thus fairly easily increase productivity. The availability of labour in LDCs also presented an opportunity which, with the right technology, might be turned to advantage. The Green Revolution does perhaps suggest that concerted effort of the developed countries on the question might at least contribute to the technological solution.

What have been described as the second generation problems of the Green Revolution are now coming increasingly to the fore, illustrating the dangers of this method of technological advance. The seed revolution was in large part a landlord biased revolution, according to a recent United Nations document.[100]

This bias arose from the fact that it is effective only where irrigation and fertilisers are present. In the unirrigated areas, to a much larger extent in the possession of small peasants, there was no revolution. Indeed, in such regions losses ensued, as falling prices following the expansion of production reduced the gains from any given physical output. Differential access to credit and hence to new forms of irrigation, to fertiliser and to machinery, gave further bias towards landlords. The net result has been a marked worsening in the distribution of income in many rural areas. Mechanisation of the large farms, following the increased cash flow, reduced the demand for labour on such farms (partly offset by increased demand for multiple cropping) while the supply increased as poor farmers on arid lands were forced to join the landless labourers. In the Philippines wages of agricultural workers fell by 25% between 1956 and 1970. A study of 126 wheat farms in the Punjab showed that "it is clear that both relative and absolute increase in disposable income per holding was higher in the case of large sized holdings as compared to small and medium sized holdings."[101]

The Green Revolution thus illustrates a major thesis of this paper—that technical change is not neutral as between different classes, or income distributions. Even where neutral, if accompanied by policies, e.g. towards credit, which favour large scale farmers, the net effects may be to bias the system further in favour of the rich. Thus two things are needed: a biased technological change policy in favour of the small scale; and the simultaneous pursuit of similarly biased (or at least not biased in the opposite direction) policies on credit, markets etc.

A major problem is how peasant biased technical developments may be achieved. Technologies from developed countries are naturally more attuned to the problems of the large scale, more in touch with the literate and powerful, and indeed are to some extent their servants (as well as their masters). A major bias in technology towards the small scale—whether in agriculture or industry—necessary to meet the problems of income distribution and employment—inevitably and by its nature threatens the position of those currently rich and powerful. Such change is thus difficult to organise from without or from within.

The Green Revolution also emphasises the need to look beyond the first round effects at the social and other (including in this case nutritional) second round effects of introducing a radically new technology. This sort of strategic socio-economic planning must be done in advance, not as a desperate reaction.

Conclusion

In conclusion two fundamental aspects of this question must be reemphasised. One is that this is an area of circular and multiple causation, in which operation in one area alone—that of technology—may well be fruitless, while operation in other areas, without technology, may equally be unsuccessful. Secondly, the question is a dynamic one, with continuous change in the (apparent) parameters as well as in the more obvious variables, so that one has to keep running to stay in the same place. I shall discuss both these aspects briefly.

Circular and Multiple Causation

Technology is often treated as a parameter—a constraint in which the system operates. In fact it too is caused as well as causing. The nature of technological change, in terms of its economic characteristics—the capital labour ratios, scale, nature of the product—is responsive to the economic conditions in which it takes place. Whether technological innovation takes place depends on attitudes and incentives at least as much—probably more—than Government's science policy, and the formal structure and quantity of r. and d. To get appropriate technical innovations developed and introduced there must be innovating attitudes. This involves a rejection of two apparently contradictory, but in fact reinforcing attitudes, both widely held. The first is the traditionalist attitude which regards any change as unnatural; the second is the idea that technological change is essentially an imported phenomenon—for new technology society must continue to look to the advanced countries. The two attitudes taken together—and often both are present in many individuals as well as many societies—prevent the development of local technological dynamism.

A change in attitude towards local innovation is an essential precondition. Equally important, the structure of the economy should be such that appropriate technology becomes profitable. Structural factors of importance for technology include the size distribution of production units,[102] the distribution of purchasing power, and the trade orientation of the economy. Large scale production units, unequal distribution of purchasing power and trade orientation towards developed country markets tend to lead to the use of advanced country technology. In contrast production by small scale units to meet the demands of poor consumers, with fairly equal income distribution, requires the use of a different and more appropriate technology.

Structural conditions set the scene within which price incentives operate. The latter, though much emphasised by economists, are probably much less important. They are in part a product of the structure and technology of the economy: a labor-intensive, appropriate-product-producing economy will produce smaller income differentials than an economy adopting advanced country, high productivity technology in one sector of the economy. The price system, while at least in part itself emanating from the overall structure of the economy, then tends to reinforce the structure by providing incentives for further developments in a similar direction. There is thus circular causation here too.

What we know of the Chinese example is beginning to suggest that a combined attack on structural adjustment, incentives and technology rapidly yields results. Operating on technology alone may achieve something. It can increase the possibilities open to entrepreneurs, and raise productivity in the traditional sector; but it is likely to do little without coordinated structural adjustment. The alternative paths can be summed up in two cycles. Most LDC economies are now following, roughly, cycle A in Diagram 5. Attitudes towards local scientific innovations are in part causes but also a product of the import of foreign technology. Once foreign technology is established the resulting large scale units and income distribution make it extremely difficult to break out of the cycle. Cycle B in contrast is the appropriate technology

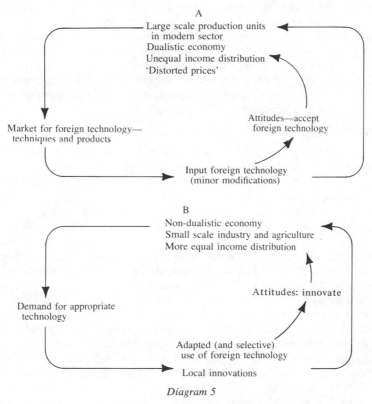

Diagram 5

development ideal. It is nowhere fully in being. China walks on two legs because of the dominance of advanced country technology in many fields. Until there are substantial advances in small scale technology, the large scale remains superior in many fields, and hence it is not possible to shift to cycle B without loss of output. But continued use of cycle A technology tends to lead to a situation where imported and large scale technology appears to be justified—because of the pattern of demands imposed on the economy by the income distribution and incentive system that tends to go with imported technology. How can one break out, and shift to cycle B?

Some have suggested changing incentives—but this is only part of the story and may not be possible without also changing the structure and technology. China has achieved a break by weakening the links between use of large scale units and income distribution, and between income distribution and production, thus making it much easier for large and small scale technology to co-exist. Direct operation on technology, which has been the central subject of this paper, increases the possibilities of shifting efficiently from A to B, but is unlikely to achieve such a shift unless accompanied by changes in structure (in particular income distribution) and incentives, and the selective import (which means positive inhibition) of foreign technology.

Dynamic Aspects

The cycles above summarise one way in which the story is dynamic. But it is also dynamic in that outside variables are continuously changing. In particular, the technology available from the developed countries gets yearly more capital intensive, the products get more and more sophisticated, and both become annually more efficient. Hence considerations of output maximisation and the availability of alternatives may require continuous import of the latest technology, which is becoming increasingly inappropriate, while population trends in LDCs mean that the need for appropriate technology becomes increasingly urgent. Thus while the circular aspects suggest that it is difficult to escape to an appropriate path of development, dynamic aspects emphasise the increasing need to do so.

The Role of Foreigners

The analysis in this paper suggests that, while the import of advanced country technology has obviously contributed a great deal, it has also been, in large part, responsible for the technology problem as described here. The import of technology here includes the import of advanced country institutions, systems of management and finance, education, products and tastes as well as actual machinery and production methods, as normally defined. To some extent, undesirable effects from this import are the direct and intentional results of advanced country policy—e.g. in promoting their own machine goods industries, and their own technological transfer—but they are also the unintended effects of the close contact between rich and poor, and of honest attempts to promote the well being of the poor countries. Whatever the motivation, it is the effects which matter. Continued and close contact with developed countries may inhibit local technological development, and may make more difficult the adoption of more appropriate paths. It is thus paradoxical that any foreign donor should try to initiate action in this field. The almost unavoidable tendency to use advanced country standards in its own operations may make any such action self-defeating. Developing countries differ greatly in resources, attitudes and structure. The poorer countries are almost certainly not able to achieve self-sustained growth; others may require scientific personnel from outside for some time to come before they can achieve scientific self-sufficiency. Countries with relatively abundant scientific and technical personnel may continue to need finance. All countries would clearly be making wasteful use of their resources if they made no use of the tremendous (and increasing) quantity of scientific and technical knowhow available from the advanced countries. Nonetheless, it would appear that the initiative should, wherever possible, pass from the rich to the poor countries, the personnel should be LDC rather than advanced, and the rich countries should direct their aid towards response to requests, and provision of finance for LDCs to purchase equipment and secure personnel from their own country and other LDCs, rather than from the rich countries themselves.

The aim should be to strengthen local institutions not dominate them and to promote local capacity for the development and selection of appropriate technology. Developing countries should not aim at scientific self-sufficiency, but they should aim at technological independence, which may be defined as the ability to make one's own choices. Dispersion of assistance to different institutions and different countries, while possibly threatening the 'efficiency' of the aid, may also prevent its advanced-country-ization.

Notes

1. The nature of the employment problem in LDCs will be discussed more below, insofar as it is relevant to the technology question. The general question has been discussed more fully in a paper prepared for the Employment Seminar, for the Ford Foundation by H. Bruton, "Economic Development and Labor Use: A Review," this book; also David Turnham, *The Employment Problem in LDCs, A Review of the Evidence* (Paris, Organisation for Economic Cooperation and Development, 1971); the three I.L.O. Mission Reports on employment—Colombia, Ceylon, and Kenya—all contain relevant and helpful analysis and statistical evidence.

2. R.S. Merrill, "The Study of Technology," in the *Encyclopedia of Social Sciences*, D.L. Sills, ed. (New York, Macmillan, 1968) quoted in UNITAR Res. Report, No. 14 (1971).

3. *Matching Employment Opportunities and Expectations: A Programme of Action for Ceylon* (Geneva, International Labour Office, 1971), see paragraphs 110 and 112.

4. Notably Turnham *op. cit.* and the I.L.O. Mission Reports.

5. See J. Harris and M. Todaro, "Migration, Unemployment and Development: A Two-Sector Analysis," *The American Economic Review*, Vol. LX, No. 1 (March, 1970).

6. See *Employment, Incomes and Equality: A Strategy for Increasing Productive Employment in Kenya* (Geneva, International Labour Office, 1972), Technical Paper No. 26.

7. See M.C. Sawyer, "Concentration in British Manufacturing Industry," *Oxford Economic Papers*, Vol. 23, No. 3 (November, 1971) and A. Armstrong and A. Silberston, "Size of Plant, Size of Enterprise and Concentration in British Manufacturing Industry, 1935-1958," *Journal of the Royal Statistical Society*, Vol. 128, Series A (1965).

8. See, for example, H.B. Chenery, "Process and Production Functions for Engineering Data," in W. Leontief, ed., *Studies in the Structrue of the American Economy* (Oxford, England, Oxford University Press, 1953); and Meir Mehav, *Technological Dependence, Monopoly and Growth* (Oxford, Pergamon Press, 1969); and "Problems of Size of Plant in Industry in Underdeveloped Countries," U.N. Bureau of Economic Affairs in *Industrialisation and Productivity*, UNIDO No. 2 (New York, 1959) and "Plant Size and Economies of Scale," *Industrialisation and Productivity*, No. 8 (New York, 1964); and C.F. Pratten, *Economies of Scale in Manufacturing Industry* (Cambridge, England, Cambridge University Press, 1971).

9. See for example the research priorities contained in the World Plan of Action, and the case studies listed by UNIDO in a background paper to the OECD Conference on Choice and Adaption of Technology, Paris (November, 1972).

10. This view of demand and products is based on that of K.J. Lancaster, in e.g. "New Approach to Consumer Theory," *Journal of Political Economy*, Vol. LXXIV, No. 2. (March-April, 1967).

11. W.E. Gustafson, "Research and Development, New Products and Productivity Change," *American Economic Review*, Proceedings, Vol. LII (May, 1962).

12. See L.H. Wortzel, "Technology Transfer in the Pharmaceutical Industry," UNITAR Research Report No. 14 (1971).

13. These consequences have been described for Ghana by M.J. Sharpston, "Uneven Geographical Distribution of Medical Care: A Ghanaian Case Study," *Journal of Development Studies* (January, 1972). Similar situation in other countries—with advanced country medical facilities largely concentrated on a minority of the people, to the neglect of the majority, are shown in Maurice King, ed., *Medical Care in Developing Countries* (Oxford, England, Oxford University Press, 1970).

14. Described by S.B. Rifkin, "Health Services in China," *Bulletin of Institute of Development Studies*, Vol. 4, No. 2/3 (June, 1972).

15. Similar complementarities in consumption were explored (in a somewhat different context) by Paul Streeten in *Economic Integration, Aspects and Problems*, 2nd ed. (Netherlands, Sythoff-Leydon, 1964), Chapter VI.

16. See R.B. Lary, *Imports of Manufactures from Less Developed Countries* (New York, National Bureau of Economic Research, 1968).

17. J. Baranson, "Diesel Engine Manufacturing in India and Japan," in *Automation in Developing Countries* (Geneva, International Labour Office, 1972), p. 66.

18. *Technology and Economics in International Development: Report of a Seminar* (Washington, D.C., Office of Science and Technology, USAID, May, 1972)—in future referred to as USAID (1), 1972.

19. H. Pack, "Employment and Productivity in Kenyan Manufacturing," mimeo (August, 1972), p. 6.

20. See, for example, G. Ranis, "Technology Employment and Growth: The Japanese Experience," in *Automation in Developing Countries, op. cit.* in future referred to as Ranis, 1972, (1), "in weaving, in contrast to spinning, the latest automatic equipment from abroad was not, in fact, invariably imported," p. 47.

21. G. Ranis, "Some Observations on the Economic Framework for Optimum LDC Utilisation of Technology," in U.S.A.I.D. (1972) (1)—referred to in future as Ranis, 1972 (2).

22. Pack, *op. cit.*, p. 12. For succeeding quotes, see pp. 6 and 12.

23. J.E. Orchard, *Japan's Economic Position* (New York, McGraw Hill, 1930), p. 255.

24. F. Stewart, "The Choice of Techniques: A Case Study of Cement Block Manufacture in Kenya," mimeo (1972).

25. See G. Winston, "Capacity Utilisation in Economic Development," *Economic Journal* (March, 1971); for other countries see the evidence in I. Little, M. Scott, T. Scitovsky, *Industry and Trade in Some Developing Countries* (Oxford, England, Oxford University Press, 1970), Chapter 3.

26. Information supplied by Unilever.

27. Ranis, 1972 (1).

28. See A.K. Sen, *The Choice of Techniques,* 3rd ed. (Oxford, Blackwell, 1968), Appendix D which shows that the Ambar Charkha produces a flow of output less than its recurring costs.

29. See R.L. Sansom, "The Motor Pump a Case Study of Innovation and Development," *Oxford Economic Papers* (March, 1969).

30. See A.U. Khan and B. Duff, "Agricultural Mechanisation Technology Development at the International Rice Research Institute," (Manila, mimeo).

31. See examples in M.M. Campos, "Adaption of Industrial Technology of the Factor Endowments and Other Requirements of Developing Countries: Some Practical Issues of the Choice of Techniques," M.A. thesis, Sussex University.

32. See e.g. "Capital Labour Ratios of Certain Industries in Some Countries: A Progress Report," (Netherlands, Netherlands Economic Institute, 1955).

33. See L.A. Doyle, *Inter-Economy Comparisons: A Case Study* (Berkeley, University of California, Institute of Business & Economic Research, 1965).

34. E.g. data from other UNIDO Manufacturing Profiles, and evidence produced by M.M. Mehta, "Capital Intensity of Manufacturing Industries in Some Selected Countries in the ECAFE Region," (Bangkok, Asian Institute for Economic Development and Planning, 1969).

35. However, Pakistan appears to be an exception according to A.R. Khan, "Capital Intensity and the Efficiency of Factor Use," *Pakistan Development Review,* X, 2 (Summer, 1970), especially Table II which shows the capital intensity of many Pakistan industries to exceed that of Japan, and in some cases that of the U.S. too.

36. Doyle, *op. cit.* found that with the same equipment (though designed for a smaller scale) numbers employed in Indonesia were 30% more than in the U.S.

37. J.E. Stepanek, *New Perspectives: Industrial Development in the Third World* (Austria, Institute of Research in Education and Development, 1972).

38. J. Tinbergen, "Choice of Technology in Industrial Planning," *Industrialisation and Productivity,* (New York, Department of Economic and Social Affairs, 1958), p. 24.

39. See W. Baer and M. Herve, "Employment in Developing Countries," *Quarterly Journal of Economics,* LXXX (February, 1966), Table II which shows substantial increases in capacity per employee in a number of countries. Gouverneur, *Productivity and Factor Proportions in Less Developed Countries* (Oxford, Clarendon Press, 1971) shows how K/L has increased over time with the adoption of advanced technology in the Congo.

40. Two United Nations Groups have recently prepared detailed comparisons of technological opportunities and choice in the textile industry: *Report of the Expert Group Meeting on the Selection of Textile Machinery in the Cotton Industry* (Vienna, UNIDO, ID/WG, 8/1, 1968); and *Choice of Technique in the Latin American Textile Industry* (Santiago, Chile, ECLA Secretariat, E/CN 12/746, 1966).

41. See *Towards Full Employment* (Geneva, International Labour Office, 1970), Chapter 2.

42. See J. Sigurdson, "Technology and Employment in China," *World Development* (forthcoming).

43. See particularly, G.K. Boon, *Economic Choice of Human and Physical Factors in Production* (Amsterdam, North Holland, 1964).

44. This point is elaborated in F. Stewart and J. Weeks, "Wages and Employment in Poor Countries," Birbeck, Department of Economics, Discussion Paper (1973).

45. See K. Marsden, "Progressive Technologies for Developing Countries," *International Labour Review,* Vol. 101, No. 5 (May, 1970). See also J.P. Ambannavar, "Changes in the Employment Pattern of the Indian Work Force: 1911-1961," *The Developing Economies,* Vol. VIII, No. 1 (March, 1970), which summarises the (negative) impact of factory methods, on traditional employment in food grain processing, vegetable oils, textiles and the leather industry.

46. See F. Stewart, "Trade and Technology," in proceedings of 1972 Cambridge Conference on Trade and Developing Countries (London, Macmillan, forthcoming).

47. E.F. Schumacher, "The Work of the Intermediate Technology Development Group in Africa," *International Labour Review*, Vol. 106, No. 1 (July, 1972).

48. Schumacher, *op. cit.*

49. See A.K. Sen, *op. cit.*

50. The argument only applies given a rather stringent set of assumptions which are explored in more detail in F. Stewart and P.P. Streeten, "Conflicts between Employment and Output Objectives in Developing Countries," *Oxford Economic Papers* (August, 1971).

51. The first of these, I.T.D.G., *Thrift and Credit Co-operatives* (London, 1970), has been published.

52. Schumacher, *op. cit.*, "The conventions clearly demonstrated that the great need was for advice on management and business methods."

53. *Appropriate Technology and Research for Industrial Development,* Report of the Advisory Committee on the Application of Science and Technology to Development on two aspects of industrial growth (New York, United Nations Department of Economic and Social Affairs, 1972), paragraph 23.

54. "Some Studies and Research Done by the I.R.E.P. on Industrialisation Problems," background paper for OECD Development Centre Conference on The Choice and Adaption of Technology, *op. cit.*

55. See, for example, R. Clark, "Aid in Uganda: Programmes and Policies," (London, Overseas Development Institute, 1966), p. 88.

56. UNIDO, "Identification of Adaptive Research Priorities: Comparative Characteristics of Different Industrial Branches," background paper for OECD Conference on Choice and Adaption of Technology, *op. cit.*, p. 1.

57. Appropriate Technology for Research for Industrial Development, *op. cit.*, paragraph 20.

58. "Industrial Information: A Pre-requisite for Appropriate Choice of Technology," paper submitted by UNIDO to OECD Study Group on Choice and Adaption of Technology, *op. cit.*

59. John Lewis, "Overview," in *Technology and Economics in International Development*, Report of a Seminar (Washington, D.C., Office of Science and Technology, USAID, 1972).

60. *World Plan of Action*, p. 177.

61. "The Role of the Research Institute in Industrial Growth," in *Appropriate Technologies for International Development* (Washington, D.C., Office of Science and Technology, USAID, September, 1972).

62. R.N. Nelson, "The Technology Gap and National Science Policy," Economic Growth Center, Yale, Discussion Paper (May, 1970).

63. See D.S. Landes, *The Unbound Prometheus* (New York, Oxford University Press, 1969).

64. USAID, "The Role of the Research Institute in Industrial Growth," *op. cit.*, p. 8.

65. J. Baranson, "Employment and Technology," mimeo (1972).

66. See, for example, N.H. Leff, *The Brazilian Capital Goods Industry, 1929-1964* (Massachusetts, Harvard University Press, 1968); and W.A. Johnson, *The Steel Industry of India* (Massachusetts, Harvard University Press, 1966).

67. H. Pack and M. Todaro, "Technological Transfer, Labour Absorption and Economic Development," *Oxford Economic Papers* (November, 1969).

68. F. Stewart, case studies, *op. cit.*

69. Schumacher, *op. cit.*

70. Draft Introductory Statement for the World Plan of Action for the Application of Science and Technology to Development, prepared by the Sussex Group, Annex II of *Science and Technology for Development, Proposals for the Second Development Decade* (New York, United Nations, 1970), paragraph 51.

71. *Ibid.*, paragraph 21.

72. J. Baranson, "Multinational Corporations and Developing Country Goals for Technological Self-Sufficiency," mimeo (1972).

73. H. Hughes and You Poh Seng, *Foreign Investment and Industrialisation in Singapore* (Madison, Wisconsin Press, 1969), p. 193.

74. L. Reynolds and P. Gregory, *Wages, Productivity and Industrialisation in Puerto Rico* (Homewood, Illinois, Richard D. Irwin, Inc., 1965).

75. Pack, *op. cit.*

76. *Op. cit.*, Technical Paper No. 16.

77. R. Hal Mason, "The Relative Factor Proportions in Manufacturing. A Pilot Study Comparing U.S. Subsidiaries and Local Counterparts in the Philippines," *The Transfer of Technology and the Factor Proportions Problem. The Philippines and Mexico* (New York, UNITAR, 1971).

78. Described by G. Helleiner, "Manufactured Exports from Less Developed Countries and Multinational Firms," *Economic Journal* (March, 1973).

79. Asian Development Bank, *Southeast Asia's Economy in the 1970's* (Harlow, England, Longman, 1971).

80. The Utrecht Pilot Plan, Philips, p. 6.

81. Estimates supplied by J. van den Brink, manager Pilot Plant.

82. "Basic Vehicle for South-East Asia," W.O. Bourke, President Ford-Asia-Pacific Inc. in *Technology and Economics in Economic Development* (Washington, D.C., USAID, May, 1972), p. 72.

83. *Ibid.*, p. 75.

84. *Loc. cit.*

85. Examples taken from "Multinational Corporations and Adaptive Research for Developing Countries," in *Appropriate Technologies for International Development* (Washington, D.C., USAID, September, 1972).

86. "Multinational Corporations and Adaptive Research," *op. cit.*, p. 50.

87. See the adaptions described by M.M. Campos, *op. cit.*

88. "Research Interests of Foreign Assistance Agencies Concerning Appropriate Technology," in *Appropriate Technologies for International Development, op. cit.*, p. 37; see also for fairly comprehensive description of such activities.

89. See P. Harper, "Soft Technology: A Proposal for Alternatives under Conditions of Crisis," paper submitted to OECD Study Group on Choice and Adaption, *op. cit.*

90. Reported in "Industrial Research as a Factor in Economic Development," Report of the Joint Study Group on Industrial Research, U.S.-Brazil Science Cooperation Programs (National Academy of Sciences, September, 1968), p. 25. For India, see e.g., A. Rahman et al, "Research and Development in Indian Drugs and Pharmaceutical Industry," *Lok Udyog* (July and August, 1970); and ICMA, "Preliminary Survey on the Status of R. and D. in Chemical Industry," (Calcutta, 1970).

91. USAID, "The Role of the Research Institute in Industrial Growth," *op. cit.*, p. 22.

92. The evidence used includes the survey of 50 institutes in LDCs conducted by the USAID and reported on in "The Role of the Research Institute in Industrial Growth," referred to above; Y. Nayudamma, "Promoting the Industrial Application of Research in an Underdeveloped Country," *Minerva,* 5 (1967); G.S. Aurora and Ward Morehouse, "The Dilemma of Technological Change. The Case of the Small Tractor," mimeo (1972); A.U. Khan and B. Duff, "Agricultural Mechanisation Technology Development at the International Rice Research Institute," paper presented to the Working Seminar on Priorities for Research on Innovating and Adapting Technologies for Asian Development, at Princeton (September, 1972); "Adapting a Developing Country to the Development of Adaptive Technologies—A Korean Case," Dr. Hyung-Sup Choi, Minister of Science and Technology, S. Korea, keynote address to the Technology and Development Institute Seminar on "Generation and Diffusion of Adaptive Technologies in Developing Countries," (Honolulu, October, 1972); and WAITRO: *Priority of Needs of Industrial Research Institutes in Developing Countries, 1972,* Publication No. 3; National Academy of Sciences, "Industrial Research as a Factor in Economic Development," *op. cit.*

93. USAID, "The Role of the Research Institute in Industrial Growth," *op. cit.*, p. 14.

94. *Ibid.*, p. 28.

95. *Ibid.*, p. 19.

96. W.P. Strassman, "Appropriate Technology in Residential Construction," mimeo (1972).

97. S. Evans, "The Korean Institute of Science and Technology. A Brief Description and Rationale," Battelle Memorial Institute (June, 1971).

98. In "The Dynamics of Technology Diffusion and Institutional Design in India," paper for the Seminar Proceeding on the Generation and Diffusion of Adaptive Technology, East-West Center (October, 1972), p. 41.

99. The term "innovative chain" and the estimates are from R.A. Charpie, *Technological Innovation—Its Environment and Management* (Washington, D.C., U.S. Department of Commerce, 1967).

100. Keith Griffin, *The Green Revolution An Economic Analysis* (Geneva, United Nations Research Institute for Social Development, 1972), p. 43.

101. Other evidence for India, of a similar nature, is contained in T. Byres, "The Dialectic of India's Green Revolution," *South Asian Review* (January, 1972); and C.R. Wharton, "The Green Revolution: Cornucopia or Pandora's Box," *Foreign Affairs* (April, 1969).

102. The relationship between size distribution of farm units and technological choice has been well documented: see e.g. K.N. Raj, "Mechanisation of Agriculture in India and Sri Lanka," *International Labour Review,* Vol. 106, No. 4 (October, 1972); and Barker, Meyers, Cristomo and Duff, "Employment and Technological Change in Philippine Agriculture," *International Labour Review,* Vol. 106, No. 2-3 (August, 1972). A similar relationship exists in industry as shown by empirical studies of industrial choice of technique.

Economics, Institutions and Employment Generation in Rural Areas

Carl Gotsch

*Harvard University
and
Ford Foundation, Beirut*

Introduction

The past few years have witnessed a large outpouring of studies on the distributive consequences of economic growth. Researchers, concerned with the long-run employment problem that is emerging in the Third World, have been unanimous in calling for rural development strategies that would reflect more closely the factor scarcities of less developed countries. For whether the calculations are done on the back of an envelope with some simple estimates of the rate of increase in the labor force and the ability of the urban areas to absorb these increases or with complicated sectoral simulation models, the answer is the same: rural areas, and particularly agriculture, will have to absorb even more people than are currently being "employed" there.[1]

Yet examples that would suggest that these pleas are being heeded and that the reforms and policies required to alter past trends are being implemented, are relatively few.[2] Indeed, it appears to even the casual observer that, with respect to admonitions regarding the importance of applied research on such subjects as more divisible agricultural technology, "correct" factor prices, asset redistribution, effective fiscal systems and labor intensive rural works programs, there continues to be a substantial gap between the technical analyses and the actual decisions being taken.

In the following paper, I have argued that this gap between technical analysis and implementation is, in large part, due to the failure to examine policy prescriptions in the context of a social system.* Despite the recent emphasis on so-called "integrated development" programs, most assessments have continued to omit a number of important institutional variables, the most notable having to do with the distribution of power and influence in the countryside. As a result, the literature is replete with examples of what Griffin has called the "fallacy of eclecticism," i.e., the indiscriminate use of bits and pieces of policies that are alleged to have been successful in other settings.[3] In some cases, the presence of unexamined institutional variables has produced extremely rapid economic and political change, frequently leading to difficult adjustment problems. More often, the presence of such unanalyzed variables, coupled with an eclectic approach, has created unfulfilled expectations and a deep scepticism regarding all efforts to initiate meaningful development.

The problem of eclecticism in policy formation in no way denies, of course, the

---

* By "social system" I shall mean both its political and economic elements.

potential value of comparative experience or the need to generalize about the development process. Indeed, the implication is quite the opposite. Only by understanding, at a deeper level, the way in which different social systems function can many of the controversies about rural development be removed from the realm of theology into that of empirical discourse. Agricultural policies and programs have habitually been disaggregated to reflect the physical environment; I shall argue that similar efforts along social and political lines are equally important to the success of rural development activities.

Structure vs. institutions. Methodologically, attempts to incorporate political and cultural considerations into an analysis of rural development programs increase the complexity of the problem by several orders of magnitude. Moreover, there is no adequate theory that can be used as a guide to rigorous hypothesis testing or data organization. To give up a focus on the intricacies of the production system in favor of the study of interest groups or social classes, however, does little to generate a broader perspective of the *interaction* of economic and political variables. Hence, I shall try to overcome the difficulty by introducing some simple schematic representations of a social structure that provide a visual image of the inter-relationships within the "system."

Structure, in the sense in which it is used in this paper, comprises the names of the variables that are to be investigated plus statements about the types of causal links that relate one variable to another. It represents a construct that is static and relatively value-free—an arrangement of the system's parts—a scheme of organization. It follows Friedrich's definition:

> Structure means, generally speaking, that there is a stable and ordered relationship of parts, such as characterizes a building, from which the term is derived . . . [It] is the static aspect of the system, its "skeleton."[4]

Much of the analysis of rural development to date has been concerned with this aspect of the problem. Although at times such essays have had the characteristics of a laundry list, they were useful contributions in that they aided the process of defining more carefully the functions that would have to be performed to achieve a particular development objective. For example, when it became apparent that the provision of new technology was an important consideration for agricultural growth, a great deal of thought was given to the organization and structure of research systems that could supply such technology.

Describing the part of a research system, however, is quite different from analyzing its actual operation in a particular social and political environment. In any dynamic system, elaboration of the organization or structure provides only a static picture of the variables and feedback mechanisms in the system; it says nothing about the system's evolution, about its "path." It is at this juncture that the nature of a society's *institutions* are important. Unlike the structure (organization) of a social system, the term institutions will be used to characterize highly value laden, relatively dynamic, *modes of behavior.* Braibanti, following a number of contemporary political scientists, argues:

> The value-laden nature of institutions is central . . . In our view, the explicitness of value absorption, accumulation, reformulation and diffusion is a fundamental difference between *institution* and *structure.* . . . [5]

Subsequently he offers a definition:

Institutions are patterns of recurring acts structured in a manner conditioning the behavior of members within the institutions, shaping a particular value or set of values and projecting value(s) in the social system in terms of attitudes or acts.[6]

Viewed in this way, the importance of the separability of structure and institution as a basis for comparative work is obvious.[7] It permits, on the one hand, the construction of a framework for data organization and the identification of certain essential functions of any type of development process. At the same time, it focuses attention on the fact that without specifying the institutional characteristics of the structure (e.g., the behavior patterns of the various organizations, the social relationships between economic actors, etc.) little can be said about the actual characteristics of the system's development path. In such a schema, different types of institutional behavior may make similar organizational forms produce radically different results, a hypothesis supported by the "perverse" character of many employment-oriented development programs undertaken during the past decade.

Institutions vs. policies and programs. Having made the distinction between structure and institutions, a further distinction is needed between institutions and policies. In the sections that follow, the latter term is used to denote the instruments by which organizations of various sorts seek to attain institutional objectives. Policies may pertain to the particular needs of an organization as in the case of making profits or expanding its influence; they may also be used to strengthen broader institutions that transcend a particular organization, e.g., discrimination in hiring that reinforces the institution of racism.[*]

With respect to the employment problem, these definitions make clear that the concern for institutions in no way denies the significance of various types of conventional economic policies in achieving or frustrating strategies of employment oriented growth. Bruton's summary of the evidence on a variety of these points, e.g. the effect of distorted factor prices, tariff and exchange policies, investment incentives, etc., on job creation, is quite persuasive.[8] The need, however, is to take a step further back and ask some additional questions: Why are the economic policies what they are? What is the likelihood that, if socially undesirable, they can be changed? Or, perhaps even more to the point, how are policies and "value-laden modes of behavior" related? To argue that the latter are "constraints" on the former is surely a static view of reality. In the real world, not only are policies constrained by institutions in any particular time period, but they are also instrumental in determining the character of the institutional constraints (the policy space) in some future period. This is nowhere better illustrated than in the work of economists who would probably consider themselves well inside the "traditional" fold. For example, in a recent paper offering a more dynamic interpretation of the two-gap model of growth and resource mobilization, Lewis again cautions against the indiscriminate use of policies aimed at protecting "infant industries," noting that the inefficient industrial structure thus established produces powerful vested interests in the continuation of socially undesirable policies.[9]

---

[*] Such a formulation would imply that economists concerned with the social efficiency of tariff and exchange policy, investment objectives, etc. have in mind the institutional "objectives" of the society as a whole. In practice, such detachment is of course rare and most policies are formulated within the objectives of a government, a union or a corporation. The oft used phrase "institutional constraints" then refers to the constraints the organization's overall institutional objectives put on the pursuit of any particular set of policies.

It seems self-evident, therefore, that analyses that do not assess the cumulative effects of policies on the strength of various groups or social classes run the grave risk of buying short-run benefits at the cost of serious institutional problems in the slightly longer run.[10]

In the sections that follow, I have tried to examine some of the relationships between structure, institutions and policies as they bear on employment in rural areas. The framework of analysis can hardly be called a model; it is beset by yet unresolved problems of definition and dimensionality. Nor can the typologies that are used be said to constitute theory; they are too crude and the indices associated with their delineation too arbitrary for that. However, where they can be shown to be roughly consistent with different schools of thought on how the problem of rural development should be approached, they help to make clear the assumptions about the rest of the system that are implicit in conventional recommendations.

Organizing Information About Rural Development and Employment

The Agricultural Production System

The most obvious place to start in assembling a structure within which to obtain a better overview of the rural employment problem is with the characteristics of the production sector. No analysis can dispense with it, for the appearance of inconsistencies between technology and the organization of resources is a fundamental force for economic and political change. Substantively, one might begin by simply examining the ways in which output is produced and incomes are generated by and distributed to the owners (controllers) of resources used. Obvious components of such an investigation would be the magnitude and ownership (control) of resources fixed to agriculture,* the technology embodied in and availability of purchased inputs, the distribution of organizational credit, the presence of marketing services, the way information regarding improved cultural practices and new technologies is disseminated, and so on.

Figure 1 illustrates these relationships graphically. The rectangles denote highly simplified state variables of the production system, the valves, points of individual decision making, and the dotted lines, influence from exogenous sources. The structure is made dynamic by including a feedback from the "income" variable to the "resources" variable, a link that is assumed to be controlled by the savings-investment decisions of individual members of the social classes among whom resources are distributed.

Investigating interactions among investment decisions affecting unit size of resources (e.g. holding size), the distribution of resources and the choice of technology provides useful insights into the dynamics of different rural situations. Ishikawa has conceptualized the problem in terms of "stable" and "unstable" technologies and holding size distributions:

> A technology is assumed to be stable (or unstable) if, under a given agrarian structure and given resource endowments of a particular society, it assures (or does not assure) to the members of each stratum of the society that level of output and income which they feel satisfactory or *at least tolerable*. Similarly, a stable (or unstable) agrarian structure could

* At a minimum, one would want to know how resources were distributed among laborers (who own only their labor power), tenants (who own labor and some capital equipment), peasant proprietors (who own labor, capital and land), and landlords (who own only land).

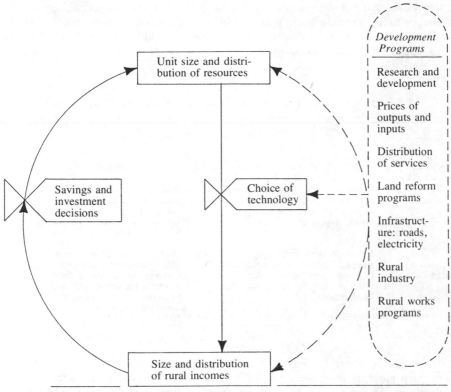

Figure 1. The Rural Production System

be conceptualized by interchanging the relation between technology and the agrarian structure in the above assumption. It follows that the stability of a technology is not obtainable unless the stability of an agrarian structure is also attained. When either a technology or an agrarian structure is unstable, it may be assumed that the interactions between the technology and the agrarian structure continue until some stable equilibrium between the two is finally attained.[11]

Ishikawa's categories invite attempts to fashion some simple typologies based on nothing more than the existence of contradictions between the technology and the structure of holding sizes.* Table 1 suggests, for example, that when the "stability" of technology is equated with a high degree of divisibility and the "stability" of the agrarian structure with relative equality in the distribution of land holdings, some fairly recognizable development situations appear. For example, in areas where such highly divisible inputs as seeds and fertilizer have been the major impetus to the "green revolution," one would expect a significant increase in the productivity of the

---

* A relatively stable technology and a relatively stable agrarian structure are presumably what characterize Schultz's "traditional" agriculture. Long periods of marginal adjustment without significant breakthroughs in productivity have removed the inconsistencies between the mode of production and the institutional arrangements to the point where the rate of return on further adjustments is below the individual's utility of consumption. As Mosher has noted, however, this equation of the absence of investment possiblities with traditional agriculture makes it possible to transform traditional agriculture only to find that after some period of time, it has again reverted to a "traditional"—albeit more productive—state.[12]

countryside, but not necessarily continuous further change in technology or the tendency to agglomerate land. Where holding sizes were relatively equal to begin with, the surplus produced by the new technology would be evenly distributed and thus would not facilitate the acquisition of land by some at the expense of others.

TABLE 1

INTERACTION OF TECHNOLOGY AND RESOURCE DISTRIBUTION

TYPE OF RESOURCE DISTRIBUTION

Type of Technology	Equal	Unequal
Divisible	Relatively stable growth process; output equally shared, increase in productivity similar on all farms; employment effects positive.	Somewhat unstable; absolute surplus of the larger farmers sufficient to permit long-run land agglomeration; employment effects positive.
Indivisible	Relatively stable but frequently stagnant; dependent on some form of organization for technology diffusion, may produce some labor displacement.	Highly unstable; large farms able to increase surpluses by cutting costs; additional funds available for investment used to increase farm size further; significant labor displacement likely.

In situations where holding sizes were initially uneven, one would expect a somewhat more unstable situation. While everyone theoretically has access to the technology, the surplus generated by the larger holdings would obviously be greater in absolute magnitude than that available for investment by subsistence farmers. Consequently, the disparity of holding sizes could be expected to increase over time, albeit at a relatively slow rate.*

The most dynamic situation, of course, is one in which both technology and the agrarian structure have unstable characteristics. Not only does the "lumpiness" of the technology suggest that significant economies of size are present, but the size distribution of holdings is such that only some farmers will be able to take advantage of the technology. They, in turn, can be expected to search for opportunities to rent land to or purchase land from small farmers as they attempt to reconcile or adjust holding size to technology. The interaction between these two conditions can be expected to create conditions in which changes in the agricultural structure may occur rather rapidly.[13] A number of areas in both developed and developing countries have experienced this latter type of development in recent years. A by no means exhaustive list would include Ethiopia, Pakistan, parts of India, the southern part of the United States, and a number of areas in Colombia, Brazil and Argentina.

Political Regimes, Bureaucracies and Development Programs

The dynamics of the adjustment process between technology and the agrarian structure provide a good deal of insight into the emergence of employment problems and employment potentials in different agricultural systems. But it leaves unanswered

---

* Where non-technique-associated constraints make access a function of farm size, caveats are, of course, in order. Evidence on this point is presented in the following section.

questions concerning the types of technology created and diffused or why the initial and continuing distribution of resources is what it is.

In most countries, both of these variables are closely identified with the activities of the state. Agricultural research, agricultural extension services, agricultural credit, land reform, the subsidization of unfamiliar inputs, etc., are all valid and necessary development activities well beyond the means of the individual farmer. Hence any structure used to organize and evaluate the potential for employment-oriented development activities must provide space for information on the make-up of the national political regime and on the characteristics and capacity of the government bureaucracy that is to be entrusted with the design and implementation of the development schemes.

The inclusion of political roles in the structure obviously complicates it immensely. For example, it raises immediately the question of how the political actors perceive what has heretofore been called simply "the employment problem."* Do they see it primarily as a poverty issue where the magnitude of the problem and its threat to regime stability is seen in terms of a relationship to some rather arbitrarily defined absolute? Or is the regime threat posed in terms of comparisons between various groups and classes inside and outside rural society? Perhaps even more significantly, do these perceptions about the problem change as attempts are made to implement employment programs? That is, does a regime responding to a poverty problem as measured in calories find that it has set in motion a dynamic process in which it must subsequently respond to relative deprivation? Is the regime's concern about agriculture even prompted by the situation of its rural constituency or are development programs primarily the outgrowth of the need to supply cheap food to a restless urban population?

Several elements of the regime's likely sources of concern have been included in Figure 2. Included also are the development programs through which decisions are made on the direction and funding of research, on the types of agricultural organizations that will be supported and on the economic policies endogenous to the structure, which relate to agriculture. In addition to the feedback loops that indicate the dynamics of political influence and resource flows, the concept of a "gap" between the actual income distribution and the distribution perceived by politicians as necessary for regime stability, has been employed to provide a mechanism for relating perception to action.

A second area of investigation to which the structure points is the relationship between the national political regime and the bureaucracy. Separating the two groups in the structure implies that in the decision-making process there may be fundamental divergencies of interest between the two. In such cases, use of the term "Government" would disguise a potential source of difference in system behavior. Horowitz, writing about nations that have recently achieved political independence, comments:

> The new political leaders differ radically from the civil service in their ideological orientation. Swept to power by the high nationalistic feeling accompanying independence; they are strongly committed to lifting their country from the stigma of colonialism. . . .
>
> Civil servants, on the other hand, tend to remain committed to the principles of

---

* As Bruton points out in detail, appropriate employment policies are highly dependent on how unemployment is defined—and in turn measured. The political formulation is no different but places an emphasis on what the regime *thinks* unemployment is.[14] In this regard I am indebted to Shahid Javed Burki for pointing out that employment programs are frequently better served by a political analysis that alters the perception of politicians regarding their actual or potential constituency than by economic analyses that indicate the value of amenities created or the extent of unemployment.

colonial-style administration . . . Training for paternalistic service, they consider themselves not only the most capable but the proper agency for national progress in the post
colonial period.[15]

This phenomenon is by no means confined, however, to countries that have
experienced lengthy colonial status. To put the bureaucrats in a pejorative light, in
many countries, politicians are subject to some manifestation of the people's will.
Consequently, they are more likely to reflect dissatisfaction with the *status quo*.
Bureaucracies, on the other hand, tend to see the perpetuation of the *status quo* as the
best strategy for the perpetuation of privileges.

In fairness to the bureaucracy, however, an equally likely scenario, also enacted
with great frequency, is one in which political activity *is* close to demagoguery and
the bureaucracy *is* the line of defense against policies that are detrimental to job
creation in the long run.

Power at the Local Level

National regimes and central bureaucracies are most often the initiators of rural
development and rural employment programs. But there is a good deal of evidence
that the forces that shape the actual performance of rural organizations are much more

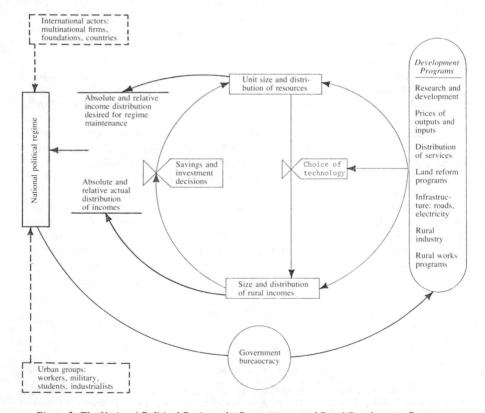

Figure 2. The National Political Regime, the Bureaucracy, and Rural Development Programs

likely to be found at the local level. Consequently, no investigation of the rural employment problem would be complete without introducing information on the characteristics of social stratification at the grassroots and its linkages to the rest of the structure.

In Figure 3, the distribution of power is seen as a function of three elements, two of which are endogenous. First, and in most situations most important, is the distribu-

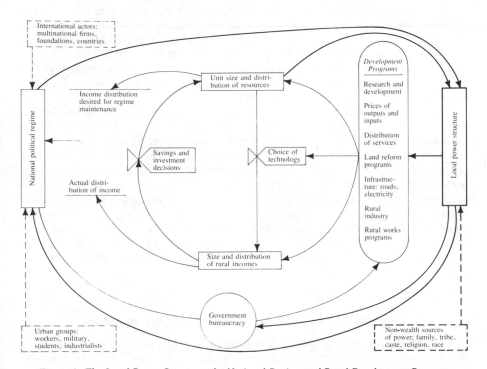

Figure 3. The Local Power Structure, the National Regime and Rural Development Programs

tion of wealth—the control over scarce resources—that exists in a particular area. In agrarian societies this means, of course, primarily land and rights to the use of the land. It is a variable encountered earlier in the description of the production process and, in capitalist countries, *is the chief link between economic and political phenomena.*

A second area of inquiry involves the extent to which national or regional political parties have sought to organize various groups or classes. Such efforts, at least in terms of conventional democratic participatory forms of mobilization, have proved to be extraordinarily difficult. However, some examples, particularly among the so-called "transitional" countries (Tanzania, Chile), do exist.

A third influence on the distribution of power stems from non-wealth sources of status: tribe, caste, family and religion. While Weber's remark that "property as such is not always recognized as a status qualification, in the long run it is, and with extra ordinary regularity," may be valid, much of the current attempt to initiate rural development clearly involves the short run in which non-wealth sources of influence may be formidable.*

Two avenues by which local power holders may seek to influence the course of rural development programs are also suggested in Figure 3. First, there is the ability to influence programs directly as they are being implemented in the field. Where are schools and roads to be built? Who is to be the demonstration farmer? Who is to be the chairman of the local cooperative? The second, but equally powerful mechanism for affecting programs and policies, is indirectly through the national regime and the higher levels of the implementing bureaucracy. Indeed, as subsequent sections dealing with rural works and land reform suggest, much of the history of such programs can best be understood by the interplay between national and local perceptions of the problem of regime stability. Of particular interest is the time lag between the initiation of programs by central governments and the marshalling in the rural areas of effective pressures for their alteration.

To emphasize again, the foregoing structure involving the agricultural production process, the make-up and role of the national political regime and its associated bureaucracy and the influence of the distribution of power among local groups is relatively value-free. These processes and these actors exist in some form in every country. What is important from an employment point of view is how the system actually behaves when different institutional parameters are associated with its structural elements. In the next section, where some of the general empirical evidence regarding the employment effects of rural development is organized within the framework described, I shall endeavor to point to unstated assumptions about these parameters—and hence about the behavior of the system as a whole—that often cast grave doubts on the feasibility of the policy prescriptions toward which the evidence points.

Technical Diagnosis and Institutional Assumptions

The following comments present in a condensed form empirical evidence regarding the relationship between certain rural development "variables" and increased employment, and summarize the more or less conventional policy conclusions that have been drawn from it.[17] In each case, some additional observations involving the institutional assumptions needed to make sure the particular proposal meets its stated objectives are appended. The focus is primarily on the countryside; the implications of adding institutional variables for overall planning and decision making are explored in a subsequent section.

The underlying model is obviously the product of a conflict oriented view of social change. Politics and programs that move beyond the analysis stage are seen to be the result of compromises between various groups, each pursuing its own self-interest. Membership in such interest groups is by no means exhaustive in that they do not sum to the total of the population. Many groups (or classes in the Marxian analysis) may be partially or totally unrepresented in the decision-making process. The corollary that

---

* There is little justification for treating this variable as being exogenous other than some concern for simplicity. As anthropologists and sociologists have pointed out for some time, one of the potentially detrimental characteristics of the commercialization of agriculture and the associated instability in the countryside, is that it undermines the cohesiveness of the rural community. Where great disparity of wealth exists that, of course, may be all to the good.[16]

they are then unlikely to be the beneficiaries of that process follows in a straightforward way.*

Agricultural Technology

Probably the most widely researched topic in the whole of the recent rural development literature is the diffusion and impact of new technology. I shall indicate only
enough of the general findings to note their implications for the employment problem.
As one might expect, these flow in a reasonably direct way from the neo-classical
production model.

Highly divisible technology. Most of the evidence of which I am aware suggests that
the effect of such highly divisible inputs as seeds, fertilizers and pesticides has been to
increase the absolute incomes of virtually all classes, although disparities of wealth
have tended to increase. New seeds, at least those involving crops traditionally grown
in the area, have spread rapidly among all segments of the farming population, but
least rapidly among small farmers and tenants.[19] (The caveat that must be made to this
finding concerns agricultural areas where climatic conditions create a high degree of
yield uncertainty. Under such conditions, small farms were less prone to adopt the
new varieties even after a lengthy period of exposure.[20]) Fertilizer adoption seems to
follow a similar pattern, i.e., a lag of several years in adoption by those in the smaller
size groups, although there is considerable evidence in the studies cited earlier that the
levels used tend to be somewhat lower among the smaller farmers. In the several cases
where this has been recorded, however, it has not been associated with differences in
yields, indicating that on small farms some substitution of labor for purchased inputs
is taking place.

In those cases where large numbers of farmers have taken part in the seed-fertilizer
revolution, the result has generally involved an increase in the absolute levels of
income/wealth for all rural residents.** The demand for the services of landless
laborers has increased both because of the increased requirements per cropped acre
associated with higher yields and the increase in labor associated with altered planting
and harvesting dates and subsequent increases in cropping intensity. Although the
available evidence in this case is limited, there is reason to think that the experience in
India is fairly common—landless laborers have had increases in real incomes on the
order of 10 percent, tenants (at least initially) 25 percent, and owner-operators, 50-60
percent.*** As suggested earlier, this kind of differential surplus generation is
sufficient to create some instability in agrarian systems that already exhibit disparity
in access to land. There is thus some basis for a long-run agglomeration of land with
what is likely to be a deleterious effect on employment. However, if such a process is
based on divisible inputs and no other forces are involved, the process is likely to
proceed rather slowly.

---

* This point raises an important issue in the role of so-called "latent groups," i.e., groups that are not
formally represented in the bargaining process but whose potential for disruptive action is perceived by the
decision makers.[18]

** Specifically exempted from this generalization are cases in which the introduction of high yielding
varieties has been accompanied by the rapid mechanization of agriculture.

***Figures given by Francine Frankel for East Punjab suggest an increase of approximately 25 percent by
landless laborers and 70 percent by landowners. She notes in addition, however, that the customary
practice of small owner-operators to rent in land has been sharply curtailed and the combination of
increased productivity on their own land plus off-farm labor has not been sufficient to maintain their
traditional incomes.[21]

Intermediate mechanical technology. A second type of technology that has received a good deal of attention is mechanical technology that is accessible to many small and medium farmers: motors, pump sets, small tubewells, small threshers and harvesters, some improved bullock implements, etc. The record with respect to the employment effects of such implements is somewhat more ambiguous than that associated with seeds and fertilizer.

Where the technology involves the pumping of additional supplies of supplementary water, it has been a more powerful stimulus to increased employment than to increased yields. As one might expect, increasing acreage under cultivation means that labor demands are likely to increase in proportion to the increase in cropped acreage, a relationship that is unlikely to hold in the case of yield increases.

This type of water producing technology, while in some sense "intermediate," nevertheless has enough lumpiness associated with it so that farmers at the small end of the holding size spectrum cannot, in most parts of the world, gain easy access to it. Moreover, as in the case of tubewells and pump sets, it is relatively immobile, making it difficult to create markets that do not contain large elements of spatial monopoly.

Small wheat and rice threshers coupled with portable electric or diesel motors of the 5-10 h.p. size have been an important element in increasing cropping intensities where the patterns of monsoons—or irrigation—have permitted additional double cropping. Somewhat more mobile than tubewells and fixed pump sets, they have on balance been a fairly neutral technology when seen in the context of the total farming system. On the one hand, they cut down on the number of hours devoted to threshing; on the other, they have permitted some shifts in the cropping pattern that have tended to increase labor use.*

It is obvious that the distributive effects of this type of small scale mechanical technology varies widely from place to place. In most areas, however, there appears to be considerable scope for redesigning relatively sophisticated machines in order to make them suitable for all but the smallest farm sizes. Not only would such redesigning enable more farmers to achieve a higher degree of control over their agricultural operations, but the extent of cooperative efforts needed to utilize such machines would be reduced significantly.

Highly indivisible mechanical technology. The greatest areas of concern regarding rural employment are those situations in which highly indivisible mechanical technology designed for use in developed countries is being introduced into developing countries with surplus labor and significant disparities of holding size. Because of its close relationship to questions of an institutional character, e.g. the size of holdings, the debate about mechanization has often been a heated one. However, there appears to be at least a limited consensus on the following points:

(1) The repeated claims that mechanization has had an impact on yields are questionable. Most research drawing this conclusion suffers from a failure to control for other inputs and the few studies that have sought to separate out various effects have found nothing to support the hypothesis. (A caveat to this conclusion might be the use of tractors to do deep tillage in dry land areas.)

(2) The argument that tractors can increase the cropping intensity and thereby increase the demand for labor must be seriously qualified. Arid areas, constrained by

---

* This does not imply, of course, that various social groups have been equally affected. In India and Pakistan, threshing is partially done by casual labor. The possibility that the bullocks used in threshing may now be used to increase cropping intensities usually involves only the farmer himself. Thus the effect is to maintain the number of hours worked by using fixed family labor more effectively.

the availability of water, offer little scope for increasing intensity. Areas in Africa and Latin America where land is relatively abundant fall into a similar category.

(3) Countries in which rapid mechanization has occurred under conditions that raise questions regarding its social desirability have almost universally pursued policies that created an artificially profitable economic climate for machines. Also, in almost every case, this was made possible by the activities of foreign aid donors whose mechanization loans removed the allocation of scarce foreign exchange from the overall planning process.

(4) There are strong reasons for believing that much of the impetus for mechanization comes from the desire to alter the basic social character of production in agriculture. Evidence from a number of countries suggests that it is seen as a means of converting a landlord-tenancy system into one in which land is personally managed and farmed with wage labor.[22] The benefits that follow from such a change are the increased security of claims to the land in the event of land reforms, the avoidance of the need to confront local institutions regarding the appropriate sharing arrangements between tenant and landlord, and the more effective exploitation of the land and water resources through effective management techniques.

With these comments on technology as background, it is easy to see why writers concerned with the employment problem place such heavy emphasis on continued progress in expanding the list of improved varieties, improving the fertilizer distribution mechanism, creating institutions for conducting research on intermediate technology, etc. Such developments have the two-fold benefit of improving the absolute incomes of the majority of the rural population while at the same time contributing to the overall growth of the agricultural economy. Where this growth in turn leads to further dynamic effects via the savings and investment of individuals or the society, additional employment in the non-agricultural sector is also a possibility. Where this employment is itself a function of the characteristics of such intermediate technology, e.g., the growth of local, small-scale manufacturing industries, the argument is virtually a complete package.[23]

Moreover, a growth strategy based on relatively divisible types of technology has considerable merit from an institutional perspective. Because of the accent on divisibility, there is only a limited connection between the distribution of resources and its adoption. Similarly, divisibility puts a minimum strain on the organizations that provide complementary services. There should be no illusion that such a strategy will do much to improve the distribution of income but, as the evidence previously cited suggests, the diffusion of this type of technology, while perhaps lagging among the smaller size groups, may even create some additional employment. Under any circumstances, it is unlikely to produce a condition of widespread rural instability.

The difficulty with implementing such a policy, of course, is that it is subject to exactly the same institutional pressures that it seeks to avoid. First, there is the fairly obvious problem of control over the importation of capital equipment from abroad. Groups that are able to resist the redistribution of land are also powerful enough to put considerable pressure on government agencies to permit equipment imports. Where considerable disparity of holding sizes exists and where the mean holding size is quite large, there will be substantial incentives to obtain technology that is consistent with such a structure.

Second, there are the more subtle phenomena associated with the direction given to indigenous research. This is partly a matter of the incentive structure (grants, status, salaries) facing researchers. It is also a matter of their training and social background. As Timmer has warned, one ought not to underrate the significance of short-sighted but sincere notions of what modern agriculture is "supposed" to look like as a determinant of research goals.[24] Individual mental sets do differ markedly and the somewhat conspiratorial view that engineers and scientists are "working for" the larger farmers should not be pushed too far.

Lastly, the argument for divisibility contains a curious ambiguity. It is by no means an unmixed blessing in areas where attempts are being made to create grassroots social and political organizations. *Provided* that the client group has some productive resources at its disposal, the need to overcome technological problems through communal activity may be a powerful focus for initial organizing efforts.[25] Where each individual cultivator, regardless of size, has access to a new technology, the possibility of using the source of increased productivity as a lever for creating consciousness and cooperation that may ultimately be used for other purposes, is limited.

Rural Development Organizations

The distinction between structure and institutions made earlier is perhaps most obvious when reviewing the evidence on the operations of organizations designed to increase output and improve the distribution of income and employment. Virtually every country has its complement of cooperatives, development banks, extension services, etc. but their presence on paper and even the quality of their staffing gives little indication of their actual role or behavior.

Figure 3 suggested that these actions may be seen as being influenced both by pressures from the national political regime and the central bureaucracy, and by the various power groups at the local level. An additional variable in their behavioral equation, institutional in a broader sense, involves the style of personal relationships within the bureaucracy at all levels. As Beteille points out, the Western system of bureaucratic organization is based on adherence to impersonal rules and norms.[26] This style of personal relations is foreign to many indigenous cultures where loyalties to tribe, caste and family are considered to be of overriding importance. The implications that the latter view holds for favoritism and discrimination is fairly evident.

Evidence concerning the actual behavior of rural organizations under these conditions is vast and cannot be summarized in much detail. However, the following might be said about those functions that figure most prominently in the development literature.

Agricultural credit. The debate over the characteristics of rural financial markets has grown more heated in recent years as the effectiveness of agricultural credit programs in improving the lot of the weaker sections of the rural community has come under increasing challenge. (Particularly sensitive to critics are the foreign aid donors who hold millions of dollars of this type of loan in their portfolios.) Two grounds are given for this disenchantment. First, there is the point that the lack of credit has not hampered many small farmers from adopting the high yielding varieties package and hence its significance as a "necessary" ingredient in rural development programs is probably overrated. Second, even if it is an important element in many situations, under existing types of delivery systems, it is not getting to those who are supposed to be the recipients of the program.

With respect to the first argument, there is some *prima facia* evidence that it is correct. However, while the availability of an institutionalized credit mechanism may not hinder the adoption of highly divisible inputs under certain favorable conditions, the rates of interest charged in the private markets surely produce an undesirable income effect. Moreover, and more important, small-scale intermediate mechanical technology will undoubtedly require medium term credit. It is here that the failure of most institutionalized credit mechanisms has been felt most clearly. Given the divergence of opinion on this issue, however, it is one of those questions to which further research could legitimately be addressed.

While there may be a divergence of opinion on the need for credit by small farmers and tenants, the verdict that they are not now the recipients of what is available is unanimous.[27] The pressures that produce this result are well known. From the top, there are explicit or implicit demands for a high rate of loan recovery. From the bottom, there are both the pressures of local social and political influence and the economies associated with lending to the larger borrowers. It has often been noted that it costs no more to lend $10,000 than to lend $100. Indeed, if investigation and supervision are included as expenses, the cost of small-scale lending is unquestionably very high.

Agricultural extension services. The situation with respect to agricultural extension services is much the same as that found with respect to agricultural credit. First, there is the question of how useful it really is. To be sure, some sort of link between the research stations and the farmers must be developed, but this varies widely with the type of crop and the type of practice that is being introduced. No blanket statement on the subject is possible.

But with respect to the distribution of extension services, the same unanimous findings cited in the case of credit also obtain, namely, that little of the available advice goes to those who might need it most. And again, the same set of pressures is at work. From the top there is the desire of the agricultural establishment to be sure that it has the support of influential local citizens in its bureaucratic battles with other sections of the government. Hence the local agent is encouraged to respond quickly and sympathetically to the needs of the well-to-do. Moreover, since he himself is usually poorly paid and without adequate transportation, the availability of a meal and transport when he visits the large farmers is an inducement that he can ill afford to ignore. Lastly, and the importance of this point should not be underestimated, medium and large farmers are prepared to undertake the procedures that are being suggested! To any field worker who sees himself as someone dedicated to creating a more modern agriculture, the self-realization that accompanies the successful introduction of a new practice is no less rewarding to him than to his counterpart anywhere else in the world. As in the case of credit, it is hard to see how the results could be anything but what they are.

Rural works programs. As both of the previous examples have suggested, where a significant disparity of economic and political power between social classes exists at the local level and where the national regime is unable, or lacks the desire, to attack these groups directly, services that are aimed at a target group of the relatively disadvantaged, are within a short time diverted to benefit those who control the community's scarce resources. This is at the root of most failures of the cooperative movement to improve the situation of the smaller farmer. As Shourie and Thomas show, it is also a frequent outcome of efforts to create employment directly.[28] To a certain extent, the distribution of benefits must necessarily follow the distribution of resources since most public works programs enhance the long-run value of the surrounding lands. However, there is more to the problem than that. Frequently, the larger farmers are also the contractors who are entrusted to organize and carry out the project. It is they who are instrumental in choosing the technology that is to be used, in siting roads and buildings, etc. Relatively little concern is likely to be evidenced in such cases for the interests of the program's intended beneficiaries.

The pattern of program implementation frequently observed in attempts to provide direct aid to the disadvantaged is instructive for the insights it gives into the dynamics of the system. Burki reports, for example, that in Pakistan the initial program for rural works was relatively well conceived and sought to provide jobs at the local level around projects whose beneficiaries were—more or less—the general populace.[29] The initial stages of project implementation were also relatively successful when measured in these terms. However, when it became apparent that substantial sums were being spent that could have been directed to activities of more direct benefit to the wealthy and politically prominent groups, a number of steps involving new project criteria, altered lines of responsibility, etc., were introduced. In the end, the original concept of benefits to the general public was all but discarded in favor of a concentration on those activities, e.g. tubewells, that were of greatest individual benefit.

A.H. Khan, in writing about recent (1970) events at the Comilla cooperative scheme in Bangladesh describes a similar dynamic.[30] Initially, the larger farmers ignored the cooperative program. For approximately 5 years, it developed largely in isolation from their influence. Because of its success, however, particularly in organizing small farmers to use intermediate and relatively indivisible technology in the form of pumps, motors and tubewells, it became evident to the traditional elites that a potential power rival existed and that by remaining aloof from the whole operation, they were creating long run problems for themselves. Then and only then did they seek to join the co-ops and to exert influence over their operations. At this writing, the struggle for the control of the co-ops continues and it is too early to know whether the solidarity of the smaller farmers will withstand the pressures being applied. However, it is interesting to note that much of the effort to undermine the Comilla program has come from the higher echelons of government as the larger farmer cum contractor sought urban allies to influence the types of programs that would be supported in the rural areas.

The divergence between structure and institutional behavior underlines a major contradiction in rural development programs. The difficulty is that nearly any organization, including the state, can be used for improving or worsening income disparity. The more effective it is, the greater the impact of its behavior—for better or worse—will be. Advocates of the creation and funding of organizations are thus faced with the same problems as the supporters of selective mechanization. How can these organizations be established in such a way that their institutional behavior does not distort the goals for which they were set up? It seems clear that without a description of the environmental conditions under which there is a strong presumption that positive results can be obtained, a case can be made for not creating organizations at all. At least with respect to the objective of creating additional employment, to do nothing is surely a policy superior to one that in fact worsens the situation.

The Distribution of Resources

One of the most direct reflections of a society's value system is to be found in the institutions surrounding the nature and distribution of rights to property. As a result, the impetus behind attempts to alter the distribution of income of rural areas have always had a two-fold thrust: economic and political.

Economic arguments for land reform have sought to elaborate its direct effects on such variables as output and the demand for labor. It has been contended, for example, that small owner-operated holdings increase the incentive to cultivate land more intensively. Included in the same category of observations is the further point that the uncertainty of various forms of tenancy provides a built-in disincentive to the undertaking of long-term investments in land and associated agricultural capital.

The second and frequently more important argument accompanying land reform seeks to make the case via the need for changing certain fundamental sources of institutional behavior. As Figure 3 suggests, the distribution of resources is an important element in the distribution of power among local groups. The latter is in turn important in determining the behavior of other sub-systems in the society. It follows from this that the ability to influence behavior elsewhere in the system may be dependent on first altering the pattern of resource control.

Of these arguments, the following might be said:

1. The direct output and employment effects of such redistributive measures as land reform are still being debated. There is a major difficulty, in assessing the empirical evidence, in untangling the short-term disruptive effects of the reforms, in those countries where some significant redistribution has taken place from the effects likely to obtain in the long run. However, the consensus appears to be that, *provided* certain minimum organizational facilities are also created to give guidance and financial assistance in the early period of the reform, the economies of scale in agriculture are not such that production need decline. Indeed, since the available evidence suggests that land utilization on small farms is more intensive than on large farms, over the long run the reform should improve the distribution of income and increase output as well.

2. There is little doubt that the control over resources has ramifications far beyond the access to lumpy technology and organizational services that accompany economies of the firm in the market. As Beteille notes:

> Inequalities of property, income and privilege and power may be cumulative or dispersed. The characteristic feature of agrarian societies is that they tend to be cumulative, creating thereby powerful ideological basis for recognition of social inequality as part of the national order. In a system of cumulative inequalities, privilege, property and power are combined in the same individuals and the socially under-privileged are also economically and politically deprived.[31]

But as Beteille himself points out, the *degree* of cumulative interaction that exists differs widely between countries and, perhaps more important from a program point of view, differs widely *within* countries. One need only think of the significantly different cultural and social stratification at the four points of the Indian compass, the nomad-sedentary split in many Middle Eastern and African countries, the Indian (mountain)-Spanish (low-land) dichotomy in Latin America, etc., to appreciate the significance of this latter point.

Even though the difficulties associated with a significant redistribution of resources in most developing countries are, at least at this stage of their development, almost insurmountable, an even more difficult problem than resource redistribution confronts many of them. Quite simply, given past and present rates of growth in the labor force, even if all the land were distributed equitably, the amount of land available per farm family is or soon will be less than that required for subsistence. Consequently, it is hard to see how a land reform alone could, even in principal, solve the employment problem. Further social reorganization is required.

One of the great strengths of some form of communal agriculture is that it makes it much easier to free part of the population *locally* from daily agricultural tasks and to make them available for various non-agricultural activities that would also benefit the communal group. The Chinese experience shows that while communes are clearly not an appropriate level for decision making with respect to agricultural tasks, they have provided a mechanism by which self-help can be organized at a level where the benefits of improving infrastructure are clearly visible.

Agricultural Price Policy

Virtually every study that has examined the employment effects of technical change has also commented on the employment effects of government price policies. These have usually been separated into discussions involving (1) the relative prices of capital and labor, (2) the relative prices of output and their effects on cropping patterns, and (3) the relative price of things agriculture buys and sells.

Considerable evidence exists that each of these relationships has in the past had an impact on the level of employment in rural areas. As indicated earlier, virtually every case of inappropriate mechanization has been accompanied by distorted input prices. Causes of distortions have ranged all the way from outright subsidies on machines to cheap credit and/or rebates on fuels and lubricants. Moreover, calculations done in the Philippines, Pakistan, India and Ethiopia, to mention but a few countries, suggest that if prices had been set that reflected the actual cost of machines to the economy, in several cases mechanization would have been strictly unprofitable and elsewhere it would undoubtedly have slowed the process considerably.

Less widely appreciated is the fact that in a number of countries, an output-pricing structure aimed at cereal self-sufficiency has had important detrimental effects on rural employment. Relative prices skewed in the direction of cereals through government support mechanisms, have discouraged diversification and further expansion of acreage under vegetables, fodder for dairying, pulses, etc. Since cereals, especially wheat, have relatively low labor requirements, such policies may affect the aggregate demand for labor significantly.

The potential in some cases for increasing employment through a rationalization of the support structure may be less important, however, than the changes in relative prices that occur when processing facilities are provided. As Desai and Schluter have pointed out in an Indian example, the installation of groundnut and sugarcane processing plants drastically altered the cropping of the surrounding areas.[32] Because of the nature of the cultural operations to be performed on these crops, aggregate labor needs increased substantially.

The adverse terms of trade between agriculture and industry as a result of inefficient import substitution policies is another potential deterrent to increased employment in rural areas. Obviously, within limits, mechanisms that permit the general economy to share in the increasing productivity of agriculture are important. But where the "squeeze" has been carried too far, i.e., to the point where agriculturalists no longer see a profit in investment in rural areas, it may be that the extraction of the surplus has become counter-productive.

The general policy prescriptions derived by economists from theory and from the empirical evidence accumulated over the past decade suggest that prices do affect rural employment in important ways. What improved pricing in agriculture might mean in situations in which prices elsewhere in the economy remain distorted, poses problems in both theory and practice. But at the very least, machines might be priced to reflect the cost of capital to the economy, output prices might reflect considerations other than simply those of growth or self-sufficiency, and there should be a continuous evaluation of the terms of trade between sectors to insure that private investment is being directed to areas where real opportunities for employment creation exist.

It will be noted immediately that when the test of political constituencies is applied to these recommendations, a much broader set of political actors is involved and something closer to the pluralistic models of political scientists in developed countries emerges. First, it is true that groups that would oppose science policies directed only at intermediate technology would also oppose removal of subsidies on capital intensive inputs. They may even find allies among the industrialists who have their own reasons for wanting cheap capital. But other groups, e.g. the military, may feel that the use of scarce foreign exchange would be better spent on tanks than on tractors. Similarly, other non-agriculturally related bureaucrats may feel that subsidies for particular items detract in an important way from their own development projects.

Second, in cases where distorted output prices subsidize an agriculture in which little opportunity to increase output rapidly through further investment exists, the urban populace provides a strong counterweight to agricultural interests.

The presence of pluralistic interests in the economy where prices are concerned in crucial. It helps to explain why strictly economic policies are frequently reasonably easy to change and why other reforms, largely isolated within the social system of rural areas, are not. Of course, in countries where rural and urban interests (or elites) are one, and there are a number in this category, the possibilities for economic reform are seriously dampened.[33] In terms of the structure outlined in Figure 3, no "negative" feedback loops exist.

Summary

The preceding section linked several important elements of an agricultural growth strategy to their effects on employment and income distribution. Policy conclusions drawn from theory and supported by this evidence were reviewed and some comments regarding the source of the difficulties in implementing the prescriptions were offered.

The argument can be summarized in a few points:

1. The characteristics of the technology to be employed in agriculture are obviously key elements in the employment picture. Most empirical studies have concluded that a general increase in the demand for labor has accompanied the adoption of such highly divisible inputs as improved varieties, fertilizer, etc. Intermediate technology (pumps, motors, small tubewells and threshers) has a somewhat more ambiguous record with respect to employment, but the means to produce additional water supplies stands out as an instrument for both increasing growth and increasing labor requirements. Premature introduction of highly indivisible inputs (tractors, combines) are perhaps the greatest threat to a rational agricultural transformation. In most cases, their introduction has involved price policies that discriminated against labor use.

2. Upon examination, the role of agricultural service organizations (credit, extension, marketing) in employment generation was somewhat problematical in situations where a reasonably divisible, well understood technology was present. However, the evidence is ambiguous enough to warrant further research. What was not ambiguous is that insofar as such programs have been justified as attempts to improve the position of the disadvantaged in imperfect capital and information markets, they

have failed. The internal pressures of bureaucrats anxious to minimize the risks of lending and the political influence of the wealthy have combined to circumvent efforts to discriminate in favor of the weaker cultivators.

3. The redistribution of resources is obviously the most sensitive parameter of social change. From an economic point of view, there is reason to think that, with even minimal efforts at helping the inexperienced and uncreditworthy recipients of land gain a foothold, land reform could have a positive effect on economic growth. Most reforms, however, are prompted by political rather than economic motives. Only by significantly altering the resource base can the system be ''opened up'' to the point where other employment generating policies are relatively easy to pursue, i.e., they move in the direction of being technical problems.

4. Prices do matter. For example, with respect to factor use, almost every case of rapid mechanization has occurred in settings in which inappropriate factor pricing was an important characteristic. Opportunities for improvement in the distribution of income may also be possible in some cases by adjusting the domestic price structure of outputs to favor comparative advantage *and* employment.

5. The difficulties of implementation range from the largely technical to the largely political. However, the effect of feedback loops is to create a mechanism in which the cumulative effects of technological change and investment decisions reinforce—and are reinforced by—the use of extra-market political and social influence.

6. However, while the cumulative effects of change on social systems—and of society on policy—are much more visible in agrarian than in industrial societies, they differ widely between and within countries. Moreover, all policy prescriptions are not affected in the same way by the characteristics of the rural society. Those that have economy-wide ramifications may be supported by such ''exogenous'' groups in the urban areas as the industrialists, workers, the military, etc. This element of pluralism is important in understanding why certain types of economic adjustment are carried out in the face of opposition from agrarian interests. (A major exception to this argument for potential reform is supplied by countries in which the interests of the rural and urban elites are represented by the same individuals.)

The challenge of such a formulation is to develop analyses that will indicate the likely effects of social and political phenomena on development programs before they proceed to the implementation stage. In order to make such an evaluation, however, it must be related to the capacity and political position of the implementing agency. It is to this broader perspective that the next section is addressed.

Rural Development in an Nth Best World

It will be obvious to the reader that permitting local power groups and institutional behavior to enter the framework within which the rural employment problem is discussed does great violence to the possibility of creating simple development typologies. The absence of simplifying theory and the potential permutations and combinations of various economic and political forces makes generalization extremely difficult. However, two aspects of the distribution of power at the local level and the characteristics of rural development programs provide an opening for further analysis. First, it is clear that both *between* and *within* countries there are wide differences in the extent and type of social stratification that exists. Secondly, programs and policies do differ widely in their distributive implications. Consequently, there is a challenge to develop what might be called a criterion of *implementability* in assessing the desirability of various types of rural development projects. That is, under what social and political circumstances is there a solid presumption that a particular proposal or activity can be implemented in substantially the form envisaged by the economic analysis?

To many, this line of questioning will appear to be static and self-defeating. It will certainly be difficult for "can do" organizations (and individuals), few of whom are willing to admit that they are as much at the mercy of their environment as they really are. Institutions are to be "created" and "changed," not submitted to. Moreover, the potentially self-serving character of decisions not to mount programs for those who are relatively powerless, is obvious. If the previous discussion of the source of difficulties in implementing rural development activities that have a distributive effect is correct, however, then a reasonably careful social and political *analysis* of the environment seems a necessary condition for implementation—if for no other reason than the fact that over the years so many well intentioned programs have in retrospect made situations worse!

The search for criteria that relate programs to their environment in terms of the ability of an implementing agency to actually carry out the activity, obviously poses a research problem of considerable magnitude. Not only must the distributive impact of development programs (about which a good deal is known) and the effects of local power structure on their implementation (about which something is known) be understood, but the perceptions and abilities of the implementing agencies must be examined as well. (About the interaction of national regimes and local political organization, relatively little is known.)

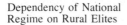

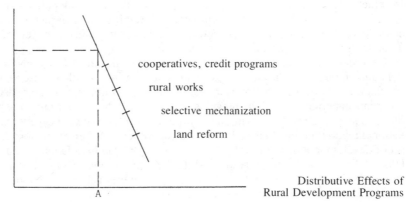

Dependency of National
Regime on Rural Elites

cooperatives, credit programs

rural works

selective mechanization

land reform

Distributive Effects of
Rural Development Programs

A

Figure 4. The Implementability of Rural Development Programs

A first approximation of what such an analysis of "implementability" might look like is shown in Figure 4. Though, as subsequent comments will indicate, it is extremely crude, it is meant to suggest that there is an inverse relation between the degree to which the national political regime is dependent upon local political elites for support and the distributive effects of the types of programs that can be implemented.

The X axis measures the distributive content of the program under the assumption that it is to be implemented and enforced in accordance with the rhetoric that accompanies its initiation.* Most innocuous are those programs that would enhance the position of smaller farmers through credit and extension programs; at the other extreme are programs that would confiscate land and lead to a redistribution of property. In the first instance, one would expect less resistance at the grassroots since the achievement of the objective, while it might mean some future income foregone to the elite groups, would involve only minor, if any, absolute economic losses. The latter (land reform) would of course be resisted mightily unless confiscated land resources were translated into substantial sums of capital. In between, one could expect to find such policies as selective mechanization where the decision not to permit the tractorization of agriculture would be vigorously—but not desperately —resisted. Various price and fiscal policies would also be found in this intermediate category.

The Y axis measures the dependency of the national regime on the local elites for regime support. As previous comments have emphasized, the notion of "local" has two implications: (1) that the decision-making processes are at the village level, and (2) that considerable geographic specificity is involved. Hence, with respect to the functioning of many rural development *projects,* "dependency" of the national regime is associated with a specific geographical area and not necessarily with an aggregate grassroots influence.

Several observations—in addition to objections involving difficulties of measurement and oversimplification—might be made about the schema in Figure 4. First, it illustrates the usual paradox of social reform, i.e., the point at which change is most needed is also the point at which the ability to mobilize resources for resistance is most concentrated. For example, those areas in which land redistribution is a necessary prelude to any attack on the employment problem are also frequently those in which the dependency factor with respect to the national political regime is greatest. This follows from the comment by Beteille cited earlier in which the cumulative character of agrarian societies, i.e., the assumption of a variety of roles by a single individual or group, was emphasized.

A second and related observation might be that Figure 4 has transformed the dynamic emphasis of the earlier systems discussion into a rather static view of the problem. It misses the fact, for example, that implementing any of the redistributive programs in period *t* would, by previous arguments, alter the distribution of power at the local level in period *t* + 1. This in turn would lower the extent of dependence by the national regime on the elites and provide a constituency for an even more ambitious set of development activities aimed at small farmers, landless laborers and the like. Ultimately, one could envisage successful efforts to establish a political organization among the disadvantaged that would permit a frontal attack on the major causes of disparity, i.e. on the distribution of resources.

The foregoing scenario has not been enacted with great frequency and the reason is not difficult to uncover. The evidence already cited discloses that very few developing countries have been able to implement *any* type of rural development program that discriminated in favor of the weaker groups. For the most part, whether it be because of a lack of political commitment, the limited capacity of the bureaucracy or whatever, the programs investigated have been shown to fall in the range indicated by point A in Figure 4.

---

*   An immediate rebuttal to this approach is that the rhetoric was never intended to become reality. This comment may often be justified. However, it is my general impression that most leaders cannot function at this level of cynicism for long.

The effect of findings of the sort just described would be translated in terms of the implementability criterion as a statement that the majority of the Third World countries at this juncture in time cannot carry out policies that depend for their success on discrimination in favor of the politically powerless. Despite the rhetoric, despite all of the hue and cry that is being raised about the need to put distribution objectives on a par with growth, it would appear that when such programs are not accompanied by rather radical political transformations in which the group to be aided is important in the *governing* structure of the ruling party, they cannot be implemented.

Employment Generation Without Redistribution

The observation that in many rural areas, policies aimed at improving the position of the underemployed by discriminating in their favor, cannot be implemented, is hardly startling. Nor does it mean necessarily that the absolute incomes of those likely to be in this class cannot be raised by politically feasible development activities. For example, under the assumption that demand constraints are not important, the availability of improved varieties and fertilizer can raise the productivity of small farmers regardless of the ability of large farmers to avoid restrictions on the introduction and utilization of tractors. The redesign of intermediate technology offers a similar proposition; decreasing the size of tubewells, motors and pump sets is not detrimental (except perhaps in some long run sense) to the rural elites as they currently exist and it makes good political sense. As indicated earlier, this type of technology, particularly where it is associated with increasing or controlling water supplies, is likely to increase the demand for labor both in agriculture and in the small-scale industry that usually accompanies its introduction. However, there should be no illusions that its introduction will improve the distribution of income. If successful, it will at best increase the absolute well-being of those at the bottom of the income ladder.

This line of argument suggests other kinds of activities that would be both implementable from a political point of view and yet provide for some likely trickle down effects in terms of employment. One of the most significant of these is rural electrification. As Mellor has noted, there is perhaps no other single incentive to the creation of additional small-scale industrial activity as powerful as the provision of a reasonably cheap energy source.[34] In agriculture as well, the costs and maintenance of electrically powered motors is far below those associated with diesel engines.*

Another kind of activity that is likely to get high marks for "implementability" is road building. To be sure, such projects are likely to benefit the owners of resources but some additional income also gets into the hands of those who work on the roads. Perhaps even more importantly, roads tend to create new market opportunities for both surplus labor and surplus commodities.**

Lastly, there is again the point that areas differ widely *within* countries and the possiblity always exists that under the right set of circumstances, i.e., a relatively egalitarian structure in the countryside and a reasonably divisible technology, farmer

---

* The Department of Agricultural Engineering at the Punjab Agricultural University, Ludhiana, India, is now experimenting with mechanical technology suitable for a 5-acre farm. It is based on a 5 h.p. electric motor that can be used to power a small tractor or removed for use on a fractional tubewell, a small thresher or maize sheller. There are energy distribution problems to be overcome but the total cost will be a fraction of the cost of similar machines powered by gasoline.

** As is well known, assessing the employment effects of roads is tricky business. New roads have also been known to wipe out traditional industries whose comparative advantage was based on high transportation costs.

organizations can be encouraged to the point where local people actually begin to take over their own futures. As Barraclough has pointed out, such pilot projects sometimes succeed and, even when they can't be implemented in the country as a whole, they serve the useful purpose of providing additional insight into what the problems really are.[35]

This latter point, i.e., the possiblity of educating those who govern about the potentials of certain types of rural development projects, is important. The previous argument on judging the possibility for implementation assumed that the perception of the national regime about its dependence on certain elites was an objective condition. Such is not the case, of course, and there is always the chance that analyses presented to the ruling elites regarding the nature of their constituency and the potential for broadening their base of support will be sufficiently persuasive to produce new responses. Indeed, such instances may be fairly common. Although those holding power tend to be inherently conservative, preserving the system's social stratification in periods of rapid technical and economic change cannot be accomplished by a slavish adherence to the past. In such situations, change is necessary to preserve the *status quo!*

Employment with Distributional Consequences

But not all areas and all countries are in the category in which the employment effects of rural development must depend largely on trickle down effects. A limited number are in a position to develop programs that either improve the absolute incomes of everyone and narrow income differences or increase the demand for labor while making some groups absolutely worse off.

The first pattern is one that would involve movements along the X axis of Figure 4 to some point short of all-out land reform. It would require two necessary conditions. First, a point already made, a national political regime must be independent enough of the local elites so that some kinds of broad-based political organizing at the grassroots level is possible. Second, the bureaucracy must have the capacity to supervise and protect the cooperative credit and marketing organizations that would need to be established, to help manage the labor unions of the landless until they were sufficiently powerful to fend for themselves, etc. What is and is not implementable in such a situation is exceedingly difficult to say. It marks a period of protracted and active struggle between an alliance of the more progressive elements in the urban areas and their disadvantaged allies in the countryside, and the power structure of the local elites. In some situations, this struggle may be relatively muted. Many areas in Africa do not have a class structure based on landed interests and thus the real difficulties of implementation lie elsewhere, e.g. in the capacity, skills and motivation of the bureaucracy. But in other countries, for example, Chile, this period has been marked by countless angry confrontations between the outside organizers, their allies and the local hacienda owners.*

What is fascinating in such situations is the question of whether or not the successful efforts in the initial phases of implementation will lead to a position from which further reforms can be initiated or whether the counterattack by the local elites will be sufficient to overwhelm the gains already made. As a previous comment indicated, a fairly common pattern is one in which some agency of the central government, usually with considerable support from urban groups, actually imple-

---

* These experiences should give some pause to those who would advocate local decision making as an important element in any rural development strategy. At least with respect to employment, the results would obviously be quite different depending on the structure of power at the local level.

ments a program whose ultimate results are not fully understood by the power holders of the countryside. Although the evidence suggests that in most rural development programs, local counter pressures have been sufficient to overwhelm these initial successes, it may still be, *provided the struggle is of reasonable duration,* that some significant increase in self-consciousness takes place among those seeking to organize. This may become the basis for the next round of activity. However, if the duration criterion is not met, i.e. the efforts are crushed quickly and effectively, the sense of powerlessness and apathy among the potential program beneficiaries is likely to increase as a result of the experience.

The most difficult efforts at employment generation from an implementability point of view are those associated with the attempt to redistribute land. Admittedly, there are so few examples of successful reform that its very requirements are hard to judge. It appears, however, that there can be no weak links in the chain. The national political regime must be firmly committed; the administrative machinery must have the capacity and the motivation to carry out the law quickly and efficiently; a power base for reform at the local level must be organized, vocal and well disciplined; and, lastly, the technical improvements necessary to increase the productivity of the newly created tenure system must be at hand. As Montgomery has noted, no matter how committed the national regime may be, if it does not have firm control of the local political and administrative structure, there is no way of forcing compliance.[36] Indeed, as other writers have pointed out, the result of tenancy legislation or rights to the use of resources under such conditions is another one of those programs that make a bad situation worse.[37] Landlords, fearing further erosion of their rights if tenants are allowed to remain, solve the problem by immediate eviction. Unless local administrative officials are sympathetic to the weaker groups, even where justice is blind, use of the courts as a remedy is usually too expensive to be much of an alternative. The result tends to be a rapid transition from the paternalism of the landlord-tenant relationship to the insecurities of wage labor before supporting institutions for this kind of social system have become functional.

The Robustness of Policy Recommendations

The previous discussion of the ability to implement conventional policy prescriptions for increasing employment opportunities suggests that they can be ranked with respect to their robustness under a variety of institutional environments.

First, nearly every society seeking to improve both its material well being and the distribution of income will find it necessary to rely heavily on a continuing flow of new yield-increasing agricultural technology. Regardless of its political climate, improved varieties, better plant protection measures, soil analyses, fertilizer availability, etc. are essential elements of a "uni-modal" development strategy.* It is in the interests of the whole agricultural community that this type of technology be generated and diffused. This does not imply that the emphasis on this type of scientific research versus other types of investment will not differ among countries with different constellations of social and political forces. However, these variations are likely to be less a matter of the overt pressures than the pattern of student training, the quality of local research leadership, etc.

The same cannot be said about selective mechanization. To be sure, an environment that offers incentives to tubewells, motors, and small threshers may be fairly easy to create. But selective mechanization means more than being *for* the kind of

---

* "Uni-modal" is a term coined by Johnston to indicate a development pattern in which various farm sizes could participate on a relatively equal footing.[38]

intermediate technology that tends to increase the demand for labor. It also means being *against* technology that does not meet these criteria. Thus policies that limit the importation of large tractor sizes, provide subsidies on small motors but not on large, etc., are unlikely to be feasible in a number of countries.

Second, many types of infrastructure are likely to be both implementable across a wide range of political environments and have a chance at generating increased employment for those at the bottom of the income ladder. I have mentioned rural electrification as being consistently positive and roads as being potentially so. Here the question is obviously what *kind* of roads, since roads that connect major rural centers open up the country to the town as well as opening up the town to the country. The need is for feeder roads that do not create competition between large urban centers and the local production of consumer goods, light machine tools, and the like.

Third, and more restricted with respect to the number of likely successes, is the implementation of rural works programs that actually improve the welfare of the group most likely to be in need of jobs. This is partly a matter of controlling the projects, to prevent the siphoning off of funds for activities that are not very labor intensive, and partly a matter of containing the power of local elites who are reluctant to permit the kind of local organizing that appears necessary for an effective program.

Fourth, and even more constraining in its institutional demands, are agricultural credit and rural service programs. Judging from the available evidence, only a small number of countries—or a small number of areas—appear to have an environment in which these programs are able to reach the target group.

Lastly, and virtually unimplementable in most developing countries at this point in time, are basic land reform programs. (The reader will by now appreciate that what is at issue is not the country's willingness to pass land reform legislation, but its ability to implement it effectively.) Tenancy reform, where this is interpreted as an effective alteration in the rights of the tenant, is in virtually the same category.

The Olympian detachment implied in these observations is not, of course, the normal perspective of the national planner or decision-maker.* First, his is an optimization problem in which he may very well concede that the ability to implement the program as it is envisaged in the economic analysis will be limited but that for political purposes, a program that *ostensibly* redistributes is a must. He is also likely to note that success or failure is a matter of degree and if he must provide some sort of benefits to certain groups, programs that give some indication of redistribution are better than those that give virtually none, even if the former turn out to be very "expensive."

So much for rural development programs. Where does economic policy of the conventional sort, e.g. factor and product pricing, fall in this spectrum? Because of the potentially large number of actors involved, it is extremely difficult to say. Some of the potential coalitions around different issues have been mentioned earlier. The point can be repeated by thinking of the problem of food grain pricing where most farmers would support high prices and most other rural residents in need of employment or at the bottom of the income ladder would favor low prices. In this they would be joined by powerful urban constituencies: labor unions, industrialists, and service workers.

Subsidies on tractors, on the other hand, would be aimed at a particular group of the larger farmers. Their opponents or allies, however, would vary depending on whether

---

* The criticism that a number of political scientists have leveled at the usefulness for policy purposes of conceptual systems guided by a highly endogenous kind of "functionalism" should be noted at this point.[39]

the policy involved imports against foreign aid, the use of own exchange reserves for imports, or local production. The result of the society-wide reflection of economic policy encountered in the last example opens up many avenues for the alteration of specific policies. The price of wheat can be raised or lowered a bit, subsidies on certain inputs can be abolished, the cost of credit adjusted by several percent, etc. These are all useful tools that can be undertaken frequently in almost every economy. (The fact that such changes are possible is probably a reason why many practicing economists have found it unnecessary to concern themselves with wider institutional problems.)

Given the plurality of interests, whether or not such marginal policy adjustments can make a significant difference in the overall rural employment situation cannot be ascertained without reference to the specific situation. For not only must the magnitude of the problem be defined, the meaning of "marginal" is conditional on the institutional structure described previously; the more the national regime is dependent on certain segments of the rural elites, the more constrained must be the economic policies that threaten the well-being of these groups. The only difference between economic policy and the types of programs mentioned earlier then is that there are powerful external checks and balances to this system that are not present in rurally isolated development programs.

Conclusion

The foregoing comments have emphasized the role of social and political institutions in implementing employment-oriented rural development programs. Lest there be a misunderstanding, however, I am definitely not arguing that *all* problems in implementation have this character. Despite the fact that the choice of technology and the location of a particular irrigation project may involve significant political and institutional considerations, there are still problems of water supply, the construction of the dam, the nature of the drainage system, etc., that must be resolved. Similarly, the fact that the provision of divisible agricultural technology shows great robustness as an agricultural strategy does not insure that the needed genetic materials for varietal improvements are at hand, that the optimal cultural practices are known, or even, to stretch the point, that the appropriate types of training and the administrative structure of an agricultural research establishment are commonly understood. To minimize these kinds of difficulties would be foolish. Large amounts of resources are currently being devoted to these technical tasks and there is good reason to believe that if more were available, they could be put to good use. Because of the nature of the problem, the work lends itself particularly to foreign assistance and one can only urge continued efforts in these areas.

However, in this process, great care should be exercised in trying to ascertain what the technical problem really is. For while it is true that there are many problems requiring "hard" knowledge for their solution, there is a link between the institutional environment and the definition of the problem. It was suggested earlier, for example, that the re-design of mechanical technology to fit small farms was a "technical" challenge. But it is obvious that in social and political environments where a great deal of the work is communally done, this "problem" loses much of its force.*

---

* A similar argument, offered by many writers from Third World countries, insists that so long as the demand structures, i.e., tastes and desires, of their countries remain linked to those of economically advanced cultures, the ability to transform their industrial sectors in the direction of small-scale, labor-intensive enterprises will be severely limited.

Lastly, the emphasis on the role of social institutions in the planning and implementation of rural development makes clear the importance of developing multi-disciplinary attitudes toward the problem. To stretch the point a bit, imagine a situation in which projects and programs had to pass an "implementability" test in much the same way that they are now required to pass scrutiny for economic benefits and costs. The need for sociologists, anthropologists, political scientists, etc., would be established overnight. To the faint hearted, this may sound preposterous. But the weight of the evidence regarding the need to confront, more honestly and openly, questions of power and privilege seems to me to be clear cut.[40] Indeed, "feasibility studies" of this type are constantly being done in an informal and unsystematic way. I submit that a large body of knowledge about human behavior and the workings of social systems exists that, if correctly approached, would permit us to do better.

Notes

1. Widely recognized references on the magnitude of the problem are David Turnham, *The Employment Problem in Less Developed Countries: A Review of the Evidence* (Paris, O.E.C.D. Development Centre, June, 1970); Robert Shaw, *Jobs and Agricultural Development,* Overseas Development Council, Monograph No. 3 (1970); Walter P. Falcon, "Agricultural Employment in Less Developed Countries: General Situation, Research Approaches and Policy Palliatives," Harvard University, mimeo (1971); and M. Yudelman, G. Butler, and R. Banerji, *Technological Change in Agriculture and Employment in Developing Countries* (Paris, O.E.C.D. Development Centre, 1971).

2. Arun Shourie's pessimistic description of the Indian experience could be easily extended to a number of other countries in Asia. Arun Shourie, "Growth and Employment," paper prepared for the Ford Foundation Seminar on Rural Development and Employment (Ibadan, April, 1973).

3. Keith Griffin, "UNDP-Global Two: Research Project on the Social and Economic Implications of the Large Scale Introduction of High Yielding Varieties of Food Grains: Policy Options" (Geneva, September, 1972).

4. Carl J. Friedrich, *Man and His Government,* as quoted in Ralph Braibanti, "The Policy Sciences and a General Theory of Political Change," (New York, The Asia Society, 1971), p. 16.

5. Ralph Braibanti, *op. cit.,* p. 13.

6. *Ibid.,* p. 14.

7. A.T. Mosher implicitly makes a similar distinction in the Preface of *Creating a Progressive Rural Structure* (New York, Agricultural Development Council, 1969), p. vi. In writing about the purpose of the book, he concludes: "It is a framework for thinking about the role of a Progressive Rural Structure and for searching for effective ways of creating it; it is *not* an operation blueprint."

8. Henry Bruton, "Economic Development and Labor Use: A Review," this book.

9. S.R. Lewis, Jr., "The Effects of Protection on the Growth Rate and on the Need for External Assistance," Research Memorandum No. 49, Center for Development Economics, Williams College (November, 1972).

10. For an argument linking policies that promote income disparity to the difficulty of creating institutions that can mobilize domestic resources in the public sector, see Richard Bird, "Income Redistribution, Economic Growth and Tax Policy," Proceedings of the Sixty-First Annual Conference on Taxation sponsored by the National Tax Association (Canada), 1968. Similar but somewhat broader arguments can be found in Mahbub ul Haq, "Employment in the 1970's: A New Perspective," *International Development Review,* XIII, 4 (1971), pp. 9-13; and Peter Dorner, "Needed Redirections in Economic Analysis for Agricultural Development Policy," *American Journal of Agricultural Economics,* 53 (February, 1971).

11. Shigeru Ishikawa, "Technological Change in Agricultural Production and Its Impact on Agrarian Structure—A Study on the So-Called Green Revolution," *Keiza Kenkyu,* Vol. 22, No. 2 (April, 1971) (my italics).

12. T.W. Schultz, *Transforming Traditional Agriculture* (New Haven, Yale University Press, 1964); and A.T. Mosher, *Promoting Agricultural Growth,* Agricultural Development Council, draft (1967).

13. For a preliminary report on a study of the quantitative effects of technological indivisibilities on income distribution in Pakistan, see Carl H. Gotsch and Shahid Yusuf, "Technological Indivisibilities and the Distribution of Income: A Mixed Integer Programming Model of Punjab Agriculture," Harvard University (October, 1973), mimeo.

14. Henry Bruton, *op. cit.*

15. Irving L. Horowitz, *Three Worlds of Development* (New York, Oxford University Press, 1972), pp. 403-404.

16. Max Weber, "Class, Status and Party" in Gerth and Mills, eds., *From Max Weber* (New York, Oxford University Press, 1946).

17. More detailed summaries of evidence and similar policy conclusions can be found in W.R. Cline, "Interrelationship Between Agricultural Strategy and Rural Income Distribution," paper presented at the conference on Strategies for Agricultural Development in the 1970's, Stanford University (December, 1971); and Keith Griffin, "Rural Development: The Policy Options," this book.

18. On the weakness of the "latent group" idea, see Mancur Olsen, *The Logic of Collective Action: Public Goods and the Theory of Groups* (New York, Schocken Books, 1968).

19. Corroborating evidence for Pakistan may be found in studies by Eckert, Hussain, the Punjab Planning & Development Department's Survey Unit, Lowdermilk and Rochin as summarized in Refugio I. Rochin, "The Impact of Dwarf Wheats on Farmers with Small Holdings in West Pakistan: Excerpts from Recent Studies," The Ford Foundation, Islamabad, mimeo (April, 1971). These results have been reinforced by survey material presented in Muhammed Naseem, "Small Farmers in the Agricultural Transformation of West Pakistan, unpublished Ph.D. thesis, University of California, Davis (1971).

Similar observations have been made in Bangladesh in LeVern Faidley and M.L. Esmay, "Introduction and Use of Improved Rice Varieties: Who Benefits? Some Observations from Comilla, East Pakistan," Michigan State University, Dept. of Agricultural Engineering (November, 1970). In the Philippines, Thamm has also indicated that where suitable ecological conditions exist, improved seeds have been taken up quickly by every cultivator class. See W.W. Thamm, *Introduction and Effects of High Yielding Varieties of Rice in the Philippines* (FAO, 1971).

In India, a survey of some 4,800 farms done under the auspices of the Intensive Agricultural Districts Program also supports the contention that, for the most part, small farmers have adopted new varieties with a minimal lag. See Carl C. Malone, "Improving Opportunities for Low-Income Farm-Occupied People: Some Indian Experience," paper presented at the Seminar on Small Farmer Development Strategies, Ohio State University (September, 1971).

General comments along the lines of the above appear in W.J. Staub and M.G. Balse, "Genetic Technology and Agricultural Development," *Science* (July 9, 1971).

20. The systematic interaction of marginal ecological environments with farm size in explaining the differential adoption of new wheat and maize varieties has received preliminary documentation in an oral presentation by Don Winklemann of CIMMYT and his collaborators at the Seminar on the Role of Social Sciences at the International Agricultural Research Center, IBRD, Washington, D.C., July 27-28, 1973. A somewhat similar argument emphasizing the general availability of adequate irrigation and drainage in explaining differences in diffusion by farm size can be found in Michael Schluter, "New Seed Varieties and the Small Farm," *Economic and Political Weekly* (India, March 25, 1972).

21. See Francine R. Frankel, "The Politics of the Green Revolution: Shifting Patterns of Peasant Participation in India and Pakistan," in Poleman and Freebairn, eds., *Food, Population and Employment: The Impact of the Green Revolution* (New York, Praeger, 1973), pp. 120-151.

22. For the details of the Pakistan case, see Carl H. Gotsch, "Tractor Mechanization and Rural Development in Pakistan," *International Labour Review,* Vol. 107, No. 2 (February, 1973).

23. An extensive discussion regarding the relationship between intermediate agricultural technology and local industry can be found in Peter Kilby and Bruce Johnston, "The Choice of Agricultural Strategy and the Development of Manufacturing," *Food Research Institute Studies in Agricultural Economics, Trade and Development,* Vol. XI (1972). For a case study in Pakistan, see Hiromitsu Kaneda and Frank Child, "Small-Scale, Agriculturally Related Industry in the Punjab," Working Paper Series, No. 11, University of California, Davis (1971).

24. C. Peter Timmer, "Choice of Technique in Indonesia," paper presented at the Harvard Development Advisory Conference, Torremolinos (1972).

25. For a description of the role of tubewells in the Comilla Project, Bangladesh, see Carl Gotsch, "Technological Change and the Distribution of Income in Rural Areas," *American Journal of Agricultural Economics* (May, 1972).

26. Andre Beteille, "The Social Framework of Agriculture," in Louis Lefeber and Mrinal Datta-Chaudhuri, *Regional Development Experiences and Prospects in South and Southeast Asia* (The Hague, Mouton & Co., 1971), pp. 114-164.

27. Considerable evidence on this point is presented in Millard F. Long, "Conditions of the Success of Small Farmer Credit Programs," paper prepared for the Spring Review on Agricultural Credit by U.S.A.I.D., Washington, D.C., (1973) mimeo. Relevant also is the summary paper for the conference prepared by Rice. E.B. Rice, "Summary of the Spring Review of Small Farmer Credit," *Small Farmer Credit Summary Papers,* A.I.D. Spring Review of Small Farmer Credit, Vol. XX (June, 1973).

28. Arun Shourie, *op. cit.;* and John Thomas, "Employment Creating Public Works Programs: Observations on Political and Social Dimensions," this book.

29. Shahid Javed Burki, "Interest Group Involvement in West Pakistan's Rural Works Program," *Public Policy,* Vol. XIX (Winter, 1971).

30. Akhter Hamid Khan, "Tour of Twenty Thanas," Pakistan Academy for Rural Development (1970).

31. Andre Beteille, *op. cit.,* pp. 146-147.

32. Guvant Desai and Michael Schluter, "Generating Employment in Rural Areas," Seminar on Rural Development for Weaker Sections, Indian Institute of Management, Ahmedbad (October, 1972) mimeo.

33. For a discussion of this "straddle" phenomenon in Latin America, see A. Eugene Havens and William L. Flinn, "Introduction: Internal Colonialism, Structural Change, and National Development" in Havens and Flinn, eds., *Internal Colonialism and Structural Change in Colombia* (New York, Praeger Publishers, 1970), pp. 3-18.

34. John Mellor, private correspondence (June, 1971).

35. Solon Barraclough, FAO/SIDA Symposium on Agricultural Institutions for Integrated Rural Development (Rome, FAO, June, 1971).

36. John Montgomery, "Land Reform Administration as a Factor in Social Change," Harvard University, mimeo, n.d.

37. Wolf Ladejinsky, "The Green Revolution in the Punjab," *Economic and Political Weekly,* Review of Agriculture (June, 1969). This point has also been underscored by Frankel, *op. cit.*

38. See Bruce Johnston and Peter Kilby, *Agricultural Strategies, Rural-Urban Interactions and the Expansion of Income Opportunities* (Paris, O.E.C.D. Development Centre, 1971).

39. For a summary of studies in this area, see R.F. Hopkins, "Securing Authority: The View from the Top," *World Politics* (January, 1972).

40. J.K. Galbraith has developed this point extensively in his Presidential Address to the American Economics Association. For the text of his remarks, see Galbraith, "Power and the Useful Economist," *American Economic Review* (March, 1973).

II

Selected Papers
on Generic Issues

The Limited Value of Employment Policies for Income Inequality

L.S. Jarvis*

*The Ford Foundation, Santiago, Chile, and
University of California, Berkeley*

A Definition of the Problem

In recent years a number of economists have expressed concern about the level of unemployment in many developing countries, and have advocated the implementation of "employment programs" as a means of improving the employment situation. The emphasis on employment has resulted from what is perceived to be a failure of past development efforts. The failure, however, is not one of insufficient growth, but rather of the insufficient improvement in social welfare brought about by growth. This distinction is important.

Most of the development strategies adopted during the last two decades sought an increase in gross national product and these strategies frequently achieved their goal. Various studies have demonstrated that the less-developed countries have grown in recent years, on average, more rapidly than did the now-developed countries at similar stages of historical development (per capita income levels), and also more rapidly than they themselves had done previously.[1] But although development strategies achieved their stated goal of higher income growth, the benefits of this growth have not been widely shared. Unemployment has continued to occur in countries achieving relatively high rates of per capita income growth, and in several of those countries whose growth rates have been particularly high the poorest groups have not even benefited absolutely and have lost ground relatively.**

Thus, while rapid growth created expectations that widespread social welfare improvements would be forthcoming within the developing countries, the results achieved in this area have been much less than hoped. The recognition of the severity of current poverty and inequality, and the fact that they have not been greatly alleviated by growth policies, have caused many economists to suggest in recent

* I have received helpful criticism and suggestions from numerous persons, among whom I would like to thank especially Peter Bell, Richard Fagen, Patricio Meller, Joseph Ramos, and Victor Tokman. I also benefited from general discussions with, and the written work of, Alejandro Foxley and Oscar Munoz, who have been concerned with similar issues within the context of the Chilean economy.

** Weisskoff estimates that in Mexico, despite a 37 percent increase in per capita gross national product between 1950 and 1963, the percentage of the total income received by the poorest 30 percent declined from 9.9 percent to 7.6 percent. The real income of this group remained essentially constant during the period. Fishlow demonstrates that Brazilian growth during the 1960s was accompanied by a deterioration in the distribution of income, and little real income growth for the poorest half of the population. Bardhan estimates that in India the percentage of rural persons whose incomes were below a constant well-defined minimum level of living rose from 38 percent to 54 percent between 1960-61 and 1968-69. In absolute numbers, this represents a rise from 135 to 230 million persons.[2]

years that growth has been overemphasized to the exclusion of distributional concerns. Programs to increase employment are advocated by some as a solution to the problem.

In this paper I shall take a discordant view by arguing that employment, although an important subsidiary issue, is not the proper focus of policy concern in the less developed countries. Instead of employment, policy should focus on income growth and income distribution. I do not wish to argue that unemployment is unimportant, or that governments should be unconcerned to ensure the full and best utilization of their population's labor services. But income growth and distribution seem better to characterize the level of individual and social welfare, and an emphasis on them is more likely to improve welfare than is an emphasis on employment per se.

I see most of the new policy emphases which have been suggested recently, including the goal of providing employment to all, as a recognition that social welfare, at least over some range of income inequality within a nation, depends more importantly on the distribution of income than on the level of income. Certainly the highly unequal distribution of income currently prevailing in many developing countries suggests that distributional questions and/or poverty ought to be receiving primary importance. If, however, the primary issue is one of income distribution or, more broadly stated, equality of opportunity, it seems better to focus attention explicitly on this objective rather than on an issue which is only indirectly related, such as employment, and which may not result in the desired solution.*

The intent of "employment policies" seems to be to increase employment and simultaneously to improve the distribution of income. As the poor earn higher discretionary incomes, they are expected to be able to bid in the marketplace for improved education, nutrition, medical care, and housing. The "employment program" is thus expected to enable the poor to obtain those necessities which are now denied them.

I think such an outcome is unlikely. The evidence which I will present shortly suggests that (what might be termed) conventional "employment policies" will not greatly affect the distribution of income, or, more importantly, the distribution of "essential" goods and services, even if these policies are applied in the best of faith. Development must bring, and stem from, the provision of better, more productive and more remunerative employment for today's lower income groups, but we should distinguish between the need to increase the productivity of workers in the lower income groups, which is necessary if the dual economy is to be eradicated (and which is a dynamic process involving numerous factors and requiring a lengthy period of time), and the problem of putting the actually unemployed to work at jobs which they will accept. A third problem is to ensure that the distribution and composition of consumption, as well as its aggregate level, are socially optimal. The latter issue forces attention directly on how to increase the current welfare of the poorer sectors of society, including precise means by which the basic goods and services they require can be provided. This is a technical question of considerable difficulty.

The other serious problem with employment programs, which is alluded to above, is that they mean different things to different persons. An examination of the different

---

* It may be argued that it is poverty, and not income inequality per se, which is most in need of attention. This view recognizes the need to guarantee each individual at least certain basic requirements, but balks at giving relative incomes themselves so great an importance, or perhaps reflects a belief that it is best not to engage in the socially disruptive process of redistribution. However, the decision to provide basic requirements to all, if taken seriously, is a decision, in fact, to engage in some redistribution. The amount of redistribution depends on the level and type of basic requirements which it is decided to provide.

groups advocating employment policies suggests a diversity of interests and logic, and a wide variety of programs seems to fall within the rubric of "employment programs." This variety, and ambiguity, may lead to confusion in policy making, and, worse, serve to cover up issues which ought to be confronted by economists, politicians and policy makers. Some may have a genuine interest in employment problems per se; others may seize upon it as a noncontroversial means of raising arguments for fundamental social reforms; and still others may use employment issues as a political stepping stone. Thus the employment issue may simply divert attention from more fundamental issues or provide an umbrella of legitimacy for other social or political concerns. Such diverse purposes are better reconciled in open discussion.

This paper now proceeds in three parts. In the first I argue that unemployment is only one aspect of the long-term disregard for equity considerations in the less developed countries wherein the sacrificing of the poorer classes' welfare has been justified as a temporary requirement of higher economic growth. The policies recently suggested to increase employment are briefly reviewed and criticized from this perspective. I argue that several of the suggested "employment policies" are in fact efficiency, not equity oriented, and ought to be taken irrespective of concern for distributional issues. For example, certain past development strategies, especially overprotectionist policies, were inefficient and resulted in less income growth (and correspondingly less employment growth) than was theoretically possible. Such policy errors should be corrected. However, although such actions might improve the distribution of income, assuming that those whose labor services are now most poorly used are most strongly affected, it is not certain that this improvement will actually occur, and particularly not in the immediate future.

Other "employment policies" are more specifically concerned with distributional issues, e.g., those which consider the tradeoff between income growth and employment creation, but these policies, even if helpful, are insufficient to solve the distributional problem. Moreover, an increasing number of the studies appearing recently on the growth-employment issue state there is no such tradeoff—the policies which maximize employment, if properly conceived, will maximize growth as well.[3] Thus, the employment focus risks making an issue which arose as a question of equity into one of efficiency, hiding and reducing the concentration on redistribution which is the only means by which the problem can be alleviated in the short run, and perhaps the only long run solution as well.*

---

* To the extent that newly recognized problems cause us to reexamine, and discard, previously accepted theories which are now shown to be inadequate or incorrect, the employment focus is clearly of benefit. This benefit certainly occurs when a new policy is designed which will provide higher growth along with greater employment. There is no reason to turn away from policies which move us closer to Pareto optimality just because one believes that distributional issues remain important. However, many of the studies which purport to have found a positive association between employment growth and income growth, emphasize the growth of manufacturing employment, not the growth of total employment. There are important differences. Ramos, for example, has provocatively suggested that

   . . . earlier development strategies have (in fact) been far more successful in generating productive employment than has been generally recognized.

He states that the critical reports which have emerged regarding low rates of employment creation

   . . . have overlooked equally significant data which indicate that the increase in open unemployment or underemployment has been accompanied by an even faster decrease in disguised unemployment or underemployment so that the net effect has been a reduction in the relative abundance of labor in most Latin American countries . . .[4]

I suspect that Ramos could be correct, but even if so, that many policy makers would still not wish to change their emphasis on employment generation. It is open urban unemployment, not underemployment in rural areas, which threatens political stability, and which employment policies are chiefly designed to arrest.

In the second part of this paper I attempt to justify more fully the assertion that employment programs, as conventionally defined, will not significantly affect the distribution of income. I do this by citing evidence on the causes of income inequality within the developing countries, and on the characteristics of the unemployed themselves, for whom direct benefits must be projected.

In the third part of the paper I discuss an alternative approach by which the current welfare of the poor can be improved more satisfactorily than with an emphasis on employment, suggesting the extensive use of public goods and publicly distributed goods. This approach is not intended to be unique, nor particularly novel, but it emphasizes the necessity to design programs which will attack consumption needs directly rather than accepting that the working of the market mechanism in the developing country will "eventually" satisfy such social needs. Governments frequently "overintervene" in the market mechanism, but rarely do they overprovide the poor with basic necessities.

A Critical Evaluation of the "Employment Policy" Approach

Higher employment is advocated to utilize resources more fully, and thereby to increase output. However, the existence of unemployment, and underemployment, is not a new phenomenon, and it had not been neglected in the literature prior to the recent interest. For example, the causes and consequences of surplus labor, and the development opportunities offered have been discussed for more than two decades. This discussion is worth mention.

The Lewis model of growth assumed that underemployment, if not unemployment, exists. Lewis emphasized the desirability of providing highly productive employment in the modern industrial sector to labor which currently has only low (or zero) productivity in the agricultural sector. He also assumed existing institutions would restrain the growth of wages for some period of time. Thus, the provision of industrial employment was not expected to create a rapid improvement in the distribution of income, nor was this improvement thought desirable, for it could only have occurred by reducing profits and thereby the rate of investment and growth.

While the Lewis model acknowledged the existence of widespread unemployment, it assumed that the fastest means to its elimination was to invest as rapidly as possible. And this rapid growth is made possible by the very existence of unemployment. Because wages are restrained, and capitalists are assumed to invest all profits, the increased productivity which results as labor is transferred from agriculture to industry can be transformed directly into the increased production of capital goods.

Whether or not the Lewis model correctly represents the situation in the majority of the less developed countries, or whether the proposed growth strategy is the best growth strategy possible, it cannot be denied that this model, and its derivations, have profoundly influenced policy making. Given this influence, it is hardly consistent to argue that today's unemployment or the skewness in the distribution of income in the LDC's was unintended. The development strategies advocated during the last twenty years have consistently sought an increase in the level of incomes, but certainly no leveling of incomes. Specific theoretical justifications have been developed to support increasing skewness of the income distribution as a means of obtaining increased savings and thereby higher investment.

The argument frequently has been made that current consumption must be sacrificed in order to obtain higher future consumption, and it is the incomes of the lower class that must be restrained, as these are the individuals who cannot be trusted independently to save and invest at a sufficient rate. A variation of this theory, the choice-of-techniques issue, has expressly justified leaving individuals unemployed as a means of restraining consumption, even though some output may be lost in the process.

It therefore seems to me ironic, and incorrect, to suggest that the current unemployment problems are the result of policy failure. The outcome was a predictable result of policies which were frequently advocated. The severity of the problem was, perhaps, underestimated, but unemployment was asserted to be a necessary evil in the short run.

It must be emphasized, however, that the choice-of-techniques issue is not an argument against employment per se. It is an argument against an improved income distribution which is assumed to lead to lower savings and, therefore, to reduced growth; the choice-of-techniques case is an argument against employment only in a second-best world where employment must be remunerative, where the poor do not save sufficiently on their own accord, and where the government does not have other instruments to achieve *ex post* the desired level of savings and investment at fuller employment. In fact, however, it would not be unfair to argue that the choice-of-techniques issue is an excuse for an unequal division of the social product, with special benefits for those in the "modern" sector, including bureaucrats, technocrats, and professionals, as well as the propertied class.*

I emphasize the roots of the current employment problem because I believe we must acknowledge its origins if we are to try effectively to alleviate it. Unemployment is only one aspect of the long-term disregard for the welfare of the poor which has been justified as being necessary to increase the rate of growth. This pursuit has been aided and abetted by conventional development strategies, most of which have been designed to be compatible with the existing social and political structure.**

If unemployment is a symptomatic rather than a fundamental problem, it is unlikely that conventional employment programs will cope adequately with the deeper problem of inequality. To demonstrate this inadequacy, however, is made difficult by the proliferation of factors (and corresponding policies) alleged to be associated with unemployment. Bruton, for example, mentions underutilization, capital formation, wage policy, import substitution, productivity growth, foreign trade, education, and population as being important factors.[6] I agree that policy changes in these areas may affect the level and composition of employment, but I believe each of these factors has as much claim to independent policy interest as does employment. Each of these policy areas has an impact on economic growth and on income distribution, and it is worth examining what the specific effects may be. However, the tendency to classify policies in terms of their employment effects seems to confuse the issue.

To permit further discussion, I have selected four general "employment policies." These policies seem to have the creation of employment as a primary goal, and each is

---

* The classical model sometimes suggests that the marginal propensity to save out of capital income is one. Although this assumption is extreme, Adelman and Morris present data for 44 developing countries suggesting that if the wealthiest 5 percent saved even one-half their income, the savings ratio would average at least 15 percent. If the wealthiest 20 percent save one-half, the savings rate would be at least 28 percent. If income skewness is justified to permit increased savings, it would appear that the wealthy classes in these countries are not doing their job. Houthakker has shown that during the 1950s an unweighted average of personal savings in 8 of the 44 countries considered by Adelman and Morris, was only 2.6 percent, and the unweighted average of domestic savings in 12 of the 44 countries was only 8.3 percent. Perhaps it is the rich whose incomes should be constrained if savings are to be increased.[5]

** Some say such compatibility is a necessary feature of "good" theory.

mentioned in the literature as being an "employment policy." I shall argue that it is not evident that any of the programs which have been advocated will create large amounts of employment in the short run. In the third section of this paper I will discuss the effect which limited employment creation is likely to have on the distribution of income.

I emphasize that I believe the rationale for changing development strategies is the necessity to deal with income inequality and its manifest effects in the immediate future. The longer run situation is much less at issue because increasing the amount of current investment should provide a larger stock of capital through time, and eventually both higher income and employment.[7] This can be made clear by reference again to the choice-of-techniques issue. The choice of the particular productive techniques, from more to less labor intensive, used to produce a particular good depends on the social rate of discount, i.e., the preference between current and future consumption. The higher are current output and employment, the lower are savings and investment, and the lower is the rate of growth of future income. Current employment can be increased in this way, but only at the expense of future output, or by changing the institutional structure to enable savings to be extracted at higher rates from the working poor.

This theory creates the basis for an "employment program." Labor-intensive techniques may be chosen, maximizing current employment at the expense of investment.* The resolution of the tradeoff, however, if it exists, depends less on the development of new economic theories than on political volition, i.e., whether policy makers are sufficiently concerned with existing unemployment to be willing to reduce the rate of aggregate growth in order to achieve more employment. Such programs may create "more" employment than policies designed to maximize the rate of investment, but any program which depends on the course of future investment for its effects cannot have a pronounced impact on employment opportunities in the short run.

A second "employment program" assumes that it is possible and profitable to develop an "intermediate" technology which is expected to conform more favorably to the less developed countries' factor endowments. To be successful, research must develop more efficient labor-intensive techniques. I doubt the importance of this approach in solving the problem immediately at hand. Economists have discussed the need for an intermediate technology for some years and yet have had practically no effect on engineering development or investment selection. I know of no reason why the result might suddenly change.** To implement this policy also requires significant time, necessitating the development of the technology as well as making the investment, and the policy must confront the choice-of-techniques problem described above.

A third "employment program" is a Keynesian effort to utilize more fully the

---

* A variation on this theme permits any subsidiary goal to receive special weight, such as encouraging regional growth at the expense of aggregate growth. As was discussed previously, recent studies have suggested that the tradeoff between growth and employment is not so great, and may not exist at all. On the other hand, these studies may merely confirm that this approach will not create much more employment than did the previous approach.

** Stewart provides an excellent summary of the problems, and the possibilities available through the development of new intermediate techniques. After reading her paper I am somewhat more optimistic than previously, and I should like to reassert that I am not opposed to such development, to the contrary. However, I would also reemphasize that the development of new technology will be slow, and is at least as much oriented toward increasing social efficiency as social equity. Such programs may or may not significantly affect the income distribution.[8]

existing stock of capital, assuming this effort will result in increased labor demand as well. The approach requires (1) a significant *ex ante* underutilization of capacity in industrial activities, (2) the existence of markets in which the increased output can be sold, and (3) the availability of the necessary complementary inputs in production. It does not require changing the labor intensity of any activity, but only the time intensity of use of the existing plant. It thus can have a faster impact than the two programs discussed previously, although it is limited in the degree to which employment can be increased by the degree to which utilization is below capacity. A direct impact on employment can be achieved only in the industrial areas of most less developed countries.

A fourth "employment program" seeks to change the composition of output toward more labor-intensive *products,* expecting that more labor can be employed to produce the same value of output, though not the same type of output. The approach requires no change in technology, but a change in the type of goods produced. This effort may involve a switch from import-substituting investment, which usually requires production of increasingly capital-intensive products, to the production of labor-intensive goods for export; or the redistribution of domestic income resulting in a different composition of internal demand; or a change in government investment priorities toward labor-intensive projects such as public works activities. Each of these approaches must face a variation of the choice-of-techniques issue. Note that the second policy suggests that a redistribution of income leads to higher employment, rather than vice versa.[9]

Several other general policies might lead toward increased employment, but I believe the strategies outlined above fairly represent the policies conventionally included when "employment programs" are discussed. Such programs are likely to have only a limited effect on employment in the short run. These programs operate gradually because they depend on future investment for their effects, or they are limited because they seek means of employing more people by using the existing capital assets more intensively, but without fundamentally changing the institutional structure.

Let us now examine more carefully what employment programs are expected to achieve beyond employment per se. Conventional employment programs assume that poverty is caused by the inability to find work and suggest that this inability, and thereby poverty, can be overcome by improving investment decisions, including altering the technology used. In contrast, I believe that the problem in many countries is not that there is no work to do, but that the work done by many is both too hard and too little remunerative—while others work little and receive much. People are poor because they have nothing to sell; they have few personal skills and abilities and control no physical capital or land. It is not at all clear that employment programs will alter this situation.

We must determine, for example, how much incomes would be changed if particular employment programs were to be enacted. Which individuals have the lowest incomes in society? Is this group composed primarily of the unemployed? Can they work? At what tasks? Are these the tasks which will be created by the proposed employment programs? One must also distinguish between the level and the distribution of income. There is no guarantee that employment programs will improve the distribution, as opposed to the level of income. They might well merely twist the distribution, making it slightly more equal at the bottom, assuming this is where the new jobs are created, while making it more unequal at the top, where the profits from the increased activity would be concentrated. This result is likely if the evidence from the cyclical experience of developed countries is acceptable as a guide.*

In arguing that conventional "employment programs" do not face up to the problem of inequality, I do not imply, of course, that employment programs will necessarily be rejected by those who have the power to influence this decision. To the contrary, the concentration of the unemployed and lower income groups in urban areas is perceived by elites, and some policy makers, as a threat to political stability. The urban unemployed are thought to be better informed than the rural poor, more conscious of their relative position in society, and more easily able to organize in defense of their own interests. For these reasons, those interested in preserving the status quo may look to an "employment program" as a means of reducing current discontent, and thereby postponing more fundamental reforms. Conventional employment programs do not threaten the rich, they require no upheaval of the existing system, and they justify the continued dominance of the technocrats who are empowered to carry out the gradual creation of jobs, often working hand in hand with the existing vested interests. Employment programs appear to be good for all. There is a harmony of interests, the rich hire the poor.

Some Causes of Income Skewness in Developing Countries

I now turn to the specific relationship between unemployment and income distribution. The factors determining income distribution are complex and I do not pretend to define all the factors involved, nor their magnitudes. Nonetheless, there is sufficient evidence available to demonstrate that if one puts the currently unemployed to work, one will not greatly change the distribution of income.

Adelman and Morris estimate that in over one-half of 44 less developed countries, the average income received by the lowest 20 percent is only one-fourth the national per capita average. Moreover, the average income received by the poorest 60 percent is less than half the national per capita average.[11] A very large proportion of the population in these countries is extremely poor.

The distribution of personal income is a weighted function of the distribution of property income and the distribution of labor income. If changes in the latter caused by employment programs do not significantly affect the former, the overall distribution of income is not likely to be greatly improved.

The distribution of property income has been estimated for relatively few less developed countries. Webb's study of Peru is a notable exception.[12] He shows that in

---

* Profit levels in the U.S. are very sensitive to cyclical changes, considerably more so, for example, than wage levels. Data regarding the income distribution in the U.S. suggests that major cyclical events may affect the distribution of income in a perverse fashion, that is, an increase in economic activity increases the share of the highest decile and decreases the share of the lower deciles. Consider the following data.[10] I have denoted years high (H) and low (L) to indicate the level of private economic activity.

Income accruing to:	Highest 10 percent	Lowest 30 percent
1929 (H)	39.0	10.0
1934 (L)	33.6	11.3
1945 (L)	29.0	10.0
1947 (H)	33.5	9.7
1950 (L)	28.7	9.0
1953 (H)	31.4	8.9
1958 (L)	27.1	9.0

During the 1960s some U.S. economists advocated a policy of high aggregate demand, even at the cost of price inflation, in order to provide greater employment for the poorer classes. This policy sought to improve the absolute, but not necessarily the relative incomes of these groups.

Peru nonlabor income (property income) is more unequally distributed than is labor income, being especially concentrated in the top decile. Webb finds that the wealthiest 1 percent in Peru receive 80 percent of property income, but only 10 percent of labor income. This group receives 31 percent of total national income: 23 percent from property and 8 percent from labor services. And the wealthiest 10 percent receive 90 percent of property income, 30 percent of labor income, and approximately 56 percent of total income.

Webb argues that the distribution of income could be significantly improved by the redistribution of property incomes. He says

> . . . a selective transfer of 5 percent of the national income, taken from the richest 1 percent and given to the poorest 25 percent, would reduce the absolute incomes of the rich by only 16 percent and would double the average income for a third of the population. If the alternative to redistribution is growth, a highly successful development effort consisting of sustained growth of 3 percent in real income at all levels would require nearly 20 years to achieve the same increase for the poorest third of the population.*

Similar estimates of the skewness of the property income distribution are available from McLure's studies of Panama and Colombia, although he is forced by his data to combine self-employment income with property income.[13] The fact that property income in McLure's studies is not completely separate from self-employment income somewhat muddles the picture, because self-employment income includes the wages received by highly paid professionals as well as the income earned by poor farmers working small plots. Nonetheless, the concentration of nonsalary income is so marked that it is unlikely that the situation could be significantly changed by removing self-employment incomes. Using Panamanian tax data, McLure makes two estimates which allocate respectively a greater and lesser income to small farmers. Depending on the estimate chosen, between 55 and 70 percent of nonsalary income accrues to the upper 10 percent of nonsalary income recipients. Nonsalary income accounts for over 40 percent of national income.

McLure's documentation of income sources also permits the determination of the concentration of income receipts from ownership of large farms and major corporations. These receipts alone amount to approximately 12 percent of national income under McLure's more conservative assumptions, and accrue almost exclusively to the upper 5 percent of property income recipients. When the property receipts from other economic sectors are included, as well as rental income and owner-occupied housing, the property income accruing to the upper 5 percent of the population amounts to approximately 25 percent of national income. If this income were distributed *equally* across *all* income recipients, the incomes of the lower 25 percent would increase by approximately 80 percent and the incomes of the second quartile by approximately 50 percent.

Are these estimates atypical of less developed countries? The data in Adelman and Morris suggest that income in Peru probably is somewhat more skewed than is the case in most other developed countries, but not so extremely as to change the basic conclusions. And the incomes in Panama and Colombia appear quite similarly distributed to those in numerous other countries.

The ownership of wealth is not the sole determinant of income differentials in developing countries, and the achievement of greater equality in the distribution of

---

* The choice of 16 percent may have been dictated by Kuznet's observation that in the United States, Sweden and the United Kingdom the shares of the upper 5 percent of the population are diminished only by between 10 and 20 percent after taxes.

property income will not produce instant income equality. However, it is clear that property incomes are sufficiently large in magnitude, and sufficiently unequally distributed, to explain a large part of the static inequality in total income receipts. Capital ownership is also a major means by which inequality is transmitted from one generation to the next.

Having discussed the role of property incomes, I now consider the extent to which income distribution could be improved if the unemployed individuals in particular age, sex, education, and sectoral categories could be employed at tasks similar to those performed by others with similar characteristics. This is, of course, only a crude indicator of the relationship between employment and income distribution, but a reasonable first step. Data on these relationships are scarce and rather crude indicators must serve at present.

Unemployment is severe in many countries, but the data presented in Turnham and Ramos suggest the aggregate rate of unemployment generally does not exceed 10 percent, and the unemployed are rarely unemployed throughout the year.[14] Moreover, the individuals who are reported as being unemployed in the less-developed countries also appear to be the most difficult to employ and those who, when they work, enjoy the lowest incomes.* They are the young, the old, the less experienced, the less educated, female, and family dependents.[15] Further, although open unemployment rates in rural areas are lower than in urban areas, the high proportion of the labor force in agriculture means a high proportion of the total unemployed are in agriculture.**

Intersectoral wage differentials among the employed rather than unemployment itself, are responsible for a large part of the labor income inequality in less-developed countries. Thorbecke and Sengupta derive the size distribution of labor income in Colombia from differences in average sectoral incomes, and find that the great differences among sectors could explain a significant portion of the total income inequality observed.[17] For example, the 60 percent of the Colombian population working in "personal services and agriculture" earn wages averaging only about one-eighth of those earned by the upper 5 percent working in "government services, finance, and utilities."

On the other hand, the wage differentials observed in the less-developed countries do not appear to be due to pure efficiency differentials. Turnham presents data for the ratio of skilled to unskilled wages in 20 less-developed countries, and the differences are marked. In Africa, the ratio is 1.57 in Nigeria and 2.87 in the Congo; in Latin America, the ratio ranges from 1.32 in Argentina to 2.09 in Chile and 2.12 in Mexico.[18] Strober also finds that even within the manufacturing sectors in the

---

* There is an exception to this rule—the "highly educated" unemployed often refuse to work at jobs which are readily available, but which do not call for the full use of their "intellectual" skills, or are otherwise unsatisfactory. In discussion at the Ford Foundation's Seminar on the Employment Process, Bogota, February 1973, Ronald Dore pointed out that a significant amount of unemployment in the less developed countries, particularly in urban areas, is cultural in nature. Individuals are unemployed only because they are unwilling to accept existing employment opportunities, having been trained for different jobs, desiring higher incomes than the available job provides, or wishing to live at a different place in the country. To be successful then, an employment program must create those jobs which will satisfy the particular individuals who are unemployed, and not just provide random new jobs. The problem is not simply one of aggregate demand, or of the availability of complementary factors, but one of matching the expectations which certain groups have come to hold. And not all the culturally unemployed are highly trained.

** Contrary to some views, studies for Chile, Colombia and Brazil suggest that the unemployed are not concentrated among recent migrants living in urban slums. Fishlow has suggested that migrants, although not especially highly qualified by urban standards, nonetheless find employment rapidly, displacing at times existing urban residents.[16]

less-developed countries, although the wage differentials are very marked, the hierarchy is not subject to explanation by such factors as " 'differences in industries' skill levels, productivity levels, changes in productivity, employment changes, labor intensities, 'female intensities,' profit levels, changes in output, product market concentrations, and unionization." She concludes that "in underdeveloped economies non-economic or accidental elements may play a significant role in wage structure formation."[19]

Thus, we may conclude that sectoral differences are not due to employment and unemployment, but to the duality of the economy, including the differences in employment opportunities (quasi-rents) available to different individuals.

Fishlow's detailed study of income distribution in Brazil suggests the same result. To study the characteristics of the poor, he groups together the 31 percent of the population in families whose total income in 1960 was below the minimum wage—a low level indeed in Brazil.* Nearly 70 percent of these poor work in the agricultural sector and nearly 10 percent more in services. He concludes: "The Brazilian problem is [not one of poverty resulting from] single-person households, the aged, families headed by females, and families whose head is not participating in the labor force [but rather] more one of low levels of productivity within the mainstream of the rural economy."**

The Role of Public Goods and Publicly Distributed Goods in Improving Social Welfare

The highly unequal distribution of income observed in less developed countries is largely due to the unequal distribution of property income and to differences among individuals in education, experience (age), intelligence (which is affected by past nutrition, health, and other environmental factors), sex, occupation, and sectoral location.

Although a redistribution of income, principally from those receiving property income and high labor incomes, is necessary if the current welfare of the poor is to be significantly improved, the solution sought must be consistent with economic growth. It also must be feasible politically. The technical and the political problems facing significant redistribution, even when redistribution is carried out dynamically with higher absolute incomes for all, are immense. Redistribution is difficult to achieve, and it is equally difficult to ensure that redistribution results in the desired improvement of social welfare ex post. The economist has a handbag of policy tools which theoretically may be utilized for income redistribution, but theory in this area often is easier to develop than to apply.

Tax and transfer policies are among the most frequently suggested approaches for affecting redistribution, yet the administrative mechanisms available in most developing countries are insufficient to the task. Few studies have been made of the

---

* The distribution of family income is a better indicator of relative welfare than is the distribution of personal income because family income is largely pooled, members enjoying similar benefits. Family income is more evenly distributed than is individual income because those earning, or reporting low incomes are frequently family dependents. However, family dependents may be the more difficult to employ at full-time occupations, and may even retire from the labor force if other family members gain additional work.

** Fishlow states that the 50 percent of the population at the bottom of the income scale in Brazil includes a sizeable proportion of retired persons or pensioners, as well as practically all rural wage earners, small artisans, and the personal services sector in the large cities. Fishlow's results confirm the fact that 13 percent of poor families have heads of households over 60.[20]

redistributive effect of current tax systems in developing countries; McLure's studies of Panama and Colombia are exceptions.[21] Neither of these studies is encouraging; the tax system seems to make almost no difference in the income distribution in either case.

Wage and price policies may also be utilized to alter the income distribution. Unfortunately, it is difficult administratively to control wages in some sectors of the economy, especially agriculture, where wages are especially low, and price controls often lead to severe distortions in the pattern of production and in the functioning of the distribution system. As a result, these policies are unlikely to form the basis for a national policy of income redistribution, particularly within the context of a private or mixed economy.

Nationalization of property, such as land reform and the socialization of industry may be a prerequisite for significant redistribution, and yet, even when the political muscle can be obtained to initiate such a program, the subsequent administrative and motivational problems can result in economic disruptions of very serious magnitude.* And certain types of property, such as human capital, cannot be nationalized effectively and must be dealt with carefully if their services are to be retained.**

Although any given single policy is likely to be insufficient in bringing about the desired improvement in the current welfare of the poorest classes in the developing countries, a set of policies, tailored to fit the particular needs and institutional structure of each country, may do much better.*** In considering different policies, however, I believe too little emphasis is generally given to the potential and advantages of using public goods and publicly distributed goods for improving the real distribution of income. The tendency to ignore this possibility stems partly from the bias imparted by the classical tradition in economics, which assumes that within the context of a competitive, well-functioning market system, it is best to effect redistribution through money incomes which subsequently allow each individual a direct voice in the determination of the goods produced for consumption. This "bias" has much to recommend it, but as I will discuss shortly, it can be exaggerated.

It is worth mentioning first, however, that most studies of income distribution have paid little attention to the real income received in the form of goods which are not purchased in the market. Fishlow makes adjustments for income received in kind when calculating the Brazilian size distribution of income, but I am unaware of any studies that make adjustments to their estimates even for the receipt of educational or

---

* Recent Chilean history exemplifies the situation wherein after the partial confiscation of the incomes of the wealthier 5 percent, it became markedly more difficult for the government to continue redistribution. While the redistribution attempted was not always undertaken in an efficient manner, efforts at further redistribution led to sharp conflicts between the "middle" income groups and the poor. These "middle" income groups, although clearly within the upper two income deciles, regarded their higher labor incomes as resulting from deserved skill differentials, and were adamantly opposed to the confiscation of their property assets (which they felt they had achieved through superior effort) and to the imposition of sharply higher taxes. Because the "middle" classes were relatively numerous and well organized, particularly in the major urban centers, their opposition was a key obstacle in the government's efforts to continue the "socialization" of Chile. The "middle" groups also included the professionals and technocrats whose cooperation was necessary to the continued operation of the country.

** International mobility presents a major problem because those individuals possessing skills which will secure them a preferred life abroad are frequently of significant technical need domestically. Although coercive techniques can be used to alleviate this problem in the short run, only the development of a system permitting personal satisfaction under more modest personal circumstances is a long-run solution, if incomes are actually to be made more equal.

***Several authors have noted the technical complexity of and the consequent need to use a multiplicity of instruments in order to effectively carry the desired benefits of "redistribution" to all the poorer groups.[22]

medical services, when' supplied by the state, let alone the variety of other public goods or publicly distributed goods which are potentially important to individual and social welfare. Data on these quantities are difficult to obtain, but I suspect that their distribution is not less unequal than the distribution of money income.*

In this context, however, I am not specifically concerned with the measurement of the existing distribution of nonprivate income, but rather with the potential for using goods and services so distributed for effecting a redistribution of real income which achieves a larger degree of current individual welfare, consistent with significant economic growth. I emphasize the need to salvage growth; decreasing the consumption of the rich is an insufficient response to the need to increase the current welfare of the poor. However, it will be possible to improve significantly the current welfare of the poorer classes and increase the growth rate as well only if the consumption "chosen" leads directly or indirectly, through higher motivation and ability, to greater investment. Fortunately, I believe many of the goods which have a large impact upon current welfare also provide a major stimulus to growth and long-term social welfare. These commodities are defined "essential" goods and services, on the grounds that their provision is essential to both short-run and long-run welfare.

It must be emphasized, however, that the provision of essential goods and services to the poorer classes requires *both* a change in the distribution of income *and* the construction of facilities to produce and distribute the goods and services to the point of consumption. In many countries, the state must play a major role in the production and distribution of these goods and services, especially in the short run, because the market mechanism works inadequately (particularly in those areas where the essential commodities are most badly needed), and because some goods can be provided efficiently only by the state, i.e., public goods. In essence, the systematic extension of certain opportunities to the populace as a whole requires that the state, for efficiency reasons, must take an active role in their provision.

The degree of state interference must depend on the sophistication, and willingness to cooperate, of the private distribution system, the capacity of the state to interfere efficiently, and the nature of the good in question, i.e., the degree of "externality" involved in its consumption. The argument relies principally on there being an actual level of externality involved in goods like housing (as where the U.S. has chosen to subsidize home ownership by a substantial amount), nutritious foods for the young, and medical care—a resultant justification to increase the consumption of these goods and services, but not consumption in general.

The goods to be singled out for government production, subsidization and/or distribution, will include public or community goods in the pure Samuelsonian sense, which must be provided by the government if an efficient allocation is to be achieved; other goods having significant positive externalities, even if not pure public goods, which require some level of subsidization; and yet other goods which fall in the "ambiguous good" category in the Head and Shoup sense, which should be supplied by the government for reasons of relative efficiency within the existing institutional structure.[23] These considerations do not imply the desirability of centralized controls over the production and distribution of all, or even most goods. The number of goods involved may be relatively small, but the impact on welfare could still be quite large. Studies are needed to determine whether there are goods and services which are "essential" in the sense defined here, and if so, to determine how these commodities

---

* A. Fishlow, in unpublished research, has calculated that in Brazil the benefits of public education, principally via controls on entry to costly university level training, are skewed toward the already wealthy. Similar results have been found for Mexico and Chile.

can be produced and distributed most efficiently. The situation could vary considerably among different countries, and even within different parts of the same country.

The relationship between employment and consumption can be introduced again at this point. The employment program approach to welfare improvement attempts to find a pattern of demand and investment which, given the existing set of social and political institutions, will fully employ the available labor. It is hoped that the resulting demand will also provide a suitable distribution of income and that the market will respond rapidly to ensure that the optimal set of goods are produced, purchased, and consumed. No guarantee of this is offered. In contrast, the income distribution approach, with an emphasis on the provision of certain goods and services, attempts to allocate real income more equally, and optimally, and having done so, to determine how to achieve the highest level of production. The latter must include the attempt to make the fullest use of the available labor resources. There is a real sense, of course, in which both approaches are required. Employment without the proper consumption pattern is insufficient, but consumption cannot occur if individuals do not produce.

However, the priority established is important. I am reminded of a lecture in which Alec Nove stated that the Soviet economy had systematically fallen short of its production goals for consumer goods industries. Although supposedly governed by a detailed plan providing for the satisfaction of production targets for both capital and consumer goods, the capital goods industries consistently had been given priority. The outcome of this process might easily have been predicted—when production difficulties in the system occurred, as they always did, they were met by drawing down the resources supposedly destined for the nonpriority consumers goods industries. The situation regarding income distribution in most countries seems to be highly similar. Development plans make use of a set of instruments to achieve certain policy goals such as growth in GNP, and income distribution, but income distribution is given, in fact, a lower priority. I am hopeful that attention to employment, as opposed to income distribution, will not result in more of the same.

Notes

1. For example, see the data provided by E. Hagen and O. Hawrylyshyn, "Analysis of World Income and Growth, 1955-1965," *Economic Development and Cultural Change*, Vol. 18, No. 1, Part 2 (1969).

2. R. Weisskoff, "Income Distribution and Economic Growth in Puerto Rico, Argentina, and Mexico," *Review of Income and Wealth*, 4 ((December, 1970), pp. 303-31; A. Fishlow, "Brazilian Size Distribution of Income," *American Economic Review*, Vol. LXII, No. 2 (May, 1972), pp. 391-402; and P. Bardhan, "On the Incidence of Poverty in Rural India of the Sixties," Discussion Paper No. 55 (New Delhi, Indian Statistical Institute, 1971).

3. See, for example, S. Morley and J. Williamson, "The Impact of Demand on Labor Absorption and the Distribution of Earnings: The Case of Brazil," Paper No. 39, Program of Development Studies, Rice University, Houston (Spring, 1973); and R. Soligo, "Factor Intensity of Consumption Patterns, Income Distribution and Employment Growth in Pakistan," Paper No. 44, Program of Development Studies, Rice University, Houston (Fall, 1973).

4. J. Ramos, "An Heterodoxical Interpretation of the Employment Problem in Latin America," paper prepared for the Ford Foundation Seminar on the Employment Process, Bogota (February, 1973).

5. See I. Adelman and C. Morris, "An Anatomy of Income Distribution Patterns in Developing Nations—A Summary of Findings," Economic Staff Working Paper No. 116 (Washington, International Bank for Reconstruction and Development, 1971); and H. Houthakker, "On Some Determinants of Saving in Developed and Under-Developed Countries," in E.A.G. Robinson, ed., *Problems of Economic Development* (London, MacMillan, 1965).

6. H. Bruton, "Economic Development and Labor Use: A Review," this book.

7. F. Stewart and P. Streeten, "Conflicts between Output and Employment Objectives in Developing Countries," *Oxford Economic Papers* (July, 1971), pp. 145-168, provide a special counter-example to this rule, but indicate the counter-example is unlikely to hold in the long run.

8. F. Stewart, "Technology and Employment in LDCs," this book. See also an excellent study by V. Tokman, *Distribucion del Ingreso, Technologia, y Empleo* (Santiago, ILO-PREALC, 1973), for a discussion of the degree to which more labor intensive techniques might be chosen to increase employment in Peru, Venezuela and Ecuador.

9. R. Soligo, "Factor Intensity of Consumption Patterns, Income Distribution and Employment Growth in Pakistan," Program of Development Studies Paper No. 44, Rice University, Houston (Fall, 1973); and S. Morley and G. Smith, "The Effects of Changes in the Distribution of Income on Labor, Foreign Investment, and Growth in Brazil, Paper No. 39, Program of Development Studies, Rice University, Houston (Spring, 1973), are two of the studies which have considered the effect which redistribution of income has on employment, growth, and other variables of policy interest.

10. G. Kolko, *Wealth and Power in America: An Analysis of Social Class and Income Distribution* (New York, Praeger, 1967).

11. I. Adelman and C. Morris, *op. cit.*

12. R. Webb, "The Distribution of Income in Peru," Discussion Paper No. 26, Program in Economic Development, Princeton University Research, Princeton (1972).

13. C. McLure, "The Distribution of Income and Tax Incidence in Panama, 1969," Paper No. 36, Program of Development Studies, Houston, 1972, and "The Incidence of Colombian Taxes," Paper No. 41, Program of Development Studies, Rice University, Houston (April, 1973).

14. D. Turnham, *The Employment Problem in Less Developed Countries* (Paris, OECD, 1971); and J. Ramos, *op. cit.*

15. D. Turnham, *op. cit.*; J. Ramos, *op. cit.*; and International Labor Organization, *Employment, Incomes and Equality: A Strategy for Increasing Productive Employment in Kenya* (Geneva, ILO, 1970).

16. See B. Herrick, *Urban Migration and Economic Development in Chile* (Cambridge, MIT, 1965); CEDE, "Encuestas Urbanas de Empleo y Desempleo," Universidad de los Andes, Faculdad de Economia, Bogota (January, 1969); and A. Fishlow (unpublished research) for Brazil.

17. E. Thorbecke and J. Sengupta, "A Consistency Framework for Employment, Output, and Income Distribution Projections Applied to Colombia," paper prepared for the International Bank for Reconstruction and Development (Washington, 1972).

18. D. Turnham, *op. cit.*

19. M. Strober, "Economic Development and the Manufacturing Earnings Hierarchy," Department of Economics Workshop Paper No. 18, University of California (Berkeley, 1971).

20. A. Fishlow, "Brazilian Size Distribution of Income," *American Economic Review*, LXII, No. 2 (May, 1972), pp. 391-402. See also the Economic Commission for Latin America, *Income Distribution in Latin America* (New York, United Nations, 1970).

21. C. McLure, *op. cit.*

22. S. Bitar, A. Foxley, R. French-Davis, and O. Munoz, *Hacia Un Desarrolo Igualitario,* unpublished manuscript (Santiago, Center for National Planning Studies, Pontifical Catholic University of Chile, 1973). See also A. Foxley and O. Munoz, "Income Distribution, Economic Growth, and Social Structure: The Case of Chile," *Journal of Development Studies* (forthcoming).

23. J. Head and C. Shoup, "Public Goods, Private Goods, and Ambiguous Goods," *The Economic Journal,* Vol. LXXIX, No. 315 (September, 1969), pp. 567-572.

Rural Development: The Policy Options*

Keith Griffin
Magdalen College
Oxford

Introduction

Any analysis of policy options for rural development must be based on certain assumptions. Ours are derived from an empirical study of the so-called green revolution. We will not attempt to defend our assumptions here but merely list them as follows: it is taken for granted (i) that technical change is not identical to progress, and that the latter has little meaning unless values are specified; (ii) that scant progress has occurred in the agricultural regions of most underdeveloped countries, in the sense that inequality has not diminished and the income of small peasants and the rural landless labour force has increased in general only slightly, and in some areas not at all; (iii) that because of the narrow class or factional support on which most governments depend, the range within which policies can be varied normally is rather restricted; but (iv) that those groups which are harmed by technical change can be expected to try to protect their interests by operating either through existing institutions or, if necessary, outside the established law. Thus the role of public policy in the processes of growth and development must be kept in perspective. Although in principle acts of government policy can be powerful, in practice they may not always be so—not because government policies are intrinsically weak, but because the capacity and willingness of governments radically to alter previous decisions is limited.

Styles of Rural Development

In discussing policy one must beware of the fallacy of eclecticism, that is, in the words of Marshall Wolfe, "the assumption that countries can borrow freely bits and pieces of policies that are alleged to have been successful in other settings." Although governments seldom are consistent in everything they do, their objectives, programmes and policies tend to have a certain coherence or internal logic which makes it difficult for them to benefit from the experience of other nations where objectives and policies may be radically different. This does not imply that the government of no country can borrow from any other, but it does imply that borrowing is likely to be most successful when it is from a similar country.

Intuition tells us that, say, Pakistan could and would borrow development policies more readily from India than from China, despite her political hostility toward India

---

*This essay is a condensed version of a chapter in my book, *The Political Economy of Agrarian Change*, (London, Macmillan, 1974).

and her friendship toward China. Similarly, North Vietnam would be more likely to emulate Chinese policies than those of the Philippines. In a sense, the Chinese ''style'' of development is incompatible with that of Pakistan, and the Cuban style is incompatible with that of, say, Guatemala. Of course, countries differ primarily in degree, not in kind; policies, objectives and ideologies are scattered along a spectrum in multi-dimensional space. Nonetheless, three distinct strategies or approaches to development in general and rural problems in particular can be detected: we shall label these the technocratic strategy, the reformist strategy and the radical strategy.

These three strategies define three points on a spectrum—viz. the extremes and the middle—and thus do not constitute a taxonomy. It is for this reason that few countries can be placed firmly under one category or another; most occupy neither an extreme position nor the mid-point, but are distributed (probably skewed right) along a continuum. It is important to recognize that the classification we propose rests on social and political considerations, namely the intended beneficiaries of agrarian policy. Evidently, it would be possible to classify strategies on a different basis, such as the interesting economic (or technological) taxonomic classification of rural strategies into uni-modal and bi-modal favoured by such authors as Bruce Johnston[1] and Eric Thorbecke. We choose not to follow them, however, because we wish to trace the connections which flow from politics, through policies, to economics and technology.

Our three strategies differ in their objectives (or the priorities they attach to various objectives), in the ideology which is used to mobilize support and action, in the dominant form of land tenure institution (and in the pattern of property rights), as well as in the way the benefits of the economic system and growth process are distributed. These differences in objectives, ideologies, institutions and distribution constitute differences in style. Differences in style, in turn, are related to the classes or factions on which the government depends for support.

Most underdeveloped countries have pursued a strategy for rural development which is located toward the technocratic end of the spectrum. The prime economic objective has been to increase agricultural output, either by incorporating more conventional inputs such as land, as in Brazil, or by encouraging farmers to adopt an improved technology, as in the Philippines. The economic system has been justified essentially in terms of a liberal capitalist ideology: emphasis is placed on competition, free markets and widely dispersed private property as sufficient conditions for achieving the objective. In practice, property ownership is highly concentrated and this is reflected in the dominant form of land tenure institutions, viz., latifundia, plantations, large corporate farms and various types of tenancy arrangements. The benefits of technical change and higher output accrue, at least in the first instance, to the landowning elite and other men of property. Inequality of income, far from being deplored, is welcomed, since it is assumed that the rich will save a large proportion of their extra income and thereby contribute to faster accumulation and growth. In other words, the concentration of income and wealth is one of the ways whereby the output objective is expected to be achieved.

The reformist strategy, on the other hand, is basically a compromise between the two extreme positions, and governments which adopt this style of development run the risk of committing the fallacy of eclecticism. Reformist governments tend to vacillate in their choice of policies and one frequently encounters inconsistencies between what a government proclaims and what it actually does. Nonetheless, this style of rural development places priority on redistributing income to some sections of the community (particularly the middle peasantry) and accordingly attributes lower priority than the technocratic strategy to increasing agricultural output. Attempts are made to reconcile greater equity with faster growth by changing agrarian institutions. Quite often, however, the reforms are partial, fragmented and incomplete, and concentrated in certain regions to the exclusion of others, with the consequence that this style creates a dualistic or bi-modal agricultural sector. This is very clear in Mexico, where a policy of redistributing land in favour of the peasantry was followed in the populous areas in the south while a policy of encouraging capital intensive farming on large holdings was pursued in the irrigated areas of the north. Similarly, in Egypt, the original thrust of the reform movement was to encourage labour intensive farming on cooperatives and small holdings, but more recently there has been a shift in favour of more capital intensive techniques on large "new farms."

The ideology associated with this style of rural development usually is nationalist and occasionally is populist. The dominant land tenure institutions tend to be family farms, but if the dualism is pronounced one may find small cooperatives and minifundia confronting large capitalist farms or neo-latifundia. In practice the beneficiaries of the strategy often are the middle peasants on family farms and large "progressive" farmers on substantial holdings. Several of the "progressive" farmers who benefit from a reformist strategy may be of urban origin, e.g. retired army officers, civil servants or politicians. The redistribution of income that occurs, thus, is largely from the upper income groups to the middle; those in the lowest deciles of the income distribution may receive higher earnings, e.g. because of greater employment opportunities, but they are unlikely to improve their relative share—or to increase their political influence.

Finally, the objective of the radical strategy is first and foremost to achieve rapid social change and a redistribution of political power. Next in priority comes a redistribution of wealth and income (in that order) and, lastly, higher production. In short, the objectives are greater mass participation, economic equality and faster growth. No conflict is seen between the first two objectives, indeed they are merely different aspects of the same thing, and these, in turn, need not conflict with the third. If there is a conflict, however, the growth objective would give way to the quest for social, political and economic equality.

The radical strategy is supported by the ideology of socialism. Agrarian socialism, particularly its Asian variant, is based on the assumption that it is possible to mobilize an untapped resource potential, namely, human labour. This involves extending the number of days worked, increasing the intensity of effort and raising the efficiency and inventiveness of labour. This can be done, however, only if social and economic inequalities are reduced, since equal sacrifices are incompatible with a system of unequal rewards. Rough equality is achieved by abolishing private property in land and establishing collectives, communes or state farms. These institutions, evidently, tend to favour small peasants and landless labourers.

Implicit in this strategy is a profound scepticism of the desirability of relying on unregulated market forces for development. Considerable emphasis is placed on the immobility and specificity of resources and great importance is attached to exploiting unique local opportunities. In contrast to the first two styles of development, the radical strategy, especially as applied in China, places relatively little emphasis on national agricultural planning, the manipulation of macro-economic aggregates or price signals. Instead more attention is concentrated on the locality; solutions to problems are sought at the local level rather than in general, national policies. Motives and attitudes, even morality, are believed to be capable of being changed (witness the search for a "new socialist man"); moreover, institutional arrangements are treated as variables and considerable experimentation with alternative means of organizing production and consumption is permitted; and if a particular locality encounters a difficulty, local initiative rather than outside assistance is expected to be relied upon.

The three styles of rural development represent, therefore, three distinct approaches to the agricultural sector and to the people who live and work within it. The major characteristics of these three styles are summarized in Table 1. A study of countries which have adopted different styles of development should be highly instructive, e.g., in determining the social and economic consequences of a particular technical change, but it is doubtful if governments following one style can or would wish to borrow policies used by countries following either of the other two styles.

TABLE 1

STYLES OF RURAL DEVELOPMENT

Development strategy	Objectives	Major beneficiaries	Dominant form of tenure	Ideology	Representative countries
Technocratic	increase output	landowning elite	large private and corporate farms, plantations, latifundia, various tenancy systems	capitalist	Philippines, Brazil, Ivory Coast
Reformist	redistribute income (and wealth); increase output	middle peasants, "progressive" farmers	family farms, cooperatives	nationalist	Mexico, Egypt
Radical	social change; redistribute political power, wealth and output	small peasants and landless labourers	collectives, communes, state farms	socialist	China, Cuba, Algeria

Salient Features of the Green Revolution

A technology is in the process of being created which will enable some tropical countries—or some farmers in some regions of tropical countries—to increase the yields from foodgrains by 50 percent or more. This new technology is commonly thought to have caused a "green revolution." The "revolution" consists of the application of a package of inputs, the most prominent of which are the new high-yielding seeds. Thus the core of the new technology is based on biological research. At present the new high-yielding seeds are largely for wheat and rice, but improved varieties of other crops have also been developed, notably, maize, sorghum (jowar) and millet (bajra). There is no reason to doubt that this process of plant improvement will continue for as far ahead as anyone may care to look.

In addition to higher yields per crop, this technology has several advantages. First, in the case of rice, it permits shorter cropping cycles and thereby enables the farmer to economize on water. Moreover, in the case both of wheat and rice, the amount of water required per unit of output is reduced. Second, the short cycles sometimes permit multiple cropping, and thus in effect economize on land. Third, under optimal conditions the new technology utilizes much more labour per unit of land and thus can increase farm employment. Finally, in principle, the new technology is rather easily disseminated since it is scale-neutral and does not require a major transformation of agricultural practices. These advantages have led some observers to predict an end to the foodgrain problem in underdeveloped countries and the beginning of an era of worldwide surplus production.

Such optimism, however, cannot at present be justified by the facts. No miracle has occurred or is likely to occur. Indeed, the new seeds have several serious disadvantages. First, the high-yielding varieties tend to be more delicate than indigenous plants and require a great deal more care on the part of the cultivator. Second, the new seeds at present available are in general less resistant to drought and flood, and thus require sophisticated irrigation and water control facilities. Third, the high-yielding varieties are somewhat more susceptible to disease and infestation by insects, and thus require protective applications of herbicides and pesticides. Fourth, the new seeds often—but not always—are more productive than local varieties even in the absence of fertilizers, but the differences are not very great unless substantial amounts of fertilizer are applied.

The response of seeds to fertilizer cannot occur in the absence of water, and for this reason irrigation and fertilizers (and perhaps pesticides as well) may be complementary in some countries. Consequently the "package" of material inputs that accompanies the new seeds may compel massive investment in industries supplying fertilizer and plant chemicals, and expenditure on irrigation works and equipment.

The complementarity among the various inputs which comprise the "green revolution" are such that many governments have concentrated their effort on particular regions (usually the more prosperous ones) and particular farmers (usually the larger ones). This tendency is particularly notable in countries pursuing a "technocratic" style of development, but it is also visible in countries which have followed a "reformist" style. In Mexico the rapid expansion of wheat output has been largely confined to large commercial farms in the northern part of the country. In Pakistan, the wheat and rice revolution has occurred largely in the prosperous areas of the Punjab, as well as in the other irrigated zones of the Indus basin. In the Philippines, Central Luzon was given priority and thus regional inequality was accentuated, since Luzon was already the most prosperous and advanced agricultural region in the country. In India the "revolution" is a bit more widespread, but it has penetrated most deeply in the Punjab and the other wheat growing areas in the north.

These examples from the four countries where the "revolution" has had the greatest impact suggest that the spatial distribution of the benefits and costs of technical change has not been even. The "green revolution," from a technical point of view, is largely a biological and chemical revolution, but from a socio-economic point of view it has largely become transformed into a commercial revolution. This is a consequence not only of the nature of the technology but also of the government policies which have been used to disseminate it. In practice the new technology has been successful primarily in the context of commercial agriculture. Moreover, the "revolution" tends to strengthen whatever commercial agriculture already exists, often at the expense of peasant farming.

In conclusion, the new technology is discriminatory, particularly when it is combined with policies typical of countries following a "technocratic" style of rural development. The technology has a differential impact. It is neutral neither as regards geographical area nor as regards social class. On the contrary, unless governments pursue a "radical" or, at least, "reformist" strategy, the "green revolution" tends to increase economic inequality and this, in turn, may aggravate social conflicts which already exist. It would be foolish to disregard its possible political implications.

Innovation and Inequality

Although the impact of the "green revolution" on total agricultural production has been relatively slight, the introduction of high yielding varieties has led to an increase in domestic supplies of some foodstuffs in several countries. If this continues, increased output is likely to result eventually in a decline in the relative price of foodgrains. At the moment, however, the governments of several countries, e.g., Pakistan and India, are supporting domestic grain prices at levels which exceed world prices by a considerable margin—while at the same time adopting policies which turn the general terms of trade against agriculture. Nonetheless, the urban areas are potentially major beneficiaries of the "green revolution." Potential benefits could be transformed into actual benefits merely by allowing domestic prices to fall to those prevailing in the world grain market.

The rural sector as a whole, on the other hand, will experience a deterioration of its commodity terms of trade if grain prices are allowed to fall. This would be of relatively little consequence to those farmers who have introduced the cost-cutting innovations, since their factoral terms of trade will have improved and their profits increased. They clearly will be better off, although they can be expected to lobby politicians for the continuation of the price support programme.

The innovating farmers have enjoyed not only high prices for their products but also low prices for their inputs. Indeed in many cases the cost of innovation has been heavily subsidized by the government, and this has supplemented price supports and further increased the incomes of large so-called "progressive" farmers.

The growth in inequality in rural areas stems in large part from the fact that small, poor peasants who have restricted access to credit, technical knowledge and the material means of production are unable to innovate as easily or as quickly as those who are landed, liquid and literate. Ownership of land, or even a secure tenancy, provides an outlet for savings, an incentive for investment and an asset on which credit can be obtained. Liquid assets, especially cash, constitute the working capital needed to purchase commercialized inputs. Moreover, liquidity enables a farmer more easily to bear risk and to time his sales and purchases to maximum advantage. Finally, literacy gives farmers access to further knowledge, although it certainly is not the only—or even perhaps the most important—means of obtaining information. Those farmers who already possess resources in the form of land, capital and knowledge are able to grasp the opportunities created by the "green revolution" and further improve their position. But those who are landless and illiterate will tend to lag behind and perhaps become further impoverished.

There is evidence from all over the underdeveloped world that it is the largest and most prosperous farmers who innovate and the middle-sized farmers who imitate. In some cases the smallest and very poor farmers subsequently introduce the new seeds and adopt a commercial pattern of production and marketing, but in many cases they do not.

Small peasant landowners who are excluded from the "green revolution" can be subjected to considerable hardship. There is a danger that ultimately they will become squeezed between their high costs and the falling prices of their output, and if this happens their incomes will decline absolutely. Many may be forced to sell their land to the larger farmers and this will lead to greater inequality in the distribution of land and an increase in the landless rural work force. In economic terms, commercialization of agriculture will be accompanied by increased specialization and division of labour. In sociological terms, it will be accompanied by increased social differentiation and the gradual polarization of the community into two broad classes, one of which possesses the means of production and derives its income therefrom, and another which owns little property and derives its income from the sale of labour services.

A rise in the number of landless workers, say, as a result of population increase or tenants and small peasants losing their land, will tend to depress rural wage rates and increase poverty in this section of the community. The decline in wages will be accentuated if the "green revolution" is accompanied by labour-saving innovations. Technological unemployment resulting from the mechanization of agriculture is unlikely to remain in rural areas; ultimately it will move to the cities and further increase the amount of underemployment in petty services. Thus rural innovation may lead to greater misery for many workers in urban areas—despite the fact that food prices may be lower.

We do not wish to imply, of course, that agricultural innovation should be resisted. On the contrary, it must be actively encouraged. But at the same time measures must be adopted to ensure that the benefits are widely shared. If the political will were present, one simple way of doing this would be to tax either the land or the income of innovating landlords. This, regrettably, is almost never done.

It must be recognized, however, that the inequitable tax and subsidy systems merely accentuate a tendency towards inequality that probably would be present in any case. This is because in countries where labour is relatively abundant improved techniques tend to raise profits and rents but not wages, so that unless property is evenly distributed the distribution of income becomes worse. There are two broad solutions to this problem. First, workers and small peasants can be organized in an attempt to obtain higher incomes without altering the distribution of wealth. Minimum wage legislation, the encouragement of rural trade unions and the promotion of various types of cooperatives are examples of policies which come under this heading—and which are usually misguided (if well intentioned) and fail. Alternatively, one can eliminate the causes of income inequality by redistributing productive wealth. In economies which are primarily agrarian, such a policy implies a redistribution of land. The first solution is essentially a "liberal" solution, while the second is essentially "radical." The two approaches are not entirely competitive—indeed government policy could well contain elements of both—but they do entail rather different consequences for the direction and pace of socio-economic change. The two approaches, in other words, imply different styles of rural development.

The basic issue which confronts all governments is whether to attempt to redistribute income while leaving the distribution of wealth intact, or to attempt to redistribute wealth directly. The former requires the government to maintain continuous pressure on wealth-holders, since they can be expected to try to regain the income produced by their assets, whereas the latter requires a single assault. A policy of redistributing wealth implies the destruction of a class by severing its connection with the means of production, whereas a policy of redistributing income merely weakens a class by appropriating part of the surplus which its assets generate.

Lines of Policy

There is no doubt that under appropriate circumstances the "green revolution" can make an important contribution towards increasing agricultural output in underdeveloped countries. The new technology, however, is neither necessary nor sufficient for achieving more rapid growth. Moreover, as we have seen, it has become reasonably clear that the introduction of high yielding varieties of foodgrains has often been associated with increased economic inequality and greater social differentiation in rural areas. Thus the "revolution" creates as well as alleviates problems, and thereby raises issues of public policy.

In the discussion which follows we shall assume that the objectives of government agricultural policy are to promote greater equality, accelerate the growth of production and ensure the efficient allocation of resources within the sector. We know from our previous discussion that many governments do not in fact pursue all these objectives, and that some governments have additional objectives. Thus our assumption will not always correspond to reality. Nonetheless, the goals we have selected are those to which many governments have aspired in their published pronouncements, and it may be useful to examine alternative means that could be used to reach declared ends.

The main policy issues are grouped under six headings: (1) the ownership and use of land, (2) factor prices, (3) agricultural surpluses and non-agricultural growth, (4) output prices and marketing, (5) government expenditure, and (6) science policy.

The Ownership and Use of Land

The major cause of inequality in the distribution of income in rural areas is inequality in the ownership of land. This is true not only because land is the most important means of production but also because ownership of land is highly correlated with ease of access to institutions (e.g. banks and the bureaucracy) and the resources they provide (e.g. credit and technical assistance). Unfortunately, as is well known, the distribution of land ownership is grossly unequal throughout much of the underdeveloped world.

In addition to its effect on the extent of poverty, land concentration also affects the distribution of political power (nationally and locally), the class structure of the society and the general cohesiveness of the rural community. These, in turn, influence the way the benefits of a particular technical change are distributed as well as the direction that will be taken by subsequent innovations.

The long-run consequences of technical change depend very much upon the institutional context in which it occurs. If one is interested in augmenting equity (both political and economic) there is a strong case for implementing a land reform. "Liberal" policies of the type mentioned earlier are clearly inferior to a "radical" solution: they do not attack the root of the difficulty, they often are slow to take effect and they usually make some problems worse. (Minimum wages, for instance, encourage the substitution of capital for labour and hence aggravate the employment problem. Similarly, the promotion of cooperatives in areas where land is unequally distributed usually is of benefit only to the more prosperous farmers.)

Land reform also is necessary on grounds of efficiency. Factor markets in underdeveloped countries are highly imperfect. Land is monopolized by a few families, particularly in North Africa, the Middle East and Latin America, but also in some Asian nations such as the Philippines. This alone is sufficient in many cases to give landowners monopsony power in the local labour market, since in a predominantly agricultural country those without land have no alternative but to offer their labour services to powerful landlords. Serfdom and debt slavery are unnecessary in most instances, although they can still be found. Credit, too, is relatively cheap to the large landowners and dear to everyone else, particularly to tenants with insecure leases.

Similarly, control over water rights by landlords can be viewed as an imperfection in the market for this input.

The imperfections are such that large landowners face a very different set of relative prices from those confronted by small-holders and tenants. Land and capital are abundant and cheap relative to labour for the big farmers, whereas the reverse is true for the small. Thus the big farmers tend to adopt techniques of production with relatively high land-labour ratios and small cultivators and tenants adopt very labour intensive techniques. These differences in techniques are a reflection of allocative inefficiency, namely, a failure of the large farmers to economize on the scarce factor of production—land, and to use intensively the plentiful factor—labour.

A striking feature of the agricultural systems of virtually all poor countries is that yields per acre rise as average farm size declines. That is, the smaller the farm, the greater the average productivity of land. Conversely, the larger the farm, the greater the average productivity of labour. Since land is usually the factor in most acute shortage, the farms with the highest yields per acre are normally the most efficient. Even in countries where the average farm is very small, such as India, it has been demonstrated that those farms which are smaller than the average are economically the most efficient.[2]

An obvious implication of this is that a land reform which resulted in smaller units of management in agriculture would both reduce inequality and increase total output. These, of course, are static or once-and-for-all gains which arise from an improvement in the allocation of resources. It is also possible to argue, however, that in certain circumstances an agrarian reform would lead to an acceleration in the rate of growth of output, i.e., to cumulative gains.

It sometimes is claimed, for example, that small farmers living near a subsistence level are inhibited by the risk of harvest failure from undertaking an innovation. It is conceivable that a land reform which increased the average size of mini- and micro-fundia, or organized production in collectives and state farms, might succeed in reducing risk and could perhaps thereby eliminate an obstacle to rapid technological change.

Another way in which agricultural growth could be accelerated would be by combining a land reform with a programme of rural public works. By now it is widely accepted that in many underdeveloped countries it is technically possible to increase the rate of rural capital formation by mobilizing underemployed labour, especially during periods of pronounced seasonal unemployment. In practice, few countries apart from China have attempted to mobilize labour on a massive scale. Small projects have been started in several nations, but they have never become a major instrument of development. One reason why few countries apart from China and North Vietnam have succeeded with this policy is that few governments have been able to raise the tax revenues necessary to finance a large investment programme. Thus real resources in the form of unemployed labour have remained idle because governments have been unable to amass the financial resources required to pay the wage bill.

The financial constraint could be overcome if it were possible to employ labour at less than the going wage rate, i.e. if it were possible to persuade workers to contribute their labour on a semi-voluntary basis. This clearly will not happen if the capital assets created by the works programme are used to increase the income and wealth of only a small number of people. No one, for instance, will work for nothing—or for less than the market wage—in order to dig a well for a large private landlord. Those who advocate tacking on a mass public works programme to an agrarian system in which large private holdings predominate are committing what we have previously described as the fallacy of eclecticism. The two policies are inconsistent and contradictory because they pertain to two quite different styles of development. On the other hand, if the agrarian system is such that the workers themselves are the direct beneficiaries of the fruits of their efforts, it may be possible to organize them on a semi-voluntary basis for rural investment projects. As long as land is unequally distributed it will be difficult to undertake massive labour intensive projects, but once property relations are altered, it should be both technically and politically possible to accelerate sharply capital formation in rural areas.

Economists and politicians of a "technocratic" persuasion would dispute this. They would argue, on the contrary, that a more egalitarian distribution of income and wealth in rural areas would conflict with faster accumulation and growth because it inevitably would reduce private savings. There are two things to be said about this assertion. First, even if household savings decline this may be offset by greater public savings generated through taxation or by greater collective effort in the manner described in the preceding paragraphs. In most of the countries following a technocratic style of rural development the bulk of the economic surplus is appropriated by a small minority who, because of their political power, are able to ensure that their incomes are lightly taxed. If incomes were more equitably distributed, however, and if political power were more widely diffused, the tax base would be broader and the political obstacles to reducing consumption via taxation for the sake of accumulation would be much diminished; at the same time, the incentive to reduce leisure in order to engage in labour intensive investment projects would be much increased. The consequences of these two effects on total capital formation cannot easily be calculated, but from what little we know of China, their importance can be considerable.

Second, it is far from certain that a reduction in inequality will in fact be accompanied by a sharp decline in household savings. (It is even less obvious that there would be a decline in household savings invested in socially productive activities.) Recent evidence suggests that excessive emphasis in the past has been placed on the level of income as the determinant of the proportion of income that a rural household saves. In several parts of Asia studies have shown that peasant cultivators—even very poor ones—save a substantial portion of their income.[3] The reason for this is not entirely clear, but one promising hypothesis is that in economies (or parts of economies) in which financial institutions are poorly developed household savings are strongly influenced by investment opportunities. That is, the saving and investment decisions coincide, and households save in order to undertake a specific investment project. One of the things that follows from this is that if land were more equally distributed, more households would have a profitable outlet for their savings and consequently the rate of rural capital formation might increase. A further corollary is that if the profitability of rural investment increases, say, as a result of an improved technology, small peasant landowners can be expected to increase their savings along with everyone else.

The "green revolution" represents an admirable opportunity to test these hypotheses, particularly in those parts of the world where the technology associated with the high yielding varieties of foodgrains has become accessible to all farmers, large and small alike. This condition is best satisfied in some of the wheat growing regions of India, and we are fortunate to have available a recent study of rural savings from this area.

A team from the Punjab Agricultural University examined the savings and investment behaviour of 72 holdings from Ludhiana District in the Punjab and 108 holdings from Hissar District in Haryana.[4] These farms were studied over a period of four years beginning in 1966-67 and terminating in 1969-70. In other words, the period of study extends from the early years of the "green revolution" in the area to the recent peak of innovative activity. During this period of rising investment opportunities net savings rose from 14.25 percent of income in Ludhiana to 24.19 percent. In Hissar, which at the beginning of the study was not as developed as Ludhiana, the rise in the savings ratio was even more dramatic, namely, from 11.53 to 33.57 percent.[5] Thus the data from these 180 holdings are consistent with our hypothesis that savings in rural areas are at least in part a function of investment opportunities.

What about our contention that small farmers may on occasion save proportionately as much as large? Once again the data from these two wheat growing districts of India do not contradict our hypothesis. The farms in the sample were divided into three size categories—small, medium, and large—and savings ratios for each category were calculated. The results are presented in Table 2. It can be seen that in

TABLE 2

NET SAVINGS AS A PERCENT OF TOTAL INCOME IN TWO WHEAT
DISTRICTS OF INDIA, 1969-1970

Size of holding	Ludhiana District, Punjab	Hissar District, Haryana
Small	16.72	34.18
Medium	26.48	35.51
Large	25.14	31.26
Average	24.19	33.57

SOURCE: A.S. Kahlon and Harbhajan Singh Bal, *Factors Associated with Farm and Farm Family Investment Pattern in Ludhiana (Punjab) and Hissar (Haryana) Districts: 1966-67 through 1969-70,* Department of Economics and Sociology, Punjab Agricultural University (Ludhiana, n.d.), p. 116.

NOTE: Small holdings are defined as 0-3.5 ha. in Ludhiana and L 0-4 ha. in Hissar; medium holdings are 3.5-6 ha. and 4-8 ha. in the two districts, respectively; and large holdings are those above 6 and 8 ha.

neither district was the savings ratio on large farms the highest, and in Hissar it was the lowest. The small farmers, on the other hand, had the lowest savings rate in Ludhiana but a very high rate in Hissar. Medium size farmers, however, had the highest rate of savings in both districts. There is nothing in this evidence, therefore, that indicates that inequality of landed wealth or of agricultural income is conducive of a high rate of savings, or that a redistribution of land necessarily would lead to a fall in the rate of accumulation. Those who wish to defend status, privilege and wealth must seek other grounds for doing so.

Factor Prices

We have stressed repeatedly that methods of cultivation and the pace of innovation are strongly affected by the ease of access to the means of production and by relative factor prices. It has been argued that factor markets in rural areas are seriously "distorted" and that factor prices fail to reflect social opportunity costs. A land reform, as suggested above, will help to correct some of these distortions, but a change in tenancy arrangements will not suffice to remove all distortions. Tenancy reform, moreover, may not be politically acceptable to most governments. Thus, for both these reasons, we should consider alternative policies which might improve the allocation of factors of production, although it should be recognized that in the absence of land reform several of the policy alternatives we examine are mere palliatives.

At present it is differences in relative factor prices which largely account for the fact that larger landowners—either directly or through their tenants—innovate more quickly than smallholder peasants. For example, in most countries the amount of credit available in rural areas is inadequate, and what little credit that is available through organized institutions tends to be rationed among those with secure titles to land and supplied at a relatively low rate of interest. The majority of the rural population must seek credit in the unorganized capital market and pay a high price for it. On grounds of equity, efficiency and growth this situation should be corrected. The rate of interest in the organized credit market in rural areas should be substantially raised in order, first, to encourage more saving in the countryside and, second, to encourage commercial banks to shift part of their lending activity from industry to agriculture. Equally important, additional credit should be supplied from government sources. The effect of these two measures would be to put pressure on the unorganized credit market to *reduce* interest rates paid by those who must have recourse to this source. Once the total supply of credit available to the agricultural sector has increased, the government should adopt policies whose purpose is to ensure that small peasants have access to the organized market on terms which are not inferior (and perhaps even superior) to those enjoyed by large landlords.

In principle, similar policies should be adopted to ensure that small owner-operators have equal or preferential access to irrigation water, technical assistance and all the other inputs which are vital to the success of the "green revolution." At present they are discriminated against in virtually all factor "markets" either in terms of price, or because of the way scarce resources are allocated by rationing, or because of restricted access to the bureaucracy.

It is sometimes thought that the new high yielding varieties of foodgrains are characterized by economies of scale, and that this explains why it is the owners of large holdings who are the most active in adopting the new technology. This hypothesis in general is not correct, as is evident from the fact that frequently large holdings are broken up into many small tenancies. Seeds, fertilizers and pesticides are complementary but highly divisible; even the smallest peasant can use them. Some types of irrigation facilities are indeed rather indivisible, and hence the scale factor is important, but large dams and canals are invariably financed by the government, and thus economies of scale in irrigation cannot explain why small peasant owners lag behind landlords. Pumping machinery and even sprayers can be rather "lumpy," but these can be supplied through cooperatives organized for the purpose or obtained by hiring. Examples of both methods of organizing the supply of lumpy inputs are common, especially the practice of relatively prosperous villagers hiring out pieces of capital equipment to their neighbours.

The technical inputs required by the "green revolution" are essentially "scale neutral," but the institutions required by the new technology often are not. Extension agents concentrate on the large farmers; credit agencies concentrate on low risk borrowers; those who sell fertilizers, pesticides and other chemical inputs concentrate on cultivators who are likely to buy the largest quantities. State organizations tend to provide services to those from whom the government seeks approval, and in most instances these are the large landowners. Unless there is "scale neutrality" in the institutions which support the "green revolution," i.e., to repeat, unless small peasants have equal access to knowledge, finance and material inputs, innovation will inevitably favour the prosperous and the secure at the expense of the poor and the insecure.

Almost all of the evidence we have seen indicates that the average productivity of labour is higher on large holdings than on small. Since land and capital are scarce relative to labour, we have concluded that average total factor productivity is greater on the small farms than on the large, and we have assumed further that what is true of the average is true on the margin as well. The implication of this analysis is that small farms should generally be encouraged relative to large farms by transferring resources from the latter to the former.

This simple policy conclusion does not necessarily remain valid, however, if some factors of production are immobile. Assume, for example, that the political system is such that it is impossible to transfer land and capital from one group of farmers to another. In this case the only mobile factor would be labour, and an improvement in resource allocation would require that labour be shifted to farms where on the margin its productivity is highest, i.e. toward the large farms. In other words, although total factor productivity may be higher on small holdings, this ceases to be relevant to policy if not all factors are mobile. Given immobility of some factors of production, efficiency requires that the remaining factors be encouraged to move where their marginal product is highest and this might imply subsidizing farms where total factor productivity is low.

A policy of subsidizing the cost of labour to large landowners—even assuming it is administratively feasible—is decidedly a ''second best'' solution, of course. In the first place, the policy does not enable the rural sector to maximize output from its given resources; it merely allows production to be somewhat higher than it might otherwise have been. That is, the policy reduces but does not eliminate inefficiency. Secondly, the policy is inegalitarian. It increases the profits of large landowners (by lowering costs) and thereby subjects small owner-operators to greater competitive pressure. Whereas a redistribution of land and capital in favour of the peasantry would lead to greater equality, a redistribution of labour in favour of landlords would result in greater inequality. (Some members of the rural proletariat would benefit, of course, but they represent a minority of the rural poor.) Thus ''second best'' policies and piecemeal reforms may improve allocative efficiency but they may also aggravate social problems. Moreover, third, to the extent that a policy of subsidizing rural wages strengthens the landowning elite, the likelihood of undertaking a major transformation of agrarian institutions is diminished, and in the long run this is contrary to the interests of the majority of the agricultural population.

Agricultural Surpluses and Non-Agricultural Growth

In several of the countries where the ''green revolution'' is now occurring, the growth of agricultural production has been adversely affected by the general policies pursued by governments anxious to encourage industrialization. A majority of underdeveloped countries, especially during the first two decades after the end of the Second World War, have provided strong incentives to import substitute manufactures, particularly consumer goods.

The effect of these policies was to turn the terms of trade against agriculture, to reduce the profitability of investment and innovation in rural areas, and to discourage production for the market, particularly the export market. The relative stagnation of agriculture which has characterized so many underdeveloped countries is due in large part to the overall growth strategy pursued by governments. It has now become painfully obvious that any strategy which hopes to transform agriculture from a technically stagnant sector to one in which rapid innovation occurs must pay particular attention to the relative commodity prices which farmers confront.

One of the consequences of turning the terms of trade against agriculture is that the income of the peasantry is reduced. The landed elite, however, need not be harmed since they can diversify their assets and shift the focus of their economic activities to the urban sector. Once they acquire a stake in manufacturing and commerce as well as in agriculture they acquire a vested interest in the status quo. The reason for this is that there is a close connection between the income of the peasantry and the urban wage rate. Low peasant incomes usually result in low wages and high profits outside of agriculture. "The fact that the wage level in the capitalist sector depends upon earnings in the subsistence sector is sometimes of immense political importance, since the effect is that capitalists have a direct interest in holding down productivity of the subsistence workers."[6] The importance of this point increases substantially once the landed elite have merged with the industrial capitalist class, because then all property owning groups have an interest in turning the terms of trade against agriculture. This tends to perpetuate low productivity and stagnation in the rural sector and low wages combined with high profits in the urban sector.

Eventually, however, the system will begin to collapse. This will occur when the subsidy required for the support and expansion of the industrial sector is greater than the resources which can be squeezed out of agriculture. When that point is reached, policy will have to be switched to favour agriculture, regardless of the nature of the regime in power.

One of the tasks of those who make policy, particularly in countries which wish to follow a radical style of rural development, is to devise a system which is able to obtain resources from rural areas for use elsewhere without turning the terms of trade against agriculture and without creating unacceptable inequalities. In capitalist economies, it is the private landlord who usually appropriates the surplus and transfers it to urban areas via unregulated, or partially regulated, markets. In socialist countries the collective amasses the surplus and transfers it to the state via compulsory delivery schemes. An alternative strategy would be to terminate the institution of private property in agricultural land and replace it by public or communal ownership. The object of "nationalizing" the land would be to replace the landlord by the state (or the local community). As owner of the land the state would be entitled to a rent, and the level of rents could be fixed so as to obtain the amount of resources necessary to fulfil government objectives. Farm management, on the other hand, need not be the direct responsibility of government, although state farms could be introduced if these were thought desirable. Relatively small farms could be created and run either cooperatively or as family enterprises. In this way efficiency and equality in rural areas could be assured without having to run the risk that too large a fraction of output would be consumed and the rate of accumulation thereby reduced.

A growing number of countries has restricted private ownership of property in land, and this has proved to be quite compatible with small scale operational holdings. The socialist countries are not unique in attributing importance to state or communal ownership of land, although their practice of organizing production in enormous state or collective farms is distinctive and more akin to large capitalist farms in North America than to the peasant systems of most of the Third World.* In

---

*It is not widely known that the U.S. government owns more than half the land in some western states. The total amount of land owned by the government is approximately 760 million acres, of which 707 million acres are leased to private individuals and corporations for livestock grazing.

Mexico, a third of the land is vested in village *ejidos,* and cultivation usually is done on individual plots, although collective farming also exists. In Algeria, the land formerly owned by French colonists has been nationalized and most production decisions are taken by the workers and their elected management committee. Traditionally in much of Africa the land was collectively owned by the tribe but farmed individually, the rights to use land being allocated by the chief. Israel, of course, has had considerable experience with the *kibbutz.* As these examples indicate, there are many ways of organizing the agricultural sector which do not require individual ownership of land.

Output Prices and Marketing

We began the previous section by arguing that a great many underdeveloped countries adopted economic policies which had the effect of turning the terms of trade against rural areas. The purpose of the policy was to encourage growth in non-agricultural activities in urban areas, and while it succeeded in doing so to a certain extent, the policy also resulted in a slow growth of agricultural production. This, in turn, created severe difficulties—including near famines in some countries—and governments have been forced to respond.

The typical response, however, has not been to turn the terms of trade sharply in favour of agriculture, but to raise the price of particular items that were in short supply. Most prominent among these items has, of course, been foodgrains. Indeed in some countries, it is difficult to tell to what extent the rise in foodgrain output is attributable to an improved technology (which lowers costs) and to what extent it is due to high domestic prices. If the introduction of high yielding seeds reduces total costs of grain production, it will raise farm profits and lead to increased output. It should not be necessary, therefore, for governments to support the "green revolution" by maintaining the domestic price of any particular commodity above that prevailing in the world at large. On the contrary, a sensible objective of government policy would be to ensure that lower costs are passed on to the community in the form of lower food prices.

We have noted that large farmers often benefit from what are in effect subsidized material inputs. If these same farmers now receive a subsidy to output as well, the consequences for income distribution and resource allocation will be serious. A policy of high support prices, first, will raise the cost of living for urban consumers, increase inequality in the cities—which in most countries already is much greater than in rural areas, accentuate demands for higher money wages and, possibly, lead to a cost-push inflation.

Secondly, support prices will induce producers to alter the composition of agricultural output. For example, there is evidence that rice production in Pakistan has been encouraged at the expense of cotton exports, and wheat acreage in India has expanded at the expense of the more nutritious high protein pulses. Indeed in most countries it seems doubtful that there is any special reason to raise the price of grains relative to other food crops and agricultural commodities; what is needed is a rise in the price of agricultural commodities as a whole relative to the price of non-agricultural commodities.

Government Expenditure

It is well known that agriculture often has been neglected and probably has received too small a share of total capital formation. A strong case can be made in general terms for reallocating more investment resources from urban to rural areas.

More specifically, the spread of the "green revolution" will require substantial investment in irrigation and transport. Much of this will have to be financed by the public sector. It will also require large investments by public and private enterprise in marketing and storage facilities, as well as in industries supplying agriculture with the necessary chemical and mechanical inputs. The private sector can be expected to respond to profit opportunities, and if the policies we have suggested are implemented, one can be confident that adequate incentives will be present and that private and social cost-benefit calculations will converge. Public investment, however, usually responds not to market signals but to political decisions. It is important, therefore, that governments that wish to promote growth and equality in rural areas should review their public expenditure policies to ensure that agricultural innovation is not obstructed by inadequate supporting institutions (e.g. irrigation water and transport). It also is the responsibility of government to ensure that new technology is widely disseminated, and that the technology is not given a class bias as a result of policy. At present, few governments have adequately discharged this responsibility.

Science Policy

Progress in agricultural science, however, has been much more encouraging. Of course, a great deal more remains to be done, but new international research institutes are being established all over the world and one can be fairly confident that our knowledge of tropical agriculture will continue to increase. Indeed research on food crops in underdeveloped areas is still a fairly recent phenomenon.

It would be wrong to imagine that international research centres could or should be a substitute for national efforts. Their role is to be a pioneer in new research activities, to gather information and material, to maintain a seed bank, and to provide a small amount of coordination. National research organizations will be necessary to undertake location-specific research. At the very least this means adapting seeds released by the international institutes to local conditions. In addition, national institutes should develop improved varieties of their own. The admirable research on rice conducted in the long established centres in Taiwan and Sri Lanka are examples of what can be done.

National research centres cannot be content with discovering new knowledge; they must also disseminate it to local cultivators. That is, research should be closely linked to extension. The research institute should run several demonstration farms in various parts of the country, and farmers should be encouraged to visit these frequently—not only so that they can learn what is happening at the institute, but also so that the scientists can learn what are the problems of the farmers. Similarly, extension agents could be trained on the demonstration farms, so that those who go out to visit the cultivators are aware of the latest research results and have seen them applied under conditions which hopefully are not too different from those which ordinary farmers confront. In this way a close connection between theory and practice, research and application can be established, and this should help to accelerate the pace of technical change and thereby raise the rate of return on research effort.

Science is a powerful instrument at the disposal of those who formulate policy. There is no doubt that it can be used to reduce poverty and inequality in rural areas and to raise the rate of growth of agricultural output. Whether it will be so used depends in large part on what are the objectives of the government and these, in turn, depend in part on which groups in the community the government relies on for support. Technology alone provides few answers to the problems that beset the underdeveloped world, although potentially it has much to contribute.

Conclusion

The great majority of people who offer economic advice to governments assume that the economic system is self-equilibrating and that there is a basic harmony of interests among the individuals and groups who comprise the system. When interests diverge it is assumed that they can be reconciled relatively easily through minor policy adjustments, and when the system moves out of equilibrium it is assumed that automatic forces tend to restore it to the previous position. This vision of the economic system is strongly entrenched in economic thought. It is reflected in Adam Smith's benevolent "hidden hand," which reconciles private self-interest with the general welfare, and in Alfred Marshall's theory of markets, which expounds the calculus of an optimising, self-adjusting economy.

Our view of the economic system is rather different. It is akin to that of Karl Marx, who saw class conflict where others imagined harmony, of Thomas Malthus, who feared a cumulative downward spiral as a result of the tendency of population to expand faster than food production, and of David Ricardo, who foresaw that mechanization could create unemployment and hardship. Our point of departure for an analysis of policy options is the assumption that interests are in conflict, that these conflicts seldom can be eliminated, and that therefore the correct choice of policy is largely a value judgement that depends upon which groups one wishes to favour. We assume, furthermore, that there is no immediate, necessary or inevitable tendency for a "countervailing power" to arise when one group finds itself at a disadvantage vis-a-vis another, and thus the possibility of cumulative movements is not ruled out. Naturally, those who are harmed by change will attempt to respond, but there is no guarantee that the response will be successful: the indigenous communities of Mindanao, for example, are in great danger of being destroyed by the forces unleashed by technical change.

Conflict can be found at many different levels, and the various groups in society can be divided in several different ways to reflect this fact. At one level there is a conflict between nations. This is an aspect of the "green revolution" to which we have devoted relatively little attention. It does arise, however, in connection with the tendency of several countries to use the new varieties as an excuse or opportunity to import substitute foodgrains at the expense of traditional rice exporting nations. In addition, there are other contexts in which international conflicts of interest can be present, e.g., a conflict between countries which wish to export agricultural machinery and agro-chemicals and those that wish to safeguard domestic employment.

The international dimension of conflict is not without interest, but the evidence we have collected appears to indicate that most of the conflicts arising from the "green revolution" are domestic in origin. A fundamental division in society is between those who own property and those who do not. The former have a common interest in keeping wage rates low and this can most easily be secured by adopting policies which restrain the rate of increase of the productivity of labour in the agricultural sector. Although a policy of low productivity in agriculture would tend to go counter to the interests of landlords, in many countries the problem has been overcome by landlords diversifying their assets and becoming industrialists as well. The "marriage of steel and rye" is a common phenomenon.

Nonetheless, there are many occasions when the interests of the agricultural sector as a whole conflict with those of non-agriculture. This is especially true when the rural areas are squeezed in order to extract resources which can be used for investment and consumption elsewhere. There are three devices which have been used to do this—by monopolizing land, by intentionally turning the terms of trade against agriculture and by imposing direct controls. Each device has different implications for resource allocation and income distribution.

The interests of agriculture and industry need not conflict, of course. Indeed in some cases growth in the one encourages growth in the other. For example, the "green revolution" has provided an enormous stimulus to small manufacturing firms in Ludhiana, India to supply agricultural implements to wheat farmers in the Punjab. Similar growth of agriculture related industries, particularly of firms producing diesel engines and irrigation pumps, can be observed in Lahore and other cities of Pakistan. Linkages between the two sectors are even more developed in Taiwan.

A possible clash of interests between sectors, however, is subordinate to a clash of interests between classes. Within agriculture, an analysis conducted in terms of a simple division between landlords and peasants will suffice for many purposes. That is a basic distinction that has to be made between those whose income is derived almost entirely from rent or profit and those who (implicitly or explicitly) derive much of their income in the form of returns to labour. Different policies can have quite different consequences for the two groups. This becomes clear, for instance, when factor prices and policies toward mechanization are discussed, as well as when the issues connected with land reform are examined.

We have argued that technical change in rural areas leads to greater specialization and division of labour and to greater social differentiation. In other words, in the course of the "green revolution" our assumption that the rural community can be divided into two groups—landlords and peasants—tends to become undermined. The peasantry ceases to be a homogeneous class (if it ever was) and the analysis has to be conducted in terms of a more sophisticated model. The minimum degree of elaboration is a division of the rural community into four classes: the landed elite, middle peasants, small peasants and agricultural labourers. The purpose of this division is to allow us to take into account the fact that conflict of interest arises not only between the landed elite and the peasantry as a whole but also among groups within the peasantry.

Middle peasants have three defining characteristics: first, they derive most (but not necessarily all) of their income from cultivation; second, their production on the farm exceeds the subsistence requirements of the household and thus a surplus is available for disposal on the market; third, their need for labour exceeds the amount available from within the household and consequently they must employ workers from off the farm. These three characteristics often will be found together, although there is no need to insist that the absence of one invalidates the concept. Small peasants and minifundistas, in contrast, have little land, often are unable even to produce the subsistence requirements of the family, and thus are forced to derive a significant proportion of their income from hiring themselves out for wage employment and engaging in other off-farm activities. Many small peasants are self-employed. The class of small peasants gradually merges into the class of landless agricultural labourers. This group, of little significance in Southeast Asia, is quite large in South Asia and in parts of Latin America. They derive their entire income from wages (received in cash or partly in kind) and may be employed either as permanent workers on a single farm, as seasonal workers in a single locality subject to lengthy periods of idleness or as roving migrant workers with no fixed abode.

Conflicts of various sorts can arise within the peasantry, of which the following are merely examples. First, agricultural labourers and small peasants are net buyers of foodgrains and thus have an interest in policies which help to keep the price of food cheap. The middle peasants, being net sellers, have an interest in maintaining high food prices and, hence, would favour price support programmes and similar measures. Second, the bottom two classes depend on wage employment for all or part of their livelihood and thus have an interest in policies which create additional work opportunities and higher wages. The middle peasants, however, hire labour and therefore have an opposing interest in low wages. Agricultural labourers would favour a rural public works programme, while middle peasants would not; the labourers would benefit from policies which enable workers to become strongly organized, whereas the middle peasantry would lose from such policies. Similarly, there would be a conflict of interest over minimum wages, the terms on which credit is provided for agricultural mechanization, and even the desirable degree of capital intensity in urban areas. What unites the middle and small peasantry is their common interest in acquiring more land from the landed elite, but in many other respects their interests differ. The landless labourers, on the other hand, are interested not in land but in higher wages, job security and better working conditions. Their interests are in evident conflict with those of the middle peasantry, but on several issues the interests of labourers and small peasants coincide. Thus, once again, different policies can have very different implications for the various classes that comprise the rural community.

Many of the policies that governments have adopted have been not only inegalitarian, they have also reduced the level of output and its rate of growth. In effect, governments have been arbiters of a "negative sum game." That is, the gains of those who have benefitted from public policy have been less than the losses of those discriminated against. This, of course, is an inevitable consequence of any policy which results in allocative inefficiency. An example of such a policy is the common practice of protecting industry and turning the terms of trade against agriculture. The losses suffered by the rural community may be substantial, whereas the additional profits reaped by industrialists may be rather small in comparison, particularly if the technical efficiency of the protected activities is rather low—as is often the case. Similarly, within agriculture, policies which subsidize labour displacing mechanization may increase the profits of landowners much less than they reduce the income of the workers; this will occur whenever factor proportions fail to reflect opportunity costs.

Unfortunately, the policies that preceded and have accompanied the "green revolution" in many underdeveloped countries have aggravated several of the problems these countries face. Supplies of some commodities have increased, but the rate of growth of total agricultural production has shown little tendency to rise. At the same time, inequality has become worse (e.g. in India), poverty sometimes has increased absolutely (e.g. in parts of Java), and employment opportunities have failed to keep up with population growth (e.g. Sri Lanka); in some cases technical change has led to such sharp social conflict that the peasantry (or part of it) has had to try to defend itself with violence (e.g. in Mindanao, Philippines). The high yielding varieties of foodgrains that have been developed—and those which are still in the pipeline—could in principle be used to alleviate many of these problems. But with the important exception of Taiwan, this has not occurred. The reason lies not in inadequate technology, but in inappropriate institutions and poor policy. The explanation for the latter, in turn, lies not in the ignorance of those who govern but in the powerlessness of most of those who are governed.

Notes

1. See, for example, Bruce Johnston and John Cownie, "The Seed-Fertilizer Revolution and Labor Force Absorption," *American Economic Review* (September, 1969).

2. L.J. Lau and P.A. Yotopoulos, "A Test for Relative Efficiency and Application to Indian Agriculture," *American Economic Review* (March, 1971). Also see M. Paglin, "'Surplus' Agricultural Labor and Development," *American Economic Review* (September, 1965).

3. Some of the evidence is summarized in Keith Griffin and A.R. Khan, eds., *Growth and Inequality in Pakistan* (London, Macmillan, 1972) commentary to Part Four.

4. A.S. Kahlon and Harbhajan Singh Bal, *Factors Associated with Farm and Farm Family Investment Pattern in Ludhiana (Punjab) and Hissar (Haryana) Districts: (1966-67 through 1969-70)* (Ludhiana, n.d.) Department of Economics and Sociology, Punjab Agricultural University.

5. *Ibid.*, p. 233.

6. W.A. Lewis, "Economic Development with Unlimited Supplies of Labour," *Manchester School of Economic and Social Studies* (May, 1954), p. 149.

Work, Incentives and Rural Society and Culture in Developing Nations

Manning Nash
University of Chicago

This discussion is restricted to comparisons and contrasts between peasant societies of Southeast Asia (really Burma and Malaya) and Latin America (really Mexico and Guatemala) because I have first-hand knowledge of these societies, and because they form analytically useful permutations. However, I hope to develop the bare bones of an apparatus that will be diagnostically useful in other cultural and economic contexts.

The Importance of Social and Cultural Variables in Subsistence Settings

Most of the peasantry of Southeast Asia operate in a dual economic framework. They are oriented at the same time to subsistence activities and to some form of cash cropping or labor export for cash wages. A subsistence-exchange ratio could be constructed on the basis of household budgets, and that ratio would be crucial in understanding the deployment of the human and other resources at the disposal of the decision-making unit, usually a domestic household with a familial or kinship core. Generally, the higher the exchange component in the income stream the less problematical the incentive structure of the peasant household, and conversely the higher the subsistence component the more problematic the economic analysis of resource allocation. In a mostly subsistence economy, or to be more accurate, in an economy minimally dependent on exchange and a ramifying specialization and division of labor, social and cultural variables must be given serious consideration; as economies become more exchange oriented, the safer and more practical it is to take the social and cultural variables and bracket them away in the limbo of ceterus paribus.

The countrysides of Upper Burma around Saigaing and of Northeast Malaya in Pasir Mas district are broadly similar in cultural and social patterns, but the gross and subtle differences highlight the role of the family, ideology, religion, and regional market integration in the deployment of peasant effort and resources.

The Kampong Economy of Northeast Malaysia

The delta region of Kelantan is a small but classic rice bowl economy. The peasants live in village clusters, here called kampong. They divide their efforts between the wet rice fields *(padi)* lying close to the kampong, the orchard crops *(dusun)* in the house compound, and the scattered patches of rubber tree stands *(getah)*. The best estimate is that 10 acres, six in rice, three in rubber, and the remaining for house and orchard would meet the customary definition of adequacy in level of living. But with the demographic density in the delta, adequacy is the expectation, not the norm. The characteristics of a long settled, dense, chiefly subsistence wet rice economy are all present: minifundia (and only a few large holdings), fragmentation of holdings, high rates of tenancy, labor intensity, and the right of any member of a household to participate in work and hence share in proceeds, so that added human inputs have diminishing marginal utility.

The peasant families of Pasir Mas eke out the subsistence base by classic means: labor export, artisan work, and marketing of primary products. The rice harvest of North Malaya occurs in the off season of the rice cycle in Kelantan, so Kelantan men migrate for the labor peak periods in Kedah and Perlis. They almost to a man return to Kelantan to work their own or others' padi fields. There is also some work, chiefly for women who also run domestic units, in the tobacco processing stations of the Malayan branch of British American Tobacco Company.

Since Kelantan is in the backwater of Malayan development, the artisan skills and crafts have not been swamped by the spread of cheap manufactures. Part of being in the periphery is the preservation of modes of dress, food, tools and ornamentation which the mass-production world does not find profitable to produce. So silverworking, batik dyeing, sawmilling, iron forging, and weaving are still part of the Kelantan scene. Some of this is proceeding to the level of cottage industry and the putting-out system, but is still a low capital, peasant means of supplementing meagre agricultural incomes.

In the marketplace of Pasir Mas are really three kinds of markets, by product, seller, and organization. There is the pasar section peopled by Malays, chiefly women, and mainly from the local district. Here primary products are sold—rice, spices, fish, fruit, prepared food, etc.—by either the producer or a woman specializing in this trade by bringing products from the kampong to the market. The pasar is a cash transaction between buyer and seller, usually many small transactions over the course of the day; there is no "clientele," and little bargaining, since the price is set by supply and demand conditions of the season and of that particular day in the actual market place. The profit is on transactions, and the skill of the seller is in winning the contest in individual encounters with largely anonymous, and fleeting, customers. Obviously this is a barely-capitalized, exchange system, and the windfall rather than planned expansion is the hope of the small pasar seller.

There is a more modern store segment of the market. This is chiefly the *rumah-kedai* (house-store) of the Chinese merchant or Indian, Pakistani, or Arab trader. Here small businesses—with credit extended, with a clientele, with account books, and with moderate capital and inventory—exists. This small business segment expands as the population increases and incomes from primary agricultural production rise. It contracts when rubber prices fall, when floods damage the rice crop, when government aid diminishes.

Finally, there is a truly modern component of the pasar—the franchises of the national and international corporations, selling refrigerators, radios, television sets, gasoline, oil, ovens, etc. These are in the hands of Chinese or Indians.

From the point of view of the Malay peasant in Kelantan, the economy has expanded slowly in a limited economic niche available to him. He responded favorably to the opportunity to tap rubber for a world market; the women moved into the pasar as that grew up from 1909 onwards with the expansion of the transportation network; and the men have migrated seasonally to the other side of the peninsula, or they have in the hundreds taken to peddling the trishaws which are still the backbone of rural transportation.

This kind of incremental and interstitial expansion within a narrow economic niche is in part related to the social organization and the culture of the kampong-based social order. Economic innovation is not built into the structure of kampong life; indeed, it is neither actively sought nor highly prized. After all, the techniques of cultivation have evolved over centuries so that, given adequate rainfall and minimal floods, the necessities of life can be reliably produced. This ecological balance is precarious and most innovations turn out in the context of the kampong to be deleterious rather than adaptive. But the ecological, technological and economic constraints on innovation are not the whole story.

There is a generalized view of the meaningful life in the kampong. For a label this ethos can be called the ''kampong ideology.'' The kampong ideology holds that rural life is the only moral, proper, and fitting human existence. A man should live in his own wood and split-bamboo house in the shade of his trees surrounded by kinsmen and neighbors. In the kampong are people with names, who are roughly equals, a sort of fraternity of farmers. This community of peers is informed by the religious teachings of Islam. The kampong is, in the insight of Boeke, ''a religious community of believers, co-resident equals engaged in sawah agriculture.''[1] Of course, this idyllic view is not the reality of kampong life. There are wealth and status differences, hostilities, enmities and factions. But it is a pervasive normative structure, and public behavior is canalized by the template of the desirable life.

The units in a Malay kampong are domestic households. At the core of the household is a kinship unit. In most long-settled kampongs all the people are in one way or another kinsmen, if anybody bothered to trace the genealogical connections. But the kin bonds are not activated in social relations beyond the second cousin degree collaterally, or three generations in depth. Everybody in the kampong is addressed by kin terms, often with a nickname following the uncle or aunt prefix, but this indicates only the generalized humanity of the person, not bonds of diffuse solidarity that active degrees of real blood *(darah)* kinship imply.

The kinship core of a household is ideally and statistically predominantly a nuclear family of husband, wife and immature offspring. This basic unit is frequently expanded with a senior generation or resident grandchildren, but infrequently by sets of married siblings in the same households. All sorts of on the ground variations exist because of the rhythm of the domestic cycle, which often includes years of wife service, and the accidents of birth, death, divorce, and multiple marriages.

Beyond the technical detail, the importance of this family structure and household composition is that a small (in terms of kinship extension) and shallow (in terms of time depth) unit is the locus of economic and social decision making. This sort of unit is engaged in maximizing two sorts of magnitudes—its present and short-run income and social status, and the possibilities of mobility for the children who are its responsibility. The unit is not hampered by the ramifying claims of a lineage, or the indivisibility of property often part of a corporate kinship structure, which are aspects of kinship most frequently discarded in the movement toward modern labor force participation.[2]

This family structure, with its kampong ideology and its views of what it can effectively maximize, deploys its human and other resources in an expectable manner. The overriding consideration is to maintain, and if possible expand, its land base in wet rice and rubber and orchard. Alienation of land through sale is the sign of dire economic straits of real social crisis for a family. The amount of land held determines the optimal size of a household in the sense of the number of hands it can most effectively use in cultivation. But any member of the household has by that membership token alone the right to participate and hence the right to share in the household's produce. In large, land-poor households there is a collective downward spiral of living aptly called "involution" by Geertz for the comparable phenomenon in Java.[3]

The kampong household knows only of one sure route of social mobility for its children—education. Completing secondary education or the university makes someone eligible for the government bureaucracy. The educated person can become a member of the "salariat" with a respected and envied town-based or city-located life style. He can *makan gaji,* literally eat salary, that is have a steady and high income, freed from the vicissitudes of flood, sun, soil, and the farmer's heavy toil.

The investment in education in Pasir Mas district is surprisingly heavy. In the district more than 90 per cent of the eligible school children are in fact school attenders and about 65 per cent of the age cohort are in secondary school. This represents a considerable outlay for the kampong families. But if a boy or girl has the skills to make it through secondary school, the family will collectively tighten its belt to put up the money to see him through. The Malay tradition of *gotong-royong* (mutual help, reciprocal labor exchange, and other connotations) is within the domestic unit a working ethic, and members of the family do not feel deprived when they knowingly reduce their wants to promote the social mobility of their more gifted members.

What has been sketched here is a sort of economic, social, and cultural structure which has grown up incrementally over a long time, adjusting, adapting, and accommodating to the modest opportunity occasions presented to it. Such structures lack the dynamism to make transformations of the basic patterns; they do not harbor a restless seed of innovation, nor do they conceive of paths to other structures. They respond to the pressures and opportunities just on the horizon, and slowly fill the niches in the economic world open to them.

These structures work until the density of population reaches the point of supersaturation of the land resources. Then comes grinding poverty, massive unemployment, drift to the cities, and a pervading atmosphere of unrest and irritation conducive to peasant risings, religious millenialism, and the empty-eyed apathy of those whose social circumstances make a mockery of hope.

The Peasant Economy of Upper Burma

Upper Burma, when I studied it in 1960-61, was an earlier, more open, more flexible phase of the involuted sawah economic structure. The point of contrasting the Burmese to the Kelantan situation is obvious: the historical moment of attempts to modernize or rationalize a rural economic structure is of equal theoretical consequence with the economic and sociocultural structure of the contemporary society. In Upper Burma in the early 60's it was still possible, with the right policy moves, to eliminate the peasantry through transformation into farmers.

The basic differences between the villages of Upper Burma and the Kelantan delta turn on religion and ethos. The nuclear family structures, the shallow and narrow kinship networks, are (apart from differences in the nomenclature of kinship) structurally and functionally similar—as they are for most of Southeast Asia, barring some of the hill tribes or the clan organized Miningkabau, Batak, Kachin, or the stem families of the Iban.

The dominant idiom for interpreting and making experience meaningful in Upper Burma is Theravada Buddhism. The canons of Burmese Buddhism as they appear to the field anthropologist are well presented in the words of Spiro and Nash.[4] What is of interest is how the social scientists have interpreted the bearing of the canons on economic and social behavior. There is some disagreement between Spiro and Hagen,[5] on the one hand, and Spiro and myself on the other. Briefly, Spiro maintains against Hagen that Burmese Buddhists are rational in the use of resources when they spend 20 to 30 per cent of their income on religious monuments and activities. He holds that, given the world view which stresses favorable rebirths gained through the accumulation of merit by devotional and religious giving, the Burmese are maximizing the magnitude most important to them. Hagen, an economist, views the heavy expenditure on religion as inhibiting capital formation, depressing the investment level, and hence hindering economic development, which is also one of the stated goals of the elite and the peasantry. The difference here is clearly that of an inside cultural view versus a social science analytical perspective.

Spiro and I differ on the sources of some behavioral and personality traits of the peasants we observed. We agree, largely, on the social and cultural regularities that characterize the Burmese, but Spiro attributes them to patterns of early socialization and child rearing in the family. I attribute them to the meaning and structure of Theravada Buddhism as refracted through the daily circumstances of life in a Burmese village. Here, it is two differing theoretical perspectives in dissonance, rather than insider versus outsider interpretations of behavior. Irrespective of the relative merits of Spiro's or my argument, the following seems to characterize the peasants of Upper Burma.

The knowledge and practice of Buddhism shapes much of the public character of the Burman and exerts a determinate influence on many aspects of the social structure. The first effect of the villagers' understanding of Buddhism is on the time horizon. Nothing can matter very much in this brief existence, wedged in among countless others. The effect of actions is very remote, so planning and sustained effort are discouraged and emphasis is placed on living in the here and now. Burmese life has the dual quality of appearing as a series of rather unconnected, immediate instances without much tie to the past, and with little concern for the future, and at the same time being filled with beginnings for projects of great energy which fizzle out and leave nothing in their wake. Burmans can and do plan, but the time horizon is always vague, and failure to do anything within a fixed period means nothing and occasions no emotions.

Many observers have noted the even tenor, the cheerfulness, and the optimism of the village Burman. These are in part derived from his Buddhism. Buddhism, according to which every man does what he can for his movement along the path to Nibban, leaves the individual feeling that any misdeed can be repaired in the future, that acts of merit can overcome acts of demerit, and that there is forever to do so. A person can only be as religious as his temperament allows him to be. He is always doing the best he can, and when he gets older, he will spend more time at merit building. Such an understanding leaves little room for guilt, anxiety, remorse or worry. And the villagers are never long sunk in any of these. As the village interprets *kan* (the moral nucleus of the balance of merit and demerit that goes from existence to existence along the chain of rebirths), it is not a fixed, implacable fate beyond the control of influence of the individual. Kan can be added to, its influence can be improved, and the good can be made to outweigh the evil. Besides, kan is not a single steady force always operating in the same direction. Sometimes the good deeds predominate and sometimes the evil predominates, and who knows but at the next venture the good may override the evil in a man's fate. Also there is always the hope that in the long run a person can accumulate enough merit to better his condition. And getting merit is so easy, so lacking in interior strain, in emotional turmoil, that cheerfulness and optimism are features which are easily fixed in the character of the Burman.

The obverse of these features is a kind of superficiality of concern, a lack of deep emotional currents, and what, from the viewpoint of a Westerner, are remarkable swings in the personality. Burmese life appears on the surface to lack deep involvements, outside of the family, and Burmans are certainly more self-concerned than other-directed. Each Burman appears as a hard, irreducible atom, only lightly tied to other people, only slightly concerned with the state of the community beyond his immediate needs. The common village saying that "there is no love like self-love" sums this up very aptly. The idea of *mehta,* universal love, is far from the villager, and the ability to identify himself with persons in the abstract is entirely absent.

This individuating effect of Burmese Buddhism, this placing of each single nucleus of kan at the center of its own universe, permits the Burman wide swings in his reactions to the world. He flares up easily, is bad-tempered and violent upon provocation, and does not cultivate interior restraint or self-discipline. If he cannot have his way, he either withdraws or lashes out violently. The art of compromise, the adjustment of interests between parties, is rare, requiring personal habits not strong in the Burmese. Burmans let each other alone very much, if there is no direct conflict between parties. A man who violates morality norma, or an official who is venal, or a monk who breaks his vows, does not get censure directly. After all, he is responsible for his own fate, all will balance out in the end, and why should I get involved and get into trouble by telling him to mend his ways? is the way a villager reasons. Gossip there is, personal rating too, but community public opinion, organized sanctions, or pressures to conform, there are not.

Buddhism, for the villager, is a costly business. The expenditure on gift giving, on ceremonial, on monk feeding is a large item in every family budget. Furthermore, when wealth is accumulated, it tends to be invested in merit-making projects rather than economic enterprise: the pagoda, the monastery, the well for the monks, a bell for a monastery, all of these are hopes and ambitions for those without wealth, and plans and projects for those with it. Buddhism thus diverts a good part of the individual and communal wealth into the channels of religious expenditure. It promotes and abets a common feature of Burmese life, display spending. Buddhism therefore is a brake on capital formation and tends to turn the local economy into one of monument building.

The extreme emphasis on the individual atomizes the society into family groupings and inhibits the formation of larger, perdurable associations. It also promotes wide areas of individual autonomy and suppresses organizations oriented to other than religious ends. As such it tends to make leadership and leaders personalistic and charismatic, rather than institutional or structural. Burmese society is marked by coalition around leaders endowed with certain powers and abilities derived from the notions of strong kan.

Concomitant with this is the egalitarian nature of the society. There are, in the village, no social classes, no large status distinctions, except those of sex and age. Buddhism can be seen to have the effect then of individuating, of leveling, of social equalizing, and with this the consequences of charismatic leaders, power coalitions, and ad hoc impermanent affiliations.

Transforming a Peasantry into a Wage Labor Force

This sketch of the world view of the villager and its social concomitants suggests an incentive structure different from that which is expected in a modern labor force. But like all world views, it is historically subject to differing emphasis on its canons, and hence to generating different motivation structures. It is my conviction that the incentive structure relevant to participation in and commitment to a roster of modern occupations is built up in the very process of participation and rarely exists anterior to that historical involvement.

From this conviction comes the obvious corollary that economic development and modernization in the rural areas advances on twin fronts. First the input of adequate modern knowledge and technology into the peasant sector (like the vaunted "green revolution"), and second the building of industry in the countryside to absorb the labor displaced by the continuing rationalization of peasant agriculture.

The implications of these activities in the countryside revolve around finding the technology that is truly of comparative advantage to the farmer, on the one hand, and structuring industry so that largely voluntary participation in the labor force will ensue.

In 1953-54, I studied the Mayan Indian community of Cantel, Guatemala. The interesting thing about Cantel and the Cantelense was that a cotton factory had been operating for more than 75 years in the midst of this Indian community, using largely local Indian labor. It was a going concern, and Cantel appeared richer and more dynamic than its neighboring Indian communities without factories.[6]

From that experience, and with comparative data from other parts of the developing world, I constructed a series of hypotheses on the variables of what is involved in the successful recruitment and commitment of a labor force from a peasant society. I shall state those hypotheses in a rather stark manner, so that I can tie together the threads of the argument in this paper.

A wage labor force which is regular, efficient, and willing to learn new skills will be recruited from peasant societies and will be maintained at wage work if:

1. the economic returns of wage labor are significantly greater than alternative opportunities in an impoverished rural area;
2. the income is translatable into customary channels of expenditure;
3. the training for wage work, the exercise of authority on the job, and the standard of output allow the recruit to adjust occupationally at his own pace;
4. new relations emerge in the context of wage work, and if these new social relations involve personal bonds;
5. a workers' organization evolves which gives wage workers some command over the job and conditions of work;
6. the institutional structure beyond the wage work situation is relatively intact so that a set of cultural norms and social relations continue to give content and meaning to work effort and coherence to personality;
7. the wage worker is not significantly differentiated socially or isolated culturally from those with whom he has the greatest frequency and depth of social interaction;
8. there are new wants tied to money wages and some social and medical services contingent on staying at wage work.

These eight sentences are arranged in order of their importance in recruiting and keeping a wage labor force, and apparently are logically adequate to account for the instances of successful labor force formation I know of.[7]

The implications of the foregoing descriptions and arguments are fairly straightforward. The first is that a knowledge of the social and cultural context is crucial to the success or failure of any innovation, economic or otherwise. The notions of compatibility, comparative advantage or utility of an innovation cannot be assessed in the abstract; they must be concretely ranged against an existing social structure and cultural pattern. This view does away with the hindering notions of "prerequisites," "barriers," "obstacles," and other such reifications that have from time to time graced the literature on economic development and cultural change. There are only well and ill-designed plans and innovations, or innovations which in fact are of comparative advantage (taking that in its widest cultural and social sense) or which are not.

Theoretically, this view shifts the onus of poverty and slow development from the peasant, his culture and his society to the elite of his nation, to the planners and to the international technocrats. The lack or slowness of economic development is not to be laid at the mythical conservatism of the peasant, or at the feet of his ignorance, or at his lack of receptivity to income-raising opportunities. The burden falls on the planners and the administrators for not seeing the structure of economic opportunity through the lens of the peasants' real choices and possibilities, and hence failing to design, present, and offer meaningful economic options.

It is no easy thing to design, package, and offer to the peasantry what they need and will accept, but neither is it mysterious or socially insuperable. What is needed is the commitment of the nation's elite to the public welfare and the technocrats willing to relax the constraints of trained incompetence to encompass the capabilities, cultures and careers of the peasantry.

Notes

1. See his interesting discussion of the village in J.H. Boeke, *Economics and Economic Policy of Dual Societies* (New York, Institute of Pacific Relations, 1953), particularly Chapter III.

2. Manning Nash, "Southeast Asian Society: Dual or Multiple," *Journal of Asian Studies,* XXIII, No. 3 (May, 1964). See also Manning Nash, "Social Prerequisite to Economic Growth in Latin America and Southeast Asia," *Economic Development and Cultural Change* (April, 1964).

3. Clifford Geertz, *Agricultural Involution: The Processes of Ecological Change in Indonesia* (Berkeley, University of California Press, 1963).

4. Manning Nash, *The Golden Road to Modernity: Village Life in Contemporary Burma* (New York, Wiley, 1965); and Melford E. Spiro, *Buddhism and Society* (New York, Harper & Row, 1970).

5. Everett E. Hagen, *On the Theory of Social Change* (Homewood, Illinois, Dorsey, 1962), especially Chapter VIII.

6. Manning Nash, *Cantel, 1944-54* (Tulane, Middle American Research Institute, 1957), No. 24, pp. 28-32.

7. Manning Nash, "The Recruitment of Wage Labor and Development of New Skills," *Annals of the American Academy of Political and Social Sciences* (May, 1956), pp. 23-31.

The Choice of Technology, Economic Efficiency and Employment in Developing Countries*

James Pickett
D.J.C. Forsyth
N.S. McBain
University of Strathclyde

This paper comprises a bald presentation of some results of an enquiry into the choice of technology in the sugar and footwear industries in Ethiopia and Ghana, and a bold examination of some implications of these results. The baldness can be justified by the need for brevity and the fact that more complete results, more fully described, will shortly be available; the boldness by the desire to focus attention on a number of issues which can stand airing in provocative form.

The paper is organized in three parts. The first provides a brief theoretical introduction (to help fix ideas); the second describes the research and presents the results; and the third considers some questions raised by the findings.

The Simple Theory of Technological Choice

In conventional economic theory, variations in capital-labour ratios are the standard response to variations in factor prices. Assuming that capital and labour are each homogenous, optimal production strategy would substitute labour for capital if the relative price of labour were to fall. From this it follows that if a given (planned) output (represented by isoquant XX in Figure 1) of a particular commodity were to be produced in two different locations with different factor price relatives, then the capital-labour ratio (given by the slope of OA) in the location where labour is relatively expensive would be greater than the capital-labour ratio (given by the slope of OB) in the location where labour is relatively cheap. In profit-maximizing equilibrium in a two-factor model the ratio of marginal products of the two factors is equal to the factor price ratio, so that P and Q in Figure 1 represent the respective equilibrium positions for the two production locations.

Given complete factor mobility, the position depicted in Figure 1 could not persist. Capital and labour would both move in search of higher returns until (ignoring transport costs) relative factor prices were the same in both locations and production was characterized by a common capital-labour ratio. In fact there are many barriers to factor movement (particularly labour mobility). Different capital-labour ratios could therefore reasonably be expected in different sub-markets, with the gap being greatest between the relatively most capital and the relatively most labour rich countries

*The research reported in this paper was undertaken by the Overseas Development Unit, (now the David Livingstone Institute of Overseas Development Studies) University of Strathclyde, and generously financed by the British Foreign and Commonwealth Office (Overseas Development Administration).

respectively. In keeping with this expectation, low wage countries would use labour-intensive and high wage countries capital-intensive methods of production. In practice, however, the expected very wide spread of capital-labour ratios in any given industry is not generally observed as between developed and developing countries. Even in the latter the casual observer is impressed by the 'sophisticated'—that is, in the general usage, capital-intensive—nature of plant and machinery, so that it seems that efforts are made to save labour even in labour rich countries.

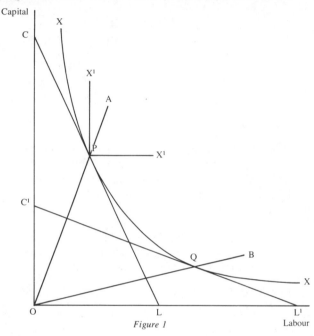

Figure 1

This contrast between expectation and reality is paradoxical since it creates a presumption that profits and employment are lower than they should be. Moreover, the inefficiency resulting from inappropriate technology need not be confined to the industry or sector in which such technology is used. In particular, the use of inefficient techniques in industry can result in non-optimum production in both industry and agriculture.

Figure 1 is a useful caricature which portrays the investment decision as comprising a fusion of independent economic and engineering elements. Not surprisingly therefore the paradoxical contrast between theory and practice has been given both technological and economic explanation. In extreme form, the technological explanation invokes completely rigid technology, in the face of which differences in relative factor prices would be irrelevant. If this explanation were valid, the production isoquant XX in Figure 1 would be replaced by the isoquant X^1PX^1. The economic explanation is basically that factor prices are distorted in developing countries. Among reasons adduced in support of this are overvalued exchange rates; generous investment allowances and other policy measures which artificially reduce the price of capital; and minimum wage laws and pressures resulting from the establishment and growth of urban trade unions which increase the price of labour.

Explanations of the paradox are considered more fully in the final section of this paper. Here it may be noted that the empirical work partially reported below suggests that there is considerable scope for technological choice in the sugar and footwear industries. Moreover available results suggest that the techniques actually used in Ghana and Ethiopia could have been replaced by more labour-intensive techniques which would also have been more profitable at factor prices as a businessman would observe them in these countries.

Some Empirical Research into the Choice of Technology

The enquiry into the choice of technology in the sugar and footwear industries in Ethiopia and Ghana basically required (a) the identification of as wide (and as dense) a range of alternative techniques of producing sugar and footwear as possible, and (b) the costing of the use of each alternative technique for given levels of output in Ethiopian and Ghanaian conditions. Field work in Ethiopia, Ghana, India, Jamaica, British Honduras, the United States and the United Kingdom provided much information on technologies (specification of plant, production machinery, manning requirements and all other associated inputs) and on capital and operating costs. This work involved visits to sugar and footwear plants, to the manufacturers of relevant capital goods, to universities and other research institutions, and (particularly in Ethiopia and Ghana) to government statistical and planning agencies.

Meticulous examination of sugar and footwear technologies has produced a conviction that the scope for choice is very great, so that technological determinism (portrayed by the isoquant X^1PX^1 in Figure 1) is ruled out. In sugar three basic systems of production have been identified: (a) the vacuum-pan or 'modern' process, (b' the Khandsari type open-pan sulphitation process, and (c) the Jaggery/vacuum-pan process. Within each system there are sub-processes, and variants are available within each sub-process. In footwear manufacturing (except for rubber boots and one shot injection-moulded shoes) there is basically one system, but still much scope for choice since there is a large number of alternative operations.

In illustration of the scope for choice, consider the vacuum-pan sugar process, in which there are at least twelve distinct sub-processes. At the plant, these are: cane handling, milling etc., clarifying, filtering, evaporating and boiling, crystallizing, centrifuging, drying, weighing and bagging, storing, general materials handling, and generating and transmitting power and steam. In Table 1 these sub-processes are numbered seriatim and the minimum number of ways in which each sub-process can

TABLE 1

SUB-PROCESSES AND THEIR VARIANTS IN VACUUM-PAN
SUGAR PRODUCTION

Sub-processes	1	2	3	4	5	6	7	8	9	10	11	12
No. of variants	4	6	2	3	2	1	5	3	6	2	2	3

be organized is shown. On the assumption that the variants of each sub-process are independent of one another, the significance of Table 1 is that there are 311,040 different ways in which vacuum-pan sugar can be produced!

It is, of course, not permissible to assume complete independence among all the production variants. The choice of crushing mill, for example, may affect the output of bagasse (fibrous cane waste). Since this is used as a boiler fuel, the choice of crusher may influence the specification of (power) boiler. Again, the choice of clarification technique will affect the quantity and character of impurities separated from the treated cane juice, and thus influence the choice of filtration equipment. Such considerations could, however, rule out eighty per cent of the independently-determined ways of making sugar and still leave over 60,000 alternatives. Some of these residual alternatives could, in certain circumstances, be technically inefficient. The general point, however, surely remains. Even if it were possible only to consider two variants for each sub-process there would still be 4,096 combinations.

The dismissal of technological determinism can be further supported. In the world as a whole, the gap between 'best' and 'worst' practice techniques (and consequently between highest and lowest capital-labour ratios) in the sugar and footwear industries is considerable; plant managers tend to be gradualist in the modernization of their factories; and machine manufacturers do not normally confine themselves to a single set of machines—thus 'manual,' semi-automatic, automatic and continuous centrifugal sugar machines are currently available (and in use). The gaps between capital-labour ratios, however, tend to correlate more highly with time of plant establishment than with plant location, so that the availability of many alternative technologies has not evidently been reflected in recently established plants in developing countries. It is therefore now necessary to examine the consequences of restricted (inappropriate) choice of techniques.

These consequences can be brought out by comparison between existing or 'synthetic' technologies representative of Ethiopian and Ghanaian practice and either techniques in use elsewhere or other 'synthetic' techniques, both adapted to Ethiopian and Ghanaian conditions. 'Synthetic' techniques have no direct counterpart in reality. They are, however, technologically feasible combinations of existing sub-processes or operations. To illustrate and provide foundation for the final part of this paper, three comparisons were made: one between two existing sugar processes, and two among three 'synthetic' shoe processes.* Discounted cash flow techniques were used to appraise the alternative technologies, and a skeletal cost-benefit analysis applied by 'adjusting' the exchange rate, using shadow wage rates, and eliminating transfer payments.

The comparison between existing processes involved an actual Ghanaian vacuum-pan and an open-pan sulphitation process. The Ghanaian factory, designed to produce sugar to normal mill-white standard, has an operating capacity of 24,000 tons per annum. It was assumed (necessarily in logic but wrongly in fact) that this level of output has been achieved since shortly after the factory was commissioned and that it will continue to be achieved for 25 years from that time. The net present value and the internal rate of return were then calculated, given the initial fixed capital investment and taking what was believed to be the most efficient manning system and the most efficient flow of current inputs. In these calculations base year prices (defined for each input as the price observed at the time the original investment appraisal was carried out) were used. The calculations were then repeated for the

---

*It should be emphasized that these comparisons are illustrative and not exhaustive. A more complete scrutiny of alternatives could, in principle, identify more profitable and more capital-intensive sugar and footwear factories than any considered in the present text. Such identification (which is unlikely for footwear and, up to levels of output which are relevant for many developing countries, sugar), would not affect either the argument that more profitable and more labour-intensive techniques could have been chosen than that currently in use in Ethiopia and Ghana, nor the view that current decision-taking is economically inefficient.

same annual output and time period for the open-pan process used in Ghanaian conditions. Adjustments were made to both sets of calculations to obtain a measure of social profitability.

Table 2 sets out the results of these calculations. From the table it can be seen that the open-pan process would have been superior to the vacuum-pan process on each of the four criteria listed. (It can also be seen that the Ghanaian factory must have been a dubious proposition on any criterion, but that is another story.) The open-pan process would not only have been more profitable than the Ghanaian factory; it would also—since the initial capital investment would have been 33 per cent of that required

TABLE 2

PRIVATE AND SOCIAL RETURNS FROM ALTERNATIVE
SUGAR TECHNOLOGIES IN GHANA

Factory	PRIVATE PROFITABILITY		SOCIAL COST-BENEFIT	
	NPV (Cedis 000 at 10 per cent)	IRR (per cent)	NPV (Cedis 000 at 10 per cent)	IRR (per cent)
Ghanaian vacuum-pan	−1,898	6.5	−1,668	8.0
Khandsari open-pan	+2,320	12.0	+5,460	13.0

for the actual factory—have used less capital and provided more employment (for 700 full-time and 3,000 seasonal workers, as compared with 476 and 219 full-time and seasonal workers required for capacity operations in the existing plant).

The shoe comparisons required the design of three 'synthetic' factories in which the production process is an amalgam of known (i.e. existing) operations conventionally used in the UK and Africa. It was assumed that three factories would each produce 300,000 pairs of shoes per annum; that they would be efficiently run and produce (men's) shoes of identical quality; that they would operate a one-shift system; and that in Ethiopia locally-produced leather would be used, but that in Ghana leather would be imported. Imported synthetic sole units were thought necessary in both countries. The period of appraisal was taken as twenty-five years.

It is convenient to designate the factories A, B and C respectively. Their salient features are that:

Factory A involves cutting the upper leather to shape on power presses, machine lasting and other machine operations such as would be found in a 'modern' factory in a developed country;

Factory B provides for hand cutting of upper leather and machine aided hand lasting of the shoes; and

Factory C involves hand cutting of uppers, hand lasting and the minimum of other machine operations consistent with the production of footwear of comparable quality to that produced in the other two factories.

The capital-labour ratios (using the crude measures of fixed capital per employee) for each of the three factories as they would operate in Ethiopia and Ghana are given in Table 3; the private and social returns (calculated in the same way as those given for sugar in Table 2) in Table 4. It is evident that Factory A is the most capital-intensive and Factory C the most labour-intensive of the three, and that on all criteria Factory C would be preferred.

As with the sugar comparisons, the most profitable shoe factory would also use less capital and employ more labour than the relevant alternatives in Ethiopia and Ghana.

TABLE 3

CAPITAL-LABOUR RATIOS IN THREE SHOE FACTORIES
IN ETHIOPIA AND GHANA

	Ethiopia (Eth.$)	Ghana (Cedi)
Fixed capital per employee in:		
Factory A	7,450	4,960
Factory B	3,670	1,870
Factory C	2,620	1,420

Thus, the initial (fixed) capital investment in Factories A, B and C respectively would be ₵693,000, ₵350,000 and ₵276,000 in Ghana, and Eth. $1,043,000, Eth. $686,000 and Eth. $512,000 in Ethiopia. The choice of Factory C rather than Factory A would increase total and unskilled labour employment by 28 and 37 per cent respectively in both countries.

TABLE 4

PRIVATE AND SOCIAL RETURNS FROM ALTERNATIVE
SHOE TECHNOLOGIES IN ETHIOPIA AND GHANA

Country and factory	PRIVATE PROFITABILITY		SOCIAL COST-BENEFIT	
	NPV (Eth.$000 at 10 per cent)	IRR (per cent)	NPV (Eth.$000 at 10 per cent)	IRR (per cent)
Ethiopia				
Factory A	Eth. $1535.8	19.6	Eth. $6873.5	55.9
Factory B	Eth. $1754.6	23.1	Eth. $7155.7	74.9
Factory C	Eth. $1783.8	24.3	Eth. $7252.0	81.7
Ghana				
Factory A	₵ 912.8	19.9	₵2615.8	34.3
Factory B	₵1075.1	24.4	₵2802.0	43.9
Factory C	₵1113.5	27.1	₵3033.5	51.5

Some Paradoxes and Their Economic Implications

The theoretical introduction to this paper created a presumption that private or public decision-makers would, in the interests of economic viability and in choosing among alternative ways of producing a given volume of a given good, select the least-cost combination of factor inputs. In the light of limited factor mobility between developed and developing countries, the same theory created the further presumption that production in the former countries would be characterized by relatively capital-intensive techniques; that in the latter countries by relatively labour-intensive processes. These presumptions are admittedly based on restrictive assumptions. These include profit-maximizing behaviour; unlimited supplies of two (and only two) homogenous factors of production; continuous possibilities for factor substitution in production; and identical production functions and effectively functioning factor-price markets in each production location.

The naive model is nevertheless useful. In particular it (implicitly) recognizes the importance of individual projects, and consequently individual project appraisal, in economic development; sees the design of such projects, as has already been pointed out, as requiring a fusion of economic and engineering elements; and suggests (realistically enough) that the investment decision at any point in time will be founded in what is then known of technological options and economic costs. Seen in this light, the naive model leads naturally to the appraisal procedures underlying the results presented in the second part of this paper. These procedures assume that decision-takers should be marginalists (in a sense to be defined presently) and that the investment decision should comprise the determination of a project life span and an attempt to maximize the discounted present value of net returns over the life time of the project. The project appraisal procedures are more realistic than the theory in their necessary recognition of the full complexity of production, and in their explicit introduction of time into the decision-taking process. As applied in the second section of the paper, the procedures are akin to theory in suggesting conscientious search among alternative techniques, and in further suggesting that this should be undertaken on the basis of economic data available at the time of decision.*

The research reported above has three significant features. It (a) records the fact that sugar and footwear production tends to be much more capital-intensive than would be expected in Ethiopian and Ghanaian conditions; (b) establishes that there is considerable scope for choice of techniques in the two industries considered; and (c) suggests that in sugar production (in Ghana) and footwear production (in Ethiopia and Ghana) labour-intensive as compared to capital-intensive processes would economize in the use of capital, yield higher net present values for given projects and provide more employment. The conjunction of (a) and (c) gives rise to a paradox and a related challenge; and (b) makes it clear that limited availability of alternative technologies cannot be advanced in explanation of the paradox. Nor, indeed, can too much be made of the obvious alternative explanation—distorted factor prices. On the one hand, the sugar and footwear comparisons yield features (a), (b) and (c) on *both* private and social criteria; on the other, Ethiopian and Ghanaian exchange rates are arguably over-valued and investment allowances arguably over-generous. Thus bad decisions could evidently be improved upon even when appraisal is based on (distorted) market prices.

Discounted cash flow techniques, and the consequent possibility of choosing on the basis of net present values, are distinctly more pleasing to economists than alternative, more homely rules (such as the payback period) for project decision. Moreover, as part of the spread of mathematical and other logical aids to decision-taking, DCF

---

*The procedures underlying the second section of the present paper are still more naive than they need be. In particular they make no allowance for product and factor price changes through time; ignore externalities; and take no account of risk and uncertainty. They also ignore questions of scale (which can arise in important but complex ways). Nor do the procedures consider the possibility that factor prices facing different decision-takers may be different. The final report on the research which underlies the present discussion will be substantially more realistic in all of these respects. It will also contain a much larger number of comparisons of alternative techniques.

techniques are being increasingly adopted. Consequently, in its strongest and most challenging form, the puzzle which has to be resolved—as a prelude to policy action—is why, given this technological flexibility and demonstrated scope for improvement even in the face of factor price distortions, appraisal of developing country projects does not produce more rational results than those now obtained.

As just formulated, the puzzle is extremely important. Its resolution bears centrally on the important and related questions of economic efficiency, employment and income distribution. There is, of course, no *a priori* reason to expect that marked improvement in project appraisal would result in efficient and full employment of all resources. To speculate no further, the underlying demographic pressures on the labour supply might be too strong to be contained in this way. At the micro-level, however, the presumption is that more rational choice of techniques would take much of the sting out of the conflict that many now see existing between growth and employment objectives; and, to paraphrase Adam Smith, what is prudent in the behaviour of a single firm can scarce be folly in the management of an entire economy.

Thus, on the assumption that the findings for sugar and footwear in Ethiopia and Ghana can stand substantial generalization to other industries and countries, it is important to ask why decision-takers have hitherto been imprudent. Many answers could be returned to this question, including denial of imprudence. Denial is considered briefly below. Here it is asserted that the explanation of imprudent decisions lies in the malign influence of the engineer and in the conceit of the economist. Less provocatively put, the investment decision, as it is widely made, is an engineering one subject to a broad economic constraint. A decision is taken, for example, to establish a plant of some given productive capacity in a developing country. Engineers trained according to developed country curricula are asked to design the plant. They produce blueprints for a limited number of alternatives, each of which is a variant on current 'best-practice' technique. The alternatives are submitted to economic (perhaps DCF) scrutiny, the most attractive chosen, and another capital-intensive, technologically inappropriate plant is established.

Two points require further explanation: the logic of engineering choice, and the failure of economists more decisively to influence the investment decision. In the present context the basic trouble with engineers is that they are professionally driven by what Schumpeter once called ''the half-artistic joy in technically perfecting the productive apparatus.''[1] Give an engineer a machine and his instinct is to improve it; give him a plant and his instinct is to automate it. From his point of view this is perfectly understandable, even laudable. The engineer's interest is in technical efficiency—in extracting the maximum amount of sucrose from a given input of sugar cane; and from this standpoint machines are often more reliable than men. At the present time there are three sugar factories in Ethiopia; the first began operations in 1952, the latest in 1969. Common to the three factories is the problem of controlling the rate of inflow of raw input to the crushing mills. In the oldest factory, three men with shovels stand on a platform seeking, as it were, to control the traffic; in the newest plant the same task is done by neat hinged steel sensing devices. These inevitably ensure a much more even flow than the best efforts of the three men.

Engineers live and work in a social context. Their social environment is, however, that of the developed country; and a standing injunction of this environment—save labour—accords well with the professional instinct of the engineer. The corresponding need of the developing country, however, is to save capital. At first sight, this accords less well with the engineer's instinct, although properly understood it could represent an exciting challenge to the engineer's professional competence. This qualification notwithstanding, it must be assumed for the present that professional instinct and training and social circumstance combine to give the engineer a strong taste for the equipment-intensive mode of production. The puzzle is why, in developing country conditions, the economist is so apparently willing to give the engineer his head.

The economist's indulgence of the engineer cannot be explained by any failure to appreciate the importance of the engineering element in production. After all, Figure 1 is part of the standard diet of the apprentice economist, so that he becomes aware of engineering influence early in his career. Figure 1 does more, however, than record the fact that there are both engineering and economic elements in the theory of production. It asserts that the economic is the predominant influence. The engineer may design as many 'plants in the air' (production isoquants) as he likes. The level of output and the techniques used to produce it are determined by factor supplies and factor prices. It is the conceit of the economist that he continues to believe in all circumstances, and as Schumpeter put it almost seventy years ago, that "actually, in practical life we observe that the technical element must submit when it collides with the economic."[2]

This conceit of Schumpeter's and *a fortiori* of his successors is worth dwelling on because it implies a view which is a distorted reflection of what actually happens when projects are appraised in developing countries. As Schumpeter saw it (and as contemporary economists at least implicitly see it),

> Every method of production in use at a given time bows to economic appropriateness. These methods consist of ideas not only of economic but also of physical content. The latter have their problems and a logic of their own, and constantly to think these through—first of all without considering the economic, and finally decisive factor—is the purport of technology.[3]

Attention to the internal logic of technology is to be encouraged:

> For then . . . measures will be worked out ready for the time when they become advantageous. And it is also useful to be constantly putting the ideal beside the actual so that the possibilities are passed by, not out of ignorance but on well-considered economic grounds.[4]

What the conceit of the economist has obscured is the fact that the technical ideal has so rapidly become the actual in developing countries that alternative possibilities have been passed by, if not out of ignorance then out of sloth and in the face of well-considered economic grounds for attending to them.

The conceit of the economist does not end with the belief that the engineer is properly under control. It runs additionally to a stubborn faith in the soundness of his theoretical insights. To repeat, the main message of Figure 1 is that the choice of techniques is determined by relative factor prices. If the choice seems inappropriate, it does not naturally occur to the economist to suspect the engineer. It does occur instinctively to him to suspect someone (governments and trade unions are the favoured culprits) of tampering with factor prices. Armed with this suspicion, the economist is apt to go charging off in an attempt to establish that the elasticity of substitution of labour for capital is high in developing countries. Most of the relevant work has been conducted at a high level of aggregation and abstraction. It has indeed been based on models more noted for their mathematical convenience than for their evident relevance to the problem on hand. The consequence has been biased (i.e.

unjustifiably high) estimates of the relevant elasticity, and cheerful policy prescription to hold down wages and make capital more expensive in a situation in which there is little hard evidence that decision-takers attend that closely to relative factor prices.[5] It has irreverently but not irrelevantly been said that ''economists use statistics as a drunk man uses a lamp post, more for support than for illumination.''

A more sober view of how matters now stand is depicted in Figure 2, which comprises two production isoquants (XPQRX and XPX^1) and three price lines (CL, C^{1}L^1 and C^{11}L^{11}). The isoquant XPX^1 reflects limited engineering vision applied to the design of a new plant; XPQRX the spectrum of feasible techniques that would be uncovered by wider search. The price line CL introduces a new element (assumption). Many plants are established in developing countries as a developed country 'turn-key' operation. In such instances casual empiricism is often employed to

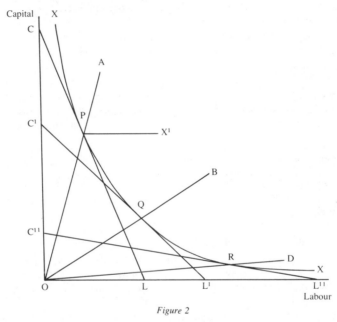

Figure 2

'determine' developing country factor prices. It is convenient to let CL represent the results of this procedure. The lines C^{1}L^1 and C^{11}L^{11} represent respectively the (distorted) market and the social view of relative factor scarcities in a developing country.

Taken together, the isoquants and price lines of Figure 2 identify three possible optimum positions on the production map. If engineering efficiency, tempered with nominal recognition that factor endowments differ in developed and developing countries, is the basis of choice, then P represents the most desirable technique (with a capital-labour ratio given by the slope of OPA). If, however, the fuller spectrum of technologies is to be considered then Q and R represent the desired positions for market and social prices respectively (with associated capital-labour ratios given by the slopes of OQB and ORD). In present circumstances, P, the least desirable is nevertheless the most likely of the three possible outcomes. Yet much of the discussion in the literature implicitly assumes that Q will be chosen and is consequently concerned with engineering the move from Q to R.

It is obvious, of course, that R is to be preferred to Q, and that both are to be preferred to P. If, however, engineering considerations dominate the choice of technique (to the extent of encouraging the view that casual allowance for developing country conditions is sufficient in making economic appraisal) the move from P to Q is logically prior to that from Q to R, unless it is thought that the gap in profitability between P and R is so great that, were it revealed, it would spontaneously overcome the engineer's predilection to plump for something approaching the 'best-practice' technique in all circumstances. There are few grounds for such a thought. There is, however, good reason to probe the decision that chooses P and to chart the requirements of the move from P to Q to R. Put differently, the policy problem is to move from a situation in which the elasticity of factor substitution is low (because of limited consideration of the alternatives) to one in which it is high (because alternative technologies are fully canvassed).

Is it possible that decision-takers are explicitly aware of the wide ranges of technical options, and the apparent economic and social benefits associated above with labour-intensive technology in developing countries? If they are, is it conceivable that they consciously reject the labour-intensive for good reason? When pressed, most decision-takers would answer yes to both questions. The supporting reasons, however, are often far from reassuring. They tend to degenerate into unsupported prejudice and assertion. Nevertheless, there is room for honest doubt. Labour-intensive technologies could be thought to be inordinately demanding of management and labour skills, and unduly sacrificial in the quality and precision of its output. On a more general level, a number of fears could be entertained on the score that the widespread use of labour-intensive techniques could retard economic progress or degrade the labour force. These are large and troubling issues. Here they will simply be considered in the light of the work reported in the second section of this paper and in the light of some general thoughts.

On management and labour skills, a general point worth making is that they can always be had at a cost (even if it is the cost of training). They can, therefore, be included in DCF calculations and so be allowed explicitly to influence the choice of techniques. Thus, in the sugar and shoe comparisons, it was assumed that top management (partly because of its capacity to delegate) would vary little with technology. Allowance was made, however, for other staff costs associated with the fact that the larger the labour force the greater the demands on the accountancy, personnel and supervisory staff. It was (realistically) assumed in both industries that skilled labour could be trained on the job. In other industries, of course, managerial costs may increase sharply with the move from capital-intensive to labour-intensive processes, and the cost of labour training may be higher. Beyond repeating that these are measurable costs, two other points should be noted. The first is that labour-intensive processes have their economies (in plant maintenance, for example) as well as their diseconomies; the second that managerial resistance to a larger rather than a smaller labour force on extra-economic grounds may be a more potent deterrent to labour-intensive technologies than genuinely and unbearably high additional costs.

The sugar and footwear comparisons were among plants thought to be capable of producing goods of comparable quality. In sugar, this threw much but not impossible weight on the skill of the sugar boilers; in shoes it required judicious combination of machine and hand operations. Fuller consideration of the sugar comparisons makes it clear that again the balance of advantage does not always lie with the capital-intensive. The skill of the open-pan sugar boiler and the vacuum-pan process can both produce a high quality, mill-white product. Demand for this product comes from fussy consumers. Less fussy consumers, bakers and confectioners (for example) would settle for a product of lower quality and lower price. No sensible relaxation of the in-built quality controls of the modern mill-white vacuum pan process could cater for this diversified demand. As it happens, the open-pan process normally yields several grades of sugar in the course of a production cycle. It is thus possible that the labour intensive technique has market advantages.

In the judgment of Sir Maurice Bowra slavery provided "a large pool of cheap and usually unskilled labour" and thus in the long run "did irreparable harm to the ancient world."[6] It stifled inventiveness, and led to the rejection of applied knowledge "by creative minds as below their proper dignity."[7] From Periclean Athens to the contemporary countries of the Third World is a long way in time and technical progress. The gibe about creative minds has nevertheless a familiar ring to it; and one interesting question in the whole set of issues that surround the pursuit of labour-intensive technology is whether it would encourage or reduce interest in applied knowledge. On such an enormous question little can be said here. The feeling can be aired, however, that labour-intensive processes, being more organically grounded in developing countries, should develop more rapidly and more wholesomely than the alternative in all directions. In particular, insofar as it creates a large and rapidly growing artisan class, the adoption of labour-intensive technology might be expected to generate a demand for education of the kind that underlay the creation of the first technical colleges, mechanics' institutes and workers' education movements in the now-developed countries.

Organically grounded technology would have other advantages. Not least of these might be the encouragement it would give to the development of an indigenous capital goods industry.

Desk-bound (or jet-set) advocates of labour-intensive processes should be universally required to face one implication of their advocacy. Intellectual and craft work apart, most work is either boring or brutal. The use of labour-intensive methods in developing countries can easily imply the substitution of brute force for machine power, and only brevity justifies the invocation of the comfortable view that this poses no particular problem as long as people are prepared to work on their own volition for whatever wage brutal labour commands.

Conclusion

This paper has been deliberately provocative, and a number of strong positions struck on the basis of what some might judge to be scanty evidence. It would, however, be unfortunate if the final impression were that it was insubstantial. Although the desire to provoke and the need to be brief may have impaired presentation, matters of substance were reported and discussed. Some recapitulation and extension is therefore in order.

What was most securely, if very partially, reported were results of research into the choice of technology in the sugar and footwear industries in Ethiopia and Ghana. This research required geographically extensive, technologically and economically minute enquiry. The results are clearly therefore not capable of generalization to other industries and (though this is less certain) other countries without specific investigation of these industries and countries. They are nevertheless such that the application of the methods evolved in the prosecution of the present research to other products and places seems a promising activity. Moreover, consideration of the results has focused on the behaviour of decision-takers in a way that identifies another fruitful line of enquiry which need not await (but could be pursued simultaneously with) further detailed industry studies. If engineering influence and economic negligence characterize the investment decision in the sugar and footwear industries in the way suggested above, there is a strong presumption that this is a general pattern of behaviour. It is certainly one that ought to be investigated and if confirmed then altered.

Further investigation would require consideration of factors which have been ignored in this paper—including, for example, the influence of market structure, forms, nationality and size of business organization on the investment decision, as well as the whole question of the costs of perceiving and disseminating a full spectrum of technologies. It is clear, however, that it is business behaviour that is to be probed. It perhaps is less clear, that it is a normative theory of business behaviour that is ultimately sought. "Nowhere," Wicksteed lets Pliny the Elder say in the frontispiece of *The Commonsense of Political Economy,* "is the nature of things more intimately revealed than in the calculus of infinitesimals."[8] In less fine language, the conventional theory from which this paper springs enjoins businessmen to bend every effort to ensure that every last penny is wisely spent. If private and public decision-takers are to achieve the results promised, as it were, on their behalf at international fora such as UNCTAD, neither personal comfort nor psychological satisfaction should divert them from the most exacting scrutiny of production possibilities.

Notes

1. J.A. Schumpeter, *The Theory of Economic Development* (Cambridge, Massachusetts, Harvard University Press, 1955), p. 13.
2. *Loc. cit.*
3. *Ibid.,* p. 14.
4. *Loc. cit.*
5. For extensive criticism of presently available estimates see C. St. J. O'Herlihy, "Capital/Labour Substitution and the Developing Countries," *Oxford Bulletin of Statistics,* Vol. 34, No. 3 (August, 1972), p. 273.
6. Sir Maurice Bowra, *Periclean Athens* (London, Weidenfeld and Nicolson, 1971), p. 81.
7. *Ibid.*
8. Philip Henry Wicksteed, *The Commonsense of Political Economy and Selected Papers and Reviews on Economic Theory,* ed. with an introduction by Lionel Robbins (London, Routledge and Kegan Paul, 1933), Vol. II, p. vii.

Appropriate Technologies: Do We Transfer, Adapt, or Develop?

Amir U. Khan

Head, Agricultural Engineering Department
International Rice Research Institute
Los Banos, Laguna, Philippines

Introduction

The problems of population growth and unemployment are of serious concern to policy makers in the developing countries of Asia. Generation of new jobs for the rapidly growing population is, therefore, an urgent issue. In recent years, this subject has been vigorously debated at both national and international levels. The transfer and adaptation of appropriate technologies to make better use of locally available resources is suggested as one solution. The objectives of employment generation and income distribution can be achieved if locally available resources of manpower, skills, materials and capital are properly utilized in the industrialization process.

So far most discussions on appropriate technologies have been based largely on considerations of supply such as labor intensity and lower capital-labor ratios. The inherent danger in following the supply approach is that the technologies chosen may not be commercially viable in the developing countries. Development policies should certainly encourage labor use in the developing countries, but the selection of technologies without due regard for market considerations could be a wasteful exercise. The marketability of products and services must be the overriding consideration in the selection of appropriate technologies for developing countries. Discussions on appropriate technology must, therefore, begin with an assessment of the primary needs of the local population, the demand for products and services to meet these needs, and a subsequent analysis of the technologies that could economically cater to these demands through an optimum use of local resources.

Expanding Existing Labor-Intensive Production

Let us look at two examples of labor-intensive technologies that have been widely mentioned as appropriate for developing countries. The handicraft industry is often recommended for developmental attention because it is labor-intensive. Products of the handicraft industry either fall in the decorative category which are usually exported, or village-craft utility products, which are used by the poorer segment of the population. Yet decorative luxury products have limited potential in the domestic markets, and the domestic demand for village-craft utility products seems likely to

223

decline as standards of living rise and products of a higher technological order find their way into the developing countries' markets.

Expansion of the handicraft industry will depend, therefore, on the unlikely growth of export markets; it is highly doubtful that the developing countries can achieve major growth in this specialty market. Moreover, traditional handicraft products have been developed through an evolutionary process and the scope for the introduction of new products to capture fresh markets appears rather limited. If this assessment is correct, the handicraft industry offers limited potential for increasing employment in the developing countries. A labor intensive industry cannot generate new employment if markets to absorb increased production cannot be found.

Another industry which is often recommended for developing countries because of its labor-intensive character is the leather goods industry. The small-scale shoe and leather goods industry has been adequately meeting domestic demands in most developing countries. More rapid growth can be achieved only through capturing new markets. It seems, however, that a rapid expansion of either the domestic or the export markets for leather goods is not an easy matter. In addition, the scarcity of raw materials for expanded production may be a serious supply bottleneck in developing countries.

The traditional sector industries are primarily craftsman-based and require skills which have been passed on through many generations. The growth of traditional sector industries may, therefore, be limited by the availability of skilled manpower. Development of craftsmanship is a slow and expensive process and cannot be attained in a short period. For this reason, the manufacture of modern-sector products, in which production operations can be broken into simpler elements that do not require a high degree of craftsmanship, may offer greater potential for the utilization of local manpower.

The Supply Potential of Production Materials

The traditionally popular production materials in the developing countries are clay, stone, leather, copper, brass, bronze, wood, straw, and other materials. The manufacture of products using traditional materials is generally well-developed in the region. Scope for a sudden expansion of markets for established products made of such materials is limited because the supply and demand for such products is fairly well-balanced. Designing new products constructed with traditional materials seems to be a logical means for generating local employment, but these materials have serious structural limitations.

The more modern materials—iron and steel, aluminum, and some synthetic materials—offer a far greater scope for utilization because substantial demand for products made of such materials exists in the developing countries, this demand is rapidly growing, and the materials offer structural flexibility.

Most ferrous materials are difficult to work manually. For this reason, the use of iron or steel as a production material has not progressed as rapidly in the developing countries. We find, however, that iron and steel are the most dominant production materials in the industrially advanced countries. The full potential for the manufacture of iron and steel products still remains to be developed and this offers the greatest opportunity and challenge in the developing regions.

It could be argued that ferrous materials are imported in most developing countries and that such an approach may not be a desirable one for countries which are faced with a chronic balance of payments problem. It must be pointed out, however, that most developing countries are already importing large amounts of manufactured iron and steel products. Substitution of some of the manufactured products with imports of basic iron and steel to be used for local production can more than offset the costs of importing raw materials.

The use of aluminum as a production material has not been fully exploited, and there is considerable scope for manufacture of aluminum products in the developing countries. The high cost of aluminum and its lower physical strength, however, restrict its use to a limited range of products.

Manufacture of products made of synthetic materials, such as plastics, requires relatively complex capital-intensive technology, which is currently being imported from the developed countries. It is doubtful that efforts to develop appropriate technologies using synthetic materials can produce significant increases in employment in the developing region.

The local production of goods based on iron and steel seems to offer great potential. The questions demanding consideration are, does a market exist for such goods? and can such goods be locally produced?

Market Potential

Increasing the purchasing power of the local population is one way to enlarge a market; however, it involves the whole process of economic development and is not something that can be achieved in a short period. In the short run, markets can be generated either through the introduction of new products which will meet the needs that are not adequately met at the moment or by a substantial reduction in prices of products that are already available.

The traditional technologies offer limited scope for either the introduction of new products or a substantial reduction in product prices. It is the author's belief that domestic and export markets for traditional sector products will grow at a rather slow pace in most developing countries and this sector will not generate new employment at the rate necessary to solve some of the urgent unemployment problems in the region.

People in the developing countries are being continuously exposed to more and more modern-sector products from the industrialized countries. Their aspiration for acquiring such products is growing rapidly even though such products are beyond the means of a majority of the people in the developing regions. Such products are beginning to find an increasing market in the developing countries. Bicycles, sewing machines, electric fans, motorcycles, scooters, and transistor radios are good examples of utility products which are finding increasing acceptance. The demand for such utility products will grow even more rapidly as benefits from the new seed fertilizer technology reach the rural masses in the developing countries.

Unfortunately, there is a widespread misconception in the industrialized countries that the developing countries need simple and somewhat primitive mechanical tools, animal-powered implements and other simple do-it-yourself gadgets. Many well-meaning international organizations have been engaged for a number of years in attempting to introduce such products of mechanical technology in the developing countries. While, on a cursory look, it may seem that there is a need for such simple products, a closer examination, however, indicates otherwise. I believe that simple products and devices are not capable of generating a commercially viable demand even when it seems that such products can meet some of the basic needs in the developing countries. This is one of the main reasons that in spite of a number of years of efforts to introduce simple devices, no significant impact has been achieved in any part of the developing world. This simplistic concept of appropriate technology needs to be changed if we are to make some meaningful progress through technological inputs in the developing countries. People in the developing countries are no longer looking for simple manual tools and gadgets but for modern sector products and mechanical devices which are capable of providing a quantum jump in their living standards. Unless appropriate technology is capable of providing demand-oriented modern-sector products through normal commercial channels, it is doubtful that it can survive the difficult environments of the developing countries.

A large number of the modern-sector products are imported from the industrialized countries which results in a severe drain on foreign exchange and hinders the development process. The low purchasing power of the people in the developing countries demands low-cost products, with different designs, specifications and standards than those in the industrialized societies both from utilitarian as well as manufacturing considerations. Simple low-cost utility products are no longer produced in the industrially advanced countries because of the high degree of sophistication of their domestic markets. It is difficult to import the available utility products from the advanced countries because of the excessively high direct and indirect costs. One finds that the selling price in the developing countries of most imported products is two to four times that in the country of manufacture. This excessively high price limits the size of the domestic market which discourages indigenous manufacture and perpetuates the dependence on imports.

In order to be relevant to the local needs in the developing countries, appropriate technologies must be intended to supply those goods the domestic demand for which is not being adequately met at this moment. It is not the author's intention here to suggest the production of expensive modern-sector luxury goods for a small wealthier segment of the population as is being done today in many developing countries, but rather to advocate the production of low-cost, day-to-day utility products that could be within the purchasing power of a large segment of the local population.

Manufacturing Potential

Many developing countries have placed heavy emphasis on the development of modern-sector, import-substituting industries. These industries have been patterned after similar industries in the industrialized countries. These developing countries are now realizing that the transfer of capital-intensive mass-production techniques is often not desirable for their low labor-cost economies. The dilemma that faces these countries is that even though a large domestic demand exists for appropriate modern-sector products, product designs which could be produced with labor-intensive methods are generally not available. Appropriate technology strategies in the developing countries must, therefore, be directed towards meeting the domestic demand for low-cost modern capital goods through labor-intensive production methods.

Much has been said about economies of scale to support capital-intensive production. There is no question that quantity production lowers unit cost in the industrialized countries. One finds, however, that this is not necessarily true in the low labor-cost economies. There is a direct correlation between economies of scale and the capital-labor ratio between alternate production methods. Thus, economies of scale tend to become less effective as more labor-intensive methods are employed.

The economic incentives and constraints that dictate capital-intensive production methods are generally not present in the low-labor cost economies; yet these are the methods being attempted in the developing regions. These efforts have often led to the erroneous conclusion that the manufacture of modern-sector products is usually uneconomic in the developing regions because the markets are small. The inference should rather be that the mechanical technologies have not been adapted to the local setting.

In reality, production of most modern-sector products can be quite economical in the developing countries if the product designs and the production processes are appropriately tailored to suit the local factor endowments. There are many interesting examples in South and Southeast Asia which support this theory. The small-scale production of power tillers, Jeepneys and the McCormick-type threshers in The Philippines, low-lift water pumps in Vietnam, air-cooled gasoline engines and power tillers in Thailand, diesel engines and machine tools in India and Pakistan are good examples which indicate that economies of scale are not as significant as suggested by many established manufacturers from the developed countries in their arguments against local production in the developing countries.

Some Case Studies

The IRRI power tiller. The development of a simple five to seven horsepower power tiller (Figure 1) was started in late 1971 by the International Rice Research Institute in The Philippines. Maximum use was made of readily available components

Figure 1.

such as engines, chains, sprockets, belts, seals, etc., in the design of this tiller. The machine was designed for production by small to medium-sized machine shops in the developing countries. The design was released for manufacture to four companies in The Philippines in June 1972. Within a period of one year, a total production of 500 tillers per month was achieved in The Philippines. It is of interest to note that this initial production is over six times the combined annual imports of all makes and sizes of power tillers in The Philippines. The locally manufactured power tillers are being marketed at about half the price of comparable power tillers being imported in The Philippines. These power tillers are being purchased by many small farmers, some of whom are going into the contract-tillage business. The tiller design was such that the local manufacturers were able to produce the machine with their existing facilities. About 80 additional workers have been employed by these companies in the production of these tillers in The Philippines. The power tillers permit faster land preparation and more intensive cultivation, which is necessary for the new high-yielding varieties and for double cropping operations.

The motor pump. Another interesting product development example is the case of a motor pump (Figure 2) which was developed in the upper region of the Mekong Delta of South Vietnam. This case has been well documented by R.L. Sampson[1] and the following is an excerpt from his publication:

Figure 2.

In 1962, Van Nam, a farmer who supplemented his income by servicing motorbicycles, invented a motor pump which was capable of lifting water from 1 to 1½ meters above the canals and ditches. Nam's invention received immediate attention of nearby residents and spread rapidly as motor dealers, acting on description of farmers, built similar models. Fifteen months after the original invention, another motor pump was invented by a Mr. Phan Van Thanh, a small engine merchant in My Tho, who had no knowledge of Van Nam's invention.

My Thanh's first model was tested on a farm in My Tho in December 1963 and it proved to be an immediate success. The farmer purchased it on the spot. Thanh's invention brought him immediate profits. By mid-1964, he had sold 600 of the new pumps. Between then and mid-1967, he had sold an average of 200 pumps per month. In early 1967, Thanh owned three imported cars, a new house, was building a hotel in My Tho for 14 million piastras, and was considered one of the town's wealthiest men, all at the age of 28.

By mid-1966, less than four years after its invention, 43 percent of the farmers in Than Cuu Nghia Village and 38 percent of those in Long Bien Dien Village owned a pump.

The Winner engine. Air-cooled gasoline engines are products which are produced in the industrialized countries with highly capital-intensive technology. Until 1967, the Thai Heng Long company was producing water pumps in Thailand; however, competition forced the company to look for new products. Mr. Praphat Thaisetahwhatkul, the general manager of the company, who has no formal engineering background, felt that he could produce air-cooled gasoline engines which were popularly used for power boats, power tillers and pumps in the country. He developed the production toolings and methods to produce engines in low volume with little capital investment. In 1967, the company started small-scale production of air-cooled engines under the brand name Winner. The engine design was an adaptation of a popular brand of imported engine. The company is now producing over 1,500 engines a month in the 10, 15, and 30 horsepower range at Amphung Muang, a small town about 40 Km. from Bangkok. The Winner engines compete favorably with the better known imported brands of engines in Thailand and they are now being exported to Indonesia and Malaysia.

The company employs nearly 200 young, unskilled farm girls with no prior manufacturing experience. The simpler operations such as machining, boring, grinding, etc., are handled by these girls, whereas the engine assembly is done by more experienced workers. The company fabricates most of its production equipment in its own foundry and machine shop. The machine tools and other production equipment were developed on a modular design to minimize capital investments. All engine components are manufactured by this company except the magneto, carburetor, connecting rod, spark plug, bearings and piston rings. The cylinder block, crankcase, flywheel-fan and fanhousing are produced by simple aluminum gravity casting methods in metal molds. The rest of the components, including the crankshaft, are fabricated by the company.

The Jeepney industry. The Jeepney industry[2] is an offshoot of the large number of surplus Jeeps that were left in The Philippines after World War II. The industry evolved through the conversion of Army Jeeps for public transport. Over the years, the simple body-building operations expanded into the manufacture of a large number of Jeepney components. Two large, four medium and over 100 small fabricators are currently engaged in the manufacture of Jeepneys in The Philippines. Those components which require very high technology in production, such as engines, transmissions, and differentials, are imported, but all other components are being locally manufactured. The sheetmetal components, such as front grills, fenders, hoods, windshield frames, tailgates, main body, and gasoline tanks, and a large number of non-sheet metal parts, such as the front axles, bumpers, chassis, rims, springs, clutch and transmission parts, batteries, and numerous other replacement parts are produced with simple production methods in numerous small shops all over the country.

The diffused character of the industry and the widespread use of labor-intensive production methods have generated many employment opportunities all over the country. In 1970, there were 120,000 Jeep-type vehicles, mostly of local origin, registered in The Philippines, representing 45.2 percent of the total car population.

These examples, the first two in which products were developed to suit local needs and the second two in which labor-intensive production methods were developed to permit manufacture of relatively complex products, illustrate some of the possibilities for low volume production in the developing countries. These examples also indicate some of the engineering inputs that would be necessary in the development of appropriate mechanical technologies for the developing countries.

Role of International Agencies

In the developed countries, product development activity in industry has played a significant role in industrial development. In the developing countries, the struggling state of the industrial sector has not permitted the allocation of many private resources to product development. To encourage industrial development, many governments have established industrial research institutes which serve specific industrial sectors. These institutes have been organized to conduct research, provide training and offer service assistance to local industries. The development of demand-oriented products for local production has, however, been largely ignored in the establishment of such institutes. It is becoming increasingly evident that these so-called industrial research institutes are essentially academic research, industrial service and training organizations rather than hardware-oriented technology and product development institutes. These institutes have thus failed to provide creative leadership in filling the product development gaps that exist in the industrial sector in most developing countries.

Most industrial research institutes in the developing countries have been organized in the public sector and are patterned after similar institutes in the industrialized countries. Generally, the industrial research institutes in the advanced countries complement the activities of the R&D departments in private industry by conducting basic and applied research. The design and development of marketable products is primarily undertaken by the companies in their own R&D departments. In the industrialized countries almost all R&D funds in industry are spent on product development rather than on research. In the developed countries, these complementary roles of the public industrial research institutes and the R&D departments in private industry have been quite successful in moving research results into the market. In the developing countries, however, the absence of product development in industry has created a serious bottleneck in transforming research into marketable forms. Technology development efforts in the developing countries must, therefore, be directed towards solving this product development bottleneck.

In the developed countries, most industrial research institutes are geared for contract research, since there are many large public and private organizations which can afford to contract out their research needs. It is doubtful that a similar contract approach could be successful in the developing countries, since most industrial organizations are small and do not have the necessary resources for contract R&D. Appropriate Technology Development Centers will, therefore, need support from the national and international agencies to provide a nuclei of products that could help to develop an industrial base in the developing regions.

The international agencies can make a significant contribution by setting up one or two regional Appropriate Technology Development Centers. The technology development centers would be distinctly different from the existing industrial research institutes and would not duplicate their functions and activities. These centers should have clear-cut objectives specifically directed towards the development and manufacture of low-cost utility products in the developing countries and it is important that these be organized to be responsive to these objectives. The centers should work independently of governments, educational institutions and manufacturing concerns in the host countries. In this manner, the centers can stay on the sharp edge of their mission while maintaining an unbiased view of all aspects of product development.

The regional centers should develop cooperative programs in other developing countries to extend and commercialize new product designs in their respective regions.

In the light of the experience gained from the international agricultural institutes, the popular argument that there are too many industrial institutions in the less-developed countries and the setting up of additional institutes would be a wasteful exercise, does not seem very valid. The number of agricultural research centers that were operating in the developing countries, prior to the establishment of the international agricultural institutes, was quite large. Yet, CIMMYT* and IRRI played a significant role in the development of tropical agriculture in a brief period of about a decade. It seems obvious that it is not the number of research institutes but the quality of each organization and its objectives, organization staff, and leadership that are significant.

Of particular significance to industrial development is the Rice Machinery Development Project which was initiated in 1967 at the International Rice Research Institute in The Philippines. With modest funding, the project has been responsible for the development of low-cost agricultural machines for improved wetland rice production in Asia. In addition to the power tiller, described earlier, a number of other machines, such as the power weeder, axial flow thresher, batch drier, and direct seeder have achieved considerable commercial success in The Philippines and some other Asian countries. The success of this IRRI/AID project points to a potential for similar work on a broader range of products to meet the basic needs of human existence in the developing countries.

Appropriate Technology Center's Objectives

The primary objective of the proposed centers should be to develop and commercialize low-cost products that could be locally manufactured to meet the basic human needs in the developing countries. These products should make an optimum use of available manpower, materials, and production technology in the developing countries. Some of the products that need to be developed to meet the primary human needs in the developing countries are:

Food: Machines and equipment for the production, processing, preserving and preparation of both animal and vegetable foods. Equipment for small-scale dryland farming is of special importance here; first because of the widespread impact it could have on the dryland agricultural regions in the developing world, and second, because no serious attempt has been made so far to cater to the equipment requirements of the small farms in the dryland areas. Agricultural machines such as power tillers, small tractors, threshers, driers and milling machines fall in this category.

Shelter: Products and equipment for facilitating the construction as well as habitation of housing structures. Equipment and machines like building hardware, brick and aggregate-making machines, wood-working equipment and low-cost household appliances, such as water heaters, evaporative refrigerators and room coolers, cooking equipment, etc., fall in this category.

Transportation: There are two major areas which require special attention. One is the development of simple low-cost vehicles such as auto rickshaws, scooters, farm trucks, low-cost power boat equipment, etc. The second is equipment for the construction and maintenance of roads, canals, dams, and other such infrastructures. This is a challenging area, since intermediate size construction equipment is not available today. Either one has to use shovels and baskets or giant earthmoving and construction equipment.

Health and sanitation: Products and equipment for household water and sanitary systems, low-cost hospital furniture and equipment, municipal sewage disposal systems, etc., fall in this category.

---
* International Wheat and Maize Improvement Center.

Rural industrial development: Development of simple production equipment that could provide increased opportunities for making a living for the rural population is badly needed. Simple equipment for the making of rope and straw products, and other cottage and village level industrial products fall in this category.

The above list is to provide a general idea of the products that could find a market in the developing regions. It is possible that the centers may see a need for other products which may fall outside the above categories. These centers should look at their regional markets to determine the products that offer the greatest potential. To the extent possible, product planners, development engineers, and production engineers at these centers should consider the factors of need, demand, available technology, materials, production facilities, etc., in arriving at the product priority decisions.

The development of a new product involves considerable investment of time and money and careful analysis in the early stages of a project is necessary to reduce the risks of failure. In industry, the product planning departments establish specifications of proposed products based on expected functional, economic, manufacturing, and sales requirements. The design and development of a product is initiated only after these factors have been evaluated and the product's commercial feasibility studied. This sequence of operations insures a reasonable degree of customer acceptance and functions as a screening process for non-promising products. Product development in the proposed centers should follow a similar analytical and screening process to insure a reasonable degree of market acceptance. These centers will require, therefore, a well-coordinated team consisting of product planners who will continuously keep abreast of present and future market needs, design and development engineers who will design and develop the products, and production engineers who will be responsible for the commercialization of the products originating in the centers.

Conclusion

The development of both the agricultural as well as the industrial sectors are essential elements of a development strategy for the developing countries. Appropriate technologies which can provide low-cost products and services to meet basic human needs can serve these two sectors simultaneously. A lack of product development activities in industry has been a serious bottleneck in the less-developed countries. International organizations can make a significant input in the development of appropriate technologies by setting up one or two small regional appropriate technology centers with clear-cut objectives to design, develop and encourage local manufacture of low-cost, day-to-day, modern utility products.

There is a widespread feeling in the industrialized countries that the technology shelf is brimming with alternative solutions. One gathers the impression in discussions on technology that it is easy to transfer technologies by merely changing economic parameters such as factor prices. The truth of the matter is that for each given set of industrial, economic and social conditions in the developing countries, there is little choice on the technology shelf. The challenge, therefore, lies in developing new technologies that are appropriate to conditions in the developing countries. To limit our strategies merely to the transfer and adaptation of existing technologies from the industrialized countries may seem to be an easier approach but it is certainly not sufficient to solve the many serious problems faced by the developing countries. The development of appropriate technologies is a far greater challenge which must be met in the most imaginative manner. This will require some international assistance since local resources and expertise for such activities are not readily available in the developing countries.

Notes

1. R.L. Sampson, "The Motor Pump: A Case Study of Innovation and Development," *Oxford Economic Papers* New Series, 21, 1 (1969), pp. 109-121.

2. P. Cabanos, "Jeepney Manufacturing in the Philippines: A Model for Developing the Agricultural Machinery Industry," *Agricultural Mechanization in Asia,* 2 (Autumn, 1971), pp. 91-97. The term "jeepney" is used in The Philippines for a variety of automotive vehicles which somewhat resemble the U.S. Army Jeeps and are used for private and public transport.

Population and Labor Force in Less Developed Regions: Some Main Facts, Theory and Research Needs

George J. Stolnitz
Indiana University

Introduction

This paper deals with some main facts and formal theory surrounding population-labor force interrelations in low-income regions. The first section focuses on trends, with considerable attention to LDC-DC comparisons; the second section deals formally with a battery of main classes of interrelations; the last section outlines a number of suggested directions for future research which have a special priority or meet a special need from policy or analytic viewpoints.

Emphasis throughout will be on supply of labor, rather than on demand or employment. Although population size and growth may have major relevance on the demand side in DC economies, whether for labor or commodities, their relevance would appear decidedly secondary in LDC contexts. Here the familiar low-productivity syndromes sustaining underdevelopment are clearly the prime forces affecting demand. Population tends much more to operate by affecting supply capacities than by determining the extent to which capacities are utilized.

As used here "LDC" or "low-income" area conforms with standard United Nations (UN) or International Labour Office (ILO) definitions, including essentially Asia, Africa and Latin America but with Japan and, typically, Temperate South America excluded (also South Africa and Israel in some compilations). With few exceptions the regions so defined consist of the world's countries having well over 50 percent of labor force in agriculture and well over 50 percent of population in rural areas. Such countries (except for a few oil-rich areas) also had reported 1967 measures of per capita GNP which were below $1,000 and nearly always far below this level.

Main Facts and Trends

A number of main population prospects confronting LDCs merit special emphasis. Although many are well known in broad terms, the often novel orders of magnitude involved and their often novel causal concomitants mark so remarkable a break between recent LDC demographic history and earlier DC history that fresh comparative perspectives are required. For this purpose, it is useful to focus on comparative DC magnitudes about 1920, when practically all DC areas had achieved far longer or sustained development than is true of practically all LDC areas today.[1]

To begin with, the population in LDCs today is over 2.5 billion, a figure which exceeds (a) total world population as recently as 1950, (b) the current DC total of

235

about 1 billion and (c) the 1920 DC total by a factor of 3 to 4. As just noted, the last comparison has interest because of its relation to economies which had already experienced a considerable history of development; conversely, nearly all but a small part of the 1970 LDC population has not yet done so. In simple numerical terms, well over 3 times as many persons today live in societies which have failed to achieve long-term development transitions as had completed such transition, or were well under way to completing it, by the 1920s.

Adding prospective growth in numbers from 1970 to 2000—between two and just over three billion according to the range of UN projections, but with growth of well over two billion seemingly almost certain barring major catastrophes—the LDC populations which have either just begun a first major development transition, or are yet to embark on it, will total at least 4.5 to 5.5 billion by the end of the century. Relative to the 1920 DC population, these end-century orders of magnitude represent multiples of six to eight, say seven in conservative, rounded terms. Even relative to the DC population in 1970, the corresponding multiple is easily likely to be five or higher.

Since the age interval 15-65 accounts for about three-fifths of total population size and change, the UN year-2000 projection (''medium'' variant) implies a rise of about 1.5 billion for this span of the main labor force ages. The rise alone is over twice the 1970 DC number in this age span and the end-century size more than five times that level. Both multiples are considerably larger, of course, relative to the corresponding DC number in 1920.

Labor force projections to the year 2000, made by ILO as of the mid-1960s, suggest an end-century LDC total of about 1.9 billion.[2] Merely the 1970-2000 rise, about 850 million, would match the total DC population as recently as 1950, be more than double the DC labor force of that year and be about one-third higher than the entire year-2000 DC labor force.*

Again using 1920-30 as a DC historical benchwork, we find that any reasonably foreseeable size of end-century LDC labor force will surely be far more than twice the entire DC population of a half-century ago and easily five times its labor force.

Subsequent ILO projections, though oriented to a ''perspectives plan'' or 15-year period rather than the futurist 30-year period of the above projections, and though using more recent bases for its assumptions, show essentially the same results for overlapping years. Interestingly, merely the 1970-85 rise in LDC labor force, projected at about 400 million, turns out to be far higher than total DC labor force in 1920-30.[3]

A further main set of interactions between population and labor force in LDC areas revolves about their urban-rural composition. Such interactions cast light, in particular, on mobility prospects or needs, given the fact that urban and rural employment often differ so radically in nature and policy issues.

Once again the same kinds of broad comparative perspectives stand out clearly, using UN urban-rural projections as a data base. Although the specific techniques underlying the UN projections are much less refined than in the case of labor force or population, with even the distinction between urban and rural open to serious

---

*   The ILO projections are relatively free from uncertainties about fertility, since a substantial part of the year-2000 15-65 age group was already born at the time the projections were made. Moreover, since the ''medium'' population projection underlying the ILO method for deriving labor force presupposes a considerable decline in LDC fertility, by over one-fourth, uncertainty on this score is more likely to center on whether the 1.9 end-result is conservative rather than excessive. Female labor force participation rates in the future, though a further unknown of some significance, would have limited effect on total labor force even if the trends proved to be out-sized compared to anticipations.

question, the main indications are unambiguous.[4] Using 20,000 as a minimum population size for defining "urban" localities leads to a projected series (consistent with the UN "medium" total population projection) which more than doubles during 1960-80 and again doubles during 1980-2000. Such "urban" size, despite its functionally conservative definition, can by 1980 be expected to exceed the entire DC population (urban plus rural) as of 1920 and would by the year 2000 be well over twice this total.*

Much the same comparisons would hold if "urban" were identified according to national definitions, a second approach used by the UN in making its urban-rural projections.

If the 1960 LDC "rural" population is defined as persons living in areas other than 20,000-plus localities, its 1.7 billion size is about 2.5 times the 1920 DC total population size and 3.5 times the DC rural population of that year. The projected 1960-2000 rise in the LDC rural population (same definition) approximately doubles these multipliers, while similar orders of magnitude are found to hold when "rural" is identified, alternatively, according to national definitions.

In the main, these LDC-DC comparisons reflect differential national rates of growth, not numbers of countries. There are, of course, many more LDC than DC entities, but this is not the main underlying factor. Rather, it is that national LDC population and labor force growth rates, the corresponding rural rates, and many or most urban rates will over the next 30 to 40 years almost surely exceed by far the DC national growth parameters of the past and, even more surely, prove to be far beyond the DC rates in prospect. The population growth rates typically anticipated in the UN regional and national projections for LDC areas tend to exceed by 50 to 100 percent margins even the maximum rates found historically over decadal or generational-length periods in Europe, the only long-settled DC region as of the nineteenth century and thereby the closest historical analogue we have today to future long-run changes under early industrialization.

In addition to dealing with LDC employment issues in comparative static terms, therefore, or even in terms of possible long-run dynamic equilibrium, we need to consider the size and variability of growth itself as possibly important explanatory elements. As yet we appear to know little about long-term processes of labor absorption under very high growth of labor supply in long-settled areas. Although size of labor force may be primary—in one sense must be so, since size and growth can always be regarded as numerical transformations of each other—growth as such may not be an unimportant additional causal factor for purposes of analyzing LDC employment and unemployment propensities.

Population-Labor Force Linkages

Among the numerous processes which can be analyzed formally in relating population trends to labor force, seven in particular are singled out for discussion below. That discussion, brief as it must be, focuses on internal distribution and ignores external migration. The seven relationships are:

1. Effects of changes in vital (birth and death) rates on labor force size and growth.
2. Comparative influence of population trends and those in labor force participation (activity) rates on future size and changes in labor force.

---

* Compared to the 1920 DC population in 20,000-plus localities, merely the 1970-2000 rise in corresponding LDC population represents a five-fold magnification and the projected end-century level, almost 1.5 billion, a seven-fold multiple.

3. Effects of age structure on aggregate activity and absorption rates.
4. Mortality or morbidity factors in relation to participation rates.
5. Fertility and female participation rates.
6. Urban-rural distribution and participation rates.
7. Sex composition effects on participation rates.

Basic Underlying Propositions

Before discussing these relationships as they may apply in LDC settings, three points of underlying interest should be made. These, in formal terms, apply to all populations, whether DC or LDC.

First, whatever the size of the population growth rate, its mortality and fertility components have separate significance. A 20 per 1,000 or two percent growth rate when crude birth and death rates are 40 and 20 per 1,000 has different implications from one arising out of a 30-10 mix and the same would be true of any other mix and size of components. The reason is age structure. Mortality declines tend to have only limited effect on age composition, partly because such declines tend to be spread, albeit unevenly, over many ages rather than a few, and partly for other technical reasons.* A fertility change, in contrast, has immediate impact on the young ages only and a continuation of such change over the long run has analogous impact, raising the proportion of young in the event of an upward fertility movement and lowering it when the movement is downward. The main reason for the substantially higher dependency ratios found in LDC regions, involving much larger proportions of population under age 15 along with much smaller proportions over 65, is their higher fertility, not their higher mortality. Most of the differences would remain if LDC death rates were to shift, whether suddenly or more gradually (the specific time path doesn't matter greatly), to DC levels.

Other things equal, future declines in LDC mortality can be expected to affect total numbers in essentially one-to-one ratio to deaths averted annually, while leaving age structure and dependency ratios essentially unchanged (the latter would be somewhat raised, if anything, by the rising fraction under 15). Fertility declines would also affect numbers in one-to-one fashion, but would in addition significantly alter age composition and dependency ratios. Hence, an equal decline in birth and death rates, while leaving the growth rate unchanged, would begin to diminish dependency immediately because of fertility effects; labor force would rise because of reduced mortality, but this would be in terms of numbers, not of relative size.

Second, neither the extent of unemployment and underemployment, nor their spatial distribution, is likely to have significant effect on mortality. Limited effects may well exist, particularly where labor underutilization is severe, but if so their visibility seems very low. Barring extreme breakdown, such as under famine or civil war conditions—and often to a surprising extent even when such conditions exist—it is government policy and action with respect to death and disease control measures which are likely to be the crucial or strategic determinants of trend. The unprecedented mortality declines found in many LDC regions over the past two or three decades have been associated with enormous ranges of variation in rates of economic growth and development, levels of living, degrees of underemployment and patterns of urban-rural distribution or redistribution. Briefly, LDC mortality levels or trends appear to be very largely exogenous to employment processes, at least over very

---

* Briefly, the effects of mortality declines on age depend on percentage changes in age-specific survival rates and such changes—unlike those in the corresponding mortality rates—tend to be of limited magnitude.

broad ranges of development and perhaps uniquely so today compared to earlier periods.

Third, the impact of fertility declines on labor force numbers involves very long lags, even when the declines are large. The point is familiar but its quantification is well worth illustrating. Using the ILO projections as example, a sudden halving of LDC fertility in 1975 (below those already posited) would only reduce male labor force by one-eighth as of the year 2000 (from about 1.28 to 1.11 billion). This would not be a trivial effect, of course, but the extreme nature of the assumption suggests that a reduction of one-twentieth or five percent would be closer to the most we can expect over the next quarter-century.

It is true that the full array of consequences might be broader than those on age structure alone, since fertility declines also might give rise to changing female activity rates, changing wage differentials by age, associated shifts in patterns of labor force entry or retirement, and changing factor proportions. However, even if some or all of these might be relevant for a fuller model of effects, it seems unlikely that the total impact from all sources would be substantially different from the above age-related effects alone.

Birth and Death Rates and the Labor Force

The foregoing illustration serves to introduce the first of the above-listed seven sets of linkages. Other things equal, a percentage change in the birth rate (or other measure of fertility) which continues over time would not lead to an equal percentage shift in size of labor force until the first affected birth cohort reached the end of its working years of life. Before such time, the effect in any earlier year would be the net result of two factors: the altered numbers of labor force within the age range already passed by this cohort, and the fraction of total labor force found in such range. To return to the previous illustration, the assumed halving of LDC fertility from 1975 onward would in the year 2000 halve the male work force under age 25 only. Since the ratio of the under-25 age group to total labor force is about one-fourth according to the ILO projection, the effect on the total is only one-eighth.

As to mortality, since its declines tend to be spread over broad spans of ages, a given percentage shift in age-specific survival rates would tend to result in an equal percentage change in labor-force size, both immediately and thereafter on an annual basis. Although it is true that such shifts are almost never equi-proportionate, the fact that they tend to be restricted in scale and have only limited impact on age structure leads to immediate effects in practice which are not very different from this theoretical guideline.

Successions or combinations of fertility or mortality changes can be similarly traced, at least in order-of-magnitude terms, by adding the effects of individual changes until the errors resulting from treating multiplicative effects additively become excessive.

Growth and Participation Rates

With respect to the comparative importance of trends in population and participation rate patterns for determining future labor-force numbers, the ILO-projected rise in LDC labor force to the year 2000 consists, in straight numerical terms, of a 90 percent contribution from the former source and 10 percent from the latter. Similar order of magnitude, according to the ILO, also held during 1950-60.[5]

Although the projections rest upon a single methodological approach, in which participation patterns are assumed to be linked with statistically identified stages of development, they attempt to stick closely to recent facts and actual trends. Moreover, the 1950-60 estimates are observations, modified only to enhance consistency in definitions. Hence, unless we see reason to expect very sharp breaks with the recent past, in which participation rates for females at all ages or for males at the younger and upper ages would move to wholly unexpected new levels, we can expect demographic factors to be the easily dominant determinants of both size and age structure of LDC labor supply. Market forces, investment levels, education and other social factors may have selective importance, but if so this would be much more visible for smaller labor force sectors than for aggregates or major sub-aggregates.

For key indicative parameters on this score, we may consult the LDC participation rates presented by ILO for 1950-2000. These show a half-century variation of only 6 points or less for either sex, with far smaller variations to 1985. Similarly constrained differences, which are found to hold in all component LDC regions, amount to minor influences on labor force trends compared to the corresponding influences from natural increase.

It follows for the long run that any fair-sized downtrend in natural increase, if sustained, can be expected to have eventually far greater impact on total labor force size than would shifting participation rates. Similar comparative impacts would seem indicated for most sex-age groups as well, though large swings in some activity rates, such as for the 15-19 and older-age groups, may occasionally enhance the relative weight of non-demographic effects.

Age Structure and Activity Rates

The influence of age structure on overall activity rates, a related but distinct effect, can best be illustrated empirically. Thus the LDC crude participation rate for males in 1960 was well below the DC rate, 54.8 to 58.3, even though the LDC rates were higher both before age 25 and after 55 and there were practically no differences at intervening ages.[6] As another example, the year-2000 ILO projections show the LDC crude rate for males rising from 51.9 to 54.6 between 1980 and 2000, at the same time as all significant shifts in age-specific rates are downward. For females, though international comparisons often reflect differences in definition as much as in the facts, a higher DC than LDC crude rate is found for 1960, 32.6 compared to 29.8, despite the fact that it is the LDC areas which have the higher rates at most ages.

Demographic factors, in the form of growth rates and age structure, tend also to dominate the relative numbers or "replacement ratio" of entries to labor force and exits from retirement and death. As of about a decade ago according to Sadie, the ratio was about 230 for "agricultural" countries (60 percent or more of labor force in agriculture), 215 for "semi-industrialized" countries (35 to 60 percent) and 170 for "industrialized" countries (under 35 percent).[7] The dynamics of labor force absorption processes portrayed by these measures make it obvious that variations in fertility far outweigh activity rate patterns in explanatory importance.

Mortality and Participation Rates

Turning next to the probable impacts of demographic trends on participation rates (to be distinguished from the comparative importance of such trends and rates on labor force), changes in mortality and morbidity appear likely to have small effect, at least in aggregate terms and as participation is measured formally. Despite the enormous mortality declines of 1950-70 in many LDC areas, overall participation rates for both males and females have moved very little. Moreover, the small movements we do find are downward, or in a direction opposite to what declining mortality as such would lead us to expect.[8] For LDC males between 15 and 65 age-specific rates have remained invariant or moved downward during this period, while beyond 65—when improved health might be expected to have especially pronounced activity effects —the male rate has moved down substantially. Both sets of patterns suggest the dominance of such factors as declining percentages in family agriculture, rising urbanization and perhaps a degree of sporadic movement toward old-age security by governments. The downtrends found correspondingly for females suggest a similar interpretation, though details of comparability complicate matters.

Possibly, however, what the figures conceal may be more important than what can be seen. Morbidity shifts associated with the recent LDC mortality declines may have had significant, if undetected, impact on quality and hourly amount of labor input, even while leaving activity rates unaffected as measured. Observations for a number of malaria-freed areas, or some of the very few analytical studies available, such as by Malenbaum,[9] suggest a possibly significant cause-effect sequence here.

Fertility and Participation Rates

A fifth topic, fertility changes in relation to female activity rates, may be considered from at least three viewpoints, all dominated by a statistical caution.

First, other things equal, a fall in fertility has the immediate effect of raising female (and also male) crude participation rates without changing size of labor force, since it increases the proportion of population in the working ages and reduces it in the young ages. Although in the long run fertility declines also result in reduced numbers in the working ages, the crude activity rate for either sex still tends to remain higher than it would have been with no decline. The reason is that the young-age proportion will continue to remain lower than it would have been if fertility had stayed unchanged.

Second, age-specific activity rates in rural areas are likely to be little changed by fertility declines. So long as family-farm agriculture is the predominant source of rural employment, place of residence and place of work tend to be the same for married women and childbearing tends to be non-competitive with labor force activity. As a result, rural (and therefore national) age-specific activity rates for women in agrarian societies tend to show small variation between about 15 and 50.[10]

Finally, in LDC urban areas, as in DC areas on a national basis, the tendency to rising female activity rates before 25 and a marked drop thereafter reflects the fact that fertility and labor force participation are competitive. In addition, it seems likely that increasing numbers of children have the effect of reducing female participation rate levels, while rising age of children seems clearly associated with return of mothers to the work force.[11] It follows that falling LDC fertility affects female national age-specific participation rates through two separable factors: the effect on urban females in the reproductive ages and the fraction of such females to the corresponding national total.

The caution noted earlier concerns the notorious degree of non-comparability of cross-national data on female labor force. Variations in female activity rates because of purely statistical reasons are often large multiples of actual behavioral differences in the rural sector, while variable inclusion of family workers in commerce and manufacturing may produce analogous distortions in non-rural sectors. The former tends, by its relative weight, to have corresponding distorting effect on national measures.

Errors may also arise in more subtle fashion. Consider two areas assumed to be experiencing large-scale urbanization. Assume also that a majority of the adult female populations in both areas were unpaid family workers on farms, but that one area counted such workers in the labor force and the other did not. Finally, suppose that fertility was falling in the former area and rising in the latter. Urbanization in the falling-fertility area would tend to lower female activity rates nationally, at least to the extent that rural-to-urban female migrants were shifted statistically from worker to non-worker status. In opposite fashion, rising fertility in the other area might appear associated with a rising activity rate as female migrants became counted as employees. Unless requisite data by sector were available, therefore, the national time series would seem to suggest a direct—rather than inverse—relation between fertility and activity changes, or at least would distort the correct relationship. Similarly, cross-national data could give rise to distortions if entire sets of areas were subject to varying time shifts in fertility and diverse practices in recording participation levels.

Urbanization and Participation

In a related way, urbanization may tend to reduce male activity rates in the young and upper adult ages. Here again, because of separation between work and family, the facts and their measures may diverge. Reporting systems which tend to overstate rural activity rates for females are likely to do the same for rural males with only marginal labor-force attachment. As a result, shifts to urban residence could lead to apparent—and, other things equal, overstated-declines in male participation rates. Correspondingly any opposite statistical bias, if one existed, would tend to understate the reducing effects of urbanization on male national rates.

For females at all ages, as suggested earlier, either type of bias may prevail. Although it seems clear that urbanization tends to raise the fraction of female labor force who work away from the family, and tends also to raise activity rates when unpaid family workers are excluded, the apparent magnitude of such effects can vary significantly, depending upon statistical conventions.

Sex Composition and Participation

A final linkage between population and labor force concerns the fact that sex ratios (males per 100 females) are high in both the urban and rural parts of nearly all main LDC regions; moreover, since internal migration tends to be male selective, the excess is higher in urban than rural sectors. With the exception of Latin America, which shows a deficit of urban males, the situation is essentially the opposite of that for DC regions, where nearly all urban and rural sex ratios are below 100.[12] The tendency is therefore for participation rates for combined sexes to be raised in most LDC regions but lowered in DC economies as a result of sex composition proper.

This tendency may diminish over the foreseeable future, as a result of mortality effects on sex composition. Since the sex ratio at birth is very nearly constant within regions, while further LDC mortality declines seem likely to be differentially favorable to females, the tendency should be to reduce the sex ratio at adult ages and thereby to reduce activity rates for combined sexes. This should hold both at individual ages and in the aggregate, though the degree of the effect on this score is likely to be secondary compared to other sources.

Research Possibilities

Each of the three research area possibilities outlined next meets the combined criteria of possessing analytic or policy importance, being insufficiently explored and providing adequate promise of feasibility.

Retrospective Projections

It would seem useful, especially in linking fertility with labor force, to develop cumulative knowledge concerning the question: "What would happen to employment today and prospectively if previous long-run fertility trends had been significantly different?" "Projections" begun well in the past for linking employment and related labor force trends with population trends over approximately quarter-century periods, or even 50 year time spans, might be involved as a basis for analyzing "the present and future."

A rationale for such an approach comes from two directions. First, a long-run orientation to population-manpower interrelations tends for that very reason to undercut attention to the question. Since changing population trends as a result of changing fertility need about quarter-century or longer periods before making significant impact on labor force, they tend to be ignored or treated as secondary by policy-makers, administrators, public opinion leaders and, not seldom, the researcher as well. The goals priority status of fertility change tends thereby to decline, even if such change could be shown to have an eventual cumulative effect exceeding that of more immediately operating causal factors.

Second and simultaneously, we have to confront the fact that our ability to analyze falls sharply when faced with future durations of several decades, if only because of exogenous shifts and shocks. In India as of 1950, there would have been no credible way of foretelling: the specific succession of good and poor harvest years that actually occurred; the droughts of the mid-1960s and appearance of the so-called Green Revolution soon afterward; the development shocks arising from the Chinese and Pakistan confrontations; the scope of the foreign exchange miscalculations that have bedeviled a succession of India's five-year plans, and so on. In Brazil similarly, the multiple major shifts in postwar development goals and the impact of exogenously-induced fluctuations in the trade, monetary and investment sectors, would have been as unpredictable a decade before the event as they were primary in impact when they appeared. Nor is there any reason to suppose that matters would be different if we tried a 25-year totally future projection today of population-employment linkages in any LDC (or DC, for that matter).

Adopting the alternative approach being suggested, that of a long-run projection starting well in the past and working forward to the present, could have two significant advantages. First, actual events would only need to be modified to the extent that they interlinked with alternative trends in fertility, the ones posited to occur if the actual ones had not happened. As a result, the "projections" would presumably have much greater immediacy and realism than would a future-oriented projection spanning a similar period of time. For example, analyzing India in 1950-75 under an assumed, counter-factual fertility decline since 1950 should provide a much more insightful and telling basis for comparing the hypothetical and actual 1975 situations than would a corresponding 1975-2000 projection of alternatives. For substantially greater accuracy could be expected in seeing how exogenous forces might interact with population-employment linkages, or in judging their comparative importance, or in specifying the dominant relations among several endogenous variables.

If these advantages have substance and can be realized in practice, retrospective projections alone could make a considerable contribution to policy formation and program implementation at one or more phases, from pre-planning of options through *ex post* evaluation.

Internal Migration Patterns

A second research area deals with population distribution. Rates of internal migration and urbanization, in contrast to fertility or mortality, are often so large or so volatile that they may match trade, income and other key economic variables in short-run magnitudes of impact on development. Compared to fertility, for example, where we are almost forced to deal with intermediate or long periods in order to achieve practical relevance, population distribution trends often feature key interdependencies with labor force in the short-run as well. Three sources of complexity in particular merit emphasis.

First, the binary or origin-destination nature of migration may introduce complications not found in other demographic areas. To assess migration effects or policy requires, or should require, comparison of at least two areas. In particular, it is not sufficient merely to point to overurbanization without allowing for possible rural overpopulation and the pressures it creates, in judging the costs and benefits of a given migration flow.

Second, externality effects add further obstacles to analysis. One such difficulty stems from the very large divergencies that tend to arise between private and social benefits or costs in, for example, the areas of transportation networks, urban infrastructure or subsidized urban housing.

Third, at a minimum for many or most LDC situations, explicit policy should focus on three locational categories, rather than on urban-rural types of dichotomies. The secondary city or hinterland town system, in addition to the large primate city and the rural sector, may well merit separate attention, if only because overurbanization and rural population pressure so often go hand in hand. To maintain merely that an LDC is overurbanized in a large-city sense loses policy relevance from employment or other viewpoints if severe rural overpopulation holds simultaneously.

Adding a third locational alternative to the usual two could at least help clarify options, whether or not any could be adopted in a practical sense. Although such addition entails tripling the number of relevant two-way comparisons, hence raises serious problems of research or policy manageability, the effort seems potentially worthwhile on several grounds. All settlement alternatives having any considerable realistic potential should merit consideration in principle; the smaller-city option has been one such; since much LDC migration is in fact multi-stage, from farm to smaller urban community to large city, rather than directly from the first to the third, an analytical need to encompass a three-way network of locations arises from the facts themselves.

In sum, we need to expand our knowledge of entire patterns of settlement locations and their development, emphasizing entire multiples as well as binary systems of settlement nodes (for example, the above three locational categories further subdivided regionally), and emphasizing also major externalities in addition to the costs and benefits as seen by household decision-makers. Such emphases, obviously, might be separable as well as joint.

As one brief illustration, much could be learned from a coordinated series of LDC surveys (census or sample) which sought to trace origin-destination mobility streams of labor force by one or more of the following: demographic characteristics; specific origin-destination sectors involved; private monetary earnings before and after migration and corresponding real earnings after adjustment for cost of living; numbers of dependents involved; associated social costs as macro-migration patterns occasioned outlays for subsidized housing, education, health facilities and other infrastructure; and others.

Productivity and Quality of Work

Third, in linking mortality trends with labor force and employment, a challenging need is to learn a great deal about productivity and quality-of-work implications. Also needed, and analytically not difficult to achieve in principle, is specific information about how mortality declines become converted through changing population size into changing manpower numbers, both in total and distributed by age, sex, regional and other main demographic characteristics. Such quantitative conversions can be carried out in rather straightforward or simulation-run fashion, possibly by graduate students as well as by more senior researchers.

More subtle mortality-labor force linkages, involving possible effects on participation rates through changing household composition, have apparently not received much research attention, but may be of secondary importance. A potentially more important set of linkages, involving the detection of lead-lag relations between mortality and fertility declines, may merit close monitoring both because of its analytic interest and because of its considerable potential interest for policy in human resource and more general development directions alike.

Notes

1. For the LDC and DC groupings by individual country, see United Nations, *World Population Prospects as Assessed in 1963*, Population Studies No. 41 (New York, 1966). An updated publication is *World Population Prospects as Assessed in 1968*, Population Studies No. 53 (New York, 1973).

2. James N. Ypsilantis, "World and Regional Estimates and Projections of Labour Force," in United Nations, *Sectoral Aspects of Projections for the World Economy. First Interregional Seminar on Long-Term Economic Projections . . .* 1966, Vol. III (New York, 1969).

3. International Labour Office, *Labour Force Projections 1965-1985,* Parts I-V (Geneva, 1971).

4. United Nations, *Growth of the World's Urban and Rural Population,* 1920-2000, Population Studies No. 44 (New York, 1969).

5. Ypsilantis, *op. cit.*

6. *Ibid.*, Tables 7 and 8.

7. Jan. L. Sadie, "Labor Supply and Employment in Less Developed Countries," *The Annals of the American Academy of Political and Social Science,* Vol. 369 (1967), Table 4.

8. Ypsilantis, *op. cit.,* Table 8.

9. Wilfred Malenbaum, "Health and Productivity in Poor Areas," in H.E. Klarman, ed., *Empirical Studies in Health Economics* (Baltimore, Maryland, Johns Hopkins Press, 1970), pp. 31-57.

10. Ypsilantis, *op. cit.,* Table 8; and Sadie, *op. cit.,* pp. 54-5.

11. See United Nations, *Methods of Analysing Census Data on Economic Activities,* Population Studies No. 43 (New York, 1969); Murray Gendell, "The Influence of Family-Building Activity on Women's Rate of Economic Activity," in United Nations, *World Population Conference: 1965,* Vol. IV (New York, 1967); John D. Kasarda, "Economic Structure and Fertility: A Comparative Analysis," *Demography,* Vol. 8, No. 3 (August, 1971); and Jan. L. Sadie, *"Demographic Aspects of Labour Supply and Employment,"* in United Nations, *World Population Conference: 1965,* Vol. I (New York, 1966).

12. United Nations, *Demographic Aspects of Manpower, Sex and Age Patterns of Participation in Economic Activities,* Population Studies No. 33 (New York, 1961).

Implementation of Policies for Fuller Employment in Less Developed Countries

Vincent M. Barnett, Jr.
Williams College

Assuming that at least the broad outlines of policies for employment consistent with growth are known or can be discovered by systematic research, what can be said about the political and administrative obstacles to the implementation of such policies?

This is, of course, but one aspect of the broader problem of plan implementation in general. Much has been written on this subject, although I sometimes think more attention has been paid to technical organizational and procedural prescriptions drawn from the experience of advanced countries than to the crucial area of organizing for informed policy choices below the level of the over-all plan and above the level of the administrative machinery for the delivery of the relevant output.

In focussing this discussion on the implementation of planning for fuller employment, it will be useful to make some assumptions as to the kinds of policies that are now perceived or may become accepted as required for this objective, with a view to looking at the implementation problems associated with their further refinement and execution. Some agreement about the nature of the unemployment problem itself is not only necessary to the devising of appropriate policies, but is also the prime prerequisite for the implementation of the policies chosen.

Some Assumptions About the Nature of the Unemployment Problem

Although it is difficult and risky to make such generalizations, I believe it can be said that there is something approaching a consensus among scholars about many aspects of the unemployment problem in developing countries. There is probably much less consensus about the appropriate policy implications of the diagnosis, and probably still less about the particular programs and the organizational and administrative steps necessary to effectuate chosen policy.

Perhaps the major points in an analysis of the nature of the unemployment problem in the developing countries would include the following kinds of generalizations:

1. Unemployment (however measured) is at too high a level in most of these countries, and is increasing. A number of countries with otherwise satisfactory growth rates continue to suffer increased unemployment.

2. Much of the increase is in urban centers, where high rates of open unemployment are added to the more typical underemployment in both urban and rural areas.

3. The transformation of rural underemployment into open unemployment in

urban centers changes both the magnitude and the political nature of the problem.

4. Industrialization, relied upon heavily to create new jobs in early development plans, has not done so as rapidly as expected; employment has lagged notably behind growth of industrial output, and the industrial job-creation rate has been greatly exceeded by increases in labor supply.

5. The major reason the industrial sector has had only limited success in job-creation lies not so much in the failure to expand industrial output as in the nature of the industrialization process; in most countries industrialization has been characterized by the adoption of relatively capital-intensive techniques and rapid expansion in the more capital-intensive industries.

6. This pattern of industrialization is a consequence in part of the ready availability of capital-intensive technologies from the developed countries, often sought by the developing countries irrespective of how inappropriate these technologies may be for the recipient country's own factor endowments, and often pushed upon the recipient country by inappropriate policies of foreign and international aid donors.

7. The effective preference for capital-intensive techniques (perhaps not a result of conscious policy) is partly explained by market imperfections leading to a misallocation of resources. Over-valued exchange rates reduce the cost of imported machinery; internal interest rate structure favors acquisition of capital by large enterprise (and government); world money markets provide capital at rates considerably below domestic rates; internal monetary and banking policies have the effect of keeping the price of capital low for these larger borrowers; and, generally, the banking and credit structure make it more difficult for smaller entrepreneurs in less capital-intensive activities to obtain credit, at least at anything like comparable rates.

8. Tax laws in many countries encourage capital intensity through such provisions as high depreciation and investment allowances.

9. Industrial wages are relatively high and rising, which tends not only to increase capital intensity but also to accelerate the migration of labor from rural to urban areas. Minimum wage provisions, government salary levels, and the wage policies of foreign firms, all exert an upward influence on industrial wage rates and result in an excessive differential between real wages in the modern urban sector and real income in agriculture.

10. Despite large and increasing unemployment of unskilled labor, there is a simultaneous shortage of skilled labor.

11. The rapid increase of the labor force in the services sector represents to a considerable degree an increase in underemployment.

12. Excessive migration of labor from agriculture and rural areas has resulted in very rapid urbanization, with urban populations in general growing at more than twice the rate of total population. Many factors contribute to this: the real wage differential in urban and rural areas; the centralization of industry; the greater availability of economic infrastructure, social services, and amenities of life in the urban areas.

13. The "push" side of this "push-pull" equation is represented by slow growth of agricultural production relative to rural population, accentuated by the fact that production gains have typically centered in relatively capital-intensive activities and large-scale commercial farms.

14. In general, rapid rural-urban migration is more significant in explaining the magnitude of the unemployment problem than the rate of industrial job-creation. Industrial employment is expanding at a high rate, but far from high enough to absorb migration from rural areas.

15. At the base of the problem lies the too-rapid growth of the labor force flowing from high population growth rates. Presently advanced countries did not have to cope during their period of rapid development with population growth rates of the magnitude now characterizing most developing countries. This aspect of the problem is, of course, irreversible in the short term. This does not make it less crucial to the ultimate mitigation of unemployment in the longer term.

Such observations about the character of the unemployment problem in developing countries (even if accepted as essentially correct) are at an excessively high level of generalization to be very useful in suggesting policies or examing implementation problems in any given country. The first step in devising policies, programs, and machinery for implementation must be a testing of such hypotheses against the empirical evidence and the particular economic, governmental, and social structure of that country. This is a research and analysis problem of the first magnitude. The institutionalizing of this kind of applied research in a manner regarded as appropriate by the country itself, and the linkage of this research activity to the governmental decision-making processes, is one of the key problems in implementing any set of effective policies with respect to unemployment.

The mere listing of hypotheses about the nature of the problem suggests certain lines of broad policy direction, again at a high level of generalization. The extent to which they would be appropriate in any given country would depend not only upon the applicability of the theoretical analysis and its empirical confirmation, but also upon the constraints which would be faced in implementing the derivative programs. These constraints will be not only administrative in the ordinary sense, but also political and social at a fundamental level—that is, having to do with the capacity of the government to carry them out in view of its own realistic power base and its continuing legitimacy. Truly viable policy options will be limited by the political leaders' perceptions of these realities, over and above their acceptance of the diagnosis or their being persuaded of what they should do if they could.

Some Assumptions About Appropriate Policies

An important concept that has emerged in recent years is the denial of the view that there must be a trade-off between growth on the one hand and income distribution (or fuller employment) on the other. If the policy of a country is to maximize future output per capita rather than present output and employment, and if capital intensity is required to achieve this goal because it increases profits, savings, and investment, then to opt for growth means to opt for more capital intensity (and more unemployment in the near-term) to the extent that there is a necessary trade-off. If, however, comparable growth rates can be achieved in fact with more labor intensity through following an appropriate set of policies, then the previously-perceived trade-off dilemma ceases to exist (or exists to a much lesser degree).

Much research remains to be done in determining the theoretical compatibility of greater income distribution and fuller employment with maximization of growth rates. But many countries are already concluding, in setting their planning goals, that maximization of growth cannot be an overriding goal. Hence, even though not enough is yet known about the theoretical possibilities of maximizing both growth and employment, political and social considerations will push toward policies based implicitly on the assumption that such compatibility exists. Increasing unemployment, heavy rural-urban migration, the politically-unsettling effects of highly visible and concentrated poverty, combine to make the choice of a lower growth rate less dangerous than the political and social consequences of growing urban poverty and unemployment. Governments will be receptive toward policy suggestions for the alleviation of unemployment, even at the possible expense of marginal increments of over-all growth; but they will not know very much about the reality of any such trade-off in their own economies, the policies necessary for a concerted attack on unemployment will be highly controversial in political practice even if widely accepted by the country's economists and other professionals, and some of these policies will present much more difficult problems of implementation than policies based upon the desirability of capital intensity.

The broad outlines of policies intended to maximize employment consistent with growth may be suggested. This subject is treated more fully in other papers prepared for the conference. The brief listing here is meant to facilitate a consideration of implementation problems, since these are ultimately meaningful only in relation to particular programs in particular countries.

1. To the extent that unemployment, though urban in its major manifestation, is rural in its major causes, policy must have a focus on rural development which can employ and otherwise contain the labor force and slow the migration to urban areas.

2. Agricultural policy should aim not only at increased output but also at increased employment through advancing the use of labor-intensive techniques on small and middle-sized farm units.

3. While the possibility of expanding employment opportunities in agriculture through labor-intensive cultivation techniques and yield-increasing inputs seems very high (on the experience, for example, of Japan and Taiwan), the effectiveness of such policies depends on the nearly simultaneous carrying out of a number of action programs which pose considerable strains on governmental administrative capacity:

   a. much more widespread and intensive agricultural education programs, including effective extension programs;
   b. more adequate rural community services, including schools and hospitals;
   c. more access roads, water facilities, land reclamation;
   d. more warehouses, local processing plants;
   e. more widespread availability of fertilizer, improved seeds, tools, animal-powered implements, and other inputs consistent with labor-intensive techniques;
   f. expansion of agricultural credit facilities;
   g. more effective agricultural research, along with better dissemination of the findings;
   h. land reform where appropriate to break up large holdings of unused or under-utilized land.

4. Industrialization policy should include the encouragement of rural-based industry and services, both those which supply inputs such as fertilizer, tools, and implements and those which process agricultural products; such encouragement will probably require improvement of rural infrastructure, upgrading rural labor skills through education, and tax or other special incentives.

5. Market distortions misrepresenting the country's factor endowment should be minimized: cost of capital for large borrowers could be increased by monetary and fiscal policies, by currency devaluation, and by removal of tax incentives such as special depreciation and tax write-offs for new plant and equipment; cost of capital might be reduced for more labor-intensive enterprises through development banks or other government lending institutions.

6. Capital-intensive technologies borrowed from abroad could be gradually

replaced by more labor-intensive technologies through engineering and scientific research; indigenous research institutions should be encouraged to focus on such problems.

7. Industrialization policy should include the encouragement of small-scale industry in general, on the ground that smaller firms tend to be more labor intensive. Implicit in such a policy would be the provision of more adequate credit facilities and the effective organization and operation of small business advisory services.

8. Training programs for unskilled labor would help reduce unemployment and help meet the shortage of skilled labor; on-the-job training and apprenticeship programs should be devised as more effective short-term responses than formal vocational education. Both the government's own public enterprises and private industrial firms could be mobilized in such programs, the latter perhaps by appropriate tax incentives.

9. The desirability of population-control programs in any long-term attack on unemployment seems clear; the decision to pursue such programs often raises religious, political, and social problems which uniquely complicate the implementation process.

10. Import substitution policies which have been widely practiced in developing countries tend to have a dampening effect on the growth of employment (because of the use of capital-intensive technology and the slower rate of growth after the substitution has been achieved), and should probably be superseded by more export-oriented policies.

11. The formal education systems in many developing countries need to be carefully reviewed and revised in the light of their current inappropriateness in meeting the country's needs, including but not limited to the needs made evident by the relationship of formal education to employment. Drastic revision of Western-oriented systems in the direction of less emphasis on higher education, more attention to vocational and technical training, more emphasis on rural formal and nonformal education, may be indicated. Both the employability of presently unskilled labor and the ability of the rural areas to retain larger numbers of their youth may depend on greatly increased emphasis on rural education.

Implementation Aspects of Various Policy Options

If economists know even as much as they think they know about the employment implications of various alternatives in economic development policy, and if governments of developing countries are increasingly concerned about the explosive potential of rising unemployment levels, why are not those governments actively pursuing the kinds of policies the economists generally agree on? This raises a whole series of rather simple questions which have, however, less-than-obvious answers. Following are some examples:

1. Why don't governments give high priority to research on employment problems which relate the economists' knowledge and insights to the situations in their own countries? Why don't they establish effective research institutions and programs and fund them adequately? Why don't they utilize universities and private business groups in such research?

2. Why don't governments revise industrial tax and other incentives to encourage labor intensity rather than continuing to facilitate the importation of capital, heavy machinery, labor-saving technology?

3. Why don't governments greatly increase the proportion of the public budget going to agriculture, rural education, and rural amenities generally as compared to public investments which tend further to encourage urban concentration?

4. Why don't governments make a big push to provide effective extension services and new seed and fertilizer technology (and improved kinds of animal-powered farm implements) to much larger numbers of small and medium sized farms?

5. Why don't governments enact necessary land reform legislation to permit the growth of more labor-intensive and productive agriculture, thus creating new jobs as well as easing political and social tensions?

6. Why don't governments establish effective incentives for the decentralization of industry and the encouragement of small-scale enterprise for the local processing of agricultural (and forest and mining and fishing) products?

7. Why don't governments recast educational systems and policies based on largely irrelevant foreign patterns so as to bring more meaningful primary education to rural areas and supplement it with nonformal job and skill-oriented education?

8. Why don't governments adopt policies aimed at restraining wage rises in urban areas and diminishing the gap between urban wages and rural real income?

9. Why don't governments require their own ministries and the various public enterprises to pursue more labor-intensive policies?

10. Why don't governments decentralize their own operations so as to give more authority (and resources) to regional, provincial, and local levels of government?

11. Why don't governments vigorously reform their own bureaucratic organization and procedures (budget, financial, personnel, reporting, over-all coordination) so as to move programs and resources into rural areas more expeditiously?

12. Why don't governments rely more heavily on taxation as an instrument of savings and investment rather than on high profits of large-scale enterprises which are typically capital-intensive and urban-based?

13. Why don't governments resist the distortion-producing effects of those foreign and international aid programs which tend to accelerate urban growth, large-scale enterprise, and the import of capital-intensive technology?

14. Why don't governments encourage and if necessary subsidize on-the-job training for intermediate technical and managerial skills in both public and private enterprise?

15. Why don't governments positively encourage the growth of service trades and other tertiary activities which hold substantial promise for the expansion of self-employment and small-enterprise activities?

16. Why don't governments mount more wide-reaching programs of publicly-organized and financed job-corps activities with substantial training components in conservation, rural road-building, water supply, and similar fields?

17. Why don't governments attack the underlying problem of the over-supply of labor with more extensive and effective population planning programs?

Much of the writing on implementation of development plans by the professional "development administration" experts seems to assume that the central problem lies in the organization and procedures of the governmental mechanism which slows or prevents the adoption and carrying out of these and other desirable policies. While attention to these kinds of problems is clearly important and of continuing concern, and while the adoption of such administrative reforms with due regard to their suitability to indigenous needs and cultural constraints is in itself a difficult challenge, there is reason to believe that their accomplishment will be hampered by the same kinds of ambivalent commitment and defective political will that impede policy changes generally. Administrative and organizational reforms on general principles of "efficiency" and "modernity" face a doubtful fate; they are likely to be meaningfully and persistently pursued only in terms of more specific goal-oriented and program-oriented decisions to which administrative problems are demonstrably related. In any case, there are probably more fundamental and less simplistic reasons for the slowness of governments in adopting and carrying out the broad range of policies implied in a far-ranging attack on unemployment and underemployment.

In fact, some of the policies outlined above require no complicated implementation machinery. Changing the incentive systems which now exist, purposely or by necessary consequence, as a result of tax, fiscal, foreign exchange, customs protection, and similar policies requires no new or elaborate structure of administrative mechanisms. It requires basically a firm and internally consistent set of political decisions taken with real commitment and pursued through the conventional processes using largely existent machinery. It requires a thorough conviction on the part of top leadership that these are the right decisions (which may be a matter of the success of the professional planners in educating their political masters) and the ability of the leaders to stand fast in the face of the pressures that will boil up when the oratory of speeches and plan documents is changed into hard decisions adversely affecting powerful individuals and groups in the society. This will vary from country to country, from leadership to leadership, and from time to time in the same country. Meaningful comment beyond a very general level is almost impossible. It is not, in fact, an implementation problem in the normal sense at all; it is a problem of the basic decision-making process in the country concerned. The rule of anticipated reactions suggests that much of the ambivalence and delay in adopting policy changes such as these may flow, not from lack of understanding of the problem, but from a judgment that the political cohesion of the government is not sufficiently strong to enable it to persevere in the pursuit of the policy. This comment can apply to governments which are superficially monolithic as well as to those whose governmental processes are more obviously subject to the play of competing political forces.

Others of the kinds of policies related to fuller employment require not only economic understanding and political commitment but also massive organizational and administrative efforts involving not only very large financial and personnel resources but managerial innovations of a high order of difficulty. The latter include programs to reach the small farmer all over the country with effective extension services, credit, rural transport, marketing, and similar facilities; reform of rural education, both formal and nonformal; programs to extend other social amenities widely to rural areas, including health and family planning; the extension of effective credit and business advisory facilities to small-scale enterprise, rural-based as well as urban; the mounting of effective research activities on labor-intensive technology and the diffusion of the results of such research throughout the economy. Each of these and numerous others present their own individual problems of implementation, as well as the overarching problem of relative priorities for insufficient budgetary, personnel, and other resources.

Both kinds of implementation problems are conditioned by a whole set of intermediate level difficulties and uncertainties—intermediate, that is, between the announcement of broad employment goals in a macroeconomic multi-year development plan, on the one hand, and the nuts-and-bolts problems of an effective governmental delivery system for specific outputs on the other. Even given the formal adoption of employment and income distribution goals as top-priority objectives alongside overall growth in a reasonably consistent plan (a commitment not always taken with complete political sincerity, or at least not always taken with a full awareness of its implications), these intermediate problems of translation into specific program and action commitments remain crucial and are typically faced with reluctance.

Is it possible to speculate usefully on why it is that this type of policy change may present special difficulties from a political and administrative point of view? I am not at all sure that there is anything unique about policies for fuller employment which sets their implementation problems apart from those of other policies for economic development. Indeed, the breadth and scope of policies discussed in relation to employment are so all-encompassing as to touch upon almost all important aspects of development. It is perhaps legitimate, however, to ponder why governments seem able to respond with more alacrity and more effectiveness when policies having adverse effects on the balance of payments or upon the level of foreign exchange reserves or upon the containment of inflation or upon a number of other financial and monetary indicators of economic health are involved than when policies having adverse effects upon prospects for maximum employment growth are called to their attention.

Political commitment. The basic political commitment to job-creation as one of the major goals of the economic development program may be weak; it may thus be easily dissipated when it comes into conflict, real or apparent, with goals of over-all growth, capital formation, financial stability, defense of the currency, attraction of foreign capital, maximization of industrial output, import substitution, modernization of productive processes, and the like.

Confidence. The state of knowledge about the interaction between employment and other economic goals may be insufficient to convince the government's own planning bodies and professional staffs of the top priority to be accorded to employment creation, or of the nature and extent of trade-offs in their own country among employment, income distribution, and economic growth.

Communication. Even if convinced, the professional staffs may not be able to communicate their conviction and their sense of urgency to the top political levels of government; the effectiveness of such channels of communication varies from government to government, but appears less than optimum in all governments.

Conflicting pressures. Even if the correctness of the emphasis on employment creation is accepted in principle at high political levels, the initial steps in instituting such programs will almost certainly raise other concerns only imperfectly foreseen at the time the political decision was made. Adverse effects on other familiar indices of economic well-being will lead to pressures for reassessment, retrenchment, retreat to "symbolic" and marginal efforts rather than a vigorous pursuit of stated employment goals. This has to do not so much with the *capacity* of the government to carry out employment programs as with recurring doubts as to *whether* they should be carried out as designed.

Compromise is likely, especially since strongly entrenched political and bureaucratic forces (Central Banks, Treasury, other economic ministries, to say nothing of private businessmen, financiers, and others) pushing their own perceived interests will bring great pressure to bear at the highest political levels. Such compromise is likely to slow or render ineffective the pursuit of the employment program before it even reaches the stage of detailed implementation. The extent of the compromise will depend on the depth of commitment at the top, the strength and cohesion of the government itself, even the personal style and effectiveness of the prime minister or other head of government.

These are matters on which useful generalization is exceedingly difficult, but even in relatively authoritarian regimes the outcome is likely to be at best repeated delays and at worst self-defeating retreat and compromise. These are things the professional and expert staffs cannot do much about except to try to provide the ammunition necessary to convince the top political leadership that things it *knows* are bad (inflation, balance of payments troubles, burgeoning budget deficits, loss of reserves, declining growth rates, diminished private investment levels) either will not happen over a reasonable period of time or are worth considerable risk because of the greater evil of intolerable unemployment levels. This typically takes some doing, and implies a confidence of the politicians in their technical and professional staffs which does not characterize most young governments.

Political survival. Some aspects of a broad employment creation program may involve even more elemental political problems, going to the heart of the cohesion and survival power of the political regime itself. Land reform in some countries, even though acknowledged as essential to the kinds of rural small-scale agricultural programs most closely linked to dampening rural-urban migration and making real inroads on unemployment, may fall or may be perceived to fall in this category.

The inability of even the relatively authoritarian regime in Ethiopia to move forward with land reform policies officially accepted by the Emperor himself may be a case in point. Indigenous planners, professional advisors and consultants, foreign donor agencies, IBRD study teams—all agree that land reform is prerequisite to real progress in the modernization of Ethiopian agriculture and the institution of labor-intensive culture on small and medium sized farms; yet legislation to this end (even with the Emperor's formal sanction) is repeatedly postponed, not only because of opposition of large land-holders and associated groups in more or less conventional political channels, but also because at least some influential leaders apparently genuinely fear that it could lead to rebellion and the dismemberment of the government. Hence, even in a regime as autocratic as the Ethiopian one (or maybe especially in a regime as essentially feudalistic as the Ethiopian one), decision in principle by the central government leadership is far from enough. The realities of political power limit and at least slow down the beginning of the process of actual implementation.

The private sector. It is probably not enough that government be convinced of the necessity and feasibility of a comprehensive and integrated program centered on job creation; in mixed-economy countries the private business and financial community must also be convinced, or at least persuaded or induced, to accept the perceived risks. Modification of the standard industrial incentive schemes in the direction of providing more inducement for decentralization, more investment in small-scale rural-based industries, adoption of labor-intensive technologies, for example, may not be enough. (I am not sure, however, that this has ever been vigorously tried.) Direct public investment in such rural industrialization projects, both for their own sake and as demonstrations that they are economically feasible, can have only a marginal—though important—effect. If sizable private investment resources are to be moved in this direction, more specific and effective inducements may have to be devised and implemented. Public guarantees of private investment in these areas, at least a theoretical possibility, would be much more difficult to formulate and administer successfully.

Basically, however, a more effective government-private sector dialogue to educate the community to the growing crisis of unemployment and the need for jointly devising feasible solutions would have to be carried out. It is precisely this kind of dialogue which is typically lacking in the policy-formulation processes in most developing countries, with adverse effects on the implementation of even much less unsettling government policies than those necessary to enlist the private sector in a full-scale attack on unemployment.

Foreign investors. The domination of the private sector by foreign investors, typical of many young countries, makes the effectuation of labor-intensive policies much more difficult. The pattern of foreign investment inherited from the pre-independence period, and perhaps more especially the process of seeking out and encouraging new foreign investment, have generally resulted in large-scale, urban-based, capital-intensive, advanced-technology oriented enterprises conducive to high profits and rapid growth of industrial output. The same can unfortunately be said of most foreign aid programs, both bi-lateral and international, at least until recently. The government which faces the task of implementing a program seeking basically to alter this pattern of investment faces the unpleasant prospect of having to say no to offers of foreign private and public investment. In its (perhaps mistaken) eagerness for more capital inflow, the government will find it difficult to hold to an investment policy which discourages or shuts off low-priced foreign capital seeking to ''modernize'' its economy with the latest and most ''advanced'' technology. Part of the educational process which must follow upon the research findings of economists and other scholars lies in the challenge to change the perceptions, attitudes, and policies of foreign investors, including aid donors.

Research needs. The obstacles to implementation flowing from inadequate attention to country-specific questions crucial to the considered formulation of employment policy decisions seem very great. Government research on such problems is typically fragmented, *ad hoc,* woefully underfinanced, and given low priority for both funds and people. Universities in most of these countries simply do not do much research useful to government planners and policy-makers; and there is an unfortunate gap of mutual suspicion and mistrust between the government and the academic community which varies from country to country but appears to be present to some degree everywhere.

In some instances this may be due primarily to differences in professional objectives, diversity of life-styles, and the presumed conflict between the theoretical and the practical; but in many cases such factors are reinforced by real hostility in stark political terms. In these instances, the government and its bureaucracy tend (with some justice) to regard the universities as the spearhead of political danger to the existing government and perhaps even to the regime. Exhortations to utilize university research resources, even if politely acknowledged, are not likely to be very productive under these circumstances.

Research of this type within the government is perhaps most frequently done, if at all, in the planning office. Here again, there are at least two obstacles to the effective organization and execution of such research (even given adequate professional staff and financial resources) pulling in both directions away from policy and program-oriented research at the intermediate level. One is the almost total preoccupation of planning offices, at least until quite recently, with macro-economic analysis and over-all plan preparation, on which much progress has been made in many countries but which does not typically get very far into specific program-related research (on employment problems or many others). The other is the tendency for the best planning office personnel (once the Plan Document is prepared) to be pulled off into very *ad hoc* fire-fighting assignments of a short-term crisis nature. I think it is a truism in the trade that planning offices tend to disintegrate once the Plan Document is approved. But this is precisely the time when such research resources as governments can muster should be focussed on the questions of specific policy and action program options left open or ambiguous in the Plan itself.

Mobilization of research talent throughout the government to work on these kinds of questions seems to present almost insuperable problems: (1) there is a relatively thin layer of trained people capable of high-quality research in these fields; (2) they are dispersed in a number of different departments and agencies; (3) they are loaded with short-term crisis assignments and day-to-day operating responsibilities incompatible with continuous and concentrated attention on research; (4) civil service rules and bureaucratic jurisdictional considerations impede their being brought together, organized, and insulated from the narrower demands of their respective agencies; (5) research functions are, in the familiar pattern, always vulnerable to retrenchment in the name of budget stringency or personnel shortage.

Perhaps these and other constraints are all derivitive of an insufficient awareness at top political levels of the indispensability of research activity in the process of plan implementation. Many governments do have central plan implementation organizations, either in the planning office itself or elsewhere, but such organizations are not typically staffed for or oriented toward operational research. The prospects for repairing this deficiency seem at best dubious in many countries; yet the very real progress in overcoming similar obstacles in organizing for over-all planning suggests that if employment creation becomes politically accepted as crucial to the success of the government, ways to bring it about can be found. It may be noted, however, that in some ways the organization and effective utilization of this kind of research presents even more difficult political and administrative problems than those raised by the over-all planning process itself, which can and typically does leave rather vague and ambiguous some of the most vital program decisions. In the case of operational research leading to choices among specific program options, so many different governmental units feel so directly and immediately involved that the problem of organizing and coordinating this research (even if all the other constraints of personnel, funding, and the like, could be met) remains a major challenge to political leadership.

Some Special Aspects of Implementation of Agricultural Programs for Employment

Increasing numbers of the less developed countries are being brought to face the proposition that labor force growth combined with limited prospects for absorption in non-agricultural sectors require that the emphasis in agricultural policy be laid on development of a labor-intensive character. Resistance to such a policy emphasis on the ground that it would substantially retard over-all growth rates is lessened by growing evidence that the "seed-fertilizer" revolution makes it feasible without excessive costs to growth, and by the accumulating experience in some countries that these highly-productive inputs can be delivered effectively to large numbers of small-scale farmers who will respond constructively. Indigenous agricultural research institutions in some countries have had considerable success in applying the findings of the "green revolution" to their own circumstances, and in experimenting with intermediate technologies based upon improved tools and animal-powered agricultural implements. Special agricultural projects demonstrating the feasibility of labor-intensive techniques and the favorable prospects that they can be delivered to small farmers and utilized by them have been accumulating useful experience. Examples are the Intensive Agricultural Development Unit (CADU) in Ethiopia, the PACCA project in Afghanistan, the Puebla Project in Mexico, and the Lilongwe Project in Malawi (for which the World Bank made its first "integrated package" loan in 1968). Most of these projects have incurred per capita costs too high to allow them to be replicated generally in the country concerned, but as research and experimentation efforts they have had some success in laying the groundwork for more modest "minimum package" programs that may be made more widely available.

In any case, economists and planners are in a position to suggest the broad outlines of a development strategy aimed at a more efficient use of a country's resources along with the creation of more jobs and the slowing of the rate of rural-urban migration. The major elements in such a strategy would include: (1) the provision of substantially larger volumes of public resources to agriculture; (2) the strengthening of agricultural research and increasing progress in making it more indigenous, both as to staffing and as to country orientation; (3) increased emphasis on intermediate technology research and on delivery systems making its results available to substantially larger numbers of users; (4) strengthening of agricultural education and extension efforts; (5) substantial expansion of rural road-construction activities utilizing labor-intensive techniques; (6) modification of existing incentive structures which favor mechanization and capital intensity in agriculture; (7) wide-ranging measures in rural education, health, and recreation to increase the general attractiveness of rural life; and (8) where relevant, effective land reform to provide the social and economic basis for longer-term rural development.

Implementation problems relate to whether a program of such magnitude can in fact be carried out and whether the benefits of the improved technologies, notably in seeds and fertilizer, can be distributed in such a way as to prevent their undue absorption by large landowners and capital-intensive enterprises. The former raises all the problems of political commitment, governmental capacity, organizational and administrative efficiency, and politically strong competing demands for limited financial resources that characterize the "implementation gap" in development administration generally. The latter would presumably be less likely to happen if factor prices were not distorted by existing incentive policies favoring capital intensity.

Each of the individual elements in such a strategy presents implementation problems about which research monographs could (and probably should) be written in the context of each country involved. General comments on some of them, based on programs and experiments with which some experience has been had, might be useful.

Research. The firm establishment and necessary expansion of agricultural research reflecting the country's own needs is likely to be impeded not only by a shortage of funds but even more importantly by a shortage of trained and experienced native research workers. A major share of the research in those countries where it is now going on is staffed by expatriates. The high turnover of expatriate professionals on short-term contract has a disruptive effect on the continuity required for effective results. The conversion of the agricultural research establishment to a basically indigenous enterprise is a long and costly process requiring careful plans for training and retention of native professional personnel. It may be objected that the quality of the research is likely to be adversely affected. But it is also true that its suitability for the country in question may be increased. And it is at least possible that its political acceptability and its consequent impact on the policy-making and administrative processes may be enhanced. The implementation gap in the full achievement of agricultural research goals is compounded by these kinds of problems, over and above the more generic ones of funding, training, coordination, and effective leadership.

Extension. Experience in most countries indicates that the single most important factor in inducing farmers to accept innovations in technology and farm practice is the presence of an adequately-staffed, well-trained extension service. The present situation in most countries is that the number of adequately-trained field-level extension workers is wholly insufficient to reach the large numbers of farm families which must be served if the effort is to be more than marginal in its effects. The comparison of the existing ratio of extension workers to farm families with the ratio suggested by FAO for Africa (one worker per 850-1000 families), or, for example, with Tanzania's stated goal of one worker for each 500 farm families by 1979, will dramatize the magnitude of the gap. Effective implementation of the necessary extension programs raises significant problems of the numbers of workers to be trained as well as the best kind of training.

Agricultural education. In most countries field-level extension workers are largely trained in the formal academic institutions specializing in agriculture. The output of these institutions, even if they were to be substantially expanded, would be far short of the numbers required to staff extension services of the reach visualized in the new agricultural strategy. Moreover, experience suggests that there is serious question whether the kind of training typically provided by the academic institutions is actually needed or is even most appropriate for the kinds of problems faced by field workers in remote rural areas. There has been some experimentation with shorter and more practical training courses for younger and formally less-well-qualified trainees in organizations outside the academic establishment.

In Ethiopia, the CADU project has had some success with such courses: they are less costly to administer; their products are less costly to employ; and the resulting staff seem more congenial to and better able to work with small-scale farmers (and to tolerate the rather austere life-style typical of remote rural field assignments). The Ministry of Agriculture has asked CADU to train extension workers for the heavy demands implicit in the expansion of the minimum package program. This would take place, of course, alongside the more conventional training programs.

In another extension program often considered one of the more successful models in less developed countries, that of the Office of Rural Development in Korea, one of the emerging problems has been that of high turnover of field staff, attributable perhaps in part to "overtraining" for the kind of work to be done. The typical agricultural college graduate (originally the source of almost all extension workers) can earn about twice as much teaching in secondary school as he can in extension work, and more than that in other available jobs in the city. As a field worker he has longer hours, harder work, and less attractive conditions of life. About half of the graduates of the agricultural colleges now take jobs outside the agricultural system. This suggests that training for effective field workers might better draw upon a more suitable clientele and offer instruction and work experience more adapted to actual working conditions in the field.

Another innovative extension program, that of the SATEC project in Senegal, achieved some substantial successes with extension workers with formal training considerably below the college level who were given well-conceived short and intensive courses in communicating the recommended package of improved practices to farmers.

In short, the implementation of greatly expanded and improved extension programs calls for a careful re-evaluation of the system of agricultural education and the introduction of rather different (and often nonformal) training programs. This is not to undervalue the continued role of the agricultural colleges and universities in the training of agricultural economists, agronomists, and other agricultural specialists for research and other middle to high level tasks in the agricultural establishment.*

Farm roads. Experience in a number of countries has shown that one of the major impediments to widespread use of improved agricultural inputs is their availability at reasonable cost. Transport charges are an important element in such costs. Fertilizer prices at the farm are particularly affected. In this respect, a comprehensive system of farm roads is essential to widespread adoption of fertilizer use by small farms. Adequate programs for rural road-building are often inhibited by high construction costs of rural roads built to the unnecessarily high specifications of central transport ministries or highway authorities and utilizing capital-intensive techniques. The cost impediment to implementation of more adequate rural road programs could be reduced by special programs for lower-specification roads built by labor-intensive techniques and utilizing surplus local labor employed at near-subsistence wages. AID's Food-for-Work program in several countries, including Ethiopia, has had some success along these lines as well as in other labor-intensive rural public works projects.

Implementation of Industrialization Policies for Decentralization and Labor-Intensity

Assuming that the general policy to encourage more labor-intensive industry and to promote both industrial dispersal and the growth of smaller firms in rural areas were adopted, what special problems of implementation would emerge?

The various tax and other governmental incentives now resulting in urban concentration and capital intensity would have to be greatly modified, but would seem to present no special problems with respect to implementation machinery as such. How effective such a changed incentive system would be is not clear, partly because it is not clear what the responses would be in either economic or political terms. It is probably easier, however, to administer a system of subsidies facilitating the use of capital and ''advanced'' technology than one which tries to hold back the march of ''progress.'' It is probably easier to administer a system of inducements resulting in (or at least not impeding) increased urbanization than one specifically aimed at employment-generating activities in rural areas.

Significantly stepped-up programs of building rural infrastructure—roads, water

---

* A draft report on nonformal education for rural development currently being prepared for the World Bank concludes, on the basis of case studies in several less developed countries, that the implementation of effective extension service is plagued almost everywhere by similar problems. These have to do with: (1) adequacy of budget; (2) staff recruitment, training, and utilization; (3) adequacy of research backstopping and soundness of recommended practices; (4) setting priorities among multiple objectives; and (5) the coordination of educational activities with essential complementary inputs and services. The report, at least in its present stage, is less clear on how these problems might be solved.

systems, schools, medical facilities—would have to be carried out to complement the incentive schemes. The usual constraints on executing public works in rural areas would come into play at a correspondingly higher level of difficulty. If, as is desirable, the public works activities were themselves to stress labor intensity, implementation problems would increase another notch. Governments, in their own activities of this kind, are among the worst offenders of the principle of labor intensity. They tend to build roads with bulldozers while unemployed villagers watch.

To the extent that government itself is the entrepreneur, it can (if it really means it and if it can effectively control its own mechanisms) make and carry out decisions along these lines. A high and fixed minimum percentage of all investments by public enterprises can be directed to the less industrialized areas, as has been done, for example, for more than twenty years in Italy under the Fund-for-the-South legislation. In many countries, such a program would raise to new levels of difficulty the already present complexities of policy-direction, control, and coordination of the activities of the rapidly proliferating number of public corporations. Goals of this kind would have to be firmly established in political terms; a clearer direction to public enterprise (and a more effective system of accountability) than is typically the case would have to be established and maintained; and severe organizational and administrative problems would have to be surmounted. Even in the relatively more successful public enterprise activities—those in the public utility and other infrastructure areas—these problems have not been satisfactorily solved in most developing countries. To instruct the growing variety of public corporations in manufacturing activities that they not only must operate "efficiently" but must experiment with labor-intensive techniques, often in "backward" areas, would surely increase the problems of coordination and accountability many times. Whether government-owned "yard-stick" enterprises could effectively demonstrate the economic efficiency of labor-intensive techniques in manufacturing and processing activities in rural areas is far from clear; but it does seem clear that governments themselves, through incentive schemes or penalties or direct intervention, must in effect subsidize the necessary experimentation. The mounting of research and analysis seeking to discover the best ways of doing this would be a vital first step in the carrying out of such a general policy.

To the question why governments don't carry out programs to decentralize industry and encourage small enterprises in rural areas, it must be said that a number of governments have indeed tried a variety of approaches to this end over a considerable period of time. Some of the nonformal training programs, including those in Nigeria, Senegal, and Thailand, have attempted to provide instruction for artisans and small entrepreneurs in rural towns. The experience with these programs has been, at best, mixed. The Mobile Trade Training Schools program in Thailand by the end of 1972 had established 54 schools located in rural towns and provincial centers. After operating in a particular town for one to three years, the equipment and staff are moved to another town. Serving primarily out-of-school rural youths and young adults, the schools utilize local community buildings and are staffed by instructors with formal qualifications meeting Ministry of Education standards. Critics have said the training offered has little relationship to the actual or potential demand in the areas in which it operates, in the absence of a reasonably adequate employment market study. An evaluation carried out in 1971, after about ten years of experience, suggested that only about half of the program's graduates had full-time or part-time employment, and even fewer were using the skills learned in the program. Moreover, most of the employed graduates had had some kind of employment before entering the MTTS.

A rather similar program in Northern Nigeria, that for Vocational Improvement Centers, was based on the government's conviction that the major impediment to the development of small-scale industries was shortage of skills and absence of training opportunities for artisans and craftsmen. With Ford Foundation assistance, the first Business Apprenticeship Training Center was opened in 1965. There are now twelve such centers, two in each of the six northern states, operating in various towns in the entire northern region. The centers have no physical facilities of their own, no full-time staff (except for a small central supervisory group), and employ their teachers on an hourly basis from local private industry, government shops, and the regular technical schools. Courses are part-time, and based on syllabi aimed at the passing of government trade tests. The success of the program in promoting small industrial enterprises in rural areas is limited, in part because the passing of the government trade test also facilitates entry into government service and larger urban-based private industries. Although the program was linked with a small industries credit scheme, few of the trainees run businesses of their own. Perhaps the major contribution of the program has been the provision of low-cost training opportunities for rural semi-skilled workers who can then move into modern-sector employment in government and larger industries. Demand for the courses has remained high.

Senegal's Rural Artisan Training Program, initiated with the help of ILO, is carefully programmed, highly formal, and of a full-time residential character. The five centers, located near small towns, and equipped with workshops, housing and boarding facilities, and staff buildings, aim at developing multipurpose artisans—in metal-working, woodworking, and home construction—well-suited to work in rural areas but not in cities. The program was plagued with problems of estimating the demand and uncertainties as to the appropriate training content. The active demand was evidently overestimated; it has proved difficult to fill the 150 places open each year. Apparently many artisans concluded that the opportunity cost of leaving their business for almost a year was too high. On the other hand, a survey of over 200 graduates at the end of 1970 showed that 153 were active at their trade in a rural area, while 24 had given up the trade and 35 had moved—mostly to urban areas.

Impressionistic conclusions from experiments such as these would be that their successful implementation requires better information about the market demand for specific skills, their structure must be flexible and low-cost, and above all, they must be complemented by a variety of other measures to increase the attractiveness of rural non-farm occupations and rural life in general. A dominant theme throughout such experiences has been that the pull of the modern urban sector is very strong indeed.

There have been efforts to combine such training programs with a wide variety of other activities to encourage small entrepreneurs in rural areas. Of all the developing countries, India has made the most extensive and diversified efforts to develop small industry in both rural and urban areas. India's activities have been more comprehensive and integrated than those, for example, in the programs referred to in Senegal and Nigeria. They combine training for both managers and employees with a wide range of complementary services for small enterprises—including in-plant consultation; assistance in the acquisition of credit, equipment, and materials; common workshops and equipment for joint use by small firms in a given area; and technical assistance on production and marketing problems.

The oldest and largest of the Indian programs comes under the Small-Scale Industry Development Organization (SSIDO) in the Ministry of Industrial Development, Company Affairs, and Internal Trade. Started in 1954, it provides training for employers and employees in a wide variety of small industries as well as a number of other services to small firms. State governments play a substantial role in carrying out the program. To promote and service small-scale industry, and to help integrate it with both the rural economy and large-scale industry, it operates training and extension services through a network of Small Industry Service Institutes and Extension Centers, backed by a central staff training and research center. In addition to its centrally important training functions, SSIDO (1) provides common testing facilities, (2) assists in product design, (3) surveys industrial opportunities and markets, (4) reviews feasibility of projects on behalf of financial institutions, (5) facilitates arrangements for subcontracting components and parts manufacture by small industries, (6) helps small firms obtain government contracts, (7) assists in procurement of scarce raw materials, and (8) seeks to promote small-scale industrial exports. While the program has had a substantial impact, recent evaluations suggest that both its training and its advisory services have declined in effectiveness. Inadequate size and quality of staff relative to the rapidly growing small industry sector in India have been major constraints; comparatively unattractive salaries and difficult working conditions have hampered recruitment of high-quality staff. Although it seems to have lost some of its early vigor and enthusiasm, the program continues to provide useful services to small industry generally. But it has developed, perhaps for reasons of administrative and bureaucratic convenience, a rather heavy urban bias.

In an effort to infuse fresh vigor into efforts at stimulating rural industry, the government in 1962 established a new Rural Industries Projects Program (RIP) to be carried out in more "backward" areas. It included, in addition to training, provisions for easy credit, common workshops, and extension services. Administration is by the state governments within general guidelines and financial resources from the national government. As of the end of 1972, the program was operating in 49 project areas in more than 34,000 villages, and reflected a rather wide variety of approaches from state to state. Much activity has been generated, but the continued implementation of the program has run into serious problems. National funding was to be phased out after an initial period (normally five years), and state governments have generally proved incapable of maintaining adequate financing. Wide dispersal of rural clientele has resulted in high unit costs, underutilization of training centers and common workshops, and strain on inadequate staffs. The low-cost credit feature has been perhaps the most popular and successful part of the program. Large numbers of small loans have been made; but screening and appraisal procedures have been such that the repayment record, on the whole, has been poor. Recently the business loan activities have been largely assumed by the State Bank of India, with a view to continuing provision of investment resources to rural small industries while improving the screening and collection procedures. With national financial support for the other activities scheduled to conclude by 1973-74, the 49 present pilot projects face a dubious future. During 1973, however, the government intends to establish and finance 50 new pilot projects. While the RIP projects have been confined to "backward" areas and communities of less than 15,000, the new projects will be located in larger rural hub-towns (perhaps up to 50,000 population) with more adequate infrastructure, in the hope that they can become growth points for surrounding areas and minimize the handicaps inherent in the earlier program. In general, the RIP experience has demonstrated that there are powerful constraints on the implementation of programs to expand small manufacturing activities in a relatively stagnant and sparsely populated traditional agrarian economy.

In addition to the central government's efforts to promote small industry, some of the Indian state governments have launched programs of their own. The Ahmedabad program, established by three public development corporations in the State of Gujarat in 1970, has introduced some innovations in efforts to train potential entrepreneurs and assist them to get started. Subsequently the State of Maharashtra established five similar centers of its own. The Ahmedabad program takes candidates with varying formal academic backgrounds who have serious entrepreneurial ambitions and specific ideas of what they would like to do. A twelve-week evening course deals with basic management skills, and is supplemented by visits to businesses and the preparation of the participant's own project for the launching of his enterprise. A special feature of the program is its stress on "achievement motivation" as developed by the Center for Research in Personality at Harvard University. By late 1971, 55 participants had completed the program, 21 had submitted their projects to financing institutions, and 13 had been granted loans. Of the 55, 31 had actually started their own factories, many without any special financial assistance. While it is too early to judge long-run prospects of success, the program has already inspired imitation in other Indian states and by the central government of India. One would suspect that its greatest impact is likely to be in urban areas.*

A Word About Government Policy-Making and Implementation

The frustration of observers (including perhaps the economists and planners themselves) that governments don't just *do* all the things the experts agree should be done flows at least in part from a somewhat simplistic view of the governmental policy-making and implementation process. It is often rather uncritically assumed that policy decisions are clearly purposive acts of unified national governments, and that governmental behavior in making choices and carrying them out can best be understood by analogy with the intelligent, well-considered, and coordinated acts of individual human beings. To understand past policies or to suggest future ones, the observer figuratively puts himself in the place of the government faced with a problem, and tries to decide how he would act under the circumstances (typically, not *all* the circumstances; the economist, for example, makes this transubstantiation *qua* economist, with a tendency to relegate other considerations to the margin where he may find it convenient to ignore them or to treat them as unfortunate non-economic constraints).

While this familiar personifying of "the government" has the advantage of reducing the actual political and organizational complexities to the comprehensible behavior of a single rational actor, and makes possible a kind of one-man national cost-benefit analysis, it obscures as well as simplifies. Most especially it obscures a frequently neglected fact of bureaucratic politics: that the "maker" of governmental policy is not one rational decision-maker, but an interacting array of large organizations and individuals who have very different views as to what the government should

---

* The data in this discussion are drawn from *Nonformal Education for Rural Development: Programs Related to Employment and Productivity,* report prepared for the World Bank by the International Council for Educational Development (October, 1972).

do on any given issue and who compete to affect both the policy decision and its implementation.*

Instead of the "unitary actor" analogy, some political scientists have suggested what they call the Bureaucratic Politics Model. This focuses on organizations and individuals within a government and the interactions among them. It sees policy as the outcome of bargaining among players positioned at different points in the governmental hierarchy. Outcomes are affected by relative bargaining power and skill, and are constrained by organizational processes and shared values. Decisions are in fact made by many actors who focus not on the single overriding national issue presumably in question but on many diverse sub-national ones as well. The various players pursue no consistent set of over-all objectives, but act in accordance with their individual views of the national interest, their organizational interest, and their own personal interests. The combination of these actions (each of which may be rational in relation to the perceptions and goals of the individual participant) may result in decisions which are clearly irrational from the perspective of the "unitary actor" analogy.

Much of what is written about the formulation and execution of economic development policy ignores or avoids untidy questions of this kind. The chasm between many academic economists and those who actually participate in governmental decision-making is typically wide from this point of view. Those who have the responsibility to act cannot ignore some bureaucratic facts of life: that various government leaders and organizations will often have sharply competitive interests as well as shared values and common interests; that broad over-all issues can seldom be disentangled from a wide variety of intersecting issues; that piece-meal, *ad hoc* "fire-fighting" types of decisions tend to preempt the time and resources necessary for wise long-term choices; and that, even so, it is often easier to come to a correct policy decision than it is to make sure that the government actually does what has been decided. All this does not make the government men any happier than it does the academic men. They are just playing in different kinds of games. Their frequent lack of patience with each other may flow from insufficient awareness of this.

In implementation as well as in policy choices, different players will see different faces of the same issue, depending on their position and their interests ("where they stand depends on where they sit"). The vigor with which they act will depend on their calculation of the importance of the stakes—national, organizational, or personal. Organizations typically seek to strengthen their autonomy, to compete for a larger share of the action, and to resist solutions that require extensive coordination with other organizations.

Those responsible for implementing policy decisions may indeed feel obliged to carry out the spirit as well as the letter of the decision. Even so, the actual results may differ substantially from what the policy-makers thought would happen. This is true partly because the actions are typically carried out by large organizations through existing routines, and partly because policy decisions do not normally specify the intended consequences in any detail. It is more likely, therefore, that those charged

---

* In this and much of the following discussion, I have made a rather free adaptation of some of the points contained in Graham T. Allison and Morton H. Halperin, *Bureaucratic Politics: A Paradigm and Some Policy Implications* (Brookings Institution Reprint No. 246, September, 1972). Although the paper deals with foreign policy and draws its primary data from U.S. experience, I find a number of its propositions provocative with respect to policy-making and implementation in general, and not inapplicable to less developed countries.

with implementation will feel that the policy decision has left them considerable leeway. Those who favored the initial decision will strive to see it faithfully implemented; those who opposed it will seek to delay implementation or to obey the letter but not the spirit, or even occasionally to ignore it. Those with experience in field-headquarters relationships in almost any field of activity are familiar with the tendency of the field to reinterpret or evade unwelcome directives from headquarters, in the hope and expectation that, having "settled" the issue, the home office will become inattentive or forgetful. If, as occasionally happens, reluctant field units are disappointed in these hopes, they can then gather evidence that vigorous implementation will result in intolerable consequences. Such watering-down of the policy decision is possible because those decisions are seldom formulated in such a way as to facilitate checking on their faithful implementation; and also because unwelcome policy decisions, once made, can be unmade or rendered relatively tolerable through interpretation.

Such a paradigm suggests that those who hope to influence policy and implementation outcomes in other governments need a bureaucratic-political map of the factors important in the outcome, including a list of individual and organizational participants and their interests. They also need to recognize that policy changes are only an early first step in a continuous process, that rapid changes in individual and organizational behavior are difficult to achieve, and that efforts should be made to minimize perceived threats to major organizational interests—particularly an organization's sense of autonomy and its ability to pursue what it regards as the essence of its functions. Such considerations suggest that if you are hoping to affect the policy and actions of governments, you would be wise (1) to seek out those individuals and organizations in that government who want to do what you want for their own reasons and, if found, to strengthen them; (2) to limit your expectations to what is reasonably achievable in the light of internal bureaucratic politics in a complicated context of personalities, organizations, and circumstances; and (3) to recognize a relatively low probability of early success.*

The applicability of any such paradigm to any particular flesh-and-blood government in less developed countries will vary widely from one to another, depending on its own political and bureaucratic structure, the political weight of its various organizational units, the degree of personalism in its decision-making processes, the style and effectiveness of its political leadership, the capacity and influence of its professional and technical staffs, and a number of other factors. But no consideration of the government's effectiveness in arriving at important policy changes or its capacity to implement them can afford to ignore such factors.

Conclusions

Much of the experience with implementation problems suggests that a major source of difficulty is the gap between the over-all planning process and the actual administrative machinery for execution of the policies which emerge from it—a gap at a middle level which might be called that of operational planning. This involves the translation of the aggregate goals and broad generalities of the Plan into concrete program policies which require more specific governmental decisions *now*—decisions that this is the operational policy choice to be followed for some

---

* From a perspective of ten years as a government bureaucrat, twenty years as a consultant to public and private agencies, and thirty years as an academic (figures which, fortunately, are not additive), I find these observations persuasive.

meaningful period of time and that administrative mechanisms will be adapted or created to give it a reasonable chance to work. An important part of those mechanisms would be some agency and procedure for the continuing evaluation of the effectiveness of the policy and its administration.

Most planning processes in developing countries are weak in this area, which lies squarely between policy and administration. Implementation is often left largely to existing ministries and departments once the broad Plan has received official sanction. But individual ministries and departments cannot, in fact, themselves make the operational policy decisions necessary to carry out the broad goals of the Plan because such decisions are typically *not* inherent in the Plan itself in any clear way, and because all of the important ones quickly overflow jurisdictional boundaries of the separate agencies. The planning agency itself typically has little direct authority at this level, although it may have considerable influence if the top political leadership uses it and values its suggestions. Hence, the general picture is often one of the planning office composing a Plan Document, the cabinet (or equivalent) sanctioning it as setting over-all goals, and the various ministries and departments being left to fight about whether particular operational policies within their respective jurisdictions best conform to those official goals. In the process, the Prime Minister's office brings such pressure, influence, attention, and direct intervention as it is organized and staffed to muster from time to time on particular issues (often by that time at the crisis state).

This suggests that there is often a missing component in the structure, or at least an inadequately developed component. It might be an inter-ministerial policy-planning committee, composed of the heads of the major economic ministries and departments, chaired by the Prime Minister or his deputy, and fully provided with professional and technical staff assistance from the Prime Minister's own office. Whether the staff would be drawn from the planning office or a separate implementation agency might be debated. In either case, there should be close cooperation and ready exchange of technical and professional personnel—a scarce resource at best.

What is essential is that the trade-offs which are typically obscured in the over-all Plan be made as clear as possible in the operational policy options presented for decision, and that both the discussion of these options and the decisions taken on them be undertaken by a *political* body on the basis of adequate professional and technical staff-work. It is only after this that the implementation problem becomes an *administrative* one in the ordinary sense of that term. Much of what is often condemned as administrative inadequacy (although that too certainly exists) is really a political incapacity or unwillingness to find effective ways of transforming Plan goals into operational policies. Once that has been done, of course, the more conventional administrative constraints begin to operate—budgetary problems, staff inadequacies, training needs, overlapping functions, bureaucratic red-tape, lack of coordination, etc. Attention to these problems is always important, but is not in itself of much help if the top policy mechanism does not succeed in providing clear guidelines and continuous conflict-resolution in a systematic way which makes the Plan goals more than official exhortations.

These considerations are perhaps of even more significance in any discussion of planning for fuller employment, because much less is known about the correct mix of policies to increase employment without an excessive slowing of over-all growth than has been learned about policies to maximize growth as such. Whether this is a necessary trade-off situation, and to what extent, has yet to be established both in general terms and with reference to any given country. It would be a political and administrative nightmare to sacrifice growth for employment and achieve neither.

Conflicting operational policies could bring this about even though it might not be implicit in the broad economic choices themselves.

Because there are such large gaps even in our theoretical knowledge about the employment effects of various possible public policy mixes, some effective applied economic research institutions need to be established (or invigorated) which can devote special and continuing attention to this problem. Such an institution would be engaged in various other problems of applied economic research as well, and its focus on employment problems would reflect the priority given that issue by the highest political authority. The institution should probably not be solely within the planning office, nor even solely within the government; it should, both organizationally and in terms of professional expertise, draw upon the universities, private research organizations if any, and the private business and financial sectors. It should be semi-autonomous, though closely related to government planning and policy-making processes and, no doubt, substantially subsidized by the government. It should provide the kind of information and knowledge that make it possible to frame options and indicate probable employment consequences of alternative policy choices. It should make available the best possible professional input as raw material for the government planning agency and the top inter-ministerial policy committees. Its organization and staffing would be a major political and administrative commitment of the government—to the extent the government was serious in its determination to make employment a major consideration in its economic growth objectives.

Because we already know that many fiscal and tax policies designed to maximize investment (both foreign and domestic), technological advance, import substitution, industrialization, and other growth goals, often tend in practice to have adverse employment effects, some governmental mechanism should be charged with a continuous review of all such policies from the employment point of view. Affirmation, modification, or reversal of such policies should be undertaken (ultimately at the highest political levels) on a systematic basis. The intermediate mechanism to facilitate this might be an interministerial committee on employment policy.

Because the government itself is a major supplier of employment, both in its ordinary governmental functions and as a public entrepreneur, it should take care to be a "model employer" in its practices regarding labor versus capital intensity. Again, broad pronouncements admonishing ministries to weigh the employment effects of their decisions, or requesting public corporations to act so as to maximize employment, do not typically have much effect. The government's own public works programs are often among the worst offenders in using capital at the expense of labor, while public corporations continue to "modernize" their processes, i.e., to stress the newest (often labor-saving) technology. There seem to be strong built-in forces against labor-intensive choices. Aside from a reluctance to accept the economic soundness of such a policy (note the argument that short-run capital intensity will accelerate growth and create more jobs over the longer-run period), there are the factors of (1) insufficient political commitment of the government itself as employer; (2) the intangible prestige connected with using the "best available" technology, especially as it may be encouraged and provided by external assistance programs; (3) the difficulties of bureaucratic and administrative accountability in getting such policies actually carried out, especially when there is a proliferation of public corporations and other agencies which are legally and administratively autonomous to a high degree.

For the public enterprise sector, this is but one aspect of the broader problem of establishing some kind of effective policy control over public corporations—a problem which has proven to be perplexing and difficult in most developing countries irrespective of employment policy issues. Control over investment decisions (the "business-like" freedom of which was one of the reasons for granting the autonomy in the first place) may be the most difficult to establish in practice. For the regular ministries, it will almost certainly require something more continuous and more effective than the routine budget process (even in countries where that is reasonably advanced), or high-level admonitions.

Because the government can always become an "employer of last resort," it should be ready with special programs for the direct hire of the unemployed (particularly unemployed youth) in large-scale conservation, reconstruction, land clearance, and similar activities. These may be attacked as relatively unproductive, and they do present serious problems of coordination and continuity, but they may be preferable to other readily available alternatives. They may also provide real training opportunities which could increase the proportion of employables among the unemployed. They will, however, provide only marginal solutions to the central problem.

As one surveys the mind-boggling array of problems concealed in the innocent and inelegant phrase "implementation of policies for fuller employment in less developed countries," one is sobered by the range of issues presented. Despite some help from general principles of development administration, the best strategies of execution as well as the best employment-maximizing policies must be devised in terms of the culture and institutions of the country involved, taking into account its own political and economic peculiarities, its own factor endowment, its own sense of its national and cultural goals and aspirations. The process will at best be halting, sporadic, and incremental. Something can be learned from other countries in similar situations; but little of decisive value will be had merely from general principles or the conventional wisdom of advanced countries. The crucial burden will in any case be borne by native administrators trained to see administrative principles in their broadest perspective but bound to adapt and apply them to the specific context of their own cultures. It is people—and for the most part *local* people—who must carry out such policies, and the recruitment, training, and effective utilization of the best of these people remains (as it always has been) the major key to the achievement of such demanding goals. The enlistment of greatly increased numbers of able young people trained in modern economics and modern administration and well-versed in their own country's political and economic life will thus remain a major imperative for some years to come.

Notes

In addition to personal experience in development planning and plan implementation in Malaysia, Ethiopia, Jordan, and Italy, and to consultation of standard works on development planning and development administration, I have drawn especially on the following:

1. Draft of Final Report on *Nonformal Education for Rural Development: Programs Related to Employment and Productivity* prepared for the World Bank by the International Council for Educational Development (October, 1972).

2. Fred Dziadek, *Unemployment in the Less Developed Countries,* USAID Discussion Paper No. 16 (June, 1967).

3. T. James Goering, "Some Thoughts on Future Strategies for Agricultural Development in Ethiopia," background paper for Ethiopian Government/World Bank Agricultural Sector Review, unpublished and labelled "for discussion only," (September, 1971).

4. Vincent M. Barnett, Jr., Paul G. Clark, and Scott Pearson, "Strategy Review of U.S. Development Assistance to Ethiopia," unpublished report to the United States Agency for International Development (August 28, 1972).

5. Graham T. Allison and Morton H. Halperin, *Bureaucratic Politics: A Paradigm and Some Policy Implications,* Brookings Institution Reprint No. 246 (September, 1972).

6. Henry J. Bruton, "Economic Development and Labor Use: A Review," this book.

III

Some Sectoral Considerations

Measurement of the Direct and Indirect Employment Effects of Agricultural Growth with Technical Change*

Raj Krishna**

Development Economics Department,
IBRD, Washington, D.C.

Introduction

It is now widely accepted that accelerated economic growth need not, by itself, solve the unemployment problems of densely populated countries. Even in agriculture, which must carry the whole labour force which cannot find non-agricultural employment, it is likely that government policies in respect of prices, farm-size structure, trade, taxation, technology and investment may not allow the full absorption of the farm labour force in spite of the availability of the new high-yield technology.[1] It is also accepted now that growth may not automatically improve the distribution of income and wealth. But apart from these weak, negative assertions the professional economists can currently offer very little empirically verified knowledge about what happens to distribution and employment when the growth of production accelerates, particularly in the agricultural sector.

Considerable time and resources would be required to fill the vast knowledge gap in this area. In this paper I shall only attack a couple of unsolved problems that arise when we try to measure the direct and indirect employment effects of the green revolution.

I shall first present a brief review of some recent attempts to project the employment effects of technical change in agriculture. The review will show that the methodology used in all these studies (with one exception) can only measure the *direct* employment effects of farm innovation. The essence of the method is the measurement of the change in the labour coefficient per hectare produced by technical change. But technical change comprises many simultaneous changes in water availability, cropping intensity, seed varieties, fertiliser use, and the degree of mechanisation of each individual operation. Therefore we face the problem of decomposing the total observed change in the labour input per hectare in crop production into the separate contribution of each of these changes. In order to solve this problem an algebraic expression which separates the employment effects of disaggregated technical changes will be developed and its use will be illustrated with Punjab wheat and

---

* This paper will also be published in the *Externalities in the Transformation of Agriculture* (Ames, Iowa, Iowa State University, forthcoming).

** The author is grateful to Narain Sinha, K.L. Sharma and Asha Hada for computational assistance.

rice data. This decomposition equation enables us to grade each individual technical change according to the magnitude of its positive or negative direct employment effect and to identify the combinations of changes which produce a positive or negative employment effect. In particular, the equation can be used to measure the true employment effect of tractorisation. This is specially important because at present, in the absence of a technique for separating different employment effects, many effects are attributed to tractorisation which are really due to other changes.

As regards indirect effects, the available literature only mentions the various chains of causation triggered by technical change.[2] But since no method has been developed for classifying and measuring the different indirect effects the net change in employment caused by technical change remains a matter of inconclusive verbal controversy.

In the third section of the paper, therefore, I use an adaptation of the basic input-output model for measuring the total indirect effects as well as each separate indirect effect. The different indirect effects are rigorously classified for the purpose of measurement.

The use of the model for projecting the net employment effects of assumed changes in coefficients is illustrated with a condensed two-sector version of the 77 x 77 coefficient matrix and national accounts of India for 1964-65.

Measurement of the Direct Employment
Effects of Innovation

Many attempts have been made recently to project the *direct* effects of the new technology on farm employment. The basic procedure in these studies is (1) to compute from field data the coefficients of labour input per hectare of each crop, grown with traditional and improved techniques, (2) to project the area in each crop, and the proportion of the area under each technique, and (3) to compute the aggregate labour input by multiplying the projected area under each crop-technique category by the relevant labour coefficient, and adding up the results.

Using this procedure, the Provisional Indicative World Plan for Agricultural Development, prepared by the FAO, predicts that in Asia and the Far East, greater intensity of land-use and higher yields will increase the number of labour days per farm family per annum by 15 percent from 227 in 1962 to 261 in 1965. Therefore, farm employment will increase, in spite of an increase in the agricultural population from 583 million to 880 million. Explaining the method used, the Indicative Plan says that:[3]

> Labour requirements per hectare were estimated crop by crop for each of six countries (Ceylon, India, Pakistan, Philippines, Thailand and West Malaysia). Distinctions were made between irrigated and non-irrigated land and in certain other cases where labour requirements were known to be different, e.g. between broadcast and transplanted rice. Labour requirements per hectare (1962 and 1985) were then multiplied by the number of hectares in each category in 1962 and the IWP proposals for 1985.

The analysis is restricted to employment in crop production and the development of land and water resources. The coefficients used are admittedly based on very meagre evidence. And the projections assume a substantial increase in multiple cropping, and the achievement of projected yields. It is also assumed that the technical innovations adopted will not displace labour.

In another study by Cownie, Johnston and Duff the farm labour force in West Pakistan (1985) is projected as the total labour force *minus* the nonfarm labour force which is assumed to grow 4.5 percent per annum. A coefficient of .08 man-year per acre is assumed for the tractor area. Bullock area employment is then computed simply as the difference between the total agricultural labour force and the tractor area employment.[4]

Billings and Singh have calculated for Punjab and Maharashtra, India, the demand for farm labour with alternative techniques and concluded that in the Punjab the demand will decline by 17 per cent and in Maharashtra it will increase by 4 per cent by 1983-84. The basic methodology, again, involves the calculation of labour requirements per acre for each crop under different technological assumptions, and the multiplication of the projected area in each crop/technique by the changing coefficients.[5]

S.V. Sethuraman has computed the direct farm employment coefficient of high-yielding varieties of wheat and rice in India as .208 man-years per acre *without mechanisation*. (1 man-year equals 240 man-days). He is perhaps the only writer who has also tried to put together some estimates of the indirect employment which may be generated in the additional production of inputs, consumption goods and investment goods demanded by farmers. This adds up to about .256 man-years per acre. Thus the total employment potential is estimated as .464 man-years per acre in high-yielding wheat and rice.[6]

All these studies have brought into focus the many complications involved in measuring the employment effects of technical change. In the first place, each individual operation required for crop production can be performed with many alternative techniques requiring labour and capital per unit of land in varying proportions. Thus (1) seed-bed preparation, (2) irrigation, (3) inter-culture, (4) harvesting and (5) threshing operations may be mechanised separately or in various possible combinations. And the change in the total labour input per hectare in a given crop will depend on the extent to which some or all of these operations are mechanised. For projecting employment, therefore, the assumed technological changes have to be disaggregated into specific changes in individual operations.

Second, the labour input is likely to be approximately proportionate to output in some operations such as threshing, and to area in other operations such as ploughing and irrigation. Let us call them output-oriented operations and area-oriented operations respectively. The change in the labour coefficient per hectare for area-oriented operations can be measured directly if the necessary technological data are available. But for measuring the change in the labour coefficient per hectare for output-oriented operations it is necessary to project not only the area but also the output per hectare. Thus yield projection becomes a necessary part of the methodology of employment projection. And the extent to which mechanisation changes the labour input for area-oriented operations and output-oriented operations has to be measured separately.

The third complication relates to the effects of irrigation and the increase in the intensity of cropping. Irrigation may increase yield without increasing the cropping intensity; or the cropping intensity may increase, due to the introduction of short-duration varieties and mechanised ploughing, with the same water availability or increases in water availability and cropping intensity may occur together. The quantitative effect on employment per hectare will be different in each case.

Finally, changes in the crop-mix alone will change the labour coefficient per hectare in crop production as a whole, because the coefficient is different for each crop. But in reality crop-mix changes accompany all the other technological changes mentioned above.

Thus even the change in the direct labour input per hectare in crop production is the resultant of a large number of simultaneous changes in the input-mix and the output-mix. In order to bring out how the net change in this coefficient will be determined let us derive the algebraic expression for it, assuming that varietal improvements, increased fertiliser. application, irrigation development, cropping intensity increases, mechanisation and crop-mix changes occur at the same time.

Direct Employment Effects: Single Crop

Consider first the derivation of the total labour input per (cropped) hectare in a single crop. The effects of changes in the cropping intensity and cropping pattern will be introduced later. Assuming that one hectare is planted with a given crop, let

w = the proportion of one hectare which is irrigated;

h = the proportion of irrigated area in the high-yielding variety;

y = basic yield per hectare on unirrigated area (old variety without chemical fertiliser);

$m_1 y$ = yield per hectare on irrigated area (old variety without chemical fertiliser);

$m_2 y$ = yield per hectare on irrigated area (high-yielding variety with chemical fertiliser);

t = proportion of area ploughed by tractor;

w_w = proportion of irrigated area, irrigated with wells;

w_c = proportion of irrigated area, irrigated with canals;

w_p = proportion of irrigated area, irrigated by pumps;

s = proportion of output mechanically threshed;

u_a = labour per hectare ploughed by bullocks;

u_a' = labour per hectare ploughed by tractors;

u_{ww} = labour per hectare irrigated with wells;

u_{wc} = labour per hectare irrigated with canals;

u_{wp} = labour per hectare irrigated with pumps;

u_w = labour per hectare irrigated with wells/canals/pumps, 1968-69;

u_w' = labour per hectare irrigated with wells/canals/pumps, 1973-74;

u_h = labour per kilogram threshed by bullocks;

u_h' = labour per kilogram mechanically threshed;

u_m = labour per hectare in inter-culture;

y^* = total yield per hectare; and

u_i = total labour per hectare in crop i.

With this notation, the rainfed area (in a single hectare) is $(1 - w)$, the irrigated area (old variety) is $w (1 - h)$ and the irrigated area (new variety) is wh. The yields in these 3 sub-sectors being y, m_1y and m_2y, the total yield y^* will be

(1) $\quad y^* = wh (m_2y) + w (1 - h) (m_1y) + (1 - w) y.$

And the total labour input is:

(2) $\quad u_i = tu_a' + (1 - t) u_a + wu_w + sy^*u_h' + (1 - s) y^*u_h + u_m$

where

(2') $\quad u_w = w_w u_{ww} + w_c u_{wc} + w_p u_{wp}.$

Substituting the value of y^* and u_w in equation (2), we can write the total labour input as a function of the 7 variable proportions w, w_w, w_c, w_p, h, t and s. The first 4 proportions represent the progress of irrigation, and h, t and s represent the progress of varietal improvement, tractor ploughing, and mechanical threshing respectively.[*] The basic yield y, the yield multipliers m_1 and m_2 and the 8 labour coefficients for specific operations will enter the expression for u_i as technological constants.

Now, we are interested in the change in $u_i = (\Delta u_i)$ between two periods produced by given discrete changes in the 7 proportions $(\Delta w, \Delta w_w, \Delta w_c, \Delta w_p, \Delta h, \Delta s$ and $\Delta t)$. Since the expression for Δu_i in algebraic symbols for all the variables and constants is tediously long, we shall write it out in a simpler form after substituting the numerical values of the 11 technological constants. The values of these constants pertain to wheat cultivation in the Punjab in 1968-69. They have been derived from a variety of sources shown in Table 1. The utmost care has been taken to see that the technological constants represent the labour-time required for each *separate* operation under assumed conditions.

Using these values we have:

(3) $\quad \Delta u_i = 271.38 \,(\Delta w) + 57.83 \,(\Delta h)$

$\qquad - 75.12 \,(\Delta t) + \left\{ 32.99 \Delta w_p + 49.42 \Delta w_c + 197.68 \Delta w_w \right\}$

$\qquad -176.46 \,(\Delta s)$

$\qquad + 115.66 \,(\Delta h) \,(\Delta w) + 98.84 \,(\Delta w) \,(\Delta w_c) + 395.37 \,(\Delta w) \,(\Delta w_w)$

$\qquad - 69.78 \,(\Delta h) \,(\Delta s)$

$\qquad - 65.98 \,(\Delta w_p) \,(\Delta w) - 140.19 \,(\Delta w) \,(\Delta s)$

$\qquad -138.55 \,(\Delta h) \,(\Delta s) \,(\Delta w).$

---

[*] It is assumed that chemical fertiliser use is confined to the irrigated area in the new variety; interculture labour input does not change; and harvesting is not mechanised.

TABLE 1

ASSUMED TECHNOLOGICAL CONSTANTS
FOR WHEAT, PUNJAB, 1968-69

Symbol (1)	Description (2)	Unit (3)	Value (4)	Source (5)
y	Basic yield per hectare on unirrigated area (old variety without chemical fertilizer)	Kg./Hec.	728.536[a]	DES, 1956[7]
m_1	Ratio of yield per hectare on irrigated area (old variety) to basic yield y	Ratio	1.662[b]	DES, 1956
m_2	Ratio of yield per hectare on irrigated area (new variety) to basic yield y	Ratio	2.974[c]	DES, 1970[8]
u_a	Labour per hectare ploughed by bullocks	Manhours/ Hec.	93.898[d]	Singh et. al., 1968[9]
u'_a	Labour per hectare ploughed by tractors	Manhours/ Hec.	18.780[e]	Billings and Singh (Maharashtra)[10]
u_{ww}	Labour per hectare irrigated with wells	Manhours/ Hec.	395.369	Singh et. al., 1968, and Billings and Singh (Maharashtra)
u_{wc}	Labour per hectare irrigated with canals	Manhours/ Hec.	98.842	Singh et. al., 1968, and Billings and Singh (Maharashtra)
u_{wp}	Labour per hectare irrigated with pumps	Manhours/ Hec.	65.977	Singh et. al., 1968, and Billings and Singh (Maharashtra)
u_w	Labour per hectare irrigated 1968-69	Manhours/ Hec.	156.190[f]	Singh et. al., 1968
u'_w	Labour per hectare irrigated 1973-74	Manhours/ Hec.	87.018[g]	Billings and Singh (Maharashtra)
u_h	Labour per kilogram threshed by bullocks	Manhours/ Kg.	0.194[h]	Singh et. al., 1968
u'_h	Labour per kilogram threshed mechanically	Manhours/ Kg.	0.048[i]	Billings and Singh (Maharashtra)
u_m	Labour per hectare in inter-culture	Manhours/ Hec.	239.687[j]	Singh et. al., 1968

NOTES: [a] 650 lbs. per acre of rainfed area in 1947-48/1951-52. There were no HY varieties and little chemical fertiliser was used in this period.

[b] 1080 lbs. per acre of irrigated area divided by 650 lbs. 1947-48/1951-52. Without HY varieties and chemical fertiliser.

[c] Wheat yield in the Punjab in 1968-69, 2167 kgs./hec. divided by basic yield y 728.536 kgs./hec. The yield in this subsector is the result of the use of the HY variety with chemical fertiliser.

d Ploughing, planking and sowing.

e 1/5 of *ua*.

f,g Bunding and irrigation. In 1968-69, the irrigated area in the Punjab irrigated by canals, wells and pumps was 54, 22 and 24 per cent respectively. The labour coefficients for these 3 modes of irrigating wheat are 40, 160 and 26.7 hours per acre respectively. (The pump coefficient is 1/6 of the well-irrigation coefficient.) Singh et. al., 1968 and Billings and Singh (Maharashtra). Therefore, using equation (2′ prime) the 1968-69 coefficient is computed as 156.190 hours per hec. For 1973-74 the coefficient is computed similarly, assuming that the canal area ratio remains the same, the pump area ratio rises to .45 and the well area ratio reduces to .01.

h Harvesting, threshing and winnowing. Singh's figure of hours per acre is converted into hours per kilogram, using his yield (1200 kg. per hec.).

i ¼ of *uh*.

j Hoeing and fertiliser application. It is assumed that technical changes do not affect this coefficient.

The first five terms of this expression can be clearly identified as:
1. the (positive) irrigation effect;
2. the (positive) variety effect;
3. the (negative) tractor-ploughing effect;
4. the irrigation technology effect; and
5. the (negative) threshing effect.

The last seven terms include the positive interaction effect of irrigation and varietal improvement, and six other interaction effects.

Assuming, for illustration, the values of w, w_w, w_c, h, w_p, t and s to be the same as those assumed by Billings and Arjan Singh for the Punjab for the interval 1968-69/1973-74 (Table 2), the *total change in the labour input turns out to be* $[-91.61]$ *hours per hectare—from 555.67 hours in 1968-69 to 464.06 hours in 1973-74.* This figure is decomposed into the 5 separate effects and the interactions in Table 3.

TABLE 2

ASSUMED CHANGES IN PROPORTIONS REFLECTING TECHNICAL
CHANGE IN PUNJAB WHEAT CULTIVATION BETWEEN
1968-69 AND 1973-74

Symbol (1)	Description (2)	Proportion in 1968-69 (3)	Proportion in 1973-74 (4)	Increase (5)
w	Proportion of one hectare which is irrigated.	.50	.56	.06
w_w	Proportion of irrigated area, irrigated with wells.	.22	.01	−.21
w_c	Proportion of irrigated area, irrigated with canals.	.54	.54	.00
h	Proportion of irrigated area in the high yielding variety.	.50	.80	.30
t	Proportion of area ploughed by tractor.	.03	.10	.07
p	Proportion of irrigated area, irrigated by pumps.	.24	.45	.21
s	Proportion of output mechanically threshed.	.50	.90	.40

SOURCE: Billings and Singh, "Farm Mechanization and the Green Revolution, 1968-84: The Punjab Case," mimeo (New Delhi, U.S.A.I.D., 1970)

TABLE 3

DECOMPOSITION OF THE CHANGE IN THE TOTAL
LABOUR INPUT PER HECTARE IN WHEAT,
PUNJAB, 1968-69 TO 1973-74

Effect	Manhours/hectare
1. Irrigation effect	+ 16.28
2. Variety effect	+ 17.35
3. Tractor-ploughing effect	− 5.26
4. Irrigation technology effect	− 34.59
5. Threshing effect	− 70.58
6. Interaction effect of irrigation and varietal improvement	+ 2.08
7. Negative interaction effects	− 16.89
Total	− 91.61

The Table shows that the positive irrigation and variety effects are roughly equal; the largest negative effect is due to the mechanisation of threshing; and the second largest negative effect is due to the shift from well-irrigation with bullocks to power pumping. The tractor-ploughing effect is relatively small.

These results are of course due to the particular values of the constants and variables relevant to this exercise. With different data on initial conditions, technological constants and rates of technical change in other areas/situations different results will be obtained.

Direct Employment Effects: Many Crops

So far we have discussed the change in the labour coefficient per hectare of a single crop. But if u_i and Δu_i have been computed for all the crops of a region according to equations (2) and (3), the variation in the employment coefficient per hectare in crop production as a whole can also be projected. Let

c = cropping intensity,

r_i = proportion of the gross cropped area in crop i,

u = labor per hectare (net) in total crop production.

Then the gross area in crop i is cr_i for every hectare of net area in all crops. Since u_i is the labor input per (gross) hectare in crop i, the total employment per (net) hectare will be:

$$(4) \quad u = c \sum_i u_i r_i$$

and the change in u will be:

$$(5) \quad \Delta u = c \sum_i (r_i \Delta u_i + u_i \Delta r_i + \Delta r_i \Delta u_i)$$
$$+ \Delta c \sum_i (r_i u_i + r_i \Delta u_i + u_i \Delta r_i + \Delta r_i \Delta u_i).$$

We can again regroup the terms in (5) into

the technology effect $= c \sum_i r_i \Delta u_i$

the crop-mix effect $= c \sum_i u_i \Delta r_i$

the intensity effect $= \Delta c \sum_i r_i u_i$

and interactions.

The decomposition of Δu according to equation (5) for all crops is not attempted here. However, for the 2-crop (wheat and rice) subsector of Punjab agriculture we can see how the technology effect, the crop-mix effect and the intensity effect can be separated.

Calculations for rice, similar to those for wheat shown in Table 1, 2 and 3 show the initial (1968-69) labour input in the Punjab to be 969.74 and the later (1973-74) input to be 946.31 hours/hec.* Thus the decrease in the labor input turns out to be 23.43 hours/hec.

Let subscripts 1 and 2 denote wheat and rice and assume that the cropping intensity increases from 1.345 to 1.390; and r_1 decreases from .84 to .81.[11]

Then the 2-crop version of equation $(4')$** gives the total labour input in both crops as 827.11 hrs./hec. in 1968-69 and 796.97 hrs./hec. in 1973-74. The decrease*** of 30.14 hrs./hec. has been decomposed in Table 4.

The table shows that with the given data for wheat and rice cultivation in the Punjab the negative technology effect is not offset by the positive crop-mix and intensity effects.

TABLE 4

SEPARATION OF TECHNOLOGY, CROP-MIX AND INTENSITY
EFFECTS ON LABOR PER HECTARE (NET) IN WHEAT &
RICE (COMBINED), PUNJAB, 1968-69 TO 1973-74

Effect	Manhours/hectare
Technology	−74.51
Crop-mix	+17.04
Intensity	+27.67
Interactions	− 0.34
Total	−30.14

---

* The coeffient is high because of the large number of irrigation operations required in the rice cultivation in the Punjab.

** $(4')$ $\quad u = c(u_1 r_1 + u_2 r_2)$

***$(5')$ $\Delta u = c(r_1 \Delta u_1 + r_2 \Delta u_2)$ (Technology)

$\qquad + c(u_1 \Delta r_1 + u_2 \Delta r_2)$ (Crop-mix)

$\qquad + \Delta c(u_1 r_1 + u_2 r_2)$ (Intensity)

$\qquad + c(\Delta u_1 \Delta r_1 + \Delta u_2 \Delta r_2)$

$\qquad + \Delta c(u_1 \Delta r_1 + u_2 \Delta r_2)$ (Interactions)

$\qquad + \Delta c(r_1 \Delta u_1 + r_2 \Delta u_2)$

$\qquad + \Delta c(\Delta r_1 \Delta u_1 + \Delta r_2 \Delta u_2)$

Tractorisation

At this stage we can conveniently consider the direct employment effect of tractorisation. In section 2 only the effect of tractor-ploughing was isolated. But it is well known that the tractor is used not only for seedbed preparation but also for "wheelwork": pumping, threshing and transport. It has also been emphasised in recent work that tractors are directly responsible for increasing the cropping intensity.[12] Therefore for measuring the total direct employment effect of tractorisation it is necessary to know the extent to which each operation is tractorised and the contribution of the tractor to the increase in the intensity of cropping. It is, of course, wrong to assume as some research workers have done [13] that the entire increase in cropping intensity is due to tractors, for irrigated nontractor farms frequently have a higher intensity of cropping than tractor farms; nor can we assume that the tractor is used to do all the pumping everywhere.* Only more detailed field investigations can reveal the extent to which the tractor is used for various purposes. If the required proportions are known the total effect of tractorisation can be computed.

Let us suppose, for example, that ploughing and threshing are entirely tractorised; and half of the pumping is done with the tractor. Then the total tractor effect on employment in wheat cultivation vide Table 3 will be

$$[-5.26 - 70.20 - (.5)(7.26)] = -79.09 \text{ hours per hectare.}$$

The total tractor effect on employment in rice cultivation can be computed from a similar decomposition table for rice** as

$$[-4.10 - (.5)(45.28)] = -26.74 \text{ hours per hectare.}$$

The change in the labor coefficient for each crop can now be broken down into the tractor effect and the non-tractor effect.

$$\Delta u_1 = \Delta u_1^t + \Delta u_1^n = -79.09 + 17.60 = -61.49 \text{ hours.}$$

$$\Delta u_2 = \Delta u_2^t + \Delta u_2^n = -26.74 + 3.32 = -23.42 \text{ hours.}$$

Rewriting (4') we have:

$$(4') \qquad u = r_1(u_1^t + u_1^n) + r_2(u_2^t + u_2^n)$$

and rewriting (5') we have:

$$(5') \quad \Delta u = c\,[r_1(\Delta u_1^t + \Delta u_1^n) + r_2(\Delta u_2^t + \Delta u_2^n)]$$

$$+ c\,[u_1\Delta r_1 + u_2\Delta r_2]$$

---

* In his careful study of tractor farms in a district of Maharashtra, India, Sapre has observed that only 21 out of 76 farmers having tractors used the tractor for irrigation because the cost of irrigation with oil engines using crude oil was 60 to 70 per cent less than the cost with tractors using diesel. He has also noted that only 54 per cent of the increase in the double cropped area can be attributed to tractors.[14]

** Not given here to save space.

$$+ \Delta c \left[r_1 u_1 + r_2 u_2 \right]$$

+ interactions.

If we attribute half of the Δc to the tractor the total tractor effect in the 2-crop economy is:

$$(6) \quad c \left[r_1 \Delta u_1^t + r_2 \Delta u_2^t \right] + \tfrac{1}{2} \Delta c \left[r_1 u_1 + r_2 u_2 \right].$$

The total change (-30.14 hours) which was decomposed in Table 4 can now be redistributed (Table 5) so as to isolate the tractor effect.

TABLE 5

SEPARATION OF THE TRACTOR EFFECT ON LABOR PER
HECTARE (NET) IN WHEAT & RICE (COMBINED),
PUNJAB, 1968-69 TO 1973-74

Effect	Manhours/hectare
Tractor technology (vide eq. 6)	−95.11
Other technology	+20.60
Crop-mix	+17.04
Intensity (non-tractor)	+27.67
Interactions	− 0.34
Total	−30.14

The importance of the decomposition equations developed in this and the foregoing sections lies in the fact that they enable us to measure correctly the separate (marginal) employment effect of each technical change as well as the total effect of any combination of particular changes, such as those associated with tractorisation, in a single-crop or a multi-crop economy.

The unit of measurement in all our equations and illustrative computations has been manhours per hectare of gross area for each crop and per hectare of net area in multi-crop equations. By multiplying the projected total net crop area in any region by the labor coefficients estimated by these equations, total farm employment in the region can be projected and decomposed. Thus our equations can also serve as projection models.

These projections are obviously critical if policy-makers, concerned about the employment effects of technical changes, are to regulate the relative rates of diffusion of different innovations by appropriate pricing or other policies.

In choice models what we really need are social benefit-cost ratios of different "baskets" of innovations. But so far benefit-cost calculations have been distorted* by the failure to disaggregate technical change and its effects on labor-use and labor-cost in different situations.

It is hoped that our methodology will remedy this deficiency and lay the basis for more reliable calculations of the costs and benefits of farm innovations.

* The World Bank studies on the basis of which substantial loans have been given to India to finance tractor loans to farmers are an example.

Measurement of Indirect Effects

Indirect effects are our next concern in this paper. Ridker presents a fairly complete list of the various indirect effects in his survey of recent work on the mechanisation of agriculture.[15] Logically the non-farm effects can be grouped into additional demands: (a) for nonfarm current inputs (fertiliser, pesticides, transport, marketing, and repairing services etc.); (b) for nonfarm consumption goods; and (c) for nonfarm investment goods (construction, equipment etc.). There are also induced (d) input, (e) consumption, and (f) investment demands on the farm sector itself. All these effects on demand (output) and the corresponding employment effects are recognised in the literature but since no method has been developed for measuring them, it is impossible to say whether the initial employment effects (assuming them to be negative) are offset by the indirect positive effects or not. And the direction of the net change in employment due to technical change remains uncertain. Fortunately the input-output technique can be adapted to measure all the indirect effects.

The Model for Measuring Indirect Effects

There are at least three reasons for resorting to input-output economics for the measurement of the indirect employment effects of agricultural growth accompanied by technical changes.

First, indirect effects are, by definition, macro effects external to, or occurring outside, the sector in which primary technical change takes place. Therefore we can measure them only with a macro model.

Second, change in a major sector like agriculture, which accounts for half or more of national product and employment in many developing economies must affect all the important aggregate magnitudes in the economy, namely, income, consumption, investment and employment. Initial changes in these macro magnitudes will in turn change aggregate magnitudes in the agricultural sector. Therefore there can be no separate sub-model of the determination of agricultural employment alone. Any model which determines farm employment must also determine all important macro variables at the same time. And even if the focus is on the projection of farm employment, the use of a macro model is indispensable.

Third, macro data *are* available in the form of national accounts and inter-sectoral transactions. In theoretical models production and demand relations may be specified in presumably more realistic linear or non-linear forms but multisectoral production, exchange and demand data are available in a form which only permits fixed coefficient specifications. However, this limitation can be overcome in two well-known ways. Sensitivity analysis can be used to study the effects of changing production and demand coefficients over specified ranges. And more satisfactory sub-models can be used to project parts of the data which are fed into the basic input-output model exogenously.

These improvements will require more work in the future. In this paper I only demonstrate the applicability of an input-output model for measuring and separating the direct and indirect employment effects of growth and technical change in the farm sector.

In the open Leontief model, if the final demand vector D and the input-output co-efficient matrix A are given, the equilibrium output vector X is computed as:

(7) $X = A^*D$ where $A^* = (I - A)^{-1}$.

If the employment-output coefficient vector U is also given, employment required in each sector to produce D is given by the vector:

(8) $L^d = \hat{U}D$

where $\hat{U}$ is the diagonal matrix of the elements of U.
The total, direct plus indirect, employment in each sector is:

(9) $L = \hat{U}X = \hat{U}A^*D$

and the aggregate employment is:

(10) $N = U'X = U'A^*D.$

The sector-wise *indirect* employment is:

(11) $L - L^d = \hat{U}(X - D)$

and the total indirect employment is:

(12) $N - N^d = U'(X - D).$

Abstracting from its composition, gross value added in each sector, defined as the difference between its gross output and its purchases from other sectors is:

(13) $V = (I - A'\hat{i})X.$

Since final demand is

(14) $D = (I - A)X,$

aggregate value added and the aggregate final demand are equal:

(15) $i'D = i'V.$

Now, when we wish to isolate the output and employment effects of growth with innovation in one sector we should specify the elements of our data which are supposed to change exogenously.

A growth rate for the output of the innovating sector j must be specified. If growth is accompanied by innovation, the material input-vector A_j and the labor input element j in vector U must change. The change in A_j will also change the ratio of gross value added to gross output v_j.

The gross value added may be divided into wages and gross profit.* A profitable innovation will at least increase the share of gross profit in gross output. If the share of wages also increases the ratio of gross value added to gross output will increase. If, however, the innovation displaces labour, the share of wages will fall; if the increase in the share of profit is more than the decrease in the share of wages, the share of gross

---

*   All quantities are valued at constant base-year prices.

value added to gross output will increase; and if the increase in the share of profit is less than the decrease in the share of wages the share of value added in output will decrease. Thus workers as well as owners, or owners alone, will have greater gross income available for expenditure.

Some assumptions are necessary about the distribution of this additional expenditure between the output of different sectors. We can then predict the new (comparative-static) equilibrium values of the variables of the system, i.e., output, income, final demand and employment, in the innovating sector, other sectors, and the economy as a whole. These new values will reflect the sectoral as well as the economy-wide "multiplier" effects of an exogenously given rate of growth in sector j, accompanied by technical change.

The logic of the procedure may be clearly brought out with a two-sector example. Let the first sector be agriculture and the second "nonagriculture."

Then, in any period,

(16) $X_1 = a_{11} X_1 + a_{12} X_2 + D_1$,

(17) $X_2 = a_{21} X_1 + a_{22} X_2 + D_2$,

(18) $V_1 = (1 - a_{11} - a_{21}) X_1$,

(19) $V_2 = (1 - a_{12} - a_{22}) X_2$, and

(20) $N = u_1 X_1 + u_2 X_2$.

It is, of course, implied by these relations that

(21) $V_1 + V_2 = D_1 + D_2$.

Given D_1, D_2 and the coefficients, a_{ij} and u_j, the five relations (16) to (20) determine X_1, X_2, V_1, V_2, and N.

But, alternatively, we can specify X_1 and D_1 exogenously* and determine X_2, D_2, V_1, V_2 and N. For analysing the effects of growth in X_1, with technical change, this specification is more appropriate.

Let us assume a growth rate g in agricultural output X_1. Innovations in the farm sector change a_{11}, a_{21} and u_1. The coefficients of the nonfarm sector a_{12}, a_{22} and u_2 remain unchanged. Then in the second period**:

(22) $X_1^1 = (1 + g) X_1^0$.

(23) $V_1^1 = (1 - a_{11}^1 - a_{21}^1) X_1^1 = (1 - a_{11}^1 - a_{21}^1)(1 + g) X_1^0$.

(24) $\Delta V_1 = [(1 + g)(1 - a_{11}^1 - a_{21}^1) - (1 - a_{11}^0 - a_{21}^0)] X_1^0$.

For the demand effects of increased income in sector 1 and of the secondary increase in the income of sector 2 we can specify:

---

*   Only a part of D is exogenous. See below.

** The initial values have superscript 0 and the second period values have superscript 1.

(25) $D_1 = m_{11} V_1 + m_{12} V_2$

where m_{11} and m_{12} are marginal propensities to spend income originating in sectors 1 and 2 on the output of sector 1. Then:

(26) $D_1^1 = D_1^0 + m_{11}\Delta V_1 + m_{12} (1 - a_{12} - a_{22}) (X_2^1 - X_2^0)$.

Implicitly, since there are only 2 sectors,

(27) $D_2^1 = D_2^0 + (1 - m_{11}) \Delta V_1 + (1 - m_{12}) (1 - a_{12} - a_{22}) (X_2^1 - X_2^0)$.

The new equilibrium value X_2^1 is given by the second-period version of equation (16):

(16) $(1 - a_{11}^1) (1 + g) X_1^0 = a_{12}^1 X_2^1 + D_1^0 + m_{11} \Delta V_1 + m_{12} (1 - a_{12} - a_{22})(X_2^1 - X_2^0)$.

Here ΔV_1 is known from (24); and all quantities other than X_2^1 are constants. Given X_1^1, V_1^1, D_1^1 and X_2^1 from equations (22), (23), (26) and (16) respectively, equations (17), (19) and (20) for the second period will determine D_2, V_2 and N.

It should be noted that in equations (25) and (26) only a part of the increase in final demand is exogenous: the part directly due to the increase in output and income in that sector $(m_{11}\Delta V_1)$. The other part, due to the induced increase in output (income) in sector 2, remains endogenous because the model itself determines X_2^1 and its income and demand effects.

In the empirical exercise presented below three variations of the above model have been tried: (1) technical change takes place in the farm sector (a_{11}, a_{21}, v_1 and u_1 change)* *without* growth; (2) growth occurs *without* technical change; and (3) growth occurs *with* technical change.

The three variations give us, respectively, the pure "substitution effect" of technical change, the pure "scale effect" of growth, and the net total effect (substitution effect *plus* scale effect) of growth with technical change on employment.

Since, in our assumptions about technical change, it displaces labour initially, the substitution effect on employment is negative. The pure scale effect is, of course, positive. And the net total effect turns out to be positive but smaller than the pure scale effect.

Empirical Illustration

The basic data used in the exercise are given in Table 6. They include the X, V, D and L vectors for India in the base year 1964-65, and the coefficients A, U, v and m. The 77 x 77 input-output table of the Indian Statistical Institute for that year has been condensed into a 2-sector table by grouping sectors into a composite farm sector and a composite nonfarm sector to get X, V, D, and v. The derivation of L and U is explained in Appendix A and that of m in Appendix B.

The rate of growth of agricultural output assumed in two of the three variations of the exercise is 5 percent.

---

* v is the ratio of gross value added to gross output.

$v_1 = (1 - a_{11} - a_{21})$.
$v_2 = (1 - a_{12} - a_{22})$.

TABLE 6

BASIC DATA, INDIA, 1964-65

Variable (1)	Unit (2)	Value (3)	Coefficient (4)	Value (5)
X_1	Rs. Crores* 1960-61 Prices	8990.7	a_{11}	0.124395
X_2	"	19229.7	a_{12}	0.108358
V_1	"	7377.0	a_{21}	0.055090
V_2	"	10832.1	a_{22}	0.328341
D_1	"	5788.6	v_{22}	0.820515
D_2	"	12420.5	v_2	0.563301
L_1	Crores of Manyears	6.0238	u_1	0.000670
L_2	"	2.1153	u_2	0.000110
			m_{11}	0.4587
			m_{12}	0.3322

SOURCE: Computed from tables in N.R. Saluja, "Structure of Indian Economy: Inter-Industry Flaws and Pattern of Final Demands 1964-65," *Sankhya* (June, 1968).

*1 Crore = 10 million

Technical change is reflected in changes in the coefficient vectors (elements) relating to sector 1 in A, U and v. The method used to compute these changes requires some explanation. Field studies of the effects of the new technology in some areas of India furnish data on each item of the cost of cultivation per acre of a few crops in these areas. The data distinguish between samples of farmers using new technology and farmers sticking to the traditional technology. Since the region and the crop-year are the same for each body of data, and therefore prices may be assumed to be the same, the cost structure of the traditional and progressive farmers may be assumed to differ primarily due to technical change.

The items of cost for each class of farmers are grouped as follows:

1. material input from agriculture, including expenditure on seed and animal labor;
2. material input from nonagriculture, including chemical fertiliser, pesticides, cost of irrigation and use of equipment;*
3. the cost of human labor including family and hired labor; and
4. return to capital including the rent of land, interest, and net profit.

Profit is calculated as gross output *minus* the total of all other costs per acre. The sum of (3) and (4) is value added. The percentage changes in the material input from agriculture, the material input from non-agriculture, labor cost, return to capital,

---

* Depreciation of equipment is included here because the wear and tear of farm equipment is real nonfarm input. Farmers make no specific provision for depreciation which can properly be included in gross value added.

value added and gross output per acre, caused by technical change, have been computed from the sub-totals of these items for traditional and progressive farmers. By dividing the percentage change in each input by the percentage change in output we get the elasticity of each input with respect to output. When output increases by .05, input i is supposed to increase by $(0.05)e_i$, where e_i is the elasticity of input i with respect to output. Thus we get the new input levels due to 5 percent growth in the output of the base period, accompanied by technical change, and compute the new coefficients in A, U and v.

The cost data were available in the required detail, separately for traditional and innovating farmers, only for wheat, rice and maize in two areas of India (Appendix C). The elasticities computed from each available body of data have been averaged, and the average elasticities have been used to compute the changes in A, U and v. Ideally, of course, we ought to have data on changes in the cost structure of every product caused by technical change, representative of the whole country, and on the proportion of the output of every product affected by technical change. But in the absence of these data we use the average of the elasticities computed from whatever cost data we have. Implicitly this procedure assumes that input changes of the order indicated by these average elasticities take place over the whole gross cropped area as output grows.

The results of the computations for each variation of the exercise are shown in Table 7. The growth rate of each of the quantities $X_1, X_2, (X_1+X_2), V_1, V_2, (V_1+V_2), D_1, D_2, (D_1+D_2), L_1, L_2$ and (L_1+L_2) are also shown.

TABLE 7

PROJECTED EFFECTS OF TECHNOLOGICAL CHANGE
AND/OR 5 PERCENT AGRICULTURAL GROWTH, INDIA

VARIABLE	UNIT	INITIAL VALUE (1964-65)	INNOVATION *WITHOUT GROWTH*		5 PERCENT FARM OUTPUT GROWTH		5 PERCENT FARM OUTPUT GROWTH	
			Projected value	Growth rate	Without Innovation Projected value	Growth rate	With Innovation Projected value	Growth rate
(1)	(2)	(3)	(4)	(5)	(6)	(7)	(8)	(9)
X_1	Rs. Crores 1960-61 Prices	8990.7	8990.7	.0000	9440.23	.0500	9440.23	.0500
X_2	"	19229.7	19427.4	.0103	19989.17	.0395	20213.00	.0511
X_1+X_2	"	28220.4	28418.1	.0070	29429.40	.0428	29653.24	.0508
V_1	"	7377.0	7249.49	−.0037	7745.85	.0500	7716.96	.0461
V_2	"	10832.1	10943.47	.0103	11259.92	.0395	11386.00	.0511
V_1+V_2	"	18209.1	18292.96	.0046	19005.77	.0428	19102.97	.0491
D_1	"	5788.6	5817.56	.0050	6099.93	.0538	6128.56	.0587
D_2	"	12420.5	12475.40	.0044	12905.84	.0391	12974.40	.0446
D_1+D_2	"	18209.1	18292.96	.0046	19005.77	.0437	19102.97	.0491
L_1	Crores Manyears	6.4373	6.1766	−.0405	6.7592	.0500	6.4854	.0075
L_2	"	2.6537	2.6809	.0103	2.7585	.0395	2.7893	.0511
L_1+L_2	"	9.0911	8.8575	−.0257	9.5177	.0469	9.2748	.0202

It will be seen from Table 7 that in the case of technical change without growth agricultural employment falls by 4 percent, in proportion to the decline in the employment coefficient. But total employment declines only 2.6 percent because of the induced growth of 1 percent in the nonagricultural sector.

In the second case of agricultural growth without innovation, the main result is that 5 percent growth in agricultural output is consistent with 3.95 percent growth in nonagricultural output. Changes in sectoral employment are of the same order, and therefore aggregate employment increases by 4.7 percent.

When agricultural growth occurs with technical change, 5 percent growth in agricultural output induces a slightly higher—5.11 percent—growth in the nonagricultural sector. Employment in the nonagricultural sector also grows 5.11 percent, but labour displacement causes farm employment to grow less than 1 percent, and therefore growth in aggregate employment is only 2 percent.

This result implies that if the labor force is growing at a rate exceeding 2 percent, unemployment will increase in spite of the fact that farm output grows 5 percent and induced nonagricultural growth is even higher. Thus when labour-displacing technical changes are taking place in agriculture, growth in employment, due to direct as well as induced output growth, may not always be sufficient to absorb the whole increase in the labour force. This conclusion is in sharp contrast with the usual theoretical expectation that the immediate negative employment effect of labour-displacing technical change in a sector will be more than offset by the positive indirect employment effects of output growth in this and other sectors.

Whether the theoretical expectation materialises or not depends on the particular constellation of the relevant parameters: the growth rate, the changes in input coefficients, and the marginal propensities to spend out of sectoral incomes.

The particular result in our exercise is subject to the limitations of available data on these coefficients and propensities. But it shows that the indirect employment effects *can* be computed; and even when they are taken into account, total employment growth *can* fall short of labour force growth.

Decomposition of Employment Growth

We can also decompose the total (direct and indirect) employment growth into the separate contributions of the different causes mentioned above.

Denoting intermediate demand $R = X - D$, employment in the second period is:

$$(28) \quad L_1^1 + L_2^1$$

$$= u_1^1 X_1^1 + u_2 X_2^1$$

$$= u_1^1 D_1^1 + u_1^1 R_1^1 + u_2 D_2^1 + u_2 R_2^1$$

and in the base period,

$$(29) \quad L_1^0 + L_2^0 = u_1^0 D_1^0 + u_1^0 R_1^0 + u_2 D_2^0 + u_2 R_2^0$$

Therefore

(30) $\Delta(L_1 + L_2)$

$$= (L_2^1 + L_2^1) - (L_1^0 + L_2^0)$$

$$= u_1^0 (\Delta D_1) + (\Delta u_1) D_1^0 + (\Delta u_1)(\Delta D_1) + u_1^0 (\Delta R_1)$$

$$+ (\Delta u_1) R_1^0 + (\Delta u_1)(\Delta R_1) + u_2 (\Delta D_2) + u_2 (\Delta R_2)$$

$$= (\Delta u_1) X_1^1 + u_1^0 (\Delta D_1) + u_1^0 (\Delta R_1) + u_2 (\Delta D_2) + u_2 (\Delta R_2)$$

The terms in the last equation can be identified and named as five economically important effects:

1. the pure labour displacement effect $\quad = (\Delta u_1)(X_1^1)$,
2. the farm final demand effect $\quad\quad\quad = u_1^0 (\Delta D_1)$,
3. the farm input demand effect $\quad\quad\quad = u_1^0 (\Delta R_1)$,
4. the nonfarm final demand effect $\quad\quad = u_2 (\Delta D_2)$, and
5. the nonfarm input demand effect $\quad\quad = u_2 (\Delta R_2)$.

It should be noted that these five effects cover all the major negative and positive effects which growth and technical change in the farm sector may generate. The grouping of terms in equation (30) enables us to measure them separately.

Using the results of the last case in Table 7 (5 percent farm output growth with innovation) the total employment increase, 1,837,970 manyears, can be decomposed as in Table 8.

TABLE 8

DECOMPOSITION OF TOTAL EMPLOYMENT
GROWTH DUE TO 5 PERCENT FARM OUTPUT
GROWTH WITH TECHNICAL CHANGE, INDIA
(BASE 1964-65)

Effect (1)	Manyears (2)	Percent (3)
(1) Pure labour displacement effect	−2,737,670	−148.9
(2) Farm input demand effect	784,490	42.7
(3) Farm final demand effect	2,434,180	132.4
(4) Nonfarm final demand effect	764,390	41.6
(5) Nonfarm input demand effect	592,580	32.2
Total	1,837,970	100.00

The negative labour displacement effect is counter-balanced by positive effects of which the strongest is the agricultural final demand effect; the next strongest is the agricultural input demand effect; and next in order are the nonfarm final demand and input demand effects.

This ordering of effects is, of course, partly due to the assumed marginal propensities to spend. The propensities to spend on agricultural output are much higher than the propensities to spend on nonfarm output; therefore, the farm final demand effect is very large. The relative magnitude of input and final demand coefficient also causes the two final demand effects to be relatively larger than the two input demand effects.

Summary and Conclusions

In summary, we have shown that recent studies of the employment effects of innovation and growth in agriculture have only tried to measure the direct effects; but the input-output technique can be used to measure the indirect as well as the direct employment effects and to separate the negative labour displacement effect and each of the positive effects viz. additional final input demands in the growing sector and the additional final and input demands induced in other sectors.

Thus verbal arguments about the positive and negative employment effects of agricultural growth accompanied by labour-displacing technical change can be clinched. And the aggregate as well as the separate employment effects of any growth-technology-demand mix can be computed. With one set of assumptions, based on Indian data, it turns out to be quite possible that even after all the positive effects counter-balancing the initial negative effects of technical change on employment are taken into account, aggregate employment growth may fall short of the growth of the labour force, and unemployment may continue to increase. The normal expectation of growth with innovation producing full employment turns out to be contingent on a number of conditions which a developing economy may not fulfill.

The policy conclusions of these results are obvious. If policy-makers do not want unemployment to increase they should establish, with appropriate measures, a growth-innovation-demand mix, which can be shown, with actual computations, to be capable of increasing employment at a higher rate than the rate of growth of the labour force.

The methodology for projecting the various employment effects of *any* given mix has been developed and illustrated with the currently available data. The task now is to use it for actual projections with more broad-based and reliable data.

Notes

1. See, for example, W.A. Lewis, "The Causes of Unemployment in Less Developed Countries and Some Research Topics," *International Labour Review* (May, 1970); Robert d'A. Shaw, *Jobs and Agricultural Development*, Monograph Number Three (Washington, D.C., Overseas Development Council, 1970); B.F. Johnston and J. Cownie, "The Seed Fertilizer Revolution and Labor Force Absorption," *American Economic Review* (September, 1969); W.F. Falcon, "Agricultural Employment in Less Developed Countries: General Situation, Research Approaches, and Policy Palliatives," mimeo (Washington, D.C., IBRD, 1971); S. Reutlinger, et al, "Agricultural Development in Relation to the Development Problem," mimeo (Washington, D.C., IBRD, 1971); and Erik Thorbecke, "Unemployment and Underemployment in the Developing World," mimeo (February, 1970).

2. See R.G. Ridker, "Agricultural Mechanization in South Asia," *Development Digest* (January, 1971).

3. U.N. Food and Agricultural Organization, *Provisional Indicative World Plan for Agricultural Development*, Vols. 1 and 2 (Rome, 1970), p. 658.

4. B.F. Johnston, J. Cownie and B. Duff, *The Quantitative Impact of the Seed-Fertilizer Revolution in West Pakistan: An Exploratory Study* (Stanford, Food Research Institute, 1970).

5. M.H. Billings and A. Singh, "The Effect of Technology on Farm Employment in India," *Development Digest* (January, 1971).

6. S.V. Sethuraman, "A Note on the Implications of Agricultural Development and Investment in the Indian Economy," mimeo (New Delhi, U.S.A.I.D., 1971).

7. Government of India, Directorate of Economics & Statistics, *Quinquennial Average Yield Per Acre of Principal Crops in India: 1947-48 to 1951-52* (New Delhi, 1956).

8. Government of India, Directorate of Economics and Statistics, *Estimates of Area and Production of Principal Crops in India, 1969-70 (Summary Tables)* (New Delhi, November, 1970).

9. I. Singh, R.H. Day and S.S. Johl, *Field Crop Technology in the Punjab, India* (Madison, Social Systems Research Institute, University of Wisconsin, 1968).

10. M.H. Billings and A. Singh, "Agriculture and Technological Change in Maharashtra (1968-1984)," mimeo (New Delhi, U.S.A.I.D., no date).

11. M.H. Billings and A. Singh, *Farm Mechanisation and the Green Revolution, 1968-84: The Punjab Case,* mimeo (New Delhi, U.S.A.I.D., 1970).

12. R.G. Ridker, *op. cit.* and Sapre, *A Study of Tractor Cultivation in Shahada,* Mimeograph Series No. 7 (Poona, Gokhale Institute, 1969).

13. C.H.H. Rao, *The Impact of Tractorization on Farm Employment,* mimeo (January, 1972).

14. Sapre, *op. cit.*

15. Ridker, *op. cit.*

Appendix A

The Computation of Employment in the Base Year and Labour-output Coefficients

Labour-output coefficients are calculated for each sector of the Indian Statistical Institute input-output table for 1964-65 (at 1960-61 prices) from data derived from the following sources.

For 15 industrial sectors the total employment is divided by the value of gross output given in Government of India, Central Statistical Organisation, *Annual Survey of Industries, 1965,* Vol. I (New Delhi, 1969). The definitions of these sectors correspond very closely to the definitions of *ASI* sectors.

For the nonagricultural sectors not included in the *Annual Survey of Industries* and agricultural sectors other than crop production the figures on employment and gross output have been taken from a variety of other sources.

For the crop production sectors, "foodgrains" and "other agriculture" labour days per acre were calculated separately for the individual crops, wheat, rice, pulses, jowar, ragi, gram, maize and bajra, from data given in *Studies in the Economics of Farm Management* of various crop-years. Labour per acre is multiplied by the gross cropped area in each crop in 1964-65 given in Government of India, Directorate of Economics and Statistics, *Area, Production and Yield of Principal Crops in India, 1950-51 to 1968-69* (New Delhi, 1970) to estimate total employment in each crop.

The value of gross output of each crop is available in Government of India, Directorate of Economics and Statistics, *Brochure of Revised Estimates of the National Product, 1960-61 to 1965-66* (New Delhi, 1970). The labour-output coefficient is therefore computed by dividing the total estimated employment in mandays by the gross output of 1964-65 in 1961 prices. The mandays are divided by 250 to estimate manyears of full employment. A manyear has been treated as equal to 250 mandays because in the industrial sector covered by the *Annual Survey of Industries* the average number of days of work per person turns out to be 250 days.

The aggregate labour-output ratio for all the crops for which separate labour-land ratios are available is applied to other crops for which such ratios are not available.

Appendix B

Computation of Propensities to Spend

The model requires marginal propensities to spend on the output of each of the two sectors out of gross income generated in each of the two sectors (m_{11} and m_{12}).

The total expenditure is divided only into two parts: consumption and investment. The total marginal propensities to spend on agricultural output out of agricultural income and nonagricultural income are computed as:

(1) $m_{11} = s_1 \left[(a_{11}/(a_{11} + a_{21})) \right] + (1 - s_1) d_{11}$

(2) $m_{12} = s_2 \left[(a_{12}/(a_{12} + a_{22})) \right] + (1 - s_2) d_{12}$

where s_1 and s_2 are the saving rates of the two sectors, d_{11} and d_{12} are marginal propensities to spend on agricultural goods out of the total consumption expenditure of the agricultural and nonagricultural sectors respectively, and a_{ij} are the input-output coefficients.

Rural and urban saving rates for 1962-63, available in the *Reserve Bank of India Bulletin* (March, 1965), are treated as marginal propensities to spend on investment out of agricultural and non-agricultural income respectively. 1962-63 is the last year for which separate rural and urban saving rates are available in the Reserve Bank of data.

Investment expenditure is broken up into expenditure on agricultural and nonagricultural output on the assumption that the proportion of each in the total investment expenditure is the same as the proportion of expenditure on current inputs to the total material input. Thus $a_{11}/(a_{11} + a_{21})$ and $a_{12}/(a_{21} + a_{22})$ are the proportions spent on agricultural output out of the investment expenditure of the agricultural and nonagricultural sectors respectively. This is a strong assumption but in the absence of precise data there is no better alternative.

The proportion of income not spent on investment is regarded as spent on consumption. *National Sample Survey* data on rural and urban consumption expenditure in 1963-64 is used to break up the consumption expenditure of the agricultural and nonagricultural sectors into expenditure on agricultural and nonagricultural output. Expenditure on foodgrains, milk and milk products is assumed to be the expenditure on agricultural output. The rest of the consumption expenditure is assumed to be spent on nonagricultural output.

The basic coefficients derived from the above sources are as follows:

$$s_1 = 0.0339 \qquad\qquad d_{11} = 0.4505$$
$$s_2 = 0.1502 \qquad\qquad d_{12} = 0.3471$$

Since there are only two sectors, $m_{21} = 1 - m_{11}$ and $m_{22} = 1 - m_{12}$.

Appendix C

Changes in the Composition of the
Input Vector Due To Technical Change

1	WHEAT (T) 2	WHEAT (M) 3	WHEAT (T) 4	WHEAT (M) 5	PADDY (T) 6	PADDY (M) 7	MAIZE (T) 8	MAIZE (M) 9
Material input from agriculture	.25	.11	.22	.11	.17	.05	.15	.05
Material input from nonagriculture	.04	.06	.02	.20	.05	.11	.05	.09
Return to human labour	.14	.07	.22	.15	.20	.06	.36	.10
Return to capital	.57	.76	.54	.54	.58	.78	.44	.75
(a) Non-profit	.08	.04	-	-	.06	.02	.03	.02
(b) Profit	.49	.72	-	-	.52	.76	.41	.73
Gross output	1.00	1.00	1.00	1.00	1.00	1.00	1.00	1.00

(T) : Traditional technique
(M) : Modern technique

SOURCES: For wheat (Columns 2 and 3) (U.P.), Paddy (U.P.) and Maize (U.P.): S.P. Dhondyal, "Cost and Effectiveness of Modern Technology on Farm Production and Farm Income," *Indian Journal of Agricultural Economics* (April-June, 1968).

For wheat (Columns 4 and 5) (Punjab): Bhagat Singh, "Economics of Tractor Cultivation: A Case Study," *Indian Journal of Agricultural Economics* (January-March, 1968).

Employment Creating Public Works Programs: Observations on Political and Social Dimensions*

John Woodward Thomas
Harvard University

Introduction

The problem of unemployment in developing nations resembles the Mafia; everybody knows it exists and that it is a serious problem but there is little agreement about its precise dimensions or the effectiveness of various policies and programs designed to eliminate it. While the economist's admonition to policy makers to "get prices right" is a sound prescription, there are serious institutional obstacles to correcting economic distortions by policy fiat, particularly in the short run. Influential groups have important interests in subsidies to capital and neither government construction agencies nor productive enterprises change their operating procedures willingly. Yet unemployment is a pressing economic and political problem that in many cases demands rapid alleviation. In such situations, special employment creating public works programs, which enable the government to organize the unemployed quickly and to direct their labor to the construction of needed public facilities, appear to offer a welcome policy option. Such programs are drawing increasing interest from both developing nations and aid donors.

The concept underlying labor intensive public works is not new. Moghul princes constructed tombs and mosques in northern India and Christian kings carved churches out of rock in the Ethiopian highlands at times when factor prices were not a concern. British colonial administrators established "test" work relief programs in times of famine and the United States utilized public works during its most serious economic depression. Depending on the interpretation of stated objectives, between 15 and 18 developing nations have established special public works programs with employment as a primary objective in the past two decades.

Despite this recurrence, relatively little is known about the real effects of public works. There have been no comparative studies published. Country studies have tended to emphasize economic issues.[1] Uncertainty exists however, about the efficacy of public works programs for dealing with unemployment and the factors which are crucial in determining their outcomes. This paper attempts to broaden the focus of analysis with comparative observations of the political and social environ-

*This paper is a preliminary product of a larger comparative study of employment creating public works programs being carried out at Harvard University with financial support from the World Bank. I wish to acknowledge the contributions of Shahid Javed Burki, Carl H. Gotsch, Richard M. Hook, John D. Montgomery and Barbara P. Thomas whose ideas and comments have considerably improved this paper. I am also grateful for the opportunity to have presented an earlier version of this paper to the SEADAG Conference on Emergency Employment Creation Programs in Baguio, Philippines, August 1973.

ment in which public works programs operate. These are based on the available literature and data and first-hand knowledge of four public works type programs.*

The Objectives of Public Works Programs

By definition the primary objective of the special public works programs being discussed here is employment creation. This implies the mobilization of the relatively unskilled and underemployed who are inevitably members of low income groups. While regimes have other important objectives in these programs, such as, asset creation or the slowing of rural urban migration, the basic redistributive objective of augmenting the incomes of those low on the income scale is generally paramount. However, the manner and intensity of the pursuit of these redistributive objectives varies greatly from country to country. The two critical factors influencing this are

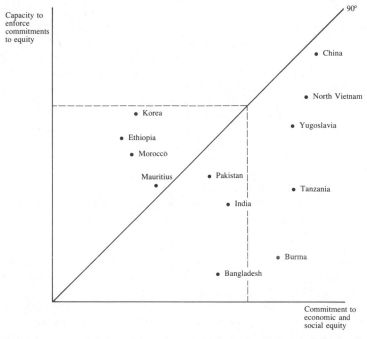

Figure 1. Commitment to Equity and Capacity to Enforce Commitments in a Selection of Countries

first, the regime's commitment to an equitable distribution of income and second, its capacity to move the country toward this goal without major conflict and opposition. There are major differences between countries and regimes in the areas of commitment and capacity. Figure 1 attempts to illustrate how some countries might be compared on such a scale and points up the very considerable differences between commitment to equity and capacity to enforce this commitment. The nature and objectives of the regime undertaking a public works program is significant because it

---

*The emphasis in this paper on political and social dimensions of public works is not intended to diminish the importance of economic factors. Detailed economic analysis plays a central role in the Harvard study of public works programs. This paper attempts to examine previously neglected political aspects and to suggest that there is an important interrelationship between these and economic factors.

has an important relationship to how a public works program is designed and its ultimate outcome.

In the upper right of Figure 1 are located countries which are both sufficiently determined and powerful to enforce a policy of full employment and a relatively equitable distribution of income. Such governments are capable of overpowering opposing political forces and organized interests in the process of structuring society at all levels. When such countries utilize labor intensive public works to broaden employment opportunities, the political responses do not significantly affect their operation.

Lower and to the right of Figure 1 are regimes which put primary emphasis on distributional objectives and on their enforcement but where the ensuing conflicts between central governments and other interests have not been definitely settled. Other countries which fall to the right of the 90° line are concerned about inequities and have declared their intention to carry out social reforms through democratic methods. When undertaking programs like public works with a reform dimension, the emergence of political opposition and well articulated economic interest groups is inevitable in these countries. The sponsoring regime usually responds in an ad hoc manner, sometimes through political accommodation, sometimes by seeking methods to enforce its reform objectives.

Finally, some regimes take action to deal with unemployment only when it reaches proportions where it threatens the stability of the regime. Overall social and economic reforms are not the primary goal and public works are viewed as a palliative that helps alleviate a pressing domestic problem. These countries would generally be placed above the 90° line in Figure 1 with capacity exceeding commitment. These governments do not want to confront distributional issues directly; their objective is to maintain a balance among internal political forces.

This paper limits its observations to two broad groups of countries. The first is those which are publicly committed to change but are dependent upon a diverse coalition of internal groups for support. If the changes initiated threaten the interests of these groups, and the regime is not able to strengthen its supporting coalition by obtaining the support of the target beneficiaries of the proposed changes, the program may be expected to mutate. (This process is described in more detail later in the paper.) In these countries commitment to equity generally exceeds capacity to enforce it. Second are those countries which initiate programs consistent with and supportive of the interests of the local power structure. Such programs will probably perform in a relatively predictable way but will not bring about any basic income redistribution or alteration of the existing structure of society. In these countries capacity to enforce objectives usually exceeds the regime's commitment to equity. Countries to be considered here would generally fall within the dotted line in Figure 1.

To the nations being considered here, there appear to be multiple attractions to initiating public works programs to alleviate unemployment. Such programs can be implemented rapidly; they are flexible as to location; they are highly divisible; and they can frequently be phased to coincide with peak and slack employment seasons. Moreover the impact of such programs is highly visible. Labor groups constructing roads, reforesting hills or digging irrigation channels heighten the impression that the government is acting to create employment and promote development. They can employ the poorest unskilled laborers on projects that directly affect the entire populace of their locality, and they have a rapid payoff without visibly diminishing the benefits of any other group, especially when foreign aid is available to support the program. They are also perceived in some cases as a means of mobilizing resources by generating local contributions. This self help approach appears to provide a low cost approach to rural development.

Many alternative means of increasing employment opportunities appear slower. Government construction agencies, with a pool of engineering talent, capital equipment and beneficial relationships with private contractors, will resist conversion to labor intensive technologies.[2] Public and private industrial units adopt technologies in response to many considerations and attempts to create employment by relative changes in factor prices are slow and imperfect.[3] With conflict and delay inherent in changing existing technologies, public works programs offer concerned governments an apparently easier and more rapid means of creating new jobs.

In the countries with which this paper is concerned, public works programs are perceived as one means of reducing unemployment and redistributing income without prior structural reform. However, if successful, they will alter the structure in significant though not fundamental ways. This raises an important political question. In a system where the governing regime is maintained by a coalition of interests, as in most of these countries, can a public works program generate enough new support to offset the political losses incurred through the program? Can an existing equilibrium of political interests be upset and a new more equitable one established without substantial changes of basic power relationships or economic structures? This is an issue that makes an investigation of the political and social effects of public works intrinsically interesting. These programs represent a mid-range of government initiative, more reformist than production oriented efforts, such as irrigation projects or agricultural extension, but less extreme than those which reallocate scarce resources, such as ownership of land or capital. Only as we begin to gain some understanding of the factors that determine the performance of such programs is it possible to judge the feasibility of this approach to reform.

The Performance of Public Works Programs

Governments' statements of objectives of reform programs are rarely matched by actual accomplishments. Public works are no exception. Consequently, in the absence of comparative studies or comparable data, it is difficult to determine exactly what various programs have accomplished. All that can be done at this stage is to compare the four programs the author has been able to observe at first-hand.* The four are: the East Pakistan (Bangladesh) Works Program, Pakistan's Rural Works Program, the Travail pour Tous program in Mauritius and the Food for Work Program of Tigre Province, Ethiopia. The first two make a particularly interesting comparison because they were initiated under the same national political regime, were similar in concept, objectives and to a lesser extent in administrative design, but were implemented in strikingly different environments and with noticeably different results. The programs in Mauritius and Ethiopia are much newer but offer a basis for comparison from first-hand observations.

The performance of these four public works programs is compared in Table 1 under five categories. First is the creation of employment for unskilled or semiskilled workers at the low end of the income scale. Comparisons are based on proportion of total expenditure utilized for wage payment. Second, is the social productivity of the projects carried out. For the productivity comparisons, an attempt was made to

---

*By early 1974 members of the Harvard public works study will have visited fourteen countries to observe and collect data on their special public works programs. Preliminary drafts of this comparative analysis will be available sometime in 1974.

estimate the approximate ratio of benefits to costs from data available or from existing studies. Third, is the degree of equity in the distribution of program benefits. Four indicators of distributive justice are utilized: a) employment created (same as item 1); b) public participation in project selection to indicate how broadly community interest was served; c) relative equality of land holding in vicinity of projects providing returns to land owners (irrigation, roads, reforestation); and d) the percentage of project expenditure on social services (schools, clinics). Fourth, is the political support generated for the national or intermediate political leadership initiating the program. Fifth, is the effect on the attitudes of low income target groups toward national development programs.

Subsequent sections will amplify the comparisons. However, several salient points emerge which should be noted here. 1. The performance in creating employment is either very good or very bad. This suggests that only when unemployment is acute and nations determine that employment creation is the top priority, do they really achieve this objective. Otherwise, the labor intensity of projects is quickly diluted. 2. The social productivity of projects in these countries is similar. The labor-capital mix does not seem to affect productivity. A negative correlation between productivity and the development of infrastructure appears to exist. In both East Pakistan and Ethiopia where infrastructure was relatively less developed, productivity was slightly higher. 3. The detailed distribution-of-benefits ranking for relative equality of land holding and extent of public participation in project choice are identical and these correlate closely with the total distribution rankings. Since equality of land holding affects participation more than the reverse, this must be a factor of considerable importance. 4. In those countries in which there are few distributive benefits from public works, the alienation of the lower income groups is a consistent political effect, undoubtedly because they see public works as one more way of extracting work from them. 5. An averaging of political effects produces a mean rating of 3. This suggests that the political benefits anticipated by regimes are more illusory than real. Perhaps most important is that the gap between anticipated results and actual performance of public works programs is substantial. If public works are to be an effective means of employment creation, redistribution, development, and increasing political support, it is necessary to examine the factors affecting performance to see why this gap exists. Understanding of the reasons might lead to new alternatives for improving the performance of public works programs.

Public Works: The Political Economy of Reform

To analyze the reasons for the gap between anticipated and actual performance, it is necessary to understand the objectives of those responsible for public works programs. The economic objectives of governments are usually fully articulated in plan documents, official requests for foreign aid and reports of program performance. That unemployment and a skewed income distribution are problems with political as well as economic consequences is clear. In reacting to these problems, regimes have political objectives which are frequently as important as the economic objectives but which generally remain unarticulated.

The Travail pour Tous program in Mauritius was motivated in part by a clear cut political challenge. The 4-Year Development Plan for 1971-1975 stated:

> The immediate task on which the success of the entire long-term development programme depends is a constructive programme for dealing with the present unemployment situa-

tion. The Travail pour Tous programme is, therefore, *the number one priority in the country's development plan.* (emphasis in original)[4]

This priority is quite consistent with the serious economic problem of unemployment which confronts the nation. However, the Labor Government draws most of its support from the rural Indo-Mauritians who represent a slight majority of the nation's population. The only strong opposition party, the Mouvement Militant Mauritian (MMM) draws support from the "general population" of mixed French, African or

TABLE 1

COMPARISON OF PERFORMANCE OF FOUR PUBLIC WORKS PROGRAMS[1]

	E. Pakistan/ Bangladesh (1962-1970)	Ethiopia Tigre Province (1970-1972)	Mauritius (1970-1972)	Pakistan (1964-1968)
1. Employment	1	5	1	4
2. Project's social productivity	3	3	4	4
3. Distribution of benefits[2]	2	5	3	4
4. Political support for initiating leadership	1 (1962-1966) 4 (1967-1970)	2	2	3
5. Support of low income groups for development programs	2 (1962-1966) 5 (1967-1970)	5	?	4

SOURCES: *East Pakistan* - Thomas, John Woodward, *The Rural Public Works Program and East Pakistan's Development,* Unpublished Ph. D. Thesis, 1968; Notes and data collected by author, 1969-70.

Ethiopia - Notes and data collected by author in June and July 1972; Bruce, Colin, *Cost-Benefit Analysis of a Tigre Agricultural Development Unit,* (mimeo 1972); Kowalczyk, Gary, *Economic Feasibility Study of Small Scale Irrigation in Tigre Province,* (mimeo 1972).

Mauritius - *4-Year Plan for Social and Economic Development,* Vol. II, pp. 90-97; author's calculation of benefits while participating in IBRD evaluation mission; labor productivity calculation by Emile Costa of ILO, manpower economist in IBRD economic mission to Mauritius, November 1971.

West Pakistan - Thomas, John W., *The Rural Public Works Program and East Pakistan's Development,* Unpublished Ph. D. Thesis, 1968; Pickering, A.K., *Report of the Rural Works Programme in West Pakistan, 1963-1969,* Lahore, Pakistan: Development Advisory Service, Harvard University, July 1969; unpublished data collected by S.J. Burki; unpublished statistics on Rural Works Programme—West Pakistan Statistical Office, Lahore.

NOTES: [1] In Item 1, 1 and 3 rankings range from 1-excellent performance to 5-unsatisfactory performance. In Items 4 and 5 rankings range from 1-strongly increased support to 5-strongly diminished support.

[2] All four programs have the important distributional benefit of increasing public investment in low income rural communities.

Employment Ratings:
1. An average of over 60% of program expenditure (including food commodities) spent on labor
2. 50-60% of expenditures on labor
3. 40-50% of expenditures on labor
4. 30-40% of expenditures on labor
5. Less than 30% of expenditures on labor

Estimated Productivity Ratings:
1. Benefits exceed cost
2. Benefits $\geq$ costs
3. Benefits and costs approximately equal
4. Benefits $\leq$ costs
5. Costs exceed benefits

Distribution of Benefits Ratings:

	E.P./Bangl.	Ethiopia	Mauritius	Pakistan
Employment	1	5	1	4
Public participation in project choice	2	5	4	4
Relative equality of landholding in vicinity of projects	2	5	4	4
Percent of expenditure on social services	4	5	2	2
Average	2	5	3	4

Political and Development Program Support Ratings:
Based on: (1) Election results in East Pakistan (1965), Mauritius (1972) and Pakistan (1965).
(2) Overt acts of opposition to program or facilities constructed by it in local communities in East Pakistan (1969) and Ethiopia (1971).
(3) Interviews with national and local officials in Ethiopia and Pakistan.

Chinese descent who are primarily urban. In 1970-71, the MMM effectively mobilized urban workers and unemployed in its support, organized a major dock strike which threatened the nation's sugar exports, and won large concessions for workers. The MMM then announced a new effort to organize rural sugar estate workers and declared its intention to call a strike on sugar estates if workers' conditions were not improved. Simultaneously, the MMM scored unanticipated successes in the local council elections in rural constituencies which were considered Labor strongholds. These gains, in addition to the MMM's urban support put it in a strong electoral position and inspired the Labor controlled Assembly to postpone the next election until 1976. In this environment of eroding support, particularly in the Labor Party's traditional rural strongholds, the initiation of a major new effort to alleviate rural unemployment must be interpreted as having strong political motivations.

Political considerations may play a dominant role in determining the character of a program. In Korea, after the student revolution removed Syngman Rhee from power in April 1960, the Democratic Government decided that the new political activism could best be utilized by channeling it into national development through a National Construction Service (NCS). This public works type program was to combine the talents of college graduates and rural underemployed in an attack on rural poverty. The expectancy and enthusiasm with which the program was launched in 1961 is captured in this description of its origins:

> The NCS program was born in urgent response to the call of the nation newly established after the bloody Student Revolution in April 1960. There was a bustling energy and willingness to work hard among the people. The masses were spearheaded by intellectuals and students ready to be guided by the nation's new leaders. The NCS strongly appealed to the growing tide of the rapidly-awakening people, especially the young people, through stressing the patriotic aspect of working on the nation's natural resource development, challenging nature's vagaries, and eliminating centuries-old rural poverty.[5]

On March 1, 1961, the day of the inauguration of the NCS, "college graduates who completed training as NCS participants marched along the main boulevards of Seoul with shovels on their shoulders, symbolizing the dignity of labor and their taking up the spiritual revolution to challenge the nation's poverty."[6]

Despite the widespread expectations created, and enthusiasm for the NCS, the military dominated regime of General Park which replaced the Democratic Government in 1962 terminated the program after one year of operation. While the Program had encountered some administrative problems and its termination is sometimes credited to these, it is clear that these were not as important as fundamental political considerations. The emphasis on mobilization of the populace for participation in the NCS was a political style and concept more appropriate to a government born of a popular uprising than to its successor which emphasised stability and "disciplined" development efforts. The Park regime did not wish to terminate public works entirely, however, probably because of the expectations created. Instead, it decided to replace the NCS with its strong political overtones, with a low profile Self-Help Work Program to finance individual village projects on a matching grant basis. This approach was more consistent with the style of the new government. With both regimes, political objectives were paramount in determing the structure and objectives of the public works type programs.

It is perfectly logical for regimes to insure that public works programs be consistent with their broad political objectives and approaches. Beyond that, however, more narrow political considerations also seem to intrude regularly.

In East Pakistan, the Works Program was, from its inception in 1962 until 1966, under the firm direction of the Secretary of Basic Democracies and Local Government. A cardinal rule of the Program was that the size of the annual allocation of funds to local councils for implementation of the program was based solely on population, and that effective performance in the previous year was a prerequisite for the release of funds. The Secretary's unwillingness to let political considerations alter the standard for the allocation of funds brought him into increasing conflict with the Governor of the Province and political leaders of President Ayub's Muslim League. The conflicts resulted in the Secretary's dismissal in 1966. From 1967 on, as political loyalty to the regime, rather than population or past performance in carrying out public works, became the basis for allocating funds, the economic benefits of the program declined sharply, and ironically, as indicated in Table 1, political benefits declined as well.[7]

Mauritius represents a variation of the theme. There, the Development Works Corporation which administers the Travail pour Tous program hires the unemployed on a permanent basis. This places the Program's director in a position where he can be perceived to be commanding a large political following. If he does not behave with extreme discretion, he may become vulnerable to overt or covert accusations of self aggrandizement. Such factors have already contributed to the dismissal of one man of generally acknowledged administrative capability.

From these observations of several public works programs, it becomes quite clear that although political objectives are rarely articulated, they play a major role in both the initiation and operation of these programs, and therefore affect the results. Economic issues pertinent to public works programs must be evaluated in relation to a range of political factors for it is clear that economic objectives are altered by political considerations.

Political Response and Program Mutation*

It has been observed that a gap exists between public works program objectives and performance and that political and economic factors are interwoven in influencing results. In this section, an attempt is made to analyze the mechanism by which

*The term "mutation" as well as several other points in this section were suggested by S.J. Burki in the course of our discussions.

program mutations occur, resulting in performance at variance with expectations. Gunnar Myrdal claims, with considerable supporting evidence, that these changes are intentional.

> When policy measures have been instituted [in what he classifies as the soft states] specifically aimed at ameliorating conditions for the lower strata, they have either not been implemented and enforced or have been distorted so as to favor the not-so-poor and to discriminate against the masses.[8]

The question is who alters programs and how?

In the countries with mixed public and private economic systems considered here, control of scarce resources is closely related to political power. Public works channel resources into the rural sector with the low income underemployed as the principal target group. However, groups other than the target beneficiaries, such as land owners, traders or contractors, may perceive that the government's initiatives and the accompanying resources provide a threat to the group's interests or an opportunity to improve their situation. Either perception will probably be sufficient to cause these local elites to act to further their own interest. Since the economic position of these groups usually provides them political power at both local and national levels, they are in a good position to alter the nature of public works programs to serve their own interests. Most national governments are dependent to some degree on these local elites and will find it difficult to bypass or sustain a challenge to these interests over an extended period of time. Therefore, the employment and distributive objectives of public works may be seriously eroded by the efforts of local elites to divert more program benefits to themselves.

There are several important decision points at which pressure for mutation can be applied: the choice of projects, the choice of technology, the choice of project implementation agent, the establishment of wage rates, or the selection of employees. Over some period of time, these pressures may succeed in altering programs, since the rural poor usually provide an inadequate political counterforce in defense of their own interests.

The changing standard for allocation of Works Program funds to local councils in East Pakistan illustrates the operation of these forces. From the time of partition in 1947, when the Hindu land owners fled Pakistan leaving their land to the Muslim peasants, the rural areas have been characterized by broadly distributed small holdings and a moderately egalitarian social and economic structure. When the public works program was applied to this social system, a relatively broad distribution of benefits was possible. Yet, as Bertocci also points out, "local economic and political power brokers have had a way of always showing up in the official organs serving the extension of state power to the rural areas of East Bengal."[9]

In the first years of the public works program, the diffuse nature of the social structure meant that "brokers" were slow to emerge. During the election of 1965, the ruling Muslim League showered its attentions on the local councillors who as Basic Democrats, served as Presidential and National Assembly electors. The result was a growing sense of political power among local councillors who increasingly demanded that their political loyalty should be the basis for public works allocations, rather than project performance. In 1965, when the Ayub regime scored an unexpected electoral victory in rural East Pakistan, the credit was widely attributed to the impact of the Works Program.[10] Paradoxically, this demonstration of the political impact of the equity and performance oriented program caused the regime to begin seeing it as a means of obtaining political support which made them more willing to manipulate the standards for political purposes. By the end of 1966, this view, supported by local elites, prevailed. The program director was dismissed for not responding to local political demands and the standard for allocating funds to local councils changed. From 1967 on, the leakage of funds out of the program increased, and performance declined. By 1969, the same levels of funding were producing far fewer projects. These were carried out primarily by contractors and the project mix had shifted toward construction of bridges and buildings with a much lower labor component.[11] The principal beneficiaries were no longer the rural poor but the local contractors, the larger farmers, and the small town dwellers, the groups from which the Basic Democrats were drawn.

In East Pakistan, the egalitarian structure slowed the process of mutation. Those attempting to keep the program operating in a manner consistent with its original objectives could utilize political competition, and enforce broad participation in project decisions at the local level to help insure the realization of these goals.[12] The emergence of power brokers and the reversal of this pattern of benefit distribution

TABLE 2

CHANGES IN THE PAKISTAN RURAL WORKS PROGRAM

Funds	1963-1964	1964-1965	1965-1966
Spent by			
District Councils	28.4	41.2	55.2
Tehsil Councils	-	7.7	5.7
Union Councils	71.6	50.7	35.7
Other uses	-	0.4	3.4
Paid to			
Contractors for implementation of projects	45.4	59.0	75.2
Spent by local councils on			
Skilled labor	11.7	n.a.	2.5
Unskilled labor	17.0	n.a.	3.5
Total	28.7	12.5	6.0

SOURCE: John W. Thomas, "The Rural Public Works Progam in East Pakistan," in Falcon & Papanek, eds., *Development Policy II—The Pakistan Experience* (Cambridge, Mass., Harvard University Press, 1971), p. 223.

took considerable time. Once popular participation had been invoked, the process of reversal was costly in terms of rural frustration, both in the sense of loss of support for local leadership and of alienation of the rural populace from the regime.[13]

In Pakistan, the distribution of economic assets, particularly land and political power are highly skewed and program mutation was much more rapid. Large land owners, rural contractors, and small town tradesmen quickly shaped the program to serve their own interests. Table 2 illustrates the rapid shift in the level of decision making and implementation of projects from the lowest level, the Union Council, to the much larger District Council controlled by large land owners and civil servants and the concurrent shift of implementation, from the work carried out by councils, to contractors, with a resulting rapid reduction of labor intensity and employment creation.

This rapid shift took place because these elites of rural Pakistan had a well developed sense of group interest and proven means of acting upon it, including powerful representation at the top levels of government. Given this capacity to wield their power, the regime lacked the capacity to enforce its distributive objectives on the rural system. The result was a public works program that within two to three years, served the interests of rural elites more than it served those of the target groups of rural unemployed.

In West Pakistan the program had few political effects. For the rural elites who already supported the regime, their influence over the Rural Works Program only reconfirmed their ability to control the rural environment. The political status of the regime was little enhanced or diminished. For the tenants, landless and other unemployed, the program only deepened their cynicism about government programs which benefit only the elite, and increased their alienation.

In the provincial program in Tigre Province, Ethiopia, political response took place but fell short of mutation because the program was not aimed at redistributing income but at increasing returns to the holders of scarce resources, land and water. The program is relatively new and results from the initiative of the politically powerful and influential Provincial Governor. The Governor gave the road construction program his personal supervision and took ultimate decision and administrative responsibility himself. He was interested in action and results, and though short of funds, got both through "voluntary" contributions of capital, supplies, equipment and labor. The program is a clear product of the Governor's drive and ambition, and serves the development of the province, which is one of the most densely populated and arid in Ethiopia, and has the lowest per capita income. The focus is on asset creation not employment or distribution, and the results reflect this emphasis.

In this case, low income groups are neither the target nor the real beneficiaries of the program. The real beneficiaries are the owners of land served by the roads and those on whose land conservation and water management projects are carried out, and the distribution of land ownership is highly skewed. The small farmers, tenants and landless laborers are expected by local leaders and authorities to work on road and reforestation projects, and have been paid (only in grain provided under the U.S. Food for Peace Program) an amount about 25% lower than the current wage rate. In several reforestation projects where laborers were terracing and planting trees on land that was not their own, trees were planted upside down. This phenomenon occurred with enough frequency that it can only be assumed to be a deliberate attempt to subvert the program's goals by those being forced to work at wages lower than a minimum acceptable standard on projects from which they gained few benefits.[14] This action forced authorities on some projects to pay a cash wage in addition to grain payments, a precedent which will undoubtedly have to become standard practice if projects are to continue. As a result of this process, returns to labor will be increased but the primary beneficiaries will remain the local elite who control scarce resources.

The phenomena of political response and program mutation are common to employment creating public works programs. They are not, however, homogenous phenomena. They vary in terms of groups responding, the character and effectiveness of the response, and the time necessary to make the response effective. If these responses can be anticipated and programs planned in ways that will counter, accommodate, or otherwise deal with them, the prospects of public works programs achieving the desired objectives may be increased.

Factors Influencing the Results of Public Works Programs

Seeking indicators to anticipate potential responses to public works programs is a difficult and hazardous task. An initial attempt is made here with the qualification that these indicators require considerably more testing before their relative importance can be assessed with accuracy. The following represents a first step in the direction of identifying the crucial determinants of response.

1. The first major factor influencing the outcome of a public works program is the level and strength of commitment to enforcing the program's reform objectives. In the countries which have a commitment to equity which is not matched by their capacity for enforcement, reform objectives generally motivate the initiation of public works programs. However, over a period of time, these run counter to the existing distribution of economic and political power at the local level. When local forces react and attempt to mutate the program in their own interest, the response of the regime is crucial. If the regime is too dependent on local support to be able to reinforce its original objective and to run the risk of alienating a significant portion of its supporting coalition, mutation will take place. If however, the regime acts to reinforce the public works program and its reform objectives, and is prepared to confront the opposition this incurs, some favorable change in the distribution of economic and political resources may occur. Other regimes without a significant commitment to equity do not begin with reform objectives, but establish programs consistent with the existing distribution of power and the result is neither mutation nor reform. The conclusion that there is no substitute for the government's determined commitment to equitable objectives is reinforced by experience in agrarian reform where "the effects of agrarian reform, their extent and intensity, stem from the forces that create the reform in the first place more than the reform itself."[15] The nature and degree of government's support for each of the objectives of public works provide a useful indicator of potential success. Without high level, continuous political support, there is no chance that public works programs will have the reform-type benefits which are usually considered part of their purpose.

2. The distribution of economic assets and political power at the level at which the public works program is implemented is a second major factor influencing the outcome. The more equal the distribution of resources, particularly of land, the more likely it is that all members of the community will be benefited by the program and will share an interest in assuring the program's success. Conversely, a highly skewed distribution of relevant assets and articulate special interest groups at the local level usually lead to strong forces to mutate the program in the interest of non-target groups. The distribution of political power frequently parallels that of economic assets, and the more broadly this is shared, the more chance there is that there will be a common interest and desire to see mutually agreed upon goals fulfilled. Broad political participation and competition at the local level are beneficial to the objectives of public works.

There is also evidence that at the other extreme, where societies are highly stratified and strong class or group identifications exist, a public works program which supports and organizes the low income group may promote that group's ability and willingness to defend its interests in the distributional objectives of the program. Such an outcome is more likely if the sponsoring regime is willing to reinforce public works investment with considerable organizational effort in order to develop a workable mechanism to insure participation of the poor, or if the program is combined with a substantial element of ideological activism. In some instances, public works may provide the catalytic outside force that enables the target, low income group to begin acting in defense of its own interest.

3. There are two corollaries to the preceding proposition. The first is that there are some countries where public works have a very low probability of success. Nations with clear social stratifications but little group identity among the poor are poor risks. When powerful rural interests are well established, dominating and controlling low income groups with little fear of challenge, prospects for creating a successful public works program are so low that such an undertaking should probably not be considered. Identifying countries where programs should not be undertaken is just as important as being able to define those where there is some prospect of success.

The second is that it is not always necessary to think in terms of country-wide programs. Most countries are not homogenous in social structure or in location of low income groups. The prospects for a successful public works program may be greatly enhanced if programs are located in carefully chosen areas. Careful selection of regions where low income groups are partially organized and have shown capacity to wield political power in their own interest, or where local elites have only weak ties to national government may considerably improve the program's chances of achieving its goals.

4. In those cases where the process of program mutation is likely to occur with resultant shift in benefits away from target groups, programs may still be justified if the time lags can be predicted and if programs can be terminated or reorganized once they have been altered. In both East and West Pakistan, public works programs were ultimately transformed but the time this process took and the resulting benefits differed substantially in the two areas. In West Pakistan, after one year, serious inroads were being made on the program and after three years, the process was total. The result was few benefits to the target groups. In East Pakistan, there were five years of substantial benefits before the program was vitiated. These lags are of importance and much can usually be achieved if they are of sufficient duration.

Therefore, in appraising the potential net impact of a public works program, it is necessary to anticipate the speed and strength with which disruptive forces will move to distort it from its original purposes, and the minimum time needed to establish irreversible gains or minimum benefits. When these are known, there becomes a possibility of making progress, despite the process of mutation.

5. In analyzing responses to public works, the size of public works allocations may be important. There are clearly thresholds of significance that are necessary to activate responses from various social groups. If the program is so small that it does not affect the interests of the more powerful groups in important ways, they may not find it worthwhile to attempt to alter it. Yet, it may still provide important benefits for the target beneficiaries. Therefore, some knowledge as to the size of public works allocations at which local elites become concerned can be an important factor in program planning.

6. Requiring matching grants for public works usually results in a local contribution in the form of voluntary labor. This is usually counter-productive in terms of potential redistribution and it decreases labor productivity drastically. This form of local contribution is more common in highly stratified societies. The reasons are obvious. Unskilled laborers are those with the least political power and can usually be made to "contribute" their time. This, of course, results in a perverse distribution of income with public works making no payments to labor and projects' benefits accruing to holders of other scarcer resources. For precisely this reason, after a year's experience, East Pakistan eliminated the local contribution requirement from its

Works Program procedures. In extreme cases, self-help can be counterproductive as in the Ethiopian reforestation projects where deliberate efforts were made to subvert the project. Almost inevitably, the self-help concept when applied in public works takes the form of voluntary labor. The result is a negation of the employment creation and redistributive objectives of the program, while increasing the target group's resistance to the program and political alienation.

7. Political benefits are a legitimate aim of public works programs but they rarely result from direct payoffs for political loyalty. Some political scientists have argued that public works as pork barrel can help develop a loyal party structure at the local level, as was the case in the United States in the 19th century, and that such a use of public works funds with its attendant corruption is justifiable.[16] Where unemployment is a serious economic condition and action is needed to alleviate poverty, payoffs to local political representatives of the regime's party in return for support are likely to have adverse political effects as they did in East Pakistan in 1968-69. In other words, the pork barrel is a poor model for political development, and public works programs are a poor vehicle for it. In countries where much of the population does not participate in the political system but where unemployment is sufficiently serious that it poses a threat to political stability, public works cannot promote that stability unless they treat the basic condition.

However, the enforcement of performance standards and other economic criteria in the operation of the program may bring substantial support for the regime. If new employment raises rural incomes, and projects stimulate the rural economy, the short-term effect may be to quiet unrest and mobilize new groups in support of the existing regime. As a result, political benefits may be inversely correlated with attempts to manipulate the program for political support.

Conclusion

This paper suggests that the operation and effects of employment generating public works programs must be understood in an interrelated political, social and economic environment. A gap between objectives and performance has been observed and the question raised as to whether the implicit reform objectives of public works programs—employment creation, productive projects, moderate redistribution of income and positive political effects—can be effectively implemented. No clear cut answer to that question is provided. Instead, an attempt is made to develop a conceptual framework for understanding the process of mutation and change in public works programs. This process is seen as resulting from the perception, by various groups, of potential effects of the program which could affect their welfare, and their response to these. When this process of response and change is understood, it may then be possible to deal with it. Several factors affecting or determining the nature and intensity of response have been suggested.

Implicit in this attempt to identify factors is the expectation that reform will be possible, although it is fully acknowledged that this will be very difficult and may prove impossible. If reform is to be attempted, it is necessary to understand the way in which objectives are thwarted and to seek new ways to accomplish them. This process has been graphically described by one participant in U.S. attempts to improve the status of low income groups as being similar to a game of American football. One side carries out a play which may result in a gain or loss of ground. It will, however, be quickly stopped by the opposition and the team must devise a new strategy or play and try again. The initiative switches back and forth. It is a lengthy and bruising battle which either side may eventually win, but only with repeated efforts and constantly changing strategy is there any chance of success.

This paper has attempted to analyze the strategy of the groups who resist the reforming objectives of public works and to delineate some of the conditions which may affect the nature and strength of that resistance. Whether public works can succeed in dealing with the problems they are designed to solve is uncertain, but if there is to be any progress in this direction, this type of analysis will have to be pursued, refined and strengthened.

Notes

1. See for example, Rajaona Andriamananjara, "Labor Mobilization: The Moroccan Experience," (Ann Arbor, Michigan, Center for Research on Economic Development, University of Michigan, Discussion Paper #15, April, 1971); John Woodward Thomas, "The Rural Public Works Program in East Pakistan," in W.P. Falcon & G.F. Papanek, eds., *Development Policy II - The Pakistan Experience* (Cambridge, Mass., Harvard University Press, 1971); and Abdessatar Grissa, *Agricultural Policies and Employment-Case Study of Tunisia* (Paris, OECD Development Centre Studies, Employment Series No. 9, 1973).

2. John Woodward Thomas, "Development Institutions, Projects and Aid in the Water Development Program of East Pakistan," (mimeo, March, 1972) gives a fuller analysis of one such established system.

3. Louis T. Wells, "Economic Man and Engineering Man: A Field Study of Choice of Technology for Light Manufacturing in Indonesia," *Public Policy* (Summer, 1973), explores the reason why, despite factor prices that reflect relative scarcities in Indonesia, technologies are less labor intensive than economic considerations would suggest.

4. Government of Mauritius, *4-Year Plan for Social and Economic Development* (Port Louis, 1971), p. 29.

5. Daniel Kie-Hong Lee, *National Construction Service—A Case Study of Korea's Experience in Utilization of Underemployed Manpower Resources* (Bangkok, Thailand: Asian Institute for Economic Development and Planning, United Nations, March, 1969), p. 68.

6. *Ibid.*, p. 33.

7. John Woodward Thomas, "The Rural Public Works Program in East Pakistan," *op. cit.*, p. 225.

8. Gunnar Myrdal, *The Challenge of World Poverty* (New York, Vintage Books, 1970), p. 220.

9. Peter J. Bertocci, "Microregion, Market Area and Muslim Community in Rural Bangladesh," mimeo (February, 1973), p. 3.

10. The New York Times (January 3, 1965), p. 2 reported, "the failure of any real anti-Ayub vote to emerge in East Pakistan is viewed as a triumph for the three year old Rural Works Program, which has pumped much needed funds into farm communities and brought many improvements in rural life."

11. A survey conducted by the author in 1969 of four thanas, in which intensive research on the impact of the Works Program had been carried out in 1967, provided plentiful evidence for these statements.

12. See John Woodward Thomas, "The Rural Public Works Program and East Pakistan's Development," Unpublished Ph. D. Thesis (1968), pp. 150-159 for a description of the politicization of the program at the local level.

13. See issues of the *Dacca Observer* or *Morning News* of March 1969 when the anti-Ayub turmoil was at its height and law enforcement in the rural areas was non-existent, for a description of killing by local mobs of those Basic Democrats who had been most flagrant in their corruption and misuse of funds.

14. Reported to the writer by Todd Crawford, co-author of Habteab Dagnewrand and Todd Crawford, "Summary of Findings Concerning the Food for Work Reforestation Program in Tigre and Welo Provinces," mimeo (September, 1972). This paper contains a good discussion of factors affecting performance of projects in Tigre Province.

15. Robert LaPorte, Jr., James F. Petras, Jeffrey C. Rinehart, "The Concept of Agrarian Reform and its Role in Development: Some Notes on Societal Cause and Effect," *Comparative Studies in Society and History* (October, 1971), p. 485.

16. Karl Von Vorys has made this argument both verbally and, in 1967, in private correspondence with Iqbal Leghari.

Education and Employment in Developing Nations*

Edgar O. Edwards *Ford Foundation*
Michael P. Todaro *Rockefeller Foundation***

Introduction

The idea that conventional education in abundance beyond literacy is an unmitigated social good and an engine for development deserves challenge. That challenge is taking the form in developing countries of growing open unemployment in urban areas, reaching in the 1960s percentages such as 13.6 in Bogota, 7.9 in Venezuela, 15.0 in Ceylon, 9.8 in Malaya, 11.6 in the Philippines, 11.5 in Kenya, and 11.6 in Ghana.[1] Moreover, the average level of education among the unemployed and underemployed appears to be rising, suggesting that the growing investment in educational systems is increasingly an investment in idle human resources. The prospects, therefore, given present employment patterns, surging educational enrollments and rapid population growth are not encouraging. In the face of these facts, the further rapid expansion of formal education beyond literacy levels without constructive efforts to create meaningful employment opportunities is likely to generate political as well as educational unrest.

Obviously the numbers being educated in developing countries exceed the employment opportunities available to them when they emerge from the educational system. Yet educational ministries with the implicit endorsement of donor agencies continue to press for the expansion of educational opportunities on the tacit assumption that so long as the private demand for educational places exceeds the supply, expansion is socially justified. But the signals reported above on employment suggest that the demand for education is itself excessive and a supply of education which responds exclusively to that signal may lead to a serious misallocation of development resources. It is our contention that an educational supply responsive to demand may not have been inappropriate in the 1950s and early 1960s when shortages of educated manpower were general but to continue to adjust supply to demand through the 1970s and 1980s when opportunities for education already exceed requirements

* An earlier version of the paper was presented at a conference of heads of donor agencies on Education and Development Reconsidered, Bellagio, May 1972. This version has appeared in *World Development*, Vol. I, Nos. 3 & 4 (March-April, 1973), under the title, "Educational Demand and Supply in the Context of Growing Unemployment in Less Developed Countries."

** The authors acknowledge the thoughtful comments of conference participants and the considered reactions of Charles Frank, James Grant, Harold Lubell, Marc Nerlove, Gus Ranis, Hans Singer, and Paul Streeten.

for it is clearly bad policy. We further contend that tinkering with educational supply alone will not sufficiently reduce the fundamental, troublesome and growing gap between the demand for post-literacy education and the supply of employment opportunities. To achieve that end more basic policy changes will be required.

The fundamental question we address is why the demand for education in developing countries is so high and growing when job opportunities are obviously scarce and growing at a distinctly slower pace. One possibility to which we feel many have given disproportionate attention is that education is wanted in significant quantities as an end in itself, as a consumption good. This may be an important factor in advanced countries but given low per capita incomes, urgent needs for other consumption goods essential for a minimum standard of living, and limited numbers of families with incomes large enough to afford education as a luxury, we are not convinced of its relative significance in developing countries. We shall argue instead that the demand for education in LDCs is primarily determined by the balance between (1) the prospects of earning considerably more income through future employment in the modern sector as perceived by the student and (2) the educational costs which the student or his family must bear. An *excess* demand for education results then from an *ex ante* rational, though *ex post* inflated, private calculation of the excess of benefits over costs of further schooling even as the numbers of educated unemployed rise.

We shall also argue that employment opportunities in the modern sector are artificially restricted largely because (1) factor prices are distorted, capital being underpriced and labor being overpriced, favoring labor-saving methods of production, (2) technologies are often borrowed from advanced countries where labor is a relatively scarce resource, (3) job specifications require excessive education partly in emulation of advanced-country standards and partly because the educational system is itself overproducing, and (4) excessive resources are devoted to education, diverting them from more productive, employment-creating investment opportunities elsewhere in the economy, one of which is clearly the provision of more complementary resources with which those educated who would otherwise be unemployed can work.

On the other hand, the demand for additional post-literacy education is inflated because (1) the income differential between modern and traditional sector employment is artificially high even when modified by the existing probability of employment, (2) perceived employment probabilities may be exaggerated because of the visible success of predecessors in the system and the temporary surfeit of employment opportunities as expatriates are replaced following independence, (3) employers give preference to the better educated even though additional education adds only marginally to productivity, and (4) the portion of the costs of education which is borne privately is usually nominal. Moreover, the demand for education may be even greater at higher levels because of the artificial stimulus created by government financial policies which reduce the proportion of total costs borne by the individual as he moves up the educational ladder. In addition to stimulating excess demand for higher education, these policies also raise serious questions of equity since often the higher education of the rich is subsidized out of public revenues extracted from the poor through regressive tax systems. These several factors suggest that privately perceived benefits may exceed the private costs of education even though the net *social* benefits are very low or even negative, and this divergence is likely to be greater at higher than at lower educational levels.

Unlike the demand for education, which is essentially privately determined, and the supply of employment opportunities in the modern sector, which is partly privately determined, the supply of educational opportunities is almost universally a government responsibility, an important political variable, and a natural focus of government policy, often to the neglect of educational demand and employment considerations. In most developing countries today it would appear that demand-for-education exceeds the supply-of-educational-opportunities which in turn greatly exceeds the supply-of-employment-opportunities. The advancing educational level of the unemployed in most LDCs makes it clear that opportunities for education exceed opportunities for employment; the continuing need to ration places in educational systems suggests that the demand for education outruns enrollment capacities.

Despite these basic inequalities little has been done in most LDCs either to temper the demand for education toward more realistic levels or to create more jobs through changes in public policies. Instead policies have focused on the supply of school places, the manipulation of which within the bounds given above has little to do with reducing the gap between the demand for education and opportunities for using it productively.

In the present circumstances of most developing countries, as opposed to earlier periods when education could not meet employment needs, the supply of educational opportunities acts as a 'decoy' variable which at one extreme leaves many dissatisfied because they are locked out of the educational system and at the other spews out growing numbers of educated unemployed. When educational capacity is geared to employment opportunities, it creates an enormous and complex problem of rationing educational opportunities; when it is accommodated to educational demand, it compels the rationing of job opportunities. In either case, the practicalities of rationing imply the ascendancy of favoritism and political ferment.

It has often been politically expedient to minimize the rationing of education and to undertake instead, though at a later date, the rationing of jobs. Indeed, for the latter task the educational system itself can be used as a rationing device. Jobs in the modern sector can be, and in most countries are, allocated (not necessarily equitably) to those with the most advanced education, leaving others less fortunate educationally to fend for themselves on the periphery of the urban sector or in the subsistence setting of the traditional economy.

Taking these several factors into account, we feel that developing countries have overexpanded conventional educational opportunities at levels above that necessary to ensure literacy. A continuation of this policy, therefore, must be looked upon most critically by both national governments and international donor agencies. We feel that greater weight should be given to prospective employment opportunities in planning the rate of educational expansion. It should be recognized, however, that this can only be a partial solution since it does not come to grips with what we perceive to be the basic issue, namely, that the private demand for education continues to outrun opportunities for productive employment.

The Private Demand for Education as a 'Derived Demand' from High-Income Modern-Sector Employment Opportunities

In this section we will focus on an aspect of education in developing nations which has been largely neglected by scholars, educational planners and donor agencies alike. The attention of these individuals and organizations has been devoted almost exclusively to the question of how to most effectively *supply* sufficient educational services to meet a set of perceived manpower needs. Implicit in this approach has been the assumption that the demand for education by individuals was not an important concern so long as it exceeded the available supply at any point in time.[2] The immediate need was to expand the supply in order to build up national human capital. So long as the supply of educational places lagged behing *both* manpower needs and the demand for education, increasing that supply was a proper response.

Although this supply-oriented approach may have been appropriate in the circumstances of a shortage of educated manpower in the 1950s and 1960s, it is becoming increasingly less valid in the 1970s and may become totally inappropriate in the 1980s. The supply of educational services is already running ahead of the economic need for educated manpower in many countries and the gap is widening. In these circumstances the benefits of further rapid growth of educational services are questionable. Consequently, it is crucial that government planning and education ministries as well as international donor agencies begin to take a critical look at the factors influencing the private demand for education. The linkage between the availability of new employment opportunities and the role of the educational system in the development process, is, in our opinion, most readily crystallized on the demand rather than on the supply side of the education equation.

The basic premise upon which our argument will be constructed concerns the relationship between the level and growth of productive employment opportunities and the demand for education. In simple form this premise states that to a large extent individual students and their families view education as a passport for entry into the modern, urban, industrialized economy with its disproportionately-high-paying employment opportunities. Clearly, some education is demanded for its own sake as a consumption good. We do not feel, however, that this represents a substantial proportion of the demand for education in developing countries. Much of what is perceived by many analysts as a demand for status and prestige is in reality derived from economic opportunities. To the extent that education beyond literacy is desired as a means of achieving status and prestige unrelated to economic opportunities, it should be perceived as a luxury and, in poor countries, might on these grounds be taxed, certainly not subsidized.*

The investment demand for education can be seen as a demand 'derived' from high-income employment opportunities in the modern sector. In fact, in almost all nations of Africa, Asia and Latin America, entry into modern-sector public and private jobs is predicated upon successful completion of the requisite years of education associated with particular jobs, often irrespective of whether or not such education requirements are really necessary for satisfactory job performance.[3]

Clearly, if our premise about the relationship between the demand for education and the availability of expanded employment opportunities in the modern sector is at all realistic, the interrelationships between the 'employment problem' and the 'educational system' are much more intimate than one might first suspect. Central to these relationships is the individual's perception of the close linkage between his educational attainment and his employment opportunities. Individuals may correctly view the private benefits (i.e., lifetime expected income-earning opportunities) of an education as greatly exceeding the private costs (i.e., school fees plus 'opportunity costs' of income-generating alternatives foregone while in school) so that in spite of widespread and growing unemployment among the more educated, they would continue to desire entry into and passage through the educational system. The problem arises when these 'private' benefit-cost calculations diverge substantially

---

* While it is operationally difficult to identify *ex ante* those who seek education purely for the prestige it confers, family wealth above some level might be used as a proxy for purposes of taxation.

from 'social' benefit-cost calculations—i.e., when what is good and rational from the individual's economic calculations is undesirable and irrational in terms of national resource allocation. Where private benefits exceed the private costs of education but the same calculation from a social viewpoint leads to a smaller or even negative result, there are powerful economic and political forces pressing that society to misallocate its human and financial resources to an overexpansion of the school system, exacerbating the problem of the educated unemployed.

Eventually, of course, one could conceive of unemployment rates among the educated reaching such substantial proportions that people will start to question the utility of the heavy investment of time and money in an educational process which gets increasingly stretched out and for which the tangible rewards are becoming more and more uncertain.* Being content with an eventual adjustment of this kind seems to us politically and economically unwise. We address instead the problem of identifying a less painful and more practical approach. Consider the following illustrative analysis.

We begin by assuming that the demand for an education sufficient to qualify an individual for entry into modern-sector employment opportunities is related to or determined by the combined influence of the following four variables:

1. The wage and/or income differential between jobs in the 'modern' sector (M) and those outside the modern sector (family farming, rural and urban self-employment, etc.) which for simplicity we can designate as the 'traditional' sector (T). Entry into modern-sector jobs is dependent initially on the level of completed education whereas income-earning opportunities in the traditional sector do not have any fixed educational prerequisites. If we designate W_M as the modern-sector wage and W_T as the traditional-sector wage, then the greater the modern-sector/traditional-sector income differential, $W_M - W_T$ (or, for all practical purposes, we might call this the urban-rural income differential), the greater will be the demand for education. Thus, our first relationship states that the demand for education is positively related to the urban-rural or modern-traditional wage differential. Since we know from empirical studies that these differentials can be very sizeable in most developing nations, one might reasonably expect the demand for education to be greater than it would be if differentials were smaller.

2. The *probability* of success in finding modern sector employment (P_M). Closely related to the wage differential as a variable affecting the demand for education on the income side is the probability that an individual who successfully completes the necessary schooling for entry into the modern-sector labor market *will in fact* get that high-paying urban job. Clearly, if urban or modern-sector unemployment rates among the educated are growing and/or if the supply of, say, secondary-school graduates continually exceeds the number of new job openings for which a secondary graduate can qualify, then we need to modify the 'actual' wage differential $W_M - W_T$, and instead speak about an 'expected' income differential $P_M W_M - W_T$ where P_M refers to the probability or likelihood that a school graduate will be successful in securing the high-paying modern-sector job. Since the probability of success is inversely related to the unemployment rate—i.e., the more people with appropriate qualifications who seek a particular job, the lower will be the probability that any one will be successful—we can argue that the demand for education through, say, the

---

* It is interesting to note in this context that in countries such as Tanzania, Kenya and Nigeria where school fees are sizeable and employment opportunities are stagnating empty primary-school places in significant numbers appear to be emerging for the first time. See Sabot, *op. cit.*

secondary level will be *inversely* related to the current unemployment rate among secondary school graduates.*

3. The direct private costs of education (C_1). We refer here to the current out-of-pocket expenses of financing a child's education. These expenses include school fees, books, clothing and related costs. We would expect that the demand for education would be inversely related to these direct costs—i.e., the higher the school fees and associated costs, the lower would be the private demand for education, everything else being equal.

4. The indirect or 'opportunity costs' of education (C_2). An investment in a child's education involves more than just the direct, out-of-pocket costs of that education especially when the child passes the age at which he can make a productive contribution to family income, whether in 'kind' or monetarily. For example, by proceeding on to secondary school, a graduate of primary school is in effect foregoing the income which he could expect to earn as a primary school graduate during the course of his years spent receiving a secondary education. These opportunity costs must also be included as a variable affecting the demand for education. One would expect the relationship between these opportunity costs and demand again to be inverse—i.e., the greater are the opportunity costs, the lower will be the demand for education.

Although there certainly are a number of other important variables, many of which are non-economic, including such factors as cultural traditions, social status, education of parents, and size of family which influence the demand for education, we believe that by focusing on the four variables described above, important new insights can be gained on the relationship between education and employment.

Suppose we have a situation in country X where the following conditions prevail:

(a) The modern-traditional or urban-rural wage gap, $W_M - W_T$, is of the magnitude of, say, 100 per cent for primary versus non-primary school graduates—that is, statistics show that primary-school graduates can earn starting salaries that average twice as much as a non-primary graduate can make outside the modern sector.

(b) The rate of increase of opportunities for remunerative employment for primary-school graduates is slower than the rate at which new primary graduates enter the labor force—that is, the number of primary-school leavers entering the labor market exceeds the number of jobs arising in the same period for which a primary education is the 'normal' qualification. The same may be true at the secondary level and even the university level in countries such as India, Egypt, Pakistan, and more recently, Ghana, Nigeria and Kenya.

(c) Employers, faced with an excess of applicants, tend to select by level of education since once an employer knows that there is an excess supply of more productive secondary-school leavers, he will employ them first at the going wage, even in jobs 'normally' performed by primary-school leavers, who get the residue only.

(d) Trade unions, supported by the political pressure of the educated, tend to bind the going wage to the level of educational attainment of job holders rather than to the minimum educational qualification required for the job.

(e) School fees are often very nominal or even non-existent and, in many cases, the state bears a larger portion of the student's costs at each successive level.

---

* In fact, since most expectations for the future tend to be based on a 'static' picture of the employment situation that now prevails, we might anticipate that with a worsening employment picture individuals will tend to overestimate their expected incomes and demand even more education than is justified in terms of 'correct' private calculations.

Under the above conditions, which we believe conform closely to the realities of the employment and education situation of most developing nations, one should expect that the demand for education will be exaggerated since the anticipated private benefits are so large compared to the alternative of little or no schooling and since the direct and indirect private costs are so low. However, as job opportunities for the uneducated diminish, individuals must safeguard their position by acquiring a primary education. This may suffice for a while but the internal dynamics of the employment demand/supply process leads to a situation in which job prospects for those with a primary education begin to decline. This in turn creates a demand for secondary education. But the demand for a primary education must also increase concurrently since some who were previously content with no education are now being 'squeezed' out of the labor market.

The irony is that the more unprofitable a given level of education becomes as a *terminal* point, the more demand for it increases as an *intermediate* stage or precondition to the next level of education! This puts great pressure on the government in conjunction with international donor agencies to expand educational facilities to meet the growing demand. If they cannot respond fast enough, the people may do so on their own, as evidenced, for example, by the Harambee school movement in Kenya.[4]

The upshot of all this is the chronic tendency for developing nations to expand their educational facilities at a rate which is extremely difficult to justify either socially or financially in terms of optimal human and physical capital resource allocation. Each worsening of the employment situation calls forth an increased demand for (and supply of) more education at all levels. Initially the uneducated swell the ranks of the unemployed. However, over time there is an inexorable tendency for the average educational level among the unemployed to rise as the supply of school graduates continues to exceed the demand for middle and high level manpower. The better educated must, after varying periods of unemployment during which aspirations are scaled downward, take jobs requiring lower levels of education. The diploma and degree become requirements for employment, not the education they were intended to signify.

Governments and private employers strengthen the trend by continuously upgrading formal educational entry requirements for jobs which were previously filled by those less educated; excess educational qualification becomes formalized and may resist downward adjustment. Moreover, to the extent that trade unions succeed in binding going wages to the educational attainments of job holders, the going wage for each *job* will tend to rise (even though worker productivity in that job has not significantly increased) and existing distortions in wage differentials will be magnified stimulating further the demand for education.

As a result of this 'educational displacement phenomenon,' those who for some reason are unable to continue their education will fall by the wayside as school leavers while the others continue to overqualify themselves through more years of education. In the extreme case, one gets a situation like that of contemporary India where the higher education system is in effect an 'absorber of last resort' for many who otherwise would be among the educated unemployed. The problem is that this is a terribly expensive form of unemployment compensation and, short of retaining people in school until retirement, these great masses will eventually have to emerge into a world of tight labor markets with the result that unemployment will become more visible among those highly educated and highly vocal.

Finally, it should be pointed out that many individuals tend to resist what they see as a downgrading of their job qualifications. Consequently, even though on the demand-for-labor side employers will attempt to substitute the more educated for the less educated for a given job, on the supply side there will be many job seekers whose expectations exceed the emerging realities of the labor market. They might prefer to remain unemployed for some time rather than accept a job which they feel is 'beneath' them. It follows that as a result of these 'frictional' effects and 'lags' in adjustment on the supply side, unemployment will exist at all levels of education even though it is concentrated at lower levels and, in general, is inversely related to educational attainment.

The inexorable attraction of higher and higher levels of education is even more costly than this simple picture suggests. Typically in developing countries, the social cost of education increases rapidly as we climb the educational ladder while the private costs increase more slowly or indeed may decline. This widening gap between social and private costs provides an even greater stimulus to the demand for higher education than it does for lower levels so that demand is increasingly exaggerated as higher levels are considered. But educational opportunities can be accommodated to these distorted demands only at full social cost. As demands are generated progressively through the system, the social cost of accommodation grows much more rapidly than the places provided. More and more resources must be misallocated to educational expansion and the potential for creating new jobs must diminish.

Must this scenario of the growing masses of educated unemployed be a necessary manifestation of the development process? We think not. We would argue that to a large degree the problem has been artificially created by inappropriate public and private policies with regard to wage differentials, educational selectivity, the pricing of educational services, etc. As a result, private perceptions of the value of education exceed its social value which takes account of rising unemployment.[5] As long as artificial and non-market incentives in the form of disproportionate expected benefits and subsidized costs are established which place a premium on the number of years one spends 'getting an education,' the individual will decide that it is in his best private interests to pursue a lengthy formal education process even though he may be cognizant that jobs are becoming more scarce and unemployment rates are rising. Unless the several price 'signals' are made to conform more closely to social realities, the misallocation of national resources (in this case too much education) will persist and possibly grow.

The phenomenon of a distorted wage- and price-structure misallocating human resources into superfluous years of formal education (as opposed to, say, literacy training in conjunction with the provision of minimum technical or entrepreneurial skills) is analogous to the phenomenon of factor-price distortions biasing production decisions towards more capital-intensive processes than are appropriate from the viewpoint of national resource endowments. In the latter case, policies which artificially cheapen capital goods below their intrinsic 'economic' value while causing the price of labor to rise above its market value create incentives for producers to economize on labor even though labor is the most abundant national resource and there is widespread unemployment. A social benefit-cost calculation would undoubtedly dictate that a more labor-intensive technology be utilized. But since most decisions in developing nations are still based on private rather than social calculations, the net result will be a misallocation of resources from a national point of view.

In the case of education, a proper functioning reward- and cost-structure would be one which develops and allocates human resources in accordance with the needs and opportunities in various segments of the economy. For example, the very high wage premiums paid to workers in the modern urban sector in conjunction with the lock-step process in which scarce jobs are allocated on the basis of ever increasing educational attainment leads directly to three obvious misallocations of human resources. First, the output of the educational system being greatly in excess of that which the economy can absorb, many emerge from it seeking jobs for which they may be educationally qualified but which have been pre-empted by others with even more education. They become temporarily unemployed for whatever period is necessary for their aspirations and status requirements, partly perhaps instilled in them by the educational system itself, to adjust to the stinging realities of the modern sector. 'Frictional' unemployment of this kind may in the aggregate be both substantial and growing as the numbers and durations involved increase and represents a serious waste of a nation's educated human resources. Indeed, some analysts speak of the educated unemployment problem almost exclusively as a manifestation of 'great expectations.'

Second, those who adjust their sights downward and secure modern-sector employment normally must take jobs for which they are 'overeducated' in terms of the number of years spent in the educational stream. Those who fail to get modern-sector jobs at all swell the ranks of the permanently unemployed or become self-employed in the traditional sector with little opportunity to contribute productively to the society which invested so heavily in their education. The combined effect of the overpaid and thus over-educated employed and the impoverished and unproductive educated unemployed represents, in our opinion, a serious misallocation of scarce national resources. For example, the resources spent on expanding the educational system might have been spent instead on needed public works projects providing employment opportunities to the school leavers as well as those with less education.

The third misallocation associated with the educational/high-wage bias of modern-sector employment policy relates to the built-in urban/rural distortion which this policy creates. Since almost all modern-sector jobs are in fact 'urban' jobs, since these jobs pay vastly higher wages than the rural alternatives, and since education serves as an initial screening mechanism for access to these jobs, there is a natural tendency for those with more education to migrate to the cities. Two recent studies of rural-urban migration in Kenya and Tanzania clearly showed that (1) the average income earned by an urban migrant varies directly with levels of educational attainment, (2) the probability of securing a salaried urban job is higher, the higher the level of educational achievement and, that as a result of (1) and (2), (3) the propensity to migrate to the cities varies directly with years of completed education—i.e., there was a disproportionately large percentage of urban migrants with levels of educational completion in excess of average levels for their age group in the nation as a whole.[6] The net effect of this phenomenon is the drawing away of young talent from rural areas where development needs are so great and where trained and educated manpower are in such short supply. This urban/rural middle- and high-level manpower misallocation is accentuated by the fact that much of this youthful talent is being wasted in urban areas as a result of limited employment opportunities and rising unemployment. However, as long as the wage structure continues to place such a premium on urban jobs, it will remain in the best private interests of the educated unemployed to stay in the cities in the hope of someday being successful in the 'urban job lottery' even though from a social productivity outlook their contributions might be much higher in rural areas.

Manipulating the Supply of Educational Opportunities as a Policy Variable

In the preceding section it has been assumed that the supply of educational opportunities accommodates itself to the apparent demand for them. Indeed, the rapid expansion of educational facilities at post-compulsory levels during the 1960s concomitant with the growing numbers of educated unemployed suggests that the satiation of demand was the principal objective of education even though it was not usually fully realized in practice.

We think the reasons for this pattern of governmental behavior are essentially self-evident and in the circumstances practically irresistible. Given heavily subsidized or free education on the one hand and unrealistic income differentials between the modern and traditional sectors on the other, a substantial gap between the demand for education and the supply of employment opportunities is inevitable. Manipulating the supply of educational opportunities within these limits is not likely to close the gap, though for reasons we have given its accommodation to demand is likely to widen it.

Instead the manipulation of educational supply changes the visible nature of the problem confronting governments without altering materially its basic dimensions or underlying causes. If governments opt for educational policies which seek to satisfy demand, as they apparently do, they leave for themselves at a later date the problem of rationing job opportunities in the modern sector among the many who are educationally qualified. So far this problem has seemed to be politically tractable though as the average educational level among the unemployed rises and their numbers grow, as they are almost certain to do with present policies, the size of it may overwhelm the rationing mechanism commonly employed.

That rationing mechanism is the educational system itself. Jobs in the modern sector typically are allocated to those with higher levels of educational attainment, those less fortunate educationally being relegated to the unemployed or dispatched to the fringes of the modern sector or the search for subsistence in more traditional settings. The rationing device has the appealing political merit of being apparently objective, relatively untainted by obvious favor, and patently dependent for its operation on many private as well as public decisions. But its operation does not relieve unemployment or improve the allocation of resources beyond ensuring that those most overeducated are indeed employed. So the magnitude of the problem is left to grow and the apparent fairness of the mechanism for rationing scarce jobs is unlikely to provide continuing and effective political cover for an increasingly explosive situation.

But the need to ration employment seems to be preferred in developing countries to a scarcity of school places and the consequent need to ration educational opportunities, since it is politically expedient to yield to current pressures rather than anticipate future problems. As a result, educational supply increases rapidly swelling enrollments and proliferating instructional activities. The pressures for expansion which stem directly from the burgeoning demand for education would in the extreme lead toward open formal education which undoubtedly has merits in advanced countries with full employment and incomes high enough to justify on social grounds the demand for education as a consumption good. It tends to equalize opportunities and to eliminate private and political favor as criteria for educational advancement. But the cost of such effects in poor countries with inadequate job opportunities, low incomes and essentially free education as privately perceived is enormous financially and economically, and politically as well if unemployment grows more rapidly as a consequence.

In addition to forces on the demand side which stimulate overall educational expansion there are pressures from alternative suppliers of education which lead public education to proliferate the activities for which it is responsible. Many types of specialized education and training which might more efficiently be given in or near the work place may nevertheless find their way into socially expensive vocational training schools or polytechnic colleges. The private business sector and public enterprises who might better perform these services to tailored needs may favor socially inefficient public institutions simply because a poorer quality product at zero private cost is preferable to a better one whose full costs must be borne privately. If, in addition, the public institutions overproduce, as we have argued, the misallocation of resources to public education is increased.

Does this dismal picture of growing unemployment and overblown educational systems suggest that another built upon an educational supply adjusted to employment opportunities would be substantially happier? Probably not, in the extreme, though educational overqualification for the limited jobs available should diminish and more jobs could indeed be created with the funds saved on education. So long as education remains essentially privately free and modern-sector jobs are relatively lucrative, the demand for education must be excessive. The problem of rationing severely limited educational places is an enormous one and even if it could be and were accomplished objectively the mechanism would be open to charges of favoritism. Moreover, the demands of those locked out of the educational system at every stage beyond literacy would likely be politically influential, and even if the limitation of supply was socially advantageous, investment in education would continue to be excessive.

Clearly the unsettling conditions associated with either extreme of educational supply policy when it is the only policy variable are cause for alarm. Within these extremes, however, and as compared with the educational supply policies most governments appear to be pursuing, we feel greater reluctance to expand education in response to demand is in order and would have a number of beneficial effects. Such a policy would reduce the gap between educational supply and job opportunities by reducing the former and releasing some resources for the expansion of the latter, slowing the rates of increase in the degree of overeducation for jobs and the numbers of educated unemployed. The widening of the gap between the demand for and supply of educational places would bring pressures on governments to reconsider their rationing devices and hopefully to increase the share of educational costs which must be borne privately, particularly by those seeking education at higher levels. It should be recognized, however, that giving greater weight to prospective employment opportunities in planning educational expansion can only be a partial solution since it does not come to grips with what we perceive to be the basic issue, namely, that the demand for education continues to outrun opportunities for productive employment.

There is simply no solution to the imbalance between educational demand and productive job opportunities to be found in the manipulation of educational supply alone. The pressures must build until policy attention is turned to the more fundamental issues of tempering demand to more realistic proportions and generating more modern-sector employment opportunities.

Some Policy Considerations for Governments

We have alluded at several points in this paper to the desirability of excluding from our considerations education to the level of literacy. We regard the minimum verbal and quantitative skills associated with literacy as essential for (1) informal self-learning, (2) further formal education, and (3) communication and the transmission of basic technical, economic, cultural, social and political information. It is thus a fundamental basis for national cohesion, internal mobility, family health and effective self-employment in traditional settings. The economic productivity of universal education to the level of literacy is itself persuasive justification for such a policy. We do not, however, argue that it need be free for all; indeed school fees may be a strong force influencing family size where the desire for education is strong. But we do argue that once the basic skills for communication and self-learning have been provided, formal public educational opportunities should in the circumstances of poor countries be geared more closely to the minimum educational requirements of the jobs which can be created. For such a policy to be effective it must be supported by constructive efforts to curtail excessive educational demands on the one hand and to expand productive employment opportunities on the other.

To temper the demand for education toward more realistic levels we suggest that governments of LDCs should strive to bring the private calculations of the benefits and costs associated with education closer to the social benefits and costs by:

1. Making the beneficiary (as opposed to his family or society as a whole) bear a larger and rising proportion of his educational costs as he proceeds through the system (with appropriate subsidies for the able poor at low levels of education and through loan programs at higher levels of education) as the most effective, practical means of rationing available places.

There are three principles in this recommendation. First, the share of educational costs borne privately should be substantially larger than is typically the case in developing countries today. This would have the effect of reducing the demand for education beyond literacy across the board. Second, the rate of educational subsidy should decline as an individual advances in the educational system. Thus the private demand for education would be curtailed more at higher levels where it is socially most expensive and where most of the overeducation in terms of educational requirements for jobs takes place. A policy of declining subsidies would also respond to the valid criticism that current programs involving rising subsidies are antiegalitarian and in fact represent a subsidy of the rich by the poor. Third, the private share of educational costs should, insofar as possible, fall on the beneficiary, *not* on his family or friends. It is *his* future earnings which will be increased. Ideally, he should pay for his education out of those future earnings. This suggests, of course, that private educational costs should be financed directly out of a student's own resources or indirectly through loans repaid either by financial levies against his future income or by social contributions of his expertise, such as service in rural areas. We feel that such arrangements are especially desirable and feasible at all levels of education beyond secondary. Below those levels the burden of private costs would likely continue to fall on the family in which case a system of subsidizing the able poor would be necessary.*

---

* Clearly it would be desirable to *select* students on the basis of ability and to *finance* them in accordance with the three principles discussed above. Until more appropriate tests and other criteria for selection are devised, however, the relative favoritism implicit in the above financing system (enabling some to buy educational opportunities regardless of ability) represents in our opinion an unavoidable cost of a second-best solution.

2. Reducing income differentials between the modern and traditional sectors and within the modern sector to ensure a more realistic appraisal of the prospective benefits of education.

It would carry us too far from the field of education to consider means in detail here. We only note that these means are much more extensive than direct, sharp and unrealistic cuts in modern-sector money wages and include more time-consuming processes of holding the line on average and minimum wages in the modern sector while productivity and prices adjust upward, purposive efforts to change the terms of trade between the modern and traditional sectors, and greater attention to rural as opposed to urban infrastructure needs.

3. Ensuring that minimum job specifications do not overvalue education.

Students should not be encouraged to seek levels of education which overqualify them for the jobs they can realistically expect to obtain. It is essential for that purpose that the economic system not exaggerate educational prerequisites to employment. Governments can take direct action on this matter within the civil service where a large share of modern-sector employment is to be found.[7]

4. Ensuring that wages are related to jobs and not to educational attainments.

If the other policies are effective, this becomes essentially an interim measure. So long as overeducation is increasing and those emerging from the system must accept jobs which realistically require progressively lower educational qualifications, the tendency, particularly in teaching and the civil service, to tie salaries to levels of education simply increases rates of overpayment stimulating even more students to follow the same socially misguided path.

To increase the supply of modern-sector job opportunities we suggest that governments should:

1. Reduce factor-price distortions to the extent that these enter into employment decisions in both the public and private sectors.

2. Give more careful consideration to improving rural infrastructure and to the possible location of new modern sector activities in areas where wages have not yet reached the distorted levels typical of established urban centers.

3. Allocate a larger share of development budgets to productive employment-creating activities and less to educational expansion than has been the pattern in the last decade.

This is not to say that funds spent on education do not create employment but only that some of the funds so spent in the past might have been more usefully allocated to other more productive, labor-intensive activities, including the provision of complementary resources for the productive employment of the educated. Education beyond literacy should compete for funds on these criteria, not on the notion that it is a privileged activity exempt from such considerations.

We feel that, over the next decade at least, reasonable efforts along these lines will leave a residual rationing problem in education of substantial magnitude. Dealing with this on the basis of merit rather than favor will be a continuing challenge to the governments of LDCs. We do not deal with it here.

Some Implications for International Donor Agencies

The past policies of international donor agencies with respect to educational expansion were intended to be responsive to the diverse manpower needs of developing nations. However, circumstances are changing rapidly, and donor postures should now be framed in the light of needed national policies such as those identified in the preceding section. Shortages of educated manpower are rapidly being overcome and a general extension into the future of present rates of growth in educational supply will surely produce new and hopeful school leavers greatly in excess of the new employment opportunities for which they must compete. Consequently it is now a matter of considerable importance that donor agencies re-examine their educational assistance policies. The rate of future educational expansion appropriate to realistic appraisals of manpower needs can for the most part be met out of national resources. Moreover, substantial outside support even for lower levels of education where expansion continues to be justified may simply free national educational resources for the less economically justifiable expansion of higher levels.

To the extent that LDCs can and will finance needed educational expansion of traditional kinds out of their own resources, donor agencies are given an opportunity to be more selective and innovative in their own contributions to educational development. We would give priority to the following kinds of activities.

1. Systematic and controlled pilot experimentation with educational innovations emanating from research efforts. Given the risks and costs associated with experimentation, it is unlikely that developing nations will be able or willing to bear the cost of systematic experimentation.

2. Intensified and expanded applied research, particularly in the developing countries themselves, on alternative educational and informational delivery systems appropriate to the diverse employment needs and opportunities of these nations. Special attention should be given to those opportunities outside of the modern sector, a sector towards which Western-type industrial training and higher educational systems are presently oriented.

3. Improvement and extension of educational planning as a means of incorporating labor market considerations into plans for educational expansion.

4. Selective assistance to overcome unanticipated manpower scarcities and bottlenecks.

Some Specific Suggestions for Experimentation and Research

Many past efforts in the field of education have been *replicative* in intent. Perhaps future activities should be more purposefully and constructively *innovative* in outlook. Instead of seeking to emulate the best of *known* alternatives, efforts should be increasingly directed toward identifying *new* and possibly better alternatives designed to function in the often special economic, social and cultural environments of developing countries.

Of the four important general activities identified above, we would like to comment more explicitly on two, namely, controlled experimentation with educational innovations and systematic applied research on interrelationships between education and the use of human resources. The distinction between applied research and controlled experimentation is an important one, the former focusing on our limited past experience and the latter exploring new and more appropriate alternatives. Both activities are needed but possibly greater weight should be given in the future to experimentation as a more promising way of identifying improved action programs.

Experimentation. Experiments rest on contrived experience permitting the examination of educational innovations on a small scale. To have relevance for donors and the countries they serve, such experiments must be designed to yield practical programs for future action. The following examples are intended to indicate the kinds of experiments we have in mind; many other useful ones might be devised.

1. Utilizing traditional systems for transmitting knowledge. Traditional societies, whether through the community, tribe or clan, have 'educated' children in the things they need to know. We feel that educational programs have failed to capitalize on this means of instruction, substituting instead western modes of teaching which are often remote from the local milieu. There are, however, a number of instances in which the traditional process has been effectively used to transmit modern information. For example, the delivery of modern health care in East Africa was considerably facilitated by channeling it through and associating it with the traditional system, namely the medicine man and the village midwife.

An experiment could be devised covering a number of different societies in which the feasibility of transmitting relevant educational information through traditional channels is tested by comparing the performance of experimental groups (who might otherwise remain uneducated) with that of control groups from the same societies who are being educated in the conventional school system.

2. Testing for the optimal age for literacy training. The debate on this issue continues without constructive efforts at resolution. A carefully controlled experiment could be devised in several developing countries having uneducated people in all age groups in which groups of children of various ages are exposed to essentially the same curriculum to determine how quickly each group achieves literacy. The objective is to find the age group which does so at minimum cost taking into account employment alternatives. Similar experiments could be devised on pre-vocational and vocational training.

3. Testing the effectiveness of different curricula in achieving specified objectives. How best to teach literacy? How should students be prepared for rural life? How can fundamentals of preventive health be taught? How can vocational training needs best be met? Questions such as these can be the subject of controlled experiments in which groups of students, standard in other respects, are subjected to different curricula. The results will not be immediate; perhaps we should ask how much better informed we will be in ten years time.

4. Utilizing examinations as a motivating educational force. Examinations *do* influence teaching (and teachers) and *will* be with us for years to come. Can they be devised less as a terminal test and more as a motivating and directing force? An experiment could be mounted in which teachers and their students are confronted with different examinations (carefully prepared) to determine which is most effective in stimulating desirable learning traits. Conducted in several countries, the impact of cultural differences could also be identified.

5. Training teachers. Some would argue that bad teachers can destroy any curriculum. If so, innovations in teacher training may be urgently needed and controlled experiments may test these effectively before bad ones are introduced throughout the system. Several of the experiments listed above could be applied to teachers.

6. Relating universities to practical development affairs. Universities have a potential, as yet often unrealized, for becoming involved in the development process through the introduction of more relevant training programs to equip high-level manpower with the appropriate tools for problem-solving. Unfortunately, many university curricula are carbon copies of their Western counterparts. Clearly, innovations in teaching methods and content are needed. Engineering is often a case in point. For example, an experiment with engineering curricula and another on teaching practices could be devised to assist in selecting those which turn out engineers equipped and willing to deal with the practical problems of devising technologies appropriate to labor-surplus economies.

7. Sharing Work. Traditional rural societies have typically shared work, but in most urban areas in developing countries the 40-hour work-week is standard while open unemployment grows. While not a solution to the underutilization of labor, the more systematic sharing of available work would distribute income more widely, refresh skills, and possibly reduce social and political tension. Experiments with several schemes for work-sharing could enable countries to buy time for dealing with more fundamental issues.

Applied research. Systematic applied research seeking to identify, both conceptually and quantitatively, the interrelationships between education and the economy is greatly needed. The following are possible topics for such efforts.

1. The relative performance of individuals by educational level in the non-market rural and urban economy. It is now abundantly clear that the opportunities for wage employment in the modern sector of the LDCs will be considerably limited in the coming years. The vast majority in the labor force will have to find opportunities in the non-modern, non-market rural and urban sectors of the economy. The question arises as to whether or not education beyond literacy enables an individual to be more successful than his less-educated counterpart. Scattered studies have indicated that the educated do *not* have much advantage in rural societies. Systematic, comparative cross-country research on this topic would be of considerable value in assessing the impact of conventional education on non-market performance.

2. Private vs. social benefit-cost analysis. More comparative research on the differential between social and private benefits and costs of education is essential to a better understanding of the relative payoffs to investment in education versus other activities. Emphasis here should be focused on conceptual, methodological, and quantitative aspects of 'social' benefit-cost analysis.

3. The role of the family as decision-maker in allocating human resources. Much more needs to be known about the decision-making process at the family level, especially with regard to the allocation of its human resources. On what basis are decisions reached regarding who goes to school, for how long and for what purpose? Who goes to the city to seek work? Do parents view the education of their children as 'human-capital' investment or are the cultural and psychic benefits more important? Extensive cross-national survey research on these and related questions could throw important light on the determinants of educational demand, a topic which has been scarcely explored.

4. The impact of wage differentials (by education, rural-urban, modern-traditional, etc.), factor-price distortions, and the educational displacement phenomenon on the demand for secondary and higher education. Since we have discussed the above issues at length in our paper, there is no need to elaborate here other than to say that more quantitative information is needed to assess the relative 'real-world' importance of these factors on both the social demand for education and the aggregate supply of employment opportunities.

The extent to which the various international aid agencies can associate themselves with these kinds of activities will undoubtedly vary but we feel that they merit serious consideration.

Notes

1. For the most up-to-date review of cross-country data on unemployment and underemployment rates in LDCs, see D. Turnham and I. Jaeger, *The Employment Problem in Less Developed Countries: A Review of Evidence* (Paris, O.E.C.D. Development Centre, 1971).

2. Skepticism of this approach was expressed a decade ago in T. Balogh and P.P. Streeten, "The Coefficient of Ignorance," *Bulletin of the Oxford University Institute of Statistics,* 25, 2 (May, 1963), pp. 97-107, reprinted in M. Blaug, *Economics of Education I* (Baltimore, Penguin Books, Inc., 1968).

3. For discussion of selectivity by education in Africa, see A.J.M. van de Laar, *Education and Employment in Anglophone Africa,* Occasional Paper No. 10 (The Hague, Institute of Social Studies, March, 1971); R.H. Sabot, "Education, Income Distribution, and the School Leaver Problem in Tanzania," Economic Research Bureau, University of Dar es Salaam (March, 1972) mimeo; and P. Kinyanjui, "The Education, Training and Unemployment of Kenya Secondary School Leavers," Institute of Development Studies, University of Nairobi (May, 1971) mimeo.

4. For a more detailed discussion of this phenomenon see Gary S. Fields, "Private and Social Returns to Education in Labour Surplus Economies," Discussion Paper 104, Institute of Development Studies, University of Nairobi (April, 1971) mimeo; and Emil Rado, "The Explosive Model," Conference on Urban Unemployment in Africa, University of Sussex (September, 1971) mimeo.

5. For an interesting attempt to incorporate employment opportunities into estimates of rates of return to various levels of education, see Martin Carnoy and Hans Thias, "Educational Planning with Flexible Wages: A Kenyan Example," *Economic Development and Cultural Change,* 20, 3 (April, 1972), pp. 438-73.

6. M.P. Todaro, "Education and Rural-Urban Migration: Theoretical Constructs and Empirical Evidence from Kenya," Conference on Urban Unemployment in Africa, University of Sussex (September, 1971) mimeo; and R. Sabot, *op. cit.*

7. The recently published I.L.O. mission report on employment problems in Ceylon contains a number of interesting and innovative suggestions for avoiding tendencies towards excessive education by, in effect, prohibiting certain categories of students from proceeding beyond a given level of education. *Matching Employment Opportunities and Expectations: A Programme of Action for Ceylon* (Geneva, I.L.O., November, 1971).

Employment Effects of Foreign Direct Investments in Developing Countries*

Constantine V. Vaitsos
Secretariat of the Andean Common Market

Introduction

The high level of open and disguised unemployment in the Third World has been singled out as one of the main and chronic symptoms as well as causes of underdevelopment. Efforts to reduce unemployment and thus induce development relate not only to economic objectives but also to the promotion of social justice. The latter, involving among other elements a more equitable distribution of benefits, becomes also a means of achieving economic objectives since some of the key causes of unemployment are structural where growth is necessary but not sufficient to assure a sustained and equitable advancement of a society.

Foreign direct investments have been heralded as one of the major contributors not only to growth but also to development since they promote the direct and rapid introduction of an economy to the technological, managerial, capital, and other overheads of the world, alleviating some of the economic constraints that characterize underdevelopment. They have also been presented as major vehicles for entering the international market through their diverse channels and marketing outlets and thus offering the advantages that accrue from trade cum specialization. In the pages that follow, by evaluating past and present performance of foreign investors and the overall impact they have had on developing countries, we are led to question and raise serious doubts about the extent and type of employment effects that they create in their host economies.

In our analysis we need to distinguish the foreignness in the ownership and control of an enterprise. That is, one needs to ask how national firms would have acted if their decision making originated and their remuneration accrued within a particular country. One also needs to ask what would have been the results in the absence of foreign investments, in other words, what is the opportunity cost of such investments for their host developing countries. At another level of generalization there is need to explore the type of developmental effects that are generated from the characteristics of foreign investments if the latter are promoted by large transnational enterprises. Such firms do not only provide capital and enjoy control through ownership but also supply products, technology and other resources and promote specific economic as well as social or political structures to assure and advance their multiple objectives within oligopolistic markets. In this case the analysis does not rest only on the foreignness of firms but more so on the type of economic and overall organizational framework to

* This paper will also be published in C.V. Vaitsos, ed., *Tecnología para el Desarrollo* (Mexico, Fondo de Cultura Económica, forthcoming).

331

which they belong or which they represent. Nationally owned firms depending for their non-equity capital inputs on foreign sources which induce and constrain different forms of business behavior and producing similar goods and services need not have operated in a significantly different form from foreign subsidiaries.

Our conclusions need to draw distinctions and will themselves differ between foreign direct investments in the extractive versus the manufacturing sectors, between different industries in the manufacturing sector as well as between countries with different economic development or introducing activities of varying degrees of novelty for their economies. Two important omissions of the paper need to be mentioned: first, we did not explore the employment effect of foreign investors in the service sector and second, we did not deal with the influence of foreign firms on the evolution of organized labor in developing countries and the impact that this had on employment.

The analysis will be separated into four broad areas which in turn affect employment generation. They are the following:[1]

1. The effects of foreign resource availability.
2. The direct income effects and their composition.
3. The factor allocation (including factor displacement) effects.
4. The consumption structure and domestic demand effects.

The Effects of Foreign Resource Availability

Foreign investors provide resources which can meet some macro-economic needs of the host country (i.e., saving and foreign exchange) as well as micro-economic requirements (i.e., risk capital, technology including management know-how, marketing opportunities, etc.). The change in the availability of savings and foreign exchange as a result of foreign direct investments can be seen at four levels of increasing generalization.

First, they relate to the direct foreign capital contribution.

Second, they can be evaluated on the basis of their net effect after discounting future payments of dividends, royalties, interest, etc., (i.e., financial flow analysis).

Third, the import substituting and export promoting activities of foreign activities can be added to the analysis of financial flows, so as to obtain the *total direct* effects of foreign investments on resource availability.

Finally, and more correctly, one can incorporate three additional elements of analysis: (a) the possibility (or its absence) of undertaking the same or similar activities through ownership and production structures distinct from those of the existing foreign direct investment, (b) the inclusion of the indirect effects on income, consumption, import, etc., that are induced by the operations of foreign investments, and (c) the usage of local scarce resources by foreign investors thus foregoing income and balance of payments contributions elsewhere. In this form one can evaluate the *full effects* of foreign direct investments.

As far as the direct capital contribution is concerned important differences exist between the extractive and manufacturing sectors. In the former, critical contributions have been made by foreign investors whose capital requirements often exceed the savings potential of many developing countries, at least during certain periods of their economic history. For example, in the petroleum industry from the total gross investment in production activities in developing countries reported in 1964, the hosts contributed about 21% (U.S.$2.8 bil.) of the total while the rest was invested by foreign affiliates. The corresponding host country's contribution in oil refineries was 25.5% (U.S.$1.2 bil.) and in piplines 21.5%.[2] The size of foreign contributions, though, as reported in present statistics can be greatly distorted due to various accounting practices, among the most important of which is the effect on net worth of the revalorization of existing assets particularly in anticipation or during negotiations of terms with the host governments.* Also, the capitalization of intangibles or of secondhand machinery sold to subsidiaries under transfer pricing by parents can significantly inflate the corresponding financial contribution.

In the manufacturing sector the investment requirements per project are, on the average, smaller than in the extractive industries. Furthermore, the foreign contribution often amounts to a very small proportion of the total funds used by foreign subsidiaries in the host developing countries.** Even if one accounts for reinvested profits, the local contributions, basically commercial and banking credit, account for most of the funds used. The usage of scarce local capital resources in foreign manufacturing subsidiaries has become a critical element in the evaluation of their overall effects on the host economies.*** Ongoing research in some Latin American countries has indicated that foreign subsidiaries absorb about 50%-70% of the banking credit with corresponding displacement effects for local firms particularly small and medium size ones.[6] On the average, the latter are noted for their comparatively higher labor utilization.

At the macro-level the foreign contribution to capital formation is, often, very small. For example, in the 1961-1969 period foreign direct investments accounted for only 4%-5% of the total investment in Latin America.[7] Such figures are in sharp contrast to earlier economic history such as in Argentina where, before the First World War, foreign investment accounted for 50% of the then existing capital.[8]

As far as the direct balance of payments or other resources effects of foreign investment over a period of time, sound measurements should include not only registered capital inflows (investments) and outflows (profits and interest remittances) but also the net effect on export promotion and import substitution. These direct effects often show a positive balance of payments outcome.[9] This is particularly so in the extractive sector. Yet, in many cases the net capital flows calculations approach (i.e., financial analysis) constitutes a correct method of estimation for the following reasons: (a) Quite often in the manufacturing sector foreign direct investments take the form of an acquisition of already existing local firms without significantly changing their activities.[10] (b) Some of the activities pursued by foreign subsidiaries could have been pursued under different ownership structures (i.e., licensing agreements). In such cases, the export promoting and/or import substituting activities of the foreign subsidiaries are not specific or are not tied to the presence of foreign investors but were or could have been achieved under different ownership and

---

* For example, in 1964 Kennecott Co. negotiated with the Chilean government the reassessment of the book value of the El Teniente property from $69 mil. to $286 mil. as one of the conditions for accepting a 51% participation by the Chilean government in the ownership but not in the management of that particular mine.[3]

** For example, of the total of $959 mil. that was used to finance the activities of the U.S. manufacturing subsidiaries in Latin America in 1968 only 12.5% originated from the U.S. in all forms including affiliate, commercial and public loans and grants.[4]

***In a study involving 159 subsidiaries in Asia, Africa and South America local borrowing by foreign manufacturing subsidiaries proved to be "an extremely important element of the welfare analysis of foreign investments."[5]

production structures.[11] The use of such alternative hypotheses often shows that foreign direct investments in the manufacturing sector of developing countries have negative balance of payments or income effects due to the future payments abroad of returns to the foreign equity owners.

The first comprehensive study to measure the full effects of foreign subsidiaries (including indirect effects and the opportunity cost of scarce local resources) has been completed by UNCTAD in a study of 159 firms in six developing countries. Using the Little/Mirrlees project evaluation methodology,[12] it was concluded that ". . . on a fairly reasonable set of assumptions nearly 40% of the firms in the six countries taken together have negative effects on social income."[13] Another 30% of the firms studied indicated that the full social, rather than private, positive income generated for the host economy amounted to less than 10% of their sales.[14]

The net contribution on employment of foreign originated or created resources will thus depend on their size and direct utilization, the degree of promoting complementary or displacing competitive domestic activities* and the opportunity costs of such resources for the host economy. We pass now to discuss some of the direct implications of foreign investments on employment with particular reference to the composition of the income effects and the impact of the technology used.

The Direct Income Effects and their Composition

The resources made available by foreign investors imply direct income gains for the host countries in terms of government tax revenues, returns to labor and other domestic factors of production, and possible lower prices paid by the local consumers. From the national point of view such income effects mean additional gains if they result from enhanced and efficient activities; otherwise they include income redistribution effects.

Government Revenues

In the extractive industries by far the most important direct income gain of the host countries has been through government revenues. Such revenues often amount to 70%, 80% or more of the total host government receipts.** Government revenues by such exporting countries are high in absolute and relative terms. For example, in 1967, the revenues from oil for the Middle Eastern, Libyan and Venezuelan governments amounted to U.S.$4,719 mil. representing around 50% of their oil exports.[16] Yet, such figures are of limited usefulness unless compared to some other standard. For example, the principal oil producing countries before the Teheran negotiations of 1971 earned in terms of royalties and taxes something around $1 per barrel of refined oil. On the other hand, tax collectors in Western Europe (the oil importing countries) averaged about $3.50 out of each barrel. The same barrel of oil was selling in Europe for about $8.00.[17]

Developing countries are becoming increasingly aware of the possibilities and use of bargaining power in enhancing their revenues (particularly government receipts) in the extractive industries as demonstrated by the successful negotiations of OPEC in

---

* Foreign firms provide capital but in so doing might reduce domestic savings if the latter are a function of investment opportunities and foreign activities pre-empt national ones.

** It should be remembered, though, that "roughly 90% of the exports of petroleum and minerals are accounted for by countries representing less than one-fourth of the population of the developing world."[15]

the 1960s and 70s.* The study and application of bargaining power is a key element in the foreign investment model where bilateral monopoly situations often arise.**

In the manufacturing sector income tax earnings by the host developing countries are comparatively small since in various cases foreign investors have been shown to underdeclare their true profitability.[18] By remitting accrued profits through other channels (such as royalties, transfer pricing on intermediates, interest payments on interaffiliate debt, fees for overhead allocations, etc.), they are achieving considerable tax avoidance in the host countries. Recent sample studies indicate that in several manufacturing activities the rate of effective return of foreign investments in Latin America averages about 40%[19] as contrasted to the declared rate of about 12%.[20]

Whatever the size of host government earnings from the activities of foreign firms, the induced effects on employment will depend on the usage of such funds which in turn depends on the composition, type of representation and orientation of the host governments. The latter are influenced in their performance and sometimes even depend for their sheer existence on, among other factors, the presence of foreign investors in their countries as well as on the pressures that might be exerted by the governments of the home countries of the foreign affiliates.

Payments to Local Factors of Production

Extractive industry. As far as direct employment effects are concerned technological requirements in the extractive industry generally imply a very high capital intensity. Technological development has been input saving over time and particularly labor saving, rendering older processes technically inefficient.*** For example, in large scale copper mining in Chile the capital-labor ratio in 1950 was $117,500 and it has been steadily rising to reach $187,800 in 1960.[22] (In other words, the equivalent of one million dollars of investment was needed at that time to create directly, less than six jobs). The capital intensity in such cases does not depend on the foreignness (in the ownership) of the project. National enterprises have to choose similar techniques if they need to compete internationally. Nevertheless, factor utilization in certain parts of production depends on the scale of operations,† yet this also affects the international competitiveness of the industry.

---

* Over longer periods of time important gains have been obtained by copper producing countries. For example in Chile the Braden Company was paying taxes that amounted to less than 1% of gross sales value over the period 1913-24. The corresponding figure was less than 6% for 1930-39 and it reached 64% in 1953. (Data from research undertaken by M. Mamalakis in Chile.)

** In addition to market structure, important cost structure considerations are involved in making bargaining a key element in the distribution of gains. For example, M.A. Adelman has estimated that the cost of producing-developing Middle East oil amount to US ¢ 20 per barrel (including a 20% return on capital). This cost was about one-tenth of the open market price of crude oil in 1968.

***In the diagram, A denotes the combination of capital (K) and labor (L) for the production of a certain output using "older" technology, while B represents the equivalent case for the same output after the introduction of new know-how. Technique A, lying to the northeast of B in the diagram is technically inefficient since it uses more of *both* capital and labor. In relative terms the capital labor ratio in A is smaller than that of B.[21]

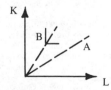

† During the period 1943-1954 although large scale mining was characterized by continuous labor displacement, labor absorption by the medium and small-scale mining "was close to spectacular as the government proceeded to promote and subsidize the Chilean-owned mining operations."[23] Yet, this applied to only parts of the industry since the extracted ore had still to be processed by capital intensive, large scale plants.

Technological change in large-scale extractive activities has resulted, even under expanding output, in progressive reduction of labor opportunities in the producing countries. In Chilean large-scale copper mining, employment was reduced from 24,777 in 1943 to 14,320 in 1954, or by about 42%.[24] Similarly in Venezuela, under conditions of increasing output, man hours of work declined in the petroleum industry from 110 mil. in 1950 to 64 mil. in 1964.[25] Despite the importance that the foreign petroleum industry has had for the Venezuelan economy (accounting in the 1960s for about 90% of the country's exports, 64% of fiscal earnings and 96% of the total investment in that industry), it provided only 1% of the country's employment.[26] In Chile, Argentina, Brazil and Mexico the labor directly employed in the combined mining and petroleum sectors accounted for 4.1%, 0.6%, 2.5% and 1.2% respectively of the economically active population in 1960.[27]

The small employment opportunities in the extractive industries are partly offset (in terms of labor income effects) by the relatively high wages paid in such sectors compared to the wage structures in the rest of the economy.* The differentials in the wage structure compensate, in a way, for the conditions of hardship and remoteness from urban centers that generally characterize the extractive industry. Nevertheless, they also create a labor aristocracy within a small part of the working class with repercussions on the economic and political fiber of the producing countries.

Import substituting activities in manufacturing. Affiliates of transnational enterprises concentrate their operations and dominate the manufacturing, import substituting industries of developing countries in areas which are generally characterized by relatively high capital intensity, yet not as high as in the extractive sector. The types of products in which such firms specialize and their scale requirements, given small internal markets and limited export activities,** imply relatively small direct employment generation. It can be inferred from available data that in the 1960s U.S. affiliates in the Latin American manufacturing industry required an investment in terms of their total assets per unit of labor employed that ranged between $35,500-$51,500.***

Compared with the rest of the manufacturing sector foreign direct investments in the developing countries provide less direct labor utilization per unit of capital

---

* In 1964 Chilean copper mine workers were earning 2.7 times as much as construction workers and 2.5 times the salary of workers in manufacturing. Similar figures existed for office personnel. Differences exist in the earnings of the Venezuelan working class but not as high as the ones noted for Chile. In the former country despite increases that almost doubled the average remuneration of workers in the petroleum industry between 1957 and 1964, the total wage bill remained constant in view of continuous labor displacements.[28]

According to studies by the OECD about 90% of the production of foreign owned firms in the manufacturing sector in developing countries was for internal sale in the host economy during the 1960s.[29]

***For the 1957-66 period employment increased in U.S. manufacturing subsidiaries by 156,000 in Latin America. During the 1959-68 decade, for which figures are available, U.S. direct investments increased by $2,679 mil. If we use a 2:1 to 3:1 relationship between local borrowing and direct investment the total investment will amount to something between $5,358 mil. and $8,037 mil. Taking the two decades as equivalent this gives a total investment-labor ratio of $35,500-51,500. The use of total assets per unit of labor rather than fixed assets presents both advantages and disadvantages as an indicator of capital intensity. The problems of measuring fixed capital which has been depreciated during previous years could be overcome if depreciation deductions are offset through the corresponding increase in other items of the balance sheet. Furthermore, total assets reflect the total foregone capital for a country for undertaking a particular activity given the availability of the same resources otherwise. Yet, total assets introduce non-technological elements such as the effect of the host government's import policies on inventory requirements, etc. The above figures were deduced from data provided by the U.S. Department of Commerce, periodic issues of *Survey of Current Business*.

committed.* For example, in Colombia for the whole manufacturing sector (including national and foreign firms) the amount of electric energy consumed per unit of labor employed increased by a factor of 1.5 between 1960 and 1967.** Yet, the industries where foreign subsidiaries concentrated indicate a much higher increase than the sector average. Energy consumption per unit of labor employed increased by a factor of 2.7 in chemical and pharmaceutical products, by 3.3 in machinery and electrical goods and by 3.7 in rubber products during the same period.[31] As noted above the basic reasons for such capital intensity rest on the type of products selected for the activities of foreign owned affiliates as well as their scale requirements.

With respect to factor utilization and substitutability, given cost differentials in developing countries as compared to the rest of the world, it has been noted that product differentiation through brand names and advertising often characterizes capital intensive production structures without significant cost inducements on factor substitution. On the contrary, quality requirements to preserve product homogeneity and identification with brand names leads to capital intensive preferences.*** Such products are characteristic of the activities of foreign manufacturing affiliates. If, though, the price elasticity of demand of a product is high, cost considerations and factor selection become more important if technological opportunities are available.[33] Even in these cases, though, the technologies selected tend to be more capital intensive than the simple cost minimization approach would have implied given multiple objectives pursued by firms and by their decision makers (i.e., organizational preferences to reduce management of larger labor force and engineering preferences to select "modern" and more "sophisticated" techniques which tend to be capital intensive.[34]

More detailed analyses have drawn a distinction between core productive activities of foreign subsidiaries related to the basic processes used and ancillary or peripheral activities such as material handling, loading and unloading as well as transport within plants, machine set-up, etc.[35] In the former case (e.g., core activities) foreign subsidiaries use basically the same capital intensive processes that characterize their production in the home countries.[36] A few exceptions exist† yet, basically minimal or no attempt is made to adapt basic processes to meet factor availability in the host developing countries.[38]

Nevertheless, in their ancillary activities foreign affiliates have been noted for changing relative factor absorption. Higher labor utilization has been experienced in such peripheral activities in comparison to practices followed in the home country plants.[39] Interestingly enough, similar higher labor utilization has been noted in some cases for foreign affiliates in ancillary activities as compared to nationally owned firms.[40] Such comparisons relate to the same product lines even if for the overall

---

* Research undertaken in Kenya by Charles Cooper reached the same conclusion noting, also, important differences on capital utilization between different industries within the manufacturing sector. For example, rough estimates on the initial cost of fixed assets per worker in Kenya were reported as follows:[30] textiles—£850-£950; can making—£2,500; cord, twine, bags—£500; tires—£23,000; assembly industries—£900.

** Energy consumption stands as a proxy for capital used rather than capital committed due to the very high excess capacity characterizing Latin American industry.

***Quality considerations assured through capital intensity become important if part of the locally produced output is directed towards exports in such differentiated products.[32]

† Some attempts have been made for scaling down production as well as for product redesign in the automotive industry as in the case of the production of a new car to meet conditions in South East Asia by Ford and General Motors.[37]

average in the manufacturing sector national firms are more labor intensive for the reasons presented in previous pages. Five explanations have been given for the higher labor absorption by foreign owned over national enterprises: (a) foreign owned firms have higher managerial skills to enable them to pursue better organizational and cost reducing operations;* (b) the financial superiority and overall resource availability of foreign firms enable them to attract scarce skilled supervisory staff (i.e., foremen) and thus use more labor intensive ancillary activities;[42] (c) foreign subsidiaries have a larger share of domestic markets and through the resulting better capacity utilization (i.e., introducing a second shift) they can increase their labor-capital ratio in their overall activities; (d) the knowledge by national firms on available technological options might be more limited and thus they could be more susceptible to pressures from equipment manufacturers; (e) foreign firms are under stronger pressures to prove their good "citizenship" and thus use relatively more local labor as a public relations gesture.

The possibilities of enhancing labor utilization when scale increases might be limited, even in the case of ancillary activities, due to output quality and organizational constraints. Thus, larger output might imply not only relative but also absolute reductions in labor utilization.[43] Such labor displacement can take place as scale of production increases regardless of the level of wages.[44]

Technological change in manufacturing industry, which is introduced in developing countries in import substituting activities, tends to be either input saving, and particularly labor saving (as in the extractive sector), or capital using and labor saving. Such a structure is the combined result of technological development which is capital biased in existing products as well as due to the introduction of new products that are capital intensive and which are promoted by transnational enterprises to maintain or enhance their share in world consumption. In the textile industry for example the total (not just fixed) captial-labor ratio has been growing as follows.

1950 (U.S.A.)	$ 8,700[45]	1960 (Brazil)	$12,700[47]
1950 (Colombia)	$ 6,200[46]	Middle 1960s	$20,000[48]

When Brazil introduced in 1961 new textile equipment in nine states of the federation it was estimated that 30% of the working force was displaced.

The relatively low government tax earnings and low labor utilization in the areas where foreign manufacturing investments take place in import substituting activities in developing countries, coupled with subsidized local capital costs, have led to a rather low contribution of such investments on reported, private, direct income effects for the host economies measured in local factor and product prices. For example, in 1966 the existing U.S. investments in manufacturing had a local direct income effect for the whole of Latin America which amounted to only about 2% of the countries' GNP. (The figure does not include the income generation effects resulting from purchases of goods or services from the local economies.)**

---

* Research in the Philippines found that foreign firms had a higher proportion of executive skilled to unskilled workers in their total work force than national firms.[41]

** In 1966 total sales of U.S. manufacturing subsidiaries amounted to a figure of about 7% of the aggregate GNP of all countries of the region. For these sales about 60% implied purchases of goods and services, 8.6% amounted to remitted profits, and additional percentage points included payments to foreign personnel and other fees remitted abroad. Thus, less than 30% of the sales value resulted in direct income effects leading to an equivalent of about 2% (7% multiplied by less than 30%) of the aggregate GNP. (Deduced from data collected by the U.S. Department of Commerce that appeared in H. May, *op. cit.*)

These income effects do not obviously imply net income gains for the host countries if goods and services are valued at international equivalents. They could imply income redistribution rather than income generation effects and in some cases they could include net income losses for the host countries given present levels of effective protection.*

Export promoting activities in manufacturing. In the latter part of the 1960s a new phenomenon began to be felt in the process of international investment and international trade of particular interest to developing countries. Vertically integrated transnational enterprises intensified their world-wide sourcing of cheap inputs locating part of their production activities in areas where the cost of local factors of production was (significantly) lower than in other parts of their world-wide activities.[50] In terms of trade this phenomenon dramatically increased the exchange of goods and services across national boundaries in certain parts of the international production structure, especially the inter-affiliate trade.** With respect to international investment theory this phenomenon raises serious questions about, and may even make obsolete, models that interpret the international location of production of transnational firms on the basis of different stages over time, like the product cycle theory.

For various developing countries like South Korea, Mexico, Pakistan, Brazil (in the 1970s), Taiwan, Indonesia, Hong Kong, etc., the export drive in manufacturing products reached significant levels in the late 1960s and early 1970s.[52] For countries like South Korea manufacturing exports presently account for 60% of their total export bill.[53] The net balance of payments and income effects, though, have to be seen in the light of the high import content of such exports and the transfer pricing policies of transnational firms in view of the high inter-affiliate trade flows. For these two reasons it has been claimed that the phenomenon observed really represents ''an illusion of trade.''[54]

In the earlier sections of the paper emphasis was placed on the high capital intensity of the activities of transnational enterprises in their import substituting and extractive activities in the LDC's. In the case of exports of processed goods, such firms develop to be important suppliers of unskilled-labor-intensive know-how. For example, the average fixed capital necessary for each unit of labor in the Taiwan export processing zone in Kaohsiung is about $1,500.[55]

Such a structure raises further issues on the repercussions of foreign firms in developing countries since the former still control the ownership, management, the marketing and technology used. They, in turn, pursue activities related to, what has been called, ''shallow development'' in the host developing economies (see below for reasons). Furthermore, such firms through their transfer pricing can separate the causes concerning the *location* of production (based on comparative production cost structures) from those related to the *values* or prices registered for the goods that are traded and produced. The latter are affected by tariff levels, absolute and relative tax differentials, political considerations on profit declarations, and government pressures on balance of payments and income effects.

---

* Research undertaken in Colombia in the pharmaceutical sector indicated that, in more than 40% of that industry, for every dollar earned by the local economy more than one dollar and a half was remitted as income through various channels by the foreign investors.[49]

** For example, Items 806.30 and 807.00 of the U.S. Tariff Schedule (for which tariffs are paid on the foreign value added for goods that originated from the U.S. rather than on the total value of the imports) indicated an increase from $953 mil. in 1966 to $1,842 mil. in 1969. The share of developing countries in such imports jumped from 7% to 22% during the same period with a sixfold increase in absolute terms.[51]

TABLE 1

AVERAGE HOURLY EARNINGS OF WORKERS PROCESSING OR ASSEMBLING
U.S. MATERIALS OVERSEAS AND IN THE UNITED STATES

	Average hourly earnings abroad (dollars)	Average hourly U.S. earnings (dollars)	Ratio of U.S. earnings to earnings abroad
Consumer electronic products			
Hong Kong	0.27	3.12	11.8
Mexico	0.53	2.31	4.4
Taiwan	0.14	2.56	18.2
Office machine parts			
Hong Kong	0.30	2.92	9.7
Mexico	0.48	2.97	6.2
Korea	0.28	2.78	10.1
Singapore	0.29	3.36	11.6
Taiwan	0.38	3.67	9.8
Semiconductors			
Hong Kong	0.28	2.84	10.3
Jamaica	0.30	2.23	7.4
Mexico	0.61	2.56	4.2
Netherlands Antilles	0.72	3.33	4.6
Korea	0.33	3.32	10.2
Singapore	0.29	3.36	11.6
Wearing Apparel			
British Honduras	0.28	2.11	7.5
Costa Rica	0.34	2.28	6.7
Honduras	0.45	2.27	5.0
Mexico	0.53	2.29	4.3
Trinidad	0.40	2.49	6.3

SOURCE: United States Tariff Commission, *Economic Factors Affecting the Use of Items 807.00 and 806.30 of the Tariff Schedules of the United States* (Washington, 1970) as cited by Helleiner (see note 50), p.45.

The basic attraction offered by developing countries to such export activities by transnational firms is obviously due to the very low wages of unskilled labor in such countries given minimum productivity rates. Table 1 presents some international comparisons on wage differentials (including supplementary compensation) for comparable job classifications.[56]

The development of this type of international sourcing by transnational firms has important repercussions for developing countries. Their comparative advantage in this case rests in specializing in unskilled labor whose wages have to stay comparatively low while importing a package of inputs (both physical and intangibles) from abroad.[57] Since skills and technology, capital, components and other goods are mobile internationally while unskilled labor is not (or is preferred not be be, due to the heavy social costs involved) transnational firms will be induced to intensify such international sourcing, diversifying their sources of unskilled labor among different developing countries to assure a continuous availability of supply, or the products of that input. It has also been suggested that since "the surplus of the product of labor over wage, resulting from the cooperation of other factors of production, accrues abroad, . . . the situation is equivalent to one in which *labor itself* rather than the *product of labor is exported*."[58]

The "shallowness" of such a development process is a result of the following reasons. The type of labor utilized represents generally the weakest and less organized part of the labor class, thus limiting possibilities for increasing labor returns unless a general shortage of labor takes place in the country, in which case opportunity cost considerations arise for the host economy. If wages increase foreign investors will tend to shift to other countries since their locational interests stem from the existence of low wages given some minimum productivity levels. The training necessary for local labor in such activities is generally very small, limiting spill-over effects.* Of critical importance is the absence of marketing knowhow effects for the host country since the goods traded are within the captive markets of affiliates. Final product promotion is handled abroad by the foreign centers of decision making.

The concentration on low wage, unskilled-labor-intensive, export promoting activities has been compared to the older enclave structures in the extractive industry. The basic difference between them, though, is that in the former the foreign investor is not very much captive once he has committed his activities in a country since the investment is very low, the shifting of activities to other nations is easy to undertake since there is no uniqueness in the local supply of inputs and the tapping of local resources did not imply the expensive discovery of previously unknown resources (as in the extractive sector). Thus, the possibility of enhancing the bargaining power of the host government to share in a more equitable distribution of the surplus involved is minimal or non-existent.

The Factor Allocation (Including Factor Displacement) Effects

The manner by which resources are being allocated and utilized influence both the size and the type of employment opportunities. The following pages discuss some of the effects of foreign investments on factor allocation and their implications on employment opportunities.

First, we refer to the creation of human capital. Foreign investors often undertake diverse training programs for their employees or even their product and service suppliers so as to improve the profitability of their investments. Such activities of on- or off-the job training improve the host country's human capital and advance the local capabilities to absorb foreign originated knowhow.

Yet, foreign investors have some important technology-retarding effects on the host country to the extent that they imply turn-key type investments. In addition to process technology or basic engineering, which characterizes the particular productive activity involved, foreign firms generally supply a series of other technical skills which are not industry specific but task specific. Such additional technological inputs include detail engineering, product design, feasibility studies, some equipment specifications and routine plant lay-out requirements, electric, civil and soil engineering, etc.

All this industry non-specific, yet task specific, knowhow is of generally limited exclusivity and in most cases implies no proprietary rights such as patents. Furthermore, once developed by undertaking a specific task in an industry they can be used in similar activities in the same or other industries with potentially significant multiplier effects in an economy. A host country by not developing many of these human resource elements, since they are supplied in a package form by the foreign investors, is foregoing opportunities not just in the particular activity for which they are

---

* It has been estimated that most of the employees working in foreign subsidiaries in the electronics industry in Southeast Asia have an on-the-job training of less than two months. (Unpublished work undertaken in Southeast Asia by Galo Cascante for the Andean Common Market). In some cases though (automotive parts, telecommunications equipment, certain types of electrical equipment and machinery) the training and resulting spill-over effects are much more important. Nevertheless, the basic technology used and the overall specifications are embodied in the imported components.

imported (where, after all, they are provided by the foreign firms) but in other productive activities. This can significantly affect the skill differentiation of a country and thus seriously limit its growth potential from local efforts. This in turn affects direct and indirect employment generation.

In the case, for example, of the Chilean copper mining sector, foreign firms generally undertook very minimal engineering activities with local consulting firms, limiting such activities to elementary tasks such as building housing camps for the miners. Yet, at the same time through the needs and policies of nationally owned firms (particularly through firms owned by the national development corporation CORFO), Chile demonstrated its ability to develop a quite competent and efficient engineering and overall consulting human resource. Quite often the usage or promotion of local technological capabilities is one of the toughest elements of negotiation with foreign investors. The latter claim lack of confidence in local skills. Yet, in so doing they restrict information and limit outsiders' training in their own activities. Such a process perpetuates the technological dependence of the host countries.[59]

In the case of Japan, local engineering capacitation in the design of oil refineries in the late 1950s proved to be critical in the development of the design of the petrochemical plants in the early 1960s. It was also basic for the particular form that the Japanese undertook in their negotiations on the importation of technology in a manner that further disaggregated the technological components in the petrochemical industry. This, in turn, promoted the advancement of additional human capital. Such cumulative or re-enforcing mechanisms of factor development were instrumental in the middle and late 1960s in adapting even process knowhow. The latter enabled the Japanese firms, together with several other governmental and business policies, to undertake export promotion, thus enhancing employment, through the partial independence from the restrictive business practices imposed by the foreign technology suppliers in the initial licensing contracts.[60]

In the petrochemicals industry, a case was studied in the Andean Pact in a large multinational, multiplan project. The payments for the technology component of this project exceeded U.S.$100 mil. Of these about 50% will go for industry non-specific direct skilled labor utilization that could to a great extent be found or developed locally. Since the other 50% covers rents for monopoly privileges, such as proprietory rights in patents, employment utilization opportunities are concentrated in the first half of the payments.[61]

Developed countries have used an infant industry strategy to advance such task-specific, yet industry non-specific, capabilities particularly through the purchasing power of the state at home and the conditions imposed by national and multinational financial institutions on the usage of capital in the rest of the world.

An area where important factor displacement exists in foreign direct investments in manufacturing activities relates to the manner of entry of such firms in their host countries. The rapid expansion and proliferation of foreign subsidiaries in many developing countries in the 1960s was undertaken to a large extent through the acquisition of existing nationally owned firms. Such acquisitions quite often did not imply an expansion or change of the activities of the acquired firms.[62] Data available on U.S.-owned manufacturing subsidiaries that established themselves in Peru and Colombia between 1958 and 1967 indicated that about one out of every three entered by acquiring existing firms.[63]

The implications of displacement effects on local entrepreneurs and the resulting reduction of locally induced activities are perhaps of greater importance than the often resulting monopoly effects of the entrance by acquisition. Local human capital is, thus, reduced to simple administrative and low management decisions while technological development is concentrated in the home country of the transnational enterprises. As a result employment opportunities stemming from future growth and expansion in new products and markets, export promotion, choice of technology, etc. are conditioned by the global interests of the foreign firms, operating in an oligopoly relation with other market sharing enterprises.

A final topic on factor allocation that we will briefly explore relates to the effective protection offered in developing countries and the role of foreign investors in this area. The initial objectives of import substitution as a road to industrialization and development were in many areas of the third world (as in Latin America) distorted by applying infant industry arguments to the operations of subsidiaries of firms such as General Motors, Philips International, Mitsubishi, ICI, etc., which dominate the protected sectors.

Government policies are often conditioned by pressures of foreign firms which pose as a condition of entry a high tariff protection and a partial or a total exclusion of other competitive products. Cost estimates upon which these pressures are often based do not discriminate between (a) infant industry considerations for the advancement and usage of *local* factors of production, (b) inefficiency considerations arising from small scale production, and (c) the purchase of *foreign*-originated goods and services sold among subsidiaries in the absence of arms-length relationships. Of the three only the first justifies protection if it will induce future efficient production. The third case implies that the higher the royalties charged by a parent to its subsidiaries, the higher the protection asked of the host government. Inter-affiliate transfer pricing is hence an important factor influencing government policies on effective protection as well as on overall price levels in the local economy.

The resulting price implications of protection have income effects on consumers and cost effects on forward-linked industries and activities (such as export promotion) all of which affect negatively employment opportunities.

The Consumption Structure and Domestic Demand Effects

Transnational enterprises producing final goods concentrate their activities—for growth, market origin of initial operations and other reasons—in families of products that are generally consumed by those in high income brackets. Through international and domestic demonstration effects, such products affect later consumption preferences of lower income brackets. The participation of foreign subsidiaries in the production of low income housing, health and hygienic needs of the mass of population, basic foods materials, elementary transportation mechanisms, etc. are quite limited and in many cases non-existent. Such areas of production activities, often reflecting the unsatisfied consumption needs of the majority of the population of developing countries, could have a far higher content of labor utilization if techniques are properly selected than the present options offered by technology in the production of goods where foreign firms specialize. The investment and income requirements of such goods *necessitate* dual and unequal structures in the host countries so that they can be locally produced and be purchased given existing levels of development and resources.

The consumption basket of a country certainly depends on many factors and among the most important ones we need to mention the existing income distribution, the extent of openness of an economy with the rest of the world, the usage of the purchasing power of the government, the magnitude of advertisement expenditures, and the structure of tariffs and excise taxes. All these factors affect the composition of consumption whether foreign subsidiaries exist or not in a country. The products involved can be imported or produced by national firms. Yet, foreign investments affect, with varying degrees, each one of these factors and hence induce directly and indirectly consumption patterns. This, in turn, can critically affect employment opportunities.

A last consideration needs to be mentioned. No *a priori* generalizations can be made with respect to the induced demand for backward-linked local industries providing goods and services, and thus creating employment, from the activities of foreign subsidiaries. It all depends on the industries involved. For example, road construction, production of machinery and equipment for use in the extractive industries, and tropical forest exploitation for the production of pulp and paper can be quite labor intensive although the products for which they serve as inputs (i.e., cars, minerals, pulp and paper) are capital intensive. Primary petrochemicals (which are highly capital intensive) can be used for the production of insecticides, fertilizers, and plastics which in turn can serve as inputs in labor intensive activities. The decision and responsibility in this area rests on the host government in promoting the type of backward links and activities that have a high labor content. Furthermore, indirect employment effects cannot be used in an unqualified way as a justification for accepting low labor content industries. Even the construction of pyramids creates indirect employment effects.

With respect to the size of such induced demand effects, aggregate statistics often overstate considerably the local content of the activities of foreign firms.[64] This is so since production and commercial relationships in the same host country by foreign affiliates, exchanging products with an originally high foreign content, greatly distort figures of what truly represents domestic inputs as distinct from those purchased domestically. (Between 1958 and 1967 out of 51 new firms of North American origin in Colombia, 20 were subsidiaries of other foreign subsidiaries already established in that country.)[65]

More careful and detailed analysis indicates a high foreign content in purchases of goods for the activities of foreign subsidiaries in host countries despite continuous policies of the governments of the latter for local backward integration. For example, for the whole of Latin America during the period 1960-65 about 45% of the expenditures on capital goods were imports. About one third of the total imports of machinery and equipment was undertaken by foreign subsidiaries generally from their parents or foreign affiliates.[66] As far as intermediates are concerned, industry samples in Colombia and Chile indicated that imported materials represented in 1968 between 50%-80% of the total materials used by firms in parts of the chemical industry, 75%-80% in pharmaceuticals and 58% in rubber products.[67] Studies undertaken by UNCTAD indicated that, in a sample of 159 firms in six LDC's, 90 had imported intermediate products that accounted for more than 20% of their sales.[68] As stated above higher local integration will not necessarily mean an appropriate employment policy given the usage of other scarce factors of production. It will all depend on the industries involved.

Concluding Remarks

The causes of unemployment are of such complexity that policies directed toward the enhancement of work opportunities in developing countries transcend through the whole developmental process and cannot be thought of as being applied piece-meal.

The issues involved raise questions that are not strictly economic but refer also, or even basically, to the overall social and political fiber of a society. Policies towards foreign direct investments and their impact, thus, should constitute only part of a more general approach towards development. The objectives themselves of the development process will define the extent and conditions under which foreign direct investment should be allowed to operate. Given the size and power of transnational enterprises, their capabilities in fomenting or displacing certain local activities and often in introducing technology and product preferences inappropriate for the conditions of the local economies, given the objectives involved in the pursuit of the firms' own global, rather than national or international, interests, and given the particular market structure within which such enterprises operate, they can be far from realizing particular development objectives of host countries especially those related to employment.

In the extractive industries the basic beneficial effect on employment can only result indirectly through the size *and* use of government revenues that are generated from the activities of foreign firms. Thus, policies directed towards the enhancement of the bargaining power of the host countries are the main element in increasing their share in the rent generated by the activities of foreign investors. Furthermore the structure and orientation of the government as well as the influence that foreign investors have on its constitution and objectives become the center of attention as far as the use of government revenues is concerned towards activities that foment employment.

In the import substituting manufacturing sector the activities of foreign wholly owned subsidiaries often have a negative net effect on social income and balance of payments considerations for the host country. This is a result basically of inappropriate import substitution policies which are to a degree influenced by the presence of foreign investors as well as the weak bargaining position of the host governments in negotiating the terms of entrance and the use of resources, both foreign as well as local, by such firms. Of perhaps even more importance in such activities is the effect that the operations of transnational enterprises have on consumption structures and preferences whether this is the outcome of their own foreign direct investments or the sale of knowhow and product licensing to nationally owned firms. Since the products that they promote have originated and are related to the needs and economic potentialities of advanced countries their introduction in the Third World *requires* dual economic structures and unequal income distribution. Inequality prompts the use of inappropriate technology to produce the goods that are consumed, while inappropriate technology further foments inequality. In the same product lines where foreign investors generally specialize, national firms do not necessarily behave differently and in some cases they might promote the direct use of less labor. In such cases the issue is not the foreignness of the ownership of the firm but the foreignness of the product and its technology to the conditions characterizing the producing country.

In the export promoting manufacturing industries in developing countries, foreign transnational enterprises have become one of the important vehicles for the introduction of unskilled labor intensive activities resulting in relatively high labor generation as compared to the uses of other scarce factors of production. Such employment generation effects, though, are conditioned by the existence of relatively very low wage rates and by specializing in unskilled labor, traditionally the weakest element in the overall class structure in the host countries. The linkages with the rest of the economy can be very limited and thus the inducing effects for other types of activities are restricted and have often been characterized as "enclave operations."

In all activities foreign investors—although bringing in technology, skills and managerial practices—displace, or pre-empt the development of, national technologies, skills, managers, and entrepreneurs. This is the combined result of the dominating role that such firms have in developing countries as well as of their use of collective units of diverse imported inputs which prevents the dynamic development of similar factors of production in the host country. Such factors are of direct use not only in areas where foreign subsidiaries specialize but of pertinence to the overall developmental process in an economy.

The most important policies that will promote the creation of further employment opportunities as a result of the activities of foreign investors can thus be summarized as follows.

First, they include the policies that will increase the bargaining power of the host economy—particularly of the government but in some cases of certain factors of production, such as labor—to improve its participation in the rents that are generated from the operations of foreign subsidiaries.

Second, they refer to policies that promote preferential treatment (during a certain period of time) of key national factors of production as well as certain institutional structures for their development.

Third, they include policies on employment that place particular emphasis on the negative effects of existing unequal income distribution (and the effects that it has on inappropriate products and technology selection) together with more strictly economic policies related to the degree and type of protection offered to the local industry as well as the overall economic links with the rest of the world. Such policies, in addition to the overcoming of internal political constraints, are conditioned by the degree of independence of host governments from influences exerted by foreign investors as well as the governments of their home countries as they try to protect and foment the interests of the affiliates of transnational enterprises.

All the above policies, which have been concluded as the key ones for the enhancement of employment opportunities in developing countries directly or indirectly related to the operations of foreign direct investors, create conditions that have traditionally been defined as inappropriate investment climates.

Notes

1. See also Simon Kuznets, "Economic Growth and the Contribution of Agriculture: Notes on Measurements," in Carl Eicher and Lawrence Witt, ed., *Agriculture and Economic Development* (New York, McGraw Hill, 1964), pp. 102-119; and Markos Mamalakis, "Contribution of Copper to Chilean Economic Development, 1920-1967: Profile of a Foreign-Owned Export Sector," in R.F. Mikesell, ed., *Foreign Investment in the Petroleum & Mineral Industries* (Baltimore, Johns Hopkins Press, 1971), pp. 387-420.

2. Data from Petroleum Department, Chase Manhattan Bank, as cited by Mikesell, *op. cit.,* p. 13. For some countries (like various of the Middle East oil producing ones) the existence of additional foreign capital in the late 1960s could be of limited interest in view of the accumulation of earnings in the government coffers from previous operations. For other countries, though, like Peru and Ecuador the late 1960s found them with critical needs for outside financing in the development of the petroleum sector.

3. See Theodore H. Moran, "Transnational Strategies of Protection and Defense by Multinational

Corporations: Spreading the Risks and Raising the Cost for Nationalization in Natural Resources," *International Organization,* Vol. 27, 2 (Spring, 1973), p. 278.

4. See D. Belli, "Sources and Uses of Funds of Foreign Affiliates of U.S. Firms, 1967-68," *Survey of Current Business* (November, 1970), pp. 14-20.

5. P.P. Streeten and S. Lall, *Evaluation of Methods and Main Findings of UNCTAD Study of Private Overseas Investment in Selected Less-Developed Countries* (Geneva, UNCTAD, TD/B/C.3/111, 1973), p. 57.

6. For the case of Argentina see Jose B. Gelbard, "Efectos Políticos de la Inversión Extranjera: El Caso Argentino," in Karl Heinz Stanzick and H.H. Godoy, ed., *Inversiones Extranjeras y Transferencia de Technología en America Latina* (Santiago, Chile, ILDIS, 1972), p. 173.

7. See F. Pazos, "El Financiamiento Externo de la América Latina, Incremento Progresivo o Disminución Gradual," *El Trimestre Económico* (April-June, 1971), Table 4.

8. See Aldo Ferrer, "El Capital Extranjero en la Economía Argentina," *El Trimestre Económico,* No. 150 (April-June, 1971), pp. 168-69.

9. See for example the study undertaken in defense of business interests in Latin America by H. May, *The Effects of United States and Other Foreign Investment in Latin America,* (New York, The Council for Latin America, 1969).

10. See work and references by G. Rosenthal, "Algunos Apuntes Sobre el Grado de Participación de la Inversión Extranjera Directa en el Proceso de Integración Económica Centroamericana," in Stanzick and Godoy, *op. cit.,* p. 343, et. seq.

11 See P. Streeten in "The Multinational Enterprise and Development," mimeo (Oxford, 1972). In the financial analysis certain adjustments need to take place for different levels of royalty payments and the usage of some local scarce factors of protection.

12. See I.M.D. Little and J.A. Mirrlees, *Manual of Industrial Project Analysis in Developing Countries* (Paris, OECD, 1969), Vol. II.

13. Streeten and Lall, *op. cit.,* p. 59.

14. *Ibid.,* p. 62.

15. Mikesell, *op. cit.,* p. 6.

16. *Ibid.,* p. 8.

17. See *Fortune* (March, 1971), p. 30.

18. For an analysis of the multiple reasons for such a behaviour, see C.V. Vaitsos, "Income Distribution, Welfare Considerations and Transnational Enterprises," in J.H. Dunning, *The Multinational Enterprise and Economic Analysis* (Hertfordshire, England, Allen & Unwin, forthcoming).

19. See Shane Hunt, "Evaluating Direct Foreign Investment in Latin America," in Luigi R. Einaudi, ed., *Latin America in the 1970's* (RAND, R-1067-DOS, December, 1972), pp. 127-146.

20. See H. May, *op. cit.,* pp. 5-6.

21. For a discussion of the theoretical implications of factor saving, capital biased, technological change see F. Stewart, "Choice of Technique in Developing Countries," in Charles Cooper, ed., *Science, Technology and Development* (London, Frank Cass, 1973).

22. See M. Mamalakis, *op. cit.,* p. 411.

23. *Ibid.,* p. 411.

24. See Mario Vera Valenzuela, *La Política Económica del Cobre en Chile* (Santiago, Universidad de Chile, 1961), p. 22.

25. See Ministerio de Minas and Hidrocarburos de Venezuela, *Petróleo y Otros Datos Estadísticos* (1964), p. 122 as cited by W.G. Harris, "The Impact of Petroleum Industry on Venezuelan Economic Development," in Mikesell, *op. cit.,* p. 153.

26. See Ruben Sáder Pérez, "La Inversión Extranjera y Petróleo: Reversión de Concesiones y Nacionalización de la Industria Petrolera en Venezuela," in Stanzick and Godoy, *op. cit.*

27. See Organization of American States, *America en Cifras: Situación Social 1960-1965* (Washington, D.C., 1970).

28. See Braden Copper Co. Department of Industrial Relations, *Análisis Sobre Remuneraciones y Beneficios Accesorios en Chile* (Santiago, 1964), pp. 324-325; and Venezuela, Ministerio de Minas and Hidrocarburos, *op. cit.,* p. 122.

29. UNCTAD, *Restrictive Business Practices* (New York, UNCTAD, TD/B/C.2/104/Rev. 1, 1971), p. 19.

30. ILO, *Employment, Incomes and Equality: A Strategy for Increasing Productive Employment in Kenya* (Geneva, ILO, 1972); and R. Hal Mason in UNITAR, *The Transfer of Technology and the Factor Proportions Problem: The Philippines and Mexico,* Research Project No. 10 (New York, 1971).

31. See Departamento Nacional de Planeación, *Algunas Observaciones a la Política del País con Relación a la Inversión Extranjera,* DNP-798 (Bogotá, September 9, 1971), p. 17.

32. See B. Baranson, "Diesel Engine Manufacturing in India and Japan," *Automation in Developing Countries* (Geneva, ILO, 1972), p. 66.

33. See W.A. Yeoman, "Selection of Production Processes for the Manufacturing Subsidaries of U.S. Based Multinational Corporations," unpublished D.B.A. thesis, Harvard Business School (Boston, 1968). Also L.T. Wells, Jr., "Economic Man and Engineering Man: Choice of Technology in a Low Wage Country," *Public Policy* (forthcoming).

34. *Ibid.*

35. For a review of the literature see F. Stewart, "Technology and Employment in LDCs," this book.

36. See H. Pack, "Employment and Productivity in Kenya Manufacturing," mimeo (August, 1972), p. 6.

37. W.O. Boorke, "Basic Vehicle for South-East Asia," U.S. AID, *Technology and Economics in Economic Development* (Washington, D.C., May, 1972).

38. See H. Hughes and You Poh Seng, *Foreign Investment and Industrialization in Singapore* (Madison, Wisconsin Press, 1969), p. 193. Also L. Reynolds and P. Gregory, *Wages, Productivity and Industrialization in Puerto Rico* (Homewood, Illinois, Richard D. Irwin, Inc., 1965).

39. See F. Stewart, *op. cit.* Also interviews in Goodyear's tire plant in India reached similar conclusions on inter-county comparisons in the practices followed by transnational firms, particularly in the area of plant material handling and transportation, substituting labor for conveyor belts. On the same subject for earlier periods see J.E. Orchard, *Japan's Economic Position* (New York, McGraw Hill, 1930).

40. See G. Ranis, *Some Observations on the Economic Framework for Optimum LDC Utilization of Technology* (Washington, U.S. AID, 1972). Also Charles Cooper in I.L.O., *Employment, Incomes and Equality, op. cit.,* pp. 449-451.

41. Mason, *op. cit.*

42. See study by Charles Cooper in I.L.O., *Employment, Incomes and Equality, op cit.,* p. 450.

43. See Pack, *op. cit.,* p. 12.

44. See F. Stewart, *op. cit.,* p. 28.

45. S. Tinbergen, *Choice of Technology in Industrial Planning, Industrialization and Productivity,* United Nations Bulletin, No. 1 (New York).

46. *Loc. cit.*

47. SUDENE, *Primeiro Plano Director de Desenvolvimiento do Nordeste,* Pres. de Rep., (Brazil, 1961).

48. United Nations, *Selección de Alternativas Tecnológicas en la Industria Textil Latinoamericana,* (Santiago, Chile, U.N. E/CN. 12/746, 1966), p. 37.

49. C.V. Vaitsos, "Transfer of Resources and Preservation of Monopoly Rents," Center of International Affairs, Harvard University, Economic Development Report 168 (1970), p. 64.

50. See G. Adam, "New Trends in International Business: World Wide Sourcing and Dedomiciling," *Acta Económica,* Vol. 7, 3-4 (1971), pp. 349-367; G.H. Helleiner, "Manufactured Exports from Less-Developed Countries and Multinational Firms," *Economic Journal* (March, 1973), pp. 21-47. Hal Lary, *Imports of Manufactures from Less Developed Countries* (New York, National Bureau of Economic Research, 1968); J. Leontiades, "International Sourcing in the LDC's," *Columbia Journal of World Business,* Vol. VI, No. 5 (September-October, 1971), pp. 19-28.

51. G.H. Helleiner, *op. cit.,* pp. 29-30; and G. Adam, "Some Implications and Concommitants of Worldwide Sourcing," *Acta Económica,* Vol. 8, 2-3 (1972), p. 310.

52. For data on growth rates of exports in manufactured products and their share in total exports from developing countries see Helleiner, *op. cit.,* p. 24.

53. For an analysis see Bela Balassa, "Industrial Policies in Taiwan and Korea," *Weltwirtschaftliches Archiv,* Band 106, Heft 1 (1971).

54. For the case of Ireland see Charles Cooper & Noel Whelan, "Science, Technology and Industry in Ireland—A Diagnosis and Some Policy Proposals," paper presented to the National Science Council (Ireland, March, 1972).

55. See Asian Development Bank, *Southeast Asia's Economy in the 1970's* (New York, Longman, 1971), pp. 306 et seq.

56. For further international wage comparisons see J.B. Thornblade, "Textile Imports from LDC's: A Challenge to the American Market," *Economic Development and Cultural Change* (January, 1971); R. d'A. Shaw, "Foreign Investment and Global Labor," *Columbia Journal of World Business* (July-August, 1971).

57. For a more generalized model see S. Hymer & S.A.Resnick, "International Trade and Uneven Development," in J.N. Bhagwati et al, ed., *Trade, Balance of Payments and Growth* (New York, Am. Elsevier, 1971), pp. 473-479.

58. See Streeten & Lall, *op. cit.,* p. 77.

59. For the case of the Venezuelan petrochemical industry and some case studies see R. Escobar and A. Sanchez, *Implementación de la Venezolanización de la Ingeniería* (Instituto Venezolano de Petroquímica, February, 1973).

60. Some original research has been done in this area by Juan Tampier on assignment by the Andean Pact to Japan.

61. See Junta del Acuerdo de Cartagena, *Resumen de los Estudios Realizados sobre Tecnología y sus Políticas* (forthcoming).

62. See G. Rosenthal for his research in the Central American countries, *op. cit.*

63. Data from J.W. Vaupel & J.P. Curhan, *The Making of the International Enterprise* (Harvard Business School, 1969) as discussed by M.S. Wionczek in "Hacia el Establecimiento de un Trato Común para la Inversión Extranjera en el Mercado Común Andino," *El Trimestre Económico,* Vol. XXXVII (April-June, 1971).

64. See, for example, U.S. Department of Commerce, U.S. Office of Business Economics, *Preliminary Data on U.S. Direct Investments in Latin American Manufacturing Enterprises, 1966* (November, 1969).

65. See M. Wionczek, *op. cit.*, p. 667.

66. F. Fanjzilber, *Elementos para la Formulación de Estrategias de Exportación de Manufacturas*, ST/ECLA/Conf. 3/L. 21 (Santiago, Chile, July, 1971), pp. 91-95.

67. C.V. Vaitsos, *Intercountry Income Distribution and Transnational Enterprises* (London, Oxford University Press, 1974), p. 90.

68. See Streeten and Lall, *op. cit.*, p. 47.

The Role of the Public Sector as an Employer

William N. Wamalwa
Chairman, Public Service Commission of Kenya

Introduction

The traditional Western approach to economic development had, as its main objective, the raising of the annual rate of growth. This is reflected in the fact that statistics on development concentrated on showing the rate of increase in the Gross National Product, per capita income, the rate of national savings, etc. This thinking has been true even where development planning has been practised. It was assumed that economic growth would almost automatically lead to increased employment opportunities.

Today, however, problems of employment are recognised by economists, planners and Government leaders as among the most intractable and urgent in the less developed countries. This realisation has come about as a result of the fact that the earlier expectation that a reasonable rate of growth would lead to increased employment opportunities has not materialised. In fact, past experience in some less developed countries, discloses that open unemployment has been growing rapidly even in countries with high rates of economic growth and investment. In the less developed countries of Africa, Asia and Latin America, open unemployment is, generally speaking, in excess of 10% of the labour force, as compared with between 3 to 6% for the more developed nations of the world.

Problems of Reckoning Public Sector Employment

Typically, the less developed countries have dual economies, a modern monetary sector existing alongside the traditional subsistence sector. In most of these countries, public sector activities constitute the largest share of the modern sector. Just how large that share is depends on the extent to which the modern sector is socialised. Public sector employment will therefore vary considerably from one country to another depending on the mixture of public and private undertakings.

There are also classification problems in determining for purposes of comparison what constitutes the public sector when reckoning employment figures. In some countries which have been reviewed in preparing this paper, the public sector comprises the orthodox civil service, local government, statutory corporations and limited liability companies which are either wholly, or substantially, owned by Government. In other countries, Government-owned industrial and commercial concerns are included in what is termed an "enterprise sector." Tanzania is a good example of this kind.

Quite apart from problems presented by variations in what constitutes the public

351

sector for purposes of reckoning employment figures, there are problems which arise from the nature of all statistical data in the less developed countries. While it is true that the reliability of data in these countries has in general terms improved quite considerably during the last decade or so, statistics, in many cases, are still fragmentary and of varying reliability. This complication arises, in part, from the fact that coverage and classifications in labour enumeration have been shifting. Additionally, in most countries, labour statistics are often not identified on a sectoral basis, i.e. by public or private sector. A third problem arises from the interdependence of the public sector and the private sector. In terms of contribution to employment opportunities, the two sectors do exercise a powerful influence on each other. What happens in the private sector does have some influence on what happens in the public sector and vice-versa. It is partly the realisation of this interdependence that, in many less developed countries, efforts have been made to embrace the private sector in development planning. This means, therefore, that the number of persons directly employed by either sector cannot, in any way, be said to be the only contribution of that sector to the total national employment. What we can determine fairly accurately is what might be termed "direct employment" by each sector; the "indirect" contribution to employment is not easy to determine.

For our purposes, public sector employment will be understood to comprise employees in the orthodox civil service, local government, statutory corporations, and industrial and commercial limited liability companies which are wholly or substantially owned by Government.

Growth of Public Sector Employment

In spite of all these measurement problems, there are a number of characteristics of public sector employment which can be fairly clearly documented. In the first place, Governments in the less developed countries are the largest single employers. Secondly, there is a general tendency for public sector employment to expand quite rapidly. Thirdly, some of this expansion of the public sector is at the expense of the private sector with the result that such expansion does not always lead to increased employment opportunities in aggregate terms. Fourthly, there seems to be a tendency towards over-employment in the public sector in relation to the functional requirements of Governments. Fifthly, in the case of countries in Asia and Africa, which have moved from a recent colonial past to sovereign status, there is the problem of youthfulness of most employees in the public sector which arises mainly from localisation efforts of the immediate post-independence era. Sixthly, there is the paradox of acute shortages of skilled, highlevel manpower in the midst of vast reservoirs of unskilled, surplus labour.

Role of Government in Development

The extent and nature of public sector employment are very largely a function of the perceived and actual role of the Government in national development. In recent years, the scope of Government participation in economic activities has enormously increased in almost all countries of the world. In the Socialist countries, the escalation of the public sector arose from an ideological commitment to ensure that all means of production are under the control of Government. For the Western countries, State intervention has been selective and varies from one country to another, but the trend has been upward. In the vast majority of these cases, the reasons for Government intervention lie in the practical realities of our times, showing clearly that "laissez-faire'' development policies of the past cannot be expected to cope adequately with the more complex situations emerging today.

For the less developed countries, Governments are, in effect, the entrepreneur. They operate in economies in which, in the majority of cases, the private sector is foreign owned as well as managed. Since the sector must operate on a profit basis and some profits must be repatriated to foreign owners, there are serious limitations on the extent to which it will voluntarily go on investing. This, coupled with the overwhelming desire for rapid development, leaves Governments with no alternative but to assume increasingly the role of the industrialist and businessman. It means not just providing the infrastructure essential for investment, but also setting up and managing industries and organising the distributive trade. Therefore, in addition to the traditional civil service, whose orthodox concern was with keeping law and order, collecting revenue and providing certain basic services, Governments in the less developed nations have had to establish vast numbers of organisations to carry out the new state functions. Inevitably, this has led to escalation in the number of people employed in the public sector. There need not be any ideological influence in this trend as the legitimacy of Governments in these relatively new nations depends, very largely, on certain specific accomplishments in a relatively short period of time.

In addition to going into new ventures, many Governments have, in pursuit of socialist policies, nationalised existing enterprises, thus adding to the number of persons employed in the public sector, although, of course, such measures in themselves, do not necessarily increase the number of persons employed in relation to the total labour force available in the population. But such measures do increase the proportion of public sector investment, and expansion may be more vigorously pursued by Government with a favorable subsequent effect on employment. Although the element of compensation involved in nationalisation means a drain on scarce national resources, such measures could be productive in the long run to the extent that they constitute a structural reform laying the foundation for more balanced development. In any event, with this type of orientation, Governments in most less developed countries, have become the largest employers.

A third factor, which has led to the rapid increase in public sector employment, in addition to nationalisation and engaging in new development ventures, is the proliferation of licenses, permits and other forms of control. Excessive control on almost every aspect of life is a major feature of the less developed countries which naturally means more employees to operate the control devices. It is not within our scope to examine the corruption that seems synonymous with these controls.

Complexity and Specialisation of Public Sector Undertakings

Today, technological skills are indispensable in our quest for accelerated economic and social advancement. Importation of new technological equipment into a less developed country entails the need to acquire new competence and skills. This need can be met in part by developing local manpower and in part by importing foreign skills. Either way, new technology brings about an increase in the number of people employed. The introduction of a computer in the Treasury, for example, means the addition to public sector employment of persons with a whole range of new skills. To the extent, however, that expatriates fill these positions, the growth in public sector employment exaggerates the extent to which jobs are being created for citizens.

In addition to the vast expansion of the public sector into new activities, Government activities and operations have, with time, grown in complexity and specialisation. The expansion into new areas has created a demand for new skills which were unknown in the traditional tasks of Governments. This, in turn, has led to the establishment of new departments, or even whole Ministries with full staff complements. The need for co-ordination of these new activities also leads to further increases in the number of personnel required.

An analysis of this rapid growth in public sector employment discloses two characteristics. The first of these is that the highest rates of growth have been in the fields of education and health services. This is hardly surprising since it is considered, in these countries, that education and health are the foundations for accelerated development. As a result of this policy orientation, these two services normally account for no less than 40% of the budget.

The second characteristic of the rapid growth in public sector employment is that it seems to have been concentrated in the intermediate and higher echelons of the hierarchy. The typical diagrammatic representation would not look like a pyramid but rather like a vase with a fairly pronounced bulge in the upper middle. This phenomenon arises from a variety of factors. Firstly, it appears inherent in the nature of Government activities. Typically, growth of public sector organisations occurs by the addition of a new activity onto an existing unit. This process involves additional personnel at the functional or operational level to discharge the new responsibilities. This, in effect, means that such growth starts at the lower levels of the organisation. However, this process leads to an increased workload in the higher echelons of the organisation and a point is reached when the original new unit attains some maturity by differentiation, thereby requiring subdivision which, in turn, necessitates additional personnel. It is at this point that an interesting phenomenon occurs: the growth at the lower levels becomes insignificant while it escalates at the higher levels. Absence of effective organisation planning in most public jurisdictions makes this growth even more pronounced.

Within the upper levels, however, trends are less clear. A study of the Indian Civil Service, between 1961 and 1965, reveals for example that the increase in the top administrative cadre of Permanent Secretary was 33%, while the next grade below, recorded 3.2%.[1] But, a study of the growth in the personnel strength in the two top administrative categories in the Kenya Civil Service shows the reverse of the Indian picture. Thus, between 1965 and 1970, the two categories, Permanent Secretary and Under Secretary, grew by 6.3% and 106.7%, respectively.[2]

Localisation Transition

In many less developed countries, public sector employment was profoundly influenced by the transitional period from colonial to independent status. This is particularly true of those countries of Asia and Africa which have become sovereign nations since the Second World War. At independence, these countries were characterised by public services manned very largely by expatriates. One of the primary objectives of the new Governments right from the outset was the replacement of the expatriates by citizens. Thus, one of the effects of independence was a rapid increase in employment opportunities for the citizens of those countries. However, in most of these countries there was a desperate shortage of qualified and experienced local personnel. As a result, therefore, Governments gave the highest priority to investment in education. Since promotional opportunities were immense, the process of localisation inevitably led to public services being manned largely by very young persons. In contrast to earlier years when persons could expect to reach the top of their careers in their late 40's, it became normal to reach those positions in the early 30's.

Those who have studied the process of localisation of personnel in new states, seem unanimous in concluding that it led to a "massive dilution of experience."[3] This dilution of experience was made worse by the unprecedented increase in the activities of the public sector, and the impatience of politicians for results.

The dilution of personnel quality and performance led to a process whereby responsibilities were pushed upwards in the organisation. Duties previously performed by junior officers had to be assumed by relatively senior officers. As pressures grew, demands for additional personnel quickly followed. In some cases, completely new organisational units with full complements of staff were created; in other cases, attempts were made to strengthen existing organisations by creating new posts and upgrading existing positions.

This transitional stage required massive investments in education. As the early investments matured, the situation of a serious overall shortage of trained manpower was transformed into a situation of selective shortages demanding a very high degree of competence in manpower and educational planning and great care in setting priorities. If no effective planning is done in this situation, a country could easily be threatened with unemployment among the relatively well-educated. When this point of maturity in investment in education is reached, there may be a tendency to reverse the situation that existed during the heyday of localisation. Job requirements are made more demanding and recruitment and selection of staff more rigorous. This is in keeping with the play of labour market forces reflecting relative abundance in the supply position.

Wage Levels and Employment

It has already been stated that among the most striking features of public sector employment are its large size and high rate of growth. To these, we must add the very large proportion of the total annual budget of Governments that goes into paying salaries and wages. In most of these countries, it is rare to find the proportion of the national budget which goes into paying salaries (or personal emoluments) being less than 40%. This high level of public expenditure on salaries reduces, to a certain extent, the amount of capital available for more productive investments which would generate more employment opportunities. It is also a fact of life, in the vast majority of these countries that the gap between the top, more skilled employees, and the less skilled employees, is very wide. Normally, this ratio is in excess of 30:1. It means that, while the level of unemployment is rising to politically and socially unacceptable limits, the major preoccupation of both employee associations and Governments is to raise the lowest wages on grounds of equity. Since the proportion of the available labour force that is actually productively employed is adversely affected by the level of going wages, efforts to escalate wages may conflict with efforts to increase employment opportunities.

However, the relationship of wages to the level of employment is not so simple and direct. In order to accelerate development, these countries require manpower with more or less the same skills as those required by the more developed countries. This means that at certain levels, the less developed countries cannot pay lower wages without encouraging and risking a brain drain. It will not make much sense to a highly qualified medical doctor in Botswana to work for a wage far below that which he considers he can obtain elsewhere. Except where emigration is highly controlled, as is the case in most Communist countries, such qualified personnel will offer their services in a country which offers the best terms of employment.

Investment Policies and Technology

For a long time, investment objectives and strategy of the less developed countries were an exact copy of those developed by the Western capitalist economic system. Investments were considered quite strictly on the basis of the return likely to be yielded. It is only in recent years that social benefits have been accepted as being an equally necessary objective of investment. However, as long as most investment in the less developed countries was by foreign private firms, there was very little that could be done to influence investment towards social benefit objectives. It is, therefore, in this connection that public sector investment can deliberately emphasize labour intensive activities.

As it has already been stated, experience shows that a high rate of economic growth does not necessarily lead to a similar increase in job opportunities. One of the many reasons for this situation is the fact that the modern industrial sector relies on technology developed in the advanced countries and which is intended to be capital intensive, rather than labour intensive. But the question is not merely whether labour intensive technology can be developed to suit the labour supply situation in the less developed countries. It is equally important and relevant to ask whether, in fact, these countries are using the most labour intensive technologies known.[4] In this connection, the public sector is well placed to use more labour intensive methods, particularly in its agricultural and construction activities, and to offer the private sector a constructive and competitive example.

Over-Employment in the Public Sector

In ideal terms, an organisation grows in response to the need to achieve goals. However, in real life, there are many other factors which determine both the size and rate of growth of an organisation. Some of these factors might, in fact, have little or no relationship to the organisational objectives to be accomplished. It is some of these extraneous factors which, in some cases, are responsible for over-employment, which is one of the most striking features of public sector employment.

In the first place, there is the human tendency highlighted by Parkinson's Law. It seems a natural human tendency that "an official wants to multiply subordinates . . . ."[5] This tendency partly springs from the notion that an executive's prestige is measured by the number of subordinates supervised. Thus, it is believed, the larger the number, the greater the prestige. Supervision of subordinates carries with it power over them and gives the supervisor a sense of prestige and achievement. This urge for a sense of greatness leads to organised pressure within public sector organisations for the establishment of additional new posts without much regard to the need for them in terms of the workload. As the organisation grows in size, so it grows in importance which, in turn, helps escalate the number of employees.

A second factor contributing to over-employment in the public sector is obsolescence of skills. With the explosion of knowledge and the rapidly changing demands of work situations, people's skills for performing tasks fall behind the job requirements. In the absence of vigorous and up-to-date training and re-training programmes, organisations begin carrying passengers. A situation develops where the people in the organisation feel that there is too much work for too few people. Demands for new posts increase. In most of these countries, because of social and political considerations, passengers have to be covered rather than fired.

Since there is almost complete lack of organisation planning in public sector bodies, ad hoc growth ensues with all of its consequences: growth being unanticipated, the organisation could become unwieldy in relation to its real workload. This situation may be aggravated by the fact that, in most of these countries, economic and social planning is done at too generalised a level. Normally, projects are not detailed enough for those responsible for resource allocation to be certain about personnel requirements. Thus, even if it were made mandatory for additional staff to be considered only in relation to work programmes, it would still not be easy to arrive at a realistic assessment of personnel content of projects.

The task of those responsible for resource allocation is made even more difficult by the absence of objective, complement-control techniques. In some countries, there is a fixed rate of annual growth in budgets which cannot be exceeded lightly. But this is not common, and even where such a system exists, determined, organised bureaucratic pressures too often have their way.

Over-employment also arises as a result of unnecessary centralisation which is another striking feature of the less developed countries. Because of the urge to control everything directly, the central offices of public sector organisations tend to be topheavy with excessively high rates of growth. This tendency also leads to faulty priority setting with the result that unimportant and non-urgent activities are given undue attention and are allocated resources, including manpower, which cannot always be justified in terms of the objectives of accelerated development.

But, in cases where staffing decisions are made by political jurisdictions, overemployment could be the direct result of patronage and nepotism. The need to reward political faithfuls and "invest" in the future, normally leads to a staff position which does not reflect the workload to be carried. The notoricty of parastatal bodies in these countries is well-documented and well-known. In the first place, persons are given jobs not on merit, but on the basis of affiliation. Secondly, since such persons often cannot adequately carry out their responsibilities, additional staff has to be hired. And the chain continues.

Another prominent feature of most developing nations is the large number of ministerial portfolios. Even in the smallest of countries, it is a rare thing to find a Cabinet of less than 20 Ministers. This escalation of the number of ministries is not always determined in terms either of workload, or task specialisation, but rather on the basis of rewarding political faithfuls and the need to reconcile sectional interests so as to preserve the integrity of the State. As a result, we find that Sudan has 27 Ministers, Zambia 24, Sri Lanka 23.

Prospects of Public Sector Employment

As the 1970s and '80s are turning out to be decades of "economic independence," Governments in the less developed countries will need to give the creation of productive employment opportunities a much higher priority than they have done in the past. The present trend of Government intervention in the direct management of national productive resources is most likely to be accelerated. This means that public sector employment will rise quite steeply beyond the current average of more than 50% of all recorded salaried employment.

To start with, employment generation should be made an important objective in national development plans. Specific targets should be established and machinery and capabilities for implementation provided. Such targets should not only reflect the level of current public sector activities, but should also be geared to stimulate economic activities. In planning all public sector investment, due regard should be given to the utilisation of available known labour-intensive methods. Priority should be given to development projects with high labour consumption, since the financing of public sector investment is such that more attention can be given to maximisation of social benefits without serious repercussions. This strategy is not being advocated as an alternative to a strategy which emphasises efficient allocation of resources aiming, inter alia, at a high economic growth rate, but rather to suggest that in seeking the social benefits associated with employment, opportunities for growth may also be increased.

In this regard, public sector investment should move into such areas as irrigation schemes which would provide needed foodstuffs, foreign exchange, and labour intensive production. The field of agriculture and rural development seems to offer more scope for increased employment than the industrial sector. This, of course, is not to suggest that the less developed countries should neglect industrialisation, but rather should seek a more employment intensive balance.

However, the nature of unemployment in these countries indicates that the very process of increasing employment opportunities leads to more people seeking employment because of the attractions of the possibility of getting a job. In this regard, it might be helpful for Governments to review the present retirement and pension arrangements. As it has already been noted, the vast majority of employees in the public sector, in most African and Asian countries are relatively young. This means that they do not have the advantage of natural turn-over of staff due to retirement. Realising the effect of this factor on morale and generation of employment opportunities, some Governments have instituted Schemes of early retirement. What this means is that the traditional Western conception of retirement must be revised so that an employee, in effect, retires from one employer into a job with another employer, or into self-employment. A scheme of this nature, if properly conceived and operated, could also assist in the struggle for ''economic independence'' by releasing fairly experienced persons to go into the private sector as entrepreneurs. In fact, in one country, where such a scheme has been introduced, the result has been the enrichment of the private sector. This is the case in Kenya where an early retirement scheme was introduced in 1968 on an experimental basis, providing for retirement after 10 years' service, or on attaining the age of 45 years. It is restricted to the higher ranks of the Civil Service. But such schemes cannot really be expected to make very much difference to the mass unemployment of the less developed countries. In the first place, job opportunities created will be negligible; and secondly, the ordinary unemployed persons will not possess the skills required for such jobs.

However, such a scheme of ''early discharge'' on a planned basis in the armed forces would seem to hold out more promise. For the vast majority of these countries, an armed force is almost synonymous with independence, national flag and national anthem. These are considered symbols of nationhood. It is, of course, legitimate that these countries should have armed forces. However, what needs to be done, and urgently, too, is a redefinition of the role of armed forces in the absence of combat situations. If it is considered essential to have these establishments, it would only be proper for them to be used for purposes of national development rather than keeping them in barracks with drill as the only activity. Quite apart from the disruption they have frequently caused (not always unwelcome, of course), this constitutes a major drain on scarce resources which could be more usefully deployed elsewhere to increase job opportunities or for other purposes. In this regard, the experience of Malaysia should be rewarding.

Equally significantly, it would be useful for all armed forces personnel to go through a course of training in general management and administration. This should be made compulsory particularly in view of the fact that most of us in the less developed countries are destined to live under armed forces rule at one time or another. If this happened, it would assist them to appreciate the intricacies of running a modern state.

There is need, not only for redefinition of the role of armed forces in the less developed countries, but also of their career pattern. In the more developed countries, the armed forces have an established position based on history and tradition. Unfortunately an established social framework which provides a stabilising influence on the armed forces is missing in most less developed countries. As a result, the concept of a career in the armed forces drives officers and men alike to engage in a search for a role and way of life in society. Against this brief background, the activities of armed forces in taking over control of governments should not be too surprising.

This situation calls for a complete rethinking of the career concept of the soldier. The change should be designed to achieve three objectives: to lessen the chances of military takeovers; to prepare the soldier for a useful civilian role; and finally, to make way for others as a means of increasing occupational opportunities.

The new concept should be that of a short career based on the assumption that active armed forces life is a young man's business. As the officer grows in experience, he should be displaced, so to speak, into normal civilian activities for which he would have been prepared during his short armed forces career. A plan of this nature would envisage a solider, for example, remaining in "active" army service for, at most, ten years.

One development, which will have a profound impact on future prospects of generating employment opportunities in the less developed countries, is the rate of population growth. The growth in the labour force is very much a function of this fact. In this connection, it is estimated by some informed sources that between 1970 and 1980 the labour force in the less developed countries will grow by more than 25%.[6] (The corresponding figure for the more developed countries for the same period is estimated at about 10%.) In the vast majority of these countries the population growth rates are above 2.5% per annum. This situation is a direct result of very high fertility rates in a situation of fairly rapidly falling death rates.

It is imperative, therefore, that, while all possible measures are taken by Governments to generate increased job opportunities, energetic efforts should also be directed towards measures designed to lower population growth rates. And, since fertility control programmes have a demonstrable impact only in the long run —normally not less than 15 years—it means that this is an urgent task that must be undertaken now. This has relevance to the role of the public sector as an employer, because population planning, like the planning of the other aspects of the economy, is rightly the responsibility of Governments. In this regard, Governments should be encouraged to make population planning, with specific targets, another major objective of economic planning.

Conclusion

It is clear that public sector employment has expanded very considerably in the past decade or so. The trend clearly points to even greater expansion in the 1970s and beyond. This trend will lead to a diminishing private sector as these countries intensify efforts at what is now popularly described as "economic independence." Because of the speed at which development is desired, and because of the fact that private investors cannot always be relied upon to invest in activities which do not promise quick returns, Governments will inevitably become the largest investors.

However, it is important for Governments in the less developed countries to approach the problem from the point of view of the totality of poverty. Salaried employment alone will not be the answer. Therefore, while efforts are made to increase job opportunities, an equal emphasis should be placed on the need to raise the level of earnings generally so that even rural self-employment can be made attractive to assist in minimising the tendency of people to drift to the urban areas.

Finally, a population policy designed to lower the rate of population growth is an essential priority as is the need for reform of the educational system to gear its products to the employment requirements of the economies of the less developed countries.

Notes

1. Indian Administrative Reforms Commission, *Report of the Study Team on Personnel Administration* (New Delhi, August, 1967), p. 19.

2. Republic of Kenya Staff List 1965 and 1970 (Nairobi, Government Printer).

3. D.N. Ndegwa, *Report of the Commission of Inquiry: Public Service Structure and Remuneration Commission* (Nairobi, Government Printer, May, 1971), p. 9. Also see Indian Administrative Reforms Commission, *op. cit.*, Chapter 2.

4. R.H. Green, "Wage Levels, Employment, Productivity, and Consumption," in J.R. Sheffield, ed., *Education, Employment and Rural Development* (Nairobi, East African Publishing House, 1967), p. 222.

5. C. Northcote Parkinson, *Parkinson's Law* (Boston, Massachusetts, Houghton Mifflin Co., 1957), p. 10.

6. D. Turnham and I. Jaeger, *The Employment Problem in Less Developed Countries: A Review of Evidence* (Paris, O.E.C.D. Development Centre, 1971), p. 1.

IV
Country Experiences

Application of Technology and its Employment Effects: The Experience in Indonesia

Mohammad Sadli
Minister of Manpower
Government of Indonesia

The Problem Setting

During the latter part of the rule of President Sukarno, because of worsening inflation and the radical brand of nationalism practised in those days, the economy was stagnating and the balance of payments worsening. The country tended to isolate itself from the West, while on the other hand significant amounts of economic aid from socialist countries and suppliers' credits from several western countries (including Japan) were disbursed in the fom of factory equipment. A number of industrial projects were under construction which, however, seldom got off the ground.

Considerable equipment was imported through the foreign exchange allocation system and the currency was much overvalued. Because foreign exchange allocation for raw materials was not plentiful, the rate of capacity utilization was low; yet new equipment was sought after since registered capacities became the basis for the (raw material) allocation system. Many old and new workers were hoarded by enterprises because they cost little and because this policy was favored by the government and the then influential communist party and its affiliated trade unions. Government departments and state enterprises were also heavily padded with new employees and workers.

This situation had an odd feature, i.e., while the economic situation was deteriorating, the distributive effects in terms of unemployment and income did not create explosive social tensions. When political tensions mounted because of culminating confrontation between the communists and their opponents, when the inflation increased and the economic situation deteriorated aggravating these tensions, the general public was not overly sensitive about distributive problems. It must be noted, however, that the communists were constantly agitating against remnants of rural landlords, petty capitalists and bureaucrats, to whom they attributed coercive and exploitative powers. Hence they always tried to maintain the image of being champions of distributive justice even at the expense of forgetting about economic growth.

All this changed since the 'New Order.' Conscious of the fact that the national pie was not growing fast enough in relation to population and that the per capita income might be shrinking, the major preoccupation of the new government became directed to making the national pie bigger, at least as a first priority.

Because of the disillusionment about the results of economic policies inspired by earlier socialistic doctrines which (because of lack of economic and political stability and lack of industrial and administrative cadres) never led to growth and efficiency,

363

the new government tried to reconstruct the economy on the principles of the market mechanism: open foreign trade, stable monetary climate, balanced government budget, limited government interference in the economy, and attraction of foreign aid and investments. The new economic system is more an incentive system than an allocative and distributional system. The price mechanism, the tax and tariff policies, the government budget, and the monetary and credit policies were used to provide a setting in which, through price signals and stability, entrepreneurs today are encouraged to invest, innovate, and produce.

After five years one can safely say that the system has worked and the economy has regained its momentum. Gross Domestic Product is now growing annually at some seven percent in real terms; exports are expanding by leaps and bounds; industrial production and other parts of the modern sector are advancing at some 10% per year; government revenues and public savings are also going up encouragingly as well as private savings; foreign aid is now coming in at a rate of over US$700 million (with some prospect of growing to US$1 billion) per year and the inflow of foreign direct investments has been gratifying (new approvals in 1972 totaled US$488 million). Most foreign observers who come to Jakarta or who write reports about the Indonesian economy have high praise for these achievements, although often indicating as well the inherent weaknesses of the situation and the large problems ahead.

No one, however, can give an accurate and credible account of how the balance sheet stands for employment and unemployment. We have the 1971 census and can compare this with the 1961 census. On this basis we are not doing badly. The ratio for unemployment in the 1971 census is below the figure in the previous census, but the culprit is the definitional system. The reference period to measure open unemployment in 1971 is shorter (i.e., one week) than the one used in the 1961 census (6 months); hence the results are incomparable. The 1971 census produced a total population figure close to 120 million, of which a little over 80 million is of working age and a little over 40 million is in the labor force. The open unemployment figure is then about one million (exactly 2.22%) and the rate in cities is more than twice that prevailing in the rural areas (i.e., 4.88% against 1.75%).

Lacking comparable statistical figures one has no ground to assess the advances or setbacks in employment since the beginning of the new policies. In 1967 and in 1970 there have been some household sample surveys (the so-called SUSENAS sample surveys) taken on a national scale and these also have produced figures for unemployment. They were based on the same reference period of one week. In orders of magnitude these unemployment ratios are the same as for the 1971 national population census and hence one could conclude that the unemployment figures have been somewhat stationary during the period of the new regime. This may be the best general conclusion, although a lot of relevant and significant properties may be concealed in these overall dimensions.

In a country like Indonesia, with a significant underemployment rate (figures of 25% are often mentioned), the balance between unemployment and underemployment can shift according to definitions and methods of interview, according to season, and according to the intensity of industrialization and urbanization. With one aggregate employment figure there can be differences in distribution between open measured unemployment, underemployment, and full employment. Also, the labor force participation rate may not be stable. Hence unemployment statistics and figures are very ambiguous. With a 7% real GDP growth rate, with a 0.5 employment elasticity with respect to output, and with a 3% growth in labor force, one could console himself that the growth rate is making a small dent in the unemployment figure, but open measured unemployment could easily grow if some of the underemployed people from the rural sector drift to the cities, attracted by the glitter of new factories. In this respect Indonesia's major unemployment worries may arrive in the near future, if the pace of industrialization quickens.

Since 1967 the market economy has certainly produced disruptive effects if judged against employment. Since 1969, when the full force of the new policies was felt, and continuing even to the present, mass dismissals of workers and business failures, and the consequent reduction of number of enterprises, became frequent phenomena. All this has been accompanied by a relative business boom with impressive gains in industrial production, growth in mining output (especially oil), and expansion in service industries, like transportation, banking, and insurance.

The market economy, the stable and free foreign exchange system, and the improvements in the balance of payments have caused the economy to change from a sellers' market to a much more competitive buyers' market. The warlike economy of empty shelves made room for a consumers' market with plenty of choice. But this turnabout exacted its victims. Industrial and other business enterprises had to purge themselves of excess personnel, while many of them could not stand the competition from imports and therefore had to liquidate. Sometimes, smart capitalist-entrepreneurs willingly closed their enterprises which were burdened by old equipment and excess labor, to venture anew in a more promising new line; for instance, liquidating an old textile mill to use the money to build a new hotel, since tourism looked like a growth industry.

The entry of foreign investments was also not free from dislocating effects, especially in the import substitution field. The existing domestic enterprises were often small, less efficient, labor intensive, and did not turn out a quality product. Often they could not stand the competition of the much more modern, larger scale, capital intensive foreign enterprises which came in with import duty privileges and tax holidays, and were out to conquer a market with aggressive advertising and selling efforts.

We have thus a comparison of two situations. Before 1967 the economy was stagnant and somewhat isolated from the outside world. New technologies were not vigorously introduced and thus were not disruptive. The social climate and policies favored protection of employment at the expense of efficiency and productivity and with consequent low real wages. After 1967, with an open and market economy and with vastly increasing imports of all goods and services, we have a growing economy in terms of output, with possibly a greater employment content in aggregate, but accompanied by a spotty record of mass dismissals and business failures. The domestic industry has become more capital and technology intensive and probably more efficient, but we still have no proof that its efficiency is great enough to enable it to compete in foreign markets. If our domestic industry does not become export-oriented and export-capable then maybe the trade-off between the old system and the new system has dubious merit. If we can produce the basket of goods we need ourselves with more employment rather than with less employment, then we would prefer this as long as we have a problem of unemployment. Admittedly, we have not taken account of the employment multiplier of the new industries, and this might be significant. With an improvement of domestic transportation and distribution, the total employment of the new industries with their backward and forward linkages might well be very important. But again, we have no statistics or results of surveys to shed light on this. In the meantime, the public debate over the merits of the new import substitution joint ventures continues.

One should bear in mind that the new technologies enter Indonesia not only in the form of factory equipment, but also in the form of organization, management, marketing techniques, etc. And apart from this hardware and software, there is now a much greater number of expatriate personnel, i.e., technicians, managers, salesmen, skilled workers, etc., who are all bearers of different value systems, different 'technologies' and different motivational drives. As to what will come out of this 'cultural shock' between indigenous and foreign entities, we can only hope for the best.

For the country there is no other effective alternative in the setting of the situation after 1966. The country had tried other policies in the past and they had failed. Hence the current task is to try to make the best of the current system. Indonesia will continue to grow as an open and stable economy, making use of a lot of foreign aid and investments. The problem is how to achieve distributive justice with at least a 7% rate of GDP growth, in terms of employment first of all, better yet also with equitable distribution of income and wealth.

Illustrative Examples in Several Sectors

In manufacturing industries. In a country where the level of industrialization is still low, the food processing and beverages industries, and the textile and garment industries are the most important in terms of output and employment. The construction and building materials industry may come next while various types of assembly industries may also occupy a significant place. The variety of technologies used in these industries is great. In textiles, for instance, there is a primitive handloom at one extreme and at the other the automatic mechanical loom requiring only one operator to tend more than 20 looms. In between there is a range of improved handlooms, powered but non-automatic, semi-automatic looms, etc. The degree of automation in the spinning plants is also quite varied.

Although a country like Indonesia has a very low wage rate (perhaps half a US dollar per day for a relatively unskilled operator) this does not automatically mean that the more labor intensive equipment will be favored by factory owners and managers. Depending upon familiar sources of supply of the machinery, depending upon financing arrangements, depending upon personal preferences, a particular set of equipment is ordered, often without adequate comparisons with lower cost alternatives. A Japanese investor may have a preference for Japanese equipment, possibly because his banks require it. Probably there is no old model or more labor intensive equipment any longer on sale, unless the investor procures second hand equipment or moves a plant from a foreign country to the new host country. Often the importation of second hand equipment is frowned upon by the officials of the receiving country, as this may be an insult to the national feelings of the officials.

Foreign managers may also prefer the management of machines rather than of men as they may be unaccustomed to the written and unwritten rules which govern labor relations in the host country. In the meantime the foreign investor can get away with inappropriate choices because his profit margins are protected by his market power. In other words, if he is secure of a certain accustomed rate of return he will not look further for a better solution for the country.

Investors' preferences and imperfect markets may not be the only culprits. The incentive system, provided by eager governments to lure new investments, may have contributed much to the distortions. These benefits usually take the form of import duty exemptions for plant equipment, raw materials, and spare parts. Tax holidays on corporate profits are also popular. All this distorts factory prices and puts a premium on capital intensity. Foreign investors also demand non-discriminatory treatment vis-á-vis domestic investors. But equal treatment for the weak and strong tends to give an advantage to the strong; hence the strong get stronger and the weak get weaker.

Fortunately, in Indonesia we have a variety of foreign investors by country of origin. Investors coming from highly developed countries tend to bring with them more advanced, i.e., more capital intensive and labor saving, technologies. Hence, there is a difference in employment content between American, European and Japanese investments on the one hand, and Hongkong, Indian and Singapore investments on the other hand. In comparison with both groups, the so-called domestic investments use more capital saving technologies.

Can advanced (i.e., capital intensive), intermediate, and more primitive technologies live side by side in one industry? Yes they can. One can find them in the textile industry and also in the beverages and food processing industry. In the soft drink industry, for instance, the advanced technology is used by the international brand and is usually based on automation; the intermediate technology is used by the national or not so international brand and is mechanical (i.e., powered) but not automated; the local, indigenous, soft drink is often manufactured with simple hand tools. The quality of the local indigenous, soft drink is much different from the foreign or national brand, and the difference is reflected in a significant price differential. The local brands may be able to survive but they certainly have no future, or room for expansion. The survival rate of these small enterprises is small and turnover is great. Their eclipse is at times accompanied by sensitive public reactions against the large predators. There are no research or survey results as yet to show to what extent establishment turnover has resulted in an overall decline of employment in this industry. What is clearly visible, though, is the increasing market share of the international brands. Some research has borne out that in terms of cost of production the intermediate technology (non-automatic) is cheaper than the advanced technology, but it is doubtful that the big (multinational) companies will be sensitive to this. The much greater market power of the international brands may have made them blind to cost differences with alternative production methods.

Sometimes the more advanced technologies break down because of deficiencies in maintenance and local repair facilities, and in certain industries (usually among national firms) one can see automatic machines standing idle. Clearly, there was a faulty investment decision; it is unfortunate that there was no correction mechanism to prevent it. In Indonesia, a lot of domestic investors must resort in varying degrees to bank financing; perhaps the banks engaged in such term lending should perform a better watchdog function.

In agriculture. As in other countries there is uncertainty as to whether or not the new high yielding varieties have brought greater employment opportunities. In terms of employment content it is calculated that the new rice varieties require more labor inputs, in terms of manweeks, in the production cycle. However, there may be dislocational effects as well. The new varieties grow well in irrigated areas. They also require more working capital for things like fertilizers and insecticides. Hence the landlords and landowning farmers stand more to gain than the landless farmers. If the production increases spoil the prices of the commodity, the marginal producers will be hit harder because they probably will not be practitioners of the new techniques. At harvest time the landlords and landowning farmers may also have an urge to pocket a greater share of the new productivity by refusing the hordes of villagers who want to help with the harvest. The harvesting could mainly be done with more efficient, i.e., labor saving techniques, costing not much in investment expenditures. Is harvest time labor really gainful employment? Maybe not, but it always has been a vehicle to distribute the social production of the village.

Nowadays, villages are humming with small, Japanese made machines milling paddy; they are called rice hullers. These innovations profit the landowners or the owners of the paddy. The rice is better polished, less broken, and hence fetches a better price. It also can be stored a little longer than the handpounded rice. Yet, many female working hours at hand pounding are foregone with consequent distributional effects. These shifts in employment and income distribution will probably never be registered in a census on account of definitions of employment, but they can shake the foundations of a village's life.

In construction and public works. This is a sector where different technologies coexist side by side and where market imperfections are so great that "market signals" are less effective, sometimes even non-existent, in preventing the utilization of inappropriate technologies. Because the output is a service, there is no competition from imports. Of course there is one form of competition checking the costs of construction and that is the tender system. This system, however, does not guarantee that the most labor intensive, or the most capital saving techniques will win. There may be at least two reasons for this; first, maybe the more capital intensive methods are just so much more efficient on the basis of current market prices; second, the competitors in the tender somehow or other may have the same bias.

Distortions in factor prices may however, be an underlying cause of a capital intensive bias. The importation of capital equipment is usually more or less subsidized, either because of an overvalued exchange rate or because there is a popular tendency in the developing countries to fix import duties of equipment at very low levels (until there is a domestic industry requiring protection). In Indonesia, as may be the case in other countries, government departments carry out a lot of construction activities. If they are not government agencies they may be semi-governmental outfits or state owned construction companies, which are not very efficiency conscious because they benefit from several kinds of (disguised) subsidies.

Away from metropolitan centers, in hinterland areas, one finds more labor intensive construction and earthmoving activities. These are carried out by local and village governments, by community groups, etc. Apparently different factor prices are relevant for different sectors of the economy. If this is the case, then a check on the costing in the more modern sector based on shadow pricing should be in order.

For village construction activities, undertaken by the "food for work program" (2 kg. bulgar wheat per day is given to participants, out of PL 480 supplies, plus a Rp. 35 per day cash supplement), it is insisted that the work be carried out by villagers and not be contracted out, as is the case in another program called the "Kabupaten Program." If contracted out there is a tendency to hire skilled earthmoving workers (with better tools) from other places, so that the employment has different distributional effects. Here we have another example of trade offs between unskilled workers and skilled workers with differing amounts of employment content measured in man-days, with different pay per man-day because of different levels of productivity. Mechanized systems will give rise to less employment in terms of man-years but maybe the aggregate wage bill will not be less. What would be a better system, one maximizing man-years or one maximizing the aggregate wage bill? These differences in labor productivity which one could observe in the construction industry (a Japanese brick layer is much more efficient than his Indonesian counterpart) may also underscore one often missing condition for more labor intensive methods of production, that is, one must have reasonable levels of labor productivity. This is probably the reason why the labor intensive electronics assembly industries first grew up in Japan, then in Hongkong, then subsequently in Korea, Taiwan and Singapore. They are now in the process of entering Indonesia, although in this latter country the wages are the lowest. Labor productivity could be achieved in this industry by training and by having a corps of good supervising and technical personnel. Hence, the missing elements for the full utilization of cheap and abundant labor should be made available first.

In trade and services. These are the traditional sectors in which most of the underemployment in urban areas is found. Not much can be said from current Indonesian experience about the relationship between technologies applied and the employment effects. The atomistic and very competitive market structure is probably a built-in safeguard against the use of very capital intensive methods of production. Department stores with high overhead costs and supermarkets are not very successful as yet in Jakarta, let alone in other places. The very few small supermarkets recently springing up in Jakarta cater more to the foreign community. The large, Japanese-war-reparations-built (but government owned) Sarinah Department store is virtually bankrupt. A current phenomenon is the partitioning out of the larger Chinese shops to individual operators who occupy their own counters. Hence, small scale and personnel-intensive operations are the dominant features in trade and distribution. Only the foreign and the state banks indulge in big and expensive buildings; on the other hand the more than hundred private banks are small and are housed in much less pretentious buildings. That the foreign banks are much more efficient and faster growing is another story. The competition between the state banks and the private banks is not completely on even terms; the state banks can fall back more easily on the Central Bank and the deposits guarantee system of the State gives them additional protection. The mechanization and the automation of the banks are continuing, especially among state banks. The local private banks can less afford such innovations. The impact of this process on efficiency and employment is something about which little information is available. Since salary levels in the banking sector are significantly higher than average, it may well be that mechanization and computerization are a foregone conclusion.

Policy Instruments and Variables

In the setting of a market economy the first option of the government to direct the allocation of resources is to influence the price mechanism through (indirect) taxes, other fiscal policies, and subsidies. Plan conscious governments of developing countries are not *laissez faire* oriented although they are committed to upholding a market economy system. They do interfere by changing the price signals, but not always with an employment orientation. To encourage capital investments, to foster industrialization, capital is often made cheaper, and the expected rate of return made higher, by import duties exemption or reduction (on capital goods), by tax holidays, and by low rates of interest for term lending. This is what has happened in Indonesia. This incentive system worked. Investors recognized the welcome signals and responded. Now that the planning community has become more employment oriented, one begins to wonder, has the government given unnecessary incentives? Has it thereby prejudiced employment? We are not sure. Capital-labor ratio is one thing, but to have employment one must have capital investment first. Maybe a capital-oriented incentive system would be the right thing to have in a particular period of time where capital is the critical bottleneck. When the investment momentum is gained and bandwagon effects have taken place, the incentive system could gradually be shifted toward other objectives. As a compromise the price system could be made more neutral, that is, not biased either way. In Indonesia the current exchange rate of Rp. 415 to the US dollar is probably not overvalued and therefore not biased. Domestic rates of interest are high. This in itself is good, but medium term investment credit is made available at lower than market rates of interest and hence may slightly favor capital intensity.

The foreign sector does not respond to these domestic signals. They have access outside to lower rates of interest. The import duty exemptions for capital equipment make them unaware of the real cost of capital. Short of abrogating the special incentives to enter, what could be done to influence their choices of technology? Often the local manager is more sensitive to the needs of the host country, but he does not make the design decisions. His influence is greater at later stages of the operation. Making headquarters' officers of multi-national companies more sensitive and more accommodating to the needs of the developing host country is one exercise for which ways and means (or communication and persuasion) must be found. The influence of the World Bank Group, the UN agencies, OPEC, and other government bodies could be effective if properly mobilized and applied. Apart from this kind of international action, some national remedies could be tried. Could the choice of technologies be made one of the specified entry requirements for foreign or multi-national firms? Of course this could be done, although this is an infringement of the free market system. As a one-time interference the measure may not be too bad. Indonesia so far has refrained from doing so as it is not sure how to determine the appropriate technologies. Should the government insist on "intermediate technologies," and if so what are they? Should the government encourage the importation and use of second hand equipment? How good is the technical competence of government officials in the determination of technologies used in the private sector? If things go sour who should take the blame? Another policy alternative is to follow the advice of foreign experts: clean up your price system (i.e., correct the biases) and leave things to the investing parties (they know best). If markets are perfect, this may work; but they are not.

In Indonesia ever since the colonial administration, the excises on "white" cigarettes are higher than for the "native," i.e., clove cigarettes. The intention was to protect the labor intensive, handrolled cigarettes. This differential tax could be applied to more goods with clear distinctions in the methods of production. By this differential tax the two commodities could coexist and the decline of the inferior technology delayed, thereby easing the unemployment effects of the transition.

Other countries apply other policies, such as making certain (labor intensive) technologies exclusive for the production of certain commodities, such as sarongs, towels, etc. Indonesia does this for batik which requires the wax process. Batik patterns may not be printed. One realizes, however, that by doing so Indonesia is giving up a widening market opportunity abroad, which is now exploited by other neighboring countries.

Another means of protection is the granting of government orders to enterprises which contribute more to the welfare of the country. In the late fifties and early sixties the military, for instance, did order its supplies from domestic (national) textile mills and refrained from importing. This "buy domestically" preference is no longer strong; moreover the products purchased by government are not such as to automatically help employment in the less modern labor intensive industries.

There is now an effort to educate government departments of the employment effects of their decisions and their activities. In this respect it is gratifying that from international agencies, such as the World Bank and the ILO, from foreign governmental agencies, e.g., AID, and other parties, similar concern is expressed and policies have been formulated to promote greater employment effects in the implementation of various aid projects. Since foreign aid is a major source of financing for development projects we stand a good chance that soon government departments will be imbued with an employment promotion spirit.

The employment effects of the development budget can be augmented by choice of projects. A significant portion of the Indonesian development budget is spent on employment-oriented or employment-creating public works and rural development projects. This is a recognition of the fact that employment effects depend not only on *how* (i.e., technologies used) you do things, but also on *what* you are making and *where* you do things. Also the *who* (implements the project) may be important.

The problems of development and dissemination of so-called intermediate technologies have received serious attention. Several international circles have shown their interest, including the East-West Center, UNIDO, and the London-based Intermediate Technology Group. Domestically, the Bandung Institute of Technology and the Departments of Industries and of Manpower arc interested parties. The Department of Manpower administers the domestic Volunteer Service, under which young graduates live for two years in villages trying to act as development and modernization agents. There is certainly a need for practical, more efficient technologies than those presently practiced in the villages. Hence, "intermediate technologies" must mean better, a little more advanced, and more productive technologies than those already in use in rural areas and local industries. This is in contrast to the term "appropriate technology" which is better suited in the modern sector, and should mean that often an imported technology is less well suited to the host country needs and conditions, and that a more appropriate technology should be developed, often through adaptation.

The search for and the dissemination of intermediate technologies may require new institutions and working arrangements, certainly domestically. A link up with the international system is also required. Prior to World War II we had several research and development institutions. Their effectiveness was greater during the Dutch colonial administration, before the war, when staffing and budgets were more adequate. The famous weaving loom (the ATBM), a product of the Bandung Textile Institute, improved on the old primitive indigenous loom (the "Gedogan"). The Leather Institute, the Ceramic Institute, the Batik Institute, and maybe others, were well functioning institutions for the development of suitable technologies and their dissemination. Through lack of qualified staff and budgets these institutions have since lived an anemic life. In the development and application of better technologies one also needs a combination of inputs, and technology alone is often not enough. If the local know-how of pottery making was upgraded by modern methods, the new products would need better design and marketing in cities and hence would need additional working capital financing. The larger scale of the operation requires more management inputs, etc. Thus, a whole system has to be changed, and here is where most innovations fail. Often a new endeavor remains fragile and needs nursing and protection for a long time. There is now an effort to strengthen these institutions (they are part of the Department of Industries) through the help of UNIDO and UNDP.

The "who" dimension of the problem of technology and employment, namely, that it may make some difference who invests, is also getting a lot of attention these days. The employment effects, say of manufacturing industry investments, can be different depending upon whether the investor is an American, a Japanese, a Hong-kong Chinese, a domestic Chinese or an indigenous Indonesian. Domestic investors may use more locally made machinery and equipment in their efforts to save capital. The differences in employment effects between indigenous Indonesian and domestic Chinese investors are not clear. The indigenous Indonesians are smaller scale investors because they do not have much capital and these scale differences may have employment consequences. The Government is now thinking of rationing investment credits among the various categories of users in order to maximize employment effects and to allay feelings of social inequities.

One final word of caution. If a government is too overly concerned to direct and control the use of technologies to maximize employment, it may dampen the investment appetite in the private sector. If every factory expansion and new project requires government approval for its technologies, this may delay and stifle the investment process. Moreover, bureaucrats may not have the right idea of what is necessary and profitable for the business. Capital intensive projects, if they are really so much more efficient, may also have greater employment effects, in the longer run, permeating throughout the economy. The amount of employment you save in the short run may be much less than the employment you may gain in the longer run if the industrial structure is much more efficient. But this again is speculation. Many more empirical studies are needed to give answers to many of the now prevailing questions.

Green Revolution and Employment in Ludhiana, Punjab, India

Partap C. Aggarwal

Shri Ram Centre for
Industrial Relations and
Human Resources

Introduction

The term Green Revolution was probably frivolously coined by a journalist, or perhaps a politician. But it has such an appeal that even those who decry its appropriateness also use it for want of a better substitute. In fact, there is a tendency to attach this label to other somewhat similar changes. For instance, dairy development is referred to as a "white revolution," and an increase in the incidence of violence is called a "red revolution."

A perusal of the growing literature on the subject indicates that different writers have presented divergent views. Some have examined only the technological aspects of the Green Revolution such as the adoption of High Yielding Varieties of seeds, farm mechanization, use of chemical fertilizers and insecticides, and irrigation with pumps. Many have tried to equate the revolution itself with one or the other of these changes. For instance there are those who say that it is a "wheat revolution," and still others who call it a "fertilizer revolution" or a "tractor revolution." Then there are writers who emphasise the increasing market orientation of the cultivators, or as some have put it, a move toward "capitalist agriculture." A majority of investigators have shown concern about the current and anticipated socio-political consequences of the Green Revolution. They notice and predict drastic changes in the traditional institutions and power relationships, and caution against severe maladjustments leading to violent conflicts.

The present paper is based on a larger study[1] in which an attempt is made to see if the various economic, technological, social, and political changes attributed to the Green Revolution have in fact occurred in Ludhiana, Punjab. And if they have, in what way are they interrelated and how best can we interpret them in an integrated fashion? In other words, our concern is to study the Green Revolution as a multifaceted phenomenon. In addition we try to see how the landless labourers and their employment prospects have been affected.

Peasants, Farmers, and Revolution

Peasants. By and large the societal type encountered in the rural areas of most underdeveloped countries is what is referred to by anthropologists as "peasantry," or simply "peasant." Ethnographic studies have shown that although no two peasan-

373

tries are exactly alike, they all have remarkable similarities even when widely separated in time and space. Three basic features characterise peasant societies everywhere. These are: 1) a two-tier structure with a cultural and communication gap separating the rural from the urban, 2) subsistence orientation, and 3) pre-industrial technology.

Prior to the Green Revolution Ludhiana cultivators were peasants like their counterparts all over the country. They produced mainly for subsistence[2], and only a small fraction of their total produce was sold in the market for cash. In fact their requirement of cash was very small. Most of what they needed as consumers or producers was either produced by themselves or obtained within the village in exchange for grain. For instance, even labourers were paid in grain. Service castes, such as carpenters and blacksmiths, functioned under the traditional *Sepi* system (a variant of the *jajmani* * system) and were compensated in kind at each harvest. Economic relationships within the community were so arranged that the non-agricultural households were also assured a subsistence living.

The technology was pre-industrial. Most of the work was done manually by simple hand tools. Bullocks provided the draft power for heavier work such as ploughing, planting, irrigating and hauling. Major implements were the wooden plough, Persian wheel and simple carts. Vegetable and animal waste material was converted into compost and returned to the soil. The agricultural cycle was matched with the quality and capacity of the available inputs. For instance, only one crop a year was grown on a given piece of land.

Since Independence in 1947 the gap between the rural areas and the urban centres had progressively narrowed due to the establishment of a democratic form of government, community development, *Panchavati Raj* institutions, and improvement in the communication channels. But despite these improvements the villages in Ludhiana District remained relatively isolated until the early 60's. The three villages which we have studied lacked road links, bus services, and electricity. In fact, the villagers' need to relate with the city was so weak that these deficiencies did not much matter.

The peasant system was so well established that the villagers resisted the small innovations introduced by the Community Development Department. *Jat Sikh* cultivators of Ludhiana are regarded as one of the most enterprising communities in the world.[3] Yet as long as they remained peasants they were unable and unwilling to adopt modern technology.

Farmers. Farmers, unlike peasants, are entrepreneurs for whom agriculture is a business for profit. Even when they live in small hamlets or isolated homesteads, they are socially, politically and economically integrated with the rest of the society. They sell most of their produce in the market and use the cash proceeds to purchase consumer goods and farm inputs. Their technology is modern, and it is based on tractors, chemical fertilizers, improved seeds, and efficient management practices.

Our study shows that Ludhiana cultivators are now farmers and no longer peasants. They have adopted modern technology so completely and so effectively that in five years they have reached a top position in the world in per hectare wheat yield. More than 80 percent of what they produce is sold in the market, and almost all their

---

*A system under which various castes provided their special services to the cultivators in exchange for a fixed payment in grain at every harvest. This hereditary arrangement was prevalent throughout North India and still survives despite considerable weakening in recent years.

transactions are now monetized. Villages have become linked with the urban areas politically, economically, and socially, and the gap that earlier separated the two has been closed.

Revolution. A revolution may be defined as, "a relatively sudden set of changes that yield a state of affairs from which a return to the situation just before the revolution is virtually impossible."[4] In terms of this definition when peasants turn farmers we have a real revolution. As explained before, the Green Revolution involves a variety of changes; in fact one way of life is replaced by another. A similar type of change occurred in the now industrialised countries over a period of a century or more; its occurrence in less than a decade is quite remarkable. Judging from the experience of the West, we can safely assume that the Green Revolution is virtually irreversible.

Antecedents of the Green Revolution

Our Ludhiana study indicates that the Green Revolution is caused by a multitude of factors. Following India's Independence a variety of developments began to take place and over two decades they grew cumulatively and converged to produce a situation where a revolution became possible. Two points need to be emphasised here. One, even if a development is slow, it can grow into something substantial over a period of time. Two, a convergence of several developments can produce a qualitatively new environment where revolutionary changes may take place.

Carl Gotsch has rightly pointed out that a "minimum technical package" and "a minimum infrastructure" are needed to motivate the cultivators for change.[5] Indeed cultivators in certain areas have responded positively to such stimuli. But the problem is that there are far too many cases where fulfillment of these conditions have not produced a positive response. Highly productive wheat varieties have been virtually ignored by cultivators in many parts of India. There are examples of IADP[6] (Intensive Agricultural District Program) districts where even a massive effort did not bring about a Green Revolution. On the other hand there are non-IADP districts that have done extremely well without the benefit of special attention.

Obviously a minimum package produces results only in a suitable environment to which a variety of factors contribute. In our Ludhiana study we have listed several, but here let me illustrate the point by emphasising only two. One is indigenization of industrial technology and the second relates to power equalization.

Indigenization of technology. Before Independence Ludhiana was a sleepy provincial town, and the district as a whole was considered backward compared to the rest of the province of Punjab. Except for a few small hosiery factories, there was no industry in the district. Agriculture, too, was rather deficient by Punjab's peasant standards, and part of the reason was believed to be poor quality of land. During British rule Ludhiana's enterprising *Ramgarhia* craftsmen and Jat cultivators had to emigrate to other areas to seek better opportunities in business, government, or agriculture.

Following Independence, small industry of a wide variety developed in the district so rapidly that by the mid-sixties Ludhiana emerged as the largest small industries centre in the country.[7] The hosiery industry grew rapidly, but more significantly, an engineering goods industry developed with an enormous range of products including bicycles, scooters, sewing and knitting machines, motor parts, machine tools, diesel engines, and agricultural machinery. In 1970-71 Ludhiana had over 10,000 registered factories and probably an equal number of unregistered ones.

Four very important characteristics of Ludhiana industry might be underlined. First, it is owned and managed by local entrepreneurs and not by industrialists from other states. Much of the metal based engineering industry is owned by the Ramgarhias, many of whom earlier worked in the villages as carpenters or blacksmiths for their Jat patrons. Consequently, the Ramgarhias[8] have gained considerable economic power and social prestige. Initially most of the skilled workers were recruited from among the Ramgarhias, but the demand increased so rapidly that lower castes were also allowed to enter.

Second, most of the business enterprises are small, and they use simple, locally made machine tools. This is significant because the level of skills required in this kind of enterprise is higher than that needed in assembly line establishments. In order successfully to operate these crude machines one has to be able to manipulate them. In this way men acquired an intimate knowledge of basic technology which they can use in solving problems outside the factory.*

Third, many of the products are intended to meet local demands, particularly for agricultural machinery, sewing and knitting machines, and machine tools. Consequently, there is a great deal of interdependence between the producer and the consumer. It is not surprising that in the last seven or eight years Ludhiana's industry has responded amazingly fast and effectively to the changing and increasingly sophisticated needs of the farmers. Agricultural machines, such as the thresher and the seed drill, developed by the engineers of the Punjab Agricultural University, were almost immediately taken up for manufacturing. Also, during periods of power scarcity the production of small diesel engines was quickly expanded to meet the demand. Excluding the tractor, almost all agricultural machines are now produced in Ludhiana.

Fourth, most of the industrial workers are from the villages in the area. Many of them commute to work either by bicycle or by bus. They bring the knowledge of industrial technology into the village and thus facilitate its adoption.[9]

As industry has grown, many supporting facilities have become available in the district. For example, a large number of repair and service workshops have sprung up. They have the facilities to repair, recondition, rebuild, and service even the most sophisticated and complex machines. Furthermore, a large number of shops have been set up that supply new equipment, spare parts, tools, lubricants, and fuels. Many such shops have been established even in the rural areas.

So many machines are in use that people have become familiar with them. Earlier, when villagers did not use fast running machines, such as the diesel engine, they lacked the basic discipline necessary for machine technology. Slow-running equipment, such as the bullock cart and the Persian wheel, required very little maintenance and care. For example, a bullock cart wheel may be allowed to squeak for weeks for want of oil, but a few minutes of dry running will seriously damage a diesel engine.

The villager's knowledge of the machine is reflected in the number of new words that have been added to his vocabulary. One hears words such as bearings, nozzles, bolts and nuts, piston, pins, foundation, fan belt, fuse, and so forth. Also, many words relating to the working of the machines have come into common use such as play, *lag* or area of contact, overheating, friction, short circuit, temperature, speed, *chakkar* or rounds per minute, *phawara* or atomization, and quite a few more. We have noticed that these words are used by villagers with a great deal of understanding.

---

*This observation is based on personal experience as managing partner of a small motor parts factory in Punjab from 1958 to 1960.

Furthermore, because of proliferation of machines in the area, and an increase in the number of men who operate them, technical assistance is easily available at the village level. Many men who currently work in Ludhiana factories, or who have returned to their villages after experience in industry, are on hand to help diffuse technical knowledge.

All these changes represent indigenization of technology which is a necessary condition for rapid and successful adoption of modern equipment in agriculture. It must be pointed out that this process began soon after Independence, and by the time the Green Revolution got underway in 1965-66, indigenization of technology had already reached a fairly high level. This greatly facilitated the successful adoption of farm machinery by agriculturists in the district.

Power equalization. Major changes have occurred in the distribution of political and economic power among individuals as well as caste groups in the last two decades in Ludhiana. These changes have contributed significantly in bringing about the Green Revolution. Considering limitations of space we will briefly discuss changes only in relation to the *Jats,* the *Ramgarhias,* and the *Harijans.**

The Jats were traditionally the dominant landowning caste in Ludhiana villages. They constituted about half the population and owned virtually all of the land. Consequently, they were not only comparatively well-off but also they wielded considerable economic and political power over all other castes. Among the Jats themselves, however, the disparities were not very great. There were several reasons for this: 1) a relatively even distribution of land, 2) employment opportunities in the military, and 3) the equalitarian ethos of Sikhism. Since Independence disparities have been further reduced mainly due to a series of land reforms. Also, due to improvements in agricultural technology the incomes of Jat farmers regardless of size of holding have multiplied. As a consequence many new avenues (e.g. college education) of social advancement have opened up even for medium and small farmers.

The Ramgarhias occupied a middle position on the caste hierarchy, i.e. between the Jats above and the Harijans below. They were represented in small numbers in each village and they served the Jats as carpenters or blacksmiths under the traditional Sepi (or jajmani) arrangement. Prevailing social norms prevented them from owning land which made them completely dependent on the Jats.[10] Also, being few in number they were politically weak. During British rule a few of them migrated to Africa and Burma and did reasonably well as carpenters or contractors, but such opportunities were limited. Since Independence, however, the Ramgarhias have entered small industry as entrepreneurs and skilled workers with remarkable success. Consequently, they have gained economic power, political influence, and social prestige.

The Harijans, traditionally, were at the bottom of the caste hierarchy. They constituted 25 to 30 percent of the population in Ludhiana villages and most of them worked as agricultural labourers. Because of their large numbers only a few practiced their traditional caste occupations—shoe making and weaving. They were poor, politically weak, and socially Pariah. In the last two decades the relative gain of the Harijans has been the greatest of all caste groups.[11] First, due to increased employment opportunities in agriculture and outside, and due to a rapid rise in wages, the

---

*Harijan refers to the low castes who were traditionally the most underprivileged. They were treated as untouchables by the higher castes.

economic condition of the Harijans has vastly improved. Second, because of the large number of their votes the Harijans have gained considerable political weight at all levels, particularly at the village Panchayat level. Third, untouchability and other discriminatory practices have been abandoned amazingly fast. The Harijans can now attend the Jat's *gurdwaras* (place of worship), use village wells, participate in village meetings, and even share food with the higher castes.[12]

The Jats have emerged as a class with common economic interests. Consolidation of holdings, increasingly even distribution of land, and now very profitable new technology have involved the Jats in agriculture even more than before. Their earlier attachment to land was only on an individual basis characteristic of peasants. Their class consciousness in the present context is combined with political participation at the local, state, and the national level. The Jats constitute a large and strategic voting block. Also, due to their dominant position in the rural areas they have influence over non-Jat electorate as well. In the absence of strong urban elites in the state, the Jats have greatly influenced Punjab politics. This is indicated by the fact that most of Punjab's chief ministers and cabinet ministers have been Jats or non-Jat cultivators.

Naturally, the Punjab governments, regardless of the party in power, have heavily favored development of agricultural and small industry. At the same time big industrial houses have been kept out of the state. Punjab succeeded in this partly because the remote-controlled industry of the colonial type does not have a strong base in Punjab.* Also there are no absentee landlords whose interests are best served in peasant agriculture.[13] Punjab's Jat farmers are actual cultivators, most of whom own and plough their land, and can benefit from a more profitable technology. Naturally, they influenced the government accordingly and all governments in Punjab since Independence have been aggressively development oriented with a strong agrarian bias.

The Jat cultivators of Punjab as a class are politically very efficacious. They influence government decisions through their representatives in the Government by active lobbying. During field work in Ludhiana we noticed that even the village level political leaders, such as the *panchayat* members, had direct links with powerful individuals in the state capital. So much so that the farmers of Punjab have the confidence that they can continue to enjoy government support for development and state assistance in case of serious problems. This knowledge and confidence on the part of the farmer, in my view, has greatly facilitated the Green Revolution. Complete replacement of a time-tested technology, and a way of life, with another yet to be tried is full of hazards: the seed may not prove as productive as claimed, its disease resistance may be low, prices may fall, fertilizer and other new inputs may not be available on time, prices of tractors may rise, sufficient credit may not be available, etc. The feeling that the resources of the government can be bent to solve all these and other unforeseen problems has made the Jat cultivator willing to change fast.

Trends toward more equal distribution of power among the various caste groups have greatly boosted the morale of the hitherto underprivileged groups. The Ramgarhias for instance have acquired a higher status by their success in industry and the resulting improvement in economic and political power. In the villages they have abandoned their tradition Sepi relationship with the Jats. Most of our Ramgarhia informants said that they no longer were willing to accept Jat dominance. Of course

---

*The British and European controlled industries such as jute, tea, textiles, footwear, and engineering were located in Bengal, Bombay or Madras. None of the large Indian industrial houses like the Tatas, the Birlas, the Dalmias and the Sarabhais showed much interest in establishing plants in Punjab. This lack of interest was partly due to non-availability of mineral resources.

they could act in response to this feeling only when there were viable alternatives before them. The desire to attain a higher status coupled with attractive opportunities has impelled the Ramgarhias toward harder work, greater risk taking, and innovative behavior.

The Harijans, too, have taken full advantage of the new opportunities. They send their children to school and encourage them to seek white-collar jobs in the city. Some have purchased land and started farming. A large proportion have found lucrative opportunities in industry, construction work, and enterprises such as poultry, dairying, etc. Consequently as Dr. Randhawa writes: "Except in the harvest season, when the wages are high, able-bodied young workers are hard to come across."[14] In other words, the Harijans have improved their economic and social position by hard striving.

The point to be stressed is this. In a rigidly stratified peasant society an individual belonging to an underprivileged caste cannot change his position by his own efforts, so he sees no advantage in accepting new ideas. On the other hand members of the privileged castes also do not strive hard partly because their position is secure. But when the society begins to change, tremendous energy is released. The privileged try to become richer, and the weaker sections see new opportunities for improvement. My research in Indian villages has convinced me that no matter how rigid and old a caste system may be, the underprivileged know where they stand and they never lose the desire to improve themselves.

Employment

At last we come to the employment implications of the Green Revolution, which is the major concern of this seminar. Although we are interested in employment in general, here I speak only of the changing employment pattern of agricultural labourers in Ludhiana, Punjab. I may repeat, however, that the caste groups who traditionally provided agricultural labour were the Harijans who constituted 25 to 30 percent of the rural population and were the most underprivileged of all the castes. Nearly 50 percent of the population is made up of landowning Jats for whom the question of employment is unimportant. The remaining 20 to 25 percent are traders or artisans who are self-employed and have all been greatly benefitted by the Green Revolution. So, even though we are talking of 25 to 30 percent of the total population, we are really confronting the rural employment question in the most meaningful way.

The demand for agricultural labour. Our Ludhiana study indicates that the demand for agricultural labour per hectare of land has remained more or less constant. This observation is amply supported by other detailed studies done in the area. In fact, it has been observed that the demand for human labour per acre has gone up.[15] This is so despite the fact that a variety of labour saving agricultural machines have come into common use. Tractors have virtually replaced bullocks for seed-bed preparation, planting, and a variety of other operations. Persian wheels have gone out of vogue and power driven centrifugal pumps have taken their place. All threshing is done by threshing machines. Furthermore, a good deal of the labour required to operate these machines is provided by the farmers themselves, mainly because of reluctance to trust labourers with expensive equipment.

Some of the explanations for the per unit demand for labour remaining constant, despite increased use of labour saving machinery, are as follows. First, because of high profitability and availability of powerful machinery, additional land has been reclaimed increasing the net cropped area by nearly 20 percent. Second, cropping intensity has increased by more than 50 percent. In fact, on almost all of the land two crops are now grown in a year. Third, due to improved quality of inputs, crops need more intensive care, including more frequent irrigation, fertilizer application, weeding, and spraying.

Furthermore, our data show that the labour requirement has become more evenly spread throughout the year. This is indicated by fewer available labourers and a significant increase in the number of days each worker is employed in a year. Nevertheless, a few peak periods still remain, particularly the two harvesting seasons and weeding. Especially for the wheat crop, which is grown on more than 80 percent of the Rabi (winter crop) land, the labour demand for harvesting and weeding is very high.

Another very significant change has been that adequate and timely availability of labour has become much more crucial. In the peasant days, seed varieties required much less care compared to the new high yielding varieties. Also the peasant's investment in each crop was low and his concern was basically that of subsistence. But now his investment on each crop is high and in the form of expensive inputs such as fertilizer, machinery, and insecticides. Hence, as there is a scarcity of labour in the area, the farmers evince a great deal of anxiety. In Ludhiana District, employers now have to compete for labour. In the villages where we did field research farmers had to visit the homes of labourers in order to engage them. We learned that farmers sometimes virtually abducted labourers while the latter were on their way to someone else's field. This kind of incidents have at times led to serious tensions.

Naturally, therefore, wage rates have more than doubled in the last 5 years, and they have a tendency to rise further. According to Randhawa, wage rates increased by 46.66 percent between 1967-68 and 1969-70.[16] Furthermore, employers now compete by offering sumptuous food to the labourers. At present labourers are given two meals and three snacks in addition to the cash wage, and sometimes alcoholic drinks are provided at the end of the day. This practice of giving meals to the labourers has become established even though it increases the work of the women in the farmers' houses, and there is growing resentment against this.

All this is leading to greater mechanization of farming. Newer and more efficient machines are sought by farmers. In the last two years, for instance, due to persistent efforts of the farm lobby, harvesting combines have come to Punjab. At present they are operated by a cooperative organization on custom service basis, but the demand for them is so great that even individual farmers are acquiring them for their own use and custom work.

To ensure adequate labour supply, many larger farmers hire men on a yearly contract. In order to bind the worker, his entire annual wage is often paid in advance. The responsibility of feeding him is that of the employer. In addition he gets fringe benefits in the form of fodder for his buffalo and other farm produce.

Supply of labour. In the villages of our study nearly half of the traditionally labour households have completely abandoned agricultural work. Even in the families that still do farm labour many younger men have taken up non-agricultural employment. In fact this process began nearly a decade before the Green Revolution, but in recent years employment opportunities have increased rapidly.

A large number of erstwhile farm labourers have found employment in textile, hosiery, and engineering goods factories in Ludhiana. Some work in shoe and chappal factories. More recently new employment opportunities have come up in the building trade. This is because a great deal of the increased income of the Jat farmers is going into new brick houses. Also the government is investing large sums in rural link roads and paving of village streets. Employment opportunities have also increased in the repair and service shops for farm equipment.

Labourers have a variety of reasons for moving to non-agricultural occupations. First, wages are better and there is scope for improvement through acquisition of new skills. Second, they have the strong desire to dissociate themselves from their traditional low caste occupations. Third, they want to be free from Jat dominance. Fourth, agricultural work, particularly weeding, is extremely tedious and it lacks prestige.

Large numbers of immigrant labourers come to this area from agriculturally poor states such as Rajasthan, Eastern U.P., and Bihar. They are employed by farmers for jobs such as weeding. Their wages are usually half of the local labourers, but they are considered slow, undependable and requiring too much supervision. Hence local labourers are preferred even at higher wages. Only when local labourers are not available are immigrants employed.

Our data show that agricultural labourers are increasingly engaging in supplementary activities such as poultry, pig rearing, and dairying. Marketing of milk and eggs is getting organized and inputs such as feed, equipment, and improved stock are available with the help of the university, the various development agencies, and some privately run business establishments.

Summary and Conclusions

We have suggested that the Green Revolution can be best understood as the transformation of peasants into farmers. It is a revolution because it involves a variety of changes which have occurred rapidly and the transformation involved is likely to be irreversible.

The Green Revolution has occurred as a result of a convergence of a number of developments. While economic factors such as infrastructure development and the adoption of high yielding varieties of seed are very important, these two alone have not everywhere produced a revolution. Several other prerequisites have been noted in our larger study, but here we have stressed two of them: indigenization of technology and power equalization.

The Ludhiana experience clearly indicates that at least so far the gains of the weaker sections are quite substantial. Employment opportunities for all, including the landless labourers, have improved considerably. Even when we try to look ahead, the prospects seem encouraging. So, if employment is our concern, Green Revolution is desirable and efforts should be made to create the right conditions for it everywhere.

There is a great deal of concern that the Green Revolution will increase the disparity between the rich and the poor. If that happens, it is logical to anticipate more tensions and violence, particularly in a democratic society. Indeed, violence has at times occurred in Thanjavur and Kerala but it cannot be attributed to the Green Revolution. Ludhiana and many other Green Revolution areas have not suffered an increase in violence even though the aspiration level of labourers seems clearly to have risen. Apparently this is because the initial gains of the weaker sections are substantial and their hopes are high.

All this is not in anyway to underplay the problems of poverty and unemployment in India or elsewhere. But judging from the Ludhiana experience, we can say that the Green Revolution is likely to help solve both these problems. Also, it is sharpening our understanding of the processes of agricultural development, particularly in relation to the peasant society.

Notes

1. Partap C. Aggarwal, *The Green Revolution and Rural Labour* (New Delhi, Shri Ram Centre, 1973).

2. For an excellent account of a Punjabi peasant village see Zakiye Eglar, *A Punjabi Village in Pakistan* (New York, Columbia, 1960); and Oscar Lewis, *Village Life in Northern India* (New York, Alfred A. Knopf, 1965).

3. Malcolm Darling, *The Punjab Peasant in Prosperity and Debt* (Bombay, Oxford, 1925), p. 117.

4. Charles F. Hockett and Robert Ascher, "The Human Revolution," *Current Anthropology*, 5 (1964), p. 135.

5. See Carl Gotsch, "Economics, Institutions and Employment Generation in Rural Areas," elsewhere in this book.

6. Government of India, *Modernising Indian Agriculture: Report of the I.A.D.P. (1960-68)*, Volume I (New Delhi, Ministry of Food, Agriculture, Community Development and Cooperation, 1969).

7. A somewhat outdated, but useful account of Ludhiana's small scale industry can be found in UNESCO, *Small Industries and Social Change* (Delhi, Unesco Research Centre, 1968). Also, see *Tribune* (June 27, 1970), special supplement on Ludhiana Industries.

8. A brief but very useful account of Ramgarhia entrepreneurs is given in Satish Saberwal, "On Entrepreneurship: Everett Hagen and the Ramgarhias," to be published in a forthcoming volume under the auspices of The Institute for Social and Economic Change, Bangalore, India.

9. We noticed this during field research in Ludhiana villages. More details can be found in my book, *The Green Revolution and Rural Labour, op cit*.

10. Saberwal, *op cit*.

11. Satish Saberwal, "Status, Mobility, and Networks in a Punjab Industrial Town," in Saberwal, ed., *Beyond the Village* (Simla, Indian Institute of Advanced Study, 1972), pp. 111-184.

12. For more details see my book, *The Green Revolution and Rural Labour, op cit*. Also see Satish Saberwal's article "Receding Pollution: Intercaste Relations in Urban Punjab," to be published shortly in the *Sociological Bulletin*, Delhi.

13. According to M.S. Randhawa, *Green Revolution* (New Delhi, Vikas, 1974), 88.32% of the land area in Ferozepur district was owner cultivated in 1969-70, (see p. 165). The average land holding in Ludhiana district is only 7½ hectares. In the three villages of our study only 24 percent of the holdings were larger than 20 acres each, the largest one was 63 acres, and almost all of them were owner cultivated.

14. *Ibid.*, p. 194.

15. *Ibid.*, p. 171.

16. *Ibid.*, p. 174.

Rural Development in China, 1949-1972 and the Lessons to be Learned From It

John G. Gurley
Stanford University

The precarious position of the Chinese peasants down through the ages and the oppressive conditions under which they labored are too well known to require much comment from me. One can read at length about their diseases, their illiteracy, their superstitions and fatalistic attitudes, the natural disasters and periodic famines that all but wiped them out, in Han (206 B.C.-220 A.D.), T'ang (618-906 A.D.), or Sung (960-1279 A.D.) records, and indeed right down to yesterday.

Nevertheless, the records also reveal, if one examines them closely, an ingenious peasantry producing a substantial surplus during most of this long period, not of course for itself, but mostly for the sustenance and pleasures of a few people who made up the ruling classes—the Emperor and his family and retainers, bureaucrats, landlords, money-lenders, and military officers. This small but powerful ruling group pumped the surplus out of the countryside through taxes, rents, interest, corvée labor, enslavement, extortion, and by other means fair and foul. It may well be that, on the average over these many centuries, one third of what this peasantry produced was taken away from it for the enjoyment and support of less than two percent of the population. What was left to the peasants was usually just enough for their survival, but from time to time not enough even for that. Undernourishment was common; starvation not unusual.

Let R.H. Tawney, who with much acumen observed the Chinese peasants in the early 1930s, have the last word:

> Exaggeration is easy. Privation is one thing, poverty to the point of wretchedness—la misère—another. A sturdy and self-reliant stock may grow in a stony soil. But, when due allowance has been made for the inevitable misconceptions, it is difficult to resist the conclusion that a large proportion of Chinese peasants are constantly on the brink of actual destitution. They are, so to say, a propertied proletariat, which is saved—when it is saved—partly by its own admirable ingenuity and fortitude, partly by the communism of the Chinese family, partly by reducing its consumption of necessaries and thus using up its physical capital . . .
>
> It is true, however, that, over a large area of China, the rural population suffers horribly through the insecurity of life and property. It is taxed by one ruffian who calls himself a general, by another, by a third, and, when it has bought them off, still owes taxes to the Government; in some places actually more than twenty years' taxation has been paid in advance. It is squeezed by dishonest officials. It must cut its crops at the point of the bayonet, and hand them over without payment to the local garrison, though it will starve without them. It is forced to grow opium in defiance of the law, because its military tyrants

can squeeze heavier taxation from opium than from rice or wheat, and make money, in addition, out of the dens where it is smoked. It pays blackmail to the professional bandits in its neighborhood; or it resists, and, a year later, when the bandits have assumed uniform, sees its villages burned to the ground . . .

There are districts in which the position of the rural population is that of a man standing permanently up to the neck in water, so that even a ripple is sufficient to drown him. The loss of life caused by the major disasters is less significant than the light which they throw on the conditions prevailing even in normal times over considerable regions.[1]

Explanations of Persistent Poverty Before 1949

There were of course reasons for the persistence of this deprivation and misery. The conventional explanation is that, even with the highest efficiency in carrying out the best-intentioned policies to alleviate rural poverty, the job would have been a most difficult one for any government. During the past century, for example, successive governments had to contend with several rebellions, civil wars, the Japanese invasions, and the continued encroachment of other foreign imperialist powers on the economy. The argument continues that, when one considers all of this turmoil within the context of how widespread and deeply embedded poverty was in the society, it is no wonder that very little was accomplished.

While this argument has some validity, it represents a very narrow view of the social forces at work in this period. For the disruptive events themselves emanated partly from the failure of the Chinese authorities to alleviate the poverty. It was a two-way street. The battles that went on were fed by the rural misery, but these struggles in turn contributed to further political disintegration and so to a growing inability of governments to shore up the crumbling base.

However, even with this reformulation, the foregoing is only a part of the total story. Most of the rest of it has to do with the "best intentions" assumed above. Social scientists these days usually suppose that all governments really want economic development, and, if they do not achieve it, then it must be because the problems are unusually difficult to solve, or that solutions take a rather long time to work themselves out. Persistence and technical knowledge are what is required for success. This supposition, however, does not adequately take account of the class structures of societies, the often conflicting aims that exist among the various classes, and the class nature of "success" and "failure." When poverty is looked at from the standpoint of the ruling classes, it may not be a failure of the system at all but rather a prerequisite for the continuation of their accumulation of wealth, their privileges, and their social, political, and economic domination of the society.

This is partly because poverty is often the carcass left from wealth acquisition; or, at best, it is the stagnant backwaters of society, not yet touched by a development process that stresses private profit-making and hence efficiency and "building on the best." But poverty persists also because it is closely associated with peasant characteristics which are highly supportive of the existing class structures and hence of the privileges and wealth of the dominant classes. I refer to the peasants' illiteracy, passivity, obedience, fatalism; to their lack of awareness of the world around them and therefore to their propensity for mythical and spiritual explanations of personal hardships and disasters; to their lack of organization, their willingness to work hard for very little; to their being easy set-ups for all sorts of manipulation by their "superiors."

A thorough-going program of economic development, which is spread widely and reaches deeply into the structure of society, is a dangerous thing to ruling classes, for it tends to undermine the very attributes of the masses of people that nourish the wealthy and powerful. Such a program awakens people, and it is often best that they doze; it mobilizes people for gigantic economic efforts, and such organization can be turned into political subversion; it sweeps away illusions, but may open their eyes to the causes of their own oppression.

Furthermore, any serious economic development program that involves indus-trialization within an agrarian and commercial society threatens existing class struc-tures by creating new economic bases from which arise new social classes, and weakens the economic foundations which support the present dominant classes. Economic development stirs up the society, establishing new classes that compete with the old order, socially, politically, and economically.

These considerations were applicable to China prior to 1949. The peasant misery of that country during the century preceding the Communist victory was due not only to the inherent difficulty, during a century of violence, of raising millions of people out of abject poverty, but, more important, to the almost complete lack of interest by the Chinese governments and foreign investors in doing any such thing. The peasants remained poor in large part because poverty served a purpose; or, at best, because it did not interfere with the wealthier classes extracting the economic surplus from the countryside.

Changes in the Countryside Since 1949

That degrading and humiliating sort of peasant misery is now gone from China, which is not to say, of course, that a rural paradise has miraculously arisen. Chinese peasants are still very poor, especially by the standards of industrial countries; the struggle against nature goes on, and some Chinese peasants every now and then find them-selves on the losing end; and there are still plenty of problems to overcome and small areas of severe poverty to eliminate.

However, the overriding economic fact about people in China today is that for over twenty years, for the first time in their lives, almost all have had a decent standard of living in the basic necessities—food, clothing, housing, health care, education, culture, and recreation. There is no longer starvation; no longer infanticide, can-nibalism, selling children into virtual slavery; no longer blank ignorance. The Chinese now have what is in effect an insurance policy against pestilence, famine, and other disasters. They have all risen together; it is difficult to see that anyone has been left far behind. And the rural areas are alive with water-control projects, small industries, transportation and communication networks, and plans for everything else that promise fuller lives for the peasants, who, while not prosperous, are prospering, awake, and optimistic. Some of the gains of the Chinese economy since 1952 are shown in Table 1.

How did this happen? I shall first present some social and political, as well as economic, reasons for this rural transformation, reasons which I believe to be basic to any understanding of what has happened in China. After that, I shall turn to a closer look at the economic policies that have changed the countryside.

Prerequisites for the Transition

The Chinese peasants have been able to improve their lives over the past two decades because they carried out a revolution of blood and fire, the only way which enabled them to break the bonds that retarded their economic progress. This violent revolution

TABLE 1

SOME ECONOMIC DATA OF THE PRC
SELECTED YEARS 1952-1972
(in million metric tons unless otherwise specified)

	Grain output	Steel prod.	Crude oil	Chem. fert.	Cotton output	Indus. prod. index 1956 = 100	Cement prod.	Coal prod.	Electric power (m. rwh)
1952	154	1.4	0.4	0.2	1.3	56	2.9	67	7.3
1957	185	5.4	1.5	0.8	1.6	109	6.9	131	19.3
1959	170	10.0	3.7	2.0	1.6	182	11.0	300	42.0
1965	208	11.0	8.0	8.0	1.5	167	11.0	220	42.0
1970	240	18.0	20.0	14.0	1.7	220	13.0	300	60.0
1971	250	21.0	25.0	18.0	1.6	242	16.0	325	70.0
1972	240	23.0	29.0[a]	21.3	1.6		20.0		

SOURCES: These data come from the Joint Economic Committee's publications on the Chinese economy, various issues of the *Peking Review, China Reconstructs, The Far Eastern Economic Review,* and from the work of U.S. scholars.

NOTE: [a] *Far Eastern Economic Review* (February 19, 1973), p. 5, reports 42 million tons.

was necessary but not sufficient to transform an agrarian society into an industrial one. The following five developments, however, established a political-social-economic framework for such a transition.

1. After 1949 the Chinese Communist Party fashioned itself and a government into organs that represented the masses and *wanted* thorough-going and penetrating economic development for the purpose of improving the lives of almost everyone. This, perhaps, is the most important thing that one can say in this regard. The Communist Party did not represent and work on behalf of a small group of merchants and traders, or a class of landed proprietors and moneylenders, or foreign interests allied with domestic entrepreneurs; instead it gained victory through a nationwide revolution of peasants against domestic oppression and foreign imperialism, and it continued to be a Party representing the interests of these masses of poor people. That may not be exactly an *economic* determinant of peasant prosperity, but there is nothing more important.

2. The government and Party proved to be efficient, honest, and well-organized in carrying out its development programs. Some inefficiencies occurred, some bribes were taken, and some confusion sown, but on the whole the Party and its cadres performed remarkably well in translating plans into actions.

3. The Party demonstrated its ability to mobilize the enthusiasm and energy of the masses with worthy and inspiring goals; to educate and give good health and improved nutrition to the people, enabling them to pursue these goals. It liberated women and youth from their previous oppression, and liberated most people from debilitating beliefs in "ghosts and monsters."

4. Through land reform, nationalization of industry, and co-operativization in the countryside, along with good use of monetary and fiscal powers, the government and Party generated a high saving rate, and with a fair amount of efficiency used the saving for investment across the board, in heavy industry, light industry, and agriculture.

5. The U.S.S.R. aided China substantially during the 1950s. The bulk of this "aid" was Soviet exports for Chinese goods (rather than Chinese securities), but the Soviet goods consisted of over 150 complete industrial plants accompanied by thousands of Soviet technicians. Soviet aid was designed to establish, in a short

period of time, the industrial base for a full-scale economic development effort. It remains, despite the subsequent rancor between the two countries, as an outstanding example of how one country can help another, if it really wants to.

Specific Policies in Rural Areas, 1949-72

The developments just described established the general environment in which specific economic policies were fashioned and carried out for rural improvement. These economic policies, however, were not neatly laid out in the early 1950s, all ready for sequential implementation later on. Instead, they have had at times an *ad hoc* nature; they have been fought over at the leadership level; and some have not worked well and have had to be replaced. But, even allowing for this, the policies in general have achieved a remarkable transformation in the rural areas.

These policies can be grouped into four categories: land reform (1949-52), collectivization-communization (1955-59), capital formation for agriculture (1960-72), and the alteration of terms of trade between agriculture and industry in favor of agriculture and the peasants (1953-72). The first set of policies redistributed wealth and income from the rich to the poor, eliminated the former ruling classes, and by so doing, raised both peasant consumption and rural savings. The second set of policies raised output in the rural areas mainly by encouraging better utilization of the labor supply. The third set further boosted agricultural output by increasing capital goods and other inputs available to this sector and by establishing small industries almost everywhere in the countryside. Finally, throughout most of the period, terms of trade were steadily turned in favor of the peasants by the raising of prices paid by the State for agricultural products and the lowering of prices of many goods purchased by the peasants. Thus, the masses of peasants initially gained control; their labor was then better utilized; increasing agricultural inputs were next acquired by them; and they gradually gained throughout the period by more favorable terms of trade.

The following four sections consider, without much detail, these four sets of agricultural policies. The penultimate section illustrates, as an example of some of the above policies, the transformation of one rural county in China, Tsunhua, located about 100 miles from Peking. Finally, the possible relevance of all this for other poor countries is taken up in the last section.

The Nature and Impact of Land Reform, 1949-52

The primary objectives of the Agrarian Reform Law of 1950 were to eliminate the feudal landlord system in the countryside, improve the lives of the poor, and develop agricultural production as a precondition for the country's industrialization. Land reform not only took land from landlords and some rich peasants but took also their draft animals, farm implements, houses, and grain—and redistributed them all to middle and poor peasants. Altogether, 300 million peasants received 700 million *mou* of land* (about 45 percent of total arable land) formerly owned by perhaps 10-12 million persons; of all land redistributed, ⅔ was taken from landlords and ⅓ from rich peasants; ⅔ of this land was given to poor peasants and ⅓ to middle peasants. Many rich peasants retained much of their land and other assets (but not their hired laborers) and so, even after the reform, were on the whole still better off than the middle and poor peasants. Further, since the land reform regulations did not forbid the resale or the renting of land afterwards, some of the redistributed land gravitated back to the

---

*1 *mou* equals 1/6 acre or 1/15 hectare.

rich peasants. Landlords, on the other hand, as a class, were wiped out by mass peasant struggles against them, confiscation, and execution.

It is important to stress that land reform was not simply legislated, passed, and carried out from above, for it was much more than that. It was a revolutionary movement involving millions of peasants struggling against their former oppressors, gaining confidence and understanding in the process, and taking actions themselves against the landlords which committed them to new lives and new ways, and which made the entire movement quite irreversible. Keith Buchanan quotes Liu Shao-ch'i on this as follows:

> In carrying out the land reform our Party did not take the simple and easy way of merely relying on administrative decrees and of "bestowing" land on the peasants. For three solid years after the establishment of the People's Republic of China, we applied ourselves to awakening the class consciousness of the peasants . . . We consider the time spent was absolutely necessary. Because we had used such a method the peasant masses stood up on their own feet, got themselves organized, closely followed the lead of the Communist Party and the People's Government, and took the reins of government and the armed forces in the villages firmly into their hands . . . The broad masses of the awakened peasants held that exploitation, whether by landlords or by rich peasants, was a shameful thing. Conditions were thus created which were favourable to the subsequent socialist transformation of agriculture and helped shorten to a great extent the time needed to bring about agricultural cooperation.[2]

A few results of the land reform are shown in Table 2, which also contains definitions of terms used above.

TABLE 2

SOME RESULTS OF LAND REFORM IN CHINA
1949-1952

	Percentage of households	SHARE OF CROP AREA OWNED		AVERAGE CROP AREA OWNED	
		Before reform	After reform	Before reform	After reform
				mou	mou
Landlords	2.6	28.7	2.1	116.10	11.98
Rich peasants	3.6	17.7	6.4	35.75	26.30
Middle peasants	35.8	30.2	44.8	15.81	18.53
Poor peasants and farm laborers	57.1	23.5	46.8	6.25	12.14
Other	0.9	0.0	0.0		

SOURCE: Peter Schran, *The Development of Chinese Agriculture, 1950-1959* (University of Illinois Press, 1969), pp. 21, 22, and 25.

NOTES: Households were classified by amounts of income and wealth, sources of income, and size of household.
Landlords: Owners of land not engaged in labor, who depend on exploitation for the livelihood—that is, land rent, moneylending, hiring of labor, etc.
Rich peasants: Similar to landlords, except that exploitation chiefly took the form of hiring long-term laborers and it constituted somewhat lesser shares of their total incomes.
Middle peasants: Owned all or a portion of the land they worked, or perhaps none at all. They depended for a living wholly or mainly on their own labor.
Poor peasants: Rented land for cultivation and were exploited by others through rent and interest.
Farm laborers: Owned neither land nor farm implements; depended wholly or mainly on the sale of their labor for their living.
1 *mou* of land = 1/6 acre or 1/15 hectare.

The land reform, through its redistribution of rural assets, not only broke the domination of the landlord-gentry class and transferred power for the first time to poor and middle peasants, but it also immediately raised the consumption level of most peasants and at the same time increased rural savings available for investment. These were results principally of wealth redistribution and not of gains in total output flowing from land reform, for such gains were not substantial, though there were output gains that came from the cessation of civil strife and the reconstruction and repair of dikes, irrigation canals, and equipment. Much of the increase in rural savings was captured by the State for investment purposes. Thus, land reform contributed in a major way to the higher investment ratios of these earlier years.

The ratio of net investment to national income rose rapidly from perhaps 1-2 percent in 1949 to around 20 percent in 1953. After that, despite the cooperativization drive in the country side during 1955-56, the ratio rose very little more until 1958-59, when communes were introduced. Thus, the initial rapid increase in saving and investment came in the early years of the period 1949-57.

Land reform had much to do with this, for it redistributed wealth and hence income from the rich to the poor, and much of what was redistributed was captured by the State in savings, through taxation, profits of State enterprises, differential pricing, and private savings. The land reform eliminated the luxury consumption of the rich, raised by lesser amounts the basic consumption of the poor, and made much of the rest available to the State for investment.

Victor Lippit has computed that the income flow to the rural propertied classes, in rent, interest, and farm business profits, plus net taxes to the State, was as much as 19 percent of national income, just a decade before land reform.[3] This income flow, which was almost entirely consumed, was redirected downward, after land reform, by rural-asset redistribution to middle and poor peasants. From there it found its way into investment via several channels: self-financed investment in agriculture; increased tax payments to the State; increased profits of government and private enterprises, which wholly or partly reverted to the State budget; increased profits of State purchasing agencies (mostly grain purchases); and increased financial asset holdings of peasants, which released real resources for investment, financed by borrowed funds from the banking system. Land reform probably contributed over one-third of the total savings in 1952 (and, presumably, in later years, too) to the investment program.

It bears repeating: The Chinese land reform did not *give* land to the poor peasants. It encouraged them to organize themselves to *take* it, and in the process to crush their former oppressors. This was the prerequisite for later socialist development in the countryside, for, without it, the old class structures and wealth ownership patterns would have been regenerated by the persistence of old attitudes and of institutions favorable to the rich.[4]

Rural Collectivization and Labor Mobilization, 1952-59

After land reform, the Chinese leaders, in four stages, transformed small private holdings into large-scale communes. The first step was the encouragement of mutual aid teams, which were units of several households, the function of which was to pool privately-owned resources in order to compensate for shortages of labor and other inputs during the rush seasons of planting and harvesting. This was at first done on a temporary, seasonal basis, the teams being dissolved at the end of the planting or harvesting period, but later some of the teams were organized on a permanent, year-round basis. These permanent teams were somewhat larger than the others and often held some capital goods and animals as common property. By 1954 almost 10 million mutual aid teams, about half of them seasonal and half permanent, were in operation, and they comprised 58 percent of all peasant households.

The second stage was the formation of elementary agricultural producers cooperatives (APCs), some of which were organized as early as 1950 but most of which were formed in the second half of 1955. They comprised several mutual aid teams or around 30 to 40 households, that is, a village. Land and other capital goods continued to be privately owned, but these assets were now pooled in the APCs for use according to annual plans prepared by central management. Peasants were compensated according to their labor and their contributions of land, implements, animals, etc., labor, however, usually claiming most of the output. By early 1956, almost all peasant families were in these APCs.

The third stage, in 1956-57, saw the consolidation of elementary APCs into advanced APCs, each comprising several small villages or perhaps one large village, varying in size from 100 to 300 households. In the advanced APCs, peasants held title to a share in the collective equity, and they no longer had any private claim on their former holdings of land and other capital goods. Accordingly, net earnings were distributed to the peasants only on the basis of work done, and the earnings withheld, including those contributed by capital goods, were collectively owned. The advanced APCs, owing to their larger size, were able to withhold larger percentages of income for collective purposes. Similarly, the payment of the agricultural tax became a collective obligation, whereas it had been an individual responsibility in the elementary APCs.

In the final step, during 1958-59, people's communes were established. The commune, as the Chinese have stated, "is the basic unit of the social structure of our country, combining industry, agriculture, trade, education and the military. At the same time, it is the basic organization of social power." The communes were organized to provide larger, more efficient units for carrying out large-scale water-control projects and the building of native-type factories and workshops throughout the countryside. They were organized, moreover, to provide additional labor through the establishment of communal mess halls and other communal services which released many women from household tasks. The communes also became the basic governmental unit; they ran factories, schools, banks, controlled their own militia; and they served to weaken the patriarchal family unit and, in general, peasants' identification only with very small groups. Further, a half-wage, half-supply system was set up, which provided free supplies of many of the necessities to peasants quite aside from whether they worked or not, the remainder of income being distributed according to work done.

The communes were quickly organized during the Great Leap Forward, which was an all-out effort by the Chinese to industrialize rural areas, to build a large iron and steel industry, to grow record agricultural crops, to raise the education, health, and cultural levels of the peasants, and to catch up within 15 years to the leading industrial nations of the world.

> The objective is to build China in the shortest possible time into a great socialist country with modern industry, modern agriculture, and modern science and culture . . . To carry out our socialist construction at a high speed naturally requires constant readjustment to the relations of production and constant adaptation of the superstructure to the developing economic base. The fundamental thing, however, is to develop the productive forces rapidly . . . The objectives are to abolish exploitation of man by man, and to build a classless society in which the difference between city and country-side, between mental and manual work will disappear and the ideal of "from each according to his ability, to each according to his needs," will become the order of the day.[5]

Within a short time, over 26,000 communes were organized, each containing around 5,000 households on the average, but the range was from 1,500 to 10,000. The former advanced APCs became 500,000 production brigades within the communes, and the former elementary APCs became 3 million production teams.

To summarize, during the 1950s the basic organizational unit in the countryside was enlarged from individual peasant households, to mutual aid teams (at first temporary and later permanent), to production teams (former elementary APCs), to production brigades (former advanced APCs), and finally to communes. The basis for the distribution of income also changed from distribution according to work and asset ownership, to distribution according to work only, to distribution according to work and needs; and, at the same time, the value of a peasant's work points was based on the work done by increasingly larger groups.

Some of these advances, however, were reversed in the early 1960s, during the downturn of economic activity, when Maoist ideology waned. Communes were greatly increased in number and so reduced in size of population; decision-making authority was moved down to lower units; income distribution by need was de-emphasized; communal services were greatly reduced; and private incentives in several forms were restored.

The enlargement of rural units and the collectivization which accompanied it during the 1950s no doubt, on balance, raised the standard of living of the masses of peasants, but the policies probably did not increase by much the economic surplus from agriculture until the Great Leap Forward in 1958-59. There were both positive and negative features of this series of rural programs, but I shall concentrate only on the principal advantage gained by the economy from the rural policies just described, namely the fuller and more efficient use of the rural labor force.

Throughout the 1950s, the percentage of the rural population comprising the labor force tended to decline sharply owing to the rapid absorption of children of school age by the school system. However, since children did not work the long hours of adults or as effectively, this downward tendency was less in actual output than it was in sheer numbers of workers. In any case, it remained simply a tendency, for it was more than offset by the rapid growth of women in the labor force during the 1950s as rural collectivization and communization proceeded.

TABLE 3

RURAL POPULATION, EMPLOYMENT, AND LABOR-DAYS
1950, 1955, 1957, AND 1959

	(1) Peasant population	(2) Total employed peasants	(3) Average annual labor-days	(4) Total annual labor-days	(5) Index of Col. (4) (1952=100)
1950	479.7 m.	222.6 m.	119.0	26.5 b.	97.5
1955	523.8	243.3	121.0	29.4	108.4
1957	541.3	260.3	159.5	41.5	152.8
1959	539.6	309.1	189.0	58.4	215.0
Collectivization 1955-57	+17.5	+17.0	+38.5	+12.1	+44.4
Communication 1957-59	-1.7	+48.8[a]	+29.5	+16.9	+62.2

SOURCE: Peter Schran, *The Development of Chinese Agriculture, 1950-1959,* Chapter 3.

[a]Increase owing largely to increased mobilization of women and the part-time employment of school children.

These rural policies also induced increases in the total number of days worked each year by greatly raising the number of labor-days for each employed peasant in general and for each female in particular. The total expansion effect, coming from the increased employment of women and the greater number of days worked for each employed person, was extremely large, as can be seen in Table 3. In fact, under normal circumstances, total annual labor-days would have risen by no more than 2-3 billion from 1950 to 1959. Instead, the rise was 29 billion. Furthermore, Peter Schran believes that even this might well understate the full impact of communization in this regard.

The increased labor was employed not only in basic farm work and in subsidiary occupations, but increasing amounts of it were set to work on large-scale water-control projects, basic construction, and rural industrial efforts; and much labor was increasingly used for communal services—administration, cultural activities, medical care, education, etc. These data are in Table 4. Consequently, this mobilization of additional labor-days served to raise not only agricultural input but also capital formation in the countryside, and it also increased the communal services offered to the peasants. Instead of fiddling away their time individually during off-seasons, the peasants were mobilized into large units for community and area projects.

The gains in total labor-days worked, however, did not result in commensurate increases in total output, for other inputs did not keep pace with labor inputs, and so resulted in diminishing marginal returns to labor, the additional labor was sometimes employed inefficiently and at tasks with quite low returns, and there was some loss of incentives to work hard during 1958-59. Nevertheless, total production in the rural areas did increase considerably throughout most of the 1950s, and capital formation made some impressive gains toward the end of the period. A few indicators of rural activity during the 1950s are recorded in Table 5.

Industrialization of the Rural Areas, 1960-72

Adverse weather conditions which lasted for three years ("the worst in a century"), the pull-out of the Soviet advisers, and disincentives of peasants arising out of the extremes to which some Great-Leap policies were pushed—all of these combined in 1959-60, first to reduce agricultural output, including the commercial crops which

TABLE 4

INDICES OF THE STRUCTURE OF RURAL
EMPLOYMENT BY LABOR-DAYS
1950, 1955, 1957, AND 1959
(Total labor-days in 1952 = 100)

	Total labor-days	Farm work	Subsidiary work[a]	Corvee, basic construction	Other[b]
1950	97.5	75.2	19.2	3.1	0
1955	108.4	83.0	21.0	3.9	0.4
1957	152.8	113.4	25.8	9.7	3.8
1959	215.0	151.7	29.5	12.3	21.4

SOURCE: Peter Schran, *op. cit.*, p. 75.

NOTES: [a] Includes gathering activities, domestic handicrafts, administration, professional services, care of private plots and livestock.
[b] Includes collective affairs, communal services, and communal industry.

fed light industry, then to hit heavy industry as the Soviet advisers withdrew with their blueprints and expertise. By late 1960 and early 1961, the economy had been damaged so severely that the Chinese leadership (probably no longer dominated by Mao), in the face of a decline of national output of around 20-25 percent, altered its economic priorities to place agriculture first, light industry second, and heavy industry last. This officially changed the priorities that had been established under Soviet-type planning during the 1950s, in which heavy industry was the centerpiece and agriculture was relatively neglected so far as State investment funds were concerned.*

TABLE 5

SOME INDICATORS OF RURAL ACTIVITY
1952-1959

	Grain output (millions of metric tons)	Area of irrigation (millions of mou)	Gross value of agricultural output (billions of yuan)
1952	154	320	48.3[b]
1953	157	330	49.9
1954	161	350	51.6
1955	175	370	55.5
1956	183	480	58.3
1957	186	520	60.4 53.7[c]
1958	250 (200)[a]	1,000	67.1
1959	270 (170)[a]	1,070	78.3

SOURCE: Nai-Ruenn Chen, *Chinese Economic Statistics* (Aldine, 1967), pp. 338-39, 289, 364.

NOTES: [a] These are Western estimates, which are probably fairly accurate.

[b] Figures in this column are in 1952 prices.

[c] Figures in this column are in 1957 prices.

These new rankings, however, did not reflect any diminished interest in industrialization. Rather they served notice that the top priority would go to those industrial pursuits that directly served agriculture, either by producing modern inputs for that sector or by processing output coming from it. Industries farther out would be emphasized to the extent that they directly served these inner firms, and so on. Increasingly, as the 1960s proceeded, the countryside was expected to establish not only the small industries that directly served agriculture but also, whenever possible, small basic industries such as iron and steel making, cement making, coal mining, etc. By the end of the decade, the economy was better able than it had been to support agriculture both with the output of large-scale industry in the urban areas and with tens of thousands of small, indigenous industries throughout the countryside. Thus, the effort was redirected from the mobilization of traditional inputs (labor, natural fertilizers, draft animals, traditional tools) to the production of modern inputs such as chemical fertilizers, insecticides and pesticides, small hydroelectric plants, electric motors, rice transplanters, tractors, trucks, other machinery, and seed-improvement stations. The agricultural task of the 1960s was, in short, to industrialize and modernize the rural areas.

Some of the results of these policies are recorded in Table 6, where it may be seen

---

*However, the agricultural sector generated a substantial amount of internal saving that was used for investment.

that chemical fertilizers, both domestically produced and imported, tractors, and other inputs all rose very rapidly in the 1960s—in absolute amounts, though not necessarily in percentages, much faster than in the 1950s. The table also shows fairly good growth for a few of the output series that are available.

However, we do not have enough information to make a confident assessment regarding the impact of these increasing dosages of modern inputs on agricultural output. We do not have, for example, data on some kinds of inputs, such as threshers, harvesters, and trucks. Further, we do not know the distribution of the various inputs among the several crops (wheat, rice, cotton, etc.) nor the changes in land area devoted to each type of crop during the period. Moreover, the grain output estimates at the beginning of this period are uncertain. Consequently, the most that can be said on a general level is that grain output rose fairly rapidly during the 1960s, apparently responding to modern inputs in this decade to about the same degree as it responded to traditional inputs in the previous decade.* It is probably true that, if further institutional changes and dosages of traditional inputs had been heavily relied upon throughout the 1960s as they were in the previous decade, agricultural output would have fared much less well than it actually did.

Somewhat more detail, however, can be supplied for chemical fertilizers, which seem to have been the most important of the modern inputs during the 1960s. The Chinese leadership did not neglect chemical fertilizers during the 1950s, though after the downturn of 1959-61 they placed much more emphasis on them. The U.S.S.R. constructed several complete plants for China in the initial decade, and China imported machinery to modernize two plants inherited from the pre-1949 period. There was, as Table 6 shows, an increase in the production of these fertilizers from 1952 to 1959. In the next decade, China purchased four complete nitrogenous fertilizer plants from the Netherlands, Britain, and Italy, which were installed in 1966. She began building her own plants in 1964, and around this time set a goal of one large-scale plant for each of the 180-190 special districts and one smaller plant for each of the 2,000 plus counties in the country. In fact, as things turned out, much of the increase of chemical fertilizers during the 1960s came from the medium-and small-scale plants that were constructed throughout the countryside during this decade. Moreover, China began to import chemical fertilizers in increasingly larger volume, mostly from Japan and western Europe. By 1970 available chemical fertilizers from both domestic and foreign sources totaled more than 18 million metric tons, which was six times the level of 1959.

It is possible to relate only in an approximate way the 15 million ton increase in the supply of chemical fertilizers to the 70 million ton increase in grain output during the period 1959-70. Considering the information available on this relationship, it may be roughly accurate to say that, during this period, chemical fertilizers contributed between 40 percent and 55 percent of the increase in grain output.[6] While this is not very exact, it probably does suggest accurately that chemical fertilizers had a substantial marginal impact on grain output in the 1960s, probably more than that of any other input. This impact however, was most likely centered on rice output which is grown in areas where water is generally available. The impact on wheat and cotton output, grown mostly in the north where water supplies are unreliable, was undoubtedly less strong.

*The average annual growth rates of grain output for several periods are as follows:

1952-57	3.7%	1959-71	3.1%
1952-58	4.4	1961-71	4.2
1952-59	1.4	1965-71	3.5

As I noted previously, the countryside has been industrialized to some extent during the past decade by the establishment of thousands of small industries under local authority.[7] These industries produce and repair farm implements and machinery; they produce fertilizers, consumer goods, insecticides, building materials, rural transportation equipment; they process agricultural products and develop power sources. Such industries have been encouraged by the central government to be as self-reliant as possible by developing new sources of raw materials from their own areas, utilizing waste materials and older machinery from the larger central industries, and using relatively labor-intensive, indigenous methods of production. These rural endeavors have been fashioned into more or less integrated industrial structures in each locality for the prime purpose of serving that area's agricultural needs.

TABLE 6

SOME AGRICULTURAL INPUTS AND OUTPUTS
1952, 1959, 1965, 1970, 1971

	CHINESE PRODUCTION OF INPUTS				OTHER INPUTS		SOME OUTPUTS	
Chemical fertilizers (in MMT)	Tractors (th. of standard units)	Electric power in agr. (bil. kwh)	Inventory of mechanical pumps (mil. hrspwr.)	Area irrigated with mechanical pumps (th. hectares)	Imports of chemical fertilizers (in MMT)	Grain output (in MMT)	Sugar output (in MMT)	Cotton yield (kg per hectare)
1952	0	n.a.	n.a.	n.a.	0.1	154	0.45	232
1959	1.5	1.5[a]	3.4	646	1.0[c]	170[d]	1.1	285
1965	33.1	2.7	8.0[b]	1,520[b]	2.3	200	1.5	333
1970	62.7	4.6			4.3	240	1.7	377
1971	73.4	5.5				250		381

SOURCES: Col 1: See footnote 6 for sources.
Col 2: Joint Economic Committee, *People's Republic of China: An Economic Assessment*, p. 139.
Col 3: *Ibid.*, p. 138.
Col 4: *Ibid.*, p. 134.
Col 5: *Ibid.*
Col 6: Kang Chao, *Agricultural Production in Communist China* (University of Wisconsin, 1970), p. 151; JEC, *op. cit.*, p. 348.
Col 7: JEC, p. 121. Grain output fell to 240 in 1972.
Col 8: JEC, p. 83.
Col 9: JEC, p. 124.

NOTES: n.a. Not available   [a] 1962   [b] 1966   [c] 1961   [d] Western estimate

The advantages claimed for these local industries are: (1) they have the ability to utilize dispersed deposits of material resources; (2) they lower average capital-output ratios and shorten the gestation periods; (3) they have the ability to undertake repairing, maintenance, and processing activities, freeing large-scale capacity for jobs which the modern sector alone could do; (4) they lower the costs of urbanization and social overhead capital in general; (5) they have a capacity to create industrial consciousness among the peasantry; (6) they contribute to national defense; and (7) they ameliorate the contradictions between cities and countryside.

More generally, this rural industrialization effort has certainly had some measure of success in expanding employment opportunities in the countryside, in balancing production geographically, and in raising agricultural productivity generally.

Improvement in Agriculture's Terms of Trade

The fourth and final program that has raised living standards in the rural areas is the change in terms of trade between agricultural and industrial products in favor of the former. This improvement for agriculture has apparently been fairly constant throughout the communist period, as shown in Table 7. By the end of the 1950s, a given amount of agricultural produce was purchasing about 35 percent more industrial goods than at the beginning of the decade. By the end of the 1960s, this had almost doubled to 67 percent.

TABLE 7

TERMS OF TRADE BETWEEN AGRICULTURE AND
INDUSTRY, 1950-1970

	(1) Agricultural purchase price index	(2) Industrial retail prices in rural areas index	(3) Ratio of (1) to (2)
1950	100.0	100.0	100.0
1951	119.6	110.2	108.5
1952	121.6	109.7	110.8
1953	132.5	108.2	122.4
1954	136.7	110.3	123.9
1955	135.1	111.9	120.7
1956	139.2	110.8	125.6
1957	146.2	112.1	130.4
1958	149.5	111.2	134.4
1970	n.a.	n.a.	166.7

SOURCES: Nai-Ruenn Chen, *Chinese Economic Statistics, op. cit.*, pp. 424-25, 409. The 1970 figure is based on information in *China Reconstructs* (November, 1970), p. 4. For the same trends, see Audrey Donnithorne, *China's Economic System* (Praeger, 1967), pp. 448-49.

Over the past two decades, the government has several times raised the price at which it purchases grain from the peasants. At the present time, this purchase price is above the level at which grain is sold by the State in urban areas and in rural areas devoted mostly to industrial crops. The difference in the prices is a subsidy from the State to the cultivators of grain. Other agricultural goods have also been purchased at higher prices. On the other hand, prices of industrial products bought by the peasants remained about the same from 1951 to the end of the decade, and in the last several years many of these prices have been reduced, some greatly. For example, the general price level of medicines is 80 percent lower now than in 1950, and most of this drop occurred in the last few years. "For the same amount of wheat, a peasant can get 70 percent more salt than at the time of the birth of the People's Republic, and for the same amount of cotton, he receives 2.4 times as much kerosene."[8] Prices of fertilizers, fuel, livestock feed, electricity, and various types of equipment have been lowered.

Rural Development in Tsunhua County

Some of the agricultural policies which I have discussed up to this point will perhaps have more meaning if they are shown in actual operation in one rural locality. I attempt this as follows.

Tsunhua county is one of six counties within the special district of T'angshan, which is located in the northeastern part of Hopei Province, about 100 miles east and a bit north of Peking. The county, the size of which is about 1640 square kilometers, has a population of over half a million, though it has only one town, Tsunhua, the county seat. The land is mostly hilly, with three mountain ranges and two valleys or plains. The economic activities of the population are largely agricultural—that is, growing wheat, kaoliang, millet, other grains, fruit orchards, chestnut trees, vegetables—but there are increasing numbers of small industries in the county, and of course some people engage in various sideline occupations. Table 8 records some of the basic economic facts about the county.

The heart of the county's economy is agriculture, mostly foodgrains. Since 1949, the output of foodgrains per hectare has risen more than three-fold, or at an average annual rate of 6 percent. However, since 1958 the rate has been only 2 percent; it was rather stagnant between 1958 and 1969, but recorded substantial increases during 1970 and 1971. The Revolutionary Committee of the county attributed the stagnant period to the revisionist policies of Liu Shao-ch'i and his followers, who discouraged self-reliant policies in the county, the building of small industries, and the full use of local resources. Since 1968 or 1969, however, the leaders of the county have "organized mass activities to change the backwardness of agriculture, make substantial use of local resources and rapidly develop local industry."[9]

The county has attempted to promote agricultural development by producing its own cement, chemical fertilizers, and iron and steel for the manufacture of agricul-

TABLE 8

SOME ECONOMIC STATISTICS OF TSUNHUA COUNTY
1970-1971

Total area	164,000 hectares or 1640 sq. kms.
Cultivated area	64,000 hectares
Irrigated area	18,700 hectares
Population	550,000
Households	116,000
Labor force	about 200,000
Communes	43 (av. of 12,800 per commune)
Production brigades	691 (av. of 800 per brigade)
Production teams	2,664 (av. of 200 per team)
Grain production	3.8 tons per hectare
Value of grain production	about 50 million yuan
Value of industrial production	18 million yuan
Income from sideline occupations	22.7 million yuan

SOURCES: Jon Sigurdson, "Rural Industry—A Traveller's View," *The China Quarterly* (July-Sept., 1972); *Collective Notes of visiting economists to China during August 1972*, mimeographed by Thomas Weisskopf, Department of Economics, University of Michigan.

tural machinery and implements, and it has supported these heavy industries, especially iron and steel, with profits from light industry and sideline activities. That is, the county has attempted to industrialize mainly on its own initiative and using its own resources for the purpose of raising agricultural productivity and the living standards of the people.

In order to produce chemical fertilizers, cement, and iron and steel, the people of the county first had to locate the necessary ores and minerals. "Initially, we were aware only of the presence of gold and iron in the hills, but now local people have discovered 23 kinds of ore, helped by the geological team.''[10] They then set up the iron and steel plant—first the small blast furnace, then a converter, after that a rolling mill. The iron and steel aided in establishing the cement factory, and the latter was used largely to expand water conservancy projects.

The iron and steel plant, however, ran at a loss. So light industry and sideline activities were developed which made more than enough profits to subsidize iron and steel. The county planted tens of thousands of fruit trees, for example, then constructed a small fruit bottling factory with an annual capacity of 250 tons of bottled fruit—apples, apricots, pears, grapes, peaches, etc. This factory required sugar, so some peasants began growing sugar beets, and turned out 10 tons of sugar per year. The factory also needed glass for the bottles and so a small glass manufacturing plant was set up. The glass, of course, required pure soda, hence, this called for the establishment of a 32-ton per year soda factory. And so on and on. The result is that the county is now able to produce a complete set of machinery, such as crushers, threshers, oil presses, and machinery for digging drainage and irrigation systems, for the development of agricultural and sideline activities.

Local industries are run not only by the county but also by the communes and production brigades. At the county level, the aim of national policy is for every county to have the "Five Small Industries": iron and steel, cement, chemical fertilizer, energy (coal, electricity), and machinery. Such complete sets were established in one-half of the 2100 counties by 1971. Tsunhua was engaged in all of these activities, except that its electricity was produced outside of the county. In addition, the county runs a sulphuric acid plant, an electromechanic factory, a plastics factory, and a paper-making plant. It engages in mining operations, has a textile mill, does major repairs on agricultural machinery, and processes agricultural and sideline products—e.g., flour-milling and cotton-ginning.

The communes and the production brigades are also involved in small industries. For example, there is a three-level agricultural machinery repair and manufacturing network, which 90 percent of the counties, including Tsunhua, had established by 1971, in which the county does the manufacturing and major repairs in seven plants, the communes in 37 plants do lesser repairs and assembly, and production brigades do minor repairs in their 407 shops. The three-levels also engage in processing agricultural and sideline products. Further "Three-level county, commune, and brigade agricultural scientific networks have been rapidly expanded all over the country [including Tsunhua] in recent years. One important objective of this is to achieve a rapid seed-selection process which together with modern inputs to agriculture may quickly increase the yield per unit.''[11] Sideline occupations are engaged in by households, brigades, and communes, and they include such things as raising silkworms and bees, quarrying stones and mining ores, making mat bags, growing fruit.

In all of these enterprises, there were 12,000-15,000 of the 200,000 labor force employed. In the 39 county-run industries, employment was 5,500 in 1971; it was 2,500 in the 71 plants managed by communes; and 5,000 in the industrial units of the production brigades.* These are not large figures relative to the total labor force, but

---

*In these plants, there are three types of workers: permanent, temporary, and contract. The permanent workers are employed within the regular 8-grade wage system, ranging from Y 28 to about Y 100 per month. Temporary workers are part peasants and part workers, who rotate regularly between agriculture and industry, and who turn over half their wages to their production teams, and then at the end of the year receive income from the teams based on their agricultural work. Contract workers are hired on a 1-, 2-, or 3-year basis, and are in general treated the same way as permanent workers; they are mostly from the city, not from production teams.

there are many other workers who are in the industrial sector indirectly. In any case, employment creation is probably not the main purpose of rural industrialization. For given the increased school enrollment of children, the fact that it is unnecessary any longer for older people to remain in the labor force and work, the continuation of large-scale labor projects in water control and reforestation, the increasing numbers of people engaged in sideline occupations (in cultural activities, medical services, education, and party work), the movement of millions of people to the northwest and west and to other relatively virgin areas of the country, and the continued rising demands for just about every kind of agricultural product—given all these things, there would seem to be no significant surplus of labor in the rural areas. This, of course, is especially true during the seasonal peaks of planting and harvesting. Instead, rural industrialization is for the principal purpose of achieving mechanization in agriculture and hence greater agricultural productivity. It is also meant to narrow the differences between town and country, workers and peasants, and to widen the horizons and the abilities of the peasants.

Maoist Development Strategy and Its Relevance for Other Countries

What possible relevance has China's attempts at rural development to other underdeveloped countries? To begin to answer this, it is first necessary to specify exactly what the Maoist strategy for economic development is, within which rural development is contained. Since this strategy is an evolving one and has already taken several twists and turns, one cannot be certain of getting it right. But as of now the overall development strategy appears to consist of the following steps.

1. Destroy the feudal-landlord-bureaucrat class structure, and redistribute land, other assets, income, and power to the peasants and workers.

2. Establish socialist relations of production as soon as possible, and use the Party to educate peasants and workers in socialist values and ideals. That is, nationalize industry as soon as feasible and bring about cooperativization in the countryside without waiting for agricultural mechanization; begin transforming the superstructure into a socialist one.*

3. Establish a full planning mechanism to take the place of market-price-determined allocation of resources and distribution of incomes, and go all out for industrialization, but emphasize those industries having direct links to agriculture.

4. Achieve high rates of capital formation by encouraging savings at all levels and the use of the savings at each level for self-financed investment. Encourage rural areas, in particular, to produce whatever can be produced by small-scale, indigenous methods, to finance these investments from their own savings, and to manage these industries themselves. Capital goods that can be produced only by large-scale, modern methods should be financed and managed at higher political levels.

5. Develop and release human energy and creativity by promoting socialist values ("serve the people," selflessness, collective incentives) over bourgeois values (individualism, selfishness, materialism), by providing health-care facilities everywhere, educating as many people as possible, providing worthy goals that inspire people to work hard, and encouraging basic decision-making at the lowest possible level.

---

*This is because, if mechanization is introduced in an essentially individualistic, private-enterprise framework, the fruits of the new technology will be captured by only a few, leaving the majority of peasants resentful and ready to "break the machines." Also, capitalist development creates capitalist people. Under certain circumstances, according to Mao, it is necessary to change the superstructure in order to release the productive forces of society. See point 5.

6. Carry out a continuing revolution at all levels of society, and maintain the dictatorship of the proletariat.

It seems to me that the Maoist strategy, *considered as a whole,* probably has very little relevance to governments of most underdeveloped countries today, for it involves breaking the power of ruling classes and their foreign supporters, opting for socialism and eventually communism over capitalism, for full-scale industrialization over trade, commerce, and agrarianism, for continuing revolutionary activity over orderly procedures. Since most "third-world" countries today play more or less subordinate and dependent roles in the international capitalist system, serving the wealthier countries of that system with raw materials, oil, cheap labor, or additional markets, for them to follow China's path would mean first breaking out of this global system and then taking their chances on an all-out development effort with their own resources plus whatever aid can be obtained from socialist countries.* This may be a program favored by some classes in these poor countries, but it is hardly a prescription that would be appealing to their governments and propertied classes. Furthermore, such thoughts are anathema to the United States, as the leader of global capitalism, the duty of which is to try to prevent such breakaways through some combination of economic aid, military aid, counterinsurgency, cultivation of domestic elites, or force. The alliance between the U.S., on the one hand, and the propertied classes and elites in the poor countries, on the other, is a powerful one.

That is the overall picture. It stresses that one thing *does* depend on another in Maoist strategy, and indeed this is so in any development strategy. To make any substantial headway, the problem of underdevelopment often has to be tackled as a whole, not piecemeal. For example, in the Chinese experience, rural industrialization depended on the general acceptance of goals other than profits and efficiency. This general acceptance in turn was based on the prior inculcation of socialist values throughout the society, which were reinforced daily by the prior establishment of socialist institutions, including a full planning mechanism. These socialist relations of production could be developed only by the prior breakup of the old class structures of society. And so on.

I have emphasized the holistic view, the Maoist way. I now wish to ask whether other underdeveloped countries can benefit, to some extent at least, from separate parts of China's total experience. Some socialist policies should be adaptable to capitalist developmental programs.

It is well to recognize at the beginning that many Chinese policies for development are universally known and in fact have been acquired by China from the theoretical and practical work of bourgeois economists and other development experts, as well as from the experience of the Soviet Union. To this extent, China has learned from others, and there are, of course, no reasons why other countries cannot take advantage of the same information. I refer to policies of raising capital formation relative to consumption to attain higher growth rates, of encouraging saving for this purpose through taxation, financial institutions, and in other ways, of using relative factor supplies to good advantage, of aiming for developmental government budgets and moderate growth rates of the money supply, of utilizing aid and trade efficiently, and so on. Much of China's overall performance can be explained "simply" in terms of the very high investment and saving ratios that were attained by 1953-54 and were

---

*This is also true for the ruling classes of the major oil-producing countries, who may gain some advantages over the industrial capitalist countries but who are so greatly dependent on international monopoly capital that they (or most of them) would not dream of breaking out of this global system.

more or less maintained thereafter. (Recall, however, that to attain *these* the old class structures were overthrown by revolution. That is what lies behind "simply.") And larger shares of this total capital formation were applied to agriculture in the 1960s, which goes a long way in explaining China's recent gains in rural development. Thus, much of the story is standard fare, known to everyone.

But, while China has learned much from others, she may also be able to teach a few things. First, China has demonstrated the importance of industrialization to economic development; that the large resources initially devoted to iron and steel, machine-building, non-ferrous metals, oil, electric power, and chemicals were indispensable in establishing a base for later advances in agriculture, transportation, consumer goods, and military weapons, and in freeing the economy from its dependency on foreign direction and influence. The initial stress on heavy industry, rather than on infrastructure and consumer goods, was made possible only by socialist aid and trade. Despite the growing bitterness between the U.S.S.R. and China, no other country has ever received so much help toward full-scale industrialization as China did during the 1950s. This is something of a lesson in itself.

Second, China has shown, especially during the 1960s, *how* to industrialize without generating social problems that threaten eventually to blow the society sky high. China has involved increasing numbers of people, especially in the rural areas, in industrial activities in order to break down the potentially antagonistic relations between city and country and between workers and peasants; to spread knowledge of industrial processes as widely as possible so as to promote talent, ingenuity, confidence, and the scientific attitude among masses of workers and peasants; and to transform rural areas into self-reliant agrarian-industrial-cultural local economies, which are attractive places to live and which can, at least partly, break their dependent relationships with higher political units, including the state. This is relevant for other poor countries because it demonstrates a pattern of industrialization that does not generate severe imbalances between urban and rural areas, between rich and poor, between employed and unemployed, or between one region and another. The lesson that many developing countries are learning from their own experience is that high output growth rates are often the "good face" on an increasingly diseased body. Thus, the last annual report of the World Bank, after noting the respectable growth rates of many underdeveloped countries, went on to say: "Statistics conceal the gravity of the underlying economic and social problems, which are typified by severely skewed income distribution, excessive levels of unemployment, high rates of infant mortality, low rates of literacy, serious malnutrition, and widespread ill-health." The statistics also conceal the growing urban problems, foreign debt difficulties, social unrest, and much else in many of these countries. Perhaps the most important message that China can send to other poor people is that not one item in the above list applies to her.

The third lesson is the importance of raising work motivation and how to do it. Capitalist economists have concentrated far too much on how to reallocate economic resources to attain higher levels of national output and far too little on how to get people really interested in their work and so willing to exert great efforts to achieve their goals. I think that China has shown that the latter is much more important than the former; that people who really want to work completely eclipse the effects of nice adjustments toward more competitive markets and fine calculations regarding factor inputs.

The Maoists believe that they have inspired and enabled people to work hard by altering their work environments, changing their incentives, and providing them with education, good health, and technical training. The first point is that, in capitalist development, to raise growth rates of national output, it is necessary to do it in such a way as to reinforce the existing class structures of society and the values which support such structures. The pursuit of higher growth rates, therefore, has generally reduced many human beings to unthinking, specialized, manipulated inputs in the production process, in which hierarchical structures of capitalists and workers, bosses and "hands," mental experts and manual workers, face each other in more or less antagonistic relationships. Such alienated work environments lower the general intelligence, initiative, and willingness to work hard of broad masses of workers, which are the obvious costs of pursuing growth in the context of such sharp class alignments. The Maoists feel that the development of people as full human beings, working in a warm, egalitarian, and cooperative atmosphere, leads to the rapid development or material output; that the former is possible only in the absence of capitalist of feudal class structures; and that the latter is desirable only within the context of the former.

Thus, the Chinese lesson, in this regard, is that it is possible to increase greatly the overall productivity of peasants and workers by establishing less alienated work environments. In the absence of full-scale revolution, underdeveloped countries might benefit from China's experience by questioning their own organizations of work both in the countryside and in the cities, and by experimenting with other forms. Are existing organizations efficient from a factor productivity point of view, or are they mainly efficient in channeling part of the economic surplus to a landed aristocracy or to a capitalist class? Do work organizations exist to maintain discipline and order or do they promote energy and initiative? And, if the former, why? Are they designed to set off one group of workers against another to the benefit of the dominant class and to the detriment of factor productivity? China may have much to teach us in this regard.

Work motivation in China has also risen, according to the Maoists, because of an increase in socialist consciousness among the masses of workers and peasants, which means that collective incentives—the willingness to work hard for increasingly larger groups of people without expectation of personal gain—have gained over individual ones. Maoists believe that people are inspired and can see real meaning in their lives only if they are working for goals worthy of human beings and not merely for their own selfish, material welfare. Indeed, people throughout China *do* seem inspired in this way, for whatever reason, and seem not only completely involved in their present accomplishments but in achieving the plans for the future: "In two years, we'll have this and have a good start on that, and then . . ." Just about everyone talks this way.

Further, with regard to work motivation, it is necessary to repeat that increasing numbers of people are able to work hard and more effectively by being more literate, having better health and improved nutrition, and having more technical training.

Finally, the Chinese Communist Party has developed high motivation among its own cadres to "serve the people" in honest and incorruptible ways. The work motivation and collective incentives engendered within this large group have been of vital importance in getting policies translated into proper actions at all levels, in ways that do not dissipate the intentions of the policymakers. The CPC has for several decades now demonstrated the importance of having such cadres for the actual realization, as contrasted to the verbalization, of national goals.

China offers other lessons, too, which there is space only to mention: how to adapt education to the needs of an industrializing society; that it is not necessary for economic development to invite foreign capital into the country; the desirability of maintaining rather stable prices of important commodities over long periods of time; and so on.

The principal lesson, however, is the necessity of breaking out of all dependency relationships with advanced industrial countries and pursuing the course of self-reliance, both at the national and the local levels.

Notes

1. R.H. Tawney, *Land and Labor in China* (Boston, Beacon Press, 1966, originally published, 1932), pp. 72-3, 76-7.

2. Keith Buchanan, *The Transformation of the Chinese Earth* (New York, Praeger, 1970), p. 123.

3. Victor Lippit, *Land Reform in China: The Contribution of Institutional Change to Financing Economic Development* (unpublished manuscript, 1972).

4. See, for example, William Hinton, *Fashen: A Documentary of Revolution in a Chinese Village* (Monthly Review Press, 1966).

5. *Peking Review* (September 9, 1958).

6. This is based on Jung-Chao Lin, *China's Fertilizer Economy* (Chicago, Aldine Publishing Co., 1970), pp. 96, 106, 110-12; Kang Chao, *Agricultural Production in Communist China*, (Madison, University of Wisconsin, 1970), pp. 150-51, 236; Leslie T.C. Kuo, *The Transformation of Agriculture in Communist China* (New York, Praeger, 1972), p. 102; and Joint Economic Committee, *People's Republic of China: An Economic Assessment* (Washington, 1972), pp. 140, 348.

7. See Carl Riskin, "Small Industry and the Chinese Model of Development," *The China Quarterly* (April-June, 1971), pp. 245-73.

8. *China Reconstructs* (November, 1970), p. 4. See also the issue for (January, 1973), p. 40.

9. Thomas Weiskoff, *Collective Notes of Visiting Economists to China During August 1972*, mimeo (University of Michigan, 1972), p. 63.

10. *Ibid*.

11. Jon Sigurdson, "Rural Industry—A Traveller's View," *The China Quarterly* (July-September, 1972), p. 320.

The Transition to Socialism:
Observations on the Chilean Agrarian Reform

Alberto Valdés
Universidad Católica de Chile

Introduction

The Agrarian Reform is the heart of the agricultural program of the Unidad Popular (UP) which came into power when Salvador Allende assumed the presidency in November 1970. Chile had already experienced six years of Agrarian Reform during the previous government of President Frei. Nevertheless, the UP decided to introduce profound changes in the existing program because it was moving too slowly and because it had a discriminatory effect which created a new privileged class within the reformed sector.

In addition to "pure" ideological objectives consistent with its Marxist orientation, the agrarian reform of the UP has established goals with respect to economic growth and the distribution of income, which we shall discuss later in the paper. The parties forming the opposition to the UP regarded this massive attempt to redistribute both income and power within the rural sector as politically inevitable, since the measures were accepted to a greater or lesser extent by a majority of the Chilean population. But like other structural changes, the agrarian reform has generated socio-economic imbalances which we will subsequently examine.

Not enough time has yet passed to evaluate fully the current agrarian reform because the UP has been in power for only two and a half years. Preliminary information, however, suggests that the agrarian reform has had unexpected results in terms of agricultural production and that few of its benefits have reached the lower-income strata and seem instead to have been concentrated in a relatively modest fraction of the agricultural population. In this situation, the policy options are difficult and complex; perhaps the time has come to make a thorough revision of the current Agrarian Reform program and set in motion the necessary changes.

First we will describe the agrarian policy of the UP, which reflects a remarkably positive effort at agrarian reform. Secondly, we will examine its results in terms of production and the balance of payments. We have also included an analysis of the results, including their distributive effects, and an evaluation of the institutional implications of the program. Lastly, some reflections on future prospects are offered.

The Agricultural Program of the Unidad Popular

Chile is a country with a low population density, a temperate climate, and abundant though heterogeneous natural resources for agriculture. Its agriculture has been predominantly commercial. The country has the best agricultural cadastral survey in

Latin America, a modern tax system, and a technical assistance program which, as the ICIRA-UNDP-FAO Report[1] has pointed out, are accompanied by the best financial backing and the highest technical skills of any poor country which has instituted a massive agrarian reform program. Chile is basically an urban country, with agriculture generating about 8% of the GNP and employing around 25% of the labor force.

The basic program of the UP is clearly revolutionary in character. It seeks to create a socialist order, but within the framework of an electoral system which has seen many decades of effective political participation and whose legal system has been characterized as "bourgeois." This "but" betrays the peculiarity of Chile.

During the present stage of transition to socialism, the government claims that the economic policies pursued are not technical but essentially political in nature. Economic policy, then, is an instrument for consolidating and amplifying the power of the forces which support this transition and it is this objective which orients and directs economic strategy.[2]

The fundamental economic goal is the expansion of the so-called "social area," ending large concentrations of private property, whether in industry, banking, mining, distribution, or agriculture.

In its policy statements, the government has emphasized the redistribution of income and the productive effort necessary to back up this policy of redistribution. These objectives are guiding the short and medium-term income, monetary, foreign trade and fiscal policies, without losing sight of the necessity for enlarging the political base which cannot depend exclusively on the proletariate but must also include the middle class.

Agricultural growth was to be fostered by taking control of the land from the latifundistas, which would supposedly eliminate economic irrationality in land use and socialize the profits, permitting a change in the level and composition of investment. By expropriating with partial compensation, distributing the gains collectively or in cooperatives, and carefully preventing private ownership and any hint of individual operation, the government hoped to generate a more equal distribution of agricultural income. Moreover, the net transference to agriculture through public sector subsidies could bring about an intersectoral redistribution in favor of agriculture. Increasing production would also alleviate dependence on food imports.

The objectives of the agrarian reform program can be summarized as follows:

—a massive, rapid change in land ownership, eliminating the latifundios and stimulating the creation of socialistic forms of production—this motivated as much by ideological as by economic goals.

—improvement in the economic productivity of the sector as a result of the above, along with larger public expenditures in agriculture.

—stimulation of a change in mentality and attitude on the part of the campesino in order to create the "new man" and to bring about democratic participation on the part of campesinos at every level thereby eliminating their dependence on the landowner and the state.

—establishment of a more equitable distribution of income and the elimination of backwardness and poverty in marginal regions.

Positive Efforts by the Government

Massive land reform. When the UP assumed power in November, 1970, the land reform begun by the Christian Democrats (DC) under President Frei had created the legal means for expropriating farms above 80 Basic Hectares (a basic hectare-HRB-was defined as an area of land which was equivalent in productive capacity to one "standard" irrigated hectare), and had established a vast infrastructure for expropriation and administration.[3] The government could act without consulting the Congress, where it was in a minority.

Before Allende came to power, 1,408 farms over 80 basic hectares in size had been reassigned, comprising some 3.5 million hectares and benefitting more than 20,000 families.

The strategy of the UP was concentrated on the latifundio over 80 HRB. The goal of the UP was to transfer all remaining 3,000 to 4,000 large farms to the reformed sector by the end of 1972. This would leave unexpropriated some 20,000-30,000 medium-sized farms and around 200,000 small farms.[4]

TABLE 1

DISTRIBUTION OF ARABLE LAND AND ALLOCATION OF LABOR BY SIZE OF HOLDING

Size of holding in HRB	Area		Difference	Availability of agricultural labor 1972*
	1965 %	1972 %	%	
Less than 5	9.7	9.7	0	
5-20	12.7	13.0	+0.3	50-55
20-40	9.5	11.6	+2.1	
40-60	7.1	14.5*	+7.4	20-25
60-80	5.7	12.8**	+7.1	
More than 80	55.3	2.9***	−52.4	
Reformed sector	0.0	35.5	+35.5	18-20
Total	100.0	100.0	0.0	100.0

SOURCE: Basic information from ICIRA, UNDP and FAO, *Diagnóstico de la Reforma Agraria Chilena* (Santiago, 1972), Ch. III, p. 3 and Ch. VII, p. 9.

NOTES: *This is not necessarily the flow of labor inputs. Some of the small proprietors and their families worked seasonally on larger holdings.

**Increased by a) private subdivisions during 1965-66, and b) by "reserves" left to expropriated owners.

***The remaining 16.9 per cent (55.3−35.5−2.9) can be explained by subdivisions made after the 1965 Census.

During 1971-72 virtually all farms over 80 HRB were expropriated and by December 1972 the reformed sector contained a total of approximately 35% of the cultivable land (in HRB), including 43.2% of the total irrigated land.[5] Sixty percent of this total was expropriated and reassigned between 1971 and 1972. This enormous task of expropriation was brought about almost without violence and in a relatively orderly fashion. At this time (March 1973), no decision seems to have been made concerning the immediate future of the land remaining in private hands. The UP and the DC are, however, implicitly in agreement in reducing the minimum size of holding subject to expropriation from 80 to 40 HRB, this will require a change in the law.

Table 1 presents a comparison of the distribution of arable land by size of holding between 1965 and 1972, expressed in equivalent hectares (HRB) and includes the distribution of the labor force by farm size for 1972.

As we can see, expropriation was concentrated in the group with the greatest productive capacity. However, the largest proportion of the labor force was not to be found on these farms. Direct beneficiaries of the Agrarian Reform total 18% of the active farm population. The concentration of the agrarian reform on large farms may have been politically motivated. There is something "symbolic" about affecting the most powerful first, because among other things, it made it easier to expand expropriation later on to the remainder. This policy was also defended as leading to greater economic efficiency, since it was believed that large holdings made relatively poor use of their resources,[6] and to an improved distribution of income.

Moreover, the latifundios, together with the "monopoly" firms in the non-agricultural sector were minorities where a large part of income was concentrated. Their expropriation was intended to capture the profits of these entities, socialize them and reorient them partially from consumption to investment.

Subsidized credit and the increase in the fiscal budget for agriculture. Private investment in agriculture was practically eliminated because a) the payments made to expropriated landholders were small relative to the value of their holdings, b) the recipients of those payments had little or no incentive to invest them in agricultural pursuits, and c) those farmers whose holdings were not as yet expropriated had little to gain by investing so long as there was a threat of future expropriation.[7]

However, through public investment and credit, financial transfers worked in the opposite direction. Not only did CORA (Corporación de Reforma Agraria) invest directly in cattle and machinery, but also substantial increases in credit to the agricultural sector were effectuated by CORA, by the Banco del Estado, and by CORFO (Corporación de Fomento). The increase in the amounts of resources involved in these operations were indeed dramatic. Whereas on the average, during 1960-70, official credits to agriculture amounted to about 20% of its gross product,[8] this figure reached approximately 80% in 1972.

Although the previous rate of default on debt servicing payments by farmers in the private sector was low, the default rate on production credit extended after November 1970 had risen to 58% by 1972. In addition, credit was further subsidized by a negative differential rate of interest on agricultural loans (-55% in real terms during 1972). There was also a substantial increase in the current budget of the Ministry of Agriculture, and an increase in direct subsidies for certain key agricultural inputs.

A recent report to the Minister of Agriculture indicates that in 1972 the sum of unrecuperated credits, the subsidy on the nominal interest rate, and subsidies on the use of inputs totalled approximately E°3480 million.[9]

Adding the "current" expenses of the agrarian public sector we arrive at a figure equivalent either to 60% of the value added, or 80% of the gross output of agricultural production in 1972.[10]

The increased payments to the agricultural sector contrast sharply with its tax payments which represented only 0.75% of total tax revenues in 1972.[11]

Results

Reduced output. During the decade 1960-1970, the cumulative annual increase in output was 2.6% in livestock and 1.8% in crops.[12]

During the Allende period, the corresponding figures (on an annual basis) are the following:

	1971/72[13]	1972/73[14]
Crops	−6.8%	−22.5%
Livestock	+0.8%	− 6.4%
Total	−3.6%	−13.7%

The incomes policy of the Chilean government considerably increased the effective demand for food. Salary readjustments over and above the rise in cost of living, the increase in family allowances and the decrease in unemployment in addition to the increase in population, all brought about effective increments in the demand for agricultural goods[15] which some authors estimated at 13.7% annually in 1971 and 11.8% annually in 1972.[16] While these figures probably overestimate the underlying increase, undoubtedly there was a significant net increase of approximately 9-10% annually.[17] This figure includes the effect of official food prices which were fixed at artificially low levels.

Balance of payments pressure. The simultaneous fall in production and increase in demand, which coincided with an increase in international prices for agricultural commodities, created an untenable situation in the balance of payments.

The increase in food imports during the Allende government has been:

	Annual Variation in the Value of Imports	Physical Volume of Imports*
1971 over 1970	60%	44%
1972 " 1971	91%	43%
1973 " 1972	27%	—

*Estimates at 1965 prices from ICIRA, UNDP, FAO, (1972), Ch. IV, pp. 10-11.

As a consequence, net farm imports, which on the average used the equivalent of 18% of the total annual value of national exports during 1965-70, have increased up to more than 55% of the total value of Chile's exports (see Table 2). Undoubltedly this is generating a serious contraction in output and employment in the rest of the economy. Also, despite the increase in imports, the problem of shortages has become more acute, especially in such products as vegetable oil, rice and meat.

At the macro-level, it would seem that as the process of socialization progresses, short-run economic phenomena have political consequences which reduce the degrees of freedom of the underlying policy processes and the potential for introducing structural changes in the economy. The options open in 1973 are clearly different from those of 1971. As Bitar points out,[18] "In 1971 the economy could count on a series of reserves and resources which compensated tendencies brought about by changes in ownership and the distribution of income." Specifically, these were unused capacity in the industrial sector, stocks of raw materials, and international reserves, which were able to reactivate the economy rapidly after the 1970 election. There is no doubt now, that in 1972 these favorable elements were exhausted and short term imbalances had developed. For example, let us look at some indicators: Inflation rose from an annual rate of 27% between 1965 and 1970 to 163.3% in 1972; the highest level in the history of Chile. The net trade balance changed from +US$71 million in 1970 to −US$122 million and −US$444 million in 1971 and 1972 respectively.[19] In addition, there has been a growing deterioration in the movement of autonomous capital. Since the international reserves have been exhausted, the government has resorted to the renegotiation of the foreign debt and is searching for new sources of credit. It would seem that 1973 will bring an inevitable reduction in food imports.

TABLE 2

AGRICULTURAL FOREIGN TRADE, 1965-1973
(US$ MILLIONS, CURRENT PRICES)

| Years | Total national exports | AGRICULTURAL IMPORTS | | | Sub-Total | Net agric. exports | Net agric. imports | Agric. Imp. as % of total exp. (2) : (1) |
		Food	Agric. raw mater.	Inputs				
	(1)						(2)	
1965-70	1065	125	59	33	217	23	194	18
1971	1148	180	85	32	297	28	269	23
1972	1100	364	171	53	588	17[a]	571	52
	900[b]							63
1973	—	463[c]	—	—	(700)[d]	—	—	—

SOURCES: Basic information for the 1965-1971 period is from ICIRA, UNDP, FAO, *Diagnosis de la Reforma Agraria Chilena,* Informe al Ministro de Agricultura (Santiago, 1972), IV, Table 7, except for:

[a]Author's estimate based on Universidad de Chile, Sede Occidente, Dpto de Economía, *Comentarios sobre la Situación Económica,* 2º Semestre, Publicación Nº4 (Febrero, 1973), p. 49.

[b]*Ibid.,* p. 130. (Calculation made in January, 1973).

[c]Projection by A. Valdés and R. Mujica, *Producción e Importaciones Agropecuarias en 1973,* Programa de Post-Grado en Economía Agraria, Universidad Católica de Chile (Santiago, 1973).

[d]On the assumption that raw materials rise in the same proportion as food.

Possible Causes

Productive inefficiency in the reformed sector. Between 1965 and November 1970 the Christian Democrat government avoided giving a definite organization to the expropriated farms and decided upon a transitional format, the "Asentamiento." In 1970 the UP followed the same strategy, changing the transitional model without committing themselves to a final model for the reformed sector. We will first describe each transitional model and conclude by explaining why the organization at the farm level may be the principal reason for the decline in production and the high financial cost of the program.

In contrast to the legal point of view, which emphasizes tenure, what is important economically is who retains the profits. While the position of the DC with respect to both aspects was ambiguous, the position of the UP has been legally clear in its explicit intention to inhibit in every way possible the development of private property and to avoid the physical subdivision of farms. Ideologically, the UP discarded the creation of small farms because it considered them economically inefficient and socially alienating.

Common to all Chilean transitional models to date, the land and fixed capital belong to the State. It is hoped that at least 80% of the land will be worked collectively and the rest will be assigned individually in pasture and farming rights. Each member is required to work a minimum number of days for the collective. The campesinos are responsible for administration, with technical assistance provided by CORA, SAG and the State Bank.[20] Theoretically, at the end of the year the campesinos pay the State between 10% and 15% of the difference between the gross revenue and all non-labor variable costs of the collective farm.

In all proposed transitional models, the campesino receives an advance per day worked, generally equivalent to the minimum wage, to be made on account against the final profits of the agricultural year. This appears in the balance sheet which CORA must prepare and present to the campesinos at the end of the year.

Let us examine the differences between these models. The asentamiento, created by the DC in 1965, is a partnership between campesinos and the State, which supplies the land, capital and technical assistance. It was hoped that with strong financial and technical assistance and no change in the scale of operation, a reduction in production would be avoided, and at the same time the members would come to appreciate the advantages of joint farming. The asentamientos were organized farm by farm, maintaining the limits of the expropriated farm. Full membership was restricted to the permanent workers present at the time of expropriation and they were allowed to contract additional labor.

As one might have expected in this model, there was no incentive to incorporate new members who would compete for the profits and physical resources of the farm. Surveys have shown that before 1970, about 30% of the annual workdays of the asentamientos were supplied by non-member laborers paid a fixed wage with no share in profits. As might be expected, labor productivity among members was in general very low, average income being dependent not only on the effort of individual members but on the total effective labor input. The normal lack of discipline on the part of some members gradually contributed to the lack of incentive.

The foregoing considerations were aggravated further by the fact that CORA did not produce the required annual balance sheet for the asentamiento. As a result, members never knew how much they owed the CORA and/or the State Bank and thus there was no basis for calculating profits or charging rent for the land and fixed capital. Also, members received payment in advance for their work in the collective enterprise. These factors encouraged members to concentrate their attention on their own individual plots. Since these plots represented only a small fraction of the total area of the asentamiento, the result was an inefficient distribution of labor effort between individual and collective cultivation and a consequent loss in output. Furthermore, the insufficient initial endowment in machinery and livestock contributed to the reduction in employment and the underutilization of the land of the collective enterprise.* The acceleration of the expropriation process in 1970 led to an extraordinary demand for financing on the part of the public sector.

The experience of the asentamiento between 1965-1970 led the UP to consider the necessity of overcoming some of the shortcomings which were an inherent consequence both of the models and poor administration.

The new government decided to establish no more asentamientos and substituted them provisionally with three types of organization entitled Agrarian Reform Centers (CERA), State Farms and Campesinos' Committees. The main objectives of these new models are: a) to increase employment, incorporating as members all the workers and their families who had normally worked on the farm, thus eliminating the hiring of additional labor, b) to bring about at least a partial ''social'' division of the surplus, reducing the amount of individual land, c) to capture economies of scale by bringing together two or more farms, d) to increase the participation of members in the management of the operation and e) to give greater autonomy from the state.

In order to carry this out the CERA was created as the predominant unit and it was proposed that State Farms and Campesinos' Committees also be established.[21]

The CERA, as established by law, is a provisional entity which will last five years. Its fundamental characteristics as stated in official documents are:[22]

—greater operational size.

---

* The law enacted in 1966 and still in force permitted the removal of machinery and livestock by the expropriated owner.

—participation of all men and women over 16 years of age, with equal rights and obligations, in a General Assembly and Welfare and Control Committee.

—executive decisions to be the sole responsibility of the campesinos in the Committee.

—worker income to consist of a fixed wage and an economic incentive in the form of a share of the profits.

—the house and garden plot assigned in individual ownership.

—the surplus of the Center is to be distributed as follows: a) to the campesinos, individually, up to a maximum not greater than 20% of the total surplus, b) 10% to the formation of an internal investment fund and the rest for a community development fund.

At the end of the transition period the land would either be assigned to a cooperative formed by the workers or would continue in the hands of the State, in which case it would become a State Farm. The final organization would be determined with the participation of the campesinos.

The Campesinos' Committee, in contrast to the CERA, has a maximum duration of one year and would be established in those cases where the campesinos object to the CERA, even though some aspects of the CERA have been included in this model. It has greater flexibility in its organization and de facto operates in a similar manner to the asentamiento. The intention of the government is to transform them into CERA's after one year.

The State Farm will operate only in special cases for farms containing a greater endowment of capital in the form of orchards, forests, nurseries and breeding stock, and for farms located in very isolated regions, such as Magallanes.

In the first stage, the small farmers (up to 20 HRB) will be organized in cooperatives through which credit and technical assistance will be channeled. The aim is to strengthen through these cooperatives, collective labor, planned production and the sale of products to the State.[23]

In addition to the State Farms already mentioned, three "alternative" permanent farm models are legally available.[24]

a) Agrarian Reform Cooperatives in which campesinos are assigned individually owned family farm units.

b) Agrarian Reform Cooperatives with collective land ownership in which all land is owned by the cooperative, except the house and garden plots.

c) Mixed Agrarian Reform Cooperatives in which part of the land is assigned to individuals and the rest is in collective ownership.

In reality, what has been the change in tenure in the reformed sector? By the middle of 1972, the distribution within the reformed sector according to type of farm was the following:[25]

CERA	150 Farms
ASENTAMIENTOS	766 (138 created after Nov. 1970)
CAMPESINOS' COMMITTEES	921
STATE FARMS	27 (excluding Magallanes)

The figures speak for themselves. In spite of an intensive campaign to convince the campesinos, the majority are opposed to the establishment of any organizational form which is different in practice from the asentamiento. Thus the UP has had to make concessions and consequently none of the models operate as they were designed. Although they have avoided calling them asentamientos, a large majority operate as such. In all of them the campesinos are assigned a plot and pasture rights, and salaries are fixed so as to keep any possible surplus on the farm. Thus, the State has conserved its power only over investment decisions (machinery above all). But its power is insignificant in production plans which in any event are only paper formalities. It is a fact that no unit pays rent on land or fixed capital. In addition, the whole reformed sector is exempted from the payment of land tax. The campesino is correct in believing that he cannot be fired for not doing his job. Thus, he grasps the only tangible thing which is to assure himself of his wage advance and the use of his individual plot.

In practice it is difficult to find significant differences between the management of the CERAs and Campesinos' Committees and the original asentamientos. All of them reveal dual exploitation, collective and individual, with a clear tendency toward an increase in the latter. There are indications that in 1972 almost half of the livestock within the reformed sector belonged to individuals and no less than a third of the total production of the reformed sector was sold individually.[26] The result of this conflict between what the campesinos want and the desires of the government, which takes the form of a conflict between individual plots and collective holdings, has been that labor has tended to concentrate in the former while land and fixed capital have been allocated to the latter, with a predictable loss in output.

Price policy. From at least 1940 until the end of the 60s, agriculture received unfavorable discriminatory treatment with respect to agricultural prices. Between 1945 and 1965 the aggregate value added was significantly lower than what it could have been at existing international prices.

Today, the principal source of internal distortion, which alters the calculation of official prices, is the notorious overvaluation of the exchange rate.

This depression in official agricultural prices is aggravated by the uncertainty regarding prices of products and inputs confronting the farmer. As an example, it should be noted that the official price of fertilizer bought by farmers on credit from the government monopoly during the period May-September 1972 was fixed only in December 1972.

In a situation where there is deeply rooted inflation, fixed prices and food shortages, such as occurred in the second semester of 1972, the evolving black market confuses both the data and its interpretation for the design of a coherent price policy. To give an idea of the magnitude, we must remember that during the grain harvest from January to March 1973, the official price received by wheat growers was E°460 per 100 kilos when wheat could fetch around E°750 per 100 kilos on the black market. It is not surprising then to encounter resistance to the wheat "estanco" (government purchasing entity) by the campesinos, who are prohibited from selling to private individuals. Under these circumstances the lack of equilibrium in farm prices represents a sharp conflict between the objective of the government to aid the urban poor and control inflation and at the same time to increase agricultural production.

For any government it would appear to be political suicide to neglect the inflationary phenomena and the underlying shortages of commodities, which in 1972-73 reached a record high unprecedented in this century. The contradiction between the politico-economic situation and the government's program has increased to the extent that it threatens to erode the political support gained by the underlying structural transformations. The maintenance of this support is absolutely essential for the government. A recovery in production and agricultural productivity seems to be a vital consideration in the short run.

Inefficiencies in the provision of basic inputs. If today we were to evaluate the infrastructure for the provision of basic inputs and services to the sector, one cannot but be amazed by the determination and speed with which the present government has taken over practically all the enterprises concerned.

Basic inputs such as fertilizers and pesticides are now provided exclusively by government agencies at fixed prices. So is the case with sales of new machinery and equipment and rental services of machinery. The banking system is entirely in the hands of government agencies.

This has led to an increasing centralization in state agencies of an infinite number of decisions, substituting former private entrepreneurs by a gigantic government bureaucracy.

It is hard to understand the underlying strategy. How could anyone imagine that such a variety and volume of operations could have been performed without a drastic decline in output, by this centralized organization, developed in such a short period of time, simultaneously with the expropriation of thousands of the most productive farms?

The results are not questioned today by anyone familiar with Chilean agriculture. Fertilizers reach the farm too late. The reformed units often unexpectedly receive a brand new (Rumanian or Russian) tractor but no implements; there are no spare parts available for the older tractor; three or four days have to be spent in procedures required for the approval to buy fish meal and maize needed for the poultry, etc., etc. No wonder agricultural production has fallen nearly 20% in two years.

Although the foregoing considerations are well known to government officials, the measures proposed to resolve this vast and heterogeneous problem do not question the role of the state agencies in this respect. Instead, the solution suggested by the government is to restructure the state agencies, tighten controls on distribution and transport and eliminate the appointment of technicians based on a party quota system. These measures are probably necessary, although insufficient, to resolve the present incapacity of the public sector to provide efficiently the basic inputs for agriculture.[27]

Lack of private investment. The main argument of the government in embarking on a "drastic and rapid" land reform was precisely to avoid uncertainty in unexpropriated farms. But the political dynamics of the process induced latent expectations on the part of unexpropriated farmers. They feared that the pressures of landless campesinos would induce Parliament to reduce the minimum size for expropriation.

As a consequence of the prevailing uncertainty about a possible change in the agrarian reform law, operators of farms between 40 and 80 HRB in size, who still farm approximately 30% of the total farming area, have no other alternative but to avoid investing in activities requiring a long gestation period. Due to the high risk of expropriation, private farmers will not normally invest in what often represents the most profitable long term production plan. A notorious example is the case of dairy and fruit products.

Rural Poverty and the Agrarian Reform Program

Statistics on the distribution of personal income in Chile are particularly deficient for the agricultural sector because of the difficulties of including income in kind and the imputed cost of housing, together with adjustments for differences in the cost of living within and between sectors. The best information available suggests that first of all, it would be a serious error to work on the premise that there is a high correlation between social class, as traditionally defined, and level of income. Authors of all political leanings in Chile agree that a large proportion of the owner-operated holdings are located within the lowest income strata. Similarly, permanent farm workers on an annual contract were not and are not today among the poorest class.[28] Within the latter group, significant differences in income are partially explained by differences in productive capacity.[29]

From an active population of about 750,000 persons in agriculture, there are between 300,000 and 400,000 who are self-employed in the "minifundio" sector.[30] These include owners, non-remunerated family members and those who work seasonally off the "minifundio" (afuerino). This group possesses a very small amount of land and capital assets. They suffer from seasonal unemployment and generally face more imperfect markets for inputs and products. Moreover, this group of self-employed workers are undoubtedly the least organized and possesses very little leverage with the government compared to the permanent workers, of whom a majority are organized in unions, and the current members of the reformed sector who are organized in confederations. It must not be forgotten that the Agrarian Reform took place *after* the unionizing of the large and middle-sized farms, a process which was initiated under the Christian Democrats in 1965.

As was predictable, wage earning groups, being better organized, were the principal beneficiaries of the Agrarian Reform. It has also turned out that the poorest sector, which represents about 50% of the campesinos, is in fact today on the margin of the Agrarian Reform. Given that the process of expropriation of all farms over 80 HRB is about to be concluded, the reformed sector will in total absorb something less than 30% of the agrarian labor force. Even if the UP were able to succeed in changing the legal definition of "latifundio" from 80 HRB to 40 HRB, it would still leave untouched the poorest 50% referred to above.

Improving the welfare of the great mass of campesinos, who are at the same time the poorest, requires an increase in the productivity of land and labor as well as more realistic price policy. At the present time it appears that these components are not yet integrated in the program of the UP.

It was an explicit goal of the UP to integrate the small farmers into the agrarian reform program. By developing production relations between the reformed sector and the minifundistas, by fostering collective work of the minifundistas, through cooperatives (through which credit facilities were made available), through production planning and supervised credit, and finally by inducing them to market their products through government purchasing agencies, it was expected to allow the minifundista to share the benefits of the organization mounted for the agrarian reform. Moreover, INDAP, traditionally the Government agency serving the minifundista, was to collaborate with CORA to find ways to give access to more land to these minifundistas.

Although in 1972 there was some progress in terms of the number of minifundistas who received credit, the volume and number of beneficiaries was still low. There has been no real change in their production activities which remain isolated and unaffected by the reformed sector.

The minifundista continues to sell practically all of his output to local intermediaries, in spite of the government's efforts to establish enforced government purchasing agreements. The latter have failed mainly because of the unrealistic official price policy which is totally uncompetitive with prevailing market prices.

Between sectors, the distribution of income is very unequal. In 1972 the value added per person in agriculture was calculated at approximately E°8600 annually which is equivalent to approximately 29% of the average wage in other sectors.[31] In part this is the result of an artificial underestimation of value added in relation to a level of "neutral" protection, which can be corrected in the manner stated above. It can be argued that this discriminatory protection is compensated, at least in part, by the financial subsidies already described (credit, inputs and tax subsidies), but available information indicates that almost all the compensation is captured by units in the reformed sector who do not fall within the poorest strata.[32]

In order to reduce the gap between sectors it is necessary to raise rural income. There is no doubt that an increase in the rate of rural-urban migration will only aggravate urban unemployment. However, it will be difficult to bring about an increase in rural employment if to the real differential in income between sectors (for equivalent productive capacity), we add the urban bias in terms of public services such as education, health, etc., which can be observed in Chile today.

Given the diversity existing within the sector, the obvious scarcity of resources and the urgent necessities of thousands of poor families, we are presented with the challenging task of locating these groups, trying to identify the various causes of their poverty and the relevant restrictions in their micro-economic relations. This would enable us to design selective policies which reduce the cost of assisting the poorest fraction.

In my opinion the UP up to now, has concentrated its effort on the latifundio without helping the minifundista and/or the afuerino (except some Mapuches). In fact, it would seem that the afuerinos and the families of minifundistas have lost the traditional employment that they had on the medium and large farms. The distributional implications are that the poorest 50% are still untouched, and the prevailing tenure arrangements in the reformed sector give incentives to CERA's and Asentamientos to keep out new members.

Prospects for the Future

Agriculture in Chile was a sector neglected by governments prior to President Frei. It has never followed a strategy that emphasizes rapid technological modernization. In 1965, Frei's government was the originator of what several authors have classified a "Reformist Strategy," emphasizing some redistribution of land and income, but without a drastic alteration of the distribution of power and income in the rest of the economy.

Since the end of 1970, Chile has opted for a "Revolutionary" strategy which has emphasized an overall strategy of transition to socialism, of which the agrarian reform is only one element. As was mentioned earlier, under this government economic policy is an instrument used primarily to consolidate and widen political power. Accordingly, the "success" of land reform, given its objectives, cannot be judged exclusively in terms of production, balance of payments and inflation. However, there is no question that rural development in the Chile of today must lead to greater farm output, and soon. The prospects for the future indicate that:

a) The balance of payments constraint is likely to become increasingly severe. The ratio of net agricultural imports to total national exports has risen from an average of 18% between 1965-70 to nearly 60% in 1972, and is likely to worsen during 1973. The country desperately needs to devote more foreign exchange to investment goods and raw materials for the non-farm sector.

b) The public sector budget allocated to agriculture is increasing at a rate which seems incompatible with a reduction in the rate of inflation. The increase in the consumers' price index of 163% during 1972 has no precedent in the country, and efforts for internal stability will probably reduce the sector's budget.

c) The evolving black market system confuses both the data and their interpretation, which together with other costs makes planning a worthless exercise both at a micro and macro level. This black market is fed by both the individual plots and collective units in the reformed sector as well as from private holdings.

d) In spite of impressive achievements in terms of expropriations and credit, given the very limited capacity for labor absorption in the reformed sector, the majority of the campesinos are the "forgotten people" of the agrarian reform. While the beneficiaries of the reform have become a privileged group, the current condition of the poorest 50% of the campesinos is not really different from that prevailing before the land reform.

e) Getting out of the Asentamiento system represents a dilemma for the UP. It is becoming widely recognized that there exists a rapid trend toward a return to individual farming within the reformed sector, even in those tenure forms, which according to the law, preclude individual plots. If campesinos are to participate jointly with the State in the design of new tenure forms, to correct the current ambiguity, they could press for tenure arrangements significantly different from those contemplated in the UP's original program.

f) Finally, there is an urgent need to resolve the contradiction between the formal centralization of power (with the growing control of the state in marketing, credit, technical assistance, etc.) and the incapacity of state agencies to perform efficiently in their new functions. *Campesino participation in the state apparatus today is insignificant.* The effective incorporation of the campesinos in the management of the rural development process represents, in my opinion, the most promising road to socio-economic progress in Chilean agriculture today.

Notes

1. Instituto de la Investigación y Capacitación en Reforma Agraria, United Nations Development Fund, Food and Agriculture Organization of the U.N. (ICIRA, UNDP, FAO) Coordinador S. Baraclough, *Diagnosis de la Reforma Agraria Chilena, Nov. 1970-Junio 1972,* Informe al Ministro de Agricultura (Santiago, 1972).

2. P. Vuskovic, "La Experiencia Chilena: Problemas Económicos" in *Transición al Socialismo y Experiencia Chilena* (Santiago, Centro de Estudios Socio-Económicos (CESO)—Centro de Estudios de la Realidad Nacional (CEREN), 1972), pp. 100-103.

3. The Christian Democrats initiated expropriations in 1965 by means of the law passed in 1962. In 1967 they obtained from Congress a new law, still in effect today, which in the judgment of one of the best known UP lawyers can be characterized as follows, "In the agricultural sector there existed, at the time the government (of Allende) assumed power, sufficient legal power to bring about profound, rapid and universal changes." J.A. Vera Gallo, "Problemática Institucional en la Experiencia Chilena" in *Transición al Socialismo* (Santiago, CESO-CEREN, 1972), p. 85.

4. J. Chonchol, "La Reforma Agraria y la Experiencia Chilena" in *Transición al Socialismo* (Santiago, CESO-CEREN, 1972), p. 152.

5. ICIRA, UNDP, FAO, *op. cit.,* III, 3 and Anexo 5 and 6.

6. Comité Interamericano de Desarrollo Agrícola (CIDA), *Tenencia de la Tierra y Desarrollo Socio-Económico del Sector Agrícola: Chile* (Washington D.C., Unión Panamericana, 1964).

7. This is clearly the case for farms between 40 and 80 HRB. As early as May 1971, the Minister of Agriculture made public the agreement of the majority in Parliament to reduce the minimum size for expropriation from 80 to 40 HRB. J. Chonchol, "Quien Reemplaza al Patron de Fondo," *Panorama Económico,* 265 (December, 1971), pp. 30-31.

8. Oficina de Planeación Nacional (ODEPLAN), *Antecedentes sobre el Desarrollo Chileno 1960-70* Serie 1, N°1 (Santiago, ODEPLAN, 1971), p. 406.

9. ICIRA, UNDP, FAO, *op. cit.,* VII, p. 52.

10. The sum of the current and capital budget of the Ministries of Agriculture and Land totalled E°3850 million in 1972. Dirección de Presupuestos, Departamento de Estadísticas, *El Presupuesto Fiscal 1972, Estimación al 30/IX/72,* mimeographed, Table 4, Reg. 323. This clearly underestimates the fiscal budget

for agriculture because it does not include transfers from the banking system (eg. the Central Bank to the State Bank, ECA, etc.) nor the budgets of government agricultural entities which depend on other ministries.

11. Total tax revenue from agriculture fell from 5.7% of the gross value of output in 1965 to less than 2% in 1972. This reduction was partly explained by the fact that land values were not readjusted, (consequently lowering the cost of expropriations) and because the reformed sector was tax exempt. ICIRA, UNDP, FAO, *op. cit.*, IV, p. 16.

12. ODEPLAN, *op. cit.*, p. 103.

13. Universidad de Chile, Sede Occidente, Depto de Economía, *Comentarios sobre la Situación Económica*, 2° Semestre, Publicación N°4 (Febrero, 1973), pp. 178-181.

14. Projection from A. Valdés and R. Mujica, *Producción e Importaciones Agropecuarias en 1973*, Programa de Post-Grado en Economía Agraria, Universidad Católica de Chile (Santiago, 1973).

15. A Martínez, "La Política Económica del Gobierno Chileno," in *Transición al Socialismo* (Santiago, CESO-CEREN, 1972), pp. 123-124.

16. ICIRA, UNDP, FAO, *op. cit.*, VI, p. 7.

17. Constant prices imply that the average income elasticity for food would have risen from 0.34 to 2.80, which appears unrealistic as is shown in the study by A. Valdés and R. Mujica, *op. cit.*

18. Sergio Bitar *La Situación Económica en 1972 y sus Posibles Implicaciones Políticas*, Seminario de Coyuntura, organized by the Council of Rectors (Santiago, 1972).

19. Universidad de Chile, Sede Occidente, Depto de Economía, *op. cit.*, pp. 178-181.

20. No rigorous analyses of theoretical micro-economic models for Chilean agriculture are available. An important advance in this direction is the study in progress by R. Yrarrázabal, *Análisis Económico de las Diferentes Estructuras Prediales Resultantes de la Reforma Agraria Chilena*, Investigación N°4, Programa de Post-Grado en Economía Agraria, Universidad Católica de Chile (Santiago, 1973).

21. It is hoped that the new units will become not only production units, but social ones as well, with responsibility for directing health, housing, culture and recreation. See, for example the statement of Minister Chonchol in *Panorama Económico*, 165 (May, 1971).

22. A good summary is provided in ICIRA, UNDP, FAO, *op. cit.*

23. *Ibid.*, II, p. 4.

24. R. Yrarrázaval, *op. cit.*

25. ICIRA, UNDP, FAO, *op. cit.*, III, p. 19.

26. *Ibid.*, III, p. 8 and VII, p. 16.

27. Most relevant in this context is T. Cox, "Causas de Retroceso y de la Futura Crisis de la Agricultura Chilena," Internal Memorandum, ODEPA (Santiago, 1973).

28. A similar opinion as to who are the poorest can be found in L. Gitahy, M. Donoso and F. Encina, "Unión Organization in the Afuerino Sector," (Santiago, FEES, 1971), and in S. Bitar, Foxley, Ffrench-Davis and Muñoz, *Panorama Económico*, 274 (December, 1972), pp. 10-13.

29. A. Valdés, "Wages and Schooling of Agricultural Workers in Chile," *Economic Development and Cultural Change*, 19, N°2, (January, 1971), pp. 312-330.

30. In 1972 owners of minifundios (up to 5 HRB) and small farmers (5-20 HRB) comprised from 50 to 55% of the labour force, and it is estimated that they generated around 28% of the gross value added. ICIRA, UNDP, FAO, *op. cit.*, VII, p. 9.

31. ODEPLAN, *op. cit.*, pp. 104-105.

32. Between 1960 and 1970, approximately 90% of the agricultural population received wages that were inferior to the "Sueldo Vital" (minimum wage). The agricultural sector also had a relatively higher rate of illiteracy. *Ibid.*, pp. 105-106.

Appendix I
Seminar on the Employment Process
Bogota, Colombia
February 21-23, 1973

Participants:

1. Vincent Barnett

Department of Political Science
Williams College
Williamstown, Massachusetts 01267

2. Henry Bruton

Center for Development Studies
Williams College
Williamstown, Massachusetts 01267

3. Clovis Calvalcanti

Instituto Joaquim Nabuco de Pesquisas
Sociais
Av. 17 de Agosto 2187
50,000 Casa Forte, Recife, Pe, Brazil

4. Norman Dahl

40 Fern Street
Lexington, Massachusetts 02173

5. David Davies

Harvard University
Development Advisory Service
1737 Cambridge Street
Cambridge, Massachusetts 02138

6. Ronald Dore

Institute of Development Studies
Falmer, Brighton
BN1 9RE
Sussex, England

7. Edgar O. Edwards

The Ford Foundation
320 East 43rd Street
New York, New York 10017

8. Reed Hertford

The Ford Foundation
Apartado Aereo 51986
Bogota, Colombia

9. Lovell Jarvis

Department of Economics
University of California
Berkeley, California 94720

10. Rajni Kothari

Center for the Study of Developing Societies
29 Rajpur Road
Delhi 6, India

11. Jorge Mendez

Calle 111 2-17
Bogota, Colombia

12. Manning Nash	Department of Anthropology University of Chicago Chicago, Illinois 60637
13. Francisco Ortega	Banco de la Republica Bogota, Colombia
14. Joseph Ramos	c/o OIT (PREALC) Casilla 618 Santiago, Chile
15. Dudley Seers	Institute of Development Studies Falmer, Brighton BN1 9RE Sussex, England
16. George Stolnitz	Department of Economics University of Indiana Bloomington, Indiana 47401
17. Victor Tokman	Latin American Institute for Economic and Social Planning Casilla 1567 Santiago, Chile
18. Pravin Visaria	Department of Economics University of Bombay Bombay 32, India

Seminar Papers:

1. Vincent M. Barnett, Jr.	Implementation of Policies for Fuller Employment in Less Developed Countries
2. Henry J. Bruton	Economic Development and Labor Use
3. Clovis Cavalcanti	Some Reflections for a Study on Labor Underutilization
4. David C. Cole	The Pattern and Causes of Employment Growth in South Korea during the 1960's
5. David G. Davies	A Critical Discussion of the I.L.O. Report on Employment in Kenya
6. Ronald P. Dore	The Labour Market and Patterns of Employment in the Wage Sector of LDC's: Implications for the Volume of Employment Generated
7. Edgar O. Edwards and Michael P. Todaro	Educational Demand and Supply in the Context of Growing Unemployment in Less Developed Countries

Seminar on Technology and Employment
New Delhi, India
March 21-24, 1973

Participants:

1. Charles Bailey

   The Ford Foundation
   55 Lodi Estate
   New Delhi, India 110003

2. Arie Beenhakker

   College of Business Administration
   University of South Florida
   Tampa, Florida 33620

3. Bepini Behari

   Appropriate Technology Cell
   Ministry of Industrial Development
   Government of India
   268 Udyog Bhawan
   New Delhi, India

4. Clark Bloom

   The Ford Foundation
   320 East 43rd Street
   New York, N.Y. 10017

5. Norman Dahl

   40 Fern Street
   Lexington, Massachusetts 02173

6. Edgar O. Edwards

   The Ford Foundation
   320 East 43rd Street
   New York, N.Y. 10017

7. Peter F. Geithner

   The Ford Foundation
   320 East 43rd Street
   New York, N.Y. 10017

8. Jose Giral

   Graduate School of Chemical Engineering
   National Autonomous University of Mexico
   Mexico 10, D.F. Mexico

9. Sajuti Hasibuan

   National Development Planning Agency
   Taman Suropati
   Jakarta, Indonesia

10. Harold E. Hoelscher

    Asian Institute of Technology
    P.O. Box 2754
    Bangkok, Thailand

11. S.S. Johl

    Department of Agricultural Economics
       and Sociology
    Punjab Agricultural University
    Ludhiana, India

12. Amir U. Khan	Agricultural Engineering Department The International Rice Research Institute P.O. Box 583 Manila, Philippines
13. Timothy King	International Bank for Reconstruction and Development 1818 H Street, N.W. Washington, D.C. 20433
14. Raj Krishna	Development Economics Department International Bank for Reconstruction and Development 1818 H Street, N.W. Washington, D.C. 20433
15. E. Lartey	Institute of Standards and Industrial Research P.O. Box M 32 Accra, Ghana
16. Hahn-Been Lee	Soongjun University Seoul, Korea
17. Michael Nelson	The Ford Foundation Alejandro Dumas 42 Polanco Mexico 5, D.F.
18. O.O. Ojo	Department of Economics University of Ife Ile, Ife, Nigeria
19. V.G. Patel	Gujarat Industrial Development Corporation 3rd Floor—Fadia Chambers Ashram Road Navrangapura Ahmedabad 9, India
20. James Pickett	Overseas Development Unit University of Strathclyde McCance Building 16 Richmond Street Glasgow G1 IXQ, Scotland
21. Jon Sigurdson	Science Policy Research Unit The University of Sussex Falmer, Brighton Sussex BN1 9RF, England
22. Eugene Staley	455 Seale Avenue Palo Alto, California 94301

424

23. Joseph E. Stepanek	Industrial Services and Institutions Division United Nations Industrial Development Organisation P.O. Box 707 A-1011 Vienna, Austria
24. Frances Stewart	Institute of Commonwealth Studies Queen Elizabeth House 21 St. Giles Oxford OX1 3LA, England
25. E.C. Subbarao	Department of Metallurgical Engineering Indian Institute of Technology IIT Post Office Kanpur, U.P., India
26. Constantine V. Vaitsos	Casilla 3237 Junta del Acuerdo de Cartagena Lima, Peru
27. Robert van Leeuwen	The Ford Foundation P.O. Box 2030 Taman Kebon Sirih I/4 Jakarta, Indonesia
28. Pravin Visaria	Department of Economics Bombay University Bombay 32, India

Seminar Papers:

1. S.A. Aluko	Employment in Nigerian Small-Scale Industrial Sector
2. Charles Cooper	Science Policy and Technology Change in Underdeveloped Countries
3. Gunvant M. Desai and Michael G.G. Schluter	Generating Employment in Rural Areas
4. Edgar O. Edwards	A Synthesis of the Seminar on the Employment Process in Developing Countries
5. Jose Giral	The Need to Reorient the Development of Appropriate Technology
6. Amir U. Khan	Appropriate Technologies: Do We Transfer, Adapt, or Develop?
7. Raj Krishna	Measurement of the Direct and Indirect Employment Effects of Agricultural Growth with Technical Change

Seminar on Rural Development and Employment
Ibadan, Nigeria
April 9-12, 1973

Participants:

1. Partap C. Aggarwal   Shri Ram Centre for Industrial Relations
and Human Resources
5 Pusa Road
New Delhi 5, India

2. Charles R. Bailey   The Ford Foundation
55 Lodi Estate
New Delhi, India 110003

3. George Beckford   University of West Indies
Mona, Kingston
Jamaica, West Indies

4. Gelia T. Castillo   Department of Agricultural Education
University of the Philippines
Los Banos Unit
College, Laguna, Philippines

5. Norman Collins   The Ford Foundation
320 East 43rd Street
New York, New York 10017

6. Victor Diejomaoh   Christ's College
Cambridge CB2 3BU, England

7. Rene Dumont   Institut National Agronomique
16 rue Claude Bernard
Paris 5^e, France

8. Edgar O. Edwards   The Ford Foundation
320 East 43rd Street
New York, New York 10017

9. William Gamble   The Ford Foundation
P.O. Box 2368
Lagos, Nigeria

10. John Gerhart   Woodrow Wilson School
Princeton University
Princeton, New Jersey 08540

11. Carl H. Gotsch   The Ford Foundation
P.O. Box 2379
Beirut, Lebanon

| 12. Keith Griffin | Magdalen College |
| | Oxford, England |

13. John Gurley | Stanford University
| 907 Lathrop Avenue
| Stanford, California

14. David Heaps | The Ford Foundation
| 17 rue Margueritte
| Paris 17, France

15. Guy Hunter | Overseas Development Institute
| 160 Picadilly
| London W1, England

16. S. Reutlinger | International Bank for Reconstruction
| and Development
| 1818 H Street, N.W.
| Washington, D.C. 20433

17. Wayne Schutjer | The Ford Foundation
| P.O. Box 436
| Bangkok, Thailand

18. Roger Selley | The Ford Foundation
| P.O. Box 7470
| Accra, North Ghana

19. Alberto Valdes | Centro Internacional de Agricultura Tropical
| Apartado Aereo 67-13
| Cali, Colombia

20. Raanan Weitz | Settlement Center
| National and University Institute of Agriculture
| P.O. Box 555
| Rehovot, Israel

Seminar Papers:

1. Partap C. Aggarwal | Green Revolution and Employment in Ludhiana, Punjab, India

2. Charles R. Bailey
Norman C. Dahl
Frances Stewart | A Summary of the Seminar on Technology and Employment in Developing Countries

3. Solon Barraclough | Rural Development Strategy and Agrarian Reform

4. George L. Beckford | Comparative, Rural Systems, Development, and Underdevelopment

5. Henry Bruton | Economic Development and Labor Use

6. Gelia T. Castillo	Banana Communities: An Exploratory Social Analysis
7. Gelia T. Castillo	The Changing Filipino Rice Farmer
8. Gunvant M. Desai and Michael G.G. Schluter	Generating Employment in Rural Areas
9. Peter Dorner	Land Reform, Technology, Income Distribution and Employment: Conceptual and Empirical Relationships
10. Rene Dumont	Rural Employment in Bangladesh with Some Chinese and Vietnamese References
11. Edgar O. Edwards	Synthesis of the Seminar on the Employment Process in Developing Countries
12. John D. Gerhart	Management Problems and Rural Development in Kenya
13. Carl Gotsch	Economics, Institutions and Employment Generation in Rural Areas
14. Carl Gotsch	Agricultural Mechanization in the Punjab: Some Comparative Observations from India and Pakistan
15. Keith Griffin	Policy Options for Rural Development
16. John G. Gurley	Rural Development in China, 1949-1972 and the Lessons to be Learned from It
17. Guy Hunter	Employment in the Rural Economy/ Government and People
18. Millard F. Long	Conditions for Success of Public Credit Programs for Small Farmers
19. John Duncan Powell	Agricultural Enterprise and Peasant Political Behavior
20. Arun Shourie	Growth and Employment
21. John Thomas	Employment Creating Public Works Programs: Observations on Political and Social Dimensions
22. C. Peter Timmer	Choice of Technique in Indonesia
23. Alberto Valdes	The Transition to Socialism: Observations on Chilean Agriculture
24. Raanan Weitz and Levia Applebaum	Planning for Full Employment in Rural Areas